FIELDING'S
BAJA
CALIFORNIA

Other Fielding Titles

Fielding's Alaska Cruises and the Inside Passage
Fielding's Asia's Top Dive Sites
Fielding's Amazon
Fielding's Australia
Fielding's Bahamas
Fielding's Baja California
Fielding's Bermuda
Fielding's Borneo
Fielding's Budget Europe
Fielding's Caribbean
Fielding's Caribbean Cruises
Fielding's World and Orlando
Fielding's Diving Indonesia
Fielding's Eastern Caribbean
Fielding's England
Fielding's Europe
Fielding's European Cruises
Fielding's Far East
Fielding's France
Fielding's Freewheelin' USA
Fielding's Kenya
Fielding's Hawaii
Fielding's Italy
Fielding's Las Vegas Agenda
Fielding's London Agenda
Fielding's Los Angeles
Fielding's Malaysia and Singapore
Fielding's Mexico
Fielding's New Orleans Agenda
Fielding's New York Agenda
Fielding's New Zealand
Fielding's Paradors, Pousadas and Charming Villages of Spain and Portugal
Fielding's Paris Agenda
Fielding's Portugal
Fielding's Rome Agenda
Fielding's San Diego Agenda
Fielding's Southeast Asia
Fielding's Southern Vietnam on Two Wheels
Fielding's Spain
Fielding's Surfing Indonesia
Fielding's Sydney Agenda
Fielding's Thailand, Cambodia, Laos and Myanmar
Fielding's Vacation Places Rated
Fielding's Vietnam
Fielding's Western Caribbean
Fielding's The World's Most Dangerous Places
Fielding's Worldwide Cruises

FIELDING'S
BAJA
CALIFORNIA

by
Jack Williams
and
Patty Williams

Fielding Worldwide, Inc.
308 South Catalina Avenue
Redondo Beach, California 90277 U.S.A.

Fielding's Baja California
Published by Fielding Worldwide, Inc.

FIELDING WORLDWIDE INC.

PUBLISHER AND CEO	**Robert Young Pelton**
GENERAL MANAGER	**John Guillebeaux**
MARKETING DIRECTOR	**Paul T. Snapp**
OPERATIONS DIRECTOR	**George Posanke**
ELECTRONIC PUBLISHING DIRECTOR	**Larry E. Hart**
PUBLIC RELATIONS DIRECTOR	**Beverly Riess**
ACCOUNT SERVICES MANAGER	**Shawn Potter**
PROJECT MANAGER	**Chris Snyder**

EDITORS

Kathy Knoles   **Linda Charlton**

Catherine Bruhn

PRODUCTION

Jebbie LaVoie   **Alfredo Mercado**

Martin Mancha   **Ramses Reynoso**

Craig South

COVER DESIGNED BY **Digital Artists, Inc.**
COVER PHOTOGRAPHERS — Front Cover **Robert Young Pelton/Westlight**
Back Cover **Baja Tourist Association**
INSIDE PHOTOS **Jack Williams, Baja Tourist Association**

Inquiries should be addressed to: Fielding Worldwide, Inc., 308 South Catalina Ave., Redondo Beach, California 90277 U.S.A., ☎ *(310) 372-4474*, Facsimile *(310) 376-8064*, 8:30 a.m.–5:30 p.m. Pacific Standard Time.

Website: http://www.fieldingtravel.com
email: fielding@fieldingtravel.com

ISBN 1-56952-106-9

Printed in the United States of America

Letter from the Publisher

In 1946, Temple Fielding began the first of what would be a remarkable new series of well-written, highly personalized guidebooks for independent travelers. Temple's opinionated, witty, and oft-imitated books have now guided travelers for almost a half-century. More important to some was Fielding's humorous and direct method of steering travelers away from the dull and the insipid. Today, Fielding's travel guides are still written by experienced travelers for experienced travelers. Our authors carry on Fielding's reputation for delivering travel experiences with insight and a sense of discovery and style.

A recognized expert on Baja California, author Jack Williams has driven more than 26,000 miles of its roads and highways and twice sailed around the peninsula in his yacht. Originally published under the title, *The Magnificent Peninsula*, and now completely revised, *Fielding's Baja California* reflects his firsthand investigative method and his intimacy with this largely undeveloped, alluring land.

The concept of independent travel has never been bigger. Our policy of *brutal honesty* and a highly personal point of view has never changed; it just seems the travel world has caught up with us.

Enjoy your Baja adventure with Jack Williams and Fielding.

RYP

Robert Young Pelton
Publisher and CEO
Fielding Worldwide, Inc.

Fielding Rating Icons

The Fielding Rating Icons are highly personal and awarded to help the besieged traveler choose from among the dizzying array of activities, attractions, hotels, restaurants and sights. The awarding of an icon denotes unusual or exceptional qualities in the relevant category.

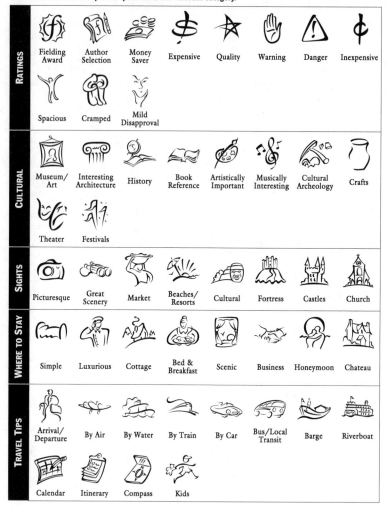

RATINGS
Fielding Award | Author Selection | Money Saver | Expensive | Quality | Warning | Danger | Inexpensive
Spacious | Cramped | Mild Disapproval

CULTURAL
Museum/Art | Interesting Architecture | History | Book Reference | Artistically Important | Musically Interesting | Cultural Archeology | Crafts
Theater | Festivals

SIGHTS
Picturesque | Great Scenery | Market | Beaches/Resorts | Cultural | Fortress | Castles | Church

WHERE TO STAY
Simple | Luxurious | Cottage | Bed & Breakfast | Scenic | Business | Honeymoon | Chateau

TRAVEL TIPS
Arrival/Departure | By Air | By Water | By Train | By Car | Bus/Local Transit | Barge | Riverboat
Calendar | Itinerary | Compass | Kids

ACTIVITIES

Downhill Skiing	X–country Skiing	Watersports	Sailing	Scuba Diving	Snorkeling/ Diving	Deep-sea Fishing	Freshwater Fishing
Swimming	Hiking	Walking	Relaxing	Golf	Tennis	Horseback Riding	General Sports
Cycling	Workout						

SPECIAL INTEREST

Nightlife	Singles	Romantic	Nude Beaches	Lecture	Spectacular Cuisine	Wine Tasting	Shopping
Cafe Stops	Gardening	Pro Sports	Mystery	Wildlife			

What's in the Stars

Fielding's Five-Star Rating System

★★★★★ Exceptionally outstanding hotels, resorts, restaurants
and attractions.

★★★★ Excellent in most respects.

★★★ Very good quality and superior value.

★★ Meritorious and worth considering.

★ Modest or better than average.

Restaurants are star-rated and classified by dollar signs as:

$ Budget

$$ Moderate

$$$ Expensive

A NOTE TO OUR READERS

If you have had an extraordinary, mediocre or horrific experience, we want to hear about it. If something has changed since we have gone to press, please let us know. If you would like to send information for review in next year's edition, send it to:

Fielding's Baja
308 South Catalina Avenue
Redondo Beach, CA 90277
FAX: (310) 376-8064
Website: http://www.fieldingtravel.com

AUTHOR'S PREFACE

The Author's Preface in the original version of *Fielding's Baja*, entitled *The Magnificent Peninsula*, presented my qualifications for producing the book. It was essentially an apology for my having had the audacity to become an author, in that my past experience in writing had been limited to business letters and the reports and other assorted jargon of the world of bureaucracy. As *The Magnificent Peninsula* met with considerable success, I am perhaps justified in withdrawing the apology. However, still included here is some background material about myself, as many readers have expressed interest in the pedigree of their guide.

I love to travel, and this activity is one of the driving forces of my life. I submit that having such an affliction is the basic requirement for writing a travel guide. By quick tally, I find I have expended some 29 months traveling in Mexico, with more than three-quarters of this time spent on the Baja peninsula or over its surrounding waters. Perhaps more importantly, I am a rover, not lingering long in any one haunt. I frequently talk to other people whose knowledge about a particular place in Baja exceeds my own, but I believe the nature and breadth of my wanderings have provided an overall perspective of Baja shared with only a relative few.

By training and experience, I am a forester, although I have now retired from that calling. Being a specialist in trees and forests may seem a strange qualification for delving into the almost totally desert environment of the Baja peninsula. In practice, many foresters find themselves engaged in the far broader task of managing land with all its surface and subsurface resources. We are fortunate in becoming familiar with geology, wildlife, botany, soils and a variety of other outdoor-oriented subjects. In addition, many of us become keen observers and interpreters of what we see, whether it be forest or desert.

At the core of my view of travel book writing is the concept that travelers need a source of information concerning the land and all its natural and man-made attributes as a basis for enjoying and appreciating what they see. As a purveyor of such material, I am an expert in very little, but in keeping with my name, I am perhaps a "Jack" of all trades concerning the great outdoors.

My post-retirement activities in Baja started in 1983 gathering data to assist another author in republishing his out-of-print boating guide. *The Magnificent Peninsula* was written as an act of frustration as I waited for this individual to produce his book. When his project still did not materialize, I produced my own *Baja Boater's Guide* in 1988. During this five-year period from 1983 to 1988, I conducted two circumnavigations of the peninsula in my sailboat, retraced this same terrain by aircraft taking more than 1000 aerial photos, and traveled approximately 20,000 miles over Baja's roads and highways.

In presenting these credentials, I have so far omitted what may be most important. I have a love affair with Mexico and the Baja peninsula. This is the catalyst that has led me to the perilous task of authorship. It is my hope that this infatuation will not overly cloud my objectivity. It is my sincere wish that these efforts will enhance your ability to plan, and to savor traveling in Mexico's magnificent peninsula. If perchance it does, or if you can offer the path to improvement, it would be a pleasure to hear from you.

—Jack Williams, P. O. Box 203, Sausalito, CA 94966

ACKNOWLEDGMENTS

Where does one begin? I have no big names to drop, but many people have made big contributions to *Fielding's Baja.* My thanks go to:

My daughter, Barbara Williams, who was the first to review the manuscript in the office and who sat at my side as we checked the "Grand Tour" in the field. The changes made at her suggestion are immense.

Ken Reimer, for contributing the poetry, a welcome touch of class.

Alan Lamb, a true friend and excellent companion during *La Patricia's* circumnavigation of the Baja peninsula and for his office and field review of the manuscript. (Putting up with the vile moods of the skipper takes a special kind of person.)

June Siringer, for a masterful job of editing a manuscript where the spelling was inspired by the political philosophy of Abraham Lincoln: "Some of the words were spelled wrong all of the time, and all of the words were spelled wrong some of the time, but mercifully all of the words were not spelled wrong all of the time"; and where the author looked upon commas as a cook looks on salt, "something to be sprinkled on at random in the process of preparation."

And a special tribute to my wife, Patricia Williams, for endless hours of help and understanding in many forms. Without her, there would have simply been no *La Patricia*, no *Fielding's Baja* and perhaps no Jack Williams.

My thanks also to Lyn Gladstone for hunches and counsel (my thin skin will never be the same); to Peter Schultz for guidance through the strange and wonderful world of printing; to Ellie Lamb for reviewing the original manuscript in the field; to my parents, Henry and Margaret Williams, whose energy and frugality produced the initial financial resources to publish the original book; and to Leland Lewis, who provided the motivation and opportunity for my venture into writing. Sometimes it is not what you do, but what you don't do that is important. Thus it was with Leland.

My gratitude to Chet Sherman, president of the *Vagabundos del Mar*, for extensive cooperation in bringing this book to the attention of the members of his fine travel club.

Finally, thanks to an endless number of travelers in Baja who have offered their counsel, to Mexican officials who have struggled with my poor Spanish in answering my questions, and to the wonderfully warm and friendly Mexican people who share their land with travelers from the north.

Thank you all.

The BAJA BOOKSHELF Offers Specialized Resource Guidebooks for the Baja Peninsula Covering

Boating

Kayaking

Fishing

Diving

Camping

Backroad Travel

The Cape Area

Wildlife

Vegetation

Geology and Biology

Mexican Real Estate

Retirement in Mexico

and Much More

TABLE OF CONTENTS

PART II:
HIGHER NEEDS

LIST OF MAPS

INTRODUCTION

Here I am at work on the book above the beach on the El Migrino Loop, south of Todos Santos. Tough work, but somebody has to do it.

Few places in the world so perfectly fit Webster's definition of a peninsula: "A portion of jutting land nearly surrounded by water." From the United States-Mexican border to Baja's tip at Cabo San Lucas is a straight-line distance of nearly 700 miles, a length greater than that of two of the world's other well-known peninsulas, Florida and the Italian boot.

This enchanting land is also unique in another manner. Baja is largely a wilderness. Except for La Paz, the border towns and the resorts at the peninsula's tip, it is little developed and lightly visited. It has always amazed me that such an area is located adjacent to one of the most densely populated metropolitan centers in the world. It is as if there were a magic line separating the

BEST OF BAJA

San Diego

TIJUANA

ROSARITO

TECATE

PUERTO NUEVO

ENSENADA

Santo Tomas

San Quintin

TIJUANA

Besides attracting hordes of shoppers and partying tourists, Tijuana is known for its Hippodrome where horses and greyhounds race. Bullfighting and jai alai are two other crowd pleasers. The bars pound with disco music all day and night.

ROSARITO BEACH

This once tranquil little village became popular when the Rosarito Beach Hotel began attracting celebrities in the 20s. Since the road between Tijuana and Rosarito was paved, tourism has increased every year. Rosarito's biggest draw is its beaches for swimming, sunning, surfing and horseback riding.

ENSENADA

The town gets most of its income from the tourists that jam the streets every weekend. Partying at Hussong's Cantina or Papas and Beer are the main activities aside from watersports, shopping and fishing. The Baja 1000 offroad race is held in Ensenada in November and 50 mile bike rides from Tijuana to Ensenada are held in April and September.

LA BUFADORA

This blowhole near Ensenada is worth an excursion. Waves rushing into an underground cavern spew 25-30 meters high. Nearby underwater pinnacles and sea caves of Punta Banda are popular with divers. The open air market nearby is cheaper than the shops in town.

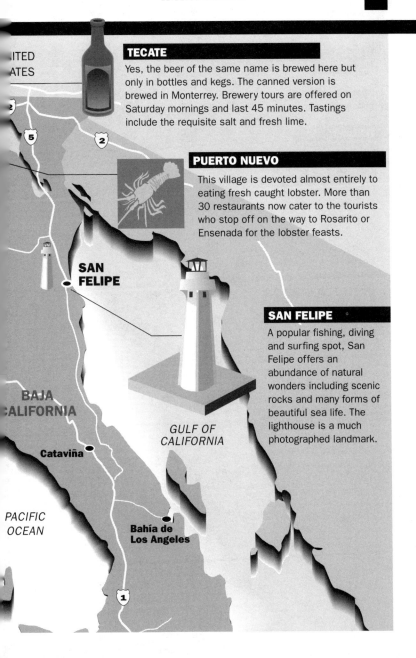

UNITED
STATES

TECATE

Yes, the beer of the same name is brewed here but only in bottles and kegs. The canned version is brewed in Monterrey. Brewery tours are offered on Saturday mornings and last 45 minutes. Tastings include the requisite salt and fresh lime.

PUERTO NUEVO

This village is devoted almost entirely to eating fresh caught lobster. More than 30 restaurants now cater to the tourists who stop off on the way to Rosarito or Ensenada for the lobster feasts.

SAN FELIPE

SAN FELIPE

A popular fishing, diving and surfing spot, San Felipe offers an abundance of natural wonders including scenic rocks and many forms of beautiful sea life. The lighthouse is a much photographed landmark.

BAJA
CALIFORNIA

GULF OF CALIFORNIA

Cataviña

PACIFIC OCEAN

Bahía de Los Angeles

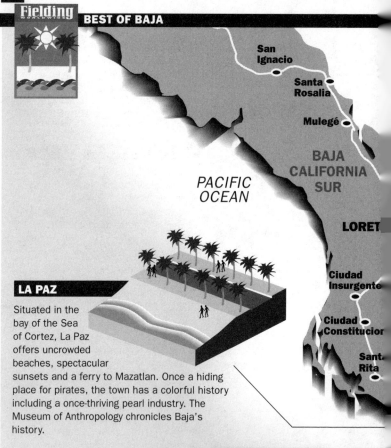

Fielding
WORLDWIDE

BEST OF BAJA

San Ignacio

Santa Rosalia

Mulegé

PACIFIC OCEAN

BAJA CALIFORNIA SUR

LORET

LA PAZ

Situated in the bay of the Sea of Cortez, La Paz offers uncrowded beaches, spectacular sunsets and a ferry to Mazatlan. Once a hiding place for pirates, the town has a colorful history including a once-thriving pearl industry. The Museum of Anthropology chronicles Baja's history.

Ciudad Insurgente

Ciudad Constitucion

Santa Rita

CABO SAN LUCAS

Long a favorite destination of fishermen, Cabo has become one of Mexico's fastest growing resort areas. Besides boating and sport-fishing, the main attractions are an underwater nature reserve and scenic Land's End Rock.

GULF OF CALIFORNIA

LORETO

Loreto's location on the Sea of Cortez has made it a favorite destination for fishermen, divers and boating enthusiasts. Collectors of sea shells will find many unusual specimens on the black, rocky beach, but watch out for giant ants!

EL BAJO

People flock here in the summer to see the giant manta rays that often let divers hitch a ride while holding onto their backs. Whale sharks and pilot whales are often seen here.

EL BAJO

MUNICIPAL HALL, SAN JOSE DEL CABO

San Jose del Cabo was founded in 1730. The architecture of this town suggests its age, however it also tells of the town's recent growth due to tourism. The completion of Highway 1 increased tourism and the town's population has grown to 11,000. The town has six large hotels, many restaurants, a golf course and shopping center.

LA PAZ

Los Barriles

Todos Santo

CABO SAN LUCAS

San Jose Del Cabo

two, and of course there is—the international border. There can be little doubt that the face of the peninsula would bear slight resemblance to what one finds today if it were a portion of the United States. Those of us who love Baja are unanimous in expressing gratitude for the presence of that border.

The Comprehensive Guidebook

It is perhaps a bit brazen for an author to maintain that his book is THE comprehensive guidebook when several other volumes on the same topic may be readily acquired. Making such a statement is a good marketing technique, but in the final analysis it will succeed only if it is true. I submit here the reasons why I believe the claim is correct, and at the same time tell you how the volume is organized and present the basic ideas on which it is founded.

Most of the space in many travel books provides descriptions of specific attractions and locales. Relatively little space is devoted to more broadly based background material concerning the total area under consideration. *Fielding's Baja* devotes approximately equal attention to these two arenas. Parts I and II provide the background. Part III, a Grand Tour through the entire peninsula, stresses and relies upon the information in Parts I and II. I believe it is the nature and use of this background material that makes the book comprehensive.

We will now move to a brief discussion of the three parts of this book.

Part I: Background and Planning

One of my principal objectives is to paint the big picture rather than to provide overly finite details that may be of limited value. I hope to bring Baja alive so that you can visualize it as a whole and obtain a grasp of its major attributes and recreational attractions. But don't be misled. This does not mean you will be reading a cluster of broad generalities. As in many subjects, even the big picture can be quite complex. So it is with Baja.

The seven chapters in Part I are designed to provide basic background information that every visitor to Baja should know. I suggest you use Part I as a planning tool to help decide if you want to go, where you want to go, how you will travel, and in what activities you will engage. Obviously it should best be read before undertaking a visit to Baja.

In Part II we will move on to a higher level of background material.

Part II: Higher Needs

Psychologists have long recognized that all human animals share certain basic needs for things such as food, safety, protection, care, gregariousness, love, respect, standing, status and self-respect. Famous psychologist Abraham Maslow stresses that these elements seem to arrange themselves in a hierarchy of importance and that the demand to fulfill a particular need usually rests on some prior satisfaction of those that fall lower on the scale. Maslow also contends that at the apex of this hierarchy there is a still higher group of needs that relate to the sheer quest for knowledge, understanding and such aesthetic factors as beauty, symmetry, simplicity and order.

As before, it appears that these higher needs only come into prominence when the basic list has been adequately serviced. I submit that it would be relatively easy to defend the proposition that most American and Canadian citizens who have the leisure and financial resources to visit Baja California have their basic needs reasonably well in hand. It follows that the fulfilling of Maslow's higher needs is an important objective for many of Baja's visitors.

It is the objective of Part II of *Fielding's Baja* to provide the data needed to gratify this human quest for knowledge, understanding and beauty. This is done by discussing subjects that relate to what is in plain view when one travels through Baja: land, vegetation, wildlife, places of historic interest, the people and their works. I suggest that its five chapters be read or reviewed a few days prior to making your trip so that its material will be fresh in mind. You can ignore Part II and still have a fine trip to Baja, but I urge you to absorb its contents in your quest for Maslow's higher ground.

Note—In writing the above paragraphs in the first version of this book I was fearful that many readers would not share my enthusiasm for the subject matter in Part II. To my pleasant surprise, these pages have proven to be the book's most popular segment. Maslow was right.

Part III: The Grand Tour

The long, craggy finger of the Baja peninsula is dominated from a transportation standpoint by the Transpeninsular Highway (Highway 1) which extends more than 1000 miles from the international border to within a mile of the famous arch at the tip of Cabo San Lucas. In Part III, the reader is taken on a Grand Tour of the Baja peninsula along the highway from north to south and is directed to dozens of side trips along the way. It also includes tours of the border towns, the San Felipe area and numerous other highways and roads.

The Grand Tour is packed with elements of real interest that will enhance your trip. Often these items are based upon the background material presented in Parts I and II. Part III goes well beyond simply keeping you from getting lost and recommending where to spend the night. It features a 30-Stop Points of Special Interest Tour and other unique features that are outlined in more detail in the introduction to Part III.

Part III is designed to be read as you make the Grand Tour. Of course, it may be perused as part of the planning phase prior to departure.

A Few Ground Rules

The preparation of this book was based on two cardinal rules.

1. I Report What I Have Seen.

This book has been written almost exclusively from my own notes and observations, supplemented in a few cases by those of trusted associates. I have reviewed the works of the authors who have preceded me but I have not pirated their accounts. In some instances I have visited coastal areas by boat but have not traveled the back roads to reach these same locations. I will alert you to these situations. In all other cases I have personally seen or investigated everything that is described. In preparing Part II, it has been necessary to base the background for much of the material on scientific literature relating to the subject in question. This is particularly true for the chapter on history. However, the specific points of interest that are noted in relation to these subjects all reflect my own observations.

2. I Concentrate On What the Traveler Can See.

A majority of the information presented relates to objects that can easily be seen while traveling in Baja. I have refrained from relating lengthy accounts of the geologic past, the activities of nocturnal or rare desert animals or other phenomena that no one is likely to see. The history chapter provides the principal exception to this rule, but even there a special effort has been made to relate the historical account to the sites where events took place and what you may visit.

It has been a constant temptation to refer to citizens of the United States as *Americans.* I am aware that Canadians and Mexicans rightly consider that they too are Americans. To avoid offending these people, the term *North Americans* is frequently used when referring to everyone who visits Baja from *north of the border.* These terms apply to the two peoples and countries of Canada and the United States collectively.

Use of the word *California* also presents a problem. For several centuries, California was everything over there west of the mainland of New Spain (Mexico). With the establishment of the Franciscan missions in what is now

California in the United States, the northern area became *Alta California* and the name Baja California was applied to the peninsula itself.

This book refers to the present state of California as Alta California, or California in the United States, in deference to our Mexican friends who might otherwise feel that the name of their land has been usurped. The peninsula as a whole is usually referred to as *Baja*, as this is a term universally used north of the border. I apologize to those in Mexico who feel that the full name Baja California is more appropriate.

It has recently come to my attention that some individuals refer to Baja California as "The Baja," meaning "The Lower." I am sure most true Baja lovers would join me in endeavoring to discourage this practice.

Finally, place names in Baja are presented in Spanish. Thus, *Bahia Escondido* is not referred to as *Escondido Bay* or *Hidden Bay*. The exceptions to this rule are the *Pacific Ocean* and the *Sea of Cortez* because they are so well known in their English versions.

Some Personal Opinions

Travel book authors, as a breed, tend to paint enchanting pictures of the realms they are describing. Their third-person descriptions sometimes take on the tone of indisputable truths or natural laws laid down by the gods. "The place has a magic charm and is a veritable heaven on earth" not because the author says so, but because that's the way it is. Descriptions and advertisements concerning Mexico frequently fall in this category. They describe a carefree land of fiestas, mariachi music, swimming pools and luxury hotels.

Therefore, let me present a few personal comments aimed at bringing a note of realism to the Baja peninsula.

First of all, I sincerely believe that Baja is magnificent. Its mountains, unique desert vegetation, coastline, people and culture appeal to thousands of Baja buffs. Others may not find it so. Baja is largely a desert. This is an inescapable reality. If deserts are an uncomfortable environment for you, *magnificent* may seem overly generous. If you have become addicted to all the finely tuned luxuries of the 20th century that are commonplace north of the border, you may be less than enchanted with Baja. What is charming, unique or challenging to one individual may be an inconvenience to others.

It is also inescapable that the living standards in Mexico are considerably below what many of us are accustomed to in the United States and Canada. A great majority of the Mexican people you will meet are fully engaged with activities lower on Maslow's scale of needs than those at its summit. The traveler can simply overlook this situation or, preferably, will adapt a frame of mind that accepts what one encounters as part of a culture that provides a foreign country with its charm. Regrettably, I know people who find what they view as poverty in Mexico is personally offensive, even when seen from the window of a luxury hotel. Should you be one of these, your travel plans might best be directed at places other than Mexico or other developing countries.

Finally, I wish to direct your attention back to a comment presented in the opening lines of this introduction. It concerns the fact that except for selected areas, Baja is relatively unvisited. (Thousands of vacationers visit Baja every year. Many return over and over, the true Baja buffs.) But their numbers are astonishingly small when one considers the enormous population living next door in the Los Angeles-San Diego area. Why isn't Baja simply overrun with tourists? I believe I know the major answer. It can be expressed in only one word: *fear.*

I have given considerable thought to bringing forth this subject. Is it wise for a travel book author to raise the potential of something negative about the area he is promoting? Obviously I have decided to do so. Proceeding otherwise would be to ignore what is all too apparent; that is, that many people are frightened to travel in Mexico. Some may fear the language barrier or the potential for becoming ill. But many more are concerned with the potential for crime and harassment from dishonest public officials. To deny that there are such officials, or to proclaim that there is no crime in Baja, would be inaccurate. But the level of anxiety experienced by the North American public is blown far out of proportion with reality.

Many negative events concerning Mexico have been in the news the past several years. There have been two prominent political assassinations, high officials have been accused of political corruption, and as I write, the former Mexican president is apparently in exile in the United States. There are ongoing problems related to the drug trade. U.S. concern about illegal immigration has reportedly angered Mexico. All these reports increase the anxiety of North Americans toward traveling in Mexico. As a result, tourism has been down in Baja the past several years.

Those of us whose task is to promote travel to Mexico often point out that fear-provoking events in the United States and other parts of the world are far, far more frequent than anything ever experienced in Baja. This is true, but, what the reader wants to know is whether it is safe to travel in Baja. I must make it clear that I can guarantee nothing. But, my many journeys to Baja support my long-held belief that the peninsula must be the safest place to travel in the two American continents.

I have discussed the fear issue with Baja buffs camped on the beaches and otherwise absorbed in the beauty and remoteness of the peninsula. Many concur that there is a fear problem, but I have been universally and firmly requested not to do anything to remedy the situation. They well know that their favorite haunts will become overwhelmed with tourists if this conceptual barrier is removed.

In closing this issue, I must note that I have stayed the night alone or with a single friend in scores of the most remote coves, beaches and villages in Baja. I have never been treated with anything but friendship and courtesy, a remarkable record considering that I sport an often unkempt beard and have never been nominated as a candidate for Mr. Neat. Thousands of foreign visitors go to Mexico without fear. I hope you will join us, but please don't tell many others. Those Baja buffs will crucify me.

Information About Baja

You may wish to consider the task of obtaining information about Baja as falling into three categories: guidebooks, newsletters and speciality books. Each of these is noted below.

Travel Guidebooks

Fielding's Baja is all that most people will need to travel in Baja. It covers a wide variety of subject matter, and it will be updated through field investigation prior to each new edition. But it is impossible to prevent changes from occurring in Baja between this field work and your reading of these pages. The best way to bridge this time gap is through obtaining newsletters published by one of two travel clubs covering the Baja beat.

Newsletters

The Discover Baja Travel Club and Vagabundos del Mar travel clubs each produce excellent monthly newsletters that report current developments and conditions in the peninsula as well as news about club activities. I recommend you join one or both of these organizations.

Specialty Books

It is impossible for this guidebook to provide in-depth coverage of all subjects related to Baja. Those desiring more detailed information are urged to look in specialty books concerning boating, fishing, camping, natural history, backroad travel and many other subjects.

PART I:
BACKGROUND AND
PLANNING

THE BIG PICTURE

This typical section of Baja's Pacific Coast features the surf pounding on rocky, sparsely vegetated cliffs. The photo was taken north of Playa los Cerritos.

Much of the world's information is best understood if presented through the art of classification. For this reason, I will be continually breaking Baja and many of its principal subjects into segments or areas. The first of these will be a vertical slice in which we will examine four zones that run more or less north-south. I say more or less because in reality, the Baja peninsula extends closer to northwest-southeast than true north and south. The four zones are (1) Baja's Pacific coast, (2) Baja's Sea of Cortez coast, (3) the interior and (4) Mexico's mainland coast (north half). The last zone may come as a surprise because it isn't a part of Baja. The reason for its inclusion will be explained in due course.

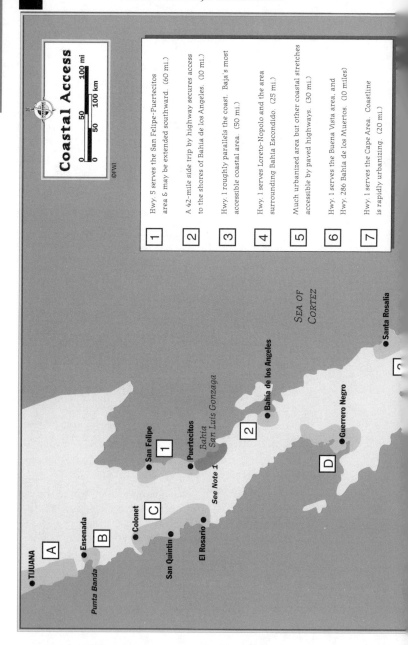

Coastal Access

0   50   100 mi
0   50   100 km

©FWI

1 | Hwy. 5 serves the San Felipe-Puertecitos area & may be extended southward. (60 mi.)

2 | A 42-mile side trip by highway secures access to the shores of Bahia de los Angeles. (10 mi.)

3 | Hwy. 1 roughly parallels the coast. Baja's most accessible coastal area. (50 mi.)

4 | Hwy. 1 serves Loreto-Nopolo and the area surrounding Bahia Escondido. (25 mi.)

5 | Much urbanized area but other coastal stretches accessible by paved highways. (30 mi.)

6 | Hwy. 1 serves the Buena Vista area, and Hwy. 286 Bahia de los Muertos. (10 miles)

7 | Hwy. 1 serves the Cape Area. Coastline is rapidly urbanizing. (20 mi.)

TIJUANA

Ensenada

Punta Banda

Colonet

San Quintin

El Rosario

San Felipe

Puertecitos

Bahia
San Luis Gonzaga

See Note 1

Bahia de los Angeles

Guerrero Negro

SEA OF
CORTEZ

Santa Rosalia

A

B

C

1

2

D

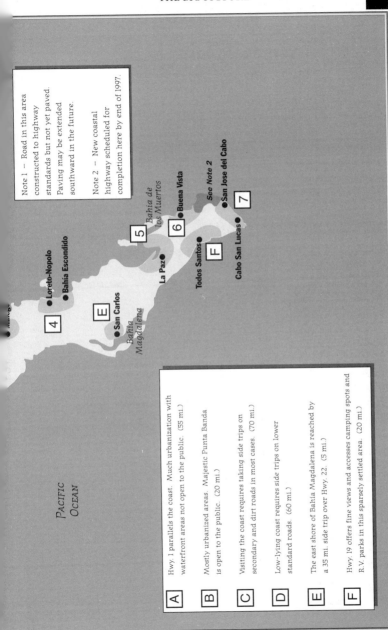

Note 1 – Road in this area constructed to highway standards but not yet paved. Paving may be extended southward in the future.

Note 2 – New coastal highway scheduled for completion here by end of 1997.

PACIFIC OCEAN

● Loreto-Nopolo
● Bahía Escondido

● San Carlos

Bahía Magdalena

4

E

Bahía de los Muertos

5

● Buena Vista

6

La Paz ●

Todos Santos ●

See Note 2
● San Jose del Cabo

F

Cabo San Lucas ●

7

A Hwy. 1 parallels the coast. Much urbanization with waterfront areas not open to the public. (55 mi.)

B Mostly urbanized areas. Majestic Punta Banda is open to the public. (20 mi.)

C Visiting the coast requires taking side trips on secondary and dirt roads in most cases. (70 mi.)

D Low-lying coast requires side trips on lower standard roads. (60 mi.)

E The east shore of Bahia Magdalena is reached by a 35 mi. side trip over Hwy. 22. (5 mi.)

F Hwy. 19 offers fine views and accesses camping spots and R.V. parks in this sparsely settled area. (20 mi.)

The Vertical Slice

Baja's Pacific Coast

Measuring a line drawn along the edge of the many projections of Baja's interface with the Pacific Ocean would disclose a largely deserted coastline of approximately 1000 miles. Inclusion of the many bays and lagoons would add hundreds of additional miles. The startling fact is how little of this shore is readily accessible to tourists who travel to Baja by conventional two-wheel-drive vehicles and whose temperaments require them to stay on the main roads. This description fits the majority of those who visit Baja by road.

Traveling from the international border to Cabo San Lucas over Highways 1 and 19 is a trip of approximately 1025 miles. I have inventoried this route in terms of coastal accessibility and found that only some 230 miles of highway provide access to the Pacific Ocean. If anything, these estimates are generous. In most places, the ocean is not visible from the highway, and side roads must be used to reach the water's edge. Conditions are similar on the Sea of Cortez coast. As the great majority of tourists traveling to Baja by road are destined for seashore areas, it is important to understand this situation.

There are several sizeable villages and many *fish camps* along those sections of the Pacific coast that are not readily accessible from the main highway. These are regularly visited by yachts making the Baja Passage and by a few land-based travelers whose equipment and interests lead them to explore the hundreds of miles of secondary and less-developed roads. These communities provide a fascinating contrast with life as we know it north of the border. Visiting them, one finds it hard to believe they are so close to the metropolitan centers of the southwestern United States.

Several other subjects must be presented to complete the big picture of the Baja peninsula's Pacific coast. The first concerns the weather. Most travel south from the border towns in Baja takes place in late fall, winter and early spring. (Most of the principal tourist areas are a bit hot during summer and early fall.) These travelers are seeking escape from a variety of adverse weather conditions north of the border. Unfortunately Baja's Pacific coast north of about Bahía Magdalena does not present a significant contrast to the weather in coastal areas of southern and central Alta California. Clearly, rain decreases as one travels south, but temperatures remain cool. Fog or low clouds often prevail. It is not the warm "swimsuit-lie-in-the-sun" weather most people envision in sunny Mexico.

The next big picture subject for the Pacific coast concerns the ocean itself. While the coast is largely deserted, there is much activity on the surface and within the ocean waters. Each year thousands of yachts cruise from San

Diego to Cabo San Lucas and beyond. Mexican fishing vessels in the 70-foot class are numerous, and these in turn are far outnumbered by shorter range, outboard-powered *pangas* engaged in fishing and lobstering. I am convinced that there is considerably more traffic on these waters than off the Pacific coast of the U.S. mainland.

Below the surface there is abundant fish life. The ocean off the central portion of the Baja peninsula is the most productive fishing area of the entire Mexican Pacific coast. These waters are also the winter home of the California gray whale, which uses Baja's protected lagoons as its calving grounds.

South of the Ensenada area there is an almost total absence of the small, tourist-owned, sportfishing boats that are commonplace in the Sea of Cortez. The reasons for this situation are the lack of launching ramps and swell and surf conditions that make launching over the beach and use of the ocean itself hazardous. Swells sweep onto the peninsula from the northwest unobstructed for thousands of miles. While they severely limit the use of small boats, they make the Pacific coast a fine area for surfing. It is also a scenic coast with its rocky outline and pounding surf. You will find the small boating and surfing situations reversed on the calmer waters of the Sea of Cortez.

Finally, as a by-product of the conditions just mentioned, the Pacific coast between Ensenada on the north, and Todos Santos on the south, has few tourist-oriented facilities. The few hotels and trailer courts are usually not visited as destinations in themselves but only as stopping points on the journey to the east coast or the peninsula's tip. The people in the towns along the Pacific side make their living from farming, cattle raising, fishing and mining. Relatively few serve the traveling public. These towns offer little of the architectural and landscaping charms common in the more tourist-oriented areas.

Baja's Sea of Cortez Coast

We will now proceed across to the eastern coast of the peninsula. The body of water between Baja California and the Mexican mainland is referred to as the Gulf of California on most maps, even those printed in Mexico. However, to most Mexicans and many North American tourists it is known as the Sea of Cortez (*Mar de Cortez*) in honor of conquistador Hernan Cortez, and that is what it will be called in this book.

Traveling south to Cabo San Lucas entirely on the Transpeninsular Highway (Highway 1) is 34 miles longer than is the combination of Highway 1 and Highway 19 through Todos Santos. Taking the former route provides access to the Sea of Cortez. An inventory of accessibility, as was done for the Pacific side, shows that 145 miles of coast are made accessible by the main highways. An additional 60 miles can be reached in the San Felipe area and this will be increased if paving of Highway 5 continues southward from Puertecitos. Fortunately, many additional miles of the coast are made accessible by secondary and less-developed roads. Also on the positive side is the fact that hundreds of miles of unroaded peninsular and offshore-island coast is available to boaters as a result of good boating conditions in the Sea of Cortez.

Campers stay on the beach north of Punta Chivato on the Sea of Cortez. The photo was taken on a windy day at an exposed location, but swells are low and gentle compared to those on the Pacific coast.

Because of the differences in the two coasts, the mileages presented are of minimal value when compared directly with each other. The key point is that relatively few miles of the main highways provide direct coastal access on either shore. Obviously the traveler needs to know where the principal tourist areas are located. This information is presented later in this chapter.

One shoreline condition applies to both coasts. Baja is a mountainous land. Where these mountains meet the sea, both coastlines are rocky, steep-faced and majestic. Beaches are small but picturesque. This situation is typical of some 75–80 percent of the Baja coasts. Vegetation is sparse and there is little soil. The mountains stand out sharply with their geologic features clearly visible. The colors and textures of their rocks are readily apparent. These coastal sections are beautiful to behold, particularly when viewed from the sea itself.

The remaining 20–25 percent of the two coasts consists of low coastal plains fronted by scores of miles of deserted beaches. Most of these are seldom visited and are on the Pacific side. In any event, you may be assured that there are miles of beautiful—although generally smaller—beaches at all of the popular tourist areas.

It is important for the traveler to realize that there are marked differences in the surf conditions between the two coasts. The Sea of Cortez lacks the pounding swells that are an ever-present condition on the Pacific side. The peninsula's picturesque rocky tip at Cabo San Lucas is generally considered to be the dividing point between the Pacific Ocean and the Sea of Cortez. The Pacific swells dissipate rapidly easterly from the cape and disappear completely approximately 50 miles to the northeast. With few swells in the Sea of Cortez, it is relatively easy to launch small boats over the beach, and swimming is far safer than on the Pacific side. While this is good news for boaters and swimmers, surfing enthusiasts will be disappointed along with those travelers who enjoy the picturesque breaking of waves on a rock-bound coast. Except during high wind conditions, the water's edge on Baja's east side takes on the characteristics of a large inland lake.

From what has been presented, you may have concluded that the Sea of Cortez coast provides home for most of the principal tourist areas in Baja; if so, you are correct.

SUMMARY COMPARISON OF PACIFIC OCEAN AND SEA OF CORTEZ

ITEM	PACIFIC OCEAN	SEA OF CORTEZ
Ocean waters	Heavy northwest swells. Boat launching difficult. Good surfing. Water is cold.	Seas flat except in high winds. Easy boat launching. Good wind-surfing and swimming.
Hotels and RV Parks	Numerous from Ensenada north. Few south of Ensenada and little-visited as destination points.	Numerous at San Felipe and in the southern half from Santa Rosalia to Cabo San Lucas.
Tourist season weather	Cool north of Bahía Magdalena, warmer to the south. Some fog. Northwest winds.	Generally warmer and dryer than the Pacific Coast. Winds from the north.
Camping	Some camping spots, but most are lightly used due to cool ocean and weather conditions.	Numerous camping spots. Many heavily used because of good ocean and weather conditions.

The Interior

A prominent backbone of mountains dominates the entire western edge of the continents of North and South America, with large "bellies" of flatter lands to the east. The mountains of Baja parallel these ranges, but in Baja the terrain is mostly backbone with relatively little "belly."

One more or less continuous chain of mountains runs the full length of the peninsula with only one brief interruption, near La Paz (See "Geologic Provinces" map). The crest of this chain rims the eastern side of the peninsula with most of the flat land found along the southern half of the Pacific coast. It is, however, important to qualify these remarks for those of you who plan to drive to Baja. While the peninsula is mountainous, traversing Baja's highways is not an arduous task for a variety of reasons that will be discussed in Chapter 3. Many of you will be exposed to artists' renditions of the peninsula's mountains on the covers and pages of maps and guidebooks. A considerable number of these are badly exaggerated and could easily frighten the faint of heart into staying home. There are many highways in the United States and Canada that traverse far more difficult terrain.

Almost all of Baja's significant cities and towns are located within a few miles of the coasts. Few are in the interior. This area's most dominant feature is man-made: the Transpeninsular Highway. By North American standards it is a modest accomplishment, but its completion in 1973 was of monumental importance for the future of Baja. It is the principal way for the tourist to travel by land to the peninsula's primary destination areas along the southern portion of the Sea of Cortez.

The interior of the peninsula also provides habitat for the best of Baja's outstanding desert vegetation. Neither coast can match the higher lands in this regard.

Mexican Mainland Coast/North Half

The area under consideration here lies directly opposite the Baja peninsula and is the eastern shore of the Sea of Cortez. (See "Transportation" map on page 35.)

Any map that depicts topography will show that most of this coastal area is composed of flat terrain. This condition extends south from the mouth of the Rio Colorado for about 1000 miles to near the town of Tepic, south of Mazatlan. While sailing along this coast, one is confronted with hundreds of miles of deserted and monotonous sandy beaches backed by sparsely vegetated, low coastal plains and marshes. From a scenic standpoint, the two Baja coastlines are hands-down winners over their mainland neighbor. The mainland highway from the United States, Highway 15, offers almost no views of the coast or the Sea of Cortez.

Still, there are some scenic areas on the mainland, the principal ones being at Bahía Kino, Guaymas and Mazatlan. These three areas, along with Puerto Penasco to the north, attract almost all the North American tourists. Guaymas, more accurately the town of San Carlos just to the north, has a large winter tourist population. It is a Mexican Phoenix, a haven for retirees and others escaping the northern winter. Mazatlan also is a fine town with excellent beaches and many tourists.

Why do so many people choose the mainland instead of Baja? It is partly a matter of transportation routes. It is closer to the mainland than to Baja from the United States intermountain west. Its cities are large and provide abundant trailer courts and hotels. Because people are attracted to other people, they feel more secure in such places. Perhaps, most importantly, Baja is remote, unknown and *over there*.

The point of this discussion is to give you the information needed to make a choice. I don't wish to downgrade the mainland, but, the scenery in Baja is better, the boating and camping areas are far more extensive, the choice of destination points is larger, the hotels are more charming, etc., etc., etc. However, should you crave the company of large numbers of your fellow North Americans in a trailer court atmosphere or at high-rise hotels, with the amenities of large nearby cities, the mainland may be best for you.

Six Principal Tourist Areas

Having sliced Baja vertically, we will now reassemble it and classify the peninsula into six principal tourist areas (See map page 25.):

> 1. **Tijuana-Ensenada Area**
>
> 2. **San Felipe-Puertecitos Area**
>
> 3. **Bahía de los Angeles**
>
> 4. **Central Coast**
>
> 5. **La Paz**
>
> 6. **The South Coast**

1. Tijuana/Ensenada Area

Poised at the international border and eager to entice North American tourists are the city of Tijuana and the smaller town of Tecate. Ensenada lies 68 miles south along the Pacific coast. Between Tijuana and Ensenada are numerous tourist-oriented subdivisions and other developments. The number of visitors to these communities is very sizeable. Tijuana boasts of being visited by more people from a foreign country than any other city in the world.

The large city of Mexicali also lies on the international border. Many people living and working in adjoining areas in the United States visit here, but it would appear that much of their activities are not related to tourism. At least in my view, Mexicali is not a tourist-oriented city.

The highlights of this area include:

(a) The most accessible area from the United States. Many visitors walk across the border to visit Tijuana. The place to go if you have only a day or two. Otherwise, head south.

(b) A bonanza for buying gifts and Mexican handicrafts of all kinds. Many of these items are typical tourist fare, but there is also much quality merchandise available.

(c) Excellent party-boat sportfishing at Ensenada.

(d) Thousands of second homes (as well as some first homes) for North Americans lie along the coast south to Punta Banda.

(e) In recent years several excellent hotels, fancy trailer courts and a golf course have been constructed along the coast between Tijuana and Ensenada. This "Between the Cities" area is thus becoming a tourist area in itself. There are very few places left for camping outside the developed trailer courts.

2. San Felipe-Puertecitos Area

San Felipe is the northernmost community along the Sea of Cortez. The town is modest in size but heavily tourist-oriented and provides all essential services. There are several good hotels. There are miles of beaches lined with housing developments, trailer courts and more modest campos. Visitation to this area will greatly increase if the paving of Highway 5 is completed south to Highway 1.

(a) The quickest way for most North Americans to hit the beach on the Sea of Cortez. It is 127 miles by highway from the border at Mexicali.

(b) Winter temperatures not as balmy as farther south, and it is hot in the summer.

(c) Many long-term trailer sites, but also a good spot for the long weekender.

(d) Puertecitos, a small town of *Norte Americano* homes, 48 miles south of San Felipe, is accessible over a paved highway.

(e) A few low hills near San Felipe provide a scenic coast, but much of the shoreline is one continuous long sandy beach backed by low coastal plains. The desert vegetation is relatively unattractive. Thus the scenery is not as good as other areas to the south, although the towering Sierra San Pedro Martir mountains are in view to the west.

(f) No nearby offshore islands, and tidal differences of up to 20 feet make small boat launching difficult.

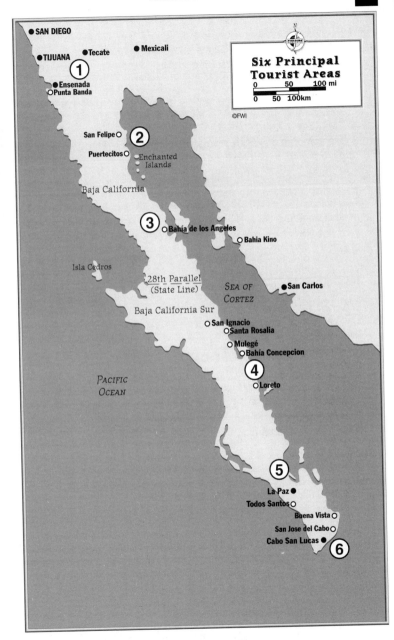

SAN DIEGO

TIJUANA ● ●Tecate ●Mexicali

①

●Ensenada
○Punta Banda

**Six Principal
Tourist Areas**

0   50   100 mi

0   50   100km

©FWI

San Felipe○ ②

Puertecitos○   ○Enchanted
                    Islands

Baja California

③ ○Bahia de los Angeles

○Bahia Kino

Isla Cedros

28th Parallel
(State Line)

SEA OF
CORTEZ

●San Carlos

Baja California Sur

○San Ignacio
○Santa Rosalia
○Mulegé
○Bahía Concepcion

④

PACIFIC
OCEAN

○Loreto

⑤

La Paz ●

Todos Santos○

Buena Vista○

San Jose del Cabo○

Cabo San Lucas ●

⑥

3. Bahía De Los Angeles

Located here is a sizeable bay with miles of beaches protected by several offshore islands. A small village offers modest services.

(a) Several hotels and RV parks. Many miles of undeveloped beaches north of the village offer camping sites.

(b) Reaching the area requires a 42-mile side trip from the Transpeninsular Highway. The total distance to Tijuana is 415 miles, making it a very long one-day trip from the border.

(c) A scenic mountainous area with a good mixture of beaches and rocky coast but with relatively unattractive desert vegetation. The nearby coast and offshore islands contain many coves and provide good boating and fishing.

(d) The least-visited of the six principal tourist areas except over the spring break-Easter Weekend, when it receives heavy visitation from north of the border.

4. Central Coast

This is one of the principal destination areas in Baja. It features one inland, and three coastal towns (San Ignacio, Santa Rosalia, Mulegé and Loreto.)

(a) Each town has its charms and all are worth exploring.

(b) The late winter and spring weather is balmy. This is what you came to Baja to experience.

(c) Several first-class hotels and other more modest ones, but fewer than farther south. Served by an international airport at Loreto.

(d) Many trailer courts and minimum facility beach-parking areas. Bahía Concepcíon is the most popular R.V. and camping area in Baja.

(e) Good combination of beaches and rocky coast backdropped by the most scenic mountains in Baja. Numerous offshore islands and coves. Fine area for fishing and overnight trips by small boat.

5. La Paz

A fine, large, modern community and the capital city of Baja California Sur. Thought by many, including myself, to be the finest large city in Mexico. Its tourist facilities are slowly increasing but at a much slower rate than at the Cape Area.

(a) Several fine luxury hotels served by an international airport, but not as fancy as at the Cape Area.

(b) City fronts the beach on a protected bay, but the main attraction here is the weather and the city itself.

(c) There are several trailer courts, but the central and south coasts are superior if your objective is to enjoy the beach and the out-of-doors.

(d) Excellent modern stores. The only really good shopping area south of the towns near the border, although there are many tourist-oriented shops at Cabo San Lucas.

(e) Good, but sometimes windy, winter weather. Winter weather not as good as in the Cape Area.

(f) Sportfishing boats are available, mostly based at nearby Bahía de los Muertos. You can use your own small boat, but other areas are better suited for such craft.

6. The South Coast

The U-shaped area capping the peninsula's southern tip has developed into three distinct zones.

The Cape Area

At the peninsula's tip and between the small communities of Cabo San Lucas and San Jose del Cabo is Baja's principal hotel, condominium and golf course area. Many developments are world-class. Construction has been going on for some 20 years and it continues at a rapid pace. Cabo is served by an international airport. There are several good trailer courts but only one is on the beach. On-your-own camping on the beach is a thing of the past.

The East Cape

On the right side of the South Coast-U is the East Cape. There are several good but modest-sized hotels, and trailer courts at and near Buena Vista. This is the place to go to experience the older Baja hotel charm without the jet-set-bustle that has developed at the Cape Area. There are many undeveloped camping sites south of Buena Vista, but an oiled highway is currently being extended from north to south along the coast, which will change the complexion of the area.

Both the Cape Area and the East Cape are famed for their marlin and other big-game fishing. This fishing is among the best in the world.

The West Cape

This section of coast was basically undeveloped until Highway 19 was completed in 1984. There is one small hotel in Todos Santos and several trailer courts and fine beach camping areas between there and the Cape. This is the area where you'll find free-lance beach campers who have been forced out of the Cape Area by urban development.

Baja's Climate

Two circumstances dominate the climate of Baja California. As is obvious to any visitor, the peninsula is an arid land. The low level of precipitation is key in determining vegetational characteristics.

Of equal but less apparent importance is the variability of the climate from one area to another, from season to season, and from year to year. Most of the time the peninsula receives no rainfall because it lies outside the normal influence of any of the major weather systems in this part of the world, but by a twist of geographic fate, it lies near the outer edge of several such systems. It is the occasional impact from these entities that creates climatic variability in Baja.

Baja lies (1) at the southern edge of the winter storms that bring plentiful rainfall to the west coast of the United States and Canada, (2) at the western perimeter of the monsoons formed over the Gulf of Mexico that bring precipitation to northern Mexico and southwestern United States in the summer, and (3) at the northeastern fringe of the region of tropical storms and hurricanes that form off the west coast of the Mexican mainland in late summer and fall.

The overall effect of these systems can be summarized by climatic zones:

1.   The air temperature along the full length of **Baja's Pacific coast** is relatively cool as the result of prevailing northwest winds that move inland over the cool waters of the Pacific Ocean.

1A.   The northern segment of the Pacific coast receives its rainfall during winter from the southern edges of the same storm systems that impact the coast of the United States and Canada. The average annual rainfall at Ensenada is about 11 inches, but from here south to Bahía Magdalena records show only three to four inches per year. The vegetation in the Vizcaino Desert at the midpoint of the peninsula is extremely scant.

1B.   Rainfall picks up along the southern Pacific coast, with Cabo San Lucas receiving an average of over nine inches per year. In contrast to area 1A, this precipitation comes mostly from high-intensity tropical storms that breed in the warm waters to the south during late summer and fall.

2.   The **Sea of Cortez coast** is much warmer than that on the Pacific side. Some of the hotels in the Cape Area close during summer. To the north, San Felipe has the highest summer temperature of any of Baja's tourist areas.

2A.   During the winter, temperatures at San Felipe are almost as chilly as at Ensenada. This coolness is aggravated by strong northerly winds funneling down the Sea of Cortez from southwestern United States. This is Baja's driest area, but what little rain does fall comes in the winter.

2B.   As on the Pacific coast, most of the rainfall comes from high-intensity tropical storms in the late fall and summer. Winter months are windy.

3.   Baja's **interior mountains** receive considerably more rainfall than either coastal area. Also, they are battered by storms in both winter and summer. The winter systems are the same as those that dampen area 1A.

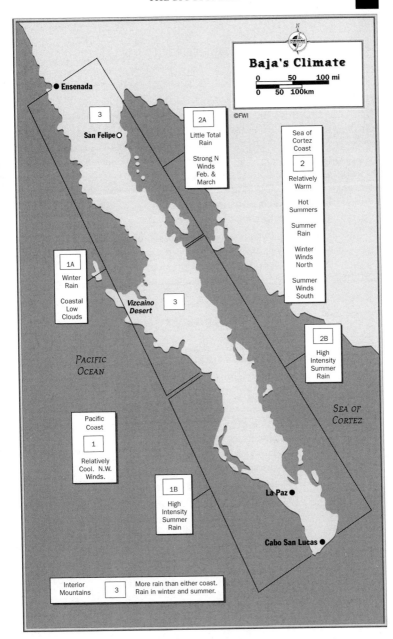

N

Baja's Climate

0   50   100 mi

0   50   100km

©FWI

● **Ensenada**

3

San Felipe ○

2A

Little Total Rain

Strong N Winds Feb. & March

Sea of Cortez Coast

2

Relatively Warm

Hot Summers

Summer Rain

Winter Winds North

Summer Winds South

1A

Winter Rain

Coastal Low Clouds

Vizcaino Desert

3

PACIFIC OCEAN

2B

High Intensity Summer Rain

SEA OF CORTEZ

Pacific Coast

1

Relatively Cool. N.W. Winds.

1B

High Intensity Summer Rain

La Paz ●

Cabo San Lucas ●

Interior Mountains

3

More rain than either coast. Rain in winter and summer.

The summer rain comes from systems in the Gulf of Mexico that also pass over the Mexican mainland and SW United States.

A final note concerning *El Niño*, an unusual warming of Pacific ocean waters off Central and North America every few years.

The winter of 1991–92 was an El Niño year. Southern California in the United States received near-record rainstorms and the Baja peninsula received abundant winter precipitation. This occurred not only in the northern area but also in the southern portions, which normally receive their rainfall in the late summer.

The result was a less than fully desirable vacation to Baja for tourists seeking endless sunshine. Travel on back roads was also hazardous due to muddy conditions. On the bright side was a wonderful display of lush desert vegetation and flowers. So keep alert to the occasional occurrence of El Niño and brace for unusual weather conditions in Baja.

In evaluating all this material, keep in mind the key factor of variability. One can only hope that you will not find yourself recovering from a trip through the arid desert one day and hiking ankle deep in the runoff from a tropical storm the next. And remember, I am not in charge of the weather. Contact You Know Who.

When to Visit

I am often asked, "When is the best time to visit Baja?" This question is best answered by asking another question, "Why do you want to visit Baja?" There are three principal answers to this latter question:

1. To Escape Bad Weather to the North

Most tourists visit Baja in the winter months (November through March). That is not when the peninsular weather is at its best, but it is when conditions at home north of the border are at their worst, and when escape is most needed. After Easter, there is a dramatic drop-off of tourism in Baja.

2. To Visit Baja for Its Own Sake

I recommend April, May and June as the best months to visit Baja. Temperatures are warm, and the often-chilly winter winds that sweep down the Sea of Cortez have ceased. Many beaches and other camping areas are uncomfortably cool and windy in the winter months. And there are far fewer other tourists with whom to contend after Easter.

3. To Get the Best Fishing

If fishing is your primary goal, go south in the summer (July through October). Air temperatures are hot and sea waters warm. The latter condition induces the game fish to migrate north into the Sea of Cortez. Summer is also the time to visit the many isolated camping and fishing areas along the cooler Pacific shore south of Ensenada.

Baja's Two States

There are two states in the Baja peninsula. The dividing line is the 28th parallel of northern latitude. (See "Six Principal Tourist Areas" map on page 25.)

There is little question that the southern state is Baja California Sur (south). Its capital city is La Paz. In contrast, there is much confusion about the name of the northern state with its capital in Mexicali. I have investigated this matter in considerable depth and can guarantee with absolute certainty that its name is *Baja California* (probably). This is the name used on state documents, stationery, license plates and many other places. Government officials have assured me that this is the proper name.

Other officials firmly attest that the name is *Baja California Norte* (north). I have seen this title on the doors of government offices and in official publications, travel guides and numerous other places. You may call it what you choose. I believe Baja California is correct.

I am advised that many Mexican citizens of Baja have solved this name complication by referring to the two states as Baja Norte (north) and Baja Sur (south). Why not.

TRANSPORTATION

This typical segment of the Transpeninsular Highway (Highway 1) is north of Bahía Concepción.

By now, the reader will have little difficulty in forecasting that it is possible to travel to Baja by land, sea or air. These alternatives will be discussed in that order.

Land Travel

Baja provides information concerning all methods of transportation, but the great majority of its readers are looking for data on the land itself and how to travel to Baja by road. Thus, much of the remainder of the book is devoted to these subjects.

The Transpeninsular Highway

The Transpeninsular Highway is Mexican Federal Highway 1 and 1-D. Officially it is La Carretera Transpeninsular Benito Juarez. It traverses the full length of the peninsula from the international border to Cabo San Lucas, a distance of 1057.468 miles to the inch. How do I know so accurately? I have consulted five references to the length of the highway, each of which is different. I have added all these offerings together and divided by five, a method I'm sure will be understood by my high school mathematics instructor who gave me a D in his subject.

The five sources provide answers from 1042 as a low to a high of 1067. For the balance of this book I will use 1059 miles, as this is the distance given on the widely used Baja map distributed by the Auto Club of Southern California. It has to be close.

Baja's citizens waited through many decades of promises by Mexico's presidential candidates before witnessing completion of the Transpeninsular Highway. At long last, on December 1, 1973, President Luis Echeverria Alvarez fulfilled his promise to build the road and dedicated its completion at the 28th parallel near Guerrero Negro. The actual completion had taken place when road building crews from north and south met the previous October near what is now named Cataviña in the plateau lands some 75 miles south of El Rosario. The president was apparently motivated to action after being treated to a trip over the old road, known to its travelers as "The Trail." By all accounts such a trip was an adventure. The new highway is a monumental leap forward.

Prior to describing Highway 1, I will repeat an opinion expressed in this book's introductory chapter. There I promised to be realistic in my descriptions of the beauty and charms of Baja, as I feel that many authors stray from reality in their use of adjectives and in their efforts to achieve literary merit. Even more disconcerting to me are those authors who create literary horror stories when providing cautionary advice. This often becomes the case when they are describing the Transpeninsular Highway. I have seen articles that would frighten even the most stout-hearted traveler into staying home. What are, in truth, reasons for caution become blown out of proportion by overly poetic adjectives and a sense of the dramatic. I will steer for the middle ground.

The Transpeninsular Highway is paved its entire distance. It is well engineered. Appropriate banking and curves allow for adequate visibility if you drive at reasonable speeds. Some 44 percent of its length is over hilly terrain, but grades (steepness) are modest and not overly demanding for vehicles

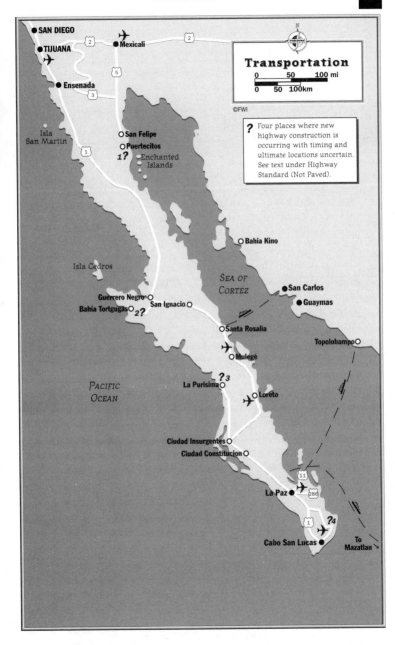

Transportation

0   50   100 mi
0   50   100km

©FWI

? Four places where new highway construction is occurring with timing and ultimate locations uncertain. See text under Highway Standard (Not Paved).

SAN DIEGO

TIJUANA

Mexicali

2

2

Ensenada

5

3

Isla San Martin

San Felipe

Puertecitos

1?

Enchanted Islands

1

Bahia Kino

Isla Cedros

SEA OF CORTEZ

San Carlos

Guaymas

Guerrero Negro

San Ignacio

Bahía Tortugas *2?*

Santa Rosalia

Topolobampo

Mulegé

?3

La Purisima

Loreto

PACIFIC OCEAN

Ciudad Insurgentes

Ciudad Constitucion

11

La Paz

286

1

?4

Cabo San Lucas

To Mazatlan

TRANSPORTATION

that are adequately powered. The remaining 56 percent passes over level ground. The highway is generally well-maintained. One frequently sees crews doing everything from cutting roadside weeds to applying new oiled surfacing. Sections of the highway may be seen in several photos in this and other chapters.

But Highway 1 does have its shortcomings, any of which can result in serious accidents or inconvenience if you violate one of two cardinal rules. These are (1) don't drive at high speeds and (2) don't drive at night. Here is a list of the negative features:

TRANSPORTATION

1. With the exception of the northerly most 80 miles, the highway is narrow. Most of it has a travel surface only 24-feet wide. Its narrowness is heightened by the almost total lack of a shoulder. There is little margin for error and if you slip off the travel surface you face the very serious threat of rolling over, particularly if you are in a recreation vehicle with a high center of gravity. Thus what is otherwise a fine highway is compromised by its lack of width.

2. Small portions of the edge of the paving tend to fall away in spots, resulting in further narrowing of the travel surface. Thus, the highway will not be a full two-lanes wide in some spots. This condition has been corrected in many places with a variety of edge-protecting techniques. However, it is still the number-one safety problem on Baja's highways.

3. A large part of Baja is open range. Thus the roadside is not fenced, and cattle and other animals may be encountered, particularly at night when they are attracted by the warmth of the road surface. I almost hit a goat on a recent field trip.

4. There are few turnouts or other places to move off the travel surface. It is not uncommon to come upon a vehicle blocking one lane of the highway while the driver is engaged in some roadside activity or correcting a mechanical problem.

5. The major arroyo crossings have been bridged; however, hundreds of the lesser crossings are designed to let water flow over the highway during storms. These dips (*vados*) provide no problem most of the time, but they can be full of water, rocks and soil during and after heavy storms.

6. There are occasional sections of potholes that can be very hard on tires if hit at high speeds. I have found that areas of potholes encountered one year have been repaired the next, but others take their place. Also, with the passage of time much of Highway 1 has received two or more layers of oiled paving. In these places the potholes only break through to the layer below and the resultant hole is only about 1 inch deep.

7. Finally, for the person of environmental sensitivity, there is one unfortunate problem with the Transpeninsular Highway. All new roads in Baja are constructed by first clearing the right-of-way of all vegetation with a bulldozer or grader. In most places various plants are returning but there is an almost total lack of the larger and more picturesque species that make the Baja desert spectacular. The vegetation is often outstanding but unfortunately is a few yards removed.

Traveling the Transpeninsular Highway can be a safe and rewarding experience if it is driven at reasonable speeds during daylight hours. Insurance industry data indicate that some 80 percent of the accidents on Baja's highways occur at night. And, what are safe speeds? A travel time estimate provided by one of the Mexican insurance companies indicates that it would take 23-3/4 hours to drive the 991 miles from Ensenada to Cabo San Lucas. This equates to 42 miles per hour. I would have estimated 40 miles per hour. You can do it faster, but you should not.

Baja's Other Roads

From 1973 until about 1983 there were few paved roads other than the Transpeninsular Highway. The location of this road appears to have been planned to connect the peninsula's principal communities over the most cost-effective route. As stressed in the second chapter, it provides little direct access to the seaside areas most sought after by tourists.

From 1983 until about 1989, many additional miles of unpaved (but otherwise highway-standard) roads were constructed along with hundreds of miles of gravel-surfaced secondary roads. This time period was clearly Baja's era of road construction. Little new highway or secondary road construction of interest to the tourist has taken place since 1989. However, there has been much road paving and landscaping in many of the peninsula's communities. As a result their appearance has been much improved. Also, sections of Highway 5 south of Mexicali and the southern most section of Highway 1 have been upgraded to four-lane divided highways.

Baja's roads may be classified rather neatly into four classes. These are described below.

Highways (Paved)

There are approximately 800 miles of main paved highways in Baja in addition to the Transpeninsular Highway. Roughly 550 miles are in the northern state of Baja California, with the remaining 250 in Baja California Sur. These figures do not include a considerable additional mileage of paved roads within the Valle de Mexicali agricultural area adjoining the international border and occasional short roads in other places.

I have driven all 800 miles of these highways and have concluded that they have all been engineered to approximately the same standards as the

Transpeninsular Highway. Thus, they are all adequate facilities and in general are safer than the Transpeninsular Highway as there is often less traffic and fewer wide trucks, buses and recreational vehicles. Most of these 800 miles of highway are shown on the "Transportation" map in this chapter.

The only totally new recreation-oriented section of paved highway to appear since 1989 is the extension of Highway 11 (north of La Paz) from Pichilingue to Tocolote.

Highway Standard (Not Paved)

In Baja, all construction work up to final paving is usually completed several years before surfacing is applied. There are about 250 miles of these roads, constructed to highway standards, but still awaiting finished grading and their oiled surface. These are the four projects shown as numbered question marks on the "Transportation" map. Following is a brief status report on these four areas:

1. San Felipe south to Highway 1—This highway has been paved south to Puertecitos for several years and is well maintained. The remaining portion has had no further improvement and has deteriorated in some places. It is very washboarded. If it is eventually completed it will provide a major new alternative route of travel from the United States to southern Baja.

2. Highway 1 to Bahía Tortugas—The oiled surface was extended westerly for 22 miles some years ago, but no further extension has occurred. The balance of the road is smoother than most of Baja's other unpaved roads.

3. Ciudad Insurgentes Northward—The oiled surface has been completed from Ciudad Insurgentes to the town of San Isidro. I am informed that a highway toll road may eventually be constructed farther northward to San Ignacio, but it is not an imminent project.

4. The East Cape—The paved surface has been completed from Highway 1, southward past La Ribera, to 10 miles north of Bahía Los Frailes. The remainder of the road south to San Jose del Cabo is often in rough condition. This section was scheduled to be completed and paved by presstime. Time will tell.

The pit-run gravel used for the subsurface of these projects is often quite coarse, as it is not intended as the final surface. Thus, some unpaved sections of these roads quickly become very rough and badly washboarded. Travel speeds are usually substantially less than over much lower-standard dirt roads. One of my traveling companions once noticed a dump truck loaded with 8- to 10-inch-diameter stones destined for someone's rock wall. He said, "There goes a load of road gravel." It's not that bad, but be prepared for a bumpy ride. As with the secondary roads described below, this class of roads are best suited for pickups and vans.

This portion of the secondary road is in steep mountain country between Loreto and the famous mission at San Javier. Most secondary roads are located on far more level terrain.

Secondary Roads (Unpaved)

A decade or so ago, one could say that there were only two standards of roads in Baja: (1) the paved highways and (2) all the others, which were of the "two tracks in the desert" variety. As previously noted, this is no longer the case. There are now hundreds of miles of dirt and gravel-surfaced roads of intermediate standard. The majority have been built to provide improved road access to Mexicans living in small towns or on ranches. In many cases these roads also serve the needs of the recreational traveler who wants to get away from the more heavily used areas. As these areas become more and more crowded, these secondary roads will become increasingly important.

These roads are 1-1/2 to two lanes in width. Some sections are wider and some are narrower. In most places, you can pass an oncoming car, but slowing down and keeping well to the right are often necessary. The surface is sometimes composed of native soil and gravel; in other places, a better grade of gravel has been imported. In all cases, the travel surface has been constructed by earthmoving equipment and is free of large rocks and similar obstacles. With few exceptions, secondary roads are those shown as "Graded Dirt Road" on the widely used Baja road map produced by the Southern California Automobile Association.

Secondary roads are infrequently graded. When recent maintenance has occurred, one can travel in the 20–40 m.p.h. range. More often you will be greeted by miles of washboarding and occasionally by rutting caused by erosion and wet-weather use. As this rough road surface is common, consider letting some of the air out of your tires to soften the washboard shock.

You will also be faced with a choice dictated by the 4–40 rule. That is, drive slowly (4 m.p.h.) to cooperate with the surface, or fly over the tops of the ridges at 40 m.p.h. Most owners of the vehicle they are driving will choose the former alternative. (You actually will average in the 10–20 m.p.h. range.) However, brace yourself for meeting some of the local citizens flying low with the fishing-co-op pickup.

These secondary roads have been *engineered*. By that I mean that the surface may have been built-up (turnpiked) above the natural terrain and there are often hard surfaced arroyo crossings and an occasional culvert. Also, there are sometimes kilometer posts and usually directional signs where these roads join the main highways. Curves and grades are modest; in most cases these roads have been constructed in areas of gentle topography. If you become alert to these characteristics of an engineered road, you can be reasonably assured that you are on the type of facility that I am describing and that washboarding will be the worst of your troubles. Be careful after storms, however, as even these engineered roads will become slick and sometimes impassable when wet.

My impression of such roads is the same as for the main highways; that is, that they all seem to have been constructed to about the same standard. To a large degree, when you have seen one, you have seen them all, and you can develop confidence in using them for recreational travel. Keep in mind that while the chief problem with the main highway system is lack of width, the weak points of secondary roads are washboarding and slick or muddy surfaces after storms.

The Grand Tour in Part III provides maps and details concerning such roads and the places they serve. These routes will be referred to as secondary roads. This term will not be used for lower standard facilities.

Other Roads (Dirt Surface)

There are thousands of miles of lower-standard dirt roads in Baja. Some have been built by a bulldozer pushing its way through the desert. Typically, the surfaces of such roads are lower than the surrounding terrain. They are not built-up as indicated for the secondary roads. Other roads simply developed as the result of vehicular use. Such roads provide access to scores of isolated ranches, fish camps and miles of coastline. They are generally unsuitable for sedans and large recreational vehicles; however, for those with vans and lightly loaded pickups, these roads offer endless possibilities. Often

Dawn at Cabo Lazaro

Dolphins frolic in the Sea of Cortez.

California grey whale, San Ignacio Lagoon

Desert and sky create a natural drama.

Roadside explorers

Uncrowded shoreside campsites are a fisherman's dream-come-true.

their travel surfaces are smoother than are those of secondary roads and un-paved highways, but they will be narrow and harbor steep trouble spots at arroyo crossings. Directional signs are rare. These roads will be referred to as *dirt roads.*

Backcountry Travel

This section concerns traveling on Baja's many secondary and lesser-standard roads. In this regard I am often asked, "Do you need four-wheel-drive in Baja?" The answer is "No." I have visited scores of isolated villages and ranches by land and sea, and seeing a Mexican with a four-wheel-drive vehicle is very unusual. The workhorse of the economy is the standard pickup truck and, until recently, all of my investigative work has been done with such a vehicle. One can go *almost* everywhere with two-wheel-drive. But keep in mind that I just said *almost* everywhere. If you have a four-wheel-drive vehicle, by all means take it to Baja, as it will add a positive new dimension to your travels.

The comments that follow have been prepared in consultation with Bob and Jean Evans, longtime members of the Vagabundos del Mar, and four-wheel-drive travelers in Baja since 1965. They report that 98 percent of their off-highway travel in Baja is in standard drive, but it is that remaining two percent that makes the difference for them. With only standard drive one must frequently stop just short of that special place to camp. A four-wheel-drive vehicle allows one to travel onto the beach, out on rocky ledges overlooking the sea, or into sandy arroyos seeking the shade of the desert's only trees. Four-wheel power allows for a steady climb up steep pitches where other vehicles have scraped deep ruts while spinning their tires. But most importantly to the Evans is the peace of mind they have in knowing that their vehicle will take them to the places they really want to go.

Repairs and Fuel

Two problems concerning travel in Baja do not relate directly to the roadways. These are vehicle repairs and fuel supplies.

Repairs

Except when driving in the heat of summer, there is little reason why a vehicle should have more repair problems in Baja than north of the border. The difficulty arises when something does happen. With the exception of Ensenada, Ciudad Constitucion, La Paz and the border cities, full-service repair facilities and parts stores are few and far between. The prudent driver will always carry spare belts, hoses, filters and a tool kit. But, sadly, our modern cars contain little under the hood that most of us can repair.

During one field trip, our transmission died. We had to be towed 100 miles to La Paz, where we spent 18 days waiting for a new transmission from the United States. It never arrived and we settled for a rebuilt model fashioned from parts from our deceased edition and those from a convenient wreck. All of this in La Paz, a city of 160,000 people that even offers an authorized agency for our make of vehicle.

I recommend that you obtain the name and phone number of an authorized dealer in the San Diego area for your make of vehicle before leaving for Mexico. Should you have a serious breakdown and need parts not available in Baja, call this agency. If they are experienced in shipping parts to Baja and can assure you of help, let them assist you. If not, your best course of action is to travel to San Diego, acquire the needed parts and bring them back to Baja personally.

On one of our previous trips, my wife and I gave a lift to a young lady whose car had serious engine trouble. We delivered her to the machine shop *(taller mecanico)* in Loreto. Its floor was the native surface and there was very little roof. Its benches and the surrounding area were littered with tools and the remains of automotive disasters of previous decades. These wrecks serve as the "parts department." We did our best for our friend but do not know how she fared.

At a similar facility in another town, I was in need of a tire-pressure gauge and asked the owner if I might borrow one. When he headed for the refrigerator I thought I had been misunderstood. Alas, the refrigerator had long outlived its original calling and now served as a tool cache, the only place in the entire facility that would remain dry in the event of rain.

The favorable news is that I have found the Baja mechanics to be good at their trade. They have to be, in a land where new cars in top running order are relatively few in number. I have also found them to be friendly and eager to help, in sharp contrast to what one often finds you-know-where. The other saving feature is the Green Angels (*Angeles Verdes*), a service of the Mexican government. They patrol the Transpeninsular, and other main highways, in their green-and-white pickup trucks. There is usually a crew of two, one of whom speaks English. They carry a limited supply of spare parts, gasoline, oil and water and perform minor repairs at no charge. Parts are sold at cost. While you may have to wait a few hours, help is always on the way.

Fuel

Mexico's fuel supplies are another subject where some travel authors rejoice in painting an unrealistically pessimistic picture. I sometimes feel that the poor conditions that were present in the past are copied from one author to the next and passed on like old wives' tales. Their most common accusation is that Mexican fuel is filled with impurities. I am sure some drivers have experienced this problem, but I have motored my diesel-powered sailboat over 10,000 miles on Mexican fuel and changed a filter only once. I have never had to change a filter in my pickup. It stands to reason that the highways would be lined with stalled vehicles if unclean fuel were a serious problem.

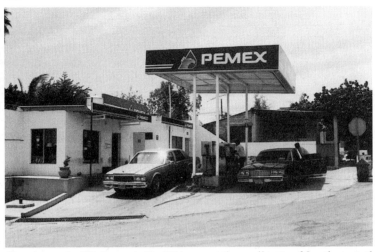

Here is a typical Baja gas station (this one at the small town of Santiago south of La Paz). The logo on the sign is the same at every station in Baja.

Also good news is the fact that gasoline and diesel prices are the same almost everywhere because fuel is sold through a government marketing monopoly. Each station bears the same sign, PEMEX *(Petroleos Mexicanos)*. If all else fails, look for the pumps. The green pump is for MAGNA SIN, a 92-octane unleaded fuel. The blue pump dispenses NOVA, which is an 82-octane regular gas containing tetraethyl lead. Diesel fuel, spelled the same in English and Spanish, comes from the red pumps.

In the past, gas stations were not always open for a variety of reasons and there was difficulty obtaining fuel along the 221-mile section of Highway 1 between El Rosario and Guerrero Negro. In recent years both of these problems have been greatly reduced, but it is still wise to never let your fuel supply drop below the halfway point. Also, in past years, many Baja gas stations did not carry unleaded gas. However, our last survey found that all but only the most remote stations had MAGNA SIN pumps.

Occasionally someone will attempt to overcharge you at a PEMEX station. Beware of pumps with inoperable or taped-over price gauges. The attendant will tell you what you owe by multiplying the number of liters pumped by the price per liter; or perhaps his version of the price per liter. Check him out.

Finally, you may be happy to find that station attendants actually pump gas for you; the self-service era has penetrated south of the border at only a few

TRANSPORTATION

stations. Young boys also often climb on your hood to wash the windows for a few pesos. Contribute to the cause.

Maps and Road Directions

The maps and directions contained in this book are fully adequate for recreational travelers using the main highways and principal secondary roads. However, I strongly recommend that you obtain the *Baja California Road Map* published by the Automobile Club of Southern California (AAA). This is an outstanding publication that is available at club offices as a free service to its members. This map shows all four classes of roads described in this chapter. Obtain road maps before going to Baja as they are hard to find once you are in the peninsula.

Railroads

Baja was linked to the Mexican mainland by railroad in 1948. This line now proceeds north from Mexicali into the United States and eventually returns to Baja at Tecate and then to Tijuana. Most of this Tecate to Tijuana segment appears to receive very little use. However, in recent years, vintage passenger cars have been used to run from the U.S. town of Campo, California southwest to Tecate. This 45-minute train ride terminates at the Tecate brewery, where it is reported that passenger's spirits are revived with samples of the brewer's output. Campo is located on California Highway 94 west of San Diego.

Trains from Mexicali make regularly scheduled runs southeastward to the Mexican mainland. The Mexicali train links up with the main line from Nogales to Mexico City at Benjamin Hill. The trip to Mexico City is scheduled to take about 48 hours, although I am advised that connection problems in Guadalajara add an extra day. En route, it passes through Guaymas, Mazatlan and Guadalajara. The line then continues east from Mexico City to the Yucatan peninsula and its Mayan ruins.

I have made this run from Mexicali as far as Guadalajara, and can recommend it for the not-too-faint-of-heart. I have also made, and can thoroughly recommend, a related side rail trip from Los Mochis to Creel near Copper Canyon. The Pullman and other passenger cars are of 1940 vintage, which actually allows you to open up the windows; there is no choking from the air conditioning. You won't see much of Baja, but Mexicali is the starting point for these railroad adventures. Train reservations may be acquired through **Romero's Mexico Service**, *1600 West Coast Highway, Newport Beach CA 92663,* ☎ *(714) 548-8931.*

Buses

Several bus companies provide frequent service between Tijuana, Mexicali and mainland Mexico along Highway 2. They operate from the *Central de*

Autobuses (Central Bus Terminal) located near the airport in Tijuana. (See "Tijuana" map on page 314). Two of these lines, *Tres Estrellas de Oro* (Three Stars of Gold) and *ABC* (Autobuses Baja California) also traverse Highway 1 from Tijuana to La Paz. The trip takes about 26 hours. The most commonly observed bus line in Baja is *Autotransportes Aguila.*

Bus service in Mexico is rated as super-deluxe, deluxe, first, second and third class. The third-class buses are affectionately referred to as "chicken buses" as they often are used to transport members of the animal kingdom other than man. Tourists are advised to utilize only the first-class or higher services. Seats on these buses are reserved, but you must acquire your reservations and tickets in person.

There are usually two drivers on the longer runs. One drives while the other rests. I have found the service and quality of Mexican buses to be very good. If I were asked to compare the overall deportment and other characteristics of the people on Mexican buses with those in the United States, I would cast my vote for south of the border.

Rental Cars

Rental cars are available in Tijuana, Mexicali, Loreto, La Paz and at the Cape. On our last visit the Los Cabos airport boasted four car agencies. The major companies are the same as those serving the United States and Canada. Reservations may be made by calling these firms' 800 telephone numbers. It is not normally possible to rent a car in Tijuana and drop it off in the southern part of the peninsula.

Tourists renting a car at La Paz or the two Cape communities can easily make the Highway 1–Highway 19 loop and return their car at the point of origin.

Car Rental Phone Numbers

Avis

☎ *(800) 331-1084*
☎ *(800) 879-2847 (in Canada)*

Budget

☎ *(800) 527-0700*
0800/188-1818 (in U.K.)

Hertz

☎ *(800) 654-3001*
☎ *(800) 263-0600 (in Canada)*
0181/679-1799 (in U. K.)

National Interrent

☎ *(800) 227-3876*
0181/950-5050 (in U.K.)

Ocean Travel

Ocean Liners

Thousands of people make the passage to Baja each year in pleasure craft of various types and sizes. At the opposite end of the ocean travel spectrum is the growing number of tourists who can now experience a few hours stopover at Cabo San Lucas while their ocean liner lies at anchor in the bay. As it has been for centuries, Cabo is a natural stopover point for vessels plying the sea. Its inner harbor provides tourist facilities at the water's edge but is too small and shallow for the large cruise vessels. Passengers make the trip to and from the anchorage in ships' launches.

During a trip to Cabo San Lucas, my wife and I encountered an elderly lady who had arrived in this manner. The lady asked how we had made our journey. We replied that we had driven in our camper. Her response was, "You mean there is some kind of giant bridge to this island?" My wife provided a brief geography lesson. In an act of great restraint, I refrained from advising her that the Spanish explorer Francisco de Ulloa discovered that the Baja peninsula was not an island in 1539.

In contrast to Cabo San Lucas, Baja's Pacific coast port city of Ensenada can accommodate ocean liners at dockside. In recent years, liners have made the run from San Pedro, California, (the port of Los Angeles) to Ensenada on a regular basis.

In 1991 a passenger dock and terminal suitable for large ocean liners was completed within the harbor of Pichilingue 10 miles from the city of La Paz in an effort to lure the ocean cruising trade to that community. To date it has had little or no use and was being used as a tuna clipper dock at press time. Contract your travel agent for details concerning ships to both Ensenada and La Paz.

The 143-foot, 80-passenger *Pacific Northwest Explorer* provided cruises into the Sea of Cortez in past years. This service was discontinued at press time but may reappear in the future.

Ferry Service

The Sea of Cortez ferry routes are shown on the "Transportation" map in this chapter. Keep in mind that this schedule periodically changes. The system offers more frequent service in the winter than it does during the summer. Also, there may be lengthy delays and cancellations of reservations when the ferries do not operate due to storm conditions or mechanical breakdowns. Fog at the entrance to the Topolobampo harbor on the Mexican mainland and constricted entrance conditions at Santa Rosalia often cause delays in the run between these two ports. Wise travelers will maintain a flexible schedule when planning to use the ferry system.

The La Paz, a typical vessel in the ferry system serving Baja, is docked at Pichilingue near La Paz.

The Santa Rosalia ferry terminal is located inside the man-made harbor at this community. The La Paz ferry docks within the natural harbor of Pichilingue located 17 km (10.5 miles) from downtown La Paz over a blacktop highway. There is also a ferry terminal inside the man-made harbor at Cabo San Lucas, but the service from there to Puerto Vallarta was discontinued in 1989.

About 1990, the ferry system was sold by the Mexican government to private interests *(Grupo SEMATUR de California)*. As a result the formerly subsidized prices have risen sharply. Rates for auto and recreational vehicles are based upon length, prices ranged from $115 to $393 between Mazatlan and La Paz; $70 to $126 between Topolobampo and La Paz; and $81 to $275 between Guaymas and Santa Rosalia. Reservations may be made by phone to any of the ferry offices or at the toll-free national (Mexico) number, ☎ *[91] (800) 6-96-96.*

The ferry system has become the lifeline for southern Baja California. Food and endless other commodities are carried by ferry on large trucks and truck containers transported from the mainland. It is thus becoming increasingly more difficult to secure ferry reservations for recreational vehicles. Passenger traffic has also increased and I have had reports of tourists having to buy tickets from scalpers at dockside.

Procedures for using the La Paz ferry are a bit complex since the ferry terminal and the La Paz reservation office are not at the same location. Using the system at Santa Rosalia is simpler as the two facilities are in one building. (See "Santa Rosalia" and "La Paz" maps for locations of the ferry offices.)

There are four passenger classes. Salon Class passengers are entitled to one of the numerous seats located throughout the ferry. Reservations are given for this general seating area. Advance reservations are required for *Turista* Class (cabins with toilet facilities outside the room) and Cabina Class (cabins with toilets). There is also a new *Especial* Class for the luxury-minded.

A temporary export permit is required for any vehicle using the ferry system. It is best to take care of this procedure at Tijuana or the other ports of entry. In La Paz, it may be obtained at the office of the *Registro Federal de Vehiculos*, located near the corner of Belisario Dominguez and 5 de Febrero.

Air Travel

Since the early 1970s, air travel has both increased and decreased in importance as a means of transportation to Baja. This seeming contradiction is explained by the fact that commercial jet travel has substantially grown due to the construction of international airports and many new hotels in the peninsula's southern half. In contrast, the completion of the Transpeninsular Highway in 1973 has considerably lowered the tourist industry's reliance on travelers who transport themselves in small private aircraft.

Commercial Air Transportation

Commercial aviation has gained in importance as the hotel industry has expanded.

Airports

There are five airports that serve modern jet aircraft. A sixth has been constructed south of Santa Rosalia but has yet to be utilized. (See "Transportation" map.) Two of these accommodate the border area at Tijuana and Mexicali, but these two cities are seldom the destination points of North Americans traveling to Mexico for recreational purposes.

The three airports in the peninsula's southern half receive nearly all the tourist traffic from the United States and Canada. The La Paz airport has been in existence for some time, while those at Loreto and Los Cabos were constructed since 1975, in tandem with major new resort facilities sponsored by FONATUR, a government tourist development agency. The Los Cabos airport has now been enlarged so it may accommodate jumbo jets

Almost all of Baja's cities and towns have airstrips, and several of these are served by propeller-driven aircraft on a scheduled or nonscheduled basis. The more prominent of these places are Ciudad Constitucion, Ensenada, Guerrero Negro, Bahía Tortugas, Mulege, Santa Rosalia, Isla Cedros and several of the larger southern hotels. Relatively few tourists use these facilities, but it is comforting to know that they are available in case of emergencies.

Airport Tax

As in most places in the world, there is an airport tax. In flying into Mexico, it somehow is magically taken care of in the cost of the ticket; however, in leaving the country one must pay the tax at an airport ticket stand, and the price may be quoted only in pesos. This system causes considerable distress to some tourists who do not understand Spanish, have no pesos left and suspect that the whole process may be a local extortion operation. It is best to find out the amount of the tax in advance and save a few pesos for that purpose. It's all quite simple, although why they don't combine the tax with the ticket price is a great mystery, except perhaps to the ticket-seller's union.

Airlines

Mexican-operated, Mexicana and Aero California are the principal regularly scheduled jet-equipped airlines serving Baja's resort areas from points in the United States. U.S. carriers join in the peninsular market from time to time. Alaska Airlines has been prominent here in recent years. The Mexican airlines fly a variety of U.S.-made aircraft, and the service is as good or better than it is north of the border. See your travel agent for details.

There are also several air charter companies based in Southern California that serve Baja. Among these are **Air Charter Express**, *6714 Avenida Andorra, La Jolla, CA 92037;* ☎ *(619) 993-5861.*

Airport Ground Transportation

Most air travelers know that getting to and from the airport is often more complex and tiring than the flight itself. At the three southern Baja airports there is ample van-type transportation to all tourist facilities. Prices are moderate and are often included in hotel accommodation packages. Taxis also are plentiful and one is required to use them to return to the airports as a concession to the taxi unions. As a result both taxis and vans run empty during half of the airport round-trip. One hotel operator informed me the government has refused permission for him to provide the hotel's own airport shuttle, but several hotel mini-buses were observed using the Los Cabos airport.

The Loreto airport is only three miles from the main resort areas. From Los Cabos airport it is about 10 miles to the San Jose del Cabo resorts and 27 miles to Cabo San Lucas. The La Paz airport is about five miles from the downtown area.

Private Flying

People flying to Baja in small private aircraft share with the ocean cruisers a means of savoring the peninsula's truly unique features. Unfortunately their choice of landing strips has been greatly reduced in recent years as the Mexican government has closed many of the smaller landing fields as a means of combatting drug traffic.

Some of the peninsula's hotels and resorts have nearby landing strips, although their number has decreased in recent years. Other small, isolated, overnight facilities that cater to the fly-in trade are beyond the scope of this book. The traveler's aircraft can often be tied down within a few yards of their lodging, and management takes special pains to attend to those who fly in. Virtually all Baja towns have a community airstrip; thus almost all of the peninsula's hotels and resorts are readily available to the small plane pilot.

RECREATIONAL VEHICLES AND CAMPING

Beach camping at Santispac on Bahía Coyote is very popular. This site directly adjoins Highway 1 and is used as a convenient stopover point.

This chapter was entitled "Camping" in the first version of this book. I have adapted the present title as the passage of time in Baja has made it evident that camping with tents and minimum facility vehicles, and the use of motorhomes and larger recreational vehicles, are two quite different activities. Likewise, for the most part, they take place at different places and provide different recreation experiences.

Recreational Vehicles

Recreational vehicles make up a significant portion of the traffic one sees on Baja's highways. While increasing numbers of tourists are traveling to Baja in private automobiles, such vehicles do not dominate the scene as they do north of the border. Recreational vehicles that travel south include bicycles, motorcycles, sport-utility vehicles, vans, pickup campers, trailers and motorhomes of all sizes. Most of you will travel to Baja in the vehicle you already own and will not venture forth to buy one based on reading this book. However, you do need to understand the relationship of your particular RV to conditions in Baja.

All of life is a compromise. The owner of an RV must choose between *accessibility* and *accommodations*. Smaller, lighter vehicles can go to far more places than their larger cousins. Obviously there are more creature comforts in the larger motorhomes and trailers. While these conditions are also true in the United States and Canada, the contrast is considerably greater in Baja. This is why the marked differences between the classes of roads were stressed in the previous chapter.

Most users of larger RVs do not stray far from paved highways and tend to congregate in developed RV parks. The risk of an accident is also increased when these large, top-heavy rigs have to pass oncoming vehicles on Baja's narrow highways. In contrast, the smaller vehicles commonly use all classes of roads. As a result, their owners can access much more of Baja and can escape the more heavily used areas that are close to the paved highways.

Remember, also, that the principal negative feature of unpaved highways and secondary roads is their rough surface. If you are willing to subject your motor home, its passengers and contents to washboard shock treatment, there is little other reason why larger rigs cannot be driven on many of these roads in dry weather. In fact, one occasionally finds them in the strangest places, although it is very unusual to see a trailer on such roads.

To complete this discussion, I need to convey a definition of *smaller RV* and *larger RV* as these terms will be used frequently throughout the book. Motorcycles, sport-utility vehicles, vans and pickup trucks with low, shell-type campers clearly fall into the former group. Most single-purpose motorhomes and trailers are clearly in the latter. My early travels on the Baja Peninsula used a 3/4-ton pickup truck with a powerful 454-cubic-inch engine. Equipped with an 8-foot cab-over camper, it fell midway between the small and large RV groups.

In the past I frequently used this pickup-camper combination on secondary and unimproved dirt roads, but occasionally found myself in places where I wish I had not ventured, due primarily to the top-heaviness of the camper.

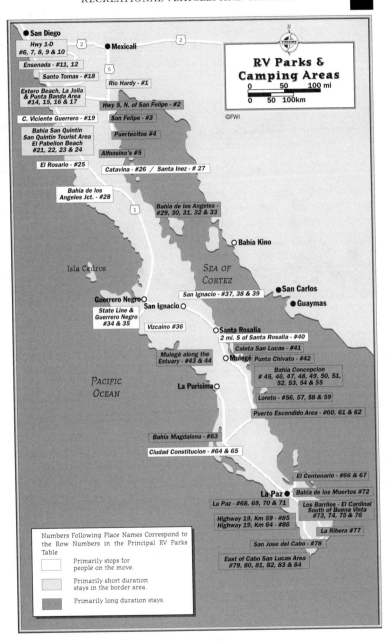

RV Parks & Camping Areas

0   50   100 mi
0   50   100km

©FWI

- San Diego
- Hwy 1-D #6, 7, 8, 9 & 10
- Mexicali
- Ensenada - #11, 12
- Santo Tomas - #18
- Rio Hardy - #1
- Estero Beach, La Jolla & Punta Banda Area #14, 15, 16 & 17
- Hwy 5, N. of San Felipe - #2
- C. Vicente Guerrero - #19
- San Felipe - #3
- Bahia San Quintin San Quintin Tourist Area El Pabellon Beach #21, 22, 23 & 24
- Puertecitos #4
- El Rosario - #25
- Alfonsina's #5
- Catavina - #26 / Santa Inez - # 27
- Bahia de los Angeles Jct. - #28
- Bahia de los Angeles - #29, 30, 31, 32 & 33
- Bahia Kino
- Isla Cedros
- SEA OF CORTEZ
- Guerrero Negro
- San Ignacio - #37, 38 & 39
- San Carlos
- State Line & Guerrero Negro #34 & 35
- San Ignacio
- Guaymas
- Vizcaino #36
- Santa Rosalia
- 2 mi. S of Santa Rosalia - #40
- Caleta San Lucas - #41
- Mulegé along the Estuary - #43 & 44
- Mulegé Punta Chivato - #42
- Bahia Concepcion # 45, 46, 47, 48, 49, 50, 51, 52, 53, 54 & 55
- PACIFIC OCEAN
- La Purisima
- Loreto - #56, 57, 58 & 59
- Puerto Escondido Area - #60, 61 & 62
- Bahia Magdalena - #63
- Ciudad Constitucion - #64 & 65
- El Centenario - #66 & 67
- La Paz Bahia de los Muertos #72
- La Paz - #68, 69, 70 & 71
- Los Barriles - El Cardinal South of Buena Vista #73, 74, 75 & 76
- Highway 19, Km 59 - #85
- Highway 19, Km 64 - #86
- La Ribera #77
- San Jose del Cabo - #78
- East of Cabo San Lucas Area #79, 80, 81, 82, 83 & 84

Numbers Following Place Names Correspond to the Row Numbers in the Principal RV Parks Table

- Primarily stops for people on the move.
- Primarily short duration stays in the border area.
- Primarily long duration stays.

For these reasons I switched to a lightweight shell-type camper. This allowed travel almost everywhere where I could enjoy camping in secluded settings. Obviously creature comforts are minimal and when I have to stay at a trailer court I am ill at ease sitting on my tailgate while large motorhomes tower over me on either side. These comments clearly illustrate the decision you need to make between *accessibility* or *accommodations* for camping in Baja.

RV Parks and Camping Areas

Map and Tables

The tables in this chapter list the principal RV parks and camping areas in Baja. Their locations are shown in an accompanying map. The site numbers on the map correspond to those in the tables.

No	LOCATION	NAME	COMMENTS
	PRINCIPAL RV PARKS AND CAMPING AREAS *Indicates Full Hookups		
1	Rio Hardy	Several Campos	Used mostly as camps for bird hunting & river fishing.
2	Hwy 5, N. of San Felipe	Many Campos on Beach	A mixed bag of beach camping and permanent sites.
3	San Felipe	12 Trailer Courts	11 in town, 1 south of town. See San Felipe map.*
4	Puertecitos	Puertecitos Resort	Parking areas adjoining the Puertecito Motel.
5	Alfonsina's Village	Villas Mar de Cortez	Beachfront Palapa area near new airstrip.
6	Hwy 1-D, Km A-22	KOA Trailer Court	Pleasant hillside location. Lots of transient spaces.*
7	Hwy 1-D, Km A-25	Oasis Hotel–RV Resort	High-class & expensive. On the beach.*
8	Hwy 1-D, Km A-71	Mal Paso Trailer Park	Parking on beach but with poor facilities.*
9	Hwy 1-D, Km A-72	Baja Seasons	High-class & expensive. On the beach.*
10	Hyw 1-D, Km A-99	San Miguel Village	Minimum facility parking on level area near beach.
11	North edge of Ensenada	California Trailer Park	Good park. Part of California Trailer Park and Motel.*
12	Ensenada, downtown	Campo Playa	Only court in downtown Ensenada. Pleasant.*
13	South edge of Ensenada	Joker Hotel & RV Park	Pleasant park along highway adjoining motel.
14	Estero Beach	Estero Beach Resort	First-class court adjoining hotel. On lagoon near ocean.*

PRINCIPAL RV PARKS AND CAMPING AREAS
* Indicates Full Hookups

No	LOCATION	NAME	COMMENTS
15	La Jolla	La Jolla Beach Camp	Permanent leased sites but with parking area for transients.
16	La Jolla	Villarino RV Park	Permanent leased sites but with parking area for transients.
17	Punta Banda Area	4 camps	See Punta Bando Area Map. Minimum facility camps.
18	Santo Tomas	El Palomar Trailer Court	Caters to weekend groups. Pleasant spot in olive grove.*
19	C. Viciente Guerrero	Don Pepes	Restaurant. A mixture of permanent and transient sites.*
20	C. Viciente Guerrero	Posada Don Diego	Restaurant. A large area used as a stopover by caravans.*
21	Bahía San Quintin	Old Mill Motel	Large area next to the Old Mill Motel.*
22	Bahía San Quintin	Muelle Viego	On bluff overlooking the bay. Pleasant—minimum facilities.
23	San Quintin Tourist Area	Cielito Lindo Motel.	Poor facilities near beach. Better park adjoining motel.
24	El Pabellon Beach	El Pabellon	Minimum facility area on the beach.*
25	El Rosario	Sinai Motel	A simple parking area behind the Sinia Motel in town.*
26	Cataviña	Government Court	A pleasant, safe, landscaped place to park but no facilities.
27	Santa Inez near Cataviña	Rancho Santa Inez	A cleared area for parking near small motel and cafe.
28	Bahía de los Angeles Jct.	Government Court	A pleasant, safe, landscaped place to park but no facilities.
29	Bahía de los Angeles	Villa Vitta RV Court	Unaesthetic court but on the beach.*
30	Bahía de los Angeles	Guerrmo's Trailer Court	Unaesthetic court but on the beach.*
31	Bahía de los Angeles	Brisa Marina RV Park	Old government park near beach. No facilities.
32	Bahía de los Angeles	Tony Resendiz	Adjoining #31.
33	Bahía de los Angeles	Playa la Gringa	At Punta la Gringa north of Bahía de los Angeles village.
34	State Line	Government Court	A pleasant, safe, landscaped place to park. Modest facilities.*
35	Guerrero Negro	Several courts in town	Parking areas adjoining motels on north side of highway into town.*

RECREATIONAL VEHICLES AND CAMPING

PRINCIPAL RV PARKS AND CAMPING AREAS
* Indicates Full Hookups

No	LOCATION	NAME	COMMENTS
36	Vizcaino	Kaadekaman	Court under development adjoining Highway 1.*
37	San Ignacio	Government Court	A landscaped parking area. Modest facilities. Near PEMEX.
38	San Ignacio	Manual Quezada RV	Pleasant parking area in palms on road into town.
39	San Ignacio	El Padrino RV Park	Pleasant park in palms on road into town.*
40	2 mi. S of Santa Rosalia	RV Park Las Palmas	Well landscaped park along highway with small restaurant.*
41	Caleta San Lucas	San Lucas RV Park	Little landscaping but directly on the water.*
42	Punta Chivato	Punta Chivato Resort	On beach east of the Punta Chivato Hotel.
43	Mulegé along the estuary	Huerta (Orchard) Court	Pleasant court in palms between highway and the estuary.*
44	Mulegé along the estuary	Maria Isabel Court	Pleasant court in palms between highway and the estuary.*
45	Bahía Concepción	Playa Punta Arena	RV parking directly on the beach. No hookups.
46	Bahía Concepción	Los Naranjos	RV parking directly on the beach. No hookups.
47	Bahía Concepción	Playa Santispac	RV parking directly on the beach. Restaurant—no hookups.
48	Bahía Concepción	Posada Concepción	A few transient sites adjoining an RV subdivision.*
49	Bahía Concepción	Los Cocos	RV parking directly on the beach. No hookups.
50	Bahía Concepción	La Burra	RV parking directly on the beach. No hookups.
51	Bahía Concepción	Playa El Coyote	RV parking directly on the beach. No hookups.
52	Bahía Concepción	Playa Buenaventura	Nice court and palapa's directly on the beach. Restaurant.*
53	Bahía Concepción	El Requeson	RV parking directly on the beach. No hookups.
54	Bahía Concepción	Playa la Perla	RV parking directly on the beach. No hookups.
55	Bahía Concepción	Playa Armenta	RV parking directly on the beach. No hookups.

PRINCIPAL RV PARKS AND CAMPING AREAS
* Indicates Full Hookups

No	LOCATION	NAME	COMMENTS
56	Loreto	Las Palmas	Pleasant court among many palms directly on the water.*
57	Loreto	Loremar RV Park	Little landscaping, directly on the water.*
58	Loreto	Villas de Loreto RV Park	Well landscaped area behind the Villas de Loreto Hotel. *
59	Loreto	El Moro RV Park	Poorly landscaped area in center of town.*
60	N. of Puerto Escondido	El Juncalito	RV parking directly on the beach. No hook-ups. Popular
61	Puerto Escondido	Tripui RV Resort	Small transient area next to permanent sites in RV Resort.*
62	S. of Puerto Escondido	Ligui (Ensenada Blanca)	RV parking directly on the beach. No hook-ups.
63	Bahía Magdalena	SE of San Carlos (No name)	RV parking directly on the beach. No hook-ups.
64	Ciudad Constitucion	Manfred's RV Trailer Park	Nicely landscaped park with Austrian restaurant.*
65	Ciudad Constitucion	Camperstre La Pila	Parking area near grassy pool area adjoining working farm.*
66	El Centenario	City View RV Park	An old government court with desert plants.*
67	El Centenario	Oasis de Aripes	A pleasant court on the water 10 miles NW of La Paz.*
68	La Paz	Casa Blanca Trailer Park	A pleasant court with pool on the highway entering La Paz.*
69	La Paz	El Cardon	A pleasant court with pool on the highway entering La Paz.*
70	La Paz	Aguamarina Trailer Ct.	A pleasant court with pool in residential area of La Paz.*
71	La Paz	La Paz Trailer Court	A pleasant court with pool in residential area of La Paz.*
72	Bahía de los Muertos	No Name	RV parking overlooking the beach. No hook-ups.
73	Los Barriles	Martin Verdugos	Very good shaded park on the beach.*
74	Los Barriles	Juanito's Garden	Fair park across road from the beach.*
75	El Cardinal	El Cardinal Resort	Park on bluff overlooking the sea. Restaurant.*
76	South of Buena Vista	Capilla Trailer Court	Good park on the beach in rural area.*

PRINCIPAL RV PARKS AND CAMPING AREAS
* Indicates Full Hookups

No	LOCATION	NAME	COMMENTS
77	La Ribera	Correcaminos	Pleasant court in mango orchard. Short walk to the beach.*
78	San Jose del Cabo	Brisa del Mar	Pleasant court, pool, restaurant on the beach.*
79	East of Cabo San Lucas	Villa Serena	Near water with fine view of the Cape. Pool, etc.*
80	Edge of Cabo San Lucas	Vista Bonita	On the Hwy entering town from the E.
81	Edge of Cabo San Lucas	El Arco	On the Hwy entering town from the E. Pool, etc.*
82	Edge of Cabo San Lucas	Cabo Cielo (Closed 1995)	On the Hwy entering town from the E. Pool, etc.*
83	Edge of Cabo San Lucas	Vagabundos del Mar	On the Hwy entering town from the E. Pool, etc.*
84	Edge of Cabo San Lucas	Club Cabo	Behind the Vagabundos del Mar.*
85	Highway 19, Km 59	San Pedrito RV Park	On fine beach. Pool in palm grove.*
86	Highway 19, Km 64	Government Court	On fine beach. Desert landscaping and active management.*

RECREATIONAL VEHICLES AND CAMPING

Changing Times

There were almost no RV parks in Baja for the first few years after the 1973 completion of the Transpenisular Highway. It was a glorious era of camping for both tenters and those with larger RVs. One could simply pull up near the beach at many places along the highway and do one's thing, which of course included substantially degrading the area's sanitary conditions. Those days are largely gone if you have a larger RV and don't wish to travel on the back roads. There are still many beach-camping spots, but you must travel farther off the highway, usually using smaller vehicles.

Most of the good places near the highway are now occupied by (1) developed RV parks or (2) camping areas. These two types of facilities are considered separately below.

RV Parks

In Baja, the term RV *park* applies to several types of facilities:

1.   Permanent mobile home subdivisions. Many of these are decades old. They lie along the Sea of Cortez from the San Felipe area south to Puertecitos, and along the Pacific coast from Tijuana south to La Jolla. In these places North Americans have leased a small site and moved in a recreation vehicle, usually adding a roof of some kind along with a vari-

ety of other attached structures. The result has usually been a community that is considerably less than luxurious. In most cases, the structures are now permanent. These are de facto recreational-vehicle second-home tracts.

The Tripui RV Park at Puerto Escondido is 16 miles south of Loreto. Note the pool, store, restaurant area at the right center. The Sierra Giganta lies in the background.

RECREATIONAL
VEHICLES AND CAMPING

In more recent years, similar places have developed farther south in Mulegé, Puerto Escondido, Los Barriles, Cabo San Lucas and Todos Santos. Some of these developments are more pleasing to the eye than those in the north. Most started out as transient parks and gradually converted to permanent residents. Where there is a mixture of permanent and transient sites, the better spots usually go to the permanent people. This arrangement best serves the economic interests of the landowner. Unfortunately the result is that the best properties are occupied most of the time by vacant improvements while the current tourist has difficulty finding a nice place to stay. This type of RV park is not shown on this chapter's map and tables.

2. During the mid-1970s the Mexican government built nine trailer courts at various places. They were nicely landscaped with desert vegetation and were enclosed with chain-link fences. Water lines were enclosed in concrete structures that made these parks look like graveyards. There were large wooden restroom buildings. Most of these parks were promptly abandoned. Today, many of them are maintained on a hit-and-miss basis by local Mexicans who often live in the restroom build-

ings. These parks are numbers 26, 28, 31, 34, 37, 66 and 86 on the "Principal RV Parks and Camping Areas" tables. Additional such parks are located at San Agustin northwest of Cataviña and at the south end of Bahía Concepcíon. They are usually closed.

3. Over the years, a sizeable number of additional RV parks have been constructed throughout Baja so that travelers are never far from a place to stay. They range in quality from super-deluxe to scroungy, with most falling some where in the middle of this range.

Camping Areas

One of Baja's most popular tourist regions lies along the eastern shore of Bahía Concepcíon south of Mulegé. In this area are located several beaches that become lined with recreational vehicles each winter season. There are few facilities except rather primitive pit toilets and trash barrels. But the RV people love them because everybody gets to park directly on the beach and the camping fee is low. I am categorizing these areas as camping areas as, in spite of their popularity, they fall below the development standards most people expect in an RV park. They are numbers 45 through 55 on the chart. There are similar places at other locations (numbers 60, 62 and 72).

Summary Comments

If you will permit me to reassemble the above noted categories of RV parks and camping areas, I will reclassify them in another manner as shown by the three groups of shadings shown in the "Principal RV Parks and Camping Areas" chart.

1. The places shown in white are *primarily stops for people on the move* along Highway 1. Several of the towns at these places offer sufficient interest to entice people to linger for several days, but most visits are for one night only.

2. The places shown in the light shading provide *primarily short duration stays in the border area.* They also serve as one-night stops for people on the move.

3. The places shown in the darker shading provide *primarily long duration stays.* These are the destination places where tourists spend many days, whether it be a week or all winter. The camping fee is paid by the day, week, month or season, but the visitor has no long-term legal rights to the site. As for item 2, these camps also serve as one-night stops for people on the move.

Where Do I Stay?

RV parks, deluxe or scroungy, are not among my favorite places. I have been known to refer to them as "parking lots with sewers." If you find me in one in the United States or Canada you will know I am desperate and could not reach a national, state or local public campground that offers a little elbow-room. In Baja, some RV parks are really very nice, but I am an isolationist and seek out a place under a tree away from the crowds. The sound of a generator in one of those large RVs with the television running is, shall we say, disturbing. So where do I stay in Baja? My list is a secret, so I will disclose it only with the explicit understanding that you will not share it with others. We must keep it a secret. Knowing that you are honorable people, here it is. The numbers are those on the "Principal RV Parks and Camping Areas" chart. Some are not on the table. Each of these places is noted in the Index at the back of this book so that you can look them up if necessary. Remember, don't tell any body else!

1. #6 KOA. Except on weekends, there are usually few people.

2. #17. One of the Ejido camps overlooking the Pacific.

3. #22. Muelle Viego. Most of the gringos stay at the Old Mill.

4. #27. Rancho Santa Inez.

5. El Tomatal. Under a few palm trees about 100 yards from the beach.

6. San Ignacio. The place by the pond used by the locals as a swimming hole.

7. Under a couple of acacia trees east of the abandoned government RV park at the south end of Bahía Concepcíon.

8. #62. Ligui. There is a little hill 100 yards east of the town of Ensenada Blanca with a great view of the water. Everybody else wants to be on the beach. So let them.

9. #72. Bahía de los Muertos on the floor of the old warehouse. Everybody else is over by the beach.

10. Playa San Pedrito. One of the best camping spots in Baja.

11. El Migrino Loop north of Cabo San Lucas.

Backcountry Camping

By the term "camping," I am here referring to staying overnight in a natural setting with the use of tents or minimum-facility vehicles such as vans and pickup trucks with camper shells.

If one visits Baja's main RV parks and beaches it is easy to conclude that the camper is now far outnumbered by the owners of larger RVs. But one still sees many smaller rigs on the highways indicating that there are still many true campers around hiding out in the lesser-known and harder-to-reach areas. The balance of this chapter is dedicated to these people.

If you are a veteran camper you will know that in most places north of the border you are not permitted to camp because you are on private land or are restricted to developed sites on public lands. In the latter areas, you will be accustomed to graceful loop roads and parking spurs all neatly lined with barriers to keep you in your place. These facilities come complete with camp tables, stoves, restrooms and a sign, or an attendant at the gate who will tell you in great detail the rules of the camp and how to pay your fee. In Baja, forget all that. Camping here is a unique experience and the rules are quite simple. They are (1) find campsite, (2) camp.

Much of the land in Mexico is federally owned, and in all cases the shoreline is open to the public. Even where the land is privately owned, no one will bother you unless you are in their front yard. Exceptions are the cities and towns and the waterfront area between San Jose del Cabo and Cabo San Lucas. In the latter place the beaches themselves are open to the public but camping is no longer possible. In other places, unless there is some obvious reason why you should not camp, you are free to do so. If someone is authorized to charge a fee, they will seek you out.

I have frequently camped in close proximity to remote seaside fish camps. One waves at the fishermen on the way in and out, but unless I initiate it, there is usually no other contact. If someone does come by, it is simply out of curiosity and to say hello. Travelers from north of the border may expect to be told, "You are on private property, get out." I have never had this happen.

Campgrounds north of the border are almost always built some distance from the feature you came to see. Camping at the edge of the stream, on the beach, or at the rim of the canyon is next to impossible. Much of this practice is justifiable, but I am also convinced that campground planners take great pleasure in separating the public from what they came to enjoy. In Baja, you may camp as near as you like to the shoreline. You may need plenty of seawater for dishwashing, and the sensible camper will not expend excess energy in carrying it too far.

On a recent trip to Baja's Pacific shore, I pulled my camper to within 10 feet of the edge of a cliff overlooking the surf pounding over a rock-lined coast. There were majestic views for 20 miles in both directions. Baja is one of the few places in North America where you can camp in this manner. I believe it is this freedom to spend time in such sites, free from the restraints placed on us by more civilized portions of our continent, that make travelers to Baja return again and again.

There are still countless uncrowded shoreside camping sites on the peninsula, but many are accessible only by secondary and lower standard dirt roads. Thus, as in many parts of the world, true campers must search out the lesser-known and harder-to-access spots to fill their needs.

NOTE

During one of our visits, we encountered the Canadian owner of a new RV Park. In his pitch to encourage me to advertise his facility, he noted that it is contrary to Mexican law to camp on the beach. Perhaps he is correct, but it is a law that is enforced in the breach.

Camping on the sand at El Requeson on the west shore of Bahía Concepción

RECREATIONAL
VEHICLES AND CAMPING

The Last 100 Yards

What follows is a discussion of the fine art of getting stuck in the sand, followed by some suggestions on how to reverse the process. As noted above, many camping spots are undeveloped, and foremost among the features that are missing are adequate roads for the last few yards to that spot that you are simply in love with only 20 feet from the ocean. In many places, you will be driving on the natural surface that has not been compacted adequately to support a vehicle. The problem is compounded by the fact that shoreline camping spots will usually be at a lower elevation than the main road. Thus, you drive downhill to your campsite but must return uphill. Spin-outs in loose sand are a frequent result, followed by "Henry, I told you this would happen."

Most people camp in one location for many days, weeks or even months, so the pain of extracting one's vehicle from a place that has provided so much pleasure may be a small price to pay. Many veterans know full well what will happen and are well-versed in the extraction process.

The prudent traveler to Baja's beaches will carry a shovel and tow chain or nylon line. Others are equipped with several buckets for carrying seawater to wet down the surface on which the drive wheels will travel. This should be done prior to moving a vehicle; however, the best method of which I am aware is to let some, or nearly all, of the air out of your tires. The increase in traction is miraculous. For this reason, don't travel in Baja without some means of pumping up your tires after returning to firmer ground. Most U.S. auto parts stores carry small, inexpensive tire pumps that operate by plugging into your vehicle cigarette lighter. Others function from engine compression and require the temporary removal of one spark plug. Don't leave home without one.

Obviously use of four-wheel-drive vehicles is the ultimate answer to the problem of "The Last 100 Yards," although sometimes even drivers of these vehicles overextend themselves and become mired down. Then one really has trouble.

Campfires

If you are expecting to hear that firewood is scarce in Baja you would be in error. As long as the land is covered with woody desert vegetation, there will be plenty of firewood. This is the situation in most of Baja. Unfortunately, the individual pieces of wood are small, and they will be well-picked-over near camping areas. The keys to success in gathering firewood in Baja are one or more large cloth or canvas sacks and a pair of gloves. Before you reach your camping site, stop near an area of heavy vegetation, wander through the desert, and fill up your sacks. Wear the gloves for protection from the ever-present thorns.

Many desert plants have dead branches near their bases, and the inside skeletal structure of dead cactus is excellent firewood. I have never had to use an ax in Baja. In most places, it's only a matter of a few minutes work to gather all the wood needed for several days. The pieces will be small, but they will be dry, full of energy and easy to gather.

Finally, keep in mind that wildfires do occur in Baja. The brushy areas in the California Vegetative Region of northern Baja are as highly flammable as similar places in southern California in the United States. Deserts can also burn, and I have seen several large devastated areas in Baja where centuries will have to pass before revegetation occurs. PLEASE BE CAREFUL WITH FIRE.

WATERSPORTS

Large sportfishing vessels lie at anchor in front of the Hotel Hacienda at Cabo San Lucas. Scores of such boats make the run from Southern California to Cabo each winter.

I really do not exaggerate in telling you that Baja, and in particular the coast of the Sea of Cortez, is a paradise for watersports. This is especially true for windsurfers and the owners of small trailerable or car-top boats who are confronted at home with the bone-chilling temperatures and heavy swells of the Pacific Ocean off the United States and Canada. North of the border, the use of small boats is limited almost exclusively to inland lakes, reservoirs, rivers and protected ocean bays. In the Sea of Cortez, deep-sea fishing and other watersports can be enjoyed in ocean waters that have mild temperatures and light swells.

Boating

Boat Classification

It is important to understand the relationship of several different classes of boats to conditions in Baja. The message is that not all boats may be transported to or used in Baja. Here are the details. (The four-boat classification system is my own creation. See "Boat Classification" table.)

Class-1

Sail and power vessels that have the fuel capacity, crew capabilities and design characteristics for ocean conditions can make the Baja Passage from San Diego around the peninsula's southern tip and into the Sea of Cortez. Hundreds make this trip every year. See the "Ocean-Cruising" section in this chapter for further discussion concerning the use of such boats.

Class-2

An unfortunate problem lies in the fact that the marinas of the United States and Canada are overflowing with boats that are either too small, have insufficient fuel capacity, or are underdesigned for the ocean passage. At the same time, they are too large to be easily trailered or launched under Baja conditions. The majority of such vessels are powerboats in the 20- to-35-foot cabin-cruiser category. They should not be taken to Baja. Please read the material to follow concerning ocean-cruising and review the description of the Transpeninsular Highway if you are inclined to ignore this advice.

Very few boats larger than this heavy trailer boat (Class-3), shown at a natural surface ramp, are towed to Baja.

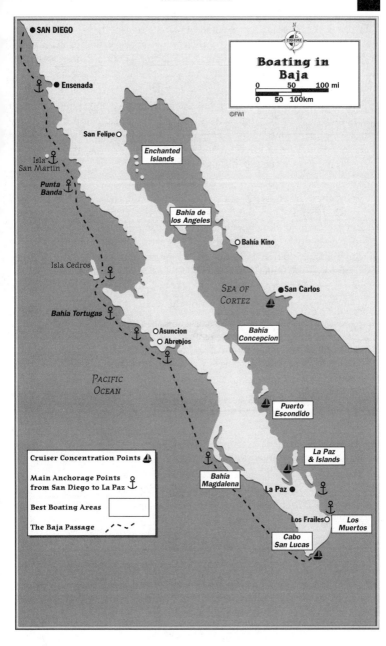

Boating in
Baja

0   50   100 mi
0   50   100km
©FWI

● SAN DIEGO

⚓
● Ensenada

San Felipe ○

*Enchanted
Islands*

Isla
San Martín ⚓

*Punta
Banda* ⚓

*Bahía de
los Angeles*

○ Bahía Kino

Isla Cedros ⚓

SEA OF
CORTEZ

● San Carlos ⛵

Bahía Tortugas ⚓

⚓

○ Asuncion
○ Abreojos ⚓

*Bahía
Concepcion*

PACIFIC
OCEAN

⛵ *Puerto
Escondido*

⚓

*La Paz
& Islands* ⛵

⚓

Cruiser Concentration Points ⛵

**Main Anchorage Points
from San Diego to La Paz** ⚓

Best Boating Areas

The Baja Passage - - -

*Bahía
Magdalena*

La Paz ●

Los Frailes ○   *Los
Muertos* ⚓

*Cabo
San Lucas* ⛵

Class-3

Two classes of boats (Classes-3 and -4) can be transported to Baja by highway. First are those that because of their weight must be floated from a trailer into the water by use of a launching ramp. There are now a sizeable number of places in Baja that have ramps, but many of these have one or more shortcomings. (See "Boat Launching Ramps" table in this chapter.)

Once in the water, these larger vessels enjoy distance and water condition capabilities greater than lightweight Class-4 boats, so I don't discourage your taking them south. Simply keep in mind that they can only be launched at a limited number of locations and that you must face the risks of towing them on the narrow Transpeninsular Highway.

Class-4

Finally, there are those boats that are light enough to be manhandled over the beach. In most cases, this involves carrying the outboard motor separately. Inflatable rubber dinghies and lightweight aluminum boats in the 13- to 17-foot range make up the majority of this class. My observation is that the great majority are carried in or on top of vans or on pickup truck racks. A few are transported by trailer.

Various types of inflatable boats are also common and in the final analysis may be the best and safest way to enjoy the water.

BOAT CLASSIFICATION

1	Oceangoing sail and powerboats having the capabilities for travel by sea.	LONG RANGE Great experience. Travel almost anywhere.
2	Boats without long-range ocean capabilities, but too big to trailer safely.	UNUSABLE IN BAJA
3	Heavy trailer boats that require a launching ramp to enter the water.	MEDIUM RANGE Sea access limited due to shortage of launching sites.
4	Light trailer or car-top boats that can be launched over the beach.	SHORT RANGE Maximum flexibility due to ease of launching.

Small Boats

By small boats, I am referring to the Class-3 and -4 vessels just described.

Small Boat Launching

Since first publishing this book in 1986, the number of boat-launching ramps in Baja has significantly increased. (See "Boat-Launching Ramps" table in this chapter.)

The ramps at about half of these locations have rough concrete surfaces that rather obviously have been poured by hand. A ready-mix concrete truck in Baja is not a common sight. Because of the difficulty in getting concrete to set after the tide comes in, some of these ramps do not extend far enough toward the water to be effective at low tide.

As previously noted, those boaters with craft that are light enough to be manhandled over the beach will be able to use their boats in far more places than those who require a ramp. Boats 18 feet and larger usually require a hard-surfaced ramp.

Other boaters abandon the boat-trailer method altogether and, after lowering their boat to the ground, maneuver it in and out of the water by hand or on various types of rollers. Also, rolling devices can be purchased that attach directly onto the hull of small boats. Many veteran Baja fishermen rely solely on lightweight 13–15 foot aluminum boats because of the ease of launching such craft over the beach.

BOAT-LAUNCHING RAMPS

GENERAL	LOCATION — SPECIFIC	COMMENTS
SAN FELIPE	Three ramps. Ruben's RV park (Motel el Cortez) Club de Pesca. See "San Felipe Area" map on page 335.	Ramps used only at high tide due to extreme fluctuation of water level.
PUERTECITOS AREA	Two ramps near north entrance to Puertecitos Cove and at Papa Fernandez Resort.	Both are concrete ramps but they are usable only at high tides.
ENSENADA	One concrete ramp near the sportfishing piers within the harbor. See "Ensenada" map on page 362.	Good concrete ramp but access may be constricted by new building construction.
ENSENADA	One ramp located at the Ensenada shipyard. See "Ensenada" map on page 362.	A good concrete ramp which is used to haul sizeable commercial fishing boats.
ESTERO BEACH	One ramp by Estero Beach Hotel, six miles south of Ensenada. See "Punta Banda Area" map, page 370.	Concrete ramp. After launching, boats must cross estero entrance bar to access the ocean.

WATERSPORTS

BOAT-LAUNCHING RAMPS

GENERAL	LOCATION SPECIFIC	COMMENTS
LA JOLLA	Two ramps at La Jolla Beach camps eight miles west of Maneadero. See "Punta Banda Area" map, page 370.	Directly on Pacific Ocean. Concrete ramps are unusable in windy weather or low tide.
LA BUFADORA	One ramp near the head of the cove east of the La Bufadora blowhole. See "Punta Banda Area" map, page 370.	Steep, concrete ramp leading to gravel beach. Constructed in bottom of a short, narrow arroyo.
PUERTO SANTO TOMAS	One ramp in arroyo bottom at the west end of the fish camp.	A steep concrete ramp. Unusable when ocean swells are heavy.
PUERTO SAN ISIDRO	One concrete ramp is at the small fish camp and resort area north of Ejido Erendira.	Ramp enters directly into the Pacific Ocean but the site is partially protected by a rocky reef.
SAN QUINTIN	Two ramps at Old Mill Motel, and Pedregal subdivision. See "San Quintin Area" map, page 383	Old Mill ramp is hard-packed natural surface plus new concrete ramp. Widely used.
BAHÍA DE LOS ANGELES	Three neighboring concrete ramps run by hotels & RV parks. See "Bahía de Los Angeles" map, page 411.	Hotel Villa Vita ramp built from a rock breakwater and reaches deeper water than the other two.
CAMPO RENE (ESTERO COYOTE)	Campo Rene resort on the shore of shallow Estero Coyote. See "Punta Eugenia Area" map, page 423.	A natural-surface (sand and shell) beach. Fishing inside the bay or access to the open Pacific.
CALETA SAN LUCAS	Ramp is inside the grounds of the San Lucas RV Park. See "Caleta San Lucas" map, page 439.	A natural surface launch area, but well protected inside the cove at Caleta San Lucas.
PUNTA CHIVATO	One ramp, 200 yards northwest of the Hotel Punta Chivato. 16-mile dirt road east from Highway 1.	Rock and concrete ramp. The hotel staff will help out if a problem arises.

WATERSPORTS

BOAT-LAUNCHING RAMPS

	LOCATION	COMMENTS
GENERAL	**SPECIFIC**	
MULEGÉ	Three ramps at RV parks & hotel on south side of estuary, ramp near lighthouse. See "Mulegé" map, page 441.	Concrete ramps (lighthouse ramp is packed sand). There is no water in the river when tide is out.
PLAYA BUENAVENTURA	Playa Buenaventura RV Park on Bahía Concepcíon. Km F-94 on Hwy. 1.	A wide concrete ramp run by the RV park. Plenty of parking and easy approach.
LORETO	Two ramps in breakwater-lined harbor and on the open water at Las Palmas RV Resort. See "Loreto" map, page 453.	Good concrete ramps. There is a large public parking area adjoining the harbor.
PUERTO ESCONDIDO	One ramp at south end of inner harbor adjacent to the entrance channel. See "Loreto-Puerto Escondido Area" map, page 465.	Good concrete ramp accessible by oiled highway. One of the most heavily used ramps in Baja.
BAHÍA MAGDALENA	One ramp, located one mile south of San Carlos on a Bahía Magdalena side lagoon. See "San Carlos" map, page 475.	A concrete ramp. Does not extend far enough at low tide, and floods at high tide. Try mid-tide.
LA PAZ	Five ramps. Fedepaz, Aquamarina RV, Marina de La Paz, Palmira marina (2 ramps). "La Paz" map, page 487.	All are good concrete ramps leading into the quiet waters of Canal de La Paz.
PICHILINGUE	Two ramps in a small cove north of Puerto Pichilingue. Off Highway 11 north of La Paz. See "La Paz Area" map, page 485.	Two good double, concrete ramps on both sides of protected cove. Marina under construction.
BUENA VISTA AREA	Beach launching at RV parks & hotels. See "Los Barriles Buena Vista Area" map, page 501.	Launch over the beach using trucks owned by RV parks and hotels.

WATERSPORTS

BOAT-LAUNCHING RAMPS

GENERAL	LOCATION SPECIFIC	COMMENTS
CABO SAN LUCAS	Two ramps in the inner harbor. One at north end and one at the south. See "Cabo San Lucas" map, page 523.	Good concrete ramps. The north ramp is operated by the marina.

Small Boat Cruising

I approach this subject with a considerable degree of trepidation, fearing that what I write might encourage the use of small boats in waters beyond their capabilities. I am proceeding simply because the cruising of small Class-3 and -4 boats in the Sea of Cortez is already a common practice. These adventures range from a simple overnight camping trip to extended voyages involving many weeks and hundreds of miles. Some utilize the heaviest possible trailer boats with on-board sleeping and cooking facilities. At the other extreme, lengthy voyages are undertaken in kayaks and small, center-board sailboats not over 12 feet in length.

Few owners of ocean-cruisers would trade their vessels for such craft, but the little fellow does have some clear advantages over the bigger boats. Most small powerboats have a greater speed than the 4- to-8 knots of the average ocean-cruiser. They can thus traverse a considerable distance in a short time taking advantage of windless periods. During some months, the wind blows heavily during all but a few hours per day. Also, small shallow-draft boats can be easily hauled onto the beach almost anywhere if the weather kicks up, and they can be anchored in coves too small or shallow to offer protection to larger vessels. These advantages open up the potential of isolated camping in scores of charming and pristine hideaways.

For the truly adventuresome, I need to note that some skippers of large trailer boats launch their vessels at Kino Bay on the Mexican mainland and make the 100-plus mile crossing of the Sea of Cortez to Bahía de los Angeles. Others launch at San Carlos and cross to Bahía Concepción. The former trip is the safer as the Midriff Islands lie en route and offer wind and sea protection and potential stopping points. Also, increasing numbers of small boat owners are launching at the ramps in Bahía de los Angeles and cruising south along Baja's eastern coast. The return trip is made by hauling the boat north on the Transpeninsular Highway.

I strongly advise that no one undertake any of these ventures in a small boat without having tested it in sea conditions similar to those encountered in the Sea of Cortez. Keep in mind that the prevailing wind during the cruising season is from the north and blows down the long axis of the peninsula.

Crossing the Sea of Cortez at right angles to these winds puts one's boat in the belly of the seas, a dangerous and uncomfortable exercise. Any of these trips should best be undertaken in April through July. The winter months are windy.

Boaters interested in small boat cruising should consider membership in the Vagabundos del Mar. This club frequently organizes such events in the Sea of Cortez and at Bahía Magdalena on the Pacific side.

Ocean-Cruising

Records at the office of the port captain at Cabo San Lucas show that more than 1000 foreign yachts check in at that port each year. Most of these vessels arrive from the United States and Canada and return north after the winter cruising season. Some spend winters at protected spots in the Sea of Cortez. A few are making longer passages to the South Pacific or are en route to or from the Panama Canal.

Many readers will not be fortunate enough to make an ocean voyage to Baja. Nevertheless, this section on ocean-cruising is presented for two reasons. First, many of you who visit Baja by land will see the cruisers' vessels at various locations. They are part of the Baja scene and you may be interested in their way of life. More importantly, this brief exposure might encourage some of you to seek an opportunity to make such a voyage. Twice in my life I quit work for four months and sailed south to sweep away the cranial cobwebs. These two trips motivated me to give up the office entrapment altogether and return for two more voyages completely around the peninsula.

There is no set way to make the passage from San Diego to Cabo San Lucas. Some cruisers simply make their way many miles offshore where the winds are stronger, and don't touch land until rounding the cape. However, the majority stay closer to land following the *Baja Passage* shown on the "Boating in Baja" map.

The "Boating in Baja" map shows several points that provide the principal anchorages along the Baja Passage. At two, there is no possibility of obtaining fuel except from other boaters. At most of the other places, fuel can be obtained only by carrying it over the beach in cans if you can persuade the local inhabitants into giving up some of their own hard-earned supply. The only reliable fueling point, and the only one actually in the business of servicing the cruiser, is Bahía Tortugas. This well-protected port and community lies approximately midway between San Diego and Cabo San Lucas. Even here, you must anchor off the pier while fuel is gravity-fed from barrels.

Bahía Tortugas is 340 miles south of San Diego. The journey from Bahía Tortugas to Cabo San Lucas is 460 miles. For this reason the rule of thumb is that you should not make the Baja Passage in a powerboat that carries fuel for less than 600 miles. This allows a reasonable margin of safety for the passages to and from Bahía Tortugas. You frequently see large, gas-guzzling sportfishing boats with 55-gallon drums lashed in their cockpits to stretch their tankage for the passage. This fuel situation is one of the principal reasons why many mid-sized powerboats (Class-2) should not be cruised to Baja. Those broad, open-to-the-sea aft cockpits are another. It is easy for a following sea to invite itself aboard.

Keep in mind that the prevailing wind is northwest along the west coast of Baja during the entire cruising season. With energy from both wind and swells coming from this direction, more or less parallel with the coast, the *downhill* voyage south is usually a delight. The return trip north is *uphill* into the wind and swells. Even sailboats make this return trip almost entirely under power. The pounding that the boat and crew takes on the way north is the price to be paid for a sunny winter in Baja. Crews to make this uphill run are often in demand, and skippers with Captain Bligh tendencies may find themselves without help.

Ocean-cruisers, like trailer-court folks, are often a gregarious breed. Thus, it is a bit ironic that people who have the transportation capabilities to visit anywhere they wish tend to congregate at certain ports once they reach the Sea of Cortez. These places are Cabo San Lucas, La Paz, Puerto Escondido and across the Sea of Cortez at San Carlos.

The two last-mentioned ports host large numbers of cruising boats whose owners have decided to spend the hot summer in Mexico. Both are well protected and are north of the tracks of the great majority of late summer hurricanes. Because of these intense tropical storms, most sensible cruisers will not venture into southern Mexican waters during summer. The safe cruising season in Baja is from December to May.

Marinas and Fuel

Until about 10 years ago the subject of marinas in Baja could have been covered in three words: "There aren't any." Now there are five locations in Baja that offer marina facilities:

Ensenada

Three small marinas are in place at the northern end of the harbor. One of these is operated in conjunction with a small craft shipyard.

Cabo San Lucas Inner Harbor

The entire inner harbor has been constructed by dredging. After a wait of more than a decade, an excellent marina was constructed about 1990. The harbor, well-protected from winter weather and Pacific swells, provides easy access to the open sea.

The Cabo San Lucas marina is in the inner harbor, which is now largely lined with hotels and condominiums, as can be seen in the upper right corner.

La Paz

Prior to 1985, there were no marinas in La Paz and obtaining fuel was not a simple task. There are now three fully functional marinas with fuel docks and launching ramps. Many large vessels are now docked all year in La Paz. An additional dredged harbor has been completed for several years but as of yet it contains no marina facilities.

The modern Marina de La Paz at La Paz.

Puerto Escondido

The area immediately inside the entrance channel to the natural harbor at Puerto Escondido has been dredged and reformed, and a major resort area with hotels, condominiums and marina awaits construction. Unfortunately it has been waiting now for more than six years with no sign of anything new happening.

Santa Rosalia

There is a small but very adequate marina inside the breakwater lined harbor at this community. Plans call for it being enlarged in the future.

There are long-range plans for marinas at many other places. In 1989, the Mexican Director of Tourism announced that marinas will be constructed every 150 miles along the Pacific coast of the country. On our last visit nothing new had occurred although the director told me such marinas are still in the offing. My only recommendation is, "Don't hold your breath."

Obtaining fuel for your boat in Baja is not a simple matter of gliding alongside the nearest fuel dock. This is particularly true along Baja's Pacific coast. With the exception of a few of the above noted marinas, the boater must obtain fuel from the land-based PEMEX stations and transport it to the launching site. Serious fishermen carry a drum of gas in the back of their pickups.

Best Boating Areas

The "Boating in Baja" map in this chapter shows the locations of what I believe are the eight best boating areas in Baja California.

Other Watersports

Windsurfing

The sport of windsurfing has rapidly gained in popularity in Baja in recent years. Windsurfers crave strong winds in the 15–30 knot range that blow parallel to the takeoff area. As noted earlier, northerly winds that meet these requirements are common along the entire Sea of Cortez coast during the winter season. When the breeze is uncomfortably strong and cool for most campers, it is just right for the windsurfers.

Individual windsurfers will be seen at many locations on the Sea of Cortez and windsurfing equipment is often for rent at the hotels on the outer harbor at Cabo San Lucas, at Nopolo and La Paz. There are, however, two areas of special interest.

The East Cape

The **Buena Vista-Los Barriles** area along Baja's East Cape has become one of the most popular windsurfing destinations in North America. The area has long sandy beaches impacted by the ideal wind conditions, and being near the peninsula's tip, air temperatures are warmer than farther north. Even so, many windsurfers prefer to wear short or full summer wetsuits when spending much time on the water.

Starting about 1987, U.S. windsurfing groups organized an annual Baja International Boardsailing Regatta at the East Cape each January. Today, this event attracts hundreds of young enthusiasts who camp on the beach north of Los Barriles, where I suspect things get a little wild.

These same organizations set up headquarters at the Hotel Playa Hermosa and Hotel Palmas de Cortez during the entire winter season. Rental equipment, instruction and repair services are readily available.

Punta San Carlos

The Sea of Cortez offers windsurfing with surf-less seas. On the Pacific shore, **Punta San Carlos** attracts expert surfers with its high winds and breaking seas. I am advised by these hardy souls that Punta San Carlos offers the best and most challenging waves on the North American coast. There are no facilities at Punta San Carlos and the trip in from Highway 1 is a rough 40 miles. The access road leaves Highway 1 about 16 miles southeast from El Rosario.

Surfing

A surfer enjoys the waves at Rosarito Beach.

I encountered a party of surfers during my last trip who complained that there was almost no published information about surfing in Baja. What is available provides the names of many surfing spots but was produced prior to 1980 and gives almost no directional material. Nearly all of these reported surfing locations are already included in the pages of *Fielding's Baja*. The accompanying "Surfing Area maps" and "Surfing Area Table" are designed to help surfers find the information they need.

I should note that I have never surfed. My closest encounter with the sport was with a surfboard projecting from the side window of a car on the narrow Transpeninsular Highway, where its owner almost forced me off the road. However, I have been to almost all of the places noted in the above referenced table and these places represent about half of the spots noted in previous publications. I have excluded many others as it is difficult to match their names with locations that are shown on any available maps. Most of those omitted lie along the heavily urbanized coast between Tijuana and Ensenada or in the Cape Area at the peninsula's tip. Many places in these areas are now difficult to access because of hotel and residential construction.

Heavy swells traveling from northwest to southeast are a daily occurrence along the entire Pacific coast of the Baja peninsula except under storm conditions, when swells come from the southwest. These swells, which are the cause of coastal surf, refract around the Cape Region as far north as Punta Colorado. There is no usable surf farther north in the Sea of Cortez. Surfing hot spots that have been reported to me are the **Islas Todos Santos**, **Punta Rosarito**, **Punta Santa Rosalillita**, **Punta Pequeña** and **Punta San Carlos**. Should readers be able to provide additional input concerning surfing in Baja, I would be happy to include it in future editions of this book.

SURFING AREA TABLE

No	NAME	COMMENTS
1	Rosarito Beach	Miles of beach fronting the town of Rosarito. Km A-34.
2	Cantamar	Town of Cantamar. Use Km-53 exit from Hwy 1-D.
3	Sand Dunes	At south end of El Descanso. Km A 53 exit from Hwy 1-D. Cantamar La Mision Area map.
4	La Fonda	Beach adjoins the La Fonda Hotel. Km A-66. Cantamar La Mision Area map.
5	Playa Mal Paso	2.5-mile beach running S from the Rio Guadalupe. Cantamar La Mision Area Map.
6	Salsipuedes	This area refers to the coast accessed at the Saldamando Campground. Km A-94.
7	San Miguel	Coast adjoins the San Miguel Village Campground near the tollgate at Km A-99.
8	Calif. Trailer Park	Coast adjoins the California Trailer Park near Km A-105 north of Ensenada.
9	Islas de Todos Santos	Islands lie 12 miles offshore from Ensenada. Hire boats at Ensenada or La Bufadora.

WATERSPORTS

SURFING AREA TABLE

No	NAME	COMMENTS
10	Ensenada Beach	7 miles of beach south of Ensenada to Estero Beach Resort. Access at resort Km B-15.
11	Estero Punta Banda	The barrier beach fronting Estero de Punta Banda. Hwy 23. "Punta Banda Area" map.
12	Boca de Santo Tomas	Beach at mouth of Rio Santo Tomas. See "Puerto Santo Tomas" Side Trip Km B-48.
13	Punta San Jose	Road leaves for Punta San Jose from the town of Santo Tomas. Km B-51
14	Punta Cabras	Point lies north of Puerto San Isidro. See "Puerto San Isidro Area" Side Trip Km B-78.
15	San Isidro	See "Puerto San Isidro Area" Side Trip Km B-78.
16	Cabo Colnett	See "Bahía Colnett" Side Trip Km B-129. Road from bay extends south to Punta Camalu.
17	Punta Camalu	See "Punta Camalu" Side Trip Km B-157.
18	Playa San Ramon	12-mile beach best accessed on road running west from Colonia Viciente Guerrero.
19	Cabo San Quintin	See "San Quintin Area" map.
20	Playa Santa Maria	Beach lines the bay in front of Cielito Lindo RV Park. See "San Quintin Area" map.
21	El Pabellon Beach	Accessed at the El Pabellon Beach RV Park. Km C-15
22	Punta Baja	See "Punta Baja" Side Trip Km C-55 and the "El Rosario Area" map.
23	Punta San Carlos	A 38-mile dirt road leaves Hwy 1 at Km C-78, 16 miles south from El Rosario.
24	Punta Canoas	A remote Pacific point. See "Pacific Coast Loop." Km C-128 and D-38.
25	Punta Blanca	A remote Pacific point. See "Pacific Coast Loop." Km C-128 and D-38.
26	Punta Maria	A remote Pacific point. See "Pacific Coast Loop." Km C-128 and D-38.
27	Punta Negra	A remote Pacific point. See "Pacific Coast Loop." Km C-128 and D-38.
28	Punta Santa Rosalillita	At fishing village of Santa Rosalillita. Km D-38.
29	Punta Rosarito	From Santa Rosalillita village drive south about nine miles on coastal road.
30	El Tomatal	See Km D-68 for 2.9-mile trip to El Tomatal and nearby Miller's Landing.
31	Bahía Tortuga	See "Punta Eugenia Area" map and Side Trip. Km E-144 to E-98.
32	Bahía Asuncion	See "Punta Eugenia Area" map and Side Trip. Km E-144 to E-98.
33	Punta San Hipolito	See "Punta Eugenia Area" map and Side Trip. Km E-144 to E-98.
34	La Bocana	See "Punta Eugenia Area" map and Side Trip. Km E-144 to E-98.

WATERSPORTS

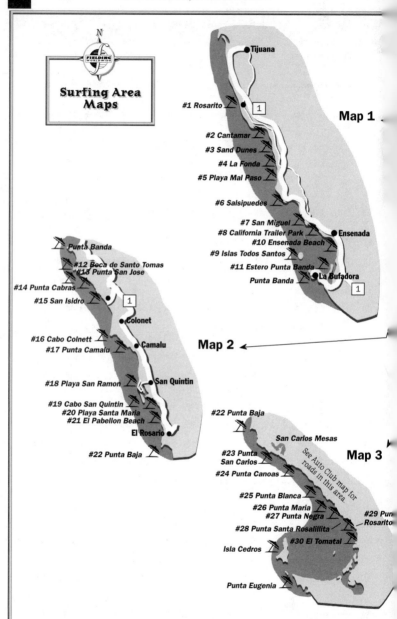

N

Surfing Area Maps

Map 1

#1 Rosarito
1
#2 Cantamar
#3 Sand Dunes
#4 La Fonda
#5 Playa Mal Paso
#6 Salsipuedes
#7 San Miguel
#8 California Trailer Park
#10 Ensenada Beach
#9 Islas Todos Santos
#11 Estero Punta Banda
Punta Banda

Tijuana
Ensenada
La Bufadora
1

Punta Banda
#12 Boca de Santo Tomas
#13 Punta San Jose
#14 Punta Cabras
#15 San Isidro
1
Colonet
#16 Cabo Colnett
#17 Punta Camalu
Camalu
#18 Playa San Ramon
San Quintin
#19 Cabo San Quintin
#20 Playa Santa Maria
#21 El Pabellon Beach
El Rosario
#22 Punta Baja

Map 2

#22 Punta Baja
San Carlos Mesas
#23 Punta San Carlos
#24 Punta Canoas
See Auto Club map for roads in this area.
Map 3
#25 Punta Blanca
#26 Punta Maria
#27 Punta Negra
#29 Punta Rosarito
#28 Punta Santa Rosalillita
Isla Cedros
#30 El Tomatal
Punta Eugenia

WATERSPORTS

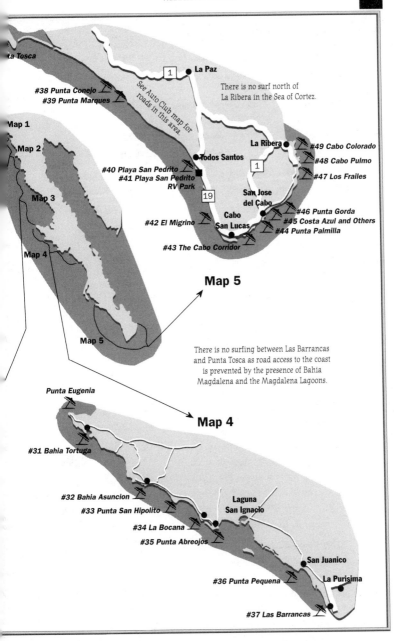

ta Tosca

#38 Punta Conejo
#39 Punta Marques

Map 1

Map 2

Map 3

Map 4

Map 5

La Paz

There is no surf north of
La Ribera in the Sea of Cortez.

See Auto Club map for
roads in this area

La Ribera

#49 Cabo Colorado
#48 Cabo Pulmo
#47 Los Frailes

Todos Santos

#40 Playa San Pedrito
#41 Playa San Pedrito
RV Park

San Jose
del Cabo

#46 Punta Gorda
#45 Costa Azul and Others
#44 Punta Palmilla

Cabo
San Lucas

#42 El Migrino

#43 The Cabo Corridor

Map 5

There is no surfing between Las Barrancas
and Punta Tosca as road access to the coast
is prevented by the presence of Bahia
Magdalena and the Magdalena Lagoons.

Map 4

Punta Eugenia

#31 Bahia Tortuga

#32 Bahia Asuncion
#33 Punta San Hipolito

Laguna
San Ignacio

#34 La Bocana
#35 Punta Abreojos

San Juanico
La Purisima

#36 Punta Pequena

#37 Las Barrancas

SURFING AREA TABLE

No	NAME	COMMENTS
35	Punta Abreojos	See Punta Eugenia Area map and Side Trip. Km E-144 to E-98.
36	Punta Pequeña	Drive 45 Km north from Km 107 on Hwy near La Purisima town of San Juanico.
37	Las Barrancas	La Barrancas lies five miles west from Km-87 on Hwy north of Ciudad Insurgentes.
38	Punta Conejo	See location on map. See Auto Club map for road details.
39	Punta Marques	See location on map. See *Auto Club* map for road details.
40	Playa San Pedrito	See map. Hwy 19 Km-57 and Km-59.
41	San Pedrito RV Park	See map. Hwy 19 Km-64.
42	El Migrino	Beach is accessed by El Migrino Loop Road. See map. Hwy 19 Km 94.
43	The CaboCorridor	Several beaches. See "The Cabo Corridor."
44	Punta Palmilla	At Hotel Palmilla. Km J-28.
45	Costa Azul and Others	Beaches line coast from Pt. Palmilla to town of La Playa. See "San Jose del Cabo" map.
46	Punta Gorda	Lies 10 miles east of town of La Playa on secondary road. New Highway anticipated.
47	Los Frailes	See "East Cape Loop" Side Trip. New Highway construction anticipated.
48	Cabo Pulmo	See "East Cape Loop" Side Trip. New Highway construction anticipated.

Kayaking

Ocean kayaking is rapidly growing in popularity in Baja. My own observations indicate that there are far more kayaks on the Sea of Cortez at any one time than there are cruising sailboats.

Ocean kayaking enthusiasts can cruise within feet of Baja's rock-bound coast and camp, fish and explore at small idyllic coves and beaches that are too confining for use by larger boats. Kayaks can easily be car-topped on conventional vehicles and launched almost anywhere. The small single seat vessels weigh a scant 50 pounds while two-person, 20-foot-long models weigh about 75 pounds. They are quite stable.

Experienced kayakers have traversed the full length of both Baja coasts. The trip from San Felipe to La Paz in the Sea of Cortez is frequently accomplished in 25 to 30 days. The most popular areas for shorter trips are the **Bahía de los Angeles**, **Puerto Escondido** and the **Bahía Concepción** areas. On the Pacific side, kayakers use **Puerto Lopez Mateos** as a base for trips into the **Magdalena** lagoons for whale-watching expeditions.

WATERSPORTS

Kayaks can carry sufficient food and gear for extended voyages, but many kayakers take advantage of package tours offered by various outfitters. In these instances, supplies are transported to prearranged camping sites by pangas, which also provide added safety for trips to islands a bit beyond the range of kayakers alone. Contact **Sea Trek**, *P.O. Box 561, Woodacre, CA,* ☎ *(415) 488-1000.* **Sea Kayak South**, *2803 Morningside Terrace, Escondido, CA 92025* ☎ *(619) 747-3615;* or **Baja Expeditions**, *2625 Garnet Avenue, San Diego, CA 92109,* ☎ *(619) 581-3311.* This latter organization also runs other types of boat trips. Kayaks may be rented for trips in Bahía Concepción from **Baja Tropicales**, *3065 Suite C, Clairemont Drive, San Diego, CA 92117,* ☎ *(619) 275-1836.*

Diving

Many locations around the Baja peninsula offer excellent sites for scuba diving. Reference to the "Water Temperatures" illustration later in this chapter will show that subtropical waters occur off the Pacific coast, while those in the Sea of Cortez are tropical. Kelp beds extend southward from the international border to about Bahía Tortugas. Whales and other marine mammals are common inhabitants off both coasts. The Sea of Cortez is host to giant whale sharks, manta rays, schools of hammerhead sharks, marlin and other large pelagic fish. These and other variables result in a wide variety of diving conditions that are difficult to duplicate anywhere in the world.

Water temperatures along the northern Pacific coast are cool enough to require wearing a 1/4-inch wetsuit year-round. Similar conditions prevail in the northern portions of the Sea of Cortez, while temperatures farther south range upwards of 90 degrees.

Much of the diving along Baja's Pacific coast is done aboard charter vessels based in San Diego. They range as far south as Isla Cedros. Many of these outfitters are based at the Commercial Basin adjacent to the Shelter Island Yacht Harbor in San Diego. Diving stores and outfitters in Baja are located at the places shown on the "Location of Diving Services" illustration. Following is a listing of those services.

La Bufadora

Dale's La Bufadora Dive, *APDO #102 Maneadero, B.C., Mexico,* ☎ *(52) 617-32092.*

Mulegé

Mulegé Divers, *On Madero Street,* ☎ *(52) 115-30059.*
Complete diving service for the Mulegé and Bahía Concepción Areas, plus the best stop for diving supplies, Baja travel books and quality gift items in the Mulegé area.

Loreto

Deportes Blazer, *Hidalgo No. 23, Col. Centro, Loreto, B.C.S., Mexico,* ☎ *(52) 113 50911; Villas de Loreto B&B & RV Park.*

La Paz

Baja Diving & Service, *A. Obregon 1665.2 La Paz, B.C.S., Mexico,* ☎ *(52) 112-21816, FAX (52) 112-28644. Other locations: La Concha Beach Resort and Marina Palmira; Baja Expeditions 2625 Garnet Avenue, San Diego, CA 92109,* ☎ *(800) 843-6967, (619) 581-3311, FAX (619) 581-6542.*

The East Cape

Vista Sea Sport, *APDO #42, Buena Vista B.C.S., Mexico 23580,* ☎ *& FAX (52) 114-10031.*

The Cape Area

Cabo Acuadeportes, *S.A. de C.V. Apartado Postal #136, Cabo San Lucas, B.C.S., Mexico 23410,* ☎ *& FAX (52) 114-30117.*

Two locations: Hacienda Beach and Chileno Beach; Cabo Diving Services, *Boulevard Marina esq. Hidalgo,* ☎ *(52) 114-30150, FAX (52) 114-31110;* Dolphin's Head, *Located at Hotel Plaza Las Glorias, Local A-6, Cabo Santa Lucas, B.C.S., Mexico,* ☎ *(52) 114-33400;* Land's End Divers, *Located at Hotel Plaza Las Glorias, Local A-5, Cabo San Lucas, B.CS., Mexico,* ☎ *& FAX (52) 114-32200.*

Fishing

One rarely encounters reports concerning fishing that do not extol the virtues of the area being discussed. Certainly this is true for Baja California. The advertisements for the Cape and East Cape hotels claim the "world's finest big-game fishing." One peninsular fishing book maintains that fishing "is unequaled anywhere in the world," and everything else one can read boasts of the outstanding qualities of the catch in a particular area. In preparing this book, I endeavored—with limited success—to determine if all of this were true. What follows results from readings in the scientific and popular literature, and my own observations.

Rating Baja's Fishing

I have been unable to find any author who makes direct qualitative comparisons of the world's fishing areas. I suspect those who claim the *world's best* for Baja may be on shaky scientific ground and could be guilty of what is known in the advertising world as *puffing* (an over-emphasis of a product's good points). Nevertheless, there are several sound reasons for believing that the fishing in the waters surrounding the Baja peninsula is of high quality.

Upwelling

There are several relatively isolated sections along the western coasts of the world's continents where the prevailing winds have the effect of forcing the surface waters offshore. The result is an upwelling of colder waters from below that bear rich concentrations of nitrates, phosphates and other nutrients. Their presence allows the development of enormous quantities of microscopic plants and animals known as plankton. Plankton, in turn, is the base of the food chain that results in large numbers of game fish.

WATERSPORTS

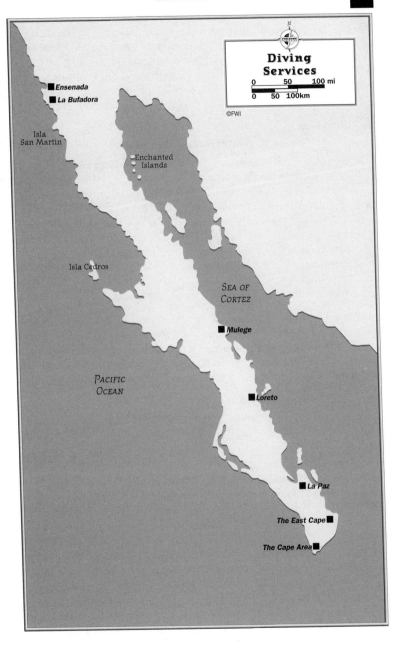

This condition exists off the north-central portion of Baja's Pacific coast. The nutrient qualities of these waters are not as high as in similar areas adjacent to Peru and at the tip of South America, but they are considerably better than average. Cool water upwelling also occurs off Baja's East Cape and in the Midriff island area east of Bahía de los Angeles due no doubt to the islands forming a constriction to the flow of tidal currents in the narrow Sea of Cortez. Upwelling conditions rarely occur on the eastern coasts of the world's continents.

Water Temperature

The world's oceans are classified into several temperature zones. Those adjoining the coasts of North America are shown on the "Water Temperature Zones" map. As can be seen, tropical waters are found in the Sea of Cortez and at the tip of the Baja peninsula. Tropical seas represent the most ideal environment for life on earth. Fish tend to be larger, more abundant, and of different species than those found in cooler waters. Baja's Pacific waters are classified as subtropical and represent a transition between the tropics and the temperate area to the north. Near the shore, they are often cooled by the upwelling noted above. And, in terms of numbers of fish, these cold Pacific waters probably outproduce the warmer Sea of Cortez.

As a result of these temperature factors, the Sea of Cortez offers the abundance of sea life common to tropical waters. It is the closest body of such waters to people living in much of western Canada and western United States. At the same time, the presence of cooler, subtropic and upwelling conditions on the Pacific side results in a wide variety of fish species being available to the Baja fisherman.

Coastal Habitat

Many species of smaller game fish thrive only where they are protected by rocky shores and reefs. As previously noted, much of Baja's coastline is mountainous and rocky. In addition, there are a considerable number of coastal islands with similar shoreline characteristics. The peninsula thus offers favorable marine environments for people who fish from, or close to, the shore.

Observation

In cruising off the coasts of Baja, one is seldom out of sight of a Mexican fishing vessel of some type. These boats do not fish hundreds of miles out to sea but near the land. There are fishing camps and villages in scores of locations. Fish processing plants are to be found in most larger communities. It is a simple matter of observation to conclude that there is abundant marine life in the surrounding waters.

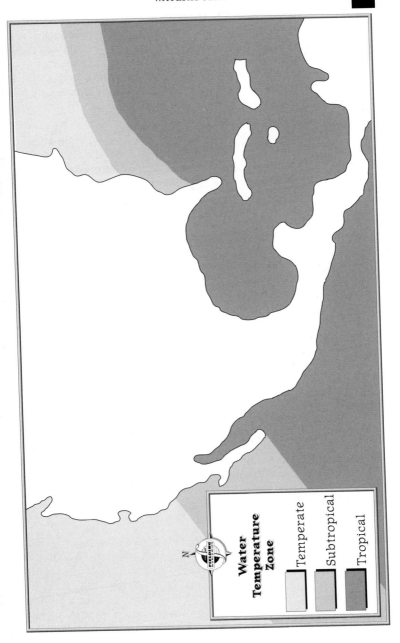

Overfishing

Sadly, this heavy commercial fishing has significantly decreased the quality of sportfishing in Baja waters in many locations. The heaviest impact has come from Mexico's own fishing vessels based at Ensenada and La Paz on the peninsula, and at Guaymas, Topolobampo and other ports on the Mexican mainland. Mexican officials have even licensed foreign fleets to fish in Baja waters, sacrificing long-term good for quick profit.

The sportfishing fleet operators at La Paz readily concede that the waters immediately adjoining their city have been fished-out, and several resort owners have asked me if there is anything I can do about the heavy commercial fishing. In spite of all this, sportfishing in Baja is still outstanding, although it is not as good as it once was in some places.

Fishing Alternatives

Fishermen have a wide range of alternatives for enjoying their sport in Baja waters, as indicated in the outline below.

—**Large charter boats**

- •**Party boats**

- •**Sportfisher charters**

- •**Extended-trip charters**

—**Medium charter boats**

—**Panga charters**

—**Fishermen-owned boats**

- •**Ocean-cruisers**

- •**Trailer boats**

- •**Large charter boats—vessels in the 40–60 foot range**

Party Boats

At many Pacific coast ports in the United States, individual fishermen may pay to join 15 to 30 others for a day's sport. Fishing gear may be rented, or you may bring your own. The advantage of such trips is their relatively low cost made possible by the large number of fishermen making each trip.

Many party boats are based in San Diego at the Commercial Basin on the north side of Shelter Island. Some of these fish in Mexican waters surrounding the Coronado Islands. Others offer more extended trips farther south. Ensenada is the only port offering true party-boat service in Baja. Fishing here is in Bahía Todos Santos and around the Islas Todos Santos. Mexican fishing licenses are usually included in the cost of the Ensenada trips. Many species caught off Ensenada are seldom taken farther north.

Sportfisher Charters

"Sportfisher" is the name applied to any number of fast, open-transom powerboats in the 40–60 foot range. They normally accommodate only two to four anglers at a time who sit in fancy chairs in the boat's stern and haul in the large glamour fish. Trips are normally on a day-basis only as overnight accommodations are limited.

Numerous sportfishers are based at Cabo San Lucas and reservations may be made at any of the local hotels or from U.S. agents in Southern California. In the past, many of these craft have been operated by U. S. skippers without formal authority from the Mexican government. I am advised that this practice may be coming to an end, but certainly sportfishing boats will be available at Cabo through one means or another. A smaller number of sportfisher vessels operate out of La Paz.

Extended-Trip Charters

There are three ports in Baja that offer oceangoing vessels large enough to provide overnight accommodations for multi-day fishing, whale-watching, and general enjoyment adventures:

Ensenada

Contact Ensenada Clipper, *8194 Havasu, Buena Park, CA 90621,* ☎ *(714) 994-1872*

San Felipe

Tony Reyes Fishing Tours, contact The Long Fin, *4010 E. Chapman Avenue, Suite D, Orange, CA 92669,* ☎ *(714) 538-8010,* or The Poseidon, *P.O. Box 974, Calexico, CA 92231,* ☎ *(619) 239-6123.* The Tony Reyes trips are six-day adventures to the Midriff Island area.

La Paz

Baja Yacht Charters, contact Frazer Charters Inc, *P.O. Box 60099, San Diego, CA 92106,* ☎ *(619) 225-0588.* The Tony Reyes vessel is moved from San Felipe to La Paz during January and February.

Medium-sized Charter Boats

Most of the larger vessels discussed above were manufactured in the United States. Dozens of smaller flybridge cruisers in the 25- to 35-foot range have been produced by small Mexican boatyards in the southern portion of the peninsula. They are less sumptuous than the U.S.-built products.

The majority of these boats make up the fishing fleets of the hotels from Cabo San Lucas to San Jose del Cabo and the Buena Vista-Los Barriles area. Another fleet operates out of the Hotel Los Arcos in La Paz. Chartering these vessels is usually less expensive. Contact any of the major hotels in the areas noted.

Some sportfishermen have purchased Mexican pangas made in La Paz. Here one is being launched at the Fishermen's Landing launching ramp at the mouth of the estuary at Mulegé.

Panga Charters

No discussion of boating in Baja would be complete without reference to the *panga*, a heavy fiberglass open-boat powered by an outboard motor. They are made in La Paz and were designed by Mac Shroyer, a former math teacher from the United States who now manages the Marina de La Paz in La Paz. They range from 18 to 24 feet in length. There is hardly a Mexican fisherman in Baja who does not operate from such a boat. About 2500 have been constructed. You will see them everywhere Mexican fishermen gather.

Most pangas are used for commercial fishing by the members of fishing co-operatives. However, more and more they are being offered for charter to sportfishermen. At La Paz, pangas make up the fishing fleet operated by Bob Butler. Contact the **Hotel Los Arcos**, or *P.O. Box 6688, Crestline, CA 92325.* In Bahía de los Angeles a small fleet is maintained by Guerrmo's Trailer Court. In most other places, one contacts the individual operators of the pangas, who will be waiting by their boats.

Concentrations of pangas available for hire may be found in the inner harbor at Cabo San Lucas; at the fisherman's landing at the small town of La Playa, one mile east of San Jose del Cabo; near the trailer courts in Loreto; immediately south of the lighthouse in San Felipe; at the mouth of the river in Mulegé, and in scores of other less-visited locations. Even if a panga fishermen is not normally in the sportfishing business, his boat can usually be hired for that purpose. Hard cash is hard to turn down.

Fisherman-Owned Boats

We will now discuss the three classes of boats brought south by tourists. The three classes are the same as presented earlier in this chapter.

Ocean-Cruisers

People coming to Baja on ocean-cruising sailboats usually engage in sport-fishing. Some of this is simply bottom-fishing from the boat when it is at anchor. More often the ship's tender is used for trolling away from the anchorage. When this occurs, the ocean-cruiser has the advantages attributable to the small Class-4 boats described below, plus the range provided by the larger mother vessel.

Trailer Boats

Small car-top and trailerable boats are taken south to Baja by the thousands. They are the Class-3 and -4 vessels noted earlier in this chapter. They range in size from small 13-foot aluminum craft to the heavy vessel on the three-axle trailer shown in the photo in this chapter. The larger boat has significant range but lacks maneuverability for fishing in shallow and restricted areas. The 13-footers have maximum maneuverability and can be launched at hundreds of places where there is no ramp. The fisherman's range is thus expanded by moving the boat around on land. The small boat's disadvantages are that it cannot be used in even moderately rough weather and it cannot safely venture far from land.

Fishing Overview

By way of background, I present the following overview material.

When to Fish

There are hundreds of varieties of game fish in the waters surrounding the Baja peninsula. They range in size from giant marlin to small rockfish and triggers. There is considerable variation in the time of year when any given species is present, and this availability also differs from section to section of the coast.

Refer to the chart "Quality of Fishing by Months," which is based on a composite of information for common game fish for all areas of the peninsula. The rating index in the chart's vertical axis is my own invention and has no significance other than to show the relative fishing quality by months of the year. It is designed to show that (1) fishing in Baja is never poor, (2) the best fishing is during the summer and early fall, and (3) the least productive months are during the winter.

In general, the peninsula-wide yearly trend shown in the chart is also encountered in most individual sections, particularly in the tropical waters of the Sea of Cortez. Clearly, the presence of many species increases as the waters become warmer during summer. However, there are numerous seasonal variations, particularly if you are interested in one particular species of fish. More data on when to fish are noted in the summaries below.

Upper Sea of Cortez Area

This is the area from north of Santa Rosalia to the mouth of the Rio Colorado. While the waters here are still classified as tropical, there is upwelling of cooler waters near the Midriff Islands lying off Bahía de los Angeles and some of the tropical fish species such as sailfish, amberjack, snappers and needlefish do not migrate this far north. By way of compensation, the northern area has several species not found farther south. These include the spotted bass and many of the mullet, tortuava, croker and corvina that spawn in the shallow waters south of the Rio Colorado.

In much of this area fishing is good year-round, but fishermen are faced with two practicalities posed by the weather. The chilly, winter, northerly winds present throughout the Sea of Cortez are particularly strong north of Santa Rosalia. Fishing in small boats can thus be both cold and dangerous during these months. In the summer, air temperatures are excessively hot, even more so than in areas to the south. From a practical standpoint, the spring and fall months constitute the best fishing periods. Boat launching is also complicated by the extreme tide fluctuations and severe currents present in these waters.

Mulegé-Loreto Area

Several of the extremes that confront the fisherman in the upper Sea of Cortez are less of a problem farther south. Winter temperatures are milder and winds, while present, are less severe. And summer temperatures, while hot, are less so than farther north. Tides and currents are not serious problems as they are to the north. However, fisherman need to be alert to the possibility of severe tropical storms that occasionally reach into this area. The U. S. Naval Weather Service records indicate the danger period is from mid-August to mid-October.

While fishing is good year-round near Caleta San Lucas, it is more seasonal in such other popular fishing areas as Punta Chivato, Mulegé, Bahía Concepcíon and the area around Puerto Escondido. This is because several of the most sought after species are migrators that come and go with the seasons. As examples, yellowtail are prevalent in the winter, while July is the big month for dorado and marlin. Consult *The Baja Catch* for details.

La Paz Area

The fishing fleet advertisements in La Paz stating that their city is Baja's all-season fishing grounds are a bit deceptive. First, fleet operators readily concede that the waters immediately off the city are badly depleted. For this reason, they transport their clients either to the northern end of the East Cape area or to the waters around the southern end of Isla Espiritu Santos.

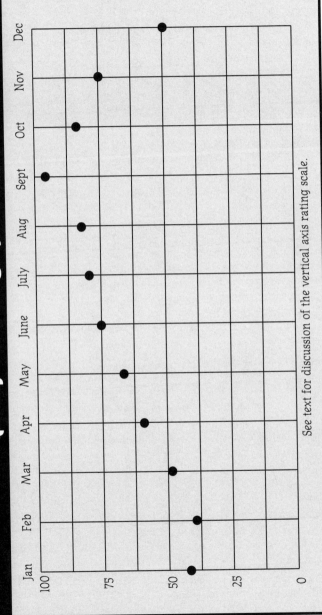

Quality of Fishing By Months

See text for discussion of the vertical axis rating scale.

Around June in this latter area they can meet the large migratory species moving north into the Sea of Cortez.

Thus, La Paz has to reach somewhat far afield to tap good fishing waters and the area is only lightly visited by fishermen in small trailerable boats.

The East Cape Area

The East Cape is that section of coast from the southern end of Isla Cerralvo south to Bahía los Frailes. The area's hotel operators boast that it is the finest fishing grounds in the world. There are four basic reasons for this high praise:

1. While Cabo San Lucas is recognized as the marlin capital of the world, this species is also one of the big draws along the East Cape.

2. The most sought-after species of fish along Baja's east coast are migrators that include marlin, tuna, dorado, roosterfish and wahoo. They move north into the Sea of Cortez in the spring and back south again in fall. Most of this migration takes place close to the Baja shore rather than on the mainland side. It passes on either side of Isla Cerralvo.

3. Ocean waters more than 1000 feet deep lie only a few miles offshore along much of the East Cape shoreline, and it is in such deep, blue-water areas that marlin thrive. Thus, lengthy trips to sea are not required to reach the large glamour species in this area. The best season is short, however, centering around six-week periods in late May and October, although some of the large species persist in some areas through the summer.

4. While the main marlin periods are limited, the East Cape also has a sizeable population of top-flight resident species so that fishing of some variety is always available.

The Cape Area

There are fewer resident fishes at the tip of the Baja peninsula than in other areas, but fishing for striped marlin and other billfish is unexcelled. They are catchable throughout the year with the best seasons centering around April and November.

As in the East Cape, the deep waters favored by marlin come close to shore at Cabo San Lucas. They may thus be caught only a few miles off the Cape, although many charter vessels take their customers to various "banks" that lie some 20–25 miles offshore. During the winter months the marlin are found on the Pacific side of the Cape and along the Sea of Cortez shore in the summer.

Small boats may be launched at the excellent ramps in the inner harbor at Cabo San Lucas, but surf conditions greatly limit over the beach launching in the Cape area. Each morning there is a mass exodus of sportfishing vessels leaving the Cabo San Lucas harbor. Some are small, fishermen-owned boats but most are various sizes of charter vessels catering to hotel clients. There is considerable fishing action at San Jose del Cabo, but simple observation will disclose that Cabo San Lucas is the fishing capital of Baja California.

Pacific Lagoons

Much of Baja's Pacific shore consists of the extremely low-lying terrain of the Continental Borderlands Province. Saltwater lagoons lie behind the barrier-beaches in many places and most have entrances to the sea protected by breaking bars. The larger lagoons support Mexican fish camps and receive light visitation from sportfishermen using small car-top boats.

The lagoons most frequently visited are Puerto San Quintin, Laguna Manuela, Laguna la Bocana, Estero Coyote, Laguna San Ignacio, and Bahía Magdalena and the extensive lagoons north of its main bay. Fishing in these places is rated from fair to excellent.

With the exception of Bahía Magdalena, these places are mostly accessed by washboarded secondary roads over level but poorly vegetated planes. Camping sites are austere and often windswept, but avid fishermen will find the lagoons a special and rewarding challenge.

Pacific Rocky Shores

The "Geologic Provinces" map on page 189 shows the mountainous, and rocky portions of Baja's Pacific coast. There is little sportfishing data on these areas as road access is poor and the launching of small boats into the heavy Pacific surf is difficult. I expect that the Punta Eugenia and Punta Abreojos area will become popular fishing areas when oiling of the highway to Bahía Tortugas is completed.

For now, sportfishing is concentrated in the Bahía Todos Santos area at Ensenada, and at various reefs and islands to the south that are accessed by three- and four-day charter trips out of San Diego and Ensenada. The Coronado Islands may also be reached by larger fisherman-owned boats out of San Diego.

Shrimp

Tourists at San Felipe and Bahía Concepcíon in the Sea of Cortez will frequently observe Mexican fishing vessels in the 40- to 60-foot class. These, in most cases, will be shrimpers and may be distinguished from more conventional fishing boats by the large array of often colorful nets hanging from booms when the boat is not actually working. Many shrimpers work at night, so you will see them anchored during the day.

Dragging for shrimp takes place in relatively shallow waters along both coasts in the northern half of the Sea of Cortez. I have also seen shrimpers working the waters of Bahía de La Paz. On the Pacific coast, shrimp boats will also be seen in Bahía Magdalena and in the shallow waters along the sandy beaches north of this bay.

Because of Mexico's economic problems, the government has decreed that shrimp must be sold on the international market in order to produce foreign currency. Many fishermen will sell shrimp to tourists, but you should recognize the illicit nature of these transactions. There are reports of shrimp being sold to tourists, who are then approached by the salesman's accomplices posing as federal officers looking for *la mordida* or "the bite," as bribery is known.

Lobster

Lobsters abound in the waters along the rocky sections of the Pacific coast and its islands. Bahía Magdalena is at the southern end of the lobstering area. Boaters must be continually alert for small buoys attached by lines to lobster traps resting on the ocean floor. As with shrimp, the taking of lobsters by anyone other than Mexican nationals is not permitted and, again, they may not be legally sold to tourists.

Fishing Licenses

All tourists 12 years or older must obtain a Mexican Sport Fishing License to fish in Mexican waters. Licenses are issued by the day, week, month or year. Fees depend upon the length of time involved and fluctuate widely according to the current exchange rate. All persons aboard a tourist's boat must have a license if the vessel is carrying fishing gear or any kind of fish or fish parts. This can become expensive for yachts carrying numerous people on extended voyages.

A fishing license must also be obtained for any boat used for fishing. Here, the fee is based on the length of the vessel.

Licenses covering all types of sportfishing are issued by the federal government *(Secretaria de Pesca)* and are valid throughout Mexico.

WATERSPORTS

RESORT AREAS
AND HOTELS

Hotel Las Rocas, Rosarito Beach, is a cliffside hotel with terraced rooms.

This chapter was entitled "Hotels" in the first version of this book. I have changed it to "Resort Areas and Hotels" as it is obviously necessary for people seeking a hotel vacation to choose a resort area before they select a specific hotel. One must also be aware that the ambience of Baja's resort areas vary markedly, one from the other, and that several new, or heavily altered areas have emerged within the past few years.

Resort Areas

The map on page 99 shows the locations of the 10 resort areas that are described below. These descriptions are obviously flavored by my personal judgments and biases. Nevertheless, I hope they are of some value. The map also indicates the names and locations of Baja's growing number of golf courses.

The first four resort areas are near the U.S. border and receive much of their use from Southern California residents escaping the jungle on weekends. They are not the places I would recommend for one's prized yearly vacation. Having said this, I am well aware that many of the hotel visits throughout Baja are limited to brief weekend and holiday-weekend visits. The flying time to the peninsula's southern resort areas is little different than that spent driving to the border areas. I have included the names of my favorite hotels in each area for what it is worth.

Tijuana

A large bustling city with few waterfront attractions or other amenities normally associated with a resort town. There are several good hotels that serve mostly business people, visitors to the golf course and bull rings, or those looking for a quick taste of Mexican culture. The **Hotel Lucerna** offers a restful atmosphere and is my favorite. The **Grand Hotel Tijuana** is more grandiose for those seeking a skyscraper atmosphere.

San Felipe

A modest-sized town on the upper end of the Sea of Cortez that is a major RV park haven for northern snowbirds. There are a few nice hotels but they serve mainly the weekend visitor. While the appearance of the community has improved considerably in recent years, it is still far from a world-class resort area and its vegetation is a bit sparse for my tastes. The **Hotel Las Misions** is the pick of the hotel crop in my view.

North Coast

(Rosarito to Ensenada)

The town of Rosarito has long been the home of several good hotels. But in recent years, several luxury establishments have been constructed along the coast to the south. One of them has a golf course. Of the four border resort areas, this is my recommendation as the best for those looking for a pleasant, coastal hotel experience. The other three are better for those wishing to explore a Mexican community. The **Rosarito Beach Hotel** would be my choice in part because of its historic background. The new ones to the south are also very nice.

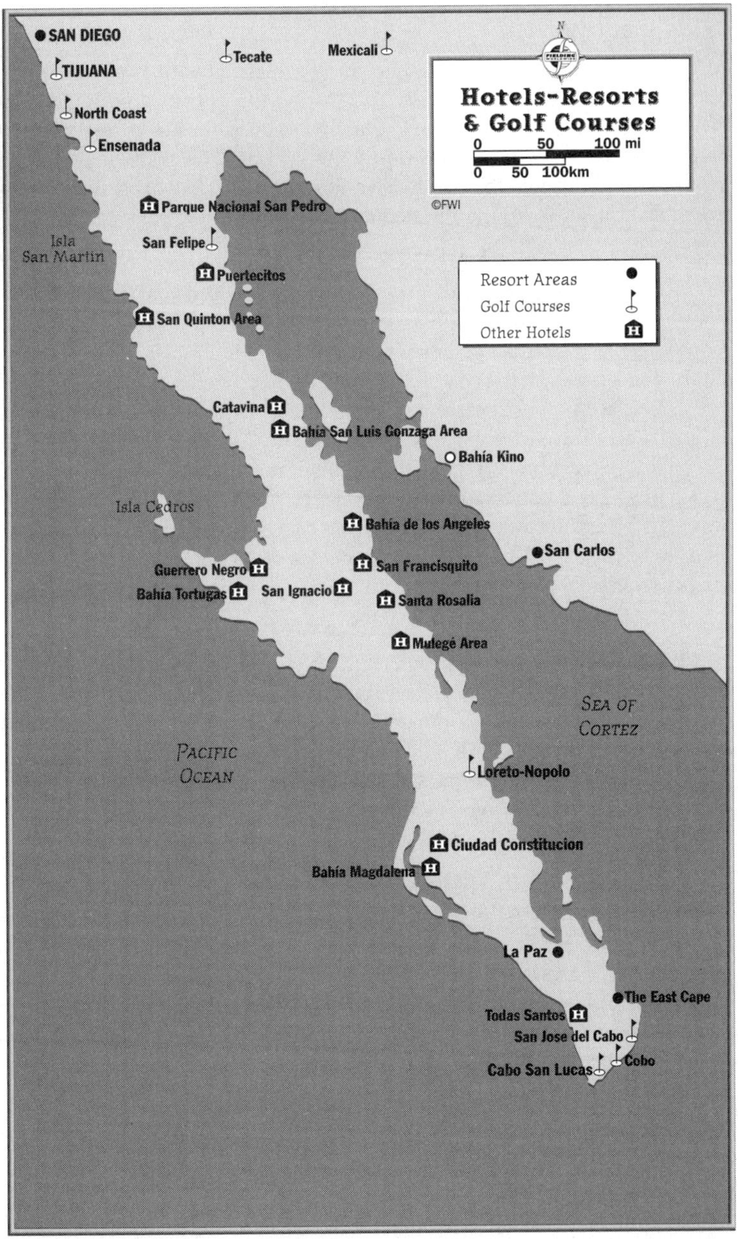

Hotels-Resorts & Golf Courses

0 50 100 mi
0 50 100km

©FWI

Resort Areas	●
Golf Courses	⚑
Other Hotels	🏨

● SAN DIEGO

⚑ TIJUANA

⚑ North Coast

⚑ Ensenada

⚑ Tecate

Mexicali ⚑

Isla San Martin

🏨 Parque Nacional San Pedro

San Felipe ⚑

🏨 Puertecitos

🏨 San Quinton Area

Catavina 🏨

🏨 Bahia San Luis Gonzaga Area

○ Bahía Kino

Isla Cedros

🏨 Bahia de los Angeles

Guerrero Negro 🏨

🏨 San Francisquito

● San Carlos

Bahía Tortugas 🏨 San Ignacio 🏨

🏨 Santa Rosalia

🏨 Mulege Area

PACIFIC OCEAN

SEA OF CORTEZ

⚑ Loreto-Nopolo

🏨 Ciudad Constitucion

Bahía Magdalena 🏨

La Paz ●

● The East Cape

Todas Santos 🏨

San Jose del Cabo ⚑

Cabo San Lucas ⚑ ⚑ Cobo

Ensenada

As with Tijuana, Ensenada is a large, busy community with few waterfront attractions or the other amenities normally associated with a resort town. It does have a clearly defined tourist area. Most visitors to its hotels are using them as a base for seeing the city. The exception is the **Estero Beach Resort Hotel** a few miles south of town on the waterfront. This is the best hotel in the area in my view. The **San Nicolas Resort Hotel** is probably the best in Ensenada proper, although the **Mission Santa Isabel** is my personal favorite.

Loreto-Nopolo

For years, the small town of Loreto was a relatively sleepy fishing village. Then in 1977 the Mexican government chose it and a nearby beach called Nopolo for development of a major resort area. This effort has largely been a failure and tourism has been minimal. But a fine, medium-sized hotel and golf course were constructed at Nopolo along with a nearby international airport. Loreto itself has now been spruced up considerably and there are several fine, small hotels. To me, the failure of the big development plans has been a blessing as Loreto and Nopolo retain a small-town atmosphere. I recommend it to your attention. Any of the hotels noted later in this chapter offer good Mexican ambience. The **Loreto Inn** at Nopolo is the fanciest, but the others offer the advantage of being directly within the community.

La Paz

La Paz is a city of 160,000 people with an international airport. It is my favorite city in Mexico. There are several very good hotels located near a bay off the Sea of Cortez. I recommend it to your attention, keeping in mind, that one visits its hotels primarily as a means of enjoying the city. While on the waterfront, it is not primarily a beach resort as are the four resort areas noted below in this listing. The **Hotel Los Arcos** is my personal favorite, but others prefer **La Concha Beach Resort**.

The East Cape

The East Cape shares the stage with Loreto-Nopolo as being Baja's low-key resort areas. Many tourists prefer its small, often isolated, beachfront hotels to the bigger, more urbanized settings of the Cape Area's three resort areas. It is served by the international airport at Los Cabos. My favorite is the **Hotel Palmas de Cortez**, but all the facilities noted in this chapter are high quality.

San Jose Del Cabo

Government development started here at the same time as that at Loreto-Nopolo, but was far more successful. A very fine hotel, now the **Presidente Inter-Continental**, was constructed on the beach. The town of San Jose was considerably modernized and a previously vacant area was developed into a golf course and major residential area for investing North Americans. The new developments are largely separated from the old Mexican town and thus are all modern and uniformly pleasing. Several other medium-sized hotels were constructed on the same beach, but they have not been overly popular. They appear to be the victims of poor lot design. I can recommend the San Jose del Cabo area but strongly advise the above noted hotel, the **La Jolla** at the western end of town, or the popular **Tropicana Inn** in the old section of town.

Its fine architectural style and great seaside location near San Jose del Cabo make the Palmilla Los Cabos one of Baja's finest hotels.

Cabo San Lucas

The fishing village at the peninsula's tip was the prime target for the government resort development that started in 1977. Here at Cabo San Lucas, the central feature was a dredged inner-harbor. Development was agonizingly slow but the harbor is finally finished. It is now filled with a high quality marina and is lined with hotels and condominiums. Other hotels and condos stretch eastward down the beach. Unlike San Jose del Cabo, the tourist attractions here are somewhat intermixed with less attractive older developments. This can be either unattractive or charming, depending on one's frame of mind. Cabo contains several world-class hotels and is regularly visited by large cruise liners. I believe the best hotels are the two that were there long before the government development, the **Hotel Finisterra** and the **Hacienda Hotel**. The **Hotel Malia** is probably the best of the newer places.

Many Baja old-timers, myself included, disparage the new Cabo and regret the passing of the old. It took so long to mature that it became fashionable to report that the place was a mess. In spite of this negative comment, I am forced to recommend it to you. Cabo has finally reached a reasonable stage of respectability and thousands of people visit and seem to enjoy themselves

Cabo Corridor

The coastal area between San Jose del Cabo and Cabo San Lucas is known as the Cabo Corridor. It is served by a 24-kilometer-long, four-lane highway. It has long been home to three of Baja's very best hotels, the **Hotel Palmilla**, **Hotel Cabo San Lucas** and **Hotel Twin Dolphin**. Then, starting about 1990, much of the intervening space began to fill with a wide range of tourist-oriented developments. The largest of these are **Cabo Real**, **Cabo del Sol** and the area adjoining the **Hotel Palmilla**. Each area is hundreds of acres in size and combines luxury hotels, golf courses and various residential developments. Much construction is still going on, but all development is uniformly first class. In this regard these areas are clearly superior to any other resort area in Baja, and to anything I have seen in the entire world. While they may lack the third-world charm of other places in Baja, they are undeniably world-class. In spite of all this grandeur, my favorite hotels in the Corridor are the original three noted above.

FONATUR

In the above descriptions of Baja's resort areas it was noted that the Mexican government was the initial developer of resort facilities at Loreto-Nopolo, San Jose del Cabo and Cabo San Lucas. The government agency responsible for this effort is FONATUR, the acronym for **Fondo National de Formento al Turismo** (translated into English as **National Fund for Tourism Development**). FONATUR was created by the federal government in 1969. Its primary function is to encourage and channel the government and private investments needed to establish new centers of tourist activities with the objectives of increasing domestic employment, generating foreign exchange and promoting regional development.

FONATUR'S initial activities were on the mainland at Cancun on Mexico's Caribbean coast and at Ixtapa on the Pacific coast north of Acapulco. Here, two essentially deserted sections of coast were converted into rows of high-rise hotels, condominiums and tourist-oriented facilities. International airports were constructed nearby.

During the mid 1970s FONATUR initiated work in the Baja peninsula. Actual construction started at Loreto in 1977, and at San Jose del Cabo and Cabo San Lucas in 1978. At all sites, early work consisted of developing such essential facilities as water and power supplies, sewage systems, and offices and housing for employees. New hotels soon followed, along with extensive networks of streets for vacation homes and condominiums. Golf courses were largely complete by 1989. So far, these developments have not included high-rise buildings; one would hope that this remains true for the future.

It is interesting to note that the newest resort developments along the Cabo Corridor are the result of private rather than government activities. This is in keeping with Mexico's marked movement away from socialism in recent years.

Hotels

I must alert you that I am in love with Baja's hotels. They are one of her major tourist attractions and provide excellent examples of the blending of man-made features with outstanding natural surroundings. The destination of most of my travels north of the border has usually been an interesting city, a national park or other enticing outdoor attraction. With few exceptions, the hotels and motels in which I have spent the night offer little more than a place to stay. When you visit Baja's fine hotels, I hope you will come to agree that they provide an end in themselves.

I am not a world traveler, but I have been fortunate in recent years to visit most of the Caribbean islands, the major South American cities, England, Spain, Portugal, Switzerland and parts of France, Italy and an assortment of lesser spots. Baja's hotels are better than anything I have seen in these places (I will concede to some excellent hotels in Hawaii). I will now briefly explain why I hold this view.

1. Location

Except in the larger cities, most of Baja's better hotels are situated directly on the water's edge, thus taking full advantage of mankind's love affair with the coast. In some cases, the front yard of your room will be an extensive white sand beach as at San Felipe, Buena Vista and San Jose del Cabo. In others, the setting blends the hotel with craggy cliffs, as at the tip of the peninsula.

Hotel locations run the gamut from busy downtown La Paz to complete isolation. In some cases, there are no other man-made features for miles in any direction. If you are less than enchanted with visiting such sardine-packed resort centers as Acapulco, Honolulu and the Florida coast, Baja will provide a welcome change.

2. Architectural Style

The designers of Baja's fine hotels have achieved an outstanding blending of structural and landscape architecture. Perhaps most importantly, almost all of Baja's fine hotels are low-rise. Three stories are usually the limit. These buildings blend with the natural environment. That Wall Street feeling is left behind. North of the border, the hotel guest is greeted by steel, lumber and sheetrock; in Baja, it is brick, native stone and tile, with palm thatching in the patio areas. These building materials, combined with the archways, tile corridors and other trappings of Spanish architecture, provide a charming change for the northern visitor.

Completing the picture are swimming pools, fountains and attractive desert landscaping. Baja's desert plants seem amazingly tolerant to being transplanted for domestic purposes. They provide peninsula hotels with instant oasis of greenery and shade. If you cannot relax in such a setting you may be beyond relaxation.

3. Uncrowded Setting

Only a few of Baja's hotels have as many as 250 rooms. The majority are much smaller. The overall ambiance is usually one of freedom and spaciousness. There is no need to rise at dawn to reserve one's lounge chair from among all the others packed at the rim of the pool, as in many other parts of the world.

Even the best hotels are seldom full except during three-day weekends and immediately prior to Christmas and Easter. (This observation spans all of my travels in Baja. It is as true today as it was 20 years ago, when Baja was far less popular than it is presently.) Reservations should be made well in advance for these peak periods. They are advisable at other times but are usually easily obtained. While this light use is not good news for management, it is pleasant for the patron who benefits by receiving better service under less hectic conditions. It seems all too obvious that there are more hotel rooms than the supply of tourists and more are being built. While this would seem to make very little economic sense for the hotel operators, it results in a relaxed and uncrowded atmosphere for the tourist.

The La Pinta Chain

In tandem with the completion of the Transpeninsular Highway in 1973 came the construction by the government of a series of *paradors* and nearby hotels. (*Parador* is derived from the Spanish word *parada*, meaning stopping place.) The paradors originally offered fuel, cafeteria-style restaurants, rest rooms, and trailer courts. Many of these facilities have been abandoned, but the hotels are all still in operation, all bearing the name **Hotel La Pinta**.

It is clear that the Mexican government wished to provide modern, first-class facilities for the deluge of tourists that were expected after completion of the highway. The paradors were to fill this need from Ensenada to the Sea of Cortez, where there were then few tourist accommodations. The onslaught came, but in the form of recreational vehicle users hellbent on making it south to the beaches in the shortest possible time. Relatively few visitors arrived in automobiles, and as a result there was only light demand for restaurants and hotels along the highway.

More recently there has been a significant increase in the number of tourists traveling Highway 1 in automobiles, and the La Pinta hotels are thus enjoying better business. They are located at, or near, San Quintin, Cataviña, Parallelo 28 near Guerrero Negro, San Ignacio and Loreto. These hotels are modest in size (25 to 65 rooms), and they were being well maintained during my most recent visit. I recommend them to you for an overnight stop.

In recent years small- to medium-sized motels have been developed in many of the towns along Highway 1. They are clean and fully usable for an overnight or longer stay, but are too numerous to include in the "Hotel Descriptions" presented in this chapter.

Fly-in Hotels

Long before completion of the Transpeninsular Highway, private hotel operators were catering to the North American tourist trade; however, many south-of-the-border cities had to be reached by air. The hotels at La Paz have long been served by an airport suitable for large commercial aircraft in addition to ferry service from the mainland. Most of the other hotels had to provide their own dirt-surface landing strips. Their patrons were thus almost exclusively people who arrived in small, privately owned aircraft.

These hotels were scattered along the coast of the Sea of Cortez from Bahía Gonzaga, on the north, all the way to Cabo San Lucas. The majority were isolated from the outside world. Some were very modest, having only a few cabins and a central dining and lounging facility. Others were, and still are, among the most luxurious resorts in all of Baja. Most of these hotels are still in operation, but many are in locations now served by main highways, and in some cases their airstrips have been closed by the Mexican government to deter drug traffic, or the land has been utilized for other purposes. The principal hotels that still have nearby airstrips and cater to the general aviation flyer are, **Hotel Punta Chivato** north of Mulegé, **Hotel Serenidad** at Mulegé, **Hotel Palmas de Cortez** as Los Barriles and **Hotel Pescadero** north of Los Barriles.

Offbeat Hotels

Finally, let's get down to some places most people have never heard of and that offer a special charm at reasonable prices. I hate to mention these hideouts because their owners may get the *big-head* and raise their prices; and then, where am I going to stay? But here they are from north to south:

The **Meling Ranch** (Parque Nacional San Pedro Martir), **La Fonda Motel & Restaurant** (Old Highway 1), **Bay-Side Motels** (Bahía San Quintin), **Las Casitas** (Mulegé), **Hotel Oasis** and **Villas de Loreto** (Loreto), **Hotel Gardinas** (La

Paz), **Hotel California** (Todos Santos), **Hotel Palomar** (Santiago) and **Hotel Mar de Cortez** (Cabo San Lucas).

In addition, I recommend that you take advantage of the services of a travel agent. Many Baja hotels offer discount rates for stays of more than two or three days, and lower airfares can frequently be obtained if travel is combined in a package with hotel reservations. These and other advantages can easily be missed if you make your own reservations. Unfortunately, travel agencies will not help you with some of the smaller, charming hotels that do not have toll-free numbers or pay agency commissions.

Finally, brace for the fact that some Baja hotels change their names and phone numbers with great regularity. You may have to do some detective work to match what you find here with what appears at your travel agency.

Hotel Descriptions

Tijuana

Hotels

Plaza las Glorias   **$46–50**   ★★

Boulevard Auga Caliente No. 11553, P.O. Box 431588, San Ysidro, CA 92173,
☎ *(800) 342-2644, FAX: (66) 863-639.*
Single: $46. Double: $50.
One block from Caliente Race Track, adjacent to Tijuana Country Club.
200 rooms, air conditioning, pool, Jacuzzi, exercise room, restaurant.
Formerly the Paraiso Radisson Tijuana, this 10-story hotel is located on Tijuana's main artery, and provides modern, if rather stark, accommodations. The bedrooms feature queen or king beds, open closets, TV, air conditioning, and small baths with tubs. Wall-sized windows fill the rooms with light. Best views overlook the golf course in back, rooms up front suffer from traffic noise. Credit Cards: V, MC.

Grand Hotel Tijuana   **$62–69**   ★★★

4500 Agua Caliente Boulevard, ☎ *(800) 472-6385, (66) 817-000, FAX: (66) 817-016*
Single: $62. Double: $69.
In Plaza Agua Caliente, adjacent to Tijuana Country Club.
422 rooms, pool, sauna, tennis courts, convention rooms, health club, nightclub.

The twin mirrored-glass towers of the Grand Hotel and Plaza Agua Caliente offices stand as a glittering city landmark. The 24-story structure houses plush "club rooms" on its upper floors, as well as an elegant French dining room, and a sky-lighted atrium with a busy cafe. Convention guests provide the hotel's main business, but travelers who desire many dining choices and a nightclub atmosphere, will appreciate the amenities. Rooms are carpeted, with small sitting areas, light-oak furnishings, and queen or king size beds, and have marble-tiled combination baths. The club rooms have large sitting areas, bath phones, complimentary continental breakfast. Views from upper levels can either be uplifting or depressing—from one side, the hotel overlooks the golf course, while the other side encompasses Tijuana's urban sprawl, including its slums. Credit Cards: AE, V, MC.

Hotel Lucerna $66–160 ★★★★

10902 Paseo de los Héroes/22320 Avenue Rodríguez, P.O. Box 437910, San Ysidro, CA, 92143. ☎ *(800) LUCERNA, (66) 342-000, FAX (66)342-400.*
Single: $66. Double: $70–80. Suites: $82–160.
In the Rio Tijuana complex.
168 rooms, nine suites, air conditioning, pool, travel agency, garden atmosphere.
Offering the most "authentic" Mexican atmosphere combined with modern amenities, this hotel is the insider's choice. Locals and visitors alike give high ratings to this hotel for its warmth, and its professional staff. The six-story hotel features a sunken lobby, an open-air cafe next to a courtyard garden with a swimming pool surrounded by plantings of palm trees. The bedrooms offer double, queen or king sized beds, cable TV, radios and baths with tubs. Most rooms have small balconies, but insist on a room that overlooks the courtyard for the best views. Rooms on the street-side are noisy. The hotel offers a French restaurant, cocktail lounge, pool, nightclub, travel agency and a tennis court. Credit Cards: MC, V.

Holiday Inn Pueblo Amigo $60–90 ★★★

921 Via Oriente/22450 Pueble Amigo, ☎ *(800) 998-6968, (66) 835-030, FAX (66) 835-032.*
Single: $60–90. Double: $60-90. Suites: $90 and up.
In the Zona Rio near the border and Avenida Revolucíon.
108 rooms, plus suites, indoor pool, sauna, exercise room, beauty salon.
Recently opened, this chain-hotel offers American-style modern facilities in the center of Tijuana's tourist area. Popular with business travelers, the hotel features standard rooms, presidential rooms and suites. All rooms feature peach, beige and green colors, and have double, queen or king-size beds with cable TV, direct-dial long-distance telephones, minibars and comfortable baths. Other amenities include meeting rooms, a business center and the Aclazar restaurant, which is popular with local business people. Credit Cards: AE, MC, V.

Real del Rio $65–105 ★★

1409 Calle J. M. Velasco ☎ *(66) 343-100, FAX (66)345-053.*
Single: $65. Double: $70. Suites: $105
In the Zona Rio.
105 rooms, two suites, air conditioning, car rental, business center, coffee shop, bar.
Basic rooms with business amenities, are available at this five-story modern hotel. Rooms feature cable TV and baths. The hotel restaurant is open from 7 a.m. to 10 p.m.

Low-Cost Lodging

La Mesa Inn ★★

50 Boulevard Diaz Ordaz, ☎ *(800) 528-1234, (66) 816-522, FAX (66)812-871.*
Single: $25-45. Double: $60.
South of the Agua Caliente Racetrack, outside main center of town
125 rooms, air conditioning, pool, bar, coffee shop.
Unpretentious but functional, this Best Western property offers down-to-earth rooms at reasonable rates. Standard rooms have TV and air conditioning. Amenities are limited to a small, shaded pool. Book ahead, because the property is popular.
Credit Cards: MC, V.

Restaurants

Boccaccio's   ★★

> 2500 Boulevard Agua Caliente, ☎ (66) 862-266.
> *Italian cuisine and seafood dishes.*
> *Hours: Daily, 1 p.m.–midnight, entrées: $10-28.*
> *Near the Tijuana Country Club.*
> Founded in 1927, but in this location since 1957, this Italian restaurant is decorated with kitschy Roman-style columns and gilded accents. The menu features seafood, including lobster, abalone, crab claws, as well as traditional pastas and steaks.

Tia Juana Tilly's   ★★★

> *Calle 7a and Avenida Revolucíon, ☎ (66) 856-024.*
> *Mexican specialties, steaks, seafood.*
> *Hours: daily, noon-midnight, entrées: $8–20.*
> *Part of the Jai Alai Palace.*
> Popular with locals as well as trendy gringos, this busy restaurant is decorated with photographs of historic Tijuana and TV screens that broadcast live sporting events. Try cochinita píbil (roast pig, red onions and oranges), or chicken molé, made with a chocolate sauces flavored with more than a dozen spices. Credit Cards: AE, MC, V.

Señor Frog's is a lively spot for lunch or dinner.

Señor Frog's   ★★

> *Pueblo Amigo Center, Paseo Tijuana, ☎ (66) 853-698.*
> *Mexican cuisine.*
> *Hours: daily noon–11 p.m., entrées: $8?10.*
> So it's part a chain eatery, but the buckets of chilled cerveza and platters of barbe-cued chicken and ribs make this a good place for a finger-licking meal after a day of bargain-hunting. Loud music and noise are trademarks, so look elsewhere for a cozy atmosphere. Credit Cards: AE, MC, V.

La Leña ★★★★

4560 Boulevard Agua Caliente, ☎ *(66) 863-752.*
Meats grilled Mexican-style
Hours: noon–11 p.m., entrées, $10-25.
Near the Auga Caliente racetrack.

Guests can watch their meal being prepared in the open kitchen, where chefs cook meats over a mesquite-fired grill. Specialties include beef dishes such as Sonoran steaks, carne asada, fillet of beef, and tripe. Mexican dishes are served with flair, and seafood also is available. La Leña has a second location at 816 Avenida Revolucíon (between Calle 4a and 5a) in the downtown area. Credit Cards: AE, MC, V.

El Tourino ★★★★

Calle 6, No. 7531, ☎ *(66) 857-075.*
Steaks and seafood.
Hours: daily, noon–10:00 p.m., entrées: $15–25.
West of Avenida Revolucíon.

Located in the heart of downtown, distant from the tourist areas, this popular establishment specializes in beef dishes served with soup or salad. Enjoy cabreria (New York steak), lobster or shrimp. Credit Cards: MC, V.

Pedrin's ★★★★★

1115 Avenida Revolucíon, ☎ *(66) 854-052.*
Seafood.
Hours: daily, noon–10:00 p.m., entrées: $15–25.
Overlooking the Jai Alai Palace.

This second-floor garden-style restaurant serves a variety of fresh seafood dishes, including cabrilla (sea bass), shrimp and grilled lobster. A branch of the renowned Pedrin's in Rosarito, this restaurant is always busy. Meals include a fried fish appetizer, fish chowder, salad, an entrée and a Kahlua and cream after-dinner drink. Credit Cards: AE, MC, V.

Nightlife

Baby Rock Disco ★

Paseo de los Heroes and Diego Rivera (66) 342-404
This eardrum -splitting disco is a favorite with the younger crowd.

Hard Rock Café ★★

520 Avenida Revolucíon, ☎ *(66) 850-206*
Hours: noon–midnight.
Between Calle 1 and 2

This Tijuana-branch of the renowned London Club isn't geared to attract those looking for the authentic Mexico, but the place is always packed. A hit with families as well as singles, you'll find the same music, menu, and interior decor here as you would at any Hard Rock Cafe.

Bar San Marcos ★★★

Calle 5 and Avenida Revolucíon, ☎ *(66) 882-794*
Hours: 6 p.m.–midnight.
In the building "Le Drugstore Tijuana" next to the Hotel Caesar.

Head here for nostalgic decor and mariachi music performed by a 10-piece band. Popular with California tourists as well as locals, Bar San Marcos features a gleaming 1940's bar and a raised platform that seats the band.

Tia Juana Tilly's   ★ ★ ★

Revolucion at Calle 7; ☎ *(66) 851-612*
Hours: 6 p.m. -midnight
The best dance spot in town for live music, cheap eats and people-watching.

Tecate

Hotels & Resorts

La Hacienda Santa Veronica $60–90   ★ ★ ★ ★

Highway 2, Tecate, 21275, ☎ *(800) 522-1517, (619) 298-4105 (U.S.).*
Single: $60. Double: $90.
Two miles east of Tecate.
87 rooms, pool, bar, tennis courts, horseback riding.
Make reservations for your stay in the U.S., because there's no phone at this ranch resort, a magnet for fans of dirt bikes and four-wheel-drive vehicles who stay the night after spending the day on the nearby dirt track. Formerly a granderia, or breeding ranch for fighting bulls, this off-the-beaten-track resort offers beginner's lessons in bull-fighting for adventurous guests. Other outdoor attractions include horseback riding in the chaparral and scrub-covered hills, volleyball, basketball or tennis on six courts. Housed in mission-style condos, rooms feature Mexican-style furnishings, fireplaces, as well as air conditioning and TV. Also on-site, you'll find a restaurant and an adjoining RV park. Credit Cards: MC, V.

Health Spa

Rancho la Puerta   ★ ★ ★ ★ ★

Highway 2, Tecate, 21275, ☎ *(800) 443-7565, (619) 744-4222 (U.S.), (65)411-55,*
FAX (65)411-08.
Singles: From $1855 per week, all inclusive. Doubles: $2970 per week, all inclusive.
Three miles west of Tecate.
80 rooms, restaurant, pool, hair salon, health club, tennis courts.
Superbly luxurious, and with the price-tag to match, this isolated, famous resort known as "The Door" has pampered the rich and famous since 1940. When the spa was founded, guests spent their nights in tents, but today's accommodations are far from rough—the Spanish-style haciendas with red-tiled roofs or glass-and-wood cottages are decorated with Mexican tiles, folk art and rustic wood. The 300 acres— much landscaped with aromatic herbs—provides a tranquil, elegant retreat, with no phones or TV to distract guests. A full-week, inclusive stay at La Puerta features a special diet and exercise regimen, with up to 30 different health-related activities a day, including opportunities to hike in the hills. Other amenities include massage, low-impact aerobics, weight-training, yoga and t'ai chi. Credit Cards: AE, MC, V.

Low-Cost Lodging

Motel El Dorado   ★ ★

1100 Avenida Juarez, ☎ *(65) 411-01, FAX (65) 413-33.*
Single: $35–40. Double: $35–40.

On the western side of Tecate.
41 rooms, air conditioning.
Clean and comfortable rooms equipped with TV, phone and air conditioning. A basic place to spend the night.

Restaurants

Plaza Jardin   ★ ★ ★

274 Andador Libertad, ☎ *(665) 434-54.*
Mexican food
Hours: 7 a.m.–10 p.m., entrées: $4–10
Near the tourist office.
Basic but hearty Mexican fare, from breakfasts to dinner selections, are served in this bustling diner. During the summer, try for one of the sidewalk tables and enjoy an inexpensive meal of tacos or rellenos while watching the street action.

El Passetto

200 Callejón Libertad, ☎ *(665) 413-61.*
Italian cuisine.
Hours: noon–11 p.m., entrées: $8–15.
West of the Plaza in an alley.
The owner makes his own wine to complement the pastas, seafood and mainstay Mexican dishes served at this popular restaurant. Enjoy live music most evenings or settle back in the attached bar, which is generally is open until midnight. Credit Cards: MC, V.

Pandarería El Mejor

331 Avenida Juárez, ☎ *(665) 400-40.*
Bakery goods and pastries
Hours: daily, 24 hours, entrees, $1–8
Between Calles Rodriguez and Portes Gil.
Pandarería means bakery—a word that will serve you well in Baja if you want to satisfy your sweet tooth or enjoy a crusty, fresh baked loaf. Many claim this bakery is the best on the peninsula. Fresh coffee is served with your purchase. No credit cards.

Mexicali

Hotels

Holiday Inn $79–103   ★ ★ ★

2220 Avenida Benito Juárez, ☎ *(800) 465-4329 (U.S.), (91) 800-00-999 (toll-free in Mexico), FAX: (65) 664-901.*
Single: $79. Double: $86. Suites: $96–103.
173 rooms, restaurant, bar, pool, one lighted tennis court.
In town center.
The business person's choice for reasonably priced, modern comfort. All rooms feature cable TV, radio and standard but well-maintained furnishings—just what you'd expect from this chain hotel. Credit Cards: AE, MC, V.

Hotel La Lucerna   ★ ★ ★ ★

2151 Calzada Juárez, ☎ *(65) 661-000*
Single: $70. Double: $75. Suites: $86–132.
Three miles outside town center.

175 rooms. air conditioning, two dining rooms, cocktails, nightclub, meeting rooms, two pools, tennis courts.

Palm trees decorate the swimming pool and intimate courtyards add a romantic touch at this popular hotel. Beautifully landscaped throughout, with a variety of room layouts, this hotel offers some rooms with private balconies that overlook the pool. All rooms have cable TV, radios and refrigerators. Credit Cards: MC, V.

Holiday Inn Crowne Plaza ★★★★

2001 Avenida de los Heroes, ☎ (800) Holiday (U.S.), (65)573-600.
Single: $110–140. Double: $110–140.
In Centro Civíco Comercial.
158 units, air conditioning, two restaurants, pool, cocktail bar.

This is Holiday Inn's upscale (and considerably more expensive) new, high-rise hotel. Rooms come with cable TV, pay-per-view movies, telephone and radio. The Crowne Plaza offers a family plan. Amenities include a spa and tennis courts. Credit Cards: AE, MC, V.

Restaurants

La Misíon Dragón ★★★

555 Lázaro Cárdenas, ☎ (65) 664-320, (65) 664-451.
Chinese cuisine.
Hours: 7 a.m.–midnight, entrées: $15–20.
One-quarter mile east of Boulevard Benito Juárez.

The first Chinese came to Mexicali in the early 1900s, as laborers to build the Imperial Canal, and today, the Chinos influence is easily seen in the more than 100 restaurants scattered throughout "Chinesca"—Mexicali's Chinatown. At La Misíon Dragón, you can enjoy excellent Chinese dishes in a setting that is a cross between a padre's mission house and an emperor's palace. This is a popular place with the locals, who flock here for big dinner parties. Credit Cards: MC, V.

El Dragón ★★★★

1830 Boulevard Juarez, ☎ (65) 662-200.
Chinese cuisine.
Hours: 11 a.m.–11 p.m., entrees: $8–20
North of the Holiday Inn.

Surrounded by fountains and gardens, the pagoda-style building that houses this "Dragón" is of one Mexicali's busiest Chinese restaurants. The lavish interior is filled floor to ceiling with traditional Chinese decor, but the real draw is the vast menu, which features many regional styles of cooking. Try a platter of chop suey and fried rice, or indulge in the "abalone special." Big portions and reasonable prices are a bonus. Credit Cards: MC, V.

Cenaduria Selecta

1510 Avenida Arista, ☎ (65) 624-047.
Mexican cuisine.
Hours: 8 a.m.–11 p.m., entrees: $8–15
Corner of Avenida Arista and Calle G.

Serving breakfast, lunch or dinner since 1945, this intimate restaurant features burritos, tacos de carne and other traditional Mexican choices. Dine in booths, and enjoy the attention from your waiter. Credit Cards: MC, V.

Los Bufalos

1616 Boulevard Jaurez, ☎ *(65) 663-116.*
Beef and seafood.
Hours: 11 a.m.–10 p.m., entrees: $12–18.
North of the Holiday Inn.

Ranch-style decor and Mexican-style steaks make this restaurant a good choice for beef-eaters. Known for carne asada and steaks, this restaurant also serves a variety of seafood and Mexican specialties. Credit Cards: MC, V.

San Felipe

Hotels & Resorts

San Felipe Marina Resort **$90+** ★ ★ ★ ★

Carretera San Felipe Aeropuerto, ☎ *(800) 777-177 (U.S.), (619) 558-0295 (U.S.), (657)715-68, FAX (657) 714-35.*
Singles: $90 and up. Double: $90 and up.
South of marina, on beach.
60 units, outdoor pool, indoor pool.

This new (and expanding) complex sits south of town, and currently offers hotel rooms, time-shares or condos. Most rooms have kitchens, with coffee makers, microwaves and refrigerators. The decor is Mexican-Mediterranean, with white-tiled floors and woven rugs, folk art accents, with the bonus of balconies or patios, most with sea views. Two pools vie with the beach for swimmers—the indoor pool is a haven on cool winter days. Next door is an RV campground. Plans for expansion include an 100-slip marina, along with resort homes and condos. Credit Cards: MC, V.

El Cortez Motel **$60–90** ★ ★ ★ ★

Avenida Mar de Cortez, ☎ *(657) 710-56, FAX (657) 710-55.*
Single: $60–90. Double: $60–90.
Five minutes walk from the malecón.
90 rooms, air conditioning, restaurant, bar, swimming

Sea views from all rooms and easy access to the boat ramp at Victor's RV Park next door make this hotel a favorite with boaters and others who love the water. Rooms are fresh and light, with white-tiled floors, white walls and pastel bed coverings, and all rooms come with TV and private bath with shower. Some have beach-front patios but these rooms are smaller. A few rooms have two bedrooms. The hotel restaurant boasts the city's best views and offers a good menu selection. Two bars, one on the beach-front and another on the second level, provide opportunities to wind down after a day in the sun. Credit Cards: MC, V.

Hotel Las Misiones **$60–90** ★ ★ ★ ★

130 Avenida Mision De Loreto, ☎ *(657) 712-80.*
Single: $60–90. Double: $60–90.
Outside town center.
183 rooms, 31 suites, three swimming pools, two tennis courts, basketball court, a bar and restaurant.

This palm-shaded resort sits on a stretch of private beach outside the bustle of town, and offers a mission-style retreat perfect for a relaxed vacation "away from it all." Linger by the palm-thatched swim-up bar or stroll the swathe of white-sand beach. Popular with group tours, the hotel offers standard rooms in a three-story building.

Some rooms have private balconies, and other choices include efficiencies, rooms with refrigerators, and suites with kitchenettes. All rooms have air conditioning, cable TV and movies. Credit Cards: MC, V.

Costa Azul   **$60–90**   ★★

Avenida Mar de Cortez and Calle Ensenada, ☎ *(675) 115-48, FAX (675) 715-49.*
Single: $60–90. Double: $60–90.
South end of the malecón.
140 rooms, pool, restaurant, bar.

This complex of three-story buildings offers superb views, although the rooms themselves are run-of-the-mill in terms of decor and furnishings. This hotel offers good deals on mid-week rates. Credit Cards: MC, V.

Restaurants

George's   ★★

336 Avenida Mar de Cortez, ☎ *(657) 710-57.*
Mexican cuisine and seafood
Hours: 7 a.m.–11 p.m., entrees: $8–18.
South of Calle Manzanillo.

A long-time favorite with Americans, this restaurant serves standard Mexican fare at reasonable prices. The margaritas pack a lot of punch, and best bets on the menu are the chiles rellenos and carne asada. Credit Cards: MC, V.

El Nido   ★★

348 Avenida Mar de Cortez Sur, ☎ *(657) 710-49.*
Steaks and seafood
Hours: noon–10 p.m., entrées: $8–15.
Near George's.

Another gringo hangout, this steak house grills its beef on mesquite coals. The menu also features seafood. The El Nido chain has locations scattered throughout the popular resort-areas in the peninsula. Credit Cards: MC, V.

El Toro   ★★★

Highway 5, ☎ *(657) 710-32.*
Mexican cuisine.
Hours: 7 a.m.–11:30 a.m., entrées: $4–8.
North of town.

Serving only breakfast, El Toro is the place where locals and those in the know come to fuel up before heading out for off-road fun in the nearby dunes. Try chorizo (spicy sausage), machaca (shredded beef), or huevos rancheros (fried eggs with green sauce), or dig into an American-style breakfast of bacon and eggs. No credit cards.

Puertecitos

Posada De Orozco   ★

Six rooms.

This facility is located near the PEMEX on the beach at the head of the cove.

The North Coast
(Tijuana to Ensenada)

The Rosarito Beach Hotel has been a favorite with Baja visitors since 1926.

Hotels & Resorts

Residence Inn by Marriott Real De Mar   **$69–169**   ★ ★ ★ ★

Highway 1-D at Km 19.5, ☎ *(800) 331-3131 (U.S.), (661) 334-53, FAX: (661) 411-42.*
Single: $69–109. Double: $69–169.
Seven miles north of Rosarito town center.
150 all-suite units, pool, whirlpool, exercise room, dining room, tennis courts.
This brand-new complex offers Marriott service and suites with fully equipped kitchens. Rooms feature golf course or ocean views, and rates include a continental breakfast and guest cocktail hour. Golf packages include a round of golf at the Real del Mar Golf Course next door. All rooms have air conditioning, phone, cable TV.
Credit Cards: MC, V.

Rosarito Beach Hotel   **$39-119**   ★ ★ ★ ★

Boulevard Juan Benito Jaurez, Rosarito, ☎ *(800) 343-8582 (U.S.), (661) 211-06.*
Single: $39–119. Double: $39–119.
In south part of town.
280 units, including suites, meeting rooms, two pools, three Jacuzzis, beach, sauna, basketball, racquetball, tennis.
Greeting guests since 1926, this venerable property has grown since its beginnings when Prohibition sent gringos south for alcohol-laced entertainment. Famous guests include Orson Welles and Rita Hayworth. Today, the typical guest will arrive on a tour bus, but the original ballrooms and lobby areas retain a nostalgic feel. A highlight is the glassed-in pool deck that overlooks the white-sand beach. Continual renovations have kept the rooms modern—rooms are offered in beach-front low-

rises or in a tower. The upper floor ocean-view rooms are the most expensive, and overall, rooms are small, with white tiled floors and standard but well-maintained furnishings. The hotel caters to both families and fiesta-loving singles, offering a pool with a slide and wading area, plus three bars. Call well in advance to find out about promotions and mid-week reduced rates. Next door is the Casa Playa Spa, housed in 1930s mansion. This full-service European-style spa offering massages, herbal wraps, sauna rooms, hot tubs and a restaurant. Credit Cards: MC, V.

Oasis Resort $30–90   ★★★★★

Highway 1-D, Km 25, ☎ *(800) 462-7472, (661) 332-55, FAX (661) 332-52.*
Single: $30–90. Double: $30–90.
Exit south-lane off-ramp only to access hotel.
100 suites, 12 RVs, 55 RV spaces. Two pools, wading pool, Jacuzzi, sauna, exercise room, tennis courts.

Stay in an ocean-view suite, or bunk down in a hotel-owned RV with maid-service to pamper you, or pull your own RV into one of this resort's 55 spaces. Open since 1992, this full-scale resort has a great beach, lots of amenities—miniature golf, a recreation room, convention facilities. A hit with families, this a lively place, so choose somewhere else for a quiet retreat. Most suites have one bedroom, all have air conditioning, cable TV and minibars. RVs have full kitchens. Credit Cards: MC, V.

La Fonda $25–60   ★★★★

On Old Highway 1, P.O. Box 268, San Ysidro, CA 92073.
Single: $25–60.
Located 0.3 mile south of La Mision exit from Highway 1-D.
80 rooms, restaurant, bar, beach.

Red-tiled roofs, banana trees and walkways edged with colorful flowers, the La Fonda epitomizes south of the border charm. This hotel draws return visits from Baja buffs, who come to enjoy La Fonda's beach and immensely popular bar/restaurant. Reservations are by mail only (allow two weeks to receive written confirmation). Rooms are basic, with no phones on the property. The restaurant has glorious ocean views and a menu filled with exotic choices, including breaded scallops and roast suckling pig. Restaurant patrons get noisy, so ask for a room far away from the bar. Apartments are also available. No Credit Cards.

Hotel Las Rocas $49–230   ★★★★

Old Ensenada Highway Km 37, ☎ *(661) 224-40, FAX (661) 224-40*
Single: $49–150. Double: $49–150. Penthouse: $230.
74 rooms and suites, beach, two Jacuzzis, bar and restaurant, tennis.
At Km 37.

White with bright blue-and-purple trim, this cliff-side hotel is built on a series of terraces, so all rooms have Pacific views. Since its opening in 1991, Las Rocas has become popular, with the big draw being the dramatically designed pool and Jacuzzi area, edged by ocean cliffs. Palms and planted gardens give the walkways a tropical feel, while rooms feature beams and rustic furniture. All rooms have telephones, satellite TV and double king size beds. Deluxe rooms, junior suites, suites and penthouse rooms are available—all suites have fireplace, minibar, refrigerator,

microwave and coffee maker. Relax after a day of touring at the open-air palapa bar.
Credit cards: MC, V.

Festival Plaza Hotel   **$50–100**   ★ ★ ★

11 Boulevard Benito Juárez, ☎ *(800) 453-8606, (661)208-42, FAX (661) 201-24*
Single: $50–100. Double: $50–100.
In Rosarito.
120 rooms, two pools, two restaurants, children's area, bar, cocktail lounge, concert stage.
For a jazzed-up experience with theme park touches, the Festival Plaza can't be beat. The eight-story building is decked out with a trellised framework meant to evoke a roller coaster, and upon entering the lobby, you are greeted by a bank of TVs, all tuned to the same cartoon. For real fun, take a spin on the hotel's own private Ferris wheel. No intimate hideaway, the party action is non-stop, with several bars, as well as a children's area in the central courtyard, which also contains a concert stage. Visit the Tequila Museum or stop by the rock-and-roll taco stand by the pool. The hotel's two swimming pools are connected by a "river" section that features boulders, waterfalls and bridges. The architecture is a mélange of wrought iron, pillars and Moorish arches, with rooms ranging in size from studios to three-bedroom apartments. Rooms have well-maintained, and have queen or king size beds, combination baths, furnished balconies and views of the pool area and ocean. Some apartments have private Jacuzzis. This property caters to both overnighters as well as time-share guests. Credit Cards: AE, MC, V.

New Port Beach Hotel   **$70–200**   ★ ★ ★ ★ ★

Old Road to Ensenada, Km 45, ☎ *(800) 582-1018, (661) 411-66.*
Single: $70–150. Double: $130–200.
South of Rosarito, near Puerto Nuevo.
147 ocean view rooms, heated pool, Jacuzzi, exercise room, tennis courts, restaurant, bar, meeting rooms.
This beach-front resort offers family packages with amenities including a children's playground and an oversize pool. The modern, red-tiled hotel building overlooks the beach just south of the picturesque village of Puerto Nuevo. The resort offers watersports, including surf-racks for surfers, as well as ample terraces for catching the sun. Rooms feature queen or king bed and have light pine furnishings and ocean views. Non-smoking rooms are available. Packages include weekend rates with welcome cocktails and daily full breakfast. Credit Cards: MC, V.

Condos and Apartments

The Grand Baja Resort   **$50–150**

Puerto Nuevo, ☎ *(800) 522-1516 (U.S.)*
Single: $50–140. Double: $75–150.
Located one block from village.
Swimming pool, tennis courts.
Guests can relax in ocean-front condominiums by the day, week, month, "or forever" at this resort situated just outside Puerto Nuevo. The red-tiled Mediterranean-style complex offers junior suites, studios, and one- and two-bedroom units, all fully furnished. Larger units have private balconies and three baths. All but the

junior suites offer kitchenettes. Amenities include 24-hour security and nearby watersports. Enjoy fresh lobster at one Puerto Nuevo's 20 restaurants, which are within easy walking distance from the resort. Credit Cards: MC, V.

Hacienda Las Glorias Bajamar $52–250   ★★★★

Bajamar Ocean Front Golf Resort, Punta Salsipuedes, ☎ *(800) 522-1516 (U.S.), (619) 298-4105.*
Single: $52–250 and up. Double: $90–250 and up.
Located at Bajamar Ocean Front Golf Resort.
81 rooms, seven suites, 20 villas; pool, Jacuzzi, golf, tennis courts.

The Hacienda Las Glorias is situated in a replica of an old Spanish hacienda, complete with flower-planted courtyards and a sparkling fountain. Part of the Bajamar Ocean Front Golf Course, which features an 18-hole PGA course and country club, this hotel is a duffer's paradise. Midweek packages include three nights and two days unlimited golf on the course. Private villas with one to three rooms also are available. Credit Cards: MC, V.

Califa $22–59   ★★★★

Old Ensenada Highway at Km 35.5, ☎ *(800) CALIFA, (661) 215-81,*
FAX: (661) 215-80.
Single: $22–59. Double: $22–59.
Six miles south of Rosarito.
60 units, 16 mobile homes with kitchens, pool, museum, restaurant.

Set on a bluff overlooking the ocean, this historic hotel offers ocean-front rooms or one-, two- and three-bedroom mobile homes that rent for up to $75 per night. Hotel rooms have cable TV, shower baths, but lack phones. Amenities include a pool and museum. One of the first resort-style hotels in the area, the Califa's staggered terraces reach nearly to the water's edge, and the hotel prides itself on offering historic ambiance at an affordable price.

Low-Cost Lodging

Motel Quinta Chica $25   ★★

Old Ensenada Highway at Km 26.8, ☎ *(661) 213-00, FAX (661) 212-15*
Single: $25. Double: $25.
Located on the south end of Rosarito.
90 rooms.

Bargain-priced beds cooled by ocean-breezes if you ask for a room that faces the free road. Rooms on the back face the busy toll road, and thus suffer from the roar of traffic. Credit cards: MC, V.

Restaurants

Los Pelicanos   ★★★★

Calle Ebano 113, ☎ *(661) 217-57.*
Steaks and seafood.
Hours: Daily 8 a.m.-midnight, entrées: $8–15.
Corner of Calle Ebano and Avenida Costa Azul.

Situated on the beach, this is one of the few restaurants in town that has an ocean view. The atmosphere is romantic and specialties include grilled steaks, fish and quail in garlic sauce. Credit Cards: MC, V.

Los Arcos ★★

777 Boulevard Benito Juárez, ☎ (661) 214-31.
Mexican cuisine.
Hours: Daily 8 a.m.–10 p.m., entrées: $2–8.
Next to the Rosarito Beach Hotel.
This tiny cafe dishes up tasty tacos, flautas, burritos, gorditas (thick corn tortillas stuffed with meat) as well as home-style Mexican breakfasts. Take it with you to munch on or dine in. Meals are served outside during summer months. No credit cards.

Mariscos de Rarito Vince's ★★★★

77 Boulevard Benito Juárez, ☎ (661) 212-53.
Seafood.
Hours: Daily 11 a.m.–11 p.m., entrées: $8–20.
In town center.
Lobster is the reason why Americans crowd this popular restaurant and deli, but other favorites include freshly grilled fish of the day. A mariachi band provides entertainment in the evening. No credit cards.

La Flor de Michocán ★★

291 Boulevard Benito Juárez, ☎ (661) 218-58.
Mexican cuisine.
Hours: 10 a.m.–9 p.m., entrées: $2–10.
Next to the Rosarito Beach Hotel.
Traditional dishes from Michoacan are highlighted at this family-run restaurant. Specialties include carnitas (marinated, pit-roasted pork), tostadas and tacos tortas (marinated pork kabobs). Dishes are served with homemade tortillas and guacamole, with hot salsa, lime slices and pickled chiles as condiments. Operated since 1950 by the same family, this restaurant offers sit-down dining or take-out, with occasional live entertainment. Carnitas are available by the kilo. Closed Wednesdays. No credit cards.

Azteca ★★★

Boulevard Benito Juárez, ☎ (661) 201-44.
American and Mexican cuisine.
Hours: Daily 7:30 a.m.–10 p.m., entrées: $8–15
In the Rosarito Beach Hotel.
This large dining rooms has views of the Pacific as well as of the Rosarito Beach Hotel pool. Locals and visitors alike enjoy the massive Sunday morning brunch, served with margarita. Also popular is the Friday night Mexican buffet, which features a weekly "fiesta" to keep things lively. The portions are hearty, off-setting the fact that the quality of the food varies.

El Nido ★★★

67 Boulevard Benito Juarez, ☎ (661) 214-31.
Mexican-style steaks and seafood.
Hours: Daily 8 a.m.–midnight, entrées: $8–15.
In town center.

Another representative of the steak house chain, this restaurant has wood-paneling and leather booths, and serves mesquite-grilled meats. Unpretentious, but tasty food is El Nido's trademark. Credit Cards: MC, V.

Ensenada Area

Hotels & Resorts

Casa del Sol $48–68   ★★★

Highway 1, Rancho Santa Inés, ☎ *(800) 528-1234, (617) 815-70.*
Single: $48–53. Double: $58–68.
On "tourist row."
48 rooms, pool, pets okay.

With a medium price range and furnished as you'd expect for a Best Western property, this motel offers no surprises. Rooms have cable TV and shower baths, but only some have air conditioning. A few have kitchens. Credit Cards: AE, MC, V.

El Cid Motor Hotel $52–72   ★★★

993 Lopez Mateos, ☎ *(617) 824-01, FAX: (617) 836-71.*
Single: $52. Double: $72.
52 rooms, pool, dining room.

This motel provides dependable lodging in large, well-furnished rooms, all housed in a three-story colonial style building. The lobby has brick arches, tiled floors and traditional pigskin furniture. Rooms feature minibars, wood mirrors and queen or king size beds. All rooms have air conditioning, carpeting, TV, small combination baths. Outside units have small balconies, but the inner rooms are quieter. Some suites have Jacuzzis. Popular with weekending San Diegans and Los Angelinos, this motel has a more comfortable feel than some of the nearby chain operated properties.Credit Cards: MC, V.

Estero Beach Resort Hotel $35–85   ★★★★★

On Highway 1, ☎ *(800) 762-2494, (617) 662-35, FAX(617) 669-25*
Single: $35–85. Double: $35–85.
6 miles south of Ensenada.
108 rooms and suites, tennis, horseback riding, boat ramp, boat rentals.

A great place for boaters and birdwatchers, this resort features hotel rooms, villas, and an RV park. If chain hotels and motor inns aren't to your liking, this resort offers a welcome alternative. A security gate fronts the property, and winding lanes are planted with flowers. Amenities are close to the beach and include a restaurant with a terrace that faces the slough. Buildings are designed with Mayan accents, and the resort has an exhibit building with a collection of Mayan vases and reproductions. The estuary and the beach are the big attractions, but tides are dangerous for children and non-swimmers. Activities include tennis, beach combing and watersports. Several gardens invite guests to stroll. Rooms are well-maintained, with the best choices at the Palenque wing (these cost more than rooms in the Tikal wing). Suites are in a two-story building that fronts the ocean. Cottages offer romantic privacy for honeymooners. The least expensive cottages have basic furnishings, small kitchenettes and open patios. Credit Cards: MC, V.

Hotel Coral & Marina **$148-314** ★★★★★

Carretara Tijuana-Ensenada KM103, Zona Playitas ☎*(800) 862-9020 or (619) 523-0064, (617) 523-0064*
Single/Double: $148-$165 Suite:$242-$314
This elegant resort features 150 spacious rooms with terraces overlooking the bay. The junior suites are worth the extra cost and include large living rooms, terraces, luxurious baths and separate bedrooms. Amenities include a restaurant, piano bar, boutique and travel agency. The full service spa includes massage, facials, sauna, gym, Jacuzzi, an indoor lap pool and an outdoor pool. Tennis courts and a game room complete the resort atmosphere. Good service and garage parking. AE MC, V.

Hotel La Pinta Ensenada **$40–60** ★★

Avenida Floresta and Boulevard Bucaneros, ☎*(800) 336-5454 (U.S.), (617) 244-900, (617) 626-01.*
Single: $40–60. Double: $45–60.
Across from post office.
52 rooms, pool.
The Mexican hotel chain has properties at various locations from Ensenada south to the Cape Area. Functional lodging at a medium price, this hotel chain offers a four-night travel booklet with pre-paid discounted rates at six selected locations. The Ensenada hotel features rooms with cable TV and shower baths.

Mision Santa Isabel **$58-74**

Blvd. Costero at Castillo; in San Diego (619)259-0686; (617) 836-16,
FAX (617) 833-45.
Single/Double: $58-$74
This neocolonial hotel, built hacienda style around a pool, offers 60 small rooms with wood-beam ceilings and baths. Restaurant and bar with mariachis on weekends. Parking.Credit Cards: MC, V

Quintas Papagayo **$60–90** ★★★★★

Highway 1, north of Ensenada, ☎ *(619) 491-682 (U.S.), (617) 441-55, (617) 445-75*
Single: $60–90. Double: $90 and up.
One mile north of town.
50 rooms, restaurant, bar, tennis courts, pool, beach.
Opened in 1947, this pretty resort features bungalows and low-rise buildings in an ocean-side setting. The personable staff works hard to make guests feel welcome, and the rooms, while rustic, are comfortably large and airy, with terra cotta tile floors and carved wood furniture. Some have fireplaces and kitchens. Patios and decks are also available. The restaurant is described below. Credit Cards: MC, V.

San Nicolas Resort Hotel **$53–85** ★★★

Avenida Lopez Mateos and Guadalupe, ☎ *(617) 619-01, FAX (617) 649-30*
Single: $53–85. Double: $53–85.
Near the Riviera Convention Center.
150 rooms, Olympic-size pool, Jacuzzi, restaurant, bar.
Outside, the hotel presents a bland facade, but inside, the decor is imaginative and fresh compared to the chain properties. The restaurant faces the pool area, which features a huge pool with a modernistic backdrop designed to look like a Mayan temple, where occasionally jets of water spray skyward for added drama. Occasion-

ally, the temple serves as a stage for folk dancing or pageants. A smaller, covered pool features a waterfall. Amenities include a cocktail lounge with a betting parlor for sports, and lounge, where most nights there is live music. Rooms are motel-standard, with well-maintained, if uninspired furnishings, and feature TV and double, queen or king size beds. Some beds have canopies and kitschy mirrored ceilings. The honeymoon suites have a private Jacuzzi. Like the El Cid, this property is a hit with Southern Californians. Credit Cards: MC, V.

Travelodge $65-82 ★★★

Blancarte 130 at Lopez Mateos; ☎ *(800) 255-3050 (617) 816-1, FAX (617) 814-5*
Single/Double; $65-$82 and often discounted

Although this is a chain hotel, its central location and well-maintained rooms make it an excellent and reasonably priced choice, particularly for those just spending a weekend in Ensenada. The 52 rooms are clean, attractively decorated and air conditioned. The pool and Jacuzzi are relaxing after a day of shopping and sightseeing. Amenities include a restaurant/bar and parking at your door. Credit Cards: MC, V.

Joker Motel $25-35 ★★★

Highway 1, Km 12.5, ☎ *(800) 22-JOKER, (617) 672-01, FAX (617) 672-01.*
Single: $25-30. Double: $24-35.
South of Ensenada, across from airport.
40 rooms, pool, Jacuzzi.

No it's not a mirage, nor is it a real castle, but the Joker Motel is an Ensenada-mainstay, perfect for travelers bound further south. An architectural mish-mash of styles and colors, this motel offers large rooms and functional furnishings, without a lot of stuffiness. Private balconies and satellite TV add to the quirky charm. Credit Cards: MC, V.

Restaurants

El Rey Sol ★★★★★

1000 Avenida Lopez Mateos, ☎ *(617) 817-33.*
French cuisine and breakfast
Hours: 8 a.m.–11:30 p.m., entrées: $15–25.
At Avenida Blancarte.

French cuisine in Mexico—yes, at the El Rey Sol, which has been serving delicious food since 1947, when Doña Pepita returned from France to open her own restaurant. Housed in a quaint building, the dining room is decorated with stained glass window and heavy oak tables and chair. The family run establishment prepares meals in a modern kitchen using fresh herbs and vegetables, many grown on the family farm in Santo Tomás. Choices include seafood, poultry and meat, and signature Mexican dishes, all served with appetizers. Pastries are baked right in the kitchen and the flour tortillas are to die for. The authentic machaca is the best in Baja. Reservations are recommended, as this restaurant is popular. Credit Cards: AE, MC, V.

Enrique's Restaurant ★★★★

Highway 1-D, ☎ *(617) 824-61.*
Continental and Mexican cuisine.
Hours: 8 a.m.–11:30 p.m., entrées: $4–18.

Located 1.5 miles north of town center.

Long a favorite with romantics, this restaurant claims it has "the smallest bar in the world." But loyal patrons come for the food, including elegant selections such as chateaubriand, quail, lobster Newburg, frog's legs and abalone prepared to order. A perfect spot for an intimate dinner.

La Embotelladora Vieja ★ ★ ★ ★ ★

Bodegras de Santo Tomás Building, Calle 7a, ☎ *(617) 408-07.*
French cuisine.
Hours: 6 p.m.–11:30 p.m., Tuesday–Sunday, entrées: $15–25.
At Calle 7a and Avenida Miramar 666.

This elegant and well-respected French restaurant is set in a converted wine-tasting room inside the Santo Tomás winery. Decorated in country-French style, the dining room has arched brick ceilings and walls lined with wine bins. Tables are intimate, with candlelight and crystal. The menu is "Baja-French," which translates into entrees that include grilled lobster in cabernet sauvignon wine sauce. Most dishes are flavored with wine, but the menu offers some dishes for teetotalers, just ask to be sure. Sample an assortment of Baja, California and French wines by the glass or bottle. A superb choice for a special dinner. Credit Cards: MC, V.

Hussong's Pelicano ★ ★ ★ ★

Highway 1, at Quinta Papagayo Beach Resort Hotel, ☎ *(617) 445-75.*
Seafood and Mexican cuisine.
Hours: 8 a.m.–11:30 p.m., entrées: $8–18.
Two miles north of town center.

Worth a visit even if you aren't staying at the resort, this seafood restaurant serves a varied selection of fresh seafood. Created and operated by Juan Hussong of Hussong's Cantina fame (see "Nightlife" below), this restaurant serves lobster, shrimp, clams, scallops and Mexican dishes, too. Open for breakfast, with a buffet brunch on Saturdays and Sundays. Credit Cards: MC, V.

Haliotis ★ ★ ★

Highway 1-D, ☎ *(617) 637-20.*
Seafood.
Hours: 1 p.m.–11 p.m., Wednesday through Monday entrées: $6–18.
On Agustin Sangines 179, 0.5 mile east of Highway 1.

Named for the Latin genus term for abalone, Haliotis specializes in this Pacific shellfish, as well as other fresh seafood dishes. The menu changes based on the season. Credit Cards: MC, V

Casamar ★ ★

987 Boulevard Lázaro Cardenas., ☎ *(617) 404017.*
Seafood.
Hours: 11 a.m.–11:30 p.m., entrées: $8–18.
In town center.

Excellent food served to the tourist crowd makes this long-established place a good bet for a meal if atmosphere isn't as important. Indulge in lobster grilled with butter and garlic, then head upstair, where on weekends a jazz band plays in the bar.

La Cueva de Los Tigres ★ ★ ★

Highway 1, ☎ *(617) 826-53.*

Continental and Mexican cuisine.
Hours: 11 a.m.–midnight., entrées: $4–18.
Located 2.5 miles south of town center, then 0.5 mile west on gravel road.

"The Tigers' Cave," prompts opinions from its guests—some say the place is over-rated, others (especially old-time Baja buffs) give the place high accolades. Located outside Ensenada, just before Estero Beach, the restaurant sits at the end of a gravel road on the beach. Menu choices include the famous abalone in crab sauce, as well as steaks and Mexican specialties. Cocktails are available in the restaurant or attached lounge. Credit Cards: MC, V.

Plaza Mexico ★★★

2184 Avenida López Mateos.
Mexican cuisine.
Hours: 8 a.m.–11:30 p.m., entrées: $4–18.
Located 1.5 miles north of town center.

A bustling patio restaurant that dishes up some of the best Mexican food, including thick, grilled steaks, carne asada, and tacos for a less expensive meal. On Friday and Saturday nights, a mariachi band plays. Enjoy a margarita with your meal, then have a sweet, jelly-filled churro—muy gusto! No credit cards.

Nightlife

Hussong's Cantina ★★★

113 Avenida Ruíz, ☎ (617) 832-10.
Hours: 11 a.m.–1 a.m.
West of Avenida Macheros

You can't go to Ensenada and skip Hussong's—an institution since 1892. No matter that it's really nothing more than a party bar that has been hyped for decades in Southern California by a steady stream of bumper stickers. Pop in (you must be 18) so you can say you saw it. Loud with gritos (shouts), frenetic and full of woozy drunks by closing, Hussong's serves beer with mariachi bands and ranchera music. Come early afternoon if you want to claim a table. Credit Cards: MC, V.

Papas and Beer ★★

Ruiz near Lopez Mateos, ☎ (617) 701-25.
Hours: 11 a.m.–1 a.m.

Just down the street from Hussong's, this party bar can get just as frenetic. A tad more upscale in decor than Hussong's, but it gets a fair share of bumper sticker and T-shirt advertising, too.Hundreds of margaritas, tequila shooters and nachos are consumed here every week. Loud recorded rock music makes conversation nearly impossible but most patrons are too drunk to care. More popular with younger revelers than Hussong's.

Parque Nacional San Pedro Martir

Resorts

Meling Ranch (San José) $110 ★★★★

Aparto Postal 1326, Ensenada, Baja California, Mexico, ☎ (619) 758-2719 (U.S.)
Double: $110, includes meals.
32 miles east of Highway 1 on road to Parque Nacional San Pedro Martir.
Accommodations for up to 12.

Founded by two pioneer families, the Melings and the Johnsons, this working cattle ranch traces its roots back to the early 1900s. Today, guests can drive or fly in, and enjoy the amenities, including a pool and dining room, horseback riding and pack trips into the mountains. The ranch house, rebuilt after the original was destroyed in the 1911 revolution, retains its historic feel. A 3500 foot airstrip lies just east of the ranch.

Mike's Sky Rancho $25–50 ★★★★

Reservations: P.O. Box 5376, San Ysidro, CA 92703, ☎ (213) 560-2119 (U.S.).
Single: $25. Double: $50.
22 miles east of Highway 3 on graded dirt road leading into the northeastern portion of Parque Nacional San Pedro Martir.
Accommodations for about 20.

Located in a valley surrounded by pine-cloaked foothills of the Sierra San Pedro Matir mountains, this isolated motel-style rancho is off-the-beaten track, and caters primarily to dirt-bikers and four-wheel-drive enthusiasts. The road is recommended for high-clearance vehicles only. The rancho offers family-style breakfasts, lunches, and dinners at prices ranging from $4 to $12 per meal. Horseback riding, fishing in the small stream that flows through the property, and hikes into the back country are some of the activities. The Olympic-size swimming pool is great for a refreshing dip. For tent campers, there are campsites are shaded by sycamores. A 6000-foot graded airstrip is maintained nearby for fly-in guests.

San Quintin Area

Hotels

Hotel La Pinta San Quintin $60–65 ★★★

West of Highway 1, San Quintin, ☎ (800) 336-5454 (U.S.), (619) 422-6900, (616) 528-78.
Single: $60. Double: $65.
From Highway 1, take paved road to outer San Quintin Bay.
56 rooms.

The Mexican hotel chain has properties at various locations from Ensenada south to the Cape Area. Functional lodging at a medium price, this hotel chain offers a four-night travel booklet with pre-paid discounted rates at six selected locations. The San Quintin hotel is situated on the beach in a pleasant, Spanish-style building. All rooms have two beds and ocean-view private balconies, as well as shower baths. Some have refrigerators. No air conditioning. Dig for your own clams, or try surf-fishing. The motel dining room is open from 7 a.m. to 10:30 p.m. Credit Cards: MC, V.

Old Mill Motel $30–60 ★★★

Bayside, eastern shore of inner bay, San Quintin ☎ (800) 479-7962 (U.S.), (619) 428-2779 (U.S.), FAX (619) 428-6269.
Single: $30–60. Double: $30–60.
Four miles west of Highway 1, take unpaved road to eastern shore of inner bay.
28 units, gasoline and diesel, RV park.

Situated on the site of a grist mill that operated from 1888 to 1914, this motel has a historic feel. Old milling machines and other relics are on display throughout the grounds and in the public areas. The grounds lead down to a secluded beach. Guests are primarily interested in hunting, fishing and other outdoor activities, but amenities include a restaurant, cocktail lounge, and clean, modern rooms. All rooms have shower baths; some rooms have kitchenettes. No air conditioning, no phones, no TV. Nearby is a year-round sport-fishing fleet with craft for hire, as well as opportunities for swimming, hiking and back-country trips. Next door is an RV park, with sites available for $15 per night. No credit cards.

Cielito Lindo Motel $40   ★ ★

Reservations: Santa Maria, Valle de San Quintin, Baja California, Mexico
Single: $40. Double: $40.
Near Hotel Pinta
14 rooms.

Large, clean rooms with two beds and combination baths provide refreshment after a day fishing or time on the road. On Saturday nights, the lounge hosts a dance. The hotel restaurant is popular (almost all San Quintin's restaurants are attached to hotels). Try the grilled crab, or lobster cocktail, or indulge in an abalone and lobster combination plate for about $12. Next door is a coffee shop. Nearby is the Cielito Lindo Trailer court. An airstrip is 200 yards east of the RV park.

Bed & Breakfast

Rancho Sereno Bed and Breakfast $45–60   ★ ★ ★

Off Highway 1, San Quintin, ☎ (909) 927-7087 (U.S.)
Single: $45–55. Double: $50–60.
1.25 miles south of military camp, then 1.5 west of Highway 1 on dirt road.
3 units, pets okay, non-smoking rooms.

This ranch house surrounded by trees offers an authentic Baja experience. No air conditioning, no phones, but there is cable TV in the recreation room—electricity is available from 8 a.m. to noon, and 5 p.m. to 9 p.m. Units come with shower baths and kitchen privileges. A full breakfast is served from 8 to 10 a.m. Fishing trips and other outdoor activities can be arranged. No credit cards.

Low-Cost Lodging

Motel Chavéz $21–28   ★

Highway 1, ☎ (619) 479-3451 (U.S.), (616) 520-05.
Single: $21. Double: $28.
1.5 miles north of the military camp.
33 units.

Very basic lodging in American-style rooms—no air conditioning, no phones. Room come with fans and shower baths. Some rooms have full kitchens. The restaurant is open 7 a.m. to 10 p.m., and there is a bar. No credit cards.

Cataviña

Hotels

Hotel La Pinta Cataviña $60–65   ★ ★ ★

Highway 1 ☎ (800) 336-5454 (U.S.), (619) 422-6900.
Single: $60. Double: $65.
One mile north of Rancho Santa Inés.
28 rooms.

The Mexican hotel chain has properties at various locations from Ensenada south to the Cape Area. Functional lodging at a medium price, this hotel chain offers a four-night travel booklet with pre-paid discounted rates at six selected locations. The Cataviña hotel is the only place in the area where you can reliably obtain a room. Situated in the heart of rugged, scenic boulder fields, the hotel is housed in a Spanish-style building with a courtyard and a small swimming pool. The rooms have cable TV, shower baths, no phone. There is no electricity from 2 to 4 p.m. A recreation room and playground are available, and the dining room is open from 7 a.m. to 10:30 a.m. Next door is an RV park, and nearby is a PEMEX station. Credit Cards: MC, V.

Bahía San Luis Gonzaga Area

Alfonsina's ★
6 rooms, restaurant (order in advance).
A line of very modest rooms along the beach at the north end of the residential development and dirt airstrip at Bahía San Luis Gonzaga. Fronted by an outstanding sand beach.

Punta Bufeo Tourist Camp ★
10 or more stone houses for lease or rent. Small restaurant and 3 small rental rooms.
Owned by Francisca Fernandez and sons. This is the northernmost of the fly-in facilities on the Sea of Cortez. It has a dirt landing strip parallel to the beach. A really isolated location with little vegetation, as is typical of the San Felipe Desert. Located near Punta Bufeo, 6 mi. north of Punta Willard. See U.S. nautical chart 21008 for location.

Papa Fernandez ★
Cabins and refreshments.
A very modest facility located near the north end of Bahía Gonzaga. The founder, Papa Fernandez, was 100 years old in 1995. The resort is now run by his son, who bears the same name.

Bahía de Los Angeles

Hotels

Villa Vitta Hotel $28–55 ★★
Highway 1, Bahía de Los Angeles, or write Jimsair, 2904 Pacific Coast Highway, San Diego, CA 92101, ☎ (619) 298-4958 (U.S.).
Singles: $28. Doubles: $55.
Adjacent to paved road in the village.
40 rooms, pool, boat rental.
This motel offers basic, clean, air-conditioned rooms, as well as a boat ramp. The restaurant is part of the motel and serves breakfast, lunch and dinner, with the emphasis on seafood. No credit cards.

Casa Diaz $25–30 ★★
Bahía de Los Angeles Antero Diaz, P.O. Box 579, Ensenada, Baja California, Mexico.
Singles: $25. Doubles: $25–30.
South end of village.
15 units.

RESORT AREAS AND HOTELS

This family-run, low-key resort has been in operation for more than 30 years. Accommodations are housed in 15 stone cabins. Hot showers are available and guests can stock up on staples at the large grocery store, or arrange in advance for meals. Fishing and bird watching trips also are available. The Diaz family also operates the area PEMEX station.

Restaurants

Las Hamacas ★★
Bahía de Los Angeles, no phone.
Seafood and Mexican cuisine.
Hours: 8 a.m.–10 p.m., entrées: $5–10
Just north of the Mini Hotel.
Seafood and basic ranchero dishes are on the menu here, as well as beer by the bottle. Purchase a paperback from the rack of used books—proceeds reportedly benefit the town museum. No credit cards.

Guillermo's ★★
Bahía de Los Angeles, no phone.
Seafood and Mexican cuisine.
Hours: 8 a.m.–10 p.m., entrees: $5–10
Adjacent to the Guillermo's Trailer Park.
Palapas provide shade in front of this small restaurant. The menu offers seafood and Mexican dishes, including shrimp, lobster and fresh fish. Relax outside with a margarita. No credit cards.

San Francisquito

Punta San Francisquito Resort ★
Write 2004 Newton Avenue, San Diego, CA 92113. *(619) 239-8872.*
11 cabins with cots, restaurant, central restroom, shower facilities.
A modest fly-in facility with poor road access. Also caters to boaters crossing the Sea of Cortez from Bahía Kino. Some visitors fly in, camp on the beach, and use the resort's rest rooms and other facilities.

Guerrero Negro

Hotels

Hotel La Pinta Guerrero Negro $60–65   ★★★
Highway 1 *(800) 336-5454 (U.S.), (619) 422-6900, (115) 713-00.*
Single: $60. Double: $65.
Near the Paralelo 28 monument.
27 rooms.
The Mexican hotel chain has properties at various locations from Ensenada south to the Cape Area. Functional lodging at a medium price, this hotel chain offers a four-night travel booklet with pre-paid discounted rates at six selected locations. Located near the Paralelo 28 monument, this single-story hotel has two-bed rooms with shower baths. No air conditioning, no phones. The dining room is open from 7 a.m. to 10:30 a.m. Adjacent is an RV park. Credit Cards: MC, V.

Hotel El Morro $26–31   ★
Boulevard Zapata, ☎ *(115) 704-14.*

Single: $26. Double: $27–31.
One mile west of Highway 1 on east side of town.
32 units.
Offering very basic rooms, this modest motel provides a utilitarian place to bunk down for the night. Rooms come with fans (no air conditioning) and shower baths. No phones. The motel restaurant is open from noon to 10 p.m. No credit cards, but traveler's checks are generally okay.

RV Park

Malarrimo $8 ★★

Boulevard Zapata, ☎ *(115) 702-50*
Sites: $8 for two people.
One mile west of Highway 1 on east edge of town.
22 sites, hookups.
This is the most popular RV park in the region, and the sites are quickly filled. The park offers flush toilets, showers and the Malarrimo Restaurant, a busy place that serves the best food in town. Abalone and shrimp are among the specialties, but other choices include octopus, clams and halibut fillets. Try a fish burrito or a dish of San Carlos shrimp. Entrées run from $4 to 15. <small>No credit cards.</small>

Bahía Tortugas

Vera Cruz Motel ★

8 rooms, restaurant, bar.
A modest motel near the PEMEX station. After having driven so many miles, even a modest establishment looks good.

San Ignacio

Hotels

Hotel La Pinta San Ignacio $60–65 ★★★

Highway 1 ☎ *(800) 336-5454 (U.S.), (619) 244-6900, (617) 626-01.*
Single: $60. Double: $65.
Two miles off Highway 1 on edge of town.
27 rooms, pool, recreation room.
The Mexican hotel chain has properties at various locations from Ensenada south to the Cape Area. Functional lodging at a medium price, this hotel chain offers a four-night travel booklet with pre-paid discounted rates at six selected locations. This single-story Spanish-style building is set in a grove of palm trees. The rooms face an interior patio. All rooms feature two beds with shower baths. No phones. Dining room is open from 7 a.m. to 10:30 p.m. Among the menu choices are beef dishes made with meat from local ranchos. Next door is a PEMEX station. <small>Credit Cards: MC, V.</small>

Low-Cost Lodging

La Posada Motel $20–25 ★★

Write: La Posada San Ignacio, Baja California Mexico
Singles: $20. Doubles: $25.
Located two blocks from the civic plaza, past Callejón Ciprés, turn left, motel is on the right.
8 rooms.

Modest but clean accommodations. Each room has two beds, a hot-water shower and a dresser. Fans provide cooling. No credit cards.

Restaurants

Restaurant Chalita   ★★

San Ignacio, no phone.
Mexican food.
Hours: 8 a.m.– 7 p.m. Mondays–Saturdays, entrées: $4–8.
On the plazuela.
Typical Mexican fare, including burritos, tacos, enchilada, and some fresh seafood. Breakfast choices include huevos rancheros. No credit cards.

Restaurant Tota   ★★

San Ignacio, no phone.
Seafood and Mexican food.
Hours: 8 a.m.–10 p.m., 6–10 p.m. Sundays, entrées: $8–15.
Near La Posada Motel beside an irrigation pond.
This family-run eatery offers fresh seafood, including lobster and crab, as well as Mexican dishes. The staff speaks some English. No credit cards.

Santa Rosalia

The Hotel Frances at Santa Rosalia is typical of many of the French-built wooden buildings in this historic town.

Hotels

Hotel El Morro $25–30   ★★

Highway 1, ☎ (115) 204-14.
Single: $25. Double: $30.
One mile south of Santa Rosalia ferry terminal.
30 units, one suite, pool.
This tourist-oriented hotel is housed in a Spanish-style building that overlooks the Sea of Cortez. The two-bed rooms feature shower baths, and some have private patios. The dining room is open Tuesday through Friday and Sunday from 7:30

a.m. to 10 p.m. Dining hours on Saturday and Monday are noon to 10 p.m. The pool is seldom clean.

Hotel Frances $20–30 ★★

Santa Rosalia, ☎ (115) 220-52.
Single: $20. Double: $30.
North of town off Calle Altamirano.
Accommodations for about 10.

This venerable, historic hotel was closed down in 1991, but has been refurbished and reopened as a bed and breakfast. The French colonial-style harkens back to the early boom days when the mines were in full operation. Unfortunately, the historic photographs that once adorned the walls are now gone. No credit cards.

Low-Cost Lodging
Hotel Blanco y Negro $10–16

Avenida Sarabia and Calle 3, ☎ (115) 200-80.
Single: $10, $12, private bath, $15, with TV. Double: $16.
Two blocks from Avenida Sarabia.
Accommodations for about 15.

This small hostel-style hotel offers rooms with shared baths, and rooms with two or three beds. One single room has a private bath. The wooden building is constructed in the French style, and the proprietors are friendly.

Restaurants
Cenaduria Gaby

Santa Rosalia, no phone.
Mexican food.
Hours: 9 a.m.–9 p.m., Mondays–Saturdays, entrées: $2–8.
Corner of Calle 5 and Avenida Progreso.

Long-established, this restaurant features delicious machaca (shredded beef), as well as enchiladas, tostadas, gorditas and burritos. Steak and chicken also are available at reasonable prices. No credit cards.

The Tokyo Cafe

Santa Rosalia, no phone.
Mexican food.
Hours: daily 7:30 a.m.–2 p.m., entrées: $2–8
Avenida Obregón between Calles 3 and 4.

No Japanese food here, just hearty Mexican standards prepared by a descendent of a Japanese laborer who came to work for El Boleo. Popular with the locals, the cafe also serves seafood. Breakfast and lunch only. No credit cards.

Mulegé Area
Hotels
Hotel Hacienda $20–25 ★★★

Francisco I, Madero 3, Mulegé Baja California, Mexico, ☎ (800) 464-8888, (115) 300-21.
Single: $20–25. Double: $20–25.
Across from town plaza.
18 units.

Popular with European tourists, this historic, two-story inn is built around a flag-stone courtyard planted with banana trees, citrus and palms. Under new management, the hotel has refurbished its once empty swimming pool and set out comfortable rockers. Rooms are offered with or without air conditioning (costs more) and feature shower baths. The lively, noisy bar makes a local favorite, the "Mulegé Milkshake," a potent drink of tequila, rum, Kalúa, milk and ice. Mountain bikes are for rent if you wish to exercise. The dining room is open from 8 a.m. to 10 p.m., and features special nights for paella and roast-pig. Trips to nearby cave paintings can be arranged. No credit cards.

Las Casitas $23–28   ★★★

Calle Madero, ☎ *(115) 300-19.*
Singles: $23–28. Doubles: $23–28.
In town center, inside hotel.
8 rooms.

Offering warm hospitality in an intimate setting, this small hotel provides basic rooms (air conditioning and shower bath), just the kind of place you'd expect to find in a sleepy Mexican town. Mulegé, of course, is no longer sleepy. No credit cards.

Hotel Terrazas $17–20   ★★

Calle Zaragoza, ☎ *(115) 300-09*
Singles: $17–20. Doubles: $17–20.
North end of Calle Zaragoza.
35 rooms.

Not as grand as it once was, this "downtown" hotel still offers spacious, clean rooms and basic if slightly worn furnishings. Rooms are quiet, with two double beds and private bath. The hot-water availability fluctuates, but console yourself with free coffee every morning. Sip your java on the second-floor palapa terrace and enjoy the view. No credit cards.

RV Parks
Playa Buenavertura $5–15   ★★

Km 94.5 Bahía Conceptión, no phone.
Sites: $5–15.
After El Coyote at Km 94.5.

This stretch of half-sand, half-rock beach is served by a market, restaurant, and an RV park with showers, toilets and sites with palapas. The more expensive sites have solid-wall palapas set on short stilts—these have cots in them for open-air sleeping. No credit cards.

Restaurants
Las Casitas   ★★★

In Las Casitas Hotel, Mulegé, ☎ *(115) 300-19.*
Steaks and seafood.
Hours: 7:30 a.m.–10 p.m., entrées: $6–15.
In town center, inside hotel.

Locals and visitors alike enjoy this hotel-restaurant's Friday night buffet, which has a mariachi band to entertain. Menu choices include meat dishes made with local beef and fresh seafood. No credit cards.

Cafe La Almeja   ★ ★

On the beach, by the river. No phone.
Mexican food.
Hours: 9 a.m.–2 p.m., entrées: $2–4.
Palapa hut on the beach.
The palm-thatched hut isn't fancy, but the food is filling and tasty. Choices include
tacos and fresh seafood. No credit cards.

Loreto-Nopolo Area

Hotels & Resorts

Hotel La Pinta Loreto   **$48–65**   ★ ★ ★

Boulevard Mision de Loreto ☎ (800) 336-5454 (U.S.), (619) 244-6900, (113) 500-36.
Single: $48–60. Double: $50–65.
On beach, one mile north of town plaza
48 rooms, pool, fishing.
The Mexican hotel chain has properties at various locations from Ensenada south to
the Cape Area. Functional lodging at a medium price, this hotel chain offers a four-
night travel booklet with pre-paid discounted rates at six selected locations. The La
Pinta Loreto is housed in brick buildings right by the beach. Rooms are large and
have shower baths and private patios. some have TVs and fireplaces. No phones.
Dining room is open from 7 a.m. to 10 p.m. Fishing trips and golf can be arranged.
Credit Cards: MC, V.

Loreto's Hotel Oasis is a small, modest hotel that blends desert landscaping and
the use of native building materials with its beachside location.

Hotel Oasis   **$45–100**   ★ ★ ★ ★

Calle de Playa at Zaragoza, Write: Postal 17, Loreto, Baja California Sur Mexico,
☎ (113) 501-12.
Single: $45–75. Double: $55–100.

On the shore of Loreto Bay, 0.5 mile south of town plaza.
35 units, pool, beach, tennis, fishing trips.

Surrounded by palms, with views of the water from most rooms, this is one Loreto's first hotels—in fact, it was once a fish camp. Today, the hotel still attracts anglers, many of whom charter fishing trips on the hotel's own fleet of pangas. Rooms are large, with two or three single beds and shower baths. Some rooms have patios. The dining room opens early—4:30 a.m. so that anglers can eat breakfast then head out to the water. Credit Cards: MC, V.

Hotel Misión de Loreto $25–60   ★★

Boulevard Mateos at Calle de Playa, ☎ *(800) 777-2664 (U.S.), (113) 500-48, FAX: (113) 506-48.*
Single: $25–60.Double: $25–60.
North end of Calle de Playa.
54 rooms, restaurant, bar, pool.

This hotel faces the beach and boasts one of the city's most popular bars. (The margaritas are the best in Loreto.) The rooms are ordinary, even drab, but this is a busy hotel—anglers favor the Misión because it is across the street from the marina. Rooms surround a courtyard and all have air conditioning and shower baths. The pool is a plus. Credit cards: MC, V.

Plaza Loreto $60–90   ★★★★

Paseo Hidalgo, ☎ *(800) 777-2664 (U.S.), (113) 508-55, FAX: (113) 508-55.*
Single: $60–90. Double: $60–90.
Next to mission church.
18 rooms, bar.

With 18 rooms available and more under construction, the Plaza Loreto is becoming a favorite with return guests who enjoy the quality of the rooms at this two-story downtown hotel. The rooms are spacious, with coffeemaker, TV and large showers. Credit Cards: MC, V.

Villas de Loreto $60–90   ★★★

Antonio Miares at the beach, ☎ *(113) 505-86, FAX (113) 505-86*
Single: $60–90. Double: $60–90.
Take Salvatierra to Madero and drive across dry riverbed, follow signs to hotel.
4 rooms, RV sites, campsites, pool.

Like a Phoenix, this hotel has risen again. With new owners, the hotel has four rooms, with more planned. Each room has a separate kitchenette and front porch. The old swimming pool and palapa bar are being renovated. Behind the hotel is an RV camp, with sites for tent campers as well. No credit cards.

Diamond Eden $70–110   ★★★

Nopoló, ☎ *(800) 472-3394 (U.S.), (113) 307-00, FAX (113) 303-77.*
Singles: $70–85. Double: $70–85. Suites: $110.
At Nopoló, 8.5 miles south on Highway 1, follow paved road to beach.
240 rooms, two restaurants, coffee shop, bar.

Formerly the Loreto Inn, this beach-side resort has views of the ocean and the scenic Sierra Giganta Mountains. Rooms and suites are housed in a three-story building with a tropical garden setting. Most rooms have private patios, all rooms have cable TV, movies, shower baths. Relax by the two pools, or play tennis or golf.

Activities include scuba diving, boating, sailboarding and horseback riding. Credit Cards: AE, MC, V.

The Diamond Eden was the first, and up to now the only, hotel to be constructed at the FONATUR resort community at Nopolo.

Restaurants

Cafe Olé ★★★

Calle Francisco Madero 14, ☎ *(113) 505-96.*
Mexican food.
Hours: 7 a.m.–10 p.m., entrées: $8–15
On the plaza.
This taqueria serves the usual tacos and burritos with flair, and for a reasonable price. Breakfast specialties include seafood omelets and huevos con nopoles (eggs with cactus). American-style burgers, ice cream and milk shakes will satisfy your junk food cravings. No credit cards.

El Super Burrito ★★★

Paseo Hidalgo, no phone.
Mexican food.
Hours: 8 a.m.–10 p.m., entrées: $8–15
Between Madero and the malecón.
Dine in or take out at this busy restaurant with the palm-thatched roof. Meats are cooked on an open grill, filling the place with the sizzle of beef. The fresh seafood dishes are the best bet, or for a less expensive meal, try the baked potatoes stuffed with cheese and meat. No credit cards.

El Nido ★★★

154 Salvitierra, ☎ *(113) 502-84.*
Mexican-grilled meats.
Hours: 8 a.m.–10 p.m., entrées: $8–20.

At town entrance.
Yet another of the chain of rancho-style steak houses, this one has a reputation for being one of the best at doing beef. Credit Cards: MC, V.

Ciudad Constitucion

Hotels

Hotel Maribel   ★

Write Maribel, Guadalupe Victoria 156, Ciudad Constitucion, B.C.S. Mexico; ☎ *(706) 832-0155.*
39 rooms.
A three-story concrete building at the corner of the main street of town (Highway 1) and Olachea Street. This corner is 2 blocks south of the junction of Highway 1 and Highway 22. A clean spot for overnight, but nothing fancy.

Hotel Casino   ★

Write Casino, Ciudad Constitucion, B.C.S. Mexico ☎ *(706) 832-0004. Located two blocks east of the Hotel Maribel on Olachea Street.*
37 rooms.
A basic motel, perhaps a bit more quiet than the Maribel, being two blocks from the traffic on the main highway.

Restaurants

Restaurant Querantana   ★ ★

Highway 1, no phone.
Mexican food.
Hours: 7 a.m.–9 p.m., entrées: $4–10
Within walking distance of Hotel Maribel and Hotel Casino.
Located in the center of town, this restaurant offers standard dishes, including tortas, tacos, burritos. No credit cards.

Bahía Magdalena

(San Carlos)

Hotel Alcatraz   ★

A small hotel entering San Carlos from Highway 22, ☎ *6-00-17, FAX 91 (113) 6-00-86.*
A pleasant place in a town that otherwise leaves a bit to be desired.

La Paz

Hotels and Resorts

La Concha Resort $85–175   ★ ★ ★ ★ ★

Km 5 Carretera a Pichilingue, ☎ *(800) 999-BAJA (U.S.), FAX: (619) 294-7366 (U.S.), (112) 163-44, FAX: (112) 262-18.*
Single: $85. Double: $85. Suites: $95–175.
Two miles north of city on the road to the ferry terminal.
129 rooms, pool, sundeck, Jacuzzi, private parking, private storage areas.
The only hotel in La Paz that sits right on the sand, La Concha is one of the most luxurious resort hotels in Baja. Once a training school for hotel employees, this three-story hotel boasts a brand-new suite tower, which has its own pool. The split-level lobby has modern-Mexican decor, a glass-encased restaurant that looks out on the heated pool, and a cabana bar on the pool terrace. The sand beach is beautiful,

Cathedral of our Lady of La Paz

Hotel Misíon de Loreto

Hotel Pamilla, Cabo corridor

Hotel Cabo San Lucas

but the water is rocky, although deep enough for swimming. Amenities include car rental, dive services (the resort maintains a full-time resident dive master), therapy pools, conference facilities, gift shop and room service. The rooms are modern, but a bit cramped—white furnishings and airy treatments make them seem bigger. All rooms have central air conditioning, sitting areas, TVs, phones, one king or two double beds and tiled baths. The views from the mini-balconies look out onto palms, the pools or the Gulf. The suites are available for rent or for sale, and contain sitting and dining areas, folk art accents, and terraces. A free shuttle carries guests to town. Credit Cards: AE, MC, V.

La Posada de Englebert $55   ★★★★

Avenida Reforma and Playa Sur, ☎ *(112) 240-11, FAX: (112) 206-63.*
Single: $55. Double: $55.
South of the defunct 13-story Gran Baja at the end of a dirt road.
26 suites, four casitas, beach.
Owned in part by singer Englebert Humperdink, this hotel is considered a hidden treasure by divers and other Baja buffs. Situated on the south end of town, the 25-year-old hotel has a tropical feel, with Spanish-Mediterranean architecture and palm-shaded terraces, all fronted by a sandy bay beach. Housed in colonial-style low-rises, the rooms are charming, with heavy furniture, wood-shuttered windows, tile floors, and hand-painted tile accents. Rooms are furnished with two double beds and large, Mexican-tiled baths. TV must be requested. The larger casitas have living rooms, bedrooms and patios. Entertainment includes strolling guitarists in the public areas, a large-screen TV in the bar, and weekend folkloric shows. Rooms are clean, even though the air always seems dusty. And yes, occasionally, Englebert drops by to inspect his property. Credit Cards: MC, V.

Hotel los Arcos $72–85   ★★★★

498 Avenida Alvaro Obregon, ☎ *(800) 347-2252 (U.S.), (112) 227-44, FAX: (112) 543-13.*
Single: $72. Double: $75. Suite: $85.
At Rosales, across from commercial beach, near town center.
130 units, 16 cabins next door, two swimming pools.
Well-known for its package vacations, and always busy, the Hotel los Arcos and the adjacent Cabanas los Arcos are used to handling tourists and groups. The Hotel los Arcos is housed in a three-story, Mediterranean-style building that has a landscaped courtyard, a small pool and a flagstone terrace. Rooms are air-conditioned, and have a sitting area, minibus, TV, twins or king bed and small bath. Rooms facing the central courtyard are the quietest. The more expensive bay-view rooms suffer from traffic noise. The hotel has an international restaurant that faces the street, a jam-packed bar that overlooks the yacht slips, and a cafe that opens early to feed anglers their breakfast before the hotel's charter boats cast off. Next door, the Cabanas los Arcos offers a more secluded, garden-atmosphere, with Tahitian-style bungalows and hotel rooms. These rooms are less expensive. Credit Cards: MC, V.

Hotel Perla $45   ★★★

1570 Malecón Alvaro Obregon, ☎ *(112) 207-77, FAX: (112) 553-63.*
Single: $45. Double: $45.

In the center of town.
102 rooms.

Located across the street from the bay, this economical but pretty hotel has undergone a recent renovation that gives it a new tiled lobby, a freshly landscaped courtyard, a bigger pool and refurbished (but rather nondescript) guest rooms. However, the open-air restaurant, La Terraza, a local favorite, still serves its guests at sidewalk tables facing the malecón. The guest rooms are clean, and all feature air conditioning, two double beds and baths with showers. Tile floors and TVs are also standard. For a comfortable night's rest close to the action on the malecón, this hotel can't be beat. Credit Cards: MC, V.

Club El Moro $75–100   ★★★

Km 2, Carretera a Pichilingue, ☎ *(112) 240-84, FAX: (112) 240-84, or (112) 270-10.*
Single: $75–100. Double: $75–100.
Outside town center.
17 suites, restaurant, bar, pool, travel services.

This vacation-ownership beach resort has white turrets and Moorish domes topping its Mediterranean-style building, and offers suites on a nightly or weekly basis. The hotel garden is tropical and lush, and guests can relax in the hot tub after a day of swimming or fishing. Rooms are richly furnished, with Mexican tiles and private balconies. The restaurant is renowned. Credit Cards: AE, MC, V.

Hotel Palmira $66   ★★

Km 2.5, La Paz-Pichilingue Road, ☎ *(800) 336-5454, (112) 240-00, FAX: (112) 539-59.*
Single: $66. Double: $66.
Opposite Marina Palmira.
120 rooms, pool, meeting facilities.

Located on the southeast portion of town, away from the main action, this resort hotel has pretty, landscaped grounds, a decent pool and tennis courts, but it sits on the highway opposite the beach. Popular with business travelers who utilize its meeting rooms, the hotel offers a restaurant, bar and disco—although nightlife activities are more plentiful in town. Rooms have air conditioning, shower baths. An acceptable choice if other resort style accommodations are completely booked. Credit Cards: MC, V.

Low-Cost Lodging

Hotel Mediterranes $25–60   ★★

Allende 36-B, ☎ *(112) 511-95, (112) 511-95.*
Single: $25–60. Double: $25–60.
Behind Trattoria La Pazta, one-half block from Boulevard Alvaro Obregón.
5 rooms.

Low-cost by La Paz standards, but offering clean, comfortable rooms, this small hotel doesn't have all the trappings of the glitzier resorts, but it offers a second-story terrace with a view of the water. More like a European villa, the hotel is suited best for guests who don't need all-night entertainment. All rooms have king-size beds, but only three are air-conditioned—fans cool the other two. Rooms have radios, but no phones. Fishing trips can be arranged. No credit cards.

Restaurants

Trattoria La Pazta ★★

36-B Allende, ☎ *(112) 511-95.*
Italian.
Hours: 1 a.m.–10 p.m., entrées: $9–18.
One-half block off Boulevard Alvaro Obregón.
Combining urban trendiness with pasta dishes made with locally-caught seafood, this restaurant draws the yuppie crowd. The dining room is sleekly minimal, with black tables, white walls and tiled floors. Pasta dishes and Swiss-style fondues are made to order. Good selection of espressos and cappuccinos. Credit Cards: AE, MC, V.

La Terraza ★★★★

Hotel Perla, Paseo Obregón, ☎ *(112) 707-77.*
International cuisine.
Hours: 1 a.m.–11 p.m., entrées: $9–18.
Facing the malecón.
A La Paz institution—the place to see and be seen—this open-air restaurant has a terrace with sidewalk-level tables that provide an ever-changing view of the malecón. Some say the food is mediocre, but the reasonably-priced, eclectic menu ranges from breakfast staples such as French toast to pastas and meats. Credit Cards: MC, V.

El Bismark ★★★★★

Santos Degollado and Avenida Altarmirano, ☎ *(112) 248-54.*
Mexican.
Hours: 8 a.m.–11 p.m., entrées: $15–20.
City center.
Home-style Mexican food served in heaping portions is this restaurant's trademark. Join the locals and try the *conhinita píbil* (marinated chunks of pork), carne asada, or fill up on a large grilled lobster. Dishes are served with homemade tortillas, beans and guacamole. Long wood tables and blaring TV make this place homey rather than elegant, but the constant stream of patrons testifies to the good food. Credit Cards: MC, V.

Restaurant Bermejo ★★★★★

498 Paseo Obregón, ☎ *(112) 227-44.*
International.
Hours: noon–10 p.m., entrées: $15–20
In the front of the Hotel Arcos.
Reservations recommended.
This elegant restaurant offers more refined cuisine than most hotel-restaurants, and the ambiance is enhanced by the view of the malecón from the dining room. Serving an array of international dishes, the restaurant's best choices are the steaks and seafood. The pasta dishes also are decent. Credit Cards: MC, V.

El Quinto Sol ★★

Calle Dominguez and Independencia, ☎ *(112) 216-92.*
Vegetarian.
Hours: 8 a.m.–10 p.m., entrées: $4–12.
Inside the market.

If you need a light meal, this small cafe serves a vegetarian-style Mexican staples and natural foods made with fresh ingredients. Try tortas, comida corrida, salads and fruit or vegetable juices. Finish with a pastry or a cup of yogurt. No credit cards.

Super Pollo

Calle 5 Febrero and Gómez Farias, no phone.
Mexican
Hours: 11 a.m.–9 p.m., entrées: $3–10.
Town center.

This chain specializes in Sinaloan-style chicken—polla asado al carbón—which is succulent grilled chicken served with tortillas and salsa so you can make your own soft tacos. Eat in or take out. Other locations as 5 de Maya and Gómez Farias, and Boulevard Forjadores and Loreto. No credit cards.

Todos Santos

Hotels and Resorts

Hotel California $35–45   ★★★★

Calle Juárez, ☎ *(800) 736-8636 (U.S.), (114) 400-02, FAX: (114) 523-33.*
Single: $35–45. Double: $35–45.
Between Morelos and Marquez de León.
16 rooms, pool, restaurant.

This thick-walled, two-story masonry building looks the way you'd imagine a small hotel in a small Mexican town should look. Upgraded in 1988, the rooms are modern but not fancy. The pool area is nicely landscaped. Management can arrange pack excursions into the Sierra de la Laguna, as well scuba diving, hunting and fishing trips. The Restaurant Las Tejitas is open for breakfast from 7:30 a.m. to 10:30 a.m., and for dinner from 6 p.m. to 9 p.m. The Tuesday seafood buffet is known for good food. No credit cards.

Restaurants

Restaurant Las Fuentes   ★★★

Degollado and Colegio Militar, no phone.
Seafood.
Hours: 7 a.m.–9 p.m., entrées: $4–10.

Stop here for fresh seafood served in an airy, romantic dining room or sit outside, surrounded by fountains. Enjoy fish or lobster and a mug of frosty beer. No credit cards.

The East Cape

Hotels and Resorts

Punta Pescadero $85–90   ★★★★

24831 Alicia Parkway, C-320, Laguna Hills, CA 92653, or P.O. Box 362, La Paz, Baja
California Sur, Mexico 23000, ☎ *(880) 426-BAJA, (114) 101-01.*
Singles: $85. Doubles: $85–90.
From Highway 1 at Km J-111 near Los Barriles, take rough dirt road 9.3 miles east.
21 rooms, restaurant, bar, pool, tennis, fishing fleet, paved airstrip.

Remote but worth it if you have a four-wheel-drive vehicle or high-clearance car, otherwise, you can fly in by private plane to reach this fishing resort. Punta Pescadero is set on 125 acres of palm trees and sandy beach, and all rooms come with ocean views and patios, as well as TV and refrigerator. Some rooms have fireplaces. Outdoor activities include watersports, fishing, scuba diving, tennis and golf. Scuba equipment is available for rent. Credit Cards: MC, V.

Hotel Playa del Sol $55–90 ★ ★ ★

Bahía de Palmas at Los Barriles, write P.O. Box 1827 Monterey, CA 93942, ☎ (800) 347-6847 (U.S.), (404) 375-4755 (U.S.).
Single: $55–60. Double: $85–90.
At Los Barriles.
21 rooms.
More modest than other resorts, but popular for watersports, especially windsurfing, this hotel offers basic rooms and a superb stretch of beach. Reservations must be made through U.S. office as there is no phone on site. Amenities include a restaurant, bar and rental fishing tackle. Closed in September. No credit cards.

Hotel Palmas de Cortez $85 ★ ★ ★

At Bahía de Palmas, write P.O. Box 9016, Calabasas, CA 93172, ☎ (818) 222-7144 (U.S.).
Single: $85. Double: $85.
South of the Hotel Playa de Sol, 0.5 mile off the highway.
32 rooms, 10 suites, pool, charter fishing fleet, airstrip.
This long-established fly-in hotel is now easily reached via Highway 1. Rooms are air-conditioned, and facilities include a restaurant, bar, pool and tennis court. You can rent windsurfing gear and fishing tackle. Trips can be arranged for dove hunting in the nearby Sierra de la Laguna. No credit cards.

Rancho Buena Vista $90–150 ★ ★ ★ ★

At Bahía de Palmas, ☎ (800) 752-3555, (U.S.), FAX: (619) 425-1832 (U.S.).
Single: $90–150. Double: $90–150.
Located 56 kilometers north of Los Cabos Airport, reached via side road from Highway 1 at Buena Vista.
80 units, pool, tennis courts, fishing fleet, spa.
This old fishing hotel has repositioned itself as a beach resort, adding a fountains, a portal entrance, bronze sculptures and a giant, free-form pool complete with swim-up bar, bridges and a palm island. Activities other than sport fishing center around the pool, which is visible from most of the tiered wings that house the rooms. The restaurant has a buffet, and meals can be eaten by the pool. Flowers, artwork and trophy-size fish mounts add to the seaside ambiance in the public areas, although the rooms themselves are rather plain. Rooms feature tiled floors, wood furnishings and two double beds (some have one double and one twin). Most rooms open up onto a common patio, but the sight of the ocean is blocked by the lush landscaping. Still, the beach is sandy and has shaded canopies, and the room rates are reasonable when compared with other local resorts. Credit Cards: MC, V.

Hotel Buenavista $85–140 ★ ★ ★ ★ ★

Bahía de Palmas, Buena Vista☎ (800) 258-8200 (U.S.), FAX: (805) 925-2990 (U.S.)
Single: $85. Double: $140.
Located 75 miles from La Paz.
60 units, seaside pool, fishing fleet.

Once a fishing camp, then a mecca for the rowdy watersports crowd, the Hotel Buenavista is returning to its roots as a destination for anglers and those in search of a tranquil seaside retreat far from the maddening phones—there are none here. Rooms are in cottages and low-rises spread throughout the spacious, landscaped grounds. Guests can enjoy fishing in the early morning hours, languid siestas throughout the afternoon, and dinners where you actually must dress up a little— men in shirts—before sitting down to a family-style meal. Play tennis or relax at the free-form pool, built right by the sea, or take a dip in the Jacuzzi. The hotel maintains a fishing fleet of 22 vessels. The airstrip was destroyed by Hurricane Kiko, so now guests arrive by car or taxi. No credit cards.

Hotel Punta Colorado $50–80 ★★★★★

South end of Bahía de Palmas, P.O. Box 9016, Calabasas, CA 93172, ☎ (800) 368-4334 (U.S.), (818) 222-5066.
Single: $50–80. Double: $50–80.
Located 10 miles east of Highway 1 via La Ribera Road (see "East Cape Loop.")
Anglers come here to fish for roosterfish, but this low-key resort also boasts large rooms and an airstrip for fly-in guests. Isolated and quiet, this moderately priced retreat is good for those who don't care for the non-stop party atmosphere of other Cape resorts. Closed during September and the first week of October.

Rancho Leonero $60–150

Bahía de Palmas, write 223 Via de San Ysidro, Suite D, San Ysidro, CA 92143, ☎ (800) 696-2164 (U.S.), (619) 428-2164 (U.S.)
Single: $60. Double: $95–150.
North of the Punta Colorado Resort, with dirt-road access.
25 rooms, restaurant, bar.
Built on a cliff overlooking the Gulf, this small hotel offers rooms with sea-views, and a locally renowned restaurant. Amenities include a fully equipped dive center, rental fishing gear, and a Jacuzzi. Credit Cards: MC, V.

Restaurants

Tío Pablo ★

In Los Barriles, no phone.
Mexican food.
Hours: 11:30 a.m. to 9 p.m., entrées: $5–12.
Palapa-style restaurant serving mostly American standards such as burgers and sandwiches. No credit cards.

Restaurant Gaviota

Highway 1 in Buena Vista, no phone.
Seafood.
Hours: 8 a.m. to 11 p.m., entrées: $5–12.
Fish tacos, antojitos, and Mexican-style breakfasts are on the menu at this low-key eatery. Enjoy a plate of seafood while the jukebox plays norteño music. No credit cards.

San Jose del Cabo

Hotels and Resorts

Presidente Inter-Continental Los Cabos $120–225   ★★★

San José del Cabo, ☎ *(114) 202-11, FAX: (114) 202-32.*
Single: $120–205. Double: $120–225.
On the beach, 1.25 miles west of town.
240 rooms, pool, tennis courts, fishing, boat rentals, disco.
The largest resort on the San José beach-front, this modern, adobe-colored complex is popular with honeymooners and couples, many of whom take advantage of vacation packages. The hotel lobby opens up to views of the large, circular pool—where most guests swim since the surf in the lagoon is often dangerously high. Decorated in a Southwestern motif, all rooms have air conditioning, white stucco walls, red-tiled sitting areas, and pine furniture. Sleeping areas are carpeted and are fitted with TVs, in-room safes, twin or double beds, dressing areas and smallish combination baths. Third-floor units have balconies, ground-floor units have patios. Activities include nearby scuba diving, tennis, and an exercise room. Bird-watching along the lagoon is worthwhile—more than 50 species of birds have been spotted. Meals are served in two seatings at a small restaurant or in a buffet-style dining room with changing themed menus. The bars are lively, and one has swim-up stools by the pool. The video disco is loud, but located away from the rooms. The large staff is friendly. Credit Cards: AE, MC, V.

Hotel Posada Real $75   ★★★

Malecón San José del Cabo, ☎ *(114) 201-55, FAX: (114) 204-60*
Single: $75. Double: $75.
On the beach, in the government-developed hotel zone.
150 rooms, pool, two Jacuzzis, fishing, boat rentals, disco.
A Best Western hotel, this beachside resort offers comfort and style at affordable rates. The complex includes two low, angled wings with views of the pool and beach—the south tower rooms offer the best ocean views and are closest to the beach. The surf is dangerous, so most guests swim in the octagonal pool, which has a swim-up shaded bar and a palapa taco stand. The two Jacuzzis are built right on the sandy beach, as is the lighted tennis court. The lobby and public areas are tiled and decorated in a tropical style, with many alcoves for private relaxation. Near the pool, the garden is planted with cactus and decorated with fountains and an artificial stream. Rooms are conventional, with brick walls, carpeting, rattan furnishings, TV, one king or two double beds and baths with tiled showers. Credit Cards: MC, V.

Moderate-Cost Lodging

Hotel Aguamarina $60–70   ★★

San José del Cabo, ☎ *(800) 897-5700 (U.S.), (114) 201-10*
Single: $60–70. Double: $60–70.
On beach, 1.5 miles west of town.
99 units, pool, beach, fishing.
This hotel offers lower rates than other area hotels, but the trade-off comes with fewer amenities. The plain, blocky building sits on a prime stretch of beach, but most rooms lack ocean views. The pool design is uninspired, the landscaping basic.

Rooms are air-conditioned, and most have TV, two double beds and small, cramped baths with tiny opaque windows. Balconies are small and shared between rooms. The staff is pleasant, but overall this property pales when compared to other area resorts. On the up side, the bar is lively if you like beer-drinking contests and the cafe serves inexpensive, but tasty breakfasts, burger lunches, and more elaborate dishes for dinners. Credit Cards: MC, V.

Fiesta Inn $85 ★ ★

Boulevard Malecón San José del Cabo, ☎ *(114) 202-11, FAX: (114) 202-32.*
Single: $85. Double: $85.
On the beach, next to the Aguamarina.
151 rooms, pool, restaurant, bar, meeting facilities.

Long and narrow, with gaily painted facades and interiors, this moderately priced Cape resort is known for its food, served in its large, rattan-furnished restaurant. The rooms are carpeted, and have a soft rose and blue color scheme, rattan furnishings, TV, open closets, and small combination baths. The surf is dangerous (red flags warn of constant currents and high tides), so the beachside pool is always busy. Guests can swim-up to the poolside bar or take time out in the bar, which is furnished with pigskin chairs. Nightlife here is limited to cocktail lounge entertainment. Credit cards: MC, V.

Tropicana Inn $52–75 ★ ★

San José del Cabo, ☎ *(114) 202-11, FAX: (114) 202-32.*
Single: $52–75. Double: $52–75.
On Boulevard Mijares, just south of town plaza.
40 units, pool.

This two-story motel isn't on the beach, but it's popular with those who appreciate the attractive, Mexican-style decor and moderate room rates. Rooms come with air conditioning, phones, cable TV and showers. The Tropicana is most famous for its restaurant (see description below). Credit Cards: AE, MC, V.

Restaurants

Damiana ★ ★ ★ ★

8 Boulevard Mijares, ☎ *(114) 204-99.*
Mexican cuisine.
Hours: 9 a.m.–11 p.m., entrées: $9–20.
East side of the plaza.

Named after the Cape Region's legendary herbal aphrodisiac, this restaurant is housed in an intimate, 18th-century hacienda-style building that is the perfect place for a special meal. The restaurant offers candlelit dining in the evening both indoors, or—most romantic of all—on the patio, where guests sit at wrought tables surrounded by tangles of bougainvillea vines and pine trees. Specialties include oysters, shrimp, lobster, abalone or steak. Don't leave without tasting the damiana liqueur. Credit Cards: MC, V.

Tropicana Bar & Grill ★ ★

30 Boulevard Mijares, ☎ *(114) 209-07.*
Mexican cuisine.
Hours: 9 a.m.–11 p.m., entrées: $10–18.

On Boulevard Mijares, just south of town plaza.

Touristy rather than intimate, the ever-popular Tropicana's menu is more American-Mexican than Baja-style. Come in the morning for coffee and Mexican pastries served at the sidewalk terrace, or stop for lunch or dinner. The extensive menu includes fajitas, chiles rellenos and grilled lobster. Drinks are potent, the bar is noisy with big screen TV, and there's dancing at night. Credit Cards: MC, V.

Pescadero del Mar   ★★★

1110 Boulevard Mauricio Castro, ☎ *(114) 232-66.*
Hours: 9 a.m.–10 p.m., entrées: $6–15
On Highway 1 just outside downtown.

Fresh fish is smoked on the premises using the mesquite-fired brick smoker, so the air is tangy with delicious aromas. You can purchase dorado, marlin, and wahoo by the kilo, or indulge in a plate of fish tacos or giant shrimp cocktails. The grilled lobster is superb. If you're a sports fisher, bring your catch here—the staff can smoke it for you to take home. No credit cards.

Nightlife

Iguana Bar   ★★

24 Boulevard Mijares, ☎ *(114) 202-66.*
Mexican cuisine.
Hours: 11 a.m.–1 a.m., entrées: $10–20.
On Boulevard Mijares, just south of town plaza.

A bar first, and a restaurant second, the Iguana bar nonetheless serves tasty seafood, chicken and ribs, as well as Mexican dishes. After dark, the place transforms into a busy nightclub with live music. No credit cards.

Cabo Corridor

Hotels and Resorts

Hotel Pamilla $130–300   ★★★★★

Highway 1, Punta Pamilla, write 4343 Von Karman Ave., Newport Beach, CA 92660
☎ *(800) 637-2226 (U.S.), FAX: (714) 851-2498 (U.S.)*
Single: $130–300. Double: $130–300.
Five miles from San José Del Cabo.
62 rooms, seven suites, two villas.

Known for its secluded, romantic atmosphere—no TVs or phones intrude here—the isolated Pamilla is a honeymooner's favorite. Situated among palm groves and landscaped shrubbery on a promontory overlooking the Gulf, this Mediterranean-style property entertains its guests with its beautiful pool and terrace. The beach below the cliffs is rocky and the surf is dangerous, however a calm, safer beach is only a short walk away. Grandly appointed and sumptuous, this hotel offers tennis, horseback riding, diving, and fishing. Two superb 18-hole Jack Nicklaus-designed courses tempt duffers. Rooms are air-conditioned, and feature knotty pine furnishings, one king or two double beds and hand-tiled baths with showers and robes. The garden units lack ocean views; 14 superior units look out on the ocean but have no terraces. There is an ample, courteous staff. Rates are higher on the weekends, and the final bill may contain surprise charges, so inquire ahead. Credit Cards: AE, MC, V.

Westin Regina Resort (Cabo Real) $195–225   ★★★★★

Highway 1, Km 22.5 ☎ *(800) 228-3000 (U.S.), (114) 290-00, FAX: (114) 290-10*
Single: $195–225. Double: $195–225.
In the Cabo Corridor.
243 rooms, three restaurants, three pools, exercise room.

Architecturally unique, the Westin Regina is perched on a cliff that tops a man-made beach. Constructed in a minimalist style, but painted with yellow, pink and adobe hues that echo vibrant desert colors, the hotel is built in tiers that step down hillsides. The main buildings curve out of the hillsides, and are accented by round towers, pillars and breezeways. One of the restaurants is housed in a cliff-top, circular building that affords stunning views. Another restaurant is designed as an open-air terrace that looks out on a waterfall, the pool and beach. At the beach, the al fresco restaurant serves light meals and snacks. Amenities include meeting rooms, tennis courts, access to two golf courses, and an exercise room. Richly luxurious, the rooms feature satellite TV, in-room safes, hair dryers, combination baths with large, walk-in showers, air conditioning and ceiling fans. Be prepared to walk—from the parking lot the lobby, from the rooms to the tennis courts, and more. The large staff is helpful and courteous. Credit Cards: AE, MC, V.

Melia Cabo Real (Cabo Real) $160–210   ★★★★★

Highway 1, Km 19.5, ☎ *(800) 336-3542 (U.S.), FAX: (305) 854-0660 (U.S.), (114) 309-67, FAX: (114) 310-03.*
Single: $160–210. Double: $160–210.
Half-way from Cabo San Lucas and San José Del Cabo.
299 rooms, two restaurants, cafe, room service, pool, exercise room, dive shop, fishing.

Although the Westin Regina overshadows the Melia Cabo Real for breathtaking architecture, the Melia's vast size makes it a major contender in the mega-resort market. Spread over a hilltop overlooking the Gulf, the hotel has a large, free-form blue pool, waterfalls, fountains, and a private beach. This hotel caters primarily to package tours—and for that market, it is top-end. The lobby highlights a pyramid sheathed with onyx, and the Mayan theme is continued in the rooms, where onyx-topped tables and tiled floors are standard. Dining options include a thatched seafood grill by the pool, a terrace restaurant and formal dining room. The two- to four-story room buildings wrap around the beach, and top-floor units have balconies (but the railings are spaced dangerously wide for babies). All rooms feature key cards, rattan furniture, mirrored walls, minibars, safes, and TVs. The combination baths are large and have dressing areas. Most rooms have landscaped patios or terraces. Amenities include tennis, golf and watersports. Credit Cards: AE, MC, V.

Hotel Cabo San Lucas $80–1000   ★★★★★

Highway 1, write P.O. Box 408088, Los Angeles, CA 90048 ☎ *(800) 733-2227 (U.S.), FAX: (213) 665-3243 (U.S.).*
Single: $80–475. Double: $80–475. Villas: $265–1000.
Located 11 miles east of Cabo San Lucas.
130 units, pool, beach, yacht anchorage.

The Cabo San Lucas is a classic resort—its layout remains largely unchanged since its opening, making it the traditionalist's choice compared to the mega-resorts that have sprung up elsewhere. The red-tiled buildings hug the curves of Chileno Bay, sprawling over 2000 acres, much of it landscaped with thick tropical growth. The resort exudes a sense of seclusion, which is enhanced by the bay vistas and surf-washed beach. Long a favorite with upscale anglers who come to fish for marlin, the resort offers yacht anchorage. Rooms are housed in haciendas decorated with wooden shutters, Mexican art, red tiled floors, and beamed ceilings. Some rooms have fireplaces and refrigerators. Activities include scuba diving and snorkeling (there is a reef just offshore), boating, horseback riding, hiking and fishing. Holiday rates are higher. Credit Cards: AE, MC, V.

The Cape Area's Hotel Twin Dolphin

Hotel Twin Dolphin   **$175–295**   ★ ★ ★ ★ ★

Highway 1, Km 12, write 1625 west Olympic Boulevard, Suite 1005, Los Angeles, CA 90015 ☎ (800) 421-8925 (U.S.), FAX: (213) 380-1302 (U.S.), (114) 318-03, FAX: (114) 318-04.
Single: $175–265. Double: $205–295.
Six miles east from San José Del Cabo.
50 units.

Catering primarily to celebrities and the very rich, the Twin Dolphin embraces a different look than most Baja resorts. Located at the end of a dusty, unmarked road off Highway 1, this special hotel has been an elite hideaway since its opening in 1977. No red tile or adobe here—instead, the buildings are sleek and modern, almost austere. Landscaped with artfully placed, xerophytic native plants, the hotel is designed with Zen-like simplicity. The large, two-story lobby is highlighted by a fountain that features sculptures of the namesake dolphins and reproductions of Baja cave paintings. Enclosed in glass, the restaurant features a marimba group nightly. Outside, guests can exercise in the open-air gym or relax on white cushions on the wide patio in front of the pool. The Jacuzzi overlooks the ocean. Sloping paths lead to the accommodations near the rocky Gulf shore. Thirteen air-conditioned cabanas house

44 deluxe rooms and six suites. Rooms have white stucco walls, heavy wood furniture, safes, minibars, king or double beds, and large baths with robes and oversize towels. All rooms have balconies or terraces. Guests do without radios, TV, or phones. Most rooms have mesmerizing views of the pounding surf. The staff is friendly and gracious. Credit cards: MC, V.

Calinda Beach $120–140 ★★★

Highway 1, just south Km J-4.5, ☎ *(114) 267-93, FAX: (114) 204-80.*
Single: $120–140. Double: $120–140.
East of San José Del Cabo.
125 rooms with balconies, restaurant, bar, three pools.

This resort's best attribute is its cliff-top views of the peninsula's rocky tip and the famed arched rock. Amenities include three swimming pools, tennis, a breakwater-protected beach, and two lighted tennis courts. The only restaurant is decorated with rattan furnishings, but the terrace looks out on the pool and the promontory. The Jacuzzi is perched on a cliffside, providing one of the best sea views in Baja. The accommodations are low, pueblo-style buildings, some set far off from the main public areas (be prepared to walk). Rooms have balconies, air conditioning, throw rugs on tile floors, fireplaces, TVs, phones and two double beds (some kings) and baths with marble showers. Oceanfront rooms cost more, but are worth it for the scenery. This hotel is not designed for disabled guests—access is practically non-existent. Credit Cards: MC, V.

Restaurants

No individual restaurants are listed for the Cabo Corridor. See Restaurants under San José Del Cabo and Cabo San Lucas.

Cabo San Lucas

Hotels and Resorts

Hotel Hacienda $99–290 ★★★★

Playa Médano, ☎ *(800) 733-2226 (U.S.), (114) 301-22.*
Single: $99–169. Double: $99–169. Cabana: $195. Townhouses: $240–290.
112 units, pool, beach, tennis courts, sailing.

One of the region's long-established resorts, this colonial-style complex is perched on the tip of a point jutting into Bahía San Lucas. The Hacienda caters to rich, international guests, but also draws locals who come for the entertainment and dining. The buildings have Old Spanish details—belltowers, arches, and stone fountains—and the theme is carried out in the hotel rooms, which are decorated with red tile floors, folk art and red marble baths. The older rooms have balconies overlooking the gardens of hibiscus and bougainvillea vines, while the newer (more expensive) units look out on the ocean. The beach cabins are right by the water's edge and feature air conditioning. The plush townhouses have wet bars, refrigerators and large baths with roomy tubs. The beach is clean and sandy, and the calm surf is safe for swimming. Guests can enjoy the restaurant's Friday night fiesta or swim in the pool, which is set in a rock deck that overlooks the water. Amenities include a dive shop, paddle-tennis and shuffleboard. Credit Cards: MC, V.

Solmar Suites   **$175–415**   ★★★★★

1 Avenida Solmar, Playa Solmar, ☎ *(800) 344-3349 (U.S.), FAX: (310) 454-1686 (U.S.), (114) 335-35, FAX: (114) 304-10.*
Single: $175–415. Double: $175–415.
At Land's End.
104 rooms, fishing fleet, dive shop, tennis court.
Once a fish camp, this hotel is now a gleaming white retreat set at the breathtaking end of the Cape. The hotel's for-hire fishing fleet is still top-notch, but landlubbers can relax on a wide Pacific-facing beach or splash in the beach-front pool. A major renovation was launched in 1992, and today, the Solmar offers studios and suites—the suites have separate sitting areas and tiled baths—but all rooms are all decorated in a modern Southwestern theme. Studios contain shower baths. Two deluxe suites (with deluxe price tags to match) are built right into the rocks at Land's End. Time-share units have kitchenettes and a private pool area, a plus since the dangerous surf is off-limits to swimmers. The hotel lobby leads to a wide terrace dining area and an airy indoor restaurant decorated with trophy-size marlin mounts and a thatched ceiling.

Hotel Melía   **$160+**   ★★★★

Playa Médano, ☎ *(800) 336-3542.161, (U.S.), (114) 310-00, FAX: (114) 304-18.*
Single: $160 and up. Double: $160 and up.
On the beach, Bahía San Lucas.
161 rooms and suites.
A venerable, luxurious hotel, the Melía offers a sheltered Pacific beach, and first-class accommodations, including three restaurants, two pools, a palm-sheltered Jacuzzi and meeting rooms. The lobby greets guests with arches that frame the views of El Arco beyond Land's End. Guest rooms are done in cool blues and offer sea views. All rooms have TV, phones, and tiled shower-baths. The hotel staff can arrange fishing charters, and other watersports, including sailing. Credit Cards: AE, MC, V.

Hotel Finisterra   **$99–148**   ★★★★★

Boulevard Marina, ☎ *(800)*
Single: $99–148. Double: $99–148.
At Land's End.
188 units,
One of the region's oldest hotels, the Finisterra has been redesigned and rebuilt into one of the most modern resorts. The older section, built at the top of a 160-foot cliff, is now connected by a bridge to the top of the new, nine-story tower. An additional 80 rooms are being added next to the new tower. At the tower's base is a large lagoon-style swimming pool set with palm trees and a terrace. The snack bar's three-tiered palapa-thatched roof juts skyward like a tropical-style Christmas tree. The new lodging have an elevator to the beach (otherwise you must take a 200-step stairway. Guests can dine on fresh seafood at the indoor restaurant or relax at the popular "Whale Watcher Bar" which overlooks the Pacific. Amenities include two tennis courts, gym, and sauna. Standard rooms are decorated with red tile floors and have TV, phone, baths with tiled showers, and semi-private terraces. Suites are spa-

cious and have marble combination baths. If booking in the older section, request an ocean-view room. Mandatory service charge: 10 percent. Credit Cards: AE, MC, V.

Moderate Cost Lodging

Mar de Cortez Hotel   **$40–90**   ★★★

Avenida Cárdenas, ☎ *(800) 347-8821 (U.S.), (408) 663-5803 (U.S.), (114) 30-32,*
FAX: (114) 302-32.
Single: $40–90. Double: $40–90.
16 rooms, restaurant and pool.
Located in center of town.

Situated on the town's main street, this small hotel is only one-half a mile from the water. Long a favorite with the fishing crowd, the Mar de Cortez is a casual place, and lacks the glitzy appointments of the mega-resorts. But the rooms are quiet (except, perhaps, in the early morning when the angler's head out) and the prices are moderate for the region. The rooms are built around a pleasant pool area, and some rooms have patios that open up onto the pool. The oldest rooms have brick ceiling, tiled floors and heavy furniture. Newer rooms are slicker, but still comfortable. Credit Cards: MC, V.

Restaurants

Mi Casa   ★★★★★

Avenida Cabo San Lucas, ☎ *(114) 319-33.*
Gourmet Mexican cuisine
Hours: 11 a.m.–11 p.m., entrées: $25–35
Opposite the plaza.

Considered to be the best Mexican restaurant in the area, Mi Casa is a Cabo San Lucas institution. Housed in a cobalt-blue building painted with a mural of a burro, the restaurant chefs prepare fresh seafood such as tuna or dorado served with Mexican sauces, as well as sophisticated meat dishes. Try the molé verde or molé poblana, which is made with an herb-spiced chocolate sauce. Roast pig or carne asada are other good choices. Guests are seated either inside or out in the back courtyard—so romantic with its candlelit tables. Credit Cards: MC, V.

El Rey Sol   ★★★★

Cabo San Lucas Area, ☎ *(114) 311-17.*
Mexican cuisine
Hours: 8 a.m.–11 p.m., entrées: $10–25
On the road to Playa Médano.

A favorite with both locals and tourists, this large brick restaurant is well-worth a stop if you have a car. Breakfasts are hearty, and lunch and dinner selections include fresh seafood dishes. The abalone is delicious, but the best deal, even though it is somewhat expensive, is the seafood combination plate, which features lobster, oysters, crab and fresh fish. The "Siete-Mares Soup" combines seven types of seafood and spices into the region's legendary cure for tequila hangovers. Credit Cards: AE, MC, V.

Peacocks/Pavo Real Restaurant   ★★★★★

Paseo Pescador near Playa Médano, ☎ *(114) 318-58.*
Gourmet International cuisine

Hours: 6 p.m.–11 p.m., entrées: $25–35
Two blocks south of Highway 1 on Paseo Pescador.
This elegant dinner restaurant features the talent of German chef Bernard Voll, who adds a European touch to all his dishes. The ever-changing menu's gourmet choices include blackened tuna with tomato-almond chutney, grilled dorado in a pecan crust, or shrimp with spinach fettuccine. The desserts are renowned, especially the tequila mousse. Credit Cards: AE, MC, V.

Taqueria San Lucas   ★ ★ ★

Avenida Hidalgos, no phone.
Mexican cuisine
Hours: 9 a.m.–11 p.m., entrées: $6–12
Between Madero and Zapata.
Known to locals and Baja buffs as "The Broken Surfboard," this tiny diner has mouth-watering fish tacos, burgers, and burritos that make a great budget-priced meal. There are few small tables outside, and the place is a must for the best breakfast deal in town. No credit cards.

BORDER INFORMATION

Shown is the entrance to Mexico at the San Ysidro-Tijuana port of entry.

In preparing this chapter it has been necessary to interview numerous government officials and visit many offices involved in entrance requirements. All too often it developed that there are differences between what the official regulations and the guidebooks say will happen and what, in fact, takes place. For this reason, be sure to read the "What Actually Happens" section later in this chapter. The saving feature is that, in practice, traveling in Baja is an extremely simple process for most people.

One overall item of advice is appropriate. Do everything possible before entering Mexico, unless your previous experience tells you to do otherwise.

This includes fulfilling the various entrance requirements and obtaining auto insurance, Mexican currency, foodstuffs and other supplies. In doing this, you can minimize peak-period crowding at the border and the complications always inherent with unfamiliar surroundings.

IMPORTANT NOTICE

In considering the recommendations for entering Mexico offered in this book, please be aware that your choice of ports of entry and travel routes in and approaching Baja may be significantly altered when, and if, the surfacing of Highway 5 is completed south of Puertocitos.

See the discussions presented in the "Baja's Other Roads" section.

Entering Mexico

Travel Zones

The requirements for U.S. and Canadian citizens who travel to Baja California differ depending on the areas to be visited. There are three travel zones:

Baja Border Zone

In 1952, the United States and Mexico reached an agreement that citizens of its respective border cities could visit the other nations' border cities for up to 72 hours without permits. The Mexican regulations refer to such visitors as *visitante locales* (local visitors) and define the area in question as the *ciudades fronterizos* (city limits).

As tourism increased, the Mexican regulations unofficially changed. A local visitor became anyone visiting the border area regardless of place of residence. On the Pacific side, the "city limits" expanded to include Ensenada and the nearby towns of La Jolla and Maneadero. For many years, the tourist card checkpoint lay adjoining Highway 1 at Maneadero, about 60 miles south of the border. As a result, some older travel books referred to a 60-mile-wide border zone. Now even the Maneadero checkpoint has disappeared. On the east coast, San Felipe is considered part of the border zone even though it is 120 miles south of the border.

Requirements in this elastic border zone are the least restrictive of the three travel zones.

Remainder of Baja

Travel requirements for the remainder of the Baja peninsula are more restrictive than for the border area, but are not as complex as those for the Mexican mainland.

Mainland Mexico

Requirements for entering mainland Mexico are the most restrictive and must be anticipated by travelers (1) entering Baja by first passing through the mainland or (2) by those planning to transport their vehicles from Baja to the mainland on the ferry system or by driving their vehicles easterly on Highway 2.

Entrance Requirements

The requirements for entering Mexico will vary depending on how you travel, and on what vehicles and other equipment you take with you. I experimented with presenting this material in narrative form, but found that something was always omitted or confusing. The end result resembled Mark Twain's incomprehensible description of how to harness a team of horses to a buggy, except that there was no humor in my product. Instead, I offer the "Entrance Requirements" table, shown below, that summarizes the regulations for the three travel zones. The numbered text sections provide additional material relating to the corresponding blocks in the table.

ENTRANCE REQUIREMENTS			
ITEM	**BAJA BORDER ZONE**	**REMAINDER OF BAJA**	**MAINLAND MEXICO**
PEOPLE	**1.** No permits required for tourist travel up to 72 hours. A passport and visa are needed for business.	**2.** For tourist travel, obtain a TOURIST CARD and have it validated after entering Mexico. A passport and visa are required for business travel.	
MOTORIZED VEHICLES	**3.** No permits required for cars, campers, motor homes, motorcycles or other motorized vehicles.		**4.** Validated permits are required. Must obtain prior to boarding any mainland-bound ferry.
TRAILERS	**5.** No permits required for recreational or boat trailers unless they exceed eight feet in width or 40 feet in length. Obtainable only in Tijuana.		**6.** Validated permits are required. Must obtain prior to boarding any mainland-bound ferry.
BOAT BY HIGHWAY	**7.** No permit is required to trailer or otherwise transport a boat into Baja by highway. A fishing license is required for the boat if it is used for fishing.		**8.** Validated permits are required. Must obtain prior to boarding any mainland-bound ferry.

ENTRANCE REQUIREMENTS

BOAT BY SEA	9.	Obtain a validated CREW LIST at the Mexican Consulate in San Diego. Also obtain TOURIST CARDS for all persons aboard. Port Captain check-in required in Mexico. A fishing license is also required for the vessel.
COMMER. AIRCRAFT	10.	No special requirements. Obtain TOURIST CARDS in advance for airports beyond the border zone. Cards will be validated by officials at the international airports. This is the easiest way to enter Mexico since the validating officials are waiting at the airports and you do not have to search for them.
PRIVATE AIRCRAFT	11.	Must land and obtain a GENERAL DECLARATION at one of Mexico's international airports and file flight plans as required by both Mexican and American authorities. Also obtain TOURIST CARDS for all persons aboard.

Block #1

More than 30 million people cross the border at Tijuana each year, making it the world's busiest international port of entry. Millions more use the other five border crossing points serving Baja. Requiring any type entrance permit for such large numbers of people would create a nightmare of paperwork. No permits of any type are required for tourist visits of up to 72 hours within the border zone. A tourist card is needed when one stays over 72 hours.

Block #2

Mexican regulations define a tourist as "any foreigner who enters the country temporarily for up to six months for recreation, health, scientific or sports activities provided they are neither remunerative or lucrative." Every tourist who visits the border zone for more than 72 hours, or who travels beyond this zone into Baja or the Mexican mainland, must carry a validated tourist card. You need a tourist card even if you have a passport. If your trip is for business you must apply for a business visa at a Mexican Consulate. As with all visas, you must have a valid passport.

Block #3

No vehicular permits are required for tourist travel within the Baja peninsula. (See further comments under "Customs Regulations" later in this chapter.)

Block #4

A **Temporary Import Permit** must be obtained if you plan to take any motorized vehicle to mainland Mexico. This includes transporting such a vehicle to the mainland via the Mexican ferry system. There is no charge for these permits. To obtain one you are required to have:

1. Proof of citizenship (the same as for obtaining a tourist card).

2.   The current registration certificate (original document, not a copy) or a notarized bill of sale for each vehicle. A notarized affidavit of authorization is also required if the vehicle is registered to a person or company other than the person applying for the permit.

3.   If you are purchasing your vehicle under a finance contract from a bank or other lending institution, you must obtain written notarized permission from the lien holder (the legal owner) authorizing you to take the vehicle into Mexico.

4.   A valid driver's license.

There is a complication if you have more than one motor vehicle, such as a motorhome pulling a small car or carrying a motorcycle. One person may obtain a permit for only one vehicle. A second person in the party may obtain a permit for the second vehicle if it is registered in that person's name. Thus, a married couple may obtain permits for two vehicles if they are registered in both their names. Also, another person in the party may obtain a permit for the second vehicle by using a notarized affidavit of authorization from the owner. In any case, all applicants must be qualified drivers. (Red tape is international.)

U.S. and Canadian Automobile Association members can obtain their Temporary Import Permits through association offices. Otherwise the permit is obtained and validated at offices inside Mexico at the border crossings or at the ferry terminals. In Tijuana, permits are obtained at the office of the *Registro Federal de Vehiculos*, which is located next to the immigration office.

Block #5

Permits are required for trailers only if they, or their load, exceed eight feet in width or 40 feet in length. Permits are obtainable only in Tijuana at the office of the federal highway police. In addition, permits are issued at the discretion of the officials.

Block #6

The requirements for taking a trailer into mainland Mexico are the same as for a motor vehicle (see "Block #4"). The trailer is included on the Temporary Import Permit of the towing motor vehicle and is obtained at the same time and place, as for a motor vehicle.

Block #7

See the "Fishing Licenses" section.

Block #8

The Temporary Import Permit covers a boat along with the vehicle that brings it into Mexico.

Block #9

The crew list must be validated at all ports visited where there is a Mexican *Capitan del Puerto* (port captain). Check-in with the immigration office is also required. The paperwork needed from a yacht operator is considerably more complex than that required of other visitors.

Block #10

The table says it all.

Block #11

Private pilots must land at one of Mexico's international airports, fill out an application form, and receive an approved document known in aviation circles as a General Declaration. Tourist cards may be obtained at the same time and place.

Tourist Cards

Obtaining a tourist card is a simple matter, but don't be dismayed to find that the document in question is not a card, nor does it bear the title tourist card, although it is universally referred to by that name. It is in fact a five by seven-inch, two-copy form that asks you in Spanish, English and French to provide the answers to 11 easily answered questions.

The tourist card may be obtained north of the border at any Mexican Consulate, offices of the Mexican Government Department of Tourism, offices of Mexican airlines, car insurance companies and at many travel agencies. It may also be obtained at the immigration offices at the ports of entry inside Mexico.

Cards are issued free upon showing proof of one's nationality. This requires that you have any of the following documents: birth certificate, passport, voter registration, naturalization letter, certificate of discharge from the armed forces, or a declaration sworn before a notary public. (Married women relying on a birth certificate also need a sworn declaration to support their change in names.) You are normally given a blank tourist card and asked to fill it out at leisure.

Children under 18 years of age who enter Mexico without *both* parents must obtain a notarized copy of the form "Permission for a Minor Child to Travel in Mexico" in order to obtain a tourist card. These forms are available at Mexican Government Tourism Offices and Consulates and must be signed by the absent parent(s).

Regulations require that the tourist card be presented for validation to Mexican immigration authorities upon entering the country. The proof-of-citizenship papers will again be required for validation and should be carried with you during your stay in Mexico.

Obtaining your tourist card *before* entering Mexico gives you a head start, but obviously the entire process of acquiring the card, filling it out and obtaining validation may be combined in one stop at the ports of entry offices.

What Actually Happens

Prior to 1980, obtaining and validating tourist cards took place at a roadside office at Maneadero on Highway 1. This station disappeared about 1980, reopened briefly a few years later, but was nowhere in sight in 1995. As a result, few people entering Baja by highway have tourist cards. Currently there is no station on Highway 5 from Mexicali to San Felipe, and few people in San Felipe have tourist cards. I am also advised that the various complications noted above concerning tourist cards and car permits rarely cause a problem. In contrast to this relaxed attitude toward tourist cards for highway travel, cards are always checked and validated at international airports during both arrival and departure.

IMPORTANT NOTICE

Early in 1992, the Mexican government announced new regulations concerning vehicles brought into Mexico from the United States. These regulations DO NOT apply to vehicles brought into Baja California. However, they will be enforced when vehicles are taken to mainland Mexico from Baja using the ferry system or when driving east on Highway 2. They are designed to deter the large numbers of vehicles that are stolen in the United States and illegally transported into Mexico.

The basic rule is that all imported vehicles must be covered by a current Mexican insurance policy or the driver must post a bond equal to the value of the vehicle. In addition, the driver must provide two photocopies of the following documents to customs inspectors: title document, driver's license, vehicle registration, insurance policy, and car rental contract in the case of rental cars.

It is the opinion of some people that this system will shortly collapse from its own weight. In that my own crystal ball is at the repair shop, I can only advise that you ask your insurance agent for the current state of affairs when you are ready for your visit.

I should also note that Mexican authorities have become strict in their enforcement of the rules concerning foreigners doing work that could be performed by a Mexican. I have heard of several persons being deported for doing home repairs and other simple tasks.

I recommend that everyone obtain tourist cards and have them validated.

Customs Regulations

The Baja peninsula is classified as a *Free Zone*, and in the past, baggage and vehicles were searched only under special circumstances. You were normally waved across the border at all points of entry. But, conditions have changed. At the Tijuana port of entry, a special lane is signed for vehicles carrying commercial products. A sampling of those using the regular lanes is stopped and inspected. RVs seem to be a prime target for this treatment. I escaped serious damage on a recent visit as the only contraband I had was a dachshund that took after the inspector. He laughed, slammed the door and moved on to more fertile ground.

Why the change? In past years, Mexican tariffs were so high that U.S. goods were rarely seen in Baja stores. Anything smuggled in and placed on sale would be easy to spot. In more recent years, trade agreements have significantly lowered, but not eliminated, these import duties, and U.S. products are much in evidence. Thus, enterprising people smuggle small quantities of this-and-that into Baja in their car trunks and under the sleeping bags. (I of course would never do such a thing, at least not anymore.) The storekeeper not only escapes the import duty but the Mexican sales tax, as such products leave no tracks entering the country.

One American told me his RV was inspected entering at Tecate, where it was discovered that his liquor supply exceeded the one-liter legal limit by about 50 bottles, but that this was easily taken care of by a small bribe. Thus, the inspection system is no doubt curtailing small-time smuggling by Mexican merchants while at the same time keeping alive the *mordida* trade between tourists with the customs inspectors.

In recent years there have been two agricultural check stations on Highway 1, one a short distance north of La Paz and the other at the line between Baja's two states. They stop northbound traffic looking for citrus fruit.

In any case, keep in mind that a tourist is one whose purpose of visit is neither remunerative nor lucrative. You should not sell items that you take to Mexico or carry supplies obviously in excess of your personal needs.

Possessing firearms is contrary to Mexican law, and officials are serious about it. The requirements for taking in firearms for hunting is a cumbersome process. Possessing and using narcotics is also against the law. There is no quicker way to get into trouble in Mexico than by violating these statutes. Mexico welcomes tourists and they are very obliging in their enforcement of the various immigration and customs laws, but they draw the line with firearms and drugs.

Pets

Most tourists don't take their pets to Baja. The potential for inconveniencing one's neighbors in camping areas is considerable, and hotels may not permit them. However, pets are often encountered in RV parks. If you take your pet to Baja you will need (1) a rabies vaccination certificate from a veterinarian and (2) a veterinarian-validated "International Health Certificate for Dogs and Small Animals." This is the title of the appropriate State of California form. The name may vary in other states.

I am advised that the above forms are valid only for 30 days from issuance and that one needs to obtain a similar document from a Mexican veterinarian to clear U.S. Customs. I asked several pet owners in Baja what actually happens and was universally advised they are always admitted home with no questions asked. This is what happened to us.

Heartworm is an internal parasite that can be fatal to small animals. It is transmitted to pets by mosquitoes. There are relatively few such insects in Baja, but they are frequently encountered in the Mulege area, where I am advised that heartworm is a problem. Heartworm may be prevented by having pets eat an inexpensive, chewable medication. Consult a veterinarian concerning the proper course of action.

Mexican Insurance

You need to give special consideration to insurance for vehicles, boats and private airplanes.

Auto Insurance

Mexican law does not recognize any insurance except that written by companies licensed in Mexico. A Mexican insurance policy guarantees that you are able to pay any potential damages and fines. If you are involved in an accident in Mexico and do not hold a policy issued by such a company, you may be held by authorities pending investigation and determination of fault. Spending time in a Mexican jail can ruin one's day.

Licensed companies are located on both sides of the border near the ports of entry. Watch for signs along the highways on the United States' side. Such companies also have offices in several larger U.S. cities. By far the least expensive insurance is obtained through membership in a travel club.

Coverage may be purchased by the day, month or on a annual basis. Daily rates are high by U.S. standards. You can hold down the amount of your premium by covering your vehicle only for the time when you will be traveling and excluding lengthy stays in trailer courts, etc. Obtaining annual insurance from one of the above noted clubs is usually the best course of action for any visit to Mexico that will last more than a few days.

Trailers and Boats

If you are towing a trailer, it must also be insured by a Mexican company or your vehicle insurance will be invalid. This coverage must also include your boat if one is being trailered.

Hull and liability insurance for seagoing yachts is a different matter. Som
yacht policies issued in the United States include travel as far south a
Ensenada as part of their regular coverage. Other companies will issue rider
for longer trips at no additional charge. In other cases, riders may involve a
considerable additional premium, and some companies simply will not pro
vide coverage for Mexican waters. The skipper's cruising experience may play
a considerable role in the insurance company's decision. No additional insur
ance is required from a Mexican company.

Private Aircraft

Liability insurance for a private aircraft must be acquired from a Mexican-
licensed company in the same manner as for a motor vehicle. In contrast to
boat and auto insurance policies, many aircraft policies issued in the United
States cover damage to the plane in Mexico. Aircraft insurance is issued by
most Mexican insurance companies.

Fishing and Hunting Licenses

Obtaining Mexican fishing licenses is discussed in the "Watersports" section of this book, while hunting licenses are included in the "Wildlife" section.

Returning to the United States

Your vehicle will be required to stop at the United States Customs Service
station located at the border. A uniformed officer is normally stationed curb-
side and will ask you several questions concerning your visit to Mexico. If
this officer believes that all is in order you will be allowed to proceed with little delay and without leaving your vehicle. If he/she should determine that
checking your vehicle is required, you will be asked to proceed to a secondary parking area where another officer will perform the inspection. This process normally takes very little time, although you may experience
considerable delay waiting your turn in line.

Mexico requires that tourist cards be surrendered when you leave the
country. Pilots of private aircraft and the skippers of oceangoing vessels normally check out at their last point of landing in Mexico and return the cards.
The U.S. customs inspectors may check for compliance and become suspi-
cious if these requirements have been ignored. In sharp contrast, persons
driving or walking home from Mexico normally retain their cards; there is no
apparent effort made to enforce the rule by either government.

Customs Regulations

The U.S. Customs Service enforces more than 400 laws for some 40 different agencies, but it is particularly concerned with (1) preventing the importation of illicit drugs, (2) enforcing the immigration laws, (3) preventing the

importation of plant and agricultural products that may harbor dangerous pests, and (4) collecting import duties on foreign goods imported for commercial use and over specified values.

To comply with these requirements, returning tourists should carry proof of citizenship. Also, wise travelers should use up their supply of fresh food supplies, or they may have to be given up at the border. The most common prohibited items are (1) raw and cooked pork, (2) raw meat of both domesticated and game fowl, (3) potatoes and (4) many fruits, including all citrus fruits. The full list of specific items that may not be brought into the United States is extensive and beyond the scope of this book. Write *"Quarantines,"* U.S. Department of Agriculture, *Federal Building, Hyattsville, MD 20782* for full details.

Each returning resident of the United States may bring back up to $400 worth of personal and household goods obtained in Mexico. These goods may not be for business purposes or for someone else. Their value includes repairs or alterations to articles taken to Mexico and being returned. You are also limited to one liter of alcoholic beverage provided you are 21 years of age or older. The exemption from duty may be used only once every 30 days. For further information, obtain Publication # 512, *Know Before You Go,* from U.S. Customs, *P.O. Box 7407, Washington, DC 20229.*

Drug Interdiction

Preventing the transportation of drugs has become a priority objective for both the United States and Mexico. During a trip to Baja in 1989, I passed through no fewer than five drug checkpoints in Mexico. On my 1992 trip there were none, while in 1995 there were two. What the future holds is anyone's guess.

At the U.S. ports of entry, checking for drugs has clearly become the priority concern. Recreation vehicles may be requested to stop at secondary checkpoints on a random basis, and trained dogs are used to sniff out violators. Customs officers also occasionally stop tourists prior to entering Mexico to inquire about guns, ammunition and large sums of cash (over $10,000). All of these are related to the drug trade.

Possession of illicit substances is a minor crime (misdemeanor), but importing them into the United States is a felony. If your vehicle is found to contain "any measurable quantity" of illegal drugs, such as one marijuana cigarette, you risk the confiscation of your vehicle and its contents.

Should you be able to pass on any helpful information to the Customs Service concerning drug trafficking, please phone them at ☎ *1 (800) BE ALERT.*

Canadian Citizens

Canadians visiting Mexico must pass through both U.S. and Canadian customs on their way home. The $400 duty-free exemption made available to U.S. citizens is not available to Canadians. U.S. regulations permit Canadians to bring in $200 worth of goods purchased in Mexico duty-free. However, I am advised that U.S. officials will normally permit Canadians to import Mexican goods if they are to be transported promptly through the country to Canada. The Canadian's declaration comes at the Canadian border. At press time, the personal exemption was $300.

Private Aircraft

The U.S. Customs Service has identified general aviation aircraft as the highest-risk vehicles for narcotics smuggling. Pilots of such planes are thus required to land at specified U.S. airports near the border for customs inspections. Brown Field southeast of San Diego, Calexico International Airport and Yuma International Airport are directly across the border from Baja. Customs officials must be notified at least one hour prior to the inbound crossing of the U.S. border. Pilots should obtain Customs Publication 513, *U.S. Customs Guide for Private Flyers*, for full information.

Returning by Sea

Skippers of yachts returning to the United States from Mexico must check in with U.S. Customs at the Harbor Police dock in San Diego.

Ports of Entry

There are six ports of entry serving Baja California. These are described in the "Ports of Entry" table. One of these, at San Luis, is in the mainland state of Sonora, but tourists may pass in either direction from Baja California to San Luis without the extra paperwork normally required to visit the Mexican mainland.

Usually it takes little time going from the United States into Mexico; however, there can be lengthy delays returning north. Keep in mind that the vast majority of this traffic consists not of tourists, but of people from the border area who live in one country and work, or shop, in the other. There is thus heavy border congestion from these commuters from 2 or 3 a.m. until mid-morning.

Aside from this commute period, U.S. customs officials at Tijuana and nearby **Otay Mesa** report that overall peak traffic periods are often unpredictable. On the average, Sunday traffic is the heaviest, followed in order by Saturday, Monday and Friday. The lightest traffic occurs on Tuesday, Wednesday and Thursday.

PORTS OF ENTRY

LOCATION	DESCRIPTION	HOURS
TIJUANA	This is the busiest port of entry. OK for entering Mexico but usually heavily congested when returning to the U.S.	24 hours
OTAY MESA	Built to relieve congestion at Tijuana. There are no adjacent communities so traffic is usually much lighter than at Tijuana.	6 a.m. to 10 p.m.
TECATE	A Mexican town of 45,000 people. No adjoining U.S. community. Traffic is usually light.	6 a.m. to midnight
MEXICALI	A large Mexican city and a busy port of entry. OK for entering Mexico but often heavily congested when returning north.	24 hours
ALGODONES	A small Mexican town with no adjoining U.S. community. Light traffic.	6 a.m. to 8 p.m.
SAN LUIS	A Mexican town of 175,000 south of Yuma, Arizona. Moderate traffic.	24 hours

Peak traffic periods at **Mexicali** also are unpredictable, but generally the busiest days are in descending order: Sunday, Saturday, Wednesday, Monday, Friday, Thursday and Tuesday. The first and 15th days of each month are also generally busy regardless of the day of the week.

San Luis reports the heaviest traffic between 10 a.m. and 8 p.m. on Sundays, when delays of from one to two hours may be encountered. November through April are the busiest months, but even here non-Sunday traffic is light except from 2 a.m. until 7 a.m., when commute workers from Mexico cross to work in agricultural fields on the U.S. side. The busiest months at nearby Algodones are similar to those at San Luis, with weekends bringing the most traffic.

At **Tecate** the busiest times occur on Sundays and holidays and on days with special events such as races and the August bull run. When traffic at Mexicali is especially heavy, Mexican authorities sometimes divert travelers to Tecate.

The U.S. freeway system tends to funnel Baja-bound tourists living along the Pacific coast to the San Diego area. Persons living east of the coastal area more readily flow towards Yuma, Arizona. The "Point of Origin" table, shown below, provides border-crossing recommendations. In all cases, it is assumed that the traveler plans to visit the main portion of the peninsula south of Ensenada via Mexico Highway 1. (NOTE—Expect significant changes in traffic patterns when and if Mexico Highway 5 is ever completed

POINT OF ORIGIN		
ITEM	**U.S. & Canadian Pacific Coast**	**Other Parts of U.S. and Canada**
ENTERING BAJA	1. Enter at Tijuana.	2. Enter at Tijuana, Tecate or San Luis.
MEXICAN TOURIST PAPERS	3. Acquire at Ensenada. Tijuana is best for car permits.	4. Acquire at Ensenada, Tecate or San Luis.
LEAVING BAJA	5. Leave at Otay Mesa or Tecate. Avoid Tijuana.	6. Tecate, San Luis, or Algodones. Avoid Tijuana and Mexicali.

Block #1

There is normally little delay in entering Mexico at Tijuana, although the spot inspections noted under "Mexican Customs Regulations" may slow you down. It is also very important to note that the Highway 1-D route around Tijuana avoids most of the city traffic.

Block #2

Car permits can be obtained, and tourist cards validated, on a 24-hour basis at Tijuana; however, there is less congestion and easier parking in Ensenada. The office hours there are 8 a.m. to 8 p.m. Monday through Friday; 8 a.m. to 3 p.m. Saturday. They are closed on Sunday.

Block #3

Avoid Tijuana at all costs. I have never returned to the U.S. at Tijuana and never intend to do so. Crossing at Tecate is the best choice. There are several twists and turns on the way to the San Diego freeway system north from Tecate, so it is best to have a highway map of the San Diego area on hand.

A somewhat easier return to the U.S. freeway system is provided by returning home at Otay Mesa, but the port of entry is a bit hard to find from the Mexican side of the border.

Block #4

Many travelers will choose to take Interstate 8 from Yuma to San Diego and enter Baja at Tijuana along with their West Coast brethren. The distance from Yuma to Ensenada via San Diego is approximately 260 miles; however, one can see more of Baja and avoid the San Diego traffic by entering Mexico at San Luis and proceeding to Ensenada via Highways 2, 5 and 3. This route is only 30 miles longer, but does involve traveling over the winding mountain highway east of Ensenada on Highway 3. As an intermediate alternative, enter at Tecate and reach Ensenada via Highway 3.

Block #5

Tecate and San Luis offer relatively congestion-free points to take care of the paperwork. Also see block #2 concerning Tijuana.

Block #6

It is really senseless not to return home via Tecate, Algodones or San Luis, and avoid Tijuana and Mexicali.

LIVING AND TRAVELING IN BAJA

The pages to follow discuss a variety of subjects about which you need to know when living and traveling in Baja.

Health Considerations

You will find that health conditions in Baja are good. It is widely reported, and it has been my experience, that tourists suffer considerably less from common intestinal disturbances (turistas) in Baja than on the Mexican mainland. Nevertheless, I shall pass on the standard fare offered to tourists everywhere in relation to this malady. Avoid overindulgence in food, beverage and exercise, and get plenty of rest, at least until your system adjusts to its changed environment. In general, avoid tap water by obtaining your needed liquids from bottled water, carbonated beverages, beer and wine. Avoid unpeeled fruits and uncooked vegetables that are the essential ingredients in salads. It is also advisable to inquire if the hotel swimming pool contains chlorinated water and avoid those that do not.

Having fulfilled this duty, I report that I know that this advice is widely ignored in Baja with few ill effects. Travelers and retirees in Baja regularly drink the tap water from many of the towns, large and small, and produce acquired at the markets is treated no differently than it would be north of the border. My best advice is to ask current residents what they do and follow your own best judgment.

Special Problems

The requirement for having had a smallpox vaccination to enter Mexico and to return to the United States was discontinued many years ago. The Anopheles mosquito, which transmits malaria, has also been eradicated from the peninsula; Baja is classified as malaria-free by the U.S. Public Health Service. This is not true for the mainland west coast from north of Mazatlan to the Guatemalan border. While there are no special medical requirements for visiting Baja, many doctors recommend vaccination for tetanus and hepatitis prior to visiting certain parts of the world. Contact your personal physician for advice.

Medical Facilities

There are well-equipped hospitals in Baja's larger cities. In recent years, government medical clinics also have been established in many of the smaller towns. These facilities prominently display the letters I.M.S.S. (*Instituto Mexicano de Seguro Social*) on the front of the building. All are equipped with radios so that air evacuation or other assistance can be summoned. In addition, two organizations in San Diego operate 24-hour, critical-care, air-transportation service throughout Baja. These are **Air-Evac International, Inc.**, ☎ *(619) 278-3822*, and **Critical Air Medicine, Inc.**, ☎ *(619) 571-8944.* If you have special health problems it may be wise to make prior financial arrangements with one of these services so that there are no delays caused by credit considerations.

The Red Cross is much in evidence in Baja. It operates ambulances and provides emergency medical treatment throughout the peninsula. Roadside volunteers are often encountered soliciting funds for this work.

Insect Pests

Troublesome insects are not usually a problem in dry desert climates. I have found this to be the most common situation in Baja. However, there are some important exceptions.

Desert insects achieve enormous increases in numbers following rain. During these periods you may be plagued by large numbers of flies, mosquitoes, gnats and "no-see-ums." The latter are particularly painful and can make life miserable. Mosquitoes can also be a problem year-round at hotels where landscape areas are kept continually moist. Take insect repellent and spray to Baja. A small section of mosquito netting used to throw over your head at night will help defeat "no-see-ums."

Currency

For decades the Mexican peso was an extremely stable currency, and from l954 to 1976 the exchange rate was 12.5 pesos per United States dollar. In September 1976, the country's spend-hearty economic policies forced a series of peso devaluations. By the end of 1992 the exchange rate was more than 3000 pesos per U.S. dollar.

Then, in January 1993, Mexico produced a new series of banknotes and coins that removed three zeros from the old peso and created the "Nuevos

Pesos" or New Pesos. It is abbreviated N$. As with the old peso, the new peso is divided into 100 centavos, but the smallest coin now minted is five cents. Cash purchases are supposed to be rounded off to the nearest multiple of five centavos. In practice, most grocery bills and similar transactions are quoted to the nearest peso.

The new peso started off with something approaching a one-to-one relationship with the U.S. dollar, but the Mexican peso crisis of early 1995 quickly reduced this to about six pesos per dollar. What you will find when you arrive in Baja is anybody's guess.

I offer the following comments and suggestions that reflect my most recent experiences:

- Mexico needs U.S. and Canadian currency. You can exchange dollars into pesos at any Mexican bank for the going rate. If you try to change these same pesos back into dollars even only two minutes later, the bank may be regrettably out of dollars. If you pay a bill in dollars, you will usually get your change in pesos. In other words, once you exchange your dollars for pesos it is often difficult to reverse the process. Prudent tourists plan ahead and spend all of their pesos before leaving Mexico. Stopping for fuel near the border, placing all your remaining pesos on top of the pump, and asking the attendant to dispense that much gasoline is one way to take care of the last centavo.

- There is no problem in exchanging or spending dollars or traveler's checks in places that are practiced in dealing with tourists, such as banks, hotels and stores in the border towns. It is often harder to use these same dollars at gas stations, food stores and other small businesses. For this reason, you should obtain a supply of pesos at a bank near your home, or at one of the border towns.

- There are often long lines at bank teller's windows. You can easily spend 20 minutes waiting only to find you are at the wrong window. Service is usually much quicker at an exchange dealer *(casa de cambio)*. You will receive slightly fewer pesos for your dollars at these places, so first check out the exchange rate at the bank and decide whether time or money is your current priority. In finding a bank, look for signs with the word *banco* (bank) or such trade names as *Banamex* or *Bancomer*.

- Canadians can exchange Canadian dollars for pesos at the major banks; however, this may not always be the case in the smaller towns. Canadian dollars also may not be as acceptable to businesspeople and individuals. The U.S. dollar is the universal solvent in Mexico and will dissolve any problem. Wise Canadians will carry some of their resources in American greenbacks.

- Always having pesos available allows you to use them to purchase an item that is priced in pesos and to receive your change in pesos. Most of us can deal with the mathematics involved in such a transaction. Using dollars in the same situation may give rise to "creative change-making" and awakens memories of grade school math tests where some of us received D's for not knowing how much change Johnny should receive in pesos when paying in dollars for a watermelon worth 4.5 pesos, when the exchange rate four days earlier was 3.75 pesos to the dollar and is increasing 0.22 pesos per day.

- Carry a pocket calculator in case you find yourself at a gas pump where the peso gauge is broken or covered over with tape and you are being told what to pay by a 12-year-old kid. I have had experiences where the mere presence of a calculator prevented mistakes in currency transactions. Have one in your hand and punch it even if you don't understand its use.

- Many businesses and hotels will also exchange dollars into pesos. My experience is that the rate at stores will be a little better than the official rate. Their managers wish to attract your business. The rates at hotels are usually lower than bank rates as most often you are paying your bill and the hotel's proprietors have already enjoyed your trade.

Spanish (Español)

Although most of us know that the language of Mexico is Spanish, it comes as a bit of a shock to find that all road and other signs immediately abandon the English language south of the border. However, even if you don't understand Spanish, you will have little trouble getting along in Baja. Almost all tourist-oriented stores in the border area employ someone who speaks English. English-speaking Mexicans rapidly diminish south of Ensenada, but there is rarely a language problem at the hotels and other tourist facilities. Menus are frequently printed in both English and Spanish and will help you to become familiar with frequently used words. What better way to learn that eggs are *huevos* than when ordering breakfast *(desayuno)*.

I suggest that you obtain an English-Spanish dictionary and a simple Spanish textbook. These items are not essential, but you can enjoy your trip more by becoming familiar with simple Spanish. Most Baja citizens are eager to help, and knowing even a little Spanish gives you common ground.

Shopping and Prices

Baja's border cities owe much of their rapid growth to the allurements they have provided over the years to residents of southern California in the United States. In the past, gambling, prostitution and alcohol (during prohibition) were the big sellers. Today, things have calmed down and just plain shopping has become a big money-gainer. Each port of entry border town has clusters of shops and stores that cater to the shopping tastes of the tourist. The same is true for Ensenada and San Felipe, farther south. The only other shopping centers of significance are La Paz and Cabo San Lucas.

These cities offer a variety of goods ranging from inexpensive baskets and similar tourist eye-catchers to more expensive silver, porcelain, perfumes, leather goods and clothing. Much of this merchandise can be obtained at prices lower than in the United States. This is particularly true for products such as tooled belts, shoes, handbags, and other items that involve considerable hand labor.

Prices are normally fixed, and marked on the merchandise, at the department stores and larger shops, but bargaining is the name of the game in many smaller establishments. This practice is a bit unfamiliar to many tourists, but you are simply paying too much if you don't participate. While there is money to be saved, bargaining often takes extra time as one needs to compare prices at different shops and engage in a sometimes protracted battle of wits with the proprietors. Having dollars rather than pesos will enhance your bargaining position. I normally despise shopping, but the sporting aspects of the bargaining process actually can make it enjoyable.

Liquor stores (signed *Vinos* and *Licores*) are plentiful. There is a wide selection of Mexican brands of beer (*cerveza*) as well as tequila, rum, brandy, gin, and vodka at prices near, or below, those in the United States. Bourbon and Scotch are scarce and expensive. Santo Tomas and other brands of wine bottled in the Ensenada vicinity are also available at reasonable prices.

Now THE BAD NEWS. In early 1989 (after the election of President Carlos Salinas de Gortari), it was apparent that prices for many commodities had roughly doubled from the previous year. This was particularly true for food. The rates paid by businesses for various government services such as power and water also rose sharply. Finally, the sales tax rate in Baja rose from six to 15 percent as it has long been on the Mexican mainland.

These price increases resulted when Mexico faced the reality that it could no longer subsidize much of what it provided for its people. Similar price escalations have occurred in other countries around the world as they back away from heavily socialized economies and move toward capitalism. And I believe there is a relationship between these policies and the recent decrease in inflation. But, for whatever reason, living in Mexico is not nearly the bargain it once was. However, some items still cost very little. Tortillas and beer both come to mind. The essentials of life are still a bargain.

At times, the peso loses much of its value in relationship to the U.S. dollar, as occurred early in 1995, and tourists believe they can travel to Mexico and secure great shopping values. This is in fact true if one is shopping at retail stores and other places frequented by the Mexican people. However, almost all establishments dealing primarily with tourists peg their prices in U.S. dollars and the traveler experiences no bargains. This is true everywhere from luxury hotels to the smallest RV parks.

Problemas

One of the most common Spanish expressions that a tourist will hear in Mexico is "*no problema,*" meaning that there is no problem, or that one's request will be complied with promptly. However, occasionally a traveler may in fact encounter a real *problema* and need assistance. Away from the larger towns, authority rests with the *delegado,* an appointed official whose office will bear the name *Delegacion Municipal,* and there are uniformed police in all but the smallest communities. Consult these officials in case of need.

Should you encounter legal difficulties, including those with public officials, contact an office of the State Tourism Department. The State of Baja California also operates the **Procuraduria General de Protection al Turista** (Office of the Attorney General for the Protection of Tourists). Call in Tijuana ☎ *(706) 684-2138* or the 24-hour hot line ☎ *(706) 685-0302;* in Ensenada ☎ *(706) 676-3686;* in Mexicali ☎ *(706) 562-5744;* and in San Felipe ☎ *7-11-55.* They act as public defenders and render free legal service.

The laws of Mexico are based on the Napoleonic Code used in much of Europe and Latin America. In these countries, one is held to be guilty until proven innocent, a somewhat frightening prospect to those of us accustomed to the opposite foundation of English law. This legal difference is a key reason why you should carry Mexican insurance for your vehicles. Failure to do so could result in your being detained pending determination of responsibility in case of an accident.

Tourists may occasionally encounter the need to part with a small bribe or tip called *la mordida* (the death bite) to avoid a problem with a public official. The Mexican government has been making a considerable effort to eliminate this practice, but it still prevails. My personal familiarities with the practice all involve situations where tourists were in violation of Mexican regulations, or wished to avoid full compliance with such requirements.

Conforming fully with Mexico's way of doing things would seem to be the simplest means of avoiding the need for *la mordida*.

Telephoning

Baja California has a modern telephone system, but the number of individual telephones is relatively small. For example, there are fewer than 100 pages of phone numbers in the single phone book covering all of the state of Baja California Sur. Each phone book also has a yellow pages section, which you may find useful in locating specific services. The phone systems for the various towns and cities are linked together by microwave radio; you will see the towers at many places along the main highways.

Calling Mexico

You may dial directly to telephones in Baja from many places in the United States and Canada. Consult the International Calling instructions in the front section of most phone books. The following examples utilize the phone number for the Estero Beach Hotel near Ensenada:

(1) 011 + 52 + 617 + 6-6235

(2) (526) 176-6235

In areas served by International Direct Distance Dialing (IDDD), *011* is the **International Access Code**, *52* the **Country Code** for Mexico, and *617* the **City Code** for Ensenada; *6-6235* is the hotel's phone number as it appears in the Mexican phone book.

The second example lists the same series of numbers in the format familiar to U.S. and Canadian citizens. This is how the numbers are shown in most travel brochures and in this book. Many of the City Codes in Baja start with 6. Thus, for practical purposes, *52 + 6* or *(526)* is what we would call the area code for these cities.

Calling Home

It is possible to dial directly to the United States and Canada from Baja by using a private telephone. Most tourists do not have access to such a telephone and will need to utilize one of the following alternatives.

1. There are phone booths on the streets in the major cities. Place a coin in the slot at the top of the phone to activate the circuit. Dial 95 for calls to the United States and Canada. I have always found that an operator answers and speaks sufficient English to complete a collect or credit card call. This is an inexpensive way to call home.

2. In the larger towns you will find long-distance offices staffed with one or more operators who will place calls for a fee. Be alert for the *larga distancia* sign.

3. Most hotels place calls for their patrons, but there is often a fee. If you are not a guest you may be refused assistance.

4. During our 1995 field trip, we encountered scores of phones located in the open at all prominent tourist facilities. They contain prominent signs reading "TO CALL THE USA—Collect or With Credit Card." You simply dial 0, an operator answers promptly and makes your call. Then when you get home your phone bill reads like the national debt. Our calls averaged over $5 per minute and we payed $10 each time we got a busy signal. This service is efficient but outrageously expensive.

5. Upon returning home from the above disaster, we contacted AT&T and were given a code number to use in direct dialing. The other long-distance companies apparently each have their own codes. You also need a credit card (calling card) from your company. We will try this method next time.

Business Opportunities

I am occasionally asked my views about starting a business in Baja. I wish to make it very clear that this subject is not within my field of expertise. However, I offer the following comments:

•   I made a quick count of non-Mexicans (mostly Americans) that I have observed with tourist-related business in Baja. The number was 25. There are no doubt others. Almost all of these people are married couples where one spouse is a Mexican. Obviously one's nationality is an important business factor. I met one Canadian who has invested a great deal of money in his business but periodically has to renew his right to remain in Mexico. On the last occasion, he was granted only a six-month extension since the immigration official was peeved over the anti-immigration movement in the United States.

•   Some of the above noted people have been in business for years and seem to be quite happy and successful. Others have suffered disasters of one sort or the other that relate not to the failure of the business itself, but to the business environment in Mexico. In several cases a land lease expired and could not be renewed at a reasonable price, and there went 10 years of hard work.

Living in Baja

Thousands of people from north of the border have purchased residential real estate in Baja. Some units are used for the buyers' personal use, and oth-

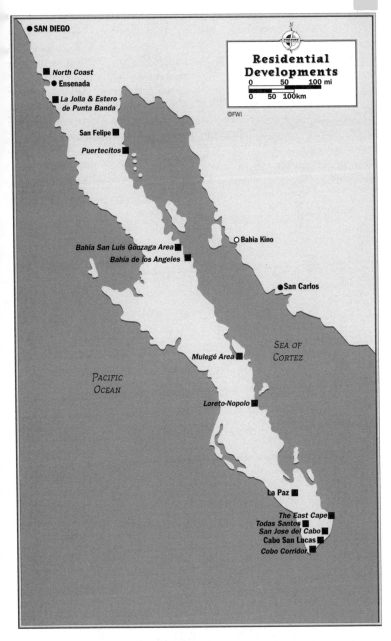

Residential Developments

0   50   100 mi

0 50 100km

©FWI

SAN DIEGO

North Coast

Ensenada

La Jolla & Estero
de Punta Banda

San Felipe

Puertecitos

Bahía San Luis Gonzaga Area

Bahía de los Angeles

Bahía Kino

San Carlos

SEA OF
CORTEZ

Mulegé Area

PACIFIC
OCEAN

Loreto-Nopolo

La Paz

The East Cape

Todas Santos

San Jose del Cabo

Cabo San Lucas

Cobo Corridor

ers are intended to be investment properties. I will limit my counsel in this regard to noting the locations of the most prominent real estate developments.

The places shown as "Residential Developments" on the map on the previous page offer relatively recent modern units. Some are fancy and expensive, others more modest. The three locations at the peninsula's southern tip are the most rapidly growing. The "Lesser Developments" are for the most part older, less auspicious places. These include the lease of space in some RV parks where the investor moves in a mobile home or trailer and adorns it with various ornaments.

Remember that buying residential real estate is a form of business enterprise, and that business in Mexico is not the same as it is north of the border.

PART II:
HIGHER NEEDS

GEOLOGY

Las Tres Virgenes volcano is north of Santa Rosalia. Note the organ pipe cactus.

Few people have training or knowledge concerning geology. Others may believe that they will have little interest in this subject. For these reasons, I am fearful that many readers may be inclined to pass over this chapter. I implore you not to do so. I make this pledge: Everything presented in this chapter is essential background material concerning features that you may readily see from the peninsula's main highways. Excluded are lengthy descriptions of geologic history and the unnecessary use of technical terms that, for the average tourist, do little more than occupy space. If technical language is necessary, straightforward definitions are provided, enhanced where possible by sketches or tables.

I sincerely hope you have been persuaded to read on and savor Baja's geologic panorama. Making such a decision would be less important were you contemplating traveling through the vast plains and prairies of the central and eastern United States and Canada, where there is relatively little geologic story to be told. Even in areas such as the Appalachian Mountains in the eastern United States, where there is much of geologic interest, the humid weather conditions and resultant dense forest vegetation tend to round over the landscape and mask the rocks and other structural features.

In contrast, geologic features are plentiful, varied and easily seen in Baja, where the land is both mountainous and arid. Perhaps the most outstanding such region in North America is the southwestern portion of the United States. I would rate this latter area as superior to Baja in both scenery and geologic interest, although the comparison may be unfair due to the tremendous size and diversity of southwestern United States. Regardless of its relative rank, the Baja peninsula is a place of fine, and at times outstanding, scenery.

In presenting this picture, I will begin with the peninsula itself and then proceed through more specific elements. As in all the chapters of Part II, the material presented here will be further amplified as individual features are encountered in Part III.

The Peninsula Is Born

Scientists estimate that the earth is some 4.5 billion years old. In comparison to this incredible age, the geologic story of Baja California is a recent one, with reliable dating going back only some 150 million years. But even at this relatively recent time, there was yet to be a peninsula. The birth of the present jagged finger of land was not to begin until 25-30 million years ago as a by-product of the formation of the famous **San Andreas Fault** and its undersea extensions both to the north and south. (See "San Andreas Fault" map.)

The San Andreas Fault is a deep, linear fracture extending from the floor of the Pacific Ocean some 25 miles north of San Francisco, south through Alta California to the mouth of the Rio Colorado, and then into the Sea of Cortez. On the floor of this body of water, this geologic phenomenon continues southward as a zone of sea floor spreading called the **Sea of Cortez Rift Zone**.

Most geologists now subscribe to the theory of plate tectonics, wherein the Earth's crust is believed to be made up of a number of massive plates that move more or less independently from each other. The San Andreas Fault and the Sea of Cortez Rift Zone are part of the boundary between the two

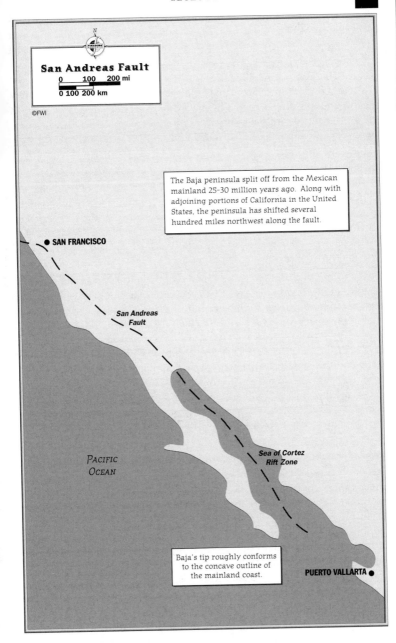

San Andreas Fault

0   100   200 mi

0 100 200 km

©FWI

The Baja peninsula split off from the Mexican mainland 25-30 million years ago. Along with adjoining portions of California in the United States, the peninsula has shifted several hundred miles northwest along the fault.

● SAN FRANCISCO

San Andreas Fault

PACIFIC OCEAN

Sea of Cortez Rift Zone

Baja's tip roughly conforms to the concave outline of the mainland coast.

PUERTO VALLARTA ●

gigantic plates that form the North American continent to the east and the Pacific plate to the west.

Millenniums ago, the Pacific plate began to slide up the California coast in a northwesterly direction. The total displacement is estimated at approximately 450 miles and is still occurring at the rate of about one inch per year. The southern portion of the plate gradually separated from the continent to open up the area now occupied by the Sea of Cortez. There is a more westerly movement toward the southern portion of the sea, which explains why the sea is wider there than to the north.

As a result, the Sea of Cortez is one of the world's youngest seas and it, and the Red Sea to the west of Africa, serve geologists as classic examples of tectonic interaction. And because of all this, the U.S. residents of southern Alta California are cast together with their Mexican neighbors in a slow and rocky boat to China. The former can take heart in knowing that the latter seem to get along quite well being separated from the mainland. It also appears that those northern California politicians who yearn to separate California into two states may eventually get their way.

The splitting and northerly movement of the peninsula has been a slow and complex event. It would appear that the journey has not been uniform and that the peninsula has been stretched in the process. In particular, the mountains at the southern tip have lagged behind the northern portion. This situation may be clearly observed at a point-of-special-interest stop in the mountains north of La Paz. This vista point overlooks the low-lying Llano de La Paz, the gap which separates the lagging mountains of the Cape region from the Sierra Giganta to the north. It would take very little rise in sea level to convert the lethargic southern tip into an island.

Baja's Backbone Mountains

Perusing the topographic maps of the world will readily show that most of our planet's mountains occur in ranges or chains rather than as isolated peaks. In western North America, many of these ranges are the result of linear masses of molten minerals welling up from below the earth's crust and solidifying into gigantic structures called batholiths. The main backbone mountains of the Baja peninsula, the Peninsular Range, are formed from part of a chain of such batholiths that stretch along the west coast of the North American continent. It is thus a close cousin of similar ranges in British Columbia, Idaho and the Sierra Nevada of Alta California.

The Sierra Nevada and Baja's Peninsular Range are similar in two basic respects. They are both formed from *fault-block batholiths*, and in both cases the block has been tilted upward unevenly to create a steep face, or *escarp-*

Baja's Peninsula Range Mountains

1 A highly simplified view of the mountains as a gigantic block of rock (a batholith) that's eastern edge is lifted along a fault in the earth's crust.

← **Fault line**

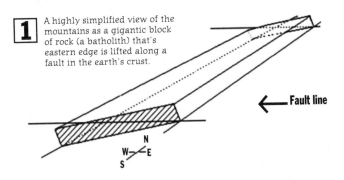

2 The same block pictured more as it looks today after being weathered by the forces of erosion.

Gentle westerly facing slope eroded by many watercourses draining from east to west into the Pacific Ocean.

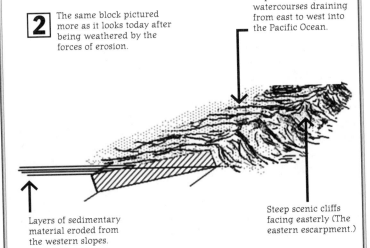

Layers of sedimentary material eroded from the western slopes.

Steep scenic cliffs facing easterly (The eastern escarpment.)

By Yves Couturier

GEOLOGY

ment, along the eastern edge. Knowledge of these very basic circumstances will allow the traveler to observe and to understand the most prominent topographic features of the peninsula.

To comprehend the makeup of a fault block batholith, see the accompanying illustration and visualize the basic structure of these mountains as a gigantic piece of lumber sawed so that it is much wider than high. A two-by 10-inch plank will do nicely. Then, because of tremendous forces developed within the crust of the Earth, a fracture or fault occurred along the eastern edge of the plank.

Over millions of years this eastern edge was raised up along the line of the fault to form a steep cliff, or escarpment. What was formerly the top of the plank now becomes the gently sloping west face of a range of mountains. The forces of erosion carve the upper eastern edge into a linear series of peaks. These same processes of erosion also dissect the westerly face, sometimes creating quite rugged topography marked by scores of watercourses running from east to west.

In the United States, the situation just described is readily apparent in the Sierra Nevada to travelers crossing the range from east to west on Interstate 80. At Reno, Nevada, the steep eastern escarpment may be seen stretching majestically both north and south. A few miles west of the city the highway climbs steeply and in a short distance crosses over the crestline at Donner Summit. The descent over the more gentle western slope extends a much longer distance, and it involves several ups and downs resulting from the forces of erosion. The highly scenic eastern escarpment of the Sierra Nevada and its series of 12,000- to 14,000-foot peaks are in clear view for hundreds of miles to the south of Reno and east of Highway 395. This situation in the United States has been described because many visitors to Baja will have traveled in this area and will now be able to relate the two geologically similar circumstances.

The geologic story of the Peninsular Range has been complicated by the linear stretching previously described, by substantial volcanic activity, and by other factors; but the dominant element is the fault-block mountain building just described. The traveler to Baja can see many evidences of this process and other related geologic events. Here is a list of the principal phenomena:

1. In general, the highest mountain peaks lie along the main crestline divide in the eastern portion of the peninsula. In many places, this divide lies so close to the Sea of Cortez that the eastern escarpment falls directly into the ocean and there are no coastal roads. For this reason, some of the peninsula's most scenic areas are not readily accessible to the tourist. They may be viewed only by the boater sailing close to the rocky coast and by passengers of small private planes flying overhead.

2. The scenic eastern escarpment of the Peninsular Range may be best seen by the land-based tourist in two places: (a) from the San Felipe area where Highways 2 and 5 traverse the flat desert lands east of the escarpment and (b) along the Sea of Cortez coast between Santa Rosalia and a point about 20 miles south of Loreto. This southerly portion of the section is the most scenic area along the Transpeninsular Highway.

Rugged mountainous areas may be visited in many other places by use of secondary and more primitive roads. Journeys to the National Parks in the Sierra de Juarez and Sierra San Pedro Martir are particularly rewarding. These side trips are described in later sections of this book.

3. The Peninsular Range mountains are crossed by the main highway system in several places, thus affording the traveler the opportunity to experience the steep eastern escarpment. A classic example lies south of Loreto. After a steep climb of some 10 miles up the steep eastern slope, the traveler might well ask "where is the other side of the mountain?" For all practical purposes, there is none. The crestline of the mountain range falls gently to the west and eventually blends into the Llano de Magdalena and the Pacific Ocean.

4. The lands lying to the west of the crestline divide are of fairly gentle overall topography. The large volumes of sediments caused by the erosion of this broad slope have been deposited to the west of the mountains resulting in the formation of some of the largest flat plains found along the west coast of the North American continent. The major areas are the Desierto de Vizcaino near the center of the peninsula and the Llano de Magdalena in the south.

Much of the Transpeninsular Highway has been located in the western and central portion of the peninsula to take advantage of this relatively gentle topography. However, the highway must cross, at right angles, the hundreds of watercourses that have been cut in an east-west direction down the west facing slope of the mountains.

5. While the eastern side of the peninsula has risen over time to form the steep eastern escarpment, the western side, south of the 28th parallel, has been subsiding for millions of years. This may be the result of the weight of erosion-deposited sediments that in places are 10 miles thick. Evidence that the land is sinking into the sea is provided by the large numbers of coastal lagoons lying between Scammon's Lagoon on the north and Bahía Magdalena on the south. Seaward from these lagoons lie long sand bars known as barrier beaches. The major areas of such beaches are shown on the map in this chapter.

Geologic Provinces

Geologists have divided the North American continent into a number of provinces. Each of these is an area of relatively homogeneous geologic features, and the dividing lines between the different provinces are in most places readily apparent to the traveler. Such geological provinces as the Sierra Nevada Mountains, the California Central Valley, the Cascade Mountains, the Willamette Valley and the Colorado Plateau are well-known to the citizens of western United States.

For the Baja peninsula, the situation is relatively simple as there are only three provinces: the Basin and Range, the Peninsular Range Mountains and the Continental Borderlands. They are shown on the "Geologic Provinces" map on page 155. This map also shows the location of various other geologic and topographic features. Most of these features, and the dividing lines between the provinces, will be pointed out in Part III.

Basin and Range Province

The Basin and Range province is that vast area of the United States and Mexico that lies roughly between the Rocky Mountains on the east, and the Sierra Nevada and Cascade Mountains on the west. It is characterized by terrain that is quite flat overall, although it is dissected by numerous, relatively short, ranges of mountains almost all running in a generally north-south direction. Highways through the province traverse flat terrain, but usually curve to skirt the edges of the mountain ranges.

The southern extremity of this large province extends into the northeastern portion of the Baja peninsula, an area referred to as the San Felipe Desert. As in the province as a whole, the terrain is flat with a scattering of mountain ranges running north and south. While much of the floor of the province in the United States is thousands of feet above sea level, in Baja the basin floor lies only a few hundred feet in elevation.

Peninsular Range Province

This province encompasses the peninsula's backbone mountain range, which is characterized by a precipitous east-facing escarpment and a much wider, overall gently sloping western portion. In the United States, the Peninsular Range Province extends into northern San Diego and western Riverside counties in southern California. Its northern boundary roughly follows Interstate 10 through San Gorgonio pass, east of San Bernardino.

The range has been divided into numerous sections, each with its own name. These are the names that are frequently shown on the maps available to travelers. The more important ones in Baja are shown on the "Geologic Provinces" map.

GEOLOGY

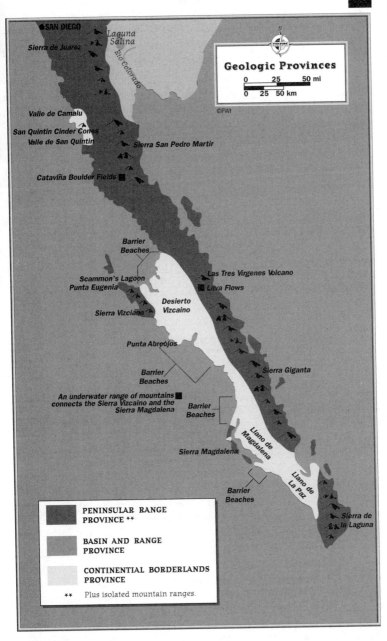

Geologic Provinces

0   25   50 mi
0 25 50 km
©FWI

SAN DIEGO
Sierra de Juarez
Laguna Salina
Rio Colorado

Valle de Camalu
San Quintin Cinder Cones
Valle de San Quintin
Sierra San Pedro Martir

Cataviña Boulder Fields

Barrier Beaches

Scammon's Lagoon
Punta Eugenia

Las Tres Virgenes Volcano
Lava Flows

Desierto Vizcaino

Sierra Vizcaino

Punta Abreojos

Barrier Beaches

Sierra Giganta

An underwater range of mountains
connects the Sierra Vizcaino and the
Sierra Magdalena

Barrier Beaches

Llano de Magdalena

Sierra Magdalena

Llano de La Paz

Barrier Beaches

Sierra de la Laguna

PENINSULAR RANGE
PROVINCE **

BASIN AND RANGE
PROVINCE

CONTINENTAL BORDERLANDS
PROVINCE

**   Plus isolated mountain ranges.

The mountains in Baja's northern half, and the Sierra de la Laguna at the southern tip, are composed primarily of granite, a plutonic rock. In contrast, the Sierra Giganta in the peninsula's southern half is made up of a volcanic rock called basalt. The differences between these two rock types will be readily apparent to the traveler. These rock types are described in more detail in the final section of this chapter.

Continental Borderlands Province

While sailing along the Pacific coast of the United States and Canada, one is impressed by the fact that virtually the entire shoreline is steep and mountainous. This situation begins to change south of the United States-Mexican border, where much of the western shoreline is backed by flat, or gently sloping, plains. These plains are located in four more or less separate areas. (See the "Geologic Provinces" map.)

In the north, a relatively small area of palms surrounds the towns of Camalu and San Quintin. To the south, the Desierto de Vizcaino, Llano de Magdalena and the Llano de la Paz are names given to sections of what is actually one continuous, largely level area. These lands are composed of deep layers of sediments eroded over geologic time from the Peninsular Range mountains to the east. The tremendous weight of these sediments is causing the western edge of the province to sink below sea level, as is evidenced by numerous saltwater lagoons and barrier beaches along the Pacific shore.

Along the western edge of this province lie two relatively minor mountain ranges, the Sierra Vizcaino and the Sierra Magdalena. Oceanographic investigations have disclosed that the two are actually linked together by a ridge of mountains lying beneath the surface of the ocean. Taken together, this system constitutes a rather significant range of mountains paralleling the main Peninsular Range.

Rock Types

The discussion of the Peninsular Range Mountains introduced several geologic terms relating to different types of rocks. At the outset, it should be noted that the terminology being presented has worldwide application. Knowing these few facts can thus be used to enhance traveling experiences anywhere on earth.

Geologists have classified the world's rocks into three great classes: *igneous*, *sedimentary* and *metamorphic*. The igneous class is further divided into two subgroups: *plutonic* and *volcanic*. Please refer to the chart above to learn the basic elements common to these classes of rock. Each of the classes will be encountered frequently while traveling through the peninsula, and many examples will be pointed out in the course of the "Grand Tour" in Part III.

You will encounter igneous-plutonic rocks (granite) in the northern portions of Baja's Peninsular Range mountains and in the Sierra de la Laguna in the extreme south. One of the most interesting points that highlights igneous-plutonic rock is in the Cataviña boulder fields south of El Rosario. Igneous-volcanic rocks (basalt) dominate the scene in the Sierra Giganta. The massive Las Tres Virgenes volcano and nearby recent lava flows are other examples of vulcanism. Volcanic cinder cones are in evidence near San Quintin. While traveling through the various sections of the Continental Borderlands, sedimentary rocks prevail and are easily seen in the highway cuts and other places.

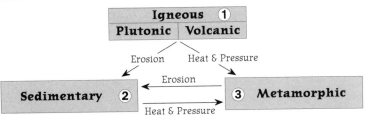

1. **IGNEOUS**—All of the earth's rocks originate as igneous rocks formed by the cooling of molten material at, or near, the surface of the earth.

   PLUTONIC—Intrusive rocks cooled slowly below the earth's surface, resulting in coarse grain, with identifiable crystals of various minerals. Light color. The most common rock is GRANITE.

   VOLCANIC—Extrusive rocks cooled rapidly at or near the earth's surface, resulting in fine grain, with no identifiable crystals. Darker color. The most common rock is BASALT.

2. **SEDIMENTARY**—Rocks made-up of (1) fragments of preexisting igneous or metamorphic rocks worn down and deposited elsewhere by the forces of erosion (running water, wind, ice flows, freezing temperatures, and gravity) or (2) by the accumulation of various organic materials. Common rocks are CONGLOMERATE, SANDSTONE, SHALE, and LIMESTONE.

3. **METAMORPHIC**—preexisting igneous or sedimentary rocks which have undergone change by being subjected to intense heat and pressure under the surface of the earth. Individual rocks are frequently banded or stratified.

VEGETATION

I have promised to be judicious in my use of superlatives, but I have to say that the desert vegetation of the peninsula is magnificent! However, as in so many other fields, appreciation of vegetative beauty can be significantly improved by understanding something about what one is viewing. With this in mind, this chapter provides material concerning the desert itself, its various plant communities, and the common characteristics of desert plants. Photographs and descriptions of many of the more interesting species are also included.

Vegetative Regions and Plant Communities

Botanists have classified the world's vegetation into easily recognizable plant communities. The Douglas fir forests of the Pacific Northwest, various areas of grasses in the Great Plains and the chaparral brushlands of southwestern United States are examples of such communities.

Norman Roberts discusses eight plant communities in his *Baja California Plant Field Guide* (Natural History Publishing, Co, La Jolla, CA:1989). These plant communities are grouped into three broad regions: (1) the California Region, (2) the Sonoran Desert and (3) the Cape Region.

The three regions are easily distinguished from each other. They are shown on the "Vegetative Regions" map. Identifying all of Robert's plant communities is a more difficult task. The map points out only the two communities that stand out best in the field.

Regional and community boundaries are distinct where there are sharp geographical changes but are more gradual elsewhere. The map and an accompanying table (See "Vegetative Regions" map, page 195, and "Points of Vegetative Significance," pages page 196) point out places where boundary changes, or other regional distinctions, are easily detected.

The Sonoran Desert Region, lying in the central portion of the peninsula is part of a far larger area classified as a true desert. The other two regions receive too much precipitation to rate this distinction. Delineating the three regions is thus basically a matter of knowing what is desert and what is not. Let us look briefly at the three regions, progressing from north to south.

California Region

This region is a continuation of the vegetational communities found to the north in Alta California. The principal plants are a number of densely growing species of shrubs, commonly referred to as *chaparral*. At the higher elevations the shrub community gives way rather sharply to forests of pinyon and Jeffrey pine and other conifers.

The California Region is not unique to Baja. The coniferous forests in Baja are little different from those that clothe the higher lands in any of southern Alta California's four national forests.

Sonoran Desert Region

There are a dozen or so major areas of desert and near-desert lands throughout the world. One is the North American Desert located in southwestern United States and northwestern Mexico. This area of more than one-half million square miles is divided into four sections, one of which is the Sonoran Desert. Approximately two-thirds of the Baja peninsula falls within the Sonoran Desert, and this area constitutes the largest of the peninsula's three vegetative regions.

The central portion of the peninsula is home to Baja's most intriguing plants. Included are a wide variety of cacti and other succulents along with the bizarre *cirio*, elephant tree and a host of others. Many of the more prominent plant species have made special adaptations to arid conditions. Their physical characteristics are thus clearly different from plants living in the California Region and other moist areas. There is also a great deal of space between the individual plants, in marked contrast to the dense brush fields to the north.

Botanists recognize four plant communities within this region. One of these, the San Felipe Desert, provides a sharp contrast to the glowing description I have just painted for the region as a whole. This community lies in the rain shadow east of the peninsula's tallest mountains along the shore of the Sea of Cortez. As a result, it is one of the driest areas in Baja and supports only low, sparse vegetation. It is easy to separate this region from its more entrancing neighbors.

The Cape Region

The vegetation of the Cape Region is also far different from what we are accustomed to north of the border. Here, there are two plant communities.

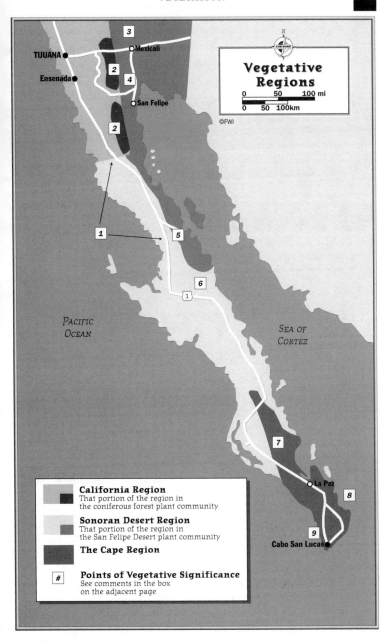

Vegetative Regions

0   50   100 mi

0   50   100km

©FWI

TIJUANA

Ensenada

Mexicali

San Felipe

PACIFIC OCEAN

SEA OF CORTEZ

La Paz

Cabo San Lucas

California Region
That portion of the region in the coniferous forest plant community

Sonoran Desert Region
That portion of the region in the San Felipe Desert plant community

The Cape Region

Points of Vegetative Significance
See comments in the box on the adjacent page

One of these, the **Oak-Pinyon Woodland**, is rarely seen by tourists as it is located at high elevations in the mountains where there are no roads. These peaks receive considerable rainfall as the result of high-intensity tropical storms and they support stands of oaks, pinyon pine and other small trees.

The Cape Region highways pass through a plant community known as an **Arid Tropical Forest**. Because these highways are at relatively low elevations, you will still see many plants to which you have become accustomed in the Sonoran Desert. However, the hallmarks of this community are (1) vegetation that is far more densely spaced than in the Sonoran Desert and (2) the presence of a variety of low-spreading trees. This area has been referred to by one leading botanist as an "impoverished tropical forest."

POINTS OF VEGETATIVE SIGNIFICANCE
(See Vegetative Regions map)

1. The segment of Highway 1 between the two arrows passes through the most impressive and picturesque vegetation in the Baja peninsula. The transition between the California Region and the Sonoran Desert is distinct near the upper arrow, where Highway 1 rapidly gains elevation south of the Rio del Rosario.

2. The two squares indicate the location of Baja's two national parks. Secondary roads lead to these parks, which lie in the coniferous forest plant community. The boundaries between this plant community and the lower elevation chaparral are clearly evident as you enter both parks.

3. At this point on Highway 3 is the most dramatic elevation change in all of Baja's highways. At the base of the grade to the east is the sparsely vegetated San Felipe Desert. At the top of the grade lies the northern fringe of the pinyon pine and juniper portion of the coniferous forest community. To the west, chaparral brush fields dominate.

4. Highway 3 again crosses the eastern escarpment of the Peninsular Range Mountains as it did at point #3. This time, the crossing is at a lower elevation, so there is no coniferous forest. The boundary between the San Felipe Desert community and the chaparral of the California Region is apparent. There is an outstanding area of barrel cactus at this point.

5. Here is another crossing of the mountain's eastern escarpment. At the base of the grade is, again, the sparse vegetation of the San Felipe Desert. To the west lies one of the most picturesque sections of the Sonoran Desert Region, with an outstanding stand of Baja's most unique plant, the *cirio* tree. The boundary between the two is easily seen.

6. In this section of the Transpeninsular Highway lies another fine area of Sonoran Desert vegetation. The plant life is enhanced by the presence of the Tres Virgenes Volcano and the lava flows emanating from its southern flank. The elephant tree is the most interesting species here.

POINTS OF VEGETATIVE SIGNIFICANCE
(See Vegetative Regions map)

7. Look for dense growth of lichens and ball moss on the larger desert plants along Highway 22 and the secondary roads between Highway 1 and the Pacific coast. Ball moss is also seen in some places along Highway 1.

8. The section of Highway 1 in the mountains on either side of the town of El Triunfo provides the best view of Cape Region vegetation. Both the denseness and presence of several species of low, spreading trees characteristic of this region's vegetation are apparent in this area.

9. The dense Cape Region vegetation is present along Highway 19 at the two places indicated by the arrows, although the stands are not as picturesque as those noted in #8.

Baja's Desert Lands

Climate

Deserts are characterized as areas receiving less than 10 inches of annual rainfall and which have generally high temperatures. In the desert, low humidity allows the sun's rays to penetrate the atmosphere easily and heat the ground far more than in moister areas. Ground temperatures 30 to 50 degrees warmer than the air are common. This same low humidity allows daytime heat to dissipate quickly; nighttime temperatures may decline as much as 50 degrees. The nighttime coolness is a key factor in the survival of both plants and animals and allows campers to enjoy cool, restful sleeping. The cheer and warmth of an evening campfire is always welcome in the desert.

It seems appropriate to ask why much of a long, narrow peninsula surrounded by water should be a desert. The answer lies in a combination of factors. At the broadest level, we find that Baja lies within a worldwide belt of high air pressure. Air is generally descending in such places, and because falling air increases in temperature, it is able to absorb rather than give up moisture.

Perhaps of more importance is the continual presence of a cell of high pressure, called the Pacific High, off the west coast of the North American continent. This high pressure cell shields the peninsula from most of the moisture-laden air masses arriving from the Pacific Ocean. As this high shifts south during the winter months it allows considerable rain to fall along the west coasts of Canada and the United States; however, this air retains little moisture when, and if, it arrives over Mexico.

Finally, the ocean off Baja's west coast is cold as the result of the upwelling of water from the depths of the sea. Air passing over these waters is chilled, and cool air can carry little moisture. As this air is warmed by contact with the land, it is able to retain, rather than dispose of, its moisture; therefore there is little rain. These circumstances combine to make Baja an extremely dry environment.

The exception to these conditions occurs near the peninsula's tip due to tropical storms, which are formed in the summer over the warm waters of the Mexican mainland to the south. Many of these storms dissipate in the Pacific Ocean, but others veer to the north and cross the southern tip of the Baja peninsula. Torrential downpours can occur, and scientists have reported witnessing continuous sheets of water one-half inch thick flowing over hundreds of acres of land.

Unfortunately, the desert's normally dry soils can absorb little water during such violent storms. As a result, areas in the Cape Region that receive considerable rainfall still support only semiarid types of vegetation. For deserts as a whole, only about three percent of the total rainfall penetrates any distance into the soil.

Humid Versus Dry Environments

There are marked contrasts between the plant communities found in humid versus dry environments. In moist areas of the world, space and light are the key factors in competition between different species of plants and among individuals within a species. These communities are frequently layered with tall trees that form a canopy over smaller trees or shrubs. The lower layers are often of a different species. Below all this vegetation will be grasses and other ground-loving plants.

With the passage of time there is often a succession of plants. Shade-tolerant species will gradually grow through the canopy of the more light-requiring varieties that preceded them. In this manner, a stand of aspen trees will gradually be replaced by conifers, but should the latter stand be destroyed by fire or disease, the succession will be repeated and aspen will return.

Finally, humid plant communities are frequently dominated by one life form such as coniferous or hardwood trees. All of these characteristics are different for desert plant communities.

In desert areas, water becomes the critical element in plant competition. As little moisture penetrates more than a few inches into the soil, most plants have a broad network of roots near the surface to quickly collect what rain does fall. These plants cannot survive if other individuals are competing in their collection area. As a result, you will see that there is only one plant in a given spot and there is no layering as is common in moister areas. (You will see some degree of layering in the Cape Region due to its more humid environment.) If desert vegetation is destroyed it tends to be replaced with the same species of plants that were displaced and there is no succession of plants as in humid areas.

Finally, desert plant communities are made up of a wide variety of species and life forms, a factor that contributes significantly to the enjoyment that can be gained from studying desert vegetation.

Soils

When you arrive in the desert area, look at the soil. There will be almost no organic material, such as the deep layers of duff found in coniferous forests or the matting of dead grass in meadow areas. There are relatively few desert plants in a given area in comparison to plant communities in moister areas, and these individuals shed very little in the way of leaves and flower parts. Much of what little organic material is produced is washed away during high-intensity storms. Desert soils tend to be high in salt content, as there is little rainfall to dissolve and carry away these materials.

VEGETATION

A CONSERVATION ETHIC FOR BAJA CALIFORNIA

There are very few natural resource managers in Mexico, and most of the environmental constraints imposed on us north of the border are not readily apparent. Also, on occasion, we tourists will see Mexican citizens conducting their affairs in ways that are not in keeping with sound conservation practices. These conditions may influence us to forget our environmental manners in Baja.

To complicate matters, Baja California is largely a desert. Deserts are particularly sensitive to disruptive, man-made change. Arid lands do not heal themselves nearly as rapidly as would be the case in areas with more moisture, as is the case where most of us live.

The conditions just noted place an added responsibility on visitors. If we are to preserve the features about Baja California that we find attractive, we must act responsibly, and do so on a voluntary basis. I recently heard a church sermon where the minister posed the question "How does one avoid doing what is wrong?" His answer was, "Just don't do it."

Avoiding environmental damage is largely a matter of using good common sense. It should be obvious that digging up sensitive plants, destroying tidepool organisms, picking up artifacts, walking about in seabird nesting areas, and throwing trash in the sea will cause long-term damage. Something inside ought to say, "Just don't do it."

Desert Plant Adaptations

It is gratifying to be able to identify specific species of plants when you see them in your travels. Material to help you do this is presented further along in this chapter. However, in the desert, it is of equal, if not greater, interest to study and observe some of the common characteristics of all desert plants.

Most living things are segregated into either the plant or animal kingdom. Each kingdom is further subdivided by phylum, class, order, family, genus and species. Individual species are named in the scientific world by combining the genus and species names. Thus, the galloping cactus must suffer through eternity being referred to as *Machaerocereus gummosus*, although you would perhaps call it something else should you be so unfortunate as to fall into one.

It would seem logical to suspect that most species of plants living in an environment as harsh as the desert would belong to a limited number of closely related genera and families. Reasoning in this way, one would assume that some particular characteristic of these select genera and families provided the key to dry-land survival. In many cases, it did not happen this way.

Ira Wiggion's classic *Flora of Baja California* notes that there are 2705 species and 884 genera of plants in Baja California. The 179 most common species described in Norman Robert's original *Field Guide* belong in 64 plant families. One can speculate that a wide variety of vegetative types were surviving contentedly in a moist environment, then, over time, they were confronted with drying climatic conditions. Those species that were to survive made certain physical and reproductive adaptations that permitted their living under desert conditions.

This process of change is termed convergent evolution and is defined as "the evolution of unrelated or distantly related groups of organisms along similar lines, resulting in the development of similar traits or features in the unrelated groups." The different types of adaptations that allow survival under dry conditions are amazingly few. As a result, many species of desert plants that look very much like each other are only distantly related.

All plants that live in the desert have to deal with surviving drought. Some species have solved the problem by simply avoiding it; they are called "evaders." Others have made the various adaptations mentioned above. These plants are "resisters."

Evaders

These are the grasses, forbs and other annual plants. They quickly germinate from seed following a rain, grow to maturity in a few weeks, produce a new crop of seed and die. They survive in the form of millions of seeds cast on the desert floor to await the next cycle. This method of existence is little different from that of annual plants in more humid regions. Because desert annuals have not made any pronounced physical adaptation to resist drought, they resemble annual species in moister climates. Grass in Baja looks much like grass in Oregon, although it may not be as tall.

Desert annuals produce a seed crop far in excess of that needed for their own reproduction. This allows many desert animals to utilize seeds as a basic source of food.

How do seeds that survive the foragers know when to germinate and when to remain dormant? The survival of the species hangs in the balance. The answer is generally believed to be that seeds have a growth-inhibiting chemical in their coats that is dissolved away when exposed to sufficient quantities of rainfall. When conditions are right, they germinate, and the traveler is treated to the colorful spectacle of the desert in bloom.

Resisters

Perennial plants live continually from year to year and gradually grow larger. They are the trees, shrubs, cactus and other species with woody superstructures that have made special adaptations to resist dry conditions. Look for evidence of these methods of adaptation in studying Baja's desert vegetation.

Water Storage

Perhaps the desert's most interesting plants are the succulents, which have developed the ability to store water. The best known are the cacti, which use their stems as reservoirs. Species such as the century plant have adapted their leaves for this purpose. Others have underground containers as part of their roots. The wide-spreading and shallow root system of the commonly seen cardón cactus is capable of soaking up hundreds of gallons of water following a rain, after which four-fifths of its weight may consist of water.

Accordion Structure

A common characteristic of many species of cactus is the accordion-like structure of the stem. As the plant takes in water, the fleshy stem quickly expands, then subsequently slowly contracts as the supply is utilized. Note the stem condition of the cacti you examine.

If you are traveling south on Highway 1, following winter rains, you will observe that the water-filled cacti in the northern portion will display broad, U-shaped spacing between their ribs. Only a few days later, you may arrive near the peninsula's tip and see that the pleats are deeply indented and V-shaped. These southern plants normally receive their moisture as the result of summer, rather than winter, storms.

Armaments

A high proportion of perennial plants in desert areas have developed thorns, leaves with sharpened points or toothed edges, and other similar armaments. Plants in other environments also contain thorns, but they are so prevalent in desert species that it is clear that thorns are an important adaptation for survival under arid conditions.

Armaments protect plants from browsing animals. Plants cannot afford to lose the food-producing foliage that took precious water to create. It is interesting to note that very few plants in the great desert in western Australia have thorns, and that this is the only one of the world's major arid areas that does not have, or has not once had, hooved, browsing animals. (Kangaroos do little browsing.) Also intriguing is the fact that some desert species that bear thorns in the wild produce no such protection when grown in the humid environment of a greenhouse.

Leaf Characteristics

If you are fortunate enough to visit Baja's desert areas following significant rainfall, you will see that the ocotillo, cirio and similar plants are greenish in color, but you will have difficulty distinguishing any leaves from a distance. The leaves are there, but they are tiny affairs no more than an inch long. Small leaf size reduces the amount of water lost through transpiration. In addition to having small leaves, these species quickly shed their foliage when the ground dries. The production of leaves is not a phenomenon one can count on at a particular time of the year.

The characteristic of having small, even minute, leaves is typical of much of Baja's perennial vegetation. Even larger trees have small leaves. The most conservative of all are the cacti, which have no leaves except for a short period in youth. Their chlorophyll is located in the main stem of the plant, as is evidenced by their green color.

Wide Spacing

As already noted, desert vegetation is widely spaced so that each individual plant has a water collecting area sufficient for its survival. Even in relatively dense areas of vegetation, it is possible to walk between the plants without being impaled by thorns. The open spaces are not filled with young plants, because they are unable to compete with their parents for moisture. Some species also seem to practice chemical warfare as their roots give off toxic substances that prevent the growth of other plants. Be particularly alert for the wide, uniform spacing of the creosote bush if you visit the San Felipe and Bahía de Los Angeles areas.

Vegetative Reproduction

It is possible to reproduce many plants by placing cuttings from their stems in moist soil or water. Many desert plants routinely reproduce in this fashion without human assistance. Look at the several species of cholla cactus common in Baja. Their stems are made up of numerous segments. The terminal segments frequently fall to the ground and take root, often producing dense cholla thickets. Also, study the galloping cactus and other species of spreading plants; notice that they are able to produce new roots at places where their stems touch the ground.

These means of vegetative reproduction allow plants to avoid the costly water and energy-consumptive process of producing seeds and permit spreading of the species in years when seed production is not possible. If you visit the FONATUR nursery at Primer Agua, near Loreto, you will see a large number of species that are being propagated by vegetative means.

Trunk Form

Many species of low trees and shrubs in Baja have a trunk or main stem that is very thick in proportion to the size of the plant. The elephant tree is the most prominent example. There are in fact two different species of plants, both commonly called elephant trees. They are so similar that close inspection is required to distinguish one from the other, yet they are members of two distantly related families.

Other Adaptations

To resist drought conditions, desert plants have made a variety of other adaptations. Some species simply surrender and die back to ground level after each rain-induced period of above-ground growth. Food and water are stored in a wide variety of underground structures related to the plant's roots. Other species have developed thick or waxy outer skins to reduce water loss, and have fewer skin pores than their related wetland cousins. Still others are found to have developed poisonous or repulsive juices to ward off browsing animals.

Endemism

An endemic species is one that is found in only one area of the world. Endemism is common in Baja because plant species have adapted to their harsh environment on an isolated peninsula. Almost 75 percent of the cactus species are endemic, as are many of the other easily observed plants. This uniqueness contributes to the peninsula's aesthetic quality.

Endemic species can also be the cause of some frustration to those who are well versed in plant identification in other areas. For many years, I referred to the abundant large cactus in Baja as a saguaro only to find that it was really the cardón. In a similar manner, the datilillo may be confused with the Joshua tree common in Alta California.

Epiphytes

Epiphytes are plants that gain physical support from other plants, poles, wires and other objects. It is unusual to find epiphytes in deserts as they have no roots and must obtain their water from the air. But while the atmosphere in most deserts is extremely dry, fog and moist air overrun much of Baja's level Pacific coastal areas. Thus the larger desert plants growing here are often heavily festooned with such species.

VEGETATION

The traveler may observe two basic types of epiphytes in Baja. Most common are lichens. These are associations of separate and distinct species o algae and fungi which live together in an intimate relationship called symbiosis. The algae provide the nourishment for the symbiotic pair, as they contain chlorophyll, and can make food using the sun's energy. The fungi, which have no chlorophyll, provide mechanical support and aid in the absorption of moisture.

While lichens are not a moss, they can best be described as looking like linear strands of moss. The Spanish moss that hangs from trees in the southeastern United States is a lichen. Sometimes the lichens are so dense as to almost obscure the branches of the host plants, making them appear quite different than they would in dryer areas.

Ball moss also is not a moss, but a perennial herb. It forms spherical clumps about six inches in diameter. This rounded shape makes for easy identification. Neither ball moss nor lichens harm the plants from which they gain support.

Common Plants

It is well beyond the scope of this book to present extensive material on the identification of individual species of plants. Included are photographs and brief descriptions of 16 common or conspicuous plants. These are all in view from the highways and can be identified with reasonable certainty when they are called to your attention in the "Grand Tour" in Part III.

Cirio

Idria columnaris

For once, a plant's scientific name imparts some information even to the amateur. In English, columnar means having the shape of a column; in Spanish, cirio means candle. Whatever language, the *cirio* is a plant shaped like a tapering column, although it often branches several times near the top. It can grow up to 60 feet high but is usually considerably shorter. Along the trunk are numerous branches smaller than the diameter of a pencil and totally out of proportion to the plant as a whole. These bear the tiny leaves that clothe the cirio in green following rain. Sometimes the cirio is referred to as a "boojum," a name inspired by the creatures mentioned by Lewis Carroll in his story, "The Hunting of the Snark."

If Baja California had a state plant, the *cirio* would have to be it, as most people would concur that it is Baja's most unique species. It is endemic to Baja except for a small colony across the Sea of Cortez along the coast south of La Libertad. The cirio is present in groves along Highway 1 from immediately south of the Rio del Rosario to the northern edge of the Vizcaino Desert (Geographic Section No. 8). It also grows along the highway to Bahía de los Angeles.

Baja's fascinating cirio backed by other Sonoran desert vegetation.

VEGETATION

Cardón

Cardón

Pachycereus pringlei

While cirio may be Baja's most unique plant, the cardón, or giant cactus, is the most widespread of the peninsula's larger plants. Cardón is a very large cactus with one main trunk, which branches from one to numerous times as the plant grows older. The branches have from 11 to 17 vertical ribs. It is a good cactus in which to check the state of expansion of an accordion structure. Don't confuse the cardón with the organ pipe, which is also many branched but has no main trunk. It is also possible to confuse the cardón with the saguaro cactus of southwestern United States, but we amateurs are blessed by the fact that the saguaro does not grow in Baja. Like the cirio, the cardón is visible immediately south of the Rio del Rosario, but unlike the cirio, it is present all the way to the tip of the peninsula. Extensive stands of cardón are called *cardónals*. An outstanding cardónal covers many square miles along the southern and eastern shores of Bahía Concepcíon.

Century plant in full bloom in the sparsely vegetated Sonoran Desert Region.

Century Plant

Various species

Throughout the Sonoran Desert Region and in the southern portion of the California Region, you see a variety of plants composed of a cluster of bayonet-like leaves. There are many species of such plants in Baja and throughout the world. Some species common to Baja bear the generic name Agave, while others are in the genus Yucca. The specimen in the picture is *Agave shawii*, commonly called the century plant. This and similar species grow slowly for years, finally pouring forth all their reserves of energy in producing an amazingly luxuriant flower stalk. After blooming, the plant dies. You can see these stalks at many places in the desert; fine samples are present immediately south of the Rio del Rosario. The century plant is a succulent because its leaves have become adapted for the storage of water. (Squeeze the leaves near their base to test the quantity of their water content.) A large number of distantly related species have developed leaves similar to the century plant, providing an excellent example of convergent evolution, and making species identification a difficult task for the amateur.

Ocotillo. Note the wide spacing of the other plants as is typical in the desert.

Ocotillo

Fouquieria splendens

The ocotillo is easily identified. It consists of numerous whip-like branches that spread out from its base. There is no main trunk. Each branch is covered with thorns, thus providing an excellent example of the extreme protective armament that has been developed by many desert plants. Using ocotillo for firewood is a challenge. The ocotillo is in the same family as the *cirio* and, like its cousin, produces a myriad of tiny leaves following rain. The plant is very sensitive to soil moisture and drops its leaves promptly at the first hint of drought. In any given year, several different crops of leaves may be produced in response to rainfall. Ocotillo is a good indicator of recent weather conditions and local soil moisture. Ocotillo is most common in the San Felipe Desert and along Highway 1 within Geographic Section No. 8. As one drives south, ocotillo comes into view shortly after crossing the Rio del Rosario.

Prickly pear. Bright flowers grow on the ends of the pads after rain.

Prickly Pear

Opuntia Species

The plant in the photo is an example of the many species of cactus that bear the name prickly pear. They are probably the most familiar cactus to tourists as they also grow in many locations north of the border. The common feature of all species is their flat, thin, pad-like stem segments, which resemble a beaver's tail. Prickly pears grow throughout Baja, but are most common in the north. The flat stem, a popular food source, may be cut up and cooked as one would prepare green beans. You will find them fresh or canned in many Mexican food stores. The Spanish name for this cactus is *nopal*, with the canned product bearing the name *nopalitos*. Many excellent specimens of this cactus are located immediately south of the Rio del Rosario. At one point in reviewing the literature for this chapter, I was seeking out what might be the common feature of all cacti. One author proudly announced, with no warning, that almost all species have no glochids in their areoles. Should you care, the areoles are the small depressions from which thorns project on the flat surface of the prickly pear stem (see photo). Glochids, tiny barbed hairs, are of course missing. Knowing all this will make you the hit of the evening at tonight's campfire.

Candelabra Cactus

Myrtillocactus cochal

This is one of Baja's endemic species. There are many excellent specimens along Highway 1 south of the Rio del Rosario. The candelabra's thick, woody branches are all nearly uniform in size and curve inward in graceful arcs toward the center of the plant. If hung upside down, it would resemble the outline of an enormous chandelier. There are six to eight ribs within each branch. Now that you are an expert in areoles (see the prickly pear cactus), note that they are spaced along the ridge lines as is the case with many other species of cactus. This cactus blooms yearlong, often during the nighttime hours. The blossoms are whitish green, with purple tinges. So, if you and the love of your life just must go for an evening walk in the desert, here is the perfect excuse.

Candelabra cactus.

Galloping Cactus

Machaerocereus gummosus

The galloping cactus is one of the most widespread species seen throughout the Sonoran Desert and Cape Region and is often present along the highways. Its individual branches are essentially the same size as those of the candelabra cactus but look like members of the latter species, but the galloping cactus branches grow randomly in all directions, often touching the ground and taking root. They can form impenetrable thickets as large as 30 feet in diameter. The galloping cactus flowers with large, fragrant white blossoms in July and August and produces a fleshy edible fruit.

Galloping cactus.

Old man cactus. Note the clusters of spines at the tops of the stems that give the plant a bearded look. It is very easy to recognize.

Old Man Cactus

Lophocereus schottii

Old man cactus branches near the base with each stem having five to seven ribs. The tip of each branch is crested with large numbers of coarse, hairlike, gray spines, giving it a whiskered look and providing the basis for its name. It is common in the area south of the Rio del Rosario.

Barrel cactus. The base of the cardón cactus to the right is growing straight up from the ground. Almost all barrel cactus lean to the south, as can be seen with this individual. This no doubt gives them minimum exposure to the sun.

Barrel Cactus

Ferocactus Species

The barrel cactus is lower growing than many of the more prominent species, but it is easy to recognize, provided you are content with identifying only the genus. There are more than 20 species in Baja. Their common feature is one cylindrical stem that resembles a barrel or similar container. Occasionally they will branch. The spines are often flattened and hooked at the end, and the upper portion of the barrel is often reddened. Notice that most plants lean to the south.

Cholla cactus. The most recent season's growth is lighter in color than the rest.

Cholla Cactus

Opuntia Species

Here is another cactus genus represented by more than 20 of species. They are widespread throughout the Sonoran Desert and Cape Regions. The cholla stems are not flat like the prickly pear, or ribbed as in many other species. In contrast, the stem is made up of numerous linearly attached segments or joints. Each joint is further divided into many, small, rounded subsections called tubercles. One of the most common species is the teddy bear cholla shown in the photo. Its silvery spines are so dense that they resemble fur at a distance, an illusion that can be promptly corrected by closer inspection. These spines are barbed at the ends and will catch on anything passing by. Joints readily break off, and if you are snared, a veritable pincushion of spines will attach themselves to your skin or clothing. Removing these with a bare hand is not recommended. You may see some of these joints lying about on the ground or rooted in vegetative reproduction.

Creosote bush. An uninspiring picture of this uninspiring but common plant.

Creosote Bush

Larrea tridentata

Creosote bush is one of the most common of Baja's desert shrubs. Most other shrubs are light green or grayish in color. The deep olive-green of the creosote bush stands out in sharp contrast. Its small leaves are often coated with a shiny, sticky substance. Small, five-petaled, yellow flowers are present throughout the year. Creosote bush is one of the most drought-tolerant of desert plants. When the more interesting vegetation disappears, creosote bush often becomes dominant. Botanists believe its roots emit a toxic substance that prevents seedlings from growing too close to the parent plants. However, the intervening spaces are usually occupied by other species. Native peoples brew a tea from the leaves. Should you be passing through creosote scrubland after a rain shower, you will have the chance to inhale the pungent aroma released from the creosote's leaves. The plant flowers with tiny yellow blossoms after periods of rain.

Datilillo

Yucca valida

The datilillo is a yucca, but it becomes a small tree in contrast to other ground-hugging plants of the same genus. The leaves are bayonet-like, although they do not store water as does the succulent century plant. The species is similar to the Joshua tree of southwestern United States. Individual plants grow in clumps and branch along the trunk.

A clump of Datilillo.

Elephant trees grow from the sterile lava flows east of San Ignacio along Highway 1. Part of PSI stop #11.

Elephant Tree

Pachycormus discolor

The elephant tree, endemic to Baja, is one of its most interesting species. Its principal characteristics are (1) the grayish-white to yellowish bark that peels off in papery layers and (2) the tree's overall shape with the trunk and main branches thick in proportion to the plant as a whole. Although found in many places along Highway 1, it is most prominent in the lava flow area east of San Ignacio. The two principal characteristics noted above are also shared by other peninsular species, some of which are only distantly related. This appears to be an example of convergent evolution, discussed earlier in this chapter. *Bursera microphylla*, also called elephant tree, or *torote*, is a good example. Its twigs and branch ends are reddish brown in contrast to the gray color of *Pachycormus discolor*, and its leaves are also much smaller.

Organ pipe cactus grows close to our campsite near Playa los Cerritos near Highway 19. Note that the vegetation is far more dense here in the Cape Region than it is in the Sonoran Desert Region.

Organ Pipe Cactus

Lemaireocereus thurberi

The organ pipe is a large, erect cactus that at first glance may be confused with the cardón. Note, however, that the organ pipe branches near ground level and has no main trunk as does the cardón. Organ pipe cactus grows only in the southern half of the peninsula. This species produces a sweet globular fruit, about the size of a tennis ball, which was the prized food of the original Indian population. Apparently they were well-fed only when the fruit was available. It is reported that once the supply was exhausted, the Indians would gather their own dried feces and collect the seeds that had passed through the intestinal tract. These were ground into meal.

Palo blanco. Note the light bark.

Palo Blanco

Lysiloma candida

Palo, meaning stick or pole in Spanish, has become the first name of a large number of small trees. Many are quite common but the *palo blanco* (white) is the one most easily identified from the highway. The trunk is quite straight, with smooth, silvery-white bark which is its identifying feature. Except for one locality across the Sea of Cortez, this species is endemic to Baja.

Palms

There are over 1100 species of palms worldwide in warm climates. The chart below will allow you to identify Baja's three basic types based on leaf and trunk characteristics.

PALMS		
Type	**Leaves**	**Trunk**
Fan	**FAN SHAPED** — Individual leaflets radiate from the ends of the stems.	**EXTREMELY ROUGH** — The bases of the dead stems remain attached to the trunk. This is true even if most of the stems have been pruned off.
Date	**PINNATE** — Individual leaflets project along both sides of the stem, similar to a bird feather.	
Coconut		**SMOOTH** — The entire dead stem falls from the trunk leaving a smooth surface

VEGETATION

WILDLIFE

Borrego Cimarron

Accounts of wildlife frequently evolve around an array of animals that people rarely view. In this vein, I will present a few nonspecific introductory remarks about desert animals, but the major portion of this chapter relates to the relatively few animals that you might actually see in your travels in the Baja peninsula.

Desert Animals

As noted in the previous chapter, desert plants have made substantial physical adaptations as a means of surviving in the harsh living conditions of the desert. Such modifications are far less pronounced in the animal kingdom.

Most desert birds and animals are quite similar to their cousins living in more humid areas. Also, the wildlife species found in Baja are essentially the same as those living in the Mexican mainland or farther north, in the United States. As is the case for many desert animals, they do tend to be smaller in size and paler in color.

Insect life in the desert is robust and peaks with the culmination of plant growth following rains. The immense supply of eggs and dormant pupae left behind by these creatures combine with the seeds of annual plants to provide basic food for birds and animals. The majority of desert mammals are seed-eating rodents.

The traveler will see relatively few land animals in Baja's deserts because most of them feed and move about only at night. Also, most species make their homes in burrows in the ground, or in large plants, where they can escape the rigorous environment.

For this reason, I suggest that you pay a visit to the zoological garden located in the small town of Santiago south of La Paz. The unlikely location of this facility may lead the traveler to expect very little. Surprisingly, this pleasant zoo, constructed in 1983, is well shaded and contains many different displays of live animals. Most are species of local Mexican mammals, birds and reptiles. Here may be your only chance to see these animals. (Every cage had occupants, including, believe it or not, a tiger.)

When you walk about in the desert you will see a variety of lizards darting about on the desert floor. Their scaled skin, which is highly resistant to drying, allows them to move about in the daytime. You will also see considerable bird life during the daylight hours, particularly near the coast. A discussion of several of the most common large birds is presented below. The concluding section describes the California gray whale, sea turtles and other marine mammals.

Hunting

Hunting by tourists is permitted in Baja. Doves are taken throughout the peninsula. The Valle de Mexicali southeast from Mexicali, with its irrigated pastures is home to a variety of dove and pheasants. Waterfowl hunting along the lower Colorado River and Laguna Salada was excellent in the past but is now greatly reduced by low-water levels resulting from upstream reservoirs. There are ongoing efforts under way to restore these lost wetlands. The Pacific coast chaparral region from Ensenada south to El Rosario produces some of the largest quail populations in North America. The Bahía San Quintín area is famous for black brant and other sea-duck hunting.

Securing permission to hunt in Mexico is a complicated process due in part to the country's strict laws concerning gun possession. The hunter is required to obtain a multiple-entry tourist card and several other documents from different Mexican agencies, including the military. A character reference also must be obtained from the hunter's local law enforcement agency.

The process is sufficiently complicated and so subject to change that you should contact the organization whose basic function is processing the documents needed to hunt in Mexico for its members: the **Mexican Hunting Association**, *6840 El Salvador St, Long Beach CA 90815,* ☎ *(310) 430-3256.* The association also publishes a newsletter concerning game regulations and other matters.

Birds

Bird Watching

Baja is an excellent place to visit for those interested in observing and studying bird life. Desert vegetation supports little of the dense foliage common in moister climates. As a result, birds have relatively little cover and are easily viewed. You will often see hawks and other large birds perched on the top of giant cactus plants. The seashore and marsh areas are alive with bird life.

Waterbirds

Many North American waterbirds (ducks, coots and similar species) breed during the summer in Alaska, Canada and northern United States. They then winter in southern United States and Mexico. These birds travel south in fairly well-defined paths called flyways. Birds using the Pacific Flyway spend the winter in Alta and Baja California and along the west coast of the Mexican mainland. A few birds migrate to the delta of the Rio Colorado, but the majority of the marsh habitat here has been destroyed by the regulatory effects of upstream reservoirs.

An exception to this Rio Colorado situation can be found along Highway 5, where the main river is joined by the Rio Hardy. During wet years, bird life is abundant here and at the nearby southern end of Laguna Salada.

The principal waterbird wintering areas in Baja are along the Pacific coast from Ensenada south to Bahía Magdalena. If you are even remotely interested in bird life, I recommend that you drive the Puerto Venustiano Carranza side trip starting at the town of Guerrero Negro. The road to the abandoned port facilities passes through several miles of outstanding saltwater marsh, which provides a home for thousands of egrets, pelicans, cranes, gulls, and many other species of marsh and seabirds. The roadbed is elevated some 10 feet above the sea level so you may look down upon the many birds.

Seabirds

The Sea of Cortez area offers the most spectacular concentrations of nesting southern seabirds on the west coast of North America. The specific species involved are listed in the following table. The majority of these birds nest primarily on the offshore islands. A few species, including osprey, herons and terns are more frequently found along the peninsular shore. There are a variety of other seabird species that visit the Sea of Cortez but which do not breed in the area. Likewise, many of the breeding varieties migrate to both north and south after the breeding season. These birds will be seen principally by those who participate in boating.

The interaction of seabirds with the boating public presents a special problem in the Sea of Cortez. The adverse effect of human disturbance on nesting seabirds is well documented. There is clear evidence that the brown pelican has abandoned its former nesting sites on Islas San Martin and Todos Santos along Baja's Pacific shore due to human disturbance. Visiting scientists have also observed damaging effects following such widely divergent visitations as individual sightseers on their own, American tourists guided by Mexicans, curious Mexican fishermen, commercial egg collectors, and even American scientists and educational tours.

Regardless of who causes the disturbance, the destructive results when nesting seabirds are flushed from their nests includes:

- Eggs and chicks may be knocked from their nests by frightened adults.

- Unprotected chicks and eggs may die from excessive heat or cold.

- Predators, mainly gulls, may eat unguarded eggs and chicks.

- Nests, and eventually entire nesting sites, may be abandoned.

If you should come upon nesting seabird colonies please observe them with binoculars from a distance. Stay at least 100 yards off when in a boat, and 300 yards away when onshore. Those desiring to seriously study seabirds should obtain a competent book on the subject.

PRINCIPAL SEABIRDS THAT BREED IN THE SEA OF CORTEZ

black storm petrel	yellow-footed gull
least storm petrel	elegant tern
brown pelican	royal tern
double-crested cormorant	sooty tern
Brandt's cormorant	noddy tern
red-billed tropicbird	American oystercatcher

WILDLIFE

PRINCIPAL SEABIRDS THAT BREED IN THE SEA OF CORTEZ

magnificent frigatebird	osprey
blue-footed booby	great blue heron
brown booby	reddish egret
Craveri's murrelet	black-crowned night heron
Heermann's gull	yellow-crowned night heron

List courtesy of Daniel W. Anderson

Five Common Birds

Following is a brief discussion of five of the common large birds seen in Baja.

Frigatebird

The frigatebird, or man-o-war bird, is unmistakable in flight. Its wingspan can exceed seven feet and is greater in proportion to the body than that of any other seabird. The wings are swept back like a World War II Navy Corvair fighter plane. The tail is deeply notched. Those with white breasts are the female.

While the pelican is a master fisherman, the frigate is basically a thief. It cannot swim or dive but makes a living largely by forcing other seabirds to disgorge or drop food that they have captured. You will see the frigate soaring in coastal areas in the southern portion of the peninsula.

WILDLIFE

The brown pelican is commonly seen on Baja's beaches and marinas. Frequently, as here, they are accompanied by seagulls ever hopeful that one of the pelicans will drop a portion of its catch.

Brown Pelican

There are pelicans north of the border, but only people who live near the coast will have seen them. In Baja the species is common along all coastal areas and if you don't see many of them, you simply aren't looking. The pelican is an unmistakable bird.

Breeding takes place locally on offshore islands. During the summer, many individuals migrate north into the United States, but their numbers have greatly decreased in recent decades. Studies conducted during the 1970s in the breeding areas of Baja's Islas de los Coronados, south of San Diego, showed that the bird's eggshells contained concentrations of DDT insecticide. The result was shell walls too thin to survive the reproductive process. Since DDT has been banned there has been a dramatic increase in pelican birthrates.

Turkey Vulture

The turkey vulture, or buzzard, is not unique to Mexico, but most people do not have the opportunity to study this bird near their homes. In Baja, you will sometimes have the opportunity of seeing groups of vultures at close range, particularly if your travels take you to a garbage dumping area. They are not pretty birds. The featherless head is small in proportion to the body and is red in color. The rest of the body is covered with black feathers. Turkey vultures are usually be observed feeding on dead animals, or rotting garbage. You will also frequently see individuals sitting on the top of a cardón cactus.

Most commonly, the turkey vulture can be seen soaring overhead. Look for the small head and two-toned wings that are held aloft clearly above the horizontal. The outer portions of the wings are lighter than the rest of the bird. It rocks unsteadily as it soars along.

Roadrunner

Bird guidebooks note that the roadrunner's call is a dove-like coo, but we all know they really go beep-beep. Baja is a good place to observe this escapee from the movie cartoons. In the films, they seem to run up and down the roads, but in the wild they emulate the chicken and always seem to be crossing the road. They are more commonly seen on the secondary and dirt roads than on the main highways.

The roadrunner is 20 to 24 inches in length, heavily streaked, has a long, narrow tail and a shaggy, rooster-like crest on the head. If a large bird runs across the road, what else can it be?

Caracara

The caracara is a large, long-legged, long-necked, dark bird whose white head is topped with a rooster-like crest. The bill is yellowish. In flight they display white markings on the wings and tail. They are a bird of prey and are commonly seen in dry desert areas in the southern half of the peninsula.

Marine Mammals

Sea Lions and Dolphins

My experience in cruising the Pacific coast clearly indicates that there are far more dolphins and sea lions in Baja's waters than in those north of the border. Unfortunately, they are infrequently seen by the tourist unless one ventures out to sea. Seeing a dolphin is simply a matter of chance, but sea lions live in colonies well known to Mexican fishermen. You can arrange for sightseeing trips at Loreto, Cabo San Lucas and other places. Ask to be shown the *lobos del mar.*

In 1995 the U.S. government imposed an embargo on Mexican tuna fish as large numbers of dolphin were being killed in the fishing process. The result was devastation of tuna fishing and packing activities at Ensenada and nearby El Sauzal on Baja's northwest coast. Fishing techniques have now been greatly improved and at press time the ban was being reconsidered.

Baja's Pacific waters also provide a home for the elephant seal, but the known colonies are all on offshore islands. If you wish to see this fascinating marine mammal, the best place to do so is at the Ano Nuevo State Reserve north of Santa Cruz in Alta California.

The massive back of the gray whale.

WILDLIFE

BAJA MARINE LIFE

The Sea of Cortez and the Pacific Ocean off Baja's west coast hold an abundant array of marine life. The Sea of Cortez is home to tropical fish, while the Pacific holds some of the larger species. The meeting of the Sea of Cortez and the Pacific provides a mixture of these two marine groups that is rarely seen.

CALIF.
ARIZ.
BAJA
MEXICO
❶
● Mulegé
❺
Pacific Ocean
❷
Sea of Cortez
❸
● La Paz
❹
● Cabo San Lucas

WILDLIFE

1. REDTAIL TIGERFISH

This is the most colorful of all the Tigerfish. Its tail is red, its body gold, and it has blue streaks across its face. The redtail tigerfish is found primarily in the Sea of Cortez.

2. WHITE SIDED DOLPHIN

The white sided dolphin is small and has a pointy snout. The dolphin almost always travels in schools, sometimes by the thousands. The white sided dolphin can be found in both the Sea of Cortez and the Pacific.

3. BOTTLENOSE DOLPHIN

The bottlenose dolphin is the most common species of dolphin in the region and will often approach and swim with divers. When fully grown these dolphins can reach 13 feet in length and weigh 600 pounds.

4. GREY WHALE

Grey whales visit the coast of Baja during their annual migration. The whales grow up to 50 feet long. While once hunted near extinction, the grey whale has bounced back and has been taken off the endangered species list.

5. BALLOONFISH

Found along reefs and sandy bottoms of Punta Concepcion and throughout the wreckage of the Mexican freighter Colima in the East Cape, balloonfish are distinguished by a dark bar over the forehead and eye, as well as long spines that cover the body. When approached by predators, balloonfish protect themselves by blowing up with water to increase their size.

Normal

Expanded

Fielding

BAJA CALIFORNIA

BAJA MARINE LIFE
(CONTINUED)

CALIF.

ARIZ.

BAJA

MEXICO

7

11

Pacific Ocean

9

Mulegé

8

Sea of Cortez

La Paz

Cabo San Lucas

10

6

6. GREEN MORAY EEL

With lengths of over five feet and gaping mouths, green moray eels can look quite intimidating. These nocturnal creatures hunt for food at night, and during the daytime hide in crevices and holes of reefs such as the ones near Mulege and Chileno beach near Cabo San Lucas.

7. CALIFORNIA SEA LION

Differentiating itself from the seal by its external ears, the California sea lion is scattered among various coastlines and islands from the Pacific to the Sea of Cortez. A few of the many prominent shoreline areas where sea lion colonies are located include: Bahía de Los Angeles, Isla San Ildefonso, Isla Los Islotes and the seamount at Las Animas. Curiosity may lead sea lions to study and very often play with divers.

8. BULLSEYE STINGRAY

Dark rings forming markings which have an appearance of a bullseye distinguish this species of stingray. They are most commonly found in the shallow and sandy areas of reefs and bays of Baja's eastern seaward side of Mulege. Bullseye stingrays are an average of two feet across.

9. MANTA RAY

The manta ray is generally found off the Pacific coast of Baja and is very approachable by divers. The ray appears to glide effortlessly through the water, with a wing span of up to 18 feet. Though rare, the ray can sometimes be seen "breaching."

WILDLIFE

10. GREEN SEA TURTLE

The green sea turtle derives its name from the color of its body fat, but is recognizable by the single pair of scales on its head, as well as its spotted green and brown shell. Turtles can be found near Isla Catalina and at Land's End where the Sea of Cortez and the Pacific meet.

11. CORTEZ ANGELFISH

Abundant throughout the Sea of Cortez, cortez angelfish can be found near reefs as deep as 100 feet. Regular sightings of cortez angelfish have occurred at Bahía de Los Angeles, El Baio and in the wreckage of the *Salvaderra* in the San Lorenzo Channel. Juvenile cortez angelfish are marked with vibrant blue and gold bands, whereas adults are striped with yellow and black.

California Gray Whale

In recent years, there has been wide public interest concerning whales in general and the California gray whale in particular. Whale-watching has become a popular pastime in many areas along the Pacific coast. The Baja peninsula plays a prominent part in this gigantic animal's life history as it is Baja' Pacific lagoons that are the primary destination of the whale's annual southern migration. The gray's basic characteristics are described in a nearby insert.

CALIFORNIA GRAY WHALE CHARACTERISTICS	
The Animal	A true mammal. Air-breathing. Warm-blooded. Nurses young on milk.
Adults	Length, 30 to 50 feet. Weight 20 to 40 tons. Average life span 30 to 40 years, occasionally 60.
Calves	Length 15 feet. Weight 1.5 tons at birth. Consume 50 gallons of milk, gain 60 to 70 pounds daily.
Migration	Travel 20 hours and 100 miles per day. A trip of 6000 miles takes six to eight weeks.
Color	Slate-gray caused by natural pigments, barnacles and barnacle scars.

Annual Migration Cycle

It was recently estimated that there are 21,000 gray whales. This population spends the summer months feeding in the Bering and Chukchi Seas off Alaska. Starting in October, the whales begin their annual southern migration to the subtropical waters of several coastal lagoons along Baja's south-central Pacific coast. Here the calves are born.

Since the gray is a bottom feeder, the whale's migration route is close to shore. As a result, whale spouts are easily seen from shore. Ocean-cruisers sail in these same waters and are frequently in company with the migration.

The "Annual Migration" chart on the following page shows that several migration phases overlap each other. Some individuals are still arriving in Baja while others are already heading back north. Pregnant females, well into their 12-month gestation period, leave Alaska early with their mission clearly in mind. Others lag behind, while males and in-season females court and mate on the way south.

By December, the whales begin arriving in the waters off northern Baja. By mid-January, most females have arrived at their destinations in the back-waters of the lagoons where most of the calving takes place. The return north occurs in reverse order. The newly pregnant females and other single whales begin north, starting in February, while the new mothers and their calves linger behind, occasionally as late as May and June. As a result, there are whales in Baja waters from December to June.

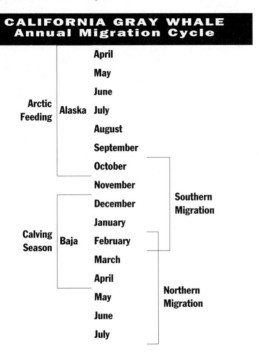

CALIFORNIA GRAY WHALE
Annual Migration Cycle

		Month	
Arctic Feeding	Alaska	April	
		May	
		June	
		July	
		August	
		September	
		October	Southern Migration
		November	
Calving Season	Baja	December	
		January	
		February	
		March	
		April	
		May	Northern Migration
		June	
		July	

Whale-Watching

The whale may be observed in a variety of ways. They are summarized as follows:

1. Viewing by boat
   - Day trips
   - Long-range trips
2. Viewing from the air
3. Viewing from land
   - Coastal observation points
   - Baja lagoons

1. **Viewing by boat**—Many Pacific coast ports in the United States offer one-day whale-watching trips in the same type of vessels normally used for sportfishing. You can frequently get close-up views of the whales on these ventures. The various fishing charter organizations noted earlier also provide whale-watching trips.

2. **Viewing from the air**—Passengers in small, private aircraft can get fine views of whales both in the ocean and in the lagoons. The Baja Bush Pilots' *Airports of Baja California* reports that landing at the dirt airstrip adjoining Laguna San Ignacio provides a ringside seat.

3. **Viewing from land**—Seaward views of Pacific waters are offered at numerous points along the southern portion of the highway between Tijuana and Ensenada. Take Highway 1, rather than 1-D, so you may easily pull off onto the side roads accessing the coastal bluffs. Also visit the Mirador vista point between Tijuana and Ensenada.

There are several good vantage points for whale watching along the road to La Bufadora on the Punta Banda peninsula. Punta Banda projects well out into the ocean, and the road is a considerable distance above the water. Another point is Punta Baja, but its elevation is not nearly as high as at Punta Banda.

During the winter of 1988–89 numbers of California gray whales migrated to the shallow waters immediately outside the harbor at La Paz. The spouts of these animals could easily be seen from many of the coastal areas.

Finally, the land-based traveler can drive to the edge of the calving lagoons at several places. In Bahía Magdalena, whales can be seen from the docks at San Carlos and boats may be rented to travel to the bay's opening into the Pacific, where whales are more common. Today, the easiest place in all of Baja to visit the whales at close range is at Puerto Lopez Mateos, which can be reached by oiled highway. Boats may be rented to visit the calving grounds inside Boca de Solidad.

There are two additional sites in the vicinity of Guerrero Negro. The first is the abandoned salt dock at Puerto Venustiano Carranza. In some years, there are no whales here as the lagoon's entrance to the sea is blocked with sand. In others, they are present and may be seen from a tour boat advertised in the area's hotels. The most famous site is Scammon's Lagoon.

Scammon's Lagoon

Scammon's Lagoon (*Laguna Ojo de Liebre*) is the largest lagoon in Baja. Its easternmost segment is called The Nursery. This area has been designated as the *Refugio Natural de la Ballena Gris* (Natural Refuge of the Gray Whale). You may camp on the shore of the lagoon in an area administered by one of the local *Ejidos*.

WILDLIFE

I recommend you visit this area not solely to see the whale, as obviously the great majority of the creatures' bodies will be below the water's surface. What you do absorb is an overall impression of a desolate area where nature is playing out the climax of a 6000-mile journey. You will see and hear four signs of the whale:

1. The backs of the whales break the surface as they move about. From your vantage point on the six-foot-high sand bar at the edge of the lagoon, you see only a small portion of the whale.

2. Occasionally, the upper 8 to 10 feet of a whale's head projects vertically from the water. This behavior is called skyhopping. Apparently the animal is simply looking about.

3. Perhaps the most common sign of the whales are the spouts, which rise up to 15 feet. What you see is largely condensation caused when a whale's warm breath cools in the sea air.

4. Accompanying the spout is an explosive "whoosh." The sounds of this breathing create an eerie feeling as evening falls at Scammon's.

If you make the trip to Scammon's, I recommend you spend the night at the lagoon's edge. Nothing that you will see is spectacular, and it takes some time to absorb what is occurring. Be sure to take your field glasses.

The Whale's Future

Because populations of whales hunted by European and Yankee whalers became depleted during the early years of the 19th century, whalers turned to the gray whale to fill their holds. By 1845, the migration route and the Baja calving lagoons had been discovered, and in 1857 Captain Charles M. Scammon first entered Laguna Ojo de Liebre. Fifteen whaling stations were eventually established along the Alta and Baja California coasts. Hunting continued until 1890, when it was abandoned because the population had been reduced to only a few thousand.

Today, the gray whale is protected under the auspices of the International Whaling Commission. In 1972, the Mexican government established sanctuaries at Scammon's Lagoon and the other principal breeding areas. As a result, the gray whale has experienced a remarkable recovery.

In the past, the animal's predictable migration pattern made it an easy mark for the hunter. These same habits have now worked to save the species because mates are easily found. As a result, breeding has flourished. By 1991, the total population was estimated to be 21,000, a number probably higher than prior to commercial whaling activities. Late in that year the U.S. National Oceanic and Atmospheric Administration proposed removing the whale from the Endangered Species list, and this action has now been taken. However, the whale is still off-limits to hunting and is protected by a variety of other statutes. The whale's recovery represents a remarkable environmental success story.

Sea Turtles

Five species of sea turtles inhabit Baja's coastal waters. For years these giant amphibians were hunted by Mexican fishermen for their meat and shells. As recently as 1988 I observed dozens of turtles being driven to market by fishermen along Baja's Pacific coast. Finally, a total ban on these activities was declared by the Mexican government in 1990. It will no doubt be some time before it is fully honored.

Why Don't You Go to Hell?

It is not too many authors who can tell their readers to "Go to Hell," but this is just what you should do if you want to see thousands of sea turtles at the turtle farm near the community of Hell on Grand Cayman Island in the Caribbean Sea. But, if you will settle for a smaller number of turtles, visit the Sea Turtle Research Station at the government RV park near the village of Bahía de los Angeles. Three species of turtles are usually kept here in concrete tanks where they are open to public viewing. The small station is managed by Mexican biologist Antonio Resendiz. Antonio and his helpers gather biological information about the turtles, educate local fisherman about the need for their protection, and take various steps to enhance turtle survival in the local area.

HISTORY

The stone church at San Javier is the best preserved of the missions established by the Jesuits in Baja.

Remote, isolated, arid and little-known. This is Baja California. One might expect to find little of historic interest in such a place. It is just the opposite. Baja boasts an amazingly rich and fascinating history beginning a scant 42 years after Columbus's first voyage to the New World in 1492 and almost a century before the pilgrims landed at Plymouth Rock in Massachusetts. Baja's history employs a cast of characters no novelist could have devised: Hernan Cortez, Juan Cabrillo, Francis Drake, Thomas Cavendish, Padres Francisco Kino and Junipero Serra, and the notorious filibuster, William Walker.

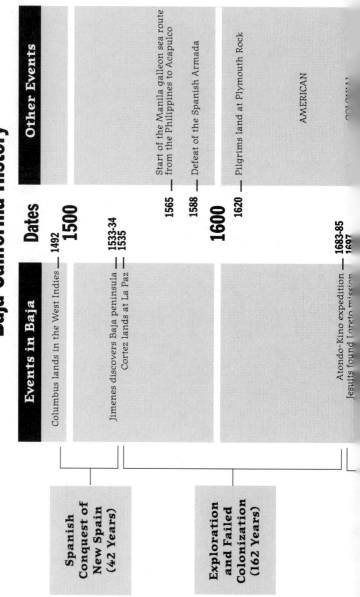

Baja California History

Events in Baja	Dates	Other Events
Columbus lands in the West Indies	1492	
	1500	
Jimenes discovers Baja peninsula	1533-34	
Cortez lands at La Paz	1535	
	1565	Start of the Manila galleon sea route from the Philippines to Acapulco
	1588	Defeat of the Spanish Armada
	1600	
	1620	Pilgrims land at Plymouth Rock
Atondo-Kino expedition	1683-85	AMERICAN
Jesuits found Loreto mission	1697	

Spanish Conquest of New Spain (42 Years)

Exploration and Failed Colonization (162 Years)

Jesuit Missionary Period (71 Years)	Franciscans and Dominicans (53 Years)	The Mexican Nation

1768 — Jesuit expulsion

1769 — Padre Serra's Journey to San Diego

1776 — Mexican Independence from Spain.

1800

1821 — United States Declaration of Independence

1822 — Oath of allegiance to Mexico signed in Loreto

1846-48 — Mexican-American War and signing of the Treaty of Hidalgo in 1848

1900

1910-1917 — Period of revolution in Mexico culminating in the Constitution of 1917

1952 — Baja California becomes a state

1974 — Baja California Sur becomes a state

(World War I–1914 to 1918)

In addition to many persons of Spanish origin, Baja's soil has witnessed th coming and going of Jesuit missionaries from Italy, as well as English adven turers, Dutch pirates, French miners. Key events that have shaped this region include war with the United States, internal revolution and incredibl amounts of land fraud. The broad aspects of this enticing drama are present ed in this chapter. Details will be interwoven as the many easily visit-ed site are encountered along the "Grand Tour" in Part III.

But first this historic stage must be set with a brief review of Baja's pre-His panic inhabitants. I must also note that much of the material presented in this chapter is based on an English translation of *A History of Lower Califor-nia* by Pablo L. Martinez.

The Prehistoric Californians

A sharp contrast existed between the Indian inhabitants of the Baja penin-sula and the native populations that the Spanish conquistadors encountered in mainland Mexico and much of South America. In these latter areas, the Aztecs, Mayas and Incas had developed highly advanced civilizations, with large cities and complex religious and cultural institutions. The Indians of southwestern United States also had well-developed, although somewhat less-advanced, civilizations. As a result of their isolated location on the Baja peninsula, the Baja California Indians were found to be among the most primitive in the Americas. This situation was to have important impacts on their interrelationships with Spanish conquerors in the centuries to come.

The early Spanish encountered three well-defined tribal groups. The most southerly were the Pericues. They inhabited the peninsula's tip north to a line drawn south of present-day Todos Santos and San Bartolo. They were to interact with the Spanish during the important early day events at San Jose del Cabo.

North of the Pericues were the Guaycuras. Their domain stretched from the line mentioned above north to Loreto. From a historic standpoint, these people were the most important as it was they who were destined to greet the early Spanish landings in the La Paz and Loreto areas, and they were to be the objects of the earliest missionary activities.

The balance of the peninsula was home to the Cochimies. The three tribal areas are shown on the "Spanish Explorations" map on page 241.

The peninsula's Indians had no written language. They lived in communal groups in the vicinity of fresh water and slept on the bare ground. Shelter was provided by holes dug in the earth, crude arrangements of branches and occasionally by caves. More commonly, the Indians slept within a low circle of stones without any roof. A fire would be kept burning during the night during winter. They cultivated nothing and lived from their native environment by hunting, fishing and gathering.

In spite of stone-age conditions, these Indians were described by the early Spaniards as strong, tall and healthy. They were good runners and swimmers. The men went nude, and painted their bodies with intricate abstract patterns. The women normally wore some form of garment made from native materials.

Their possessions were limited to a few crude cups, bowls, baskets and simple implements for fishing, hunting and warfare. For these latter activities they had mastered the use of the bow and arrow, boomerang and wooden lances. This mention of warfare leads to a discussion of several attributes of the Indians that were of particular importance in their future relationships with the Spanish.

Tribal Warfare

There appears to have been a more or less continuous state of warfare among the tribes; the males were practiced in this art. On the whole, the Indians did not transfer their hostilities toward the Spaniards. There were few organized attempts to eject the intruders. The Spaniards did not have to conquer California with force of arms as was necessary on the mainland. Nevertheless, there were armed encounters between the two parties, and the Spanish possession of firearms was a crucial advantage. In addition, the Indians' warlike behavior toward each other frequently cast the Spaniards in the role of referee.

Polygamy

As a result of battlefield mortality, there were considerably more women than men. The natural outcome was that the surviving males acquired more than one wife. Multiple wives also contributed considerably to the husband's standard of living in a culture requiring the constant gathering of food. This polygamous lifestyle was to lead to considerable conflict with the missionaries, who endeavored to enforce Christian morality.

Shamans

The California Indian had little in the way of a tribal hierarchy, except during periods of warfare. However, there was the universal presence of the shaman, or witch-doctor. These individuals, usually elderly men, had considerable influence. They functioned as healers and exercised their authority during the frequent public dances and at funeral ceremonies. The coming of Spanish missionaries threatened the authority of the shamans. As a result, the shaman became the principal obstacle to the work of the missionaries.

Language

The missionaries found the Indian languages inadequate to use for instructing their charges in Christianity and the arts of civilization. The native tongues were very basic, and there were significant dialect differences among the tribes and subtribes. The Indians were thus taught Spanish, a process that was duplicated in many other areas and had far-reaching consequences for the Americas. It explains, in part, why today Spanish is the native tongue in most of Mexico and South America.

Historic Overview

The historic pageant of Baja California commences with Columbus's landing in the West Indies in 1492 and ends with the achievement of statehood by Baja California Sur in 1974. It is divided into five historic periods that correspond to the five remaining sections in this chapter. Each section begins with a small chart summarizing additional dates and events. The full-page chart also indicates the chronological relationship of Baja's history to other well-known world events.

It is perhaps a natural tendency for those of us who live in the highly developed areas of the United States and Canadian Pacific coast to surmise that the historic events in these areas must surely have preceded those in a land as remote as Baja California. As can be seen, it was just the reverse. Civilization on the Pacific coast was to flow from south to north. The founding of the Loreto mission on the east coast of the Baja peninsula preceded the first Alta California mission by 72 years.

Spanish Conquest of New Spain (42 Years)

Columbus's discovery of the islands of the Caribbean Sea promptly engendered Spanish colonization. The first colony was on the island of Haiti, then called Espanola. By 1511, there were settlements on the islands of Jamaica, Cuba and Puerto Rico. Among the earliest settlers was the 19-year-old Hernan Cortez, who arrived in 1505. He proceeded to earn his living from ranching and mining.

SPANISH CONQUEST OF NEW SPAIN	
1492–1502	Columbus's four voyages to the West Indies.
1519	Cortez lands at Vera Cruz to conquer New Spain (Mexico).

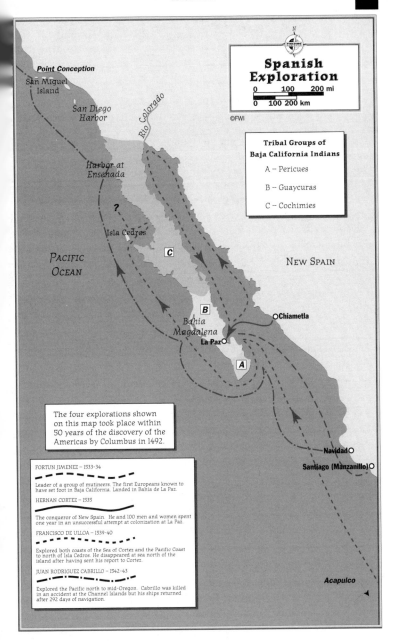

Spanish Exploration

0   100   200 mi
0 100 200 km

©FWI

Tribal Groups of Baja California Indians

A – Pericues

B – Guaycuras

C – Cochimies

Point Conception

San Miguel Island

San Diego Harbor

Rio Colorado

Harbor at Ensenada

?

Isla Cedros

PACIFIC OCEAN

C

NEW SPAIN

B

Bahia Magdalena

OChiametla

La Paz O

A

The four explorations shown on this map took place within 50 years of the discovery of the Americas by Columbus in 1492.

NavidadO

Santiago (Manzanillo)O

FORTUN JIMENEZ – 1533-34

Leader of a group of mutineers. The first Europeans known to have set foot in Baja California. Landed in Bahía de La Paz.

HERNAN CORTEZ – 1535

The conqueror of New Spain. He and 100 men and women spent one year in an unsuccessful attempt at colonization at La Paz.

FRANCISCO DE ULLOA – 1539-40

Explored both coasts of the Sea of Cortez and the Pacific Coast to north of Isla Cedros. He disappeared at sea north of the island after having sent his report to Cortez.

JUAN RODRIGUEZ CABRILLO – 1542-43

Explored the Pacific north to mid-Oregon. Cabrillo was killed in an accident at the Channel Islands but his ships returned after 292 days of navigation.

Acapulco

SPANISH CONQUEST OF NEW SPAIN

1522	Cortez conquers the Aztecs and founds Mexico City.
1532	Failed Mendoza expedition.
1533–34	Baja Peninsula discovered by mutineer Fortun Jimenez.

In time, reports of golden cities in the interior of Mexico reached the islands, and Cortez resolved to lead an expedition of conquest. After many intrigues, he boldly sailed for the mainland in 1519 leading a force of 11 ships, more than 800 Spaniards and Cuban Indians, 16 horses and 14 cannons. Upon landing, he founded the first Spanish city in Mexico at Vera Cruz. He promptly scuttled his ships to prevent the desertion of his forces. In a series of adventures that would fill a novel, he brutally captured the Aztec capital of Tenochtitlan in 1522, with the estimated loss of 100,000 of its inhabitants.

In the decade to follow, Cortez and his men ravaged the land in all directions, accumulating great wealth and enslaving the native populations. Mexico City was constructed on the site of Tenochtitlan. During this period, Cortez operated largely on his own initiative, with his own resources, and only marginally within the auspices of the Spanish government.

This same methodology was also employed by Cortez's bitter rival Nuno de Guzman, a fellow Spaniard who had amassed great wealth by illegal slave trading in the Caribbean Islands. During 1530–31, Guzman conquered vast areas of land northwest of Mexico City and established a personal empire. This action established Guzman as the master of the lands on the Mexican coast opposite the southern tip of the Baja peninsula.

During this same period, the King of Spain gradually moved to gain control of the actions of his freewheeling conquistadors.

The world was aware that Magellan had circled the globe in 1522, passing through a strait at the southerly tip of the South American continent. Cortez longed to explore to the northwest along the recently discovered Pacific Ocean in order to discover a similar passage above the North American continent. However, he was blocked from doing this by land by the presence of Guzman.

Cortez thus reached agreement with the Spanish crown that he would, at his own expense, undertake seaborne explorations of the Pacific coast. To this end, Cortez established a shipbuilding station on the Pacific coast near the mouth of the Rio Balsas, about 100 miles north of present-day Acapulco. Native porters endlessly transported the rigging, ironwork and similar materials needed for the ships across the mountains of Mexico from Vera Cruz.

The stage was thus set for the discovery of the Baja peninsula. In 1532, Cortez dispatched the first of four expeditions into the Pacific. The first was under the command of Diego Hurtado de Mendoza, Cortez's cousin. Mendoza sailed north and penetrated the Sea of Cortez; however, the expedition was never to return. It met its end at the hands of Indians, Guzman or both.

Undaunted, Cortez sent forth a second group of two ships that departed from present-day Manzanillo on October 29, 1533. The two ships soon parted company. The first discovered the Revilla Gigedo Islands, which lie some 400 miles off the Mexican coast, and then returned to the mainland at Acapulco.

The second vessel was placed under the command of Diego de Becerra, a captain of tyrannical nature. As a result, Becerra was soon set upon and killed by many of his crew under the leadership of the pilot Fortun Jimenez. After depositing the non-mutinous crew members on the Mexican mainland, Jimenez and the others fled to the north and stumbled upon the Baja peninsula. They became the first Europeans known to have set foot on this land.

Baja was thus discovered through accident by a group of mutineers. The date of the discovery is unknown but probably took place either late 1533 or early 1534. The spot of the landing was subsequently determined to be Bahía de La Paz.

It is reported that Jimenez and most of his crew were killed by the Indians as a result of their attempts to violate the Indian women. The survivors sailed across the gulf to the mainland, where they fell into the hands of Guzman. There they passed on stories of their discovery of what was then believed to be an island. Of equal importance was their report of the abundance of pearls. This news would increase Cortez's desire to continue with his exploratory efforts.

Exploration and Failed Colonization (162 Years)

Angered at the interference of Guzman and by the failure of the two expeditions he had dispatched, Cortez chose to lead the next effort himself. This expedition differed from the previous two in that Cortez was aware of his destination, the Island of California. It was to be the only serious effort to actually conquer and colonize the new land until 162 years later.

Three new ships were constructed and loaded with 300 men and 130 horses. Many of the men took along their families, among them 37 women. In May 1535, Cortez landed at Bahía de La Paz and named it Santa Cruz. There he was to find evidences of the Jimenez mutineers and the pearls that they had reported. It is now believed that the actual location of Santa Cruz was at Pichilingue, 14 miles north of present-day La Paz.

ORIGIN OF THE NAME CALIFORNIA

The name "California" was first encountered in the diary of one of the people who accompanied Francisco de Ulloa on his exploratory voyage. For centuries its origin was a mystery. It was surmised that it had been derived from the Latin words "calida formax," meaning hot furnace. Then in 1862 a New England clergyman, Edward Hall, came upon a Spanish novel "The Adventures of Explandian," which was known to be popular during the years of the conquest of Mexico. It describes a fantastic island inhabited by Amazons: "It is known that to the right of the Indies there exists an island called California very near the side of the Terrestrial Paradise...and was peopled by black women, among whom there was not a single man....Their weapons were all of gold...because in all the island there was no metal except gold."

This story flourished along with other legends of golden cities in the unknown lands beyond New Spain. It is now the opinion of most historians that the seafarers of the day came to mix these prevailing legends with the tale of California from the "Adventures" and applied the name to the newly discovered "island" to the west. In any event, from then on, the land from the tip of the peninsula north was to be known as California.

Cortez's colonization efforts were to prove unproductive. He did build a church and houses for the colonists. It has also been reported that he made exploratory trips into the interior of the peninsula. However, there were apparently no efforts made to raise crops, and the colony had to be supplied by ship from across the gulf. After a year and the death by starvation of many of the colonists, the colony was deemed a failure. Cortez returned to Mexico and shortly ordered the others to follow.

In Mexico, Cortez encountered Antonio de Mendoza, the first of a long line of viceroys of New Spain appointed by the king. From this time forward, adventurers such as Cortez and Guzman were to have far less of a free hand, and decisions affecting the Baja peninsula would emanate largely from the viceroys at Mexico City.

HISTORY

EXPLORATION AND FAILED COLONIZATION

1535	Cortez lands at La Paz.
1539–1540	Ulloa expedition.
1542–1543	Cabrillo expedition.
1565	Start of the galleon sea route from Manila to Acapulco.
1578	Drake circles the world.

EXPLORATION AND FAILED COLONIZATION

1586	Cavendish in Baja.
1596–1602	Viscaino expeditions.
1615	Pichilingue pirates.
1644	Gonzalez expedition.
1663	Bernal expedition.
1683–1685	Atondo-Kino expedition.

Francisco de Ulloa

For his part, Cortez remained obsessed with the desire to press forward by sea to the northwest. Without the approval of the viceroy, he dispatched his fourth and final expedition under the command of Francisco de Ulloa. Ulloa's orders were to press as far north as possible. He left Acapulco in July 1539, and accomplished an amazing feat of navigation. (See the "Spanish Explorations" map in this chapter.)

Ulloa sailed the full length of the Sea of Cortez, exploring both coasts, stopping at La Paz both going and coming. He anchored at the mouth of the Rio Colorado and established that the Baja peninsula was not an island, although the island myth persisted for centuries. Finally, the expedition rounded the peninsula's southern tip, and explored the Pacific coast to north of Isla Cedros. From there Ulloa sent one of his ships south to report to Cortez concerning his findings, a most fortunate decision, as nothing further was ever heard from this intrepid explorer.

At this point, it may be well to reflect that the humble California peninsula was discovered, explored and first colonized under the auspices of one of the most renowned men in the history of the New World. Although Cortez was the conqueror of Mexico, he was, in turn, largely conquered by Baja. He secured little of the riches he sought and spent a significant part of his personal fortune in the process.

While other explorers were to push even farther north up the Pacific coast, the route they discovered was not to be the one used in the northern expansion of New Spain. In the years after Cortez, great land expeditions under Coronado and others pressed north along the western edge of New Spain and into what are today the states of Arizona and New Mexico in the United States.

By the year 1600, more than 160,000 Spaniards had migrated to the New World. There were more than 200 chartered towns in New Spain. The path of this movement was on the mainland, not along Baja's Pacific coast. The

Baja peninsula was not to be settled by Europeans for more than 150 years after the era of Cortez.

The peninsula acted as a massive barrier in the path of the northerly march of European civilization. With the help of a margarita or two, it would be interesting to speculate on what would have occurred along the west coast of the United States if the Baja barrier had not existed. Certainly Alta California would have been heavily colonized by the Spanish at a far earlier date, and the course of history would have been greatly altered.

Juan Rodriguez Cabrillo

After the Ulloa expedition, Cortez returned to Spain and faded from the new world scene. In New Spain, Viceroy Mendoza was faced with the reality of the California coast and not our margarita-induced speculation. As a result, he dispatched a new expedition under the command of Juan Rodriguez Cabrillo. It was to prove to be one of the most remarkable in the history of navigation.

Cabrillo left the Mexican mainland on June 27, 1542, from the well-protected harbor at Navidad. He arrived at the tip of the Baja peninsula in early July and took on water at San Jose del Cabo. His ships were to join the hundreds that were to make this open roadstead a key stopping point along the Pacific coast. Today, the hotel **Presidente Inter-Continental** has been constructed adjacent to the stream-fed estuary that provided water to these mariners.

After this brief stop, Cabrillo rounded Cabo San Lucas, and on the 13th of July sailed by the magnificent harbor at Bahía Magdalena. In August, he arrived at Isla Cedros, the farthest point north known to have been reached by Ulloa two years earlier. From here, Cabrillo inched his way north, anchoring each night. He reached the broad, protected bay at present-day Ensenada in September; a few days later he stepped ashore near what is now San Diego. On September 28, 1542, he claimed this land in the name of Spain and became the first European known to have set foot on the west coast of what was to become the United States.

In the months to come, Cabrillo beat his way through the notoriously bad weather off Point Conception and reached as far north as Fort Ross on the California coast. After retreating south, Cabrillo met his death on San Miguel Island as the result of an accident. His second-in-command took charge, fought his way north again during winter weather, and eventually reached latitude 44 off the Oregon coast.

From there, the expedition returned to the point of origin, in Navidad, after an absence of nine and one-half months. Tragically, the results of Cabrillo's voyage were considered of little importance by the Spanish officials and no further formal efforts at exploring the peninsula were undertaken for more than 50 years.

Pirates and the Manila Galleons

The Viceroy of New Spain was ordered to shift his efforts to the Philippine Islands, which had been discovered by Magellan during his circumnavigation of the globe. Ships sent from the coast of Mexico sailed west to the islands and developed trade with the countries of the Far East. Starting in the spring of 1565, Spanish ships voyaged northeasterly from the Philippines almost to Japan to reach the prevailing westerly winds. These winds blew them west to the California coast along the northern part of the Baja peninsula and then south to Acapulco. The following winter, the galleons would return to the islands with the aid of the southeast trade winds. The ships making these circuits became known as the Manila Galleons, and their annual trips were to continue for an incredible 250 years.

The development of this important trade route was to be of special importance to the Baja peninsula. The long voyage east from the Philippines was a difficult undertaking requiring six to eight months (twice the time of the westerly leg). By the time the galleons reached the waters off California, their food and water supplies were nearly exhausted, and the crews often suffered from scurvy. There was obviously a pressing need for a coastal supply point. While this need was to go unmet for many decades, it did strongly influence future activities on the Baja peninsula.

The presence of the Manila Galleons also resulted in the Baja California cape region becoming the hiding place of pirates who would lay in wait for the annual passage of the richly laden ships. In 1578, Francis Drake entered the Pacific through the Straits of Magellan and became the first to prey on the Spanish galleons. Drake's prizes were seized in waters to the south of Baja, but he and the *Golden Hind* touched at San Jose Del Cabo to take on water, joining the illustrious ranks of those who had visited the peninsula.

Drake was followed eight years later by his fellow Englishman, Thomas Cavendish. After ravaging ships along the South American coast, Cavendish arrived in the protective shelter of the harbor of Cabo San Lucas to lie in wait for the annual trip of the Manila Galleons. On November 4, 1587, he attacked the 700-ton *Santa Ana*, which was so heavily laden that her guns had been left behind. After a fierce defense with small arms, the *Santa Ana* was captured and taken to the anchorage off San Jose del Cabo and the Spanish survivors were cast ashore.

On the 17th of November, Cavendish hosted the Spanish on board his vessel to celebrate the 17th anniversary of the coronation of Queen Elizabeth. Two days later, he set fire to the *Santa Ana*, promptly weighed anchor and arrived in England after circling the globe.

Remarkably, the stranded Spaniards, headed by Sebastian Vizcaino, were able to extinguish the fire. After performing makeshift repairs, they sailed their ship to the Mexican mainland.

Today, the site of the burning of the *Santa Ana* is in plain view from the swimming pools of the hotels that line the beach at San Jose del Cabo. From the balconies of the **Hotel Finisterra**, on the cliffs at Cabo San Lucas, one may look over the harbor where Cavendish lay in wait for his prey.

The lure of the Manila Galleons and Spanish shipping along the South American coast also attracted Dutch pirates. Sizeable fleets of these raiders entered the Pacific through the Straits of Magellan starting in 1598. The year 1615 was to witness the coming of a Dutch armada of eight well-armed ships commanded by Boris van Spilbergen. Following a victorious battle with a Spanish fleet to the south, the Dutch fleet infested the waters of the Baja peninsula in hope of capturing ships from Manila.

The men of these ships came to be known as the Pichilingues. This name was left behind on the excellent natural harbor north of La Paz, which today is the terminal for the La Paz-to-Mazatlan ferries. This obviously non-hispanic name has become a tongue twister for today's tourists.

Spanish authorities became concerned with the losses incurred at the hands of these adventurers. The need for reliable supply points on the peninsula became clearly apparent. However, these distant events were overshadowed by the defeat of the Spanish Armada in European waters the year following the sacking of the *Santa Ana*. It was thus several years before the Viceroy of New Spain obtained authority to press forward with exploration and colonization in Baja, and it was stipulated that few public funds were to be expended.

Sebastian Vizcaino

Further authorization for exploration was then awarded to Sebastian Vizcaino. This intrepid seaman made two expeditions. The first, in 1596, resulted in an effort of several months to colonize La Paz. The second, in 1602, was to see Vizcaino sail as far north as Cape Mendocino in Alta California. He visited the sites of present-day San Diego and Monterey and described the latter port as an excellent possibility for establishing a supply station for the Manila Galleons. Plans were actually made to put these recommendations into action but they were not carried out.

Vizcaino had essentially duplicated the path that Cabrillo had taken 60 years earlier, and with similar results. Little occurred as the result of either voyage. Monterey and San Diego faded from memory. They were not colonized for more than 160 years, but many of Vizcaino's geographic place names have survived. The extensive Vizcaino Desert surrounding present-day Guerrero Negro is named in his honor.

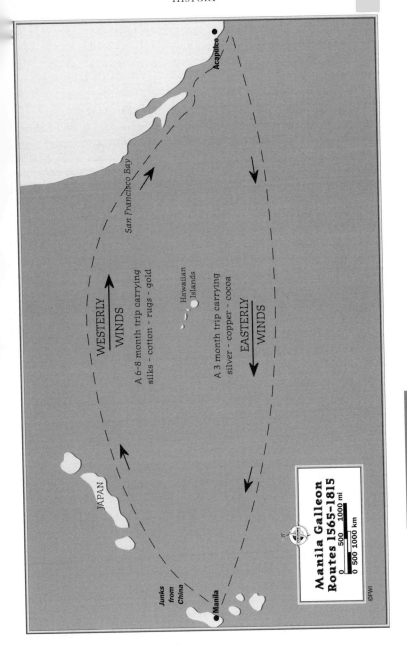

Manila Galleon Routes 1565–1815

Junks from China

Manila

JAPAN

Hawaiian Islands

San Francisco Bay

Acapulco

WESTERLY WINDS

A 6-8 month trip carrying
silks - cotton - rugs - gold

EASTERLY WINDS

A 3 month trip carrying
silver - copper - cocoa

0   500   1000 mi
0   500 1000 km

©FWI

Following the expedition of Sebastian Vizcaino, more than 80 years were to pass with only an occasional attempt at colonizing California. Brief efforts were made in 1644, under the command of Alonzo Gonzalez, and again, in 1663, under Bernardo Bernal. While these ventures seem to have been in response to various royal decrees, they do not appear to have been vigorously pursued. As in the past, little in the way of public funds was allocated to these projects; in reality they were little more than pearl fishing ventures.

It was not until 1683 that an expedition was mounted that was to have lasting effect on the colonizing of the Baja peninsula. The Spanish authorities came to realize that public funding was going to be required if colonization was to be achieved. They thus provisioned a small fleet of three ships and gave command to Isidro de Atondo y Antillon.

Atondo and Kino

In January 1683, Atondo crossed the Sea of Cortez in four days and arrived at La Paz with some 200 men. With him was the Jesuit padre Francisco Kino. Kino would irrevocably influence the future of the peninsula.

The Indians in the La Paz area had grown accustomed to the temporary presence of ships engaged in pearl fishing. In contrast, Atondo and his party obviously intended to stay. The Indians became restive. In due course, Atondo invited the native leaders to a feast and used the occasion to fall upon, and kill, 10 of their number.

This event made matters worse. Atondo was forced to abandon La Paz and return to the mainland. As a result of this tragic event, the center of colonization efforts on the peninsula was to shift to the north.

After refitting their ship, Atondo and Kino set out again and in October 1683 landed at a place far to the north of La Paz that they named San Bruno. This site is 12 miles north of present-day Loreto. At San Bruno they erected a small triangular fortification surrounding a church and other buildings. Some 10 miles inland, they found better water and established a livestock farm at a site they named San Isidro. From these bases of operations Atondo and Kino mounted four expeditions into the interior. On one, Padre Kino reached the Pacific coast and became the first European known to have crossed the peninsula on foot.

The San Bruno colony was to last for 19 months. In May 1685, supplies were exhausted and the colonists returned to the mainland. However, the aborted San Bruno colony was to give rise to the permanent settlement of Baja within a few years.

Jesuit Missionary Period (71 Years)

The Jesuits

The driving force behind the permanent colonization of the Baja peninsula was the Company of Jesus, the Jesuits, also known today as the Society of Jesus. Because of the importance of the missionary system in general, and the Jesuits in particular, it is necessary to examine them both briefly.

As the result of the Catholic Counter-Reformation in Europe, members of several religious orders accompanied the conquerors of new lands to many parts of the world. Use of the missionary system became a hallmark of Spanish colonization. It was to become an effective and economical tool for accomplishing the purposes of the kings, for the orders had their own internal administrative systems and access to sources of revenue other than the royal treasury.

Ignatius Loyola founded the Company of Jesus in 1534. Members of the order came to Mexico in 1572 and soon established extensive missions in the northwestern region. Their members were university-trained men of good family from many European countries. By the time of the Atondo colonizing effort at San Bruno, the Jesuits had more than 100 years of missionary experience in Mexico.

JESUIT MISSIONARY PERIOD	
1697	Founding of Loreto mission by Salvatierra.
1717	Salvatierra dies—succeeded by Ugarte.
1734	Pericue Indian revolt.
1742–48	Epidemics kill many Indians.
1767	Jesuits expelled from Baja.

The mission was to become an institution under Spanish law along with the *pueblo* and the *presidio*. Each mission was planned to last only 10 years. It was then to be replaced by the pueblo, with the mission lands divided between communal acreage, town-site areas and individual plots for each Indian. This transfer process was a long time coming in Baja. The presidio was the headquarters of the military establishment that accompanied the missionaries.

In Baja, each mission consisted of a central village where the missionary and any accompanying soldiers lived. Each mission had a number of outlying visiting stations, which are sometimes mistakenly referred to as missions.

HISTORY

Establishment of a mission was not done at the whim of the local priest but required following well-established rules and sequences. After securing approval for a new mission, the padre would bless the chosen site and erect the necessary buildings. Indians were attracted through gifts of food and other items. Children and any dying adults were baptized. Any receptive Indian was required to give up his wandering ways and settle down in the vicinity of the mission. The teaching of Spanish and the tenets of Christianity were to follow.

Each mission aimed at becoming self-supporting through farming and grazing, but this was difficult because of Baja's arid conditions. Heavy reliance had to be placed on supplies shipped from the mainland.

Padre Francisco Kino was of Italian birth and had been educated in mathematics at German universities, a strange background for his assignments in spreading Christianity in remote areas of the world. Upon returning to the mainland from the failed effort at San Bruno, Kino and Atondo found the viceroy unwilling to expend additional funds in colonizing the arid lands across the Sea of Cortez.

As a result, the Jesuits assigned Padre Kino to missionary efforts in the mainland northwest, where he was to become one of the most successful and famous figures in the history of Mexico and the American southwest. But before moving to these tasks, he was to transfer his enthusiasm for missionary work in California to a visiting Jesuit, Padre Juan Maria de Salvatierra. The two made a mutual promise to work toward establishing missions on the distant peninsula.

The burden of pursuing this effort was to fall to Salvatierra, but he met with continual frustration. Neither the Spanish authorities nor the leader of the Jesuits in Mexico would undertake the project. Finally, help came from none other than Father Santaella, the General of the Jesuit order, who visited Mexico in 1696. His support resulted in the order giving Salvatierra permission to enter California.

But frustration continued because the viceroy would not provide financial support for such an enterprise. Salvatierra was forced to solicit contributions from private sources. Accomplishing this, he finally secured a license to proceed on February 6, 1697. Because the Jesuits were to provide the funding, this document gave the Jesuits almost complete control over the peninsula. After additional delays, Salvatierra and his followers finally arrived on the California shore in October of that year. The Baja peninsula was never again without settlers from the Old World.

Founding of Loreto

San Bruno was the site of the Jesuit landing. Little remained of the fortifications that had been constructed 14 years earlier. Salvatierra decided to

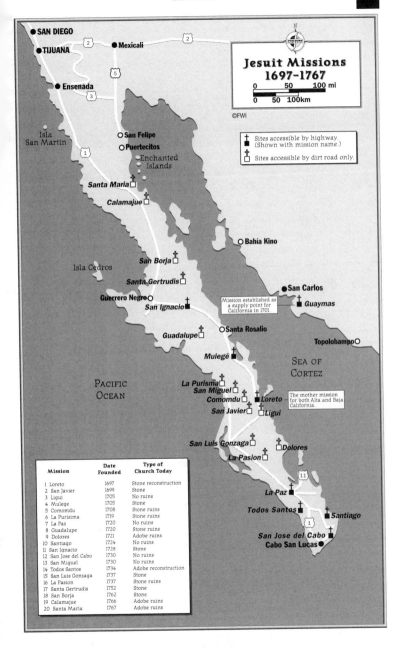

Jesuit Missions 1697-1767

0 — 50 — 100 mi
0 — 50 — 100km

©FWI

† Sites accessible by highway. (Shown with mission name.)

■ Sites accessible by highway. (Shown with mission name.)

† Sites accessible by dirt road only.

● SAN DIEGO
● TIJUANA
● Mexicali
● Ensenada

Isla San Martin

○ San Felipe
○ Puertecitos

Enchanted Islands

Santa Maria †
Calamajue †

○ Bahía Kino

Isla Cedros

San Borja †
Santa Gertrudis †
Guerrero Negro ○
San Ignacio ■

● San Carlos
■ Guaymas

Mission established as a supply point for California in 1701.

Guadalupe †
○ Santa Rosalio

Topolobampo ○

Mulegé ■

SEA OF CORTEZ

PACIFIC OCEAN

La Purisma †
San Miguel †
Comomdu ○
San Javier †
Loreto ■
Ligui †

The mother mission for both Alta and Baja California.

San Luis Gonzaga †
○ Dolores
La Pasion †

La Paz ■

Todos Santos ■
■ Santiago

San Jose del Cabo ●
Cabo San Lucas ●

Mission	Date Founded	Type of Church Today
1 Loreto	1697	Stone reconstruction
2 San Javier	1699	Stone
3 Ligui	1705	No ruins
4 Mulege	1705	Stone
5 Comomdu	1708	Stone ruins
6 La Purisima	1719	Stone ruins
7 La Paz	1720	No ruins
8 Guadalupe	1720	Stone ruins
9 Dolores	1721	Adobe ruins
10 Santiago	1724	No ruins
11 San Ignacio	1728	Stone
12 San Jose del Cabo	1730	No ruins
13 San Miguel	1730	No ruins
14 Todos Santos	1734	Adobe reconstruction
15 San Luis Gonzaga	1737	Stone
16 La Pasion	1737	Stone ruins
17 Santa Gertrudis	1752	Stone
18 San Borja	1762	Stone
19 Calamajue	1766	Adobe ruins
20 Santa Maria	1767	Adobe ruins

search for a better location for his mission because San Bruno was situated more than a mile from the coast and the water supply was brackish. In a few days a suitable place was found to the south.

On October 19, 1697, supplies from the ship began to be unloaded on the beach at the present location of Loreto. This was to be one of the most momentous events in the history of the Californias—Loreto was to become the mother mission for all those to follow in Baja and Alta California.

The settlers were able to converse with the Indians because the elements of their language had been documented by one of the padres who had accompanied the Atondo expedition. As was the missionaries' practice, a porridge of cornmeal was shared with those who had helped in the work. This act of charity was soon to cause the Indians to covet the limited food supplies.

After more than three weeks of tension, the Indians attacked the meager fortification, which consisted of a wall made up of the expedition's supplies. The settlers resorted to firearms and several Indians died that day.

During the next 70 years, the Jesuits established 20 missions (see "Jesuit Missions" map on page 253) and many more visiting stations from the tip of the peninsula north to the vicinity of Cataviña. Certain missions were to be used as bases from which new ones were founded. This stepping stone sequence was eventually to lead to the establishment of a chain of missions with its northern limit at Sonoma, north of San Francisco, in Alta California.

Additional Jesuit Missions

By the end of the first year, there were 22 Spaniards at Loreto, and the situation with the Indians had quieted to the point where Padre Salvatierra set forth in search of new mission sites. The initial efforts at expansion were located in the mountains to the west of Loreto and north along the coast to Mulegé. Father Salvatierra was also called to cross to the mainland and establish a mission at Guaymas for use as a supply point for the peninsula. By the time of Salvatierra's death in 1717, five peninsula missions were in operation.

Salvatierra's successor was Padre Juan Ugarte. Considerable progress was made under his leadership; 11 new missions were established during the next 20 years. There was also the never-ending need for financial support. Arid conditions on the peninsula resulted in very little food being raised, and the missions did not become self-supporting, as was usually the case in better agricultural areas. Supplies continued to be shipped across the Sea of Cortez.

Over the years, the peninsula's leaders wrote letters and even made trips to the mainland to plead their case with government authorities. The response was always negative. The padres' only alternative was to continue to seek out contributions from wealthy citizens on the mainland.

In the long run, they were very successful in this effort. The money and lands that were acquired were to become known as the Pious Fund. It was this fund that later became the financial basis for the founding of the future chain of missions in the United States.

The founding of the mission at San Jose del Cabo in 1730 was to be an important, although tragic, event. Within a short time of its establishment, one of the great ships inbound from Manila dropped anchor nearby. Fearing hostile Indians, the captain sent armed men ashore in search of water. To their astonishment, they were met by the padre and his charges and were provided with fresh supplies. At long last, after 165 years, the Manila Galleons had a supply point on the California coast. This good news was carried to Mexico City and Manila, and the order was given for all future sailings from the Philippines to stop at San Jose del Cabo. Sadly, this state of affairs was to be short-lived.

Indian Uprising

As previously noted, the peninsula Indians were polygamists. The Pericue Indians at the southern missions most resented the padres' efforts to change this system. Many Indians conspired against the missionaries under the leadership of the shamans. By 1733, the rebellious individuals felt they had sufficient strength and plotted to eliminate the few soldiers who guarded the missions—only one at La Paz, two at Santiago and three at Todos Santos. There were no soldiers at San Jose del Cabo.

The Indians made their move the following year by killing the soldier stationed at La Paz. Within a short time they killed the padre, two soldiers and an Indian at Santiago, and the padre at San Jose del Cabo. The padre and other surviving mission personnel from Todos Santos fled first to La Paz and then to the mission at Dolores.

Upon receiving news of the uprising, soldiers from the presidio at Loreto moved south to La Paz. They were joined by Indian soldiers from the mainland. Military action was taken against the peninsula Indians with little success. In January 1735, a ship from Manila arrived at Cabo San Lucas in search of the padre and the warm reception they were told to expect. Instead, they were greeted with violence at the hands of some 600 natives who almost succeeded in taking over the vessel.

Upon arrival in Acapulco, the galleon captain traveled to Mexico City and advised the viceroy of the situation on the peninsula. As a result, the authorities were finally moved to provide greater assistance to the struggling missionaries. As is so often the case, economically related events became to be the motivating factor. None other than the governor of mainland Sinaloa was ordered to the peninsula. Although his initial efforts were ineffective, the rebellious Indians were finally crushed by the end of 1736.

BAJA MISSIONS

The Jesuits founded missions throughout the Baja Peninsula in hopes of converting the local Indian populations. However, the Indians were driven from the land by subsequent settlers or died from European diseases. The Jesuits were looked upon with distrust by the later colonists and eventually driven out. Today many of the old missions still stand as a testament to one of the chapters in the peninsula's history.

SAN IGNACIO MISSION

Surrounded by desert, San Ignacio is an oasis. The Jesuits founded the mission in 1728, and the surrounding community developed. The mission is surrounded by a large number of date palms – San Ignacio's chief crop. San Ignacio is 90 miles southeast of Guerrero Negro along Highway 1.

MISSION SAN BORJA

The mission San Borja was founded in 1759 by Jesuits and completed in 1801. At one time the mission hosted 3000 Indians but is now abandoned. The mission is still intact and has been restored by the Mexican government. The mission is 22 miles south of the small southern Baja town of Rosarito (not the Northern tourist town). Thirteen miles south of the town bear left and follow the route to the mission. The route is only suitable for off road vehicles.

MISSION SANTA ROSALIA DE MULEGE

The Mission Santa Rosalia de Mulege was founded by the Jesuits in 1705 and completed in 1766. The mission has been restored to its orginal state. Mulege lies 38 miles south of Santa Rosalia.

MISSION NUESTRA SEÑORA DE LORETO

The town of Loreto is the oldest in Baja California. The town began in 1697 when a Jesuit padre, Juan Maria Salvatierra, arrived and founded Mission Nuestra Señora de Loreto.The original structure was destroyed by earthquakes, however the present structure dates back to 1752 and is still an active church.

MISSION DE NUESTRA SEÑORA LA PAZ

The church that lies here was built this century on the foundation of the Jesuit mission that was built in 1720. La Paz lies 134 miles south of La Ciudad Constitucion.

Mulege

Loreto

La Paz

In response to all this unrest, a new presidio was established at San Jose del Cabo with a complement of 30 soldiers. Little by little, modest buildings rose to replace those destroyed in the rebellion, but conditions would never be the same. While the Manila galleons brought silks and jewelry to the mainland, they left smallpox, measles and venereal disease in Baja.

During the years 1742 to 1748, epidemics spread throughout the peninsula, particularly in the south. Almost the entire Pericue tribe was wiped out. Some missions were abandoned, and the few remaining Indians concentrated at other points. The port of La Paz was abandoned and bore no sign of life for many years.

With the curtailment of activities in the south, the Jesuits began to push toward the north. In the final 15 years of their reign, they established four new missions in the mountains north of San Ignacio. The previous missions were located where concentrations of Indians and the best sites for agriculture and grazing were found. The majority were in places that today support substantial communities. To the north, such favorable conditions were located near the crest of the peninsular divide, which lies to the east of the Transpeninsular Highway and far from the path of today's activities.

In founding these new missions, the padres endeavored to establish "stepping stones" linking the peninsula missions with those on the Mexican mainland. Although this was never to occur, the new outposts eventually served as the supply route for the founding of a new empire of missions in Alta California.

These final years for the Jesuits were restless ones in other ways. The increase in support from Mexico City brought with it conflict between civil and Jesuit authorities. The Indians began to petition the government authorities to grant them the lands they were cultivating. Diseases continued to cause many deaths, particularly among the women, who suffered disproportionately from venereal disease. Men who had only recently ceased the practice of polygamy were now unable to find even one wife.

Jesuit Expulsion

While the Jesuit situation on the peninsula was in a deteriorating condition, the ultimate blow was to be delivered from the outside. The military-like Company of Jesus had attracted many enemies throughout the years, and there was world-wide resentment of the Jesuits' power and wealth. Even in Baja, it was believed that the Jesuits had accumulated and concealed a sizeable treasure.

These resentments peaked in Europe where the Company was expelled from Portugal in 1759, France in 1764 and finally from Spain in 1767. The Viceroy of New Spain was to receive a double-sealed package from Charles

III to be opened June 24, 1767. In this message, the king ordered all Jesuits to be arrested and sent to the port of Vera Cruz for deportation to Spain.

On the peninsula, the unhappy task of carrying out this order fell to Captain Gaspar de Portola. He and 50 soldiers arrived in San Jose del Cabo that same year and proceeded to arrest sixteen padres from the fourteen remaining missions. On February 3, 1768, the missionaries met in front of the church in Loreto, where the image of the virgin was draped in black. There the weeping inhabitants watched as the Jesuits departed for the mainland with only a few personal possessions. By July, they were imprisoned in Spain in company with Jesuits from other regions.

To the Jesuits goes the credit for bringing civilization to California. Each mission had a school. Primitive roads were constructed that ultimately connected Baja and Alta California. Regular postal service linked the missions. The first garden plants were introduced at Loreto, and in 1730 date palms were brought to San Ignacio, Loreto, Mulegé and other locations.

Most of the Jesuit missionary buildings were constructed of adobe and have not survived. The principle exception is the stone church at San Javier built between 1744 and 1758. It is located some 24 miles from Highway 1 by secondary road. Tourists staying in the Loreto-Puerto Escondido area will be well rewarded with a visit to this historic spot.

Tragically, through no fault of the padres, contact with the outside world during this period brought the diseases that were soon to almost exterminate the native peoples. Estimates of the pre-Hispanic population range from 40,000 to 50,000 persons. By the end of the Jesuit period, only some 7000 remained.

Franciscans and Dominicans (53 Years)

The Franciscans

Prior to the expulsion of the Jesuits, the Franciscan order had been responsible for missionary activity in northwestern Mexico. Now they were pressed to also take over the area vacated by the Company of Jesus on both the mainland and the Baja peninsula. There was to be little lapse in authority because the Franciscan padres sailed for California on the same ship that had just delivered their expelled predecessors to the mainland.

Fifteen priests landed at Loreto on April 1, 1768, under the leadership of Padre Junipero Serra. Each of Serra's charges was assigned to one of the 14 missions remaining in service at the time of the expulsion.

During the Jesuit period, the missionaries had been the virtual masters of life on the peninsula, which included authority over military personnel. They had discouraged the settlement of lands by immigrants from the mainland, so there was little activity outside the missions. All of this was to change dramatically. Captain Portola, who had expelled the Jesuits, had been appointed governor. He met the Franciscans and advised them that he and his soldiers would dispense justice and administer farming, grazing, and other economic activities.

The missionary system had remained in effect for more than 70 years. The change to civil authority was now to come, even though conditions on the peninsula had not advanced to the point where the transformation was fully justified.

Shortly after the arrival of the Franciscans, there came to the peninsula one Jose de Galvez, a personal agent of the King of Spain. He established himself at Santa Ana, a silver mining center near the present towns of San Antonio and El Triunfo south of La Paz. There, mining was one of the few economic activities carried out on the peninsula outside the administration of the missionaries.

Galvez carried royal orders to organize an expedition aimed at colonizing Alta California and to make changes in operations on the peninsula. From Santa Ana, he issued numerous decrees to which little attention was paid once he departed the region. However, he was successful in giving birth to the new missionary venture.

The padres had been pressing for the establishment of settlements in San Diego and Monterey for more than 150 years since these sites were discovered by Cabrillo and Vizcaino. However, the Spanish authorities showed no interest in expending effort in this direction until it became known that Czarist Russian fur trappers and explorers were working their way down the northwestern Pacific coast. They had set up outposts as far south as the Farallon Islands off San Francisco.

From his headquarters at Santa Ana, Galvez summoned Padre Serra and Captain Fernando Javier de Rivera y Moncada, commander of the presidio at Loreto. There, in this obscure hideaway in the mountains south of La Paz, the plans were drawn up for the settlement of what was to become the homes of millions of people in today's southern and central California in the United States.

Governor Portola was placed in command of the venture. He was delighted to be relieved of the political obscurity of his post in Loreto. Padre Serra was also eager to join and quickly secured release from his peninsular duties. The expedition was to be divided into four units, two by land and two by sea. In January 1769, the packet *San Carlos* weighed anchor at La Paz and sailed for San Diego. (Six years later, this same *San Carlos* became the first European ship to sail into the harbor at San Francisco.) A second vessel, the *San Antonio*, followed a month later. Both arrived at San Diego in April.

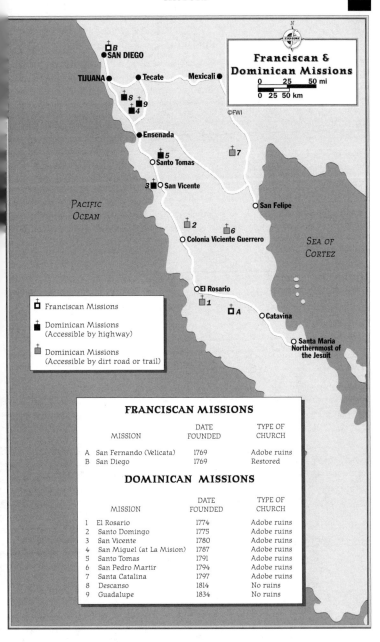

Franciscan & Dominican Missions

0   25   50 mi
0 25 50 km

©FWI

SAN DIEGO †B

TIJUANA ● ● Tecate   Mexicali ●

†8 †9
†4

● Ensenada

†5
O Santo Tomas

3 ■ O San Vicente

†7

PACIFIC
OCEAN

O San Felipe

†2   †6
O Colonia Viciente Guerrero

SEA OF
CORTEZ

O El Rosario

1   □A

O Catavina

† Franciscan Missions

■ Dominican Missions
  (Accessible by highway)

■ Dominican Missions
  (Accessible by dirt road or trail)

O Santa Maria
Northernmost of
the Jesuit

FRANCISCAN MISSIONS

	MISSION	DATE FOUNDED	TYPE OF CHURCH
A	San Fernando (Velicata)	1769	Adobe ruins
B	San Diego	1769	Restored

DOMINICAN MISSIONS

	MISSION	DATE FOUNDED	TYPE OF CHURCH
1	El Rosario	1774	Adobe ruins
2	Santo Domingo	1775	Adobe ruins
3	San Vicente	1780	Adobe ruins
4	San Miguel (at La Mision)	1787	Adobe ruins
5	Santo Tomas	1791	Adobe ruins
6	San Pedro Martir	1794	Adobe ruins
7	Santa Catalina	1797	Adobe ruins
8	Descanso	1814	No ruins
9	Guadalupe	1834	No ruins

HISTORY

The first land party was led by Captain Rivera y Moncada. It was his assign ment to visit the missions north of La Paz and collect everything that h could in the way of livestock, food and other supplies and to proceed wit these to the northernmost mission at Santa Maria. This task was successfull accomplished, although he was forced to move northwest from Santa Mari to obtain better pasturage. This was found at a place to be named Velicata After recouping there, Rivera y Moncada set out for San Diego, where he ar rived on May 14, 1769, after a journey of 50 days.

Portola and Serra led the last party and proceeded to Velicata where River y Moncada had rested. Here, Padre Serra founded Mission San Fernando the only mission to be established on the peninsula by the Franciscans. It wa to stay in operation for 49 years, providing one more link in the chain of mis sions stretching north from Loreto.

The ruins of this mission lie three miles west of the Transpeninsular High way (Highway 1), midway between the towns of El Rosario and Cataviña in what is a very remote area even today. Its location will be noted during the "Grand Tour" in Part III. It is hoped the traveler will pause briefly to honor the passage of Portola, Serra and their men on their historic journey.

The two leaders arrived in San Diego on July 1, 1769. While both land par ties had suffered great hardships, the crews of the ships that had arrived ear lier in April were in worse condition. Scurvy had claimed the lives of more than one-third of the crew on each vessel.

From this base in San Diego, Father Serra and his successors were to found 21 missions and to give birth to western civilization in what has become Cal ifornia in the United States. It is clear that the success of what has taken place in the north was predicated on events preceding it in the Baja peninsula. It is certainly ironic that the mighty giant of the north owes such an enormous debt to a place that most of its citizens know virtually nothing about.

FRANCISCANS AND DOMINICANS

1768	Franciscans arrive in Baja.
1769	Expedition to San Diego.
1772	Dominicans take over Baja missions.
1780–1782	Severe Indian epidemics.
1810–1822	Revolution against Spanish rule.
1822	Baja swears allegiance to Mexico.

Shown are ruins of the Dominican mission at Santo Domingo. Several sites similar to this one are a few miles from the Transpeninsular Highway.

The Dominicans

While Padre Serra labored to advance the cause of Christianity in Alta California, the Franciscans to the south briefly reigned. Following the Jesuits' expulsion from the Spanish domain, the Dominican order petitioned the King of Spain to obtain missionary territory in California. This request was granted, and the king ordered the peninsula to be divided equally between the Dominicans and the Franciscans.

The Franciscans, who had originally resisted their assignment to California, soon found that they were in continual disagreement with the peninsula's civil authorities. Various epidemics caused the death of some 2000 Indians in only three years, and the missions in the south were in a state of complete deterioration. It is not surprising that after some initial disagreement, the issue was resolved by providing the Dominicans with the entire peninsula, while the Franciscans received Alta California.

Dominican friars arrived in Loreto on October 14, 1772. There had been only four and one-half years of administration by the Franciscans. Inspection of the existing missions and their Indian charges made it clear to the Dominicans that their future lay to the north. Within two years, they established a new mission on the banks of the Rio del Rosario at the present town of El Rosario. The site of the buildings was to be moved down river some 28 years later. The crumbling ruins may be easily visited in a short side trip from the Transpeninsular Highway.

Within 20 years of their arrival on the peninsula, the Dominicans respond
ed to royal order by establishing five missions between Velicata and San D
ego. These served as stepping stones along the road pioneered by Junipero
Serra. The linkage with Alta California was complete. In the years to follow
four additional missions were founded in the northern portion of the penin
sula.

It should be noted that the churches that may be visited by today's travel
ers were built some years after the original missions were founded. Several
stone buildings were built by the Dominicans, but the only one still standing
is the beautiful church at San Ignacio. More recently, reconstruction at other
sites has been sponsored by the Mexican government and private groups.

Epidemics also followed the northward march of the Dominicans. Smallpox struck the northern missions from 1780 to 1782. Indians who were
moved from the north to populate the decimated southern missions often
met prompt death from disease.

A report prepared in 1786 paints this horrible picture: "The missions of
San Jose, Santiago, Todos Santos, San Javier, Loreto, Comondu, Cadego-
mo, Guadalupe and Mulegé are on the way to total extinction. The reason is
so evident that it leaves no doubt. Syphilis has taken possession of both sexes
to such a degree that mothers do not conceive, and if they do conceive, the
fetus is born with little hope of living. There are three times as many adults
who die as there are babies born." By 1800, there were no more than 4000
to 5000 Indians still living in the entire peninsula, only 10 percent of the
original population.

Changes in the peninsula's civil administration under Governor Portola
also led to the decay of the entire missionary system. These same adjustments
did bring about small increases in the number of Spaniards and *Mestizos*, and
in their hands rested the future of Baja and all of Mexico. In 1800, the estimate of their number was 700 to 800. They gained a living from cattle raising and farming. Historic accounts also frequently refer to the mining of
silver at Santa Ana (near present-day San Antonio and El Triunfo) as well as
the salt deposits on Isla Carmen. These salt mines had been worked from the
early days of the Jesuits and may be visited today by boat from Loreto or Puerto Escondido.

There were also important administrative changes made during the reign of
the Dominicans. Shortly after their arrival, a 1776 royal order separated the
provinces of Texas, New Mexico, New Viscaya, Coahuila, Sinaloa, Sonora
and the Californias into a new internal province to be governed from Arizpe
rather than Mexico City. The capital of the Californias was also to be
changed from Loreto to Monterey. Under this arrangement, peninsular
business matters had to travel from Loreto to Monterey and then to Arizpe.

Mariachis are a Baja fixture.

Mule rider surveys the majestic landscape.

Cardon cacti spotlighted by a spectactular sunset

Baja campfire at sunset

Ranchero Region

Espiritu Santo

It is a matter of considerable wonder that the state of California in the United States was once governed from what is now a small Mexican town (Arizpe) located on a side road northeast of present-day Hermosillo on the Mexican mainland. Twenty-eight years after the capital was moved to Monterey, the seat of peninsula government was to return to Loreto as the result of Baja and Alta California being separated into two provinces.

Of far more importance to Mexico were the events that took place from 1810 to 1822. Mexico was to rise in revolution against the authority of Spain, as were peoples throughout the Americas. Action began September 16, 1810, now Mexico's Independence Day. Independence was finally achieved in 1821; however, there remained some hesitancy by the peninsular people to accept the rule of the new Mexican nation. As a result, they were to come under attack from a amazingly unlikely source.

Almost two and one-half centuries after Francis Drake and Thomas Cavendish had left Baja's waters, another English adventurer appeared in the Sea of Cortez. Lord Thomas de Cochrane arrived off San Jose del Cabo with two ships on February 17, 1822. This seaman was the archenemy of Spain and had arrived after pillaging along the South American coast wherever any vestiges of Spanish authority were to be found.

A ship in the roadstead off San Jose del Cabo still flew the Spanish flag, and Cochrane used this as an excuse to sack the town. From there he turned to Loreto, where 15 days later he made a similar attack. The governor and other citizens fled, but Cochrane was repulsed by 15 men led by Ensign Jose Maria Mata. Mata took command and felt that the time had come to swear allegiance to Mexico. An official ceremony took place in July of that year at Loreto; the peninsula formally took its place in the Mexican nation.

The dominance of the mission system and the authority of Spain had come to an end. In the years ahead, events on the peninsula would reflect the political aftermath of the revolution. Civil rather than religious matters would dominate, and war would come with the United States.

The Mexican Nation

Many aspects of life were to change on the Baja California peninsula and throughout Mexico following independence from Spain. Mexican officials arrived from the mainland to rule in Loreto. In time, all the missions were converted to pueblos, many lands distributed to those who worked them, and religious affairs turned over to the secular clergy. The peninsula was divided into four municipalities, each under the authority of a mayor. In 1828, the town of Loreto was largely destroyed by heavy rains and flooding. The capital was transferred briefly to the silver mining town of San Antonio and then, in 1830, to La Paz. Loreto was to languish in obscurity for many years.

Political passions rose in the peninsula. There were Indian uprisings in the north. Uprisings of citizens and soldiers occurred at La Paz, and small battles were fought. As the influence of the clergy dissipated, economic factors and the press for land ownership were becoming important issues to the peninsula's people. Finally, as the midpoint of the 19th century approached, the peninsula was to be caught up in the fringes of war between Mexico and the United States.

THE MEXICAN NATION

1822	Baja swears allegiance to Mexico.
1830	Capital moved—Loreto to La Paz.
1846–1848	Mexican-American war in Baja.
1853	William Walker invades Baja.
1864	Baja leased to the Americans.
1883	Law to Colonization passed.
1885	Copper mining at Santa Rosalia.
1901	Founding of Mexicali.
1911	Revolutionary activity in the north.
1933	End of the Law of Colonization.
1952	Baja California becomes a state.
1974	Baja California Sur becomes a state.

The Mexican-American War

Momentous events were occurring in the outlying Mexican lands that are today a part of southwestern United States. Texas had declared itself a separate republic in the 1830s, and Mexico's General Santa Ana was defeated by the forces of Sam Houston. In Alta California, there were only scattered Mexican forces and settlers along the coast. English-speaking peoples from the east were migrating west and taking up lands.

It became clear that both England and France coveted possession of Alta California and its fabulous harbor at San Francisco. By 1837, the United States was making proposals to Mexico for the purchase of Mexican lands in the west. A mood of expansionism, manifest destiny prevailed in the United States. In 1845, James Polk was elected president, standing on a political platform advocating the annexation of Texas and the purchase of Alta California from Mexico.

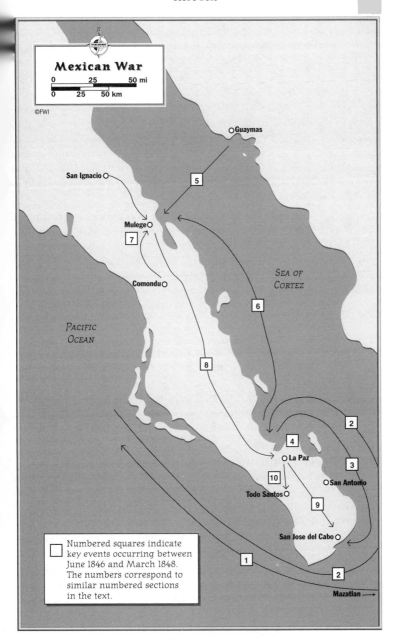

As a result of the election mandate, the United States issued, and received acceptance of, an invitation for Texas to join the Federal Union. This annexation infuriated Mexican authorities and resulted in armed conflict along the border. In addition to the issue of Texas, the United States had various grievances against Mexico and also feared the potential takeover of California by England or France. As a result, the United States declared war on May 11, 1846.

Prior to the outbreak of hostilities, the United States had been prepared to pay approximately $25 million for California, depending on the inclusion or exclusion of Baja California. This either/or proviso indicates that obtaining possession of Baja California was not a primary goal of the United States government. However, once war started, specific military steps were taken to bring the peninsula under U.S. authority.

The decisive battles of the Mexican-American War took place in mainland Mexico. Invading United States forces under the command of Zachary Taylor and Winfield Scott conducted successful campaigns. The latter general captured Mexico City on September 14, 1847. Lesser actions took place in New Mexico and Alta California. Perhaps the least known of all were the battles that took place in the Baja peninsula, where the fighting was actually heavier than it was to the north. These peninsular events are depicted on a map and are amplified below. The item numbers in the text correspond to similar numbers on the map.

1. A squadron of eight U.S. Navy ships and their marine contingents had been stationed in Pacific waters for some time. They were commanded by Commodore John D. Sloat, who was under instructions to occupy San Francisco and other Alta California ports in the event of war with Mexico. Sloat stationed his fleet at Mazatlan, where there was a U.S. consul; it was apparently the best site along the entire Pacific coast for him to receive instruction from Washington.

    On May 16, 1846, he received word that fighting had begun along the Rio Grande. While he did not know that war had been declared several days earlier, he moved his ships north along the California coast and during July took possession of Monterey, San Francisco and San Diego—without resistance.

2. After completing this assignment, some of the U.S. ships returned south to blockade the Mexican coast and take possession of additional ports. In September 1846, these ships arrived in La Paz. The U.S. commander told local authorities they were under U.S. control and secured an agreement that they would remain neutral. The U.S. forces were under orders to utilize this neutrality approach to pacify the Mexicans and to make them more receptive to a change in authority.

3. On Mar. 29, 1847, the U.S. sloop *Portsmouth* sailed to San Jose del Cabo and imposed the same arrangement.

4. Prior to the declaration of war, Congress had authorized the formation of battalions of volunteers as backup forces to the regular army. The first was to be the First Battalion of Volunteers from the state of New York. It was composed mostly of young men eager for adventure and was referred to in New York newspapers as the "Baby Regiment."

   The battalion was placed on ships and transported around Cape Horn to Alta California, where it arrived in spring 1847. The young men were assigned to guard the various towns in the region. Subsequently, two companies were ordered to La Paz, where they went ashore without incident on July 20, 1847.

5. Word reached the Mexican government of the neutral position taken by their small military force that was stationed at La Paz. In anger, they dispatched Captain Manual Pinada and a small group of officers and arms to take over military matters in the peninsula. Pinada had previous knowledge of the terrain and people of Baja. He crossed the Sea of Cortez from Guaymas and arrived at Mulegé in September 1847. Here, he organized the local people into a force to defend the peninsula.

This is an aerial view of the estuary forming the mouth of the Rio Santa Rosalia at Mulegé. This area was the site of the Mexican-American War battle between the U.S. sloop Dale *and Mexican patriots.*

6. Hearing of Pinada's arrival, the Americans dispatched the sloop *Dale* to Mulegé, where it arrived in October. The sloop's commander sent a message ashore demanding that the inhabitants preserve neutrality. Pi-

nada responded with a prideful message that he and his soldiers would defend their country until the last drop of blood was shed.

Hearing this, the U.S. commander sent boats ashore with some 60 men and a small artillery piece. This force was fired upon by Pinada and his small group of men. There followed a considerable exchange of gunfire, including some 135 canister shots from the *Dale* lying offshore. The proud Mexicans held fast, and by afternoon the Americans returned to their ship.

Having met with resistance, the *Dale* left Mulegé, leaving a smaller ship behind to provide a blockade. All this action took place at the mouth of the Rio Santa Rosalia near El Sombrerito, a small but conspicuous peak that now bears the Mulegé lighthouse. It is in plain view from Highway 1 and is within a few yards of the **Serenidad Hotel**.

7. The heroic defense of Mulegé gave rise to considerable public spirit. Pinada was able to recruit a force that Mexican historians say numbered about 300 men. They came from the pueblos of San Ignacio, Mulegé and Comondu, and later from San Antonio and Todos Santos.

8. Pinada marched his soldiers south. Part of the force was detached and sent to San Jose del Cabo. On November 16, 1847, the main body of some 180 men under Pinada attacked the New York Volunteers who had fortified themselves in buildings within La Paz. There was to follow 12 days of fierce fighting, with the Americans defending themselves with cannon fire and by tearing down buildings that were providing the Mexicans with cover. At one point these forces penetrated to within 100 feet of the fortified Americans, but Pinada finally had to withdraw due to lack of ammunition. After the fighting was over, American reinforcements arrived by sea.

9. After hearing of the Mexican successes at Mulegé, the citizens of San Jose del Cabo tore down the U.S. flag and declared an end to U.S. rule. As a result, U.S. ships arrived and left a detachment of 24 men. As at La Paz, this force was required to fortify itself in the town buildings when they were attacked by the Mexicans from Pinada's forces that had marched south from La Paz. The assault failed, and the Mexican leader, Naval Lieutenant Jose Antonio Mijares, was mortally wounded. A monument to this fallen hero may be seen in the town plaza at San Jose del Cabo.

As at La Paz, U.S. ships arrived, and the garrison was reinforced with 46 men. The Mexican forces were also reinforced by Pinada's soldiers from the north. When the U.S. ships left, the Mexicans renewed the attack in mid-January 1848. They surrounded the U.S. position and cut off all sources of water and supplies.

By mid-February, surrender seemed inevitable; but reinforcements again arrived by sea. The Mexicans attacked these newcomers. Fierce fighting and artillery fire was to occur on the way from the sea to the pueblo. In the end, the arrival of these reinforcements required the Mexicans to retire to the north.

10. During March, the U.S. forces from La Paz conducted several campaigns to put an end to the Mexican resistance. On March 27, 1848, they captured Captain Pinada in San Antonio. A few days later, a force of more than 200 Americans surrounded and captured the remaining Mexican defenders north of Todos Santos and fighting came to an end.

Much of the fighting at San Jose del Cabo and the final actions at San Antonio and Todos Santos were to take place after the signing of the peace treaty on February 2, 1848, but this information had not been received in the peninsula.

Having been victorious in the major land battles on the Mexican mainland, the United States was in a position to demand a harsh settlement. However, its proposal was not to differ greatly from that made prior to the war. Under its terms, Mexico ceded Alta California and New Mexico. In return, it received $15 million, and the United States agreed to pay various claims held by its citizens against Mexico.

The original draft of the treaty presented by the United States included the Baja peninsula within the lands to be ceded by Mexico. In its counter-proposal, Mexico asserted "The cession of Lower California ...offers great embarrassment to Mexico, considering the position of that peninsula, facing our coast of Sonora, which is separated from it by the narrow Gulf of Cortez." The United States negotiator bowed to the Mexican position. As a result, the Baja peninsula together with sufficient territory to tie it to the mainland was retained in the Mexican republic.

One can readily draw the conclusion that the principal objective of the U.S. occupation of the peninsula was that of obtaining a bargaining chip. If so, this posture was apparently not conveyed to the U.S. military commanders, who assured the Mexican citizens in the south that United States administration was there to stay. With these assurances, many Mexicans placed themselves openly on the side of the invading forces. After the peace treaty, these people were branded as traitors. When the U.S. military left the peninsula in September 1848, more than 300 of these people were taken to Monterey in Alta California to prevent their being killed by their outraged fellow Mexicans.

While they were not to prevail in the military actions on the peninsula, the Mexican forces obviously conducted themselves with valor. This is

particularly impressive when one considers that most of them were no
professional soldiers but only citizens gathered from far-flung town
where there was little knowledge of the overall motivations of the war
Hopefully, today's tourists will stop at the sites and monuments relating
to this conflict and pay homage to the combatants.

*The steam engine monument at Santa Rosalia stands as a remnant of this
historic town's heyday as a copper mining center. Other old mining machinery
is also on display nearby.*

Filibusters and Frauds

Turbulent years lay ahead for Baja. The decade following the war was to
give rise to a period of filibustering. Filibusters were lawless military adventurers who entered Mexico and Central American countries with the intent
of overthrowing the national authorities. Americans involved in these activities in Mexico had as their objective the annexing of the conquered areas
into the United States, as had occurred with Texas.

The most notorious of these individuals was William Walker. He gathered
48 armed followers in San Francisco and sailed for Mexico. On November 3,
1853, he landed at La Paz, seized control from the local authorities and declared the establishment of the Republic of Sonora. Within a few days, he
was attacked by Mexican forces and lost six men. He retreated to Cabo San
Lucas and eventually to Ensenada.

Near Ensenada there were several armed conflicts and deaths. During the
weeks to follow, Walker's men asserted their authority at San Vicente, San
Quintin and El Rosario, all towns visited by today's traveler along the
Transpeninsular Highway. From this area, Walker moved east to conquer

mainland Sonora, but in turn was defeated by the rigors of the Sonoran desert. He was forced to return to the United States, where he was captured and tried.

In the years to come, William Walker was to move his operations to several Central American countries. He was put to death in 1860 by Honduran authorities, bringing to an end the era of filibustering.

These same years saw civil war within Mexico between groups with opposing liberal and conservative political views. Baja California was firmly on the liberal side. There was some fighting in the peninsula. The year 1857 saw the establishment of a constitution for Mexico and Benito Juarez became president in 1861. Statues and other references to Juarez may be seen throughout Mexico.

In 1862, new silver mines were discovered in the historic mining district of San Antonio in the mountains south of La Paz. The area became a bonanza, and many miners came from the United States. The ruins of the smelters and other facilities may be seen at the town of El Triunfo and San Antonio and are included in Part III.

In the years to follow, some 25 to 30 mining and colonizing land frauds were known to have been perpetrated on North Americans using the claimed resources of the Baja peninsula as bait. The most outrageous of them all was instigated by none other than President Juarez himself.

As a means of obtaining badly needed funds, Juarez actually leased some two-thirds of the entire peninsula to a U.S. citizen named Jacob P. Leese. In 1864, Leese sold out to a group of New York capitalists whose object was to raise $25 million, through fraud, on a massive scale. Announcements in California newspapers read "Free lands, free commerce, homes for the poor, riches for the wealthy. For the first 1000 colonists who acquire land in Lower California a lot of 160 acres is offered absolutely free." Colonists were actually transported to the Bahía Magdalena region to till the "pure black humus soil where the grass was higher than the shoulders of a horse." The lease was cancelled within a few years because the company was unable to meet some of its near-impossible terms.

Twenty years after issuance of the lease to Jacob Leese, Mexico passed a Law of Colonization as a means of raising foreign capital. Under this 1883 law, some 30 land concessions covering vast areas of the peninsula were granted to foreigners. Few were aggressively pursued, but as a result Mexican citizens were prohibited from developing the land of their own country and economic growth was impeded. This era of concessions did not end until 1933. Because of its unsuccessful background in foreign concessions, the Mexican government today, understandably, maintains stringent control on private ownership of businesses and foreign ownership of land.

At least one of the Law of Colonization concessions was aggressively pursued. This concession was issued on July 17, 1885, for the mining of the large copper deposits found some years earlier at Santa Rosalia. It came into the hands of a French syndicate that operated the mine and smelter until 1954. Coal and coke were shipped from northern Europe in square-rigged ships to the smelter at Santa Rosalia, one of the last world ports used in the age of sail. The smelter, French buildings, port facilities and machinery provide a must stop for the traveler along the Transpeninsular Highway.

Santa Rosalia's copper operation was also to be of importance to the peninsula's history in another way. Labor conditions there have been described by one Mexican historian as "nauseating." This situation was to contribute to labor unrest and revolutionary uprisings in the future.

Activities in the North

As can be seen, historic events were concentrated in the southern portion of the peninsula up to this point. At the time of passage of the Law of Colonization in 1883, there were some 30,000 people in the entire peninsula. Only a few hundred lived in the northern portion. In this region, all of the missions had been abandoned. Ensenada was little more than a ranch, and Mexicali did not exist. But conditions were to change rapidly as the result of the land concessions issued by the federal government.

In 1884, large acreages of land in the north came under the control of New York capitalists who organized the International Company of Mexico. The usual land-promotion schemes were soon to follow, with the objective of selling land to gullible persons north of the border. However, the developers were required to make some investment in Mexico.

The town site of Ensenada was laid out, and various business enterprises sprang up. Within four years, Ensenada had a population of approximately 1400 people. Government inspectors issued such a glowing report that in 1887 the peninsula was formerly divided into two parts, and the District of the North was to have its own government, independent of La Paz.

In 1899 gold was discovered at El Alamo, southeast of Ensenada. Thousands of miners poured in from north of the border. In the United States an irrigation project was undertaken to bring water from the Rio Colorado to the Imperial Valley. Small communities sprang up along the border as an indirect result of activities in the United States. One of these was Mexicali, which was founded in 1901, and was destined to become the capital city of the state of Baja California. Within a few years after the turn of the century, it became apparent that few projects of the International Company of Mexico were to flourish, but life in the north had taken root.

NO MAN'S LAND

When Cortez and the conquistadores
To Baja California came,

They discovered a poor land
That they could not tame;

Then the missionaries tried
With the same short success,

They found very little
And they left even less;

The "civilization" they brought
For the Indians' release

Killed most of the natives
With the white man's disease.

No treasures were gained
When Spain's flag was unfurled

And the souls converted
Soon departed this world.

So Baja was abandoned,
Like a poor bastard child,

To shift for itself
and revert to the wild.

—Ken Reimer

Political Turmoil

In the minds of some North Americans, Mexico is a land of revolution and political unrest. Actually, the country has had a remarkably stable government for many decades, but its reputation in this regard suffers from its previous political turmoil at the turn of the century. This period will now be briefly reviewed.

There were small armed conflicts in the south in 1865, 1875 and in 1880. More serious unrest was to follow in both the north and south after the turn of the century. These activities reflected political turmoil in the nation as a whole, arising from the 30-year dictatorial reign of President Porfirio Diaz and from various socialist and labor-oriented movements that were present in many parts of the world. Revolution was to force Diaz to resign in 1911, and his successor also was overthrown and assassinated.

Also in 1911, revolution broke out in the newly populated areas in Baja California along the U.S.–Mexican border. This conflict was led by Mexican citizens based in the United States. Small armies of Mexicans were organized, and battles were waged with Mexican federal troops in the general area around Mexicali, Ensenada and Tijuana. For a time, Tijuana was controlled by revolutionary forces. Additional federal troops from the Mexican mainland were sent to quell the uprisings. As a result of this unrest, some 30,000 U.S. troops were sent to protect the international border.

The revolutionary forces may be labeled socialist, although historians also utilize the terms liberal and anarchist. Their leaders clearly associated themselves with labor movements in the United States that advocated strikes, boycotts and sabotage.

Added intrigue was spawned by the political activities of foreigners who owned or controlled most of the land in the peninsula. There were always the threats, some real and some invented, that a popular uprising would be used as the rationale for the purchasing, or otherwise annexing, of the peninsula by the United States, as had occurred with Texas some 65 years prior. Such an event would of course have been favored by the U.S. landowners.

Revolutionary action in the south followed the disturbances in the north by two years. It was to be more purely Mexican, without the overtones of involvement by foreigners. The leader of this "Constitutionalist Revolution" was Felix Ortega, who organized a band of armed men who fought with federal troops in many battles at La Paz and in the mountains and towns to the south. From 1913 to 1915, Ortega's forces frequently took refuge in the cape region mountains. Today's tourists drive through this same terrain on the Transpeninsular Highway between La Paz and San Jose del Cabo.

The size of the forces engaged in these battles was often considerably larger than those involved in the war with the United States 65 years earlier, and thus represents the largest military operation ever to take place on the Baja peninsula. While the federal forces prevailed, as in the north, Baja's citizens are proud that their efforts contributed to the civil liberties and land reforms gained on a national level from these revolutionary activities. The Constitution of 1917 was the result.

Summary of Activities in the South

Revolutionary activities continued on the mainland, but a relative calm prevailed in the southern peninsula. Various public works projects were undertaken starting in 1920, including the beginning of construction of the Transpeninsular Highway between La Paz and Bahía Magdalena.

One of the most important events in the history of the peninsula took place in 1933, when the national government recovered the lands that had been encumbered for 50 years in various foreign-dominated concessions. Only from this very late date could the citizens of the peninsula were able to t colonize and develop their own land.

Agricultural settlement was started at Santo Domingo, north of the highway junction at Ciudad Insurgentes. The extensive farming activities resulting from this early effort are still evident. A second agricultural effort was started at San Juan de Los Planes in 1946, and may be visited on Highway 286.

During this period of agricultural development, the peninsula suffered the tragic loss of its pearl and oyster fishing industry. Between 1936 and 1949, the oysters in the Sea of Cortez were attacked by an unknown disease. Pearl bearing oysters, which had lured the original explorers and which had been a source of wealth for 400 years, disappeared.

In its place, as a source of revenue, hotel and other tourist facilities came into being in the 1940s and tourism is now the region's principal industry. The population gradually increased, and in 1974 the southern territory proudly entered the Union. It and Quintana Roo in the Yucatan peninsula were the last two Mexican states.

Summary of Activities in the North

Following the revolutionary activities of the early 1900s, the northern territory saw a period of spectacular development. Two progressive and skilled administrators governed during most years between 1915 and 1929. The second of these, Abelardo Rodriguez, later became president of the Mexican Republic. Roads, schools and extensive other public works were developed.

Much of this activity was financed by astute taxation on gambling houses, prostitution and drug traffic centering largely in Tijuana. In 1920, the Mexicans struck it rich with the coming of prohibition in the United States. The saloons and restaurants of Tijuana contributed on a massive scale to the prosperity of the territory. Tijuana's greatest natural resource was its location adjacent to the international boundary. As in the south, the inefficient land concessions were recaptured in the 1930s, but here the process was not as simple.

Most land in the fertile Valle de Mexicali west of the Rio Colorado was owned by foreign interests under the name of the Colorado River Land Company. These lands were not farmed, as existing irrigation systems served only the Imperial Valley to the north in the United States. Company lands were used only for grazing, with the labor performed by imported Chinese and other Asians.

It required protests by local Mexicans and action by the progressive President Lazaro Gardenas to bring about removal of the foreign interests and placement of the lands in the hands of Mexican farmers. This action was completed in 1937. New villages promptly sprung up, and the population rapidly increased.

Large-scale irrigation of the valley lands followed as the result of a water treaty with the United States in 1945, and the construction of the Morelos

Dam on the Rio Colorado three years later. During these same years, construction work began on Baja's only railroad. After its completion in 1948, for the first time in history there was a land transportation link between the Baja peninsula and the Mexican mainland that did not pass through the United States.

The towering eagle statue is at the 28th parallel.

The Mexican constitution requires that a territory must have a population of 80,000 to merit admission into the national union. By 1950, there were actually more than 225,000 people. For this and other reasons, the northern territory became Mexico's 29th state on January 16, 1952.

OUR DEVELOPING COUNTRY NEIGHBOR

Statues of three of Mexico's famous men are in the civic plaza in Ensenada. On the left is Benito Juarez, a leader in the reform movement.

This chapter is concerned with Baja's people and her political, economic and social systems. Much of what is presented is of a positive nature and should provide encouragement to those interested in beneficial social change. And I hope you might concur that acquiring an understanding of a country's people may, in the final analysis, be the most important benefit derived from travel to a foreign land.

In recent years there has been much reference in the news to the Third World and to developing countries. Many of us may have a vague conception as to where these countries are located. We are perhaps most likely to think of nations in Africa, South America and Southeast Asia. We may overlook the fact that the United States has such a country on its southern doorstep, and in visiting the rural areas of Baja California we are viewing some of the last sections of Mexico to experience modernization. The states of Baja California Sur, along with Quintana Roo in southeast Mexico, were the last to receive statehood in Mexico.

Mexico and Baja California are considerably more advanced than the average Third World country. They nevertheless share many characteristics and problems in common with these nations. As a result, there is much to learn about the developing world through a trip not very far from home.

In other portions of this book, the material presented is founded on some degree of my personal experience or training. In the present chapter, I clearly tread beyond my fields of expertise. A friend once told me that I know just enough to be dangerous. Perhaps that will be the result here.

It will also be difficult to discuss the subjects of sociology, economics and politics with complete objectivity. I apologize in advance for the almost certain bias of my personal convictions. Conversely, one rarely finds two economists or politicians who agree with each other, so perhaps I am after all on sound ground. I believe that the worst course of action I could take would be to omit discussion of these subjects.

Mexico's People

Some seven to nine million Indians lived in what is present-day Mexico when Cortez arrived in 1519. (A century later, their numbers were reduced to only one million by disease and warfare.) These various Indian nations had developed some of the most brilliant civilizations in the world. Today's Mexican is the end product of the intermarriage of these people with Europeans, almost all of Spanish origin. The result has been the emergence of a new race, the *Mestizos*. These are the people you will meet in Baja. There are millions of Indians still living in Mexico, but very few of them reside in Baja.

Population Growth

Although Mexico begat a new race of people, a case can now be made that they have made too much of a good thing. Mexico's exploding population is a serious national problem that tends to cancel out the country's significant economic advances.

The population of Mexico was 13.5 million in 1900. It grew slowly during the revolutionary period and was only 15 million in 1920. Continued slow growth brought the population to 19.6 million in 1940. Then after World War II the explosion began. There were 35 million in 1960; 46 million in

1970; 67 million in 1980, and 94 million at last count. During these latter years, Mexico's population growth rate was 3.4 percent, one of the highest in the world.

During most of this period, the law, public policy, individual inclination and the influence of the Roman Catholic Church favored population growth. Perhaps influenced by the results of the 1970 census, the government came to realize that Mexico had a population problem. The year 1973 saw passage of the General Population Law, which began a series of steps aimed at integrated family planning. The result has been one of the most successful state-coordinated programs of family planning in the world.

Today, free contraceptives are supplied at government clinics; population and sex education are included in the public education system, and there is dissemination of material on these subjects on radio and television. Although abortion is prohibited by law, one in six pregnancies ends in this manner, often resulting in serious harm to the woman. The overall result of these actions has been a reduction of the population growth rate to 2.4 percent by 1984, and the national goal is to reduce it to one percent by the year 2000.

The United Nations reports that many developing countries have achieved substantial reductions in birth rates and that the most important factors involved relate to improvements in (1) family planning, (2) health and (3) education. (We will examine Mexico's progress in the last two areas in the pages to come.) Ironically, a by-product of improvements in these areas is a marked increase in life expectancy, a factor that counteracts lowering of the birth rate. This has occurred in Mexico and accounts for much of the population explosion.

In Baja, my personal observations can attest to substantial population increases in nearly all communities, both large and small, although there has been no detectable increase in the number of communities themselves. Baja is still largely a thinly populated land, although the traveler on Highway 1 must pass south of El Rosario to realize that this is true.

Immigration

Mexico's population growth is also of concern to the United States. Prior to World War II, the vast majority of immigrants into the United States came from western Europe. A quota system established by U.S. law had the effect of maintaining this European ethnic composition while minimizing the influx of peoples from other countries. Since the war, the law has changed and the country again is experiencing a wave of immigration, but this time consisting largely of peoples from Asia and Latin America. Approximately 40 percent of the total inflow into the U.S. comes from Mexico.

In the past, a great majority of this immigration from Mexico entered the United States without legal permission. This situation aroused national concern and the U.S. Immigration Reform Act was passed in 1988. Then, Proposition 187 was placed on the November 1994 ballot in California. It called for widespread reductions in the expenditure of government funds received by persons residing in the state illegally. It passed by an overwhelming majority. As I write, the new law is under court appeal, but the anti-immigration movement has spread to the national level. U.S. border surveillance has been greatly increased, and national legislation aimed at preventing illegal immigration and reducing legal entry are under consideration.

Press reports indicate that activist groups representing Latino people in the United States look on this anti-immigration movement as also being anti-Latino—more simply put, they feel it is racist. I thus anticipated that I might encounter backlash anti-American sentiment on the part of Mexicans in Baja during my last visit. This was clearly not the case. I suspect that most Mexicans have far more pressing personal concerns on their minds than U.S. politics. I personally have no trouble in distinguishing between my support for control of illegal immigration and my affection for the Mexican people. In other words, support for enforcement of the law does not translate into racism. Perhaps you might wish to test your own views on these issues as you travel in Baja.

Current birth rates in the United States have declined in recent years, and immigration now accounts for almost half of the country's population growth. If the present trends continue, a time will come in the next century when all population growth will come from immigration. I make no judgments as to whether this situation is good or bad, but it does raise questions about the future size and ethnic proportions of the United States.

Government and Politics

Although Mexico freed herself from Spanish rule in 1821, the new nation continued to be dominated by the institutions of the past. The country was ruled by authoritarian leaders. The Catholic Church controlled from one-third to one-half of the national wealth and owned nearly one-half of the land. All but 3 percent of the remaining land was vested in the hands of a mere 830, mostly absentee owners.

The *Mestizos* gradually grew to dominate the racial composition of the country and became the core of various liberal movements that culminated in the revolution of 1910. The Constitution of February 5, 1917 resulted from this struggle. Almost all of Mexico's current political and economic institutions and progress stem from this date and constitution. The Mexican citizen's civil rights guarantees are contained in the first 29 articles. Mexico's Indian, rather than her Spanish, heritage predominate after 1917.

The new constitution also severely limits the position of the Catholic Church. Today the church may not own property and priests are not permitted to vote or wear clerical garb in public. (NOTE—Press reports in early 1992 indicate that the Mexican congress has given preliminary approval to a series of constitutional reforms that would give the Church formal recognition by the government. I am sorry that I cannot update this report.)

The 96 years between Mexico's independence from Spain (1821) and enactment of her present constitution (1917) were filled with upheaval. There were wars with other nations, civil war, the loss of one-half the nation's territory to the United States, and political, economic and social degeneration. It can be seen that while western civilization was well established in Mexico far earlier than in Canada and the United States, Mexico's modern era was to get a very late and tumultuous start. Its underdeveloped status is a product of its history.

The Government

Although the Constitution of 1917 establishes a tripartite division of power among the executive, legislative and judicial branches of the government, the authority of the executive far exceeds that of the latter two. The president is elected by universal suffrage for a six-year term. (Minimum voting age is 18.) An individual may serve only one term. A recent presidential election campaign received widespread press coverage in the United States when one of the leading presidential candidates was assassinated in Tijuana. The president appoints a cabinet to oversee more than 20 ministries, or *Secretarias*. You will see this word and the names of the various ministries in numerous places in your travels in Baja California.

There are two houses of the national legislature. The Senate is composed of two individuals elected for six-year terms from each of the 31 states and the Federal District. The Chamber of Deputies is made up of more than 200 members elected for three-year terms. Each member represents a specific number of citizens. The members of both houses are barred from re-election, so there is an often disruptive turnover in both the legislature and the ministries following elections.

The state governments consist of an elected governor and a Chamber of Deputies, but the autonomy of the states is limited. The federal system is not the result of a merging compact among independent states as in the United States. In Mexico, the states have been created by the national government. Federal financing and administration of programs dominate at all levels, and the states are expected to enforce federal law. While traveling in Baja, you will see the names and acronyms of federal agencies on signs and government construction projects throughout the peninsula. (NOTE—My most recent travels in Baja indicate a reduction of a least the outward signs of the federal government. Perhaps this is merely because I have grown accustomed to Mexican conditions, but I believe it reflects the countries steady move away from socialistic tendencies over the past six to eight years.)

MUNICIPALITIES	
Municipio*	Cabacera Municipal**
Baja California	
Tijuana	Tijuana
Tecate	Tecate
Mexicali	Mexicali
Baja California Sur	
Mulegé	Santa Rosalia
Comondu	Ciudad Constitucion
La Paz	La Paz
Los Cabos	San Jose del Cabo

* Municipio: Municipality

** Cabacera Municipal: Seat of government

Each of Baja's two states is divided into municipalities similar to those of counties in the United States. The cities do not incorporate and establish separate governments. Thus, the official that tourists may refer to as the mayor of Ensenada is in fact the *Presidente Municipal* of an area of hundreds of square miles, which includes many communities other than Ensenada. The municipalities of the peninsula are shown in the table. Look for the *Palacio Municipal* (Municipal Palace) when you visit the towns which are the *Cabacera Municipal* (the Seat of Government). The Municipal boundaries are also marked by signs along the Transpeninsular Highway.

In other towns, the government building will bear the name *Delegado Municipal*. The *Delegado* (Delegate) is an official appointed by the *Presidente Municipal* to represent him in the area in question. In the smallest communities, there are *subdelegados*. Thus, the citizens of a small town find themselves governed by a *Subdelegado, Delegado, Presidente Municipal, Gobernador* and finally, *El Presidente*.

Politics

A common characteristic of developing countries throughout the world is the presence of one dominant political party. Mexico has been no exception. Since 1929, the country's government has been dominated at all levels by the *Partido Revolucionario Institucion* (Institutional Revolutionary Party). You will see the PRI symbol in many places Baja.

In reading of the immense powers of the Mexican president, and the domination of the PRI, one could easily come to the conclusion that the country's government should be classified as a dictatorship. Certainly, one party dominance has resulted in substantial government corruption. Nevertheless, the PRI has provided Mexico with a stable administration for decades. There is a minimum of domination by the military, and social programs aimed at providing a better life for the masses are in evidence everywhere.

In the past the PRI party's nominees for president, governors, and other officials was tantamount to their being elected. They often received some 90 percent of the vote, although it has been alleged that vote fraud was widespread.

The principal opposition party has been the *Partido de Accion Nacional* (National Action Party). Its acronym is PAN. PAN's agenda can best be described as "conservative" and it is supported by the business community and the Catholic Church. However, emerging in 1988 was a coalition of several liberal-leaning parties, who along with the PAN mounted a serious challenge to PRI. Vote counting fraud was again charged by the opposition parties, and the PRI candidate was eventually announced to have won with 50.5 percent of the vote. It is widely alleged that PRI actually lost the election.

It would appear that Mexico is now on the threshold a multiparty political system and several state's governors are now from opposition parties. Some may conclude that traveling in Mexico is unwise because of this political situation. I firmly believe this to be untrue. In my view the political changes occurring in Mexico are positive and will have no direct effects on foreign visitors. My travels in Baja after the 1988 and 1994 elections were no different than they were in past years.

The Military

Those who keep abreast of current events in developing countries are well aware that many nations' military establishments dominate and often overthrow the civilian authority. This was true in Mexico in the distant past, but it is generally conceded today that the military has only modest influence on the government. The last president who was also a general left office in 1942.

The Mexican army, air force and navy are assigned the responsibility of defending the independence of the country, but from a practical standpoint, their most significant mission is the preservation of internal order. The navy patrols the coastline and in general assumes the duties assigned to the Coast Guard in the United States. Over the years, the army has been called on to suppress riots and other forms of civil unrest, to control illicit drug traffic, to register firearms and to undertake similar activities. In effect, the army is assigned duties that citizens of Canada and the United States would normally associate with the civil police.

Because of their policing responsibilities, the army and navy are much in evidence to the tourist in Baja, which, from a public relations standpoint, is unfortunate. These people normally carry automatic rifles and those of us from north of the border tend to associate such weapons with trouble. A uniformed policeman with a sidearm in the United States is one thing; a soldier in brown combat fatigues and helmet carrying a machine gun, in a country where the traveler is a bit squeamish to begin with, is quite another.

My messages here are that you will frequently see the military, that its role is keeping the peace, and that you should not be concerned.

You will see the military at their encampments in many peninsula communities. There are also small detachments at recreation spots such as Puerto Escondido and Santispac. Usually there is an enlisted man on guard duty who speaks no English and who has an exaggerated view of the importance of his assignment. I have found them almost universally brusque, quick to wave their rifle about, and obviously wanting me to depart. I have also found that if you can arrange to see an officer, only courtesy and helpfulness prevail. My counsel is to avoid the military unless you have a particular need, and then ask for the brass.

Mexico's Economy

A Developing Country

A majority of the countries in the world are considered developing countries. They are endeavoring to improve the quality of life of their people through industrialization and other means. From an economic standpoint, such a country is defined as "one that has not yet reached a stage of economic development characterized by the growth of industrialization, and a level of national income sufficient to yield the domestic savings required to finance the investment necessary for further growth." This complex definition simply means that a developing country must rely on foreign investment and international borrowing to fuel its economic growth. During the 1970s and '80s, Mexico, along with Brazil, led the world in such borrowing. Mexico made rapid industrial growth and is now classified by the World Bank as a Newly Industrialized Country and as a Middle Income Developing Country.

This situation was clearly apparent in Baja during the mid-1980s. The initial field work needed to produce this book was done from about 1984 to 1988. The dominant impression that lingers in my mind from this period was that government developmental activities were everywhere. There were new roads, water lines, schools, tourist facilities and everything imaginable. And on one's next trip, many of these projects were abandoned or had received little maintenance. One had to ask, as Mexico is supposed to be a poor country, where is the money coming from for all this development? International borrowing was no doubt the answer. But, by this same period, borrowing became Mexico's curse, and the country's payments on its immense national debt threatened to collapse its economy. The situation was known as *La Crisis* (The Crisis).

Mexico apparently learned from the crisis. Developmental activities in much of Baja have clearly slowed down, and the emphasis has shifted from government to the private projects. Private developments have proceeded rapidly in the last several years in the Cape Area at the peninsula's southern tip and in the industrial areas along the U.S. border. But, the balance of Baja has experienced more moderate growth, and in some cases, little at all.

Foreign Investment

In 1973, Mexico enacted the Foreign Investment Law. It was designed to promote foreign investment, while at the same time ensuring the government's autonomy and control over the country's economy. Under this law, a foreign investor's interest in a commercial enterprise was limited to 49 percent while a Mexican national was required to own the controlling 51 percent. Mexico coveted foreign assistance, but on its own terms.

In addition, a foreigner could not own real estate within 100 kilometers of the border or 50 kilometers of the coastline. That very well excludes the desirable locations in the Baja peninsula. Foreign interest in land was secured through a trust arrangement that required that after 30 years the trust must be sold to persons or entities capable of acquiring legal title. It is understandable why Mexico would not wish to engender a recurrence of the land frauds and other negative aspects of past foreign control of its assets, but many feel that these rules inhibit, rather than encourage, investment.

As of 1991, some of Mexico's landownership laws have been changed or are in the process of change. Then, 1994 saw passage of the North American Free Trade Agreement (NAFTA). How all of these developments will effect development in Mexico is beyond my field of expertise. I suggest caution to potential investors and advise that they seek the counsel of a competent attorney not connected with persons offering land for sale or lease.

A unique form of foreign investment, the *maquiladora* program, occurs at Baja's border cities. It started two decades ago when the Mexican government permitted these cities merchants to import U.S. goods duty-free so that local citizens would not do their shopping north of the border. In due course, U.S. manufacturers established hundreds of assembly plants across the border where finished products are produced by cheap, nonunionized

Mexican labor from U.S. raw materials imported duty-free. When shipped back north, the U.S. tariff is paid only on the value added. The two chief *maquiladora* cities in Baja are Tijuana and Mexicali.

Socialism

A great majority of the world's developing nations look on their economies as socialistic. Mexico has fit this mold. Certainly, it has not been communistic as there is much private land and thousands of small private businesses, but major enterprises have been government owned or controlled. During *La Crisis* the banks were nationalized as was one of the country's airlines.

However, the winds of change have been blowing. During the past several years hundreds of government businesses have been moved into the private sector. Mexico, along with the countries of Eastern Europe, the former Soviet Union and much of Latin America that experimented with socialism are finding it prudent to move rapidly toward a capitalistic economic system. These changes appear to be meeting with success. The Inter-American Bank recently reported that Mexico and other Latin American countries had made impressive economic gains in 1991 after the "lost decade" of the 1980s.

But while change is occurring, much of socialism remains. The CONASUPO stores are government owned as is much of the land with tourism potential brokered by FONATUR. The entire fishing industry is based on government-controlled and financed cooperatives, and its modern fishing fleet has been constructed with federal funds. Government planning and control is evident to the traveler in most aspects of Mexico's social and economic systems.

It is my understanding that Canada can be classified as somewhat more socialistic than the United States, but Mexico is clearly far more socialistic than either. Travel to Baja thus gives citizens of these two countries an opportunity to view a nation different from their own. Talk to the Mexicans; see how they view their socialist country and how they view the changes that are taking place. How would you change Mexico if, suddenly, you were president? After all, you have to think about something while lying there in the sun.

Land Reform

Since the 1910 revolution, much of Mexico's land has been distributed to the people. In Baja, one principal method of accomplishing this has been the *ejido*. You will see this word on maps and on countless road signs along the highways, and it is easy to arrive at the conclusion that it means village or town. This is not the case. An *ejido* is a landholding institution established under Mexican law. There were more than 28,000 of them in Mexico in 1990.

It is the *ejido* rather than the individual that has been made the legal proprietor of the land. Land may be worked on a cooperative basis or may be distributed to individuals who acquire what are called usufructuary rights. Land may be passed on through inheritance, but it is lost if not worked for two consecutive years. The *ejido* is administered by elected officials.

But the *ejido* system has recently undergone change. In the past, ejido farmers had been unable to secure credit for seed and machinery because they did not own the land they farmed. And as farmers divided their plots among their children, the average acreage of an *ejido* holding dwindled to an unprofitable size. In Baja, there is clear evidence of areas that have been cultivated that are submarginal for such purposes.

In 1992, the Mexican constitution was amended so that *ejido* members could obtain title to their lands, and could in turn sell or lease them to others. Apparently prior law strictly prohibited the sale or lease of *ejido* property. The fact that sizeable hotels, trailer courts and residential improvements in Baja have been leased by American investors for many years is no doubt an indication that Mexicans also trade in the old adage that "A sucker is born every minute."

Ejidos engage in enterprises other than farming. Members of ejidos work in the CONASUPO stores; there is a mining ejido in the town of El Triunfo on Highway 1, south of La Paz; and ejidos run camping areas on the highway to La Bufadora, near Ensenada, and at the whale-watching site at Scammon's lagoon.

Developmental Activities

In reading about Mexico and other developing countries, it is often noted that progress has been made but that its benefits have not spread to the rural areas. While I am sure this is true to some extent in Mexico, I can attest that there are clear evidences of government-sponsored improvements in even the smallest and most remote of Baja's villages. Even at isolated fish camps the fishermen's boats are modern fiberglass pangas provided by government-sponsored cooperatives, and access may be over a newly modernized road.

The distribution of income in Mexico is held to be among the most inequitable in the world, but it is also evident, at least to this observer, that some degree of social improvement is being shared by most of Baja's citizens. It is a simple matter of observation to note that there are far more late-model cars and trucks on Baja's streets and highways than there were only a few years ago. It is widely reported that Mexico's government officials are corrupt and amass sizeable personal fortunes. All I can say is that they seem to be letting some of the country's wealth slip through their fingers and trickle down to a growing middle class.

A modern flood-control and water conservation dam is upstream from the agricultural lands at Todos Santos. It is one of scores of government projects readily seen by the traveler in Baja.

Agricultural Production

The development of Baja's agricultural lands was almost totally prevented until 1933 due to the presence of various foreign land leases. Today you will see substantial farming areas in (1) the Valle de Mexicali near the mouth of the Rio Colorado, (2) along the Pacific coast from Ensenada to south of San Quintin, (3) in the desert surrounding Ciudad Constitucion and Ciudad Insurgentes, (4) in the desert around the community of Vizcaino south of Guerrero Negro, and (5) in the plains near San Juan de los Planes southeast of La Paz. Water for irrigation comes from deep wells.

Education

Many locations have recently constructed school buildings. Often they are clearly the newest buildings in town. Sometimes there is even a school building and no community. Look for one-room school houses at crossroads along the highways.

Be alert for the *Jardin de Ninos* (Kindergarten), where attendance is optional for three years for children from ages four to six. Most of the *escuelas* (schools) will bear the name *Primaria* (Primary). Here, attendance is mandatory from ages six to 14, or until six grades are completed. Middle schools, *Secundaria* (Secondary), *Secundaria-Tecnico* (Secondary-Technical) and *Tecnico* (Technical) are less in evidence to the traveler, but are frequently seen if you drive off the main roads.

The number of new schools is impressive, as is the fact that the children are frequently well-dressed. There is an obvious pride taken in the children. Sadly, you must keep in mind that many of the people you will meet have no more than a sixth-grade education, but progress is clearly evident.

Medical Services

There are private doctors in Mexico, but most people receive medical attention at clinics and hospitals operated by the *Instituto Mexicano de Seguro Social* (Mexican Social Security Institute). Look for the large letters IMSS on the front of medical buildings. Most are new facilities in the smaller towns. Social security refers to health services in Mexico rather than to retirement pensions as in the United States.

Water and Sewage

A major water pipeline was constructed early in the 1970s from water sources in the mountains north of San Jose del Cabo, all along Highway 1 to Cabo San Lucas. FONATUR has developed a new water system from wells for Loreto and the tourist facilities at Nopolo. On a recent visit to Mulegé, I saw roads being torn up for new pipelines. In 1986, a large water line was constructed to serve the coastal towns south of Guerrero Negro. This line will replace saltwater conversion plants, which are themselves only a few years old. The ocean-cruisers always fill their tanks from city water lines at La Paz and with no ill effect. These and other signs of safe water and sewer systems are in clear evidence throughout the peninsula.

Electric Power

There are three major diesel-fueled electric power plants in Baja, all in clear view to the traveler. The northern plant is located between Highway 1-D and the coast near Rosarito, south of Tijuana. The southern plant is adjacent to the highway between La Paz and Pichilingue. The most recent plant lies a few miles inland from San Carlos near Bahía Magdalena.

Communications

Baja's telephone system has been described in some detail earlier in this book. Making international calls involves some inconveniences for the traveler. In spite of this shortcoming, the system is founded on modern microwave radio techniques. Watch for the numerous microwave radio towers along the main highways.

Conservation

I attended a lecture by an American biologist who looked upon Mexican conservation activities as a joke. In his view, Mexican politics and economic concerns held sway over environmental matters. I cannot say to what degree this is still true, but I can report the following positive observation. (1) There is a modern biological center (*Centro de Investigaciones Biologicas de Baja*

California Sur located near La Paz. Much of the center's work is concentrat ed in the Sierra de la Laguna mountains east of Todos Santos and in th Vizcaino Desert *(La Reserva de la Biosfera el Vizcaino)* region of Baja Cali fornia Sur. (2) There are two national parks in the state of Baja California. (3 The U.S. manager of the manganese processing operation at Santa Rosali informed me that the environmental regulations he must follow differ littl from those encountered in the United States.

The port city of Ensenada and its extensive port facilities were built by the Mexican government.

Transportation

Hundreds of miles of new roads were constructed in Baja during the 1980s. In recent years, road-building has been largely limited to improvement of the streets within existing communities, converting Highway 1 to four lanes from the Los Cabos Airport to Cabo San Lucas and development of a four-lane, limited-access highway along the U.S. border from Tijuana to Mexicali.

Although the standards of Baja's roads are considerably lower than those encountered north of the border, they meet the needs of the Mexican people and are an immense improvement over what was available only a few years ago. In addition, the past two decades have seen the construction of several international airports, numerous smaller airfields and port facilities at Ensenada, San Carlos, La Paz and several other places.

Summary

What is set forth here are my personal views about my observations concerning social and economic progress in Baja. First, it is evident that there as been substantial economic and social progress. Much has been accomplished between my first visit to Baja and my most recent, but perhaps progress has been a bit too swift. The leaders of developing countries are under tremendous pressures to rapidly achieve progress. If they don't, they face political upheaval. In Mexico, as in other nations, much of this progress has been financed through the borrowing of foreign capital and with the vehicle of deficit federal spending. The result in the mid 1980s was a near collapse of the Mexican economy. In February 1995 an agreement was reached with the United States to prevent the collapse of Mexico's private banks. The strict provisions gave the U.S. veto power over key elements in Mexico's economic policy.

The hand of the federal government is everywhere. It has built hotels and airfields that simple observation indicates are financial liabilities. The creation of jobs, not profitability, seems to be the objective. I have observed dozens of government projects, ranging from the ferry terminal at Puerto Escondido to the buildings in the center of the highway at the state line, that lie unused and unrepaired. The major recent airport between Santa Rosalia and Mulegé receives little use.

The Mexican people must come to grips with the question of how many non-income-producing government services they can afford to provide for themselves. We, in Canada and the United States, also face this same question, but I believe it is more aggravated in Mexico.

It is my personal view that the administration of President Salinas (1988 to 1994) recognized the shortcomings that have been noted above and moved very early in his administration to make major economic changes. Mexico also pressed hard to secure the passage of the North American Free Trade Agreement (NAFTA) with the United States and Canada. Unfortunately, many recent changes designed to produce long-term benefits have more immediate negative impacts on working people. This is occurring all over the world as countries move away from socialism to market-oriented economies.

I have come to the conclusion that one of Mexico's most pressing problems involves the construction and maintenance standards of almost everything one sees. Often the traveler can observe partially completed buildings and other structures lying unused. Concrete is often mixed by a shovel in a small depression in the sand pile with little concern for the proportions of its ingredients. The use of reinforced concrete construction in multi-storied buildings, and the total lack of structural steel, is frightening, as the country found to its sorrow in the 1985 Mexico City earthquake. Fortunately, there are few such buildings in Baja.

Much of what is completed appears to receive little maintenance. The doors of public buildings hang from their hinges, windows are broken and not repaired, letters fall from signs and are not replaced. It is as if no one in the community possesses a screwdriver, wrench or other simple hand tools and that the most common repair items from a hardware store are unavailable. Some have said that Mexicans have little desire to contribute to the upkeep of such public improvements. This lies in sharp contrast to the obvious pride they take in their persons and their own homes. Perhaps their lack of concern for public property lies in the "cradle to the grave" philosophy inherent in socialism.

NOTE

Much of the above summary material was written for the two previous editions of this book. I have left it largely intact, if for no other reason than to form a basis for reporting that conditions in Baja have improved in recent years. I do not recall seeing any new governmental white elephants in the past six years. Road maintenance is considerably improved over the past, particularly in Baja California Sur. The new four-lane highway from Tijuana to Mexicali appears to be of excellent quality. The major new resort developments in the Cape Area are first class in appearance and are well maintained. The move from government to private ownership of businesses may be having its effect. Many conditions experienced in Baja are still substantially below what one encounters north of the border, but clearly they are improving.

EL MALO Y EL BUENO
(The Bad and the Good)

This arid land, so hot and so dry,
  Where the sun always shines in a bright azure sky

On rough ragged rocks and on scorching sand,
  Offering to humans a most desolate land

Covered with cacti and thickets of thorn,
  A prickly jungle, dense and forlorn;

Where the coarse cardon commands and at its feet
  The pin-cushion cholla and the ocotillo meet;

The ridiculous roadrunner hurries about
  Pursuing a lizard that skitters in rout;

The merry mockingbird sings in his bower,
  The promiscuous hummingbird kisses each bright cactus flower

And along the shores within easy reach
  The snowy white surf caresses a golden beach.

—By Ken Reimer

PART III:
THE GRAND TOUR

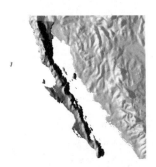

INTRODUCTION TO PART III

Now that you have completed the background and introductory materials in Parts I and II, you are ready to begin your Part III—Grand Tour—of Baja.

What is the Grand Tour? It has three basic objectives. These are to provide the following:

1. Essential travel directions needed for use of the main highways and secondary roads. The maps found in each chapter will be principal tools. The material presented is not an all-inclusive road log of everything one encounters. This is because such an exhaustive treatment simply is not necessary. It is possible for the first-time traveler to become temporarily disoriented within the larger cities, but on the open road it would really take special effort to become lost. There are very few paved side roads, and I submit that most people could find their way from Tijuana to Cabo San Lucas by adhering to only one instruction, "Stay on the blacktop and follow your nose."

2. Travel directions on recommended side trips off the main highways. The text will frequently be supplemented by large-scale local maps.

3. Special information concerning local history, vegetation, geology, etc., which builds upon the background material presented in Part II.

The Grand Tour is presented in 11 chapters. The first three cover the border towns along Highway 2, Mexicali to Highway 1, and Highway 3. The seven that follow relate to the Transpeninsular Highway. The concluding chapter describes the region accessible by Highway 19, the Pacific coast highway to Cabo San Lucas via Todos Santos.

Several other techniques are also used throughout the Grand Tour. These are as follows:

Kilometer Posts and Highway Sections

To many of us, milepost is a common word. Unfortunately few roads in the United States have them. Most U.S. highways are marked with long numbers that give the distance to the one-hundredth of a foot from the initial point of the construction survey, a place known only to God and the highway department. In Baja, the road engineers have shared their secret with travelers. Along all main highways you will find numbered white signs every kilometer. Outside of the cities, hotels and other businesses will use the nearest kilometer as their mailing address.

The Mexican highway department has divided the Transpeninsular Highway into nine sections. For the purposes of this book, these sections have been designated by the letters **A** through **J**. The kilometer post numbers begin with zero in each section. The location of each section, along with its distances in kilometers and miles, is shown in an accompanying map. In the northern state of Baja California, the numbers run consecutively from north to south. To add zest to your travels, they proceed from south to north in Baja California Sur. In this state, the south-bound traveler encounters the numbers in reverse order.

The seven chapters of this book that cover the Transpeninsular Highway begin and end at the same places as the highway sections, except that in two cases, two sections are combined in one chapter. (See the "Kilometer Post Sections" map.)

If you need to be alerted to look for some particular point of interest, the Grand Tour will reference it to the nearest kilometer post. All you need to do is watch for the proper kilometer post without the necessity of keeping track of your odometer readings from some obscure reference point. Canadian drivers should be particularly pleased with this system, as their highways and odometers utilize the metric system.

Knowledge of sectional breakpoint locations also allows you to use the posts to assess your progress all along the way. Kilometer post numbers will be printed in **BOLD TYPE**. Thus **Km D-14** refers to the 14th kilometer in section **D**. Travel distances for some of the SIDE TRIPS are given in miles when there are no kilometer posts.

Transpeninsular Highway Geographic Sections

This book segregates the Transpeninsular Highway into 19 geographic sections based on geologic and topographic aspects of the land through which it travels. There are 10 odd-numbered sections of gentle terrain and nine even-numbered ones with steeper topography. These gentle and steeper areas alternate.

The 10 gentle sections encompass 956 Km (595 miles), or 56 percent of the total length of the highway. The nine steeper areas account for the remaining 748 Km (464 miles), or 44 percent. These figures demonstrate that the highway is basically level and straight for more than half of its length, even though Baja as a whole is a mountainous land. Also, large portions of the steeper sections follow valleys or cross gently rolling plateaus that provide relatively easy driving conditions.

The 19 geographic sections are shown on a map and described in a table in this "Introduction." Kilometer post starting- and ending-points, and the length of each section also are included. By using these aids, you can look ahead to the kind of terrain through which you will be driving, and also will be more aware of the peninsula's geological story. The symbol of the mountain, shown previously, will alert you to textual material relating to these geographic sections.

Points of Special Interest Tour

I sincerely hope that you will decide to savor your trip through the peninsula and will not choose to drive through it in the shortest possible time. With this in mind, a 30-stop Points of Special Interest Tour has been prepared to guide you along the Transpeninsular Highway. These stops are listed in a table and are described in more detail in the text.

Look over the brief comments presented in the table to obtain an overall impression of the attractions included and the time involved in paying them a visit. Some of the points are adjacent to the highway. A majority require stopping and visiting a town or other feature just off the highway. A few require a more lengthy side trip, the longest being 16 miles to visit the whales at Scammon's Lagoon. Many stops on this Points of Special Interest tour also are logical places to spend the night. Thus, paying them a visit may not significantly increase your travel time.

In both text and maps, the Points of Special Interest Tour will be identified by the **PSI** symbol shown above. The text will alert you to a few of the stops that provide special problems for the larger RVs. And finally, to add a bit of sporting challenge, a specific number of points have been assigned to each of the points of special interest. The more time and effort involved in visiting a site, the more points allotted. The top score is 100 points. Rate yourself as follows:

90	**to**	**100**	**— Grande Baja Buff**
70	**to**	**89**	**— Baja Buffito**
50	**to**	**69**	**— Baja Amigo**
30	**to**	**49**	**— Posiblemente Manana**
0	**to**	**29**	**— Speed Merchant**

No fair saying "There it is!" and roaring by. You have to stop and at leas stretch your legs. There is no prize for scoring 100 points, but you know will want to shake your hand, and should we chance to meet, the *cerveza* i: on me.

GEOGRAPHIC SECTIONS ALONG THE TRANSPENINSULAR HIGHWAY

NO.	FROM	TO	DESCRIPTION	GENTLE		STEEPER	
				Km	Mi	Km	Mi
1	International Border at Tijuana.	Km (A-75) 21 mi. N of Ensenada.	Limited access freeway (Hwy.1-D) near sea level. Traverses flat areas and gentle hills along the coast.	75	47	—	—
2	Km (A-75) 21 miles N. of Ensenada.	Km (A -99) Tollgate 6 mi. N of Ensenada.	Limited access freeway (Hwy.1-D) Low mountainous section. Good views of the Pacific Ocean along southern portion.	—	—	24	15
3	Km (A -99) Tollgate 6 mi. N of Ensenada.	Km (B-25) 16 mi. S of Ensenada.	Flat lands around Ensenada. Some agriculture in southern portion. Narrow 4-lane hwy. from Ensenada to Maneadero. 2 lanes to south.	35	22	—	—
4	Km (B-25) 16 mi. S of Ensenada.	Km (B-125) at the town of Colonet.	Moderately steep mountains with numerous intermountain valleys.	—	—	100	62
5	Km (B-125) at the town of Colonet.	Km (C-41) 28 mi. S of San Quintin.	Mtns. move inland at Colonet. Hwy. passes over wide coastal plain. Southerly 17 Km. (11 mi.) is within 1/4 to 1/2 mi. of the ocean.	112	70	—	—
6	Km (C-41) 28 mi. S of San Quintin.	Km (C-55) at the town of El Rosario.	A short mountainous section involving a moderate climb to a plateau, and then a steep descent into El Rosario.	—	—	14	9
7	Km (C-55) at the town of El Rosario.	Km (C-63) at the Rio del Rosario bridge.	A short flat section along the north edge of a valley through which flows the Rio del Rosario.	8	5	—	—
8	Km (C-63) at the Rio del Rosario bridge.	Km (D-70) North edge of the Desierto de Vizcaino.	A section of high dissected plateaus, ridges and mountains. The gentle west slope of the Peninsular Range Mountains. The longest mountain section of Hwy. 1.	—	—	287	178
9	Km (D-70) North edge of the Desierto de Vizcaino.	Km (E-84) SE edge of the Desierto de Vizcaino.	Hwy. straight & level, but narrow. The most dangerous section of hwy. E of Guerrero Negro, hwy. climbs slowly to a pass through the mountains.	192	119	—	—

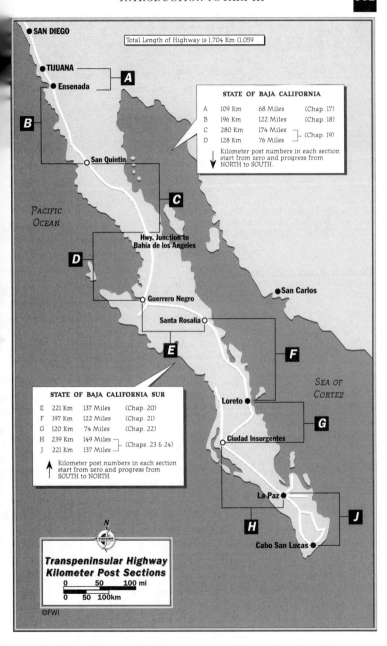

● SAN DIEGO

● TIJUANA

● Ensenada

A

B

Total Length of Highway is 1,704 Km (1,059

STATE OF BAJA CALIFORNIA

A	109 Km	68 Miles	(Chap. 17)
B	196 Km	122 Miles	(Chap. 18)
C	280 Km	174 Miles	(Chap. 19)
D	128 Km	76 Miles	

Kilometer post numbers in each section
start from zero and progress from
NORTH to SOUTH.

● San Quintin

PACIFIC
OCEAN

C

Hwy. Junction to
Bahia de los Angeles

D

● San Carlos

○ Guerrero Negro

Santa Rosalia ○

E

F

SEA OF
CORTEZ

STATE OF BAJA CALIFORNIA SUR

E	221 Km	137 Miles	(Chap. 20)
F	197 Km	122 Miles	(Chap. 21)
G	120 Km	74 Miles	(Chap. 22)
H	239 Km	149 Miles	(Chaps. 23 & 24)
J	221 Km	137 Miles	

Kilometer post numbers in each section
start from zero and progress from
SOUTH to NORTH.

Loreto ●

G

○ Ciudad Insurgentes

La Paz ●

J

H

N

*Transpeninsular Highway
Kilometer Post Sections*

0   50   100 mi

0   50   100km

©FWI

Cabo San Lucas ●

GEOGRAPHIC SECTIONS ALONG THE TRANSPENINSULAR HIGHWAY

NO.	FROM	TO	DESCRIPTION	GENTLE		STEEPER	
				Km	Mi	Km	Mi
10	Km (E-84) SE edge of the Desierto de Vizcaino.	Km (E-8) Highway 1 meets the Sea of Cortez.	Hwy.1 passes over the Peninsular Range Mountains. through a gentle pass. Eastern 27 Kms. (17 miles) has steep descent to the sea.	—	—	74	46
11	Km (E-8) Highway 1 meets the Sea of Cortez.	Km (G-83) Highway 1 leaves the Sea of Cortez.	Coastal benches and low hills between the coast and the Sierra Giganta. Near sea level in most places. South portion very scenic.	241	150	—	—
12	Km (G-83) Highway 1 leaves the Sea of Cortez.	Km (G-45) Mtns. blend with Llano de Magdalena.	Highway 1 again passes over the main Peninsular Range Mountains. Eastern 10 Km fairly steep with many curves. A scenic section.	—	—	38	24
13	Km (G-45) Mtns. blend with Llano de Magdalena.	Km (H-120) Llano de Mag. blends with plateau lands.	Highway 1 is straight and level through the Llano de Magdalena. Passes through agricultural lands near Ciudad Constitucion.	164	102	—	—
14	Km (H-120) Llano de Mag. blends with plateau lands.	Km (H-31) Plateau lands end. Start Ll. de La Paz.	A section of relatively level plateau lands formed by the gentle western slopes of the Peninsular Range Mountains.	—	—	89	55
15	Km (H-31) Plateau lands end. Start Ll. de La Paz.	Km (J-170) End Ll. de La Paz. Start Sr. de la Laguna.	Highway 1 passes over the level Llano de La Paz. This is the peninsula's lowest and narrowest section.	82	51	—	—
16	Km (J-170) End Ll. de La Paz. Start Sr. de la Laguna.	Km (J-112) Hwy. 1 meets the sea near Los Barriles.	Section through the granitic Sierra de la Laguna and its "arid tropical forest" plant community.	—	—	58	36
17	Km (J-112) Hwy. 1 meets the sea near Los Barriles.	Km (J-93) Junction with the road to La Ribera.	Section along coastal flat lands. Northern portion adjoins the Sea of Cortez coast near the resort towns of Los Barriles and Buena Vista.	19	12	—	—

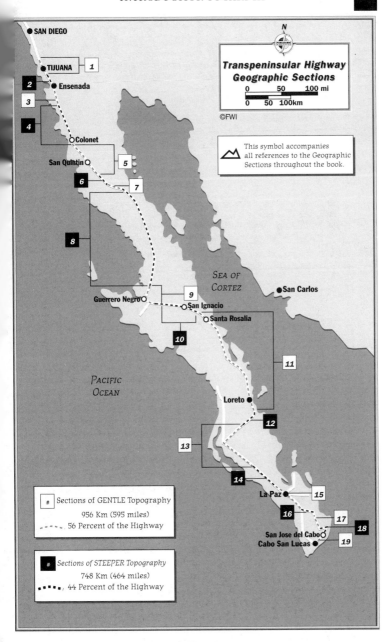

N

Transpeninsular Highway Geographic Sections

| 0 | 50 | 100 mi |

| 0 | 50 | 100km |

©FWI

This symbol accompanies all references to the Geographic Sections throughout the book.

SAN DIEGO

TIJUANA *1*

2 Ensenada

3

4

Colonet

San Quintin *5*

6

7

8

SEA OF CORTEZ

Guerrero Negro *9* San Carlos

San Ignacio

10 Santa Rosalia

11

PACIFIC OCEAN

Loreto

12

13

14

La Paz *15*

16 *17* *18*

San Jose del Cabo *19*
Cabo San Lucas

Sections of GENTLE Topography
956 Km (595 miles)
- - - - 56 Percent of the Highway

Sections of STEEPER Topography
748 Km (464 miles)
▪▪▪▪ 44 Percent of the Highway

INTRODUCTION TO PART III

GEOGRAPHIC SECTIONS ALONG THE TRANSPENINSULAR HIGHWAY

NO.	FROM	TO	DESCRIPTION	GENTLE		STEEPER	
				Km	Mi	Km	Mi
18	Km (J-93) Junction with the road to La Ribera.	Km (J-35) Hwy.1 meets the sea at San Jose del Cabo.	Highway 1 passes over low hills and plateaus lying between the Sierra de la Laguna to the west and a lesser range to the east.	—	—	60	37
19	Km (J-35) Hwy.1 meets the sea at San Jose del Cabo.	Km (J-0) Highway 1 ends at Cabo San Lucas.	A section of coastal benches and low hills at the peninsula's southern tip.	33	21	—	—

TRANSPENINSULAR HIGHWAY POINTS OF SPECIAL INTEREST TOUR
Points 29 and 30 are along Highway 19

NO.	POINT OF INTEREST	HRS	PTS	KM	COMMENTS
1	International boundary monument.	0:20	3	A-9	Historic monument near Bullring By-the-Sea at Tijuana.
2	Rosarito Beach Hotel.	0:20	2	A-34	Historic hotel, wall decorations, etc. Former 1930s gambling casino.
3	El Mirador (the vista point).	0:10	1	A-84	Fine views of coast and Islas Todos Santos. Adjoins Hwy 1-D.
4	Ensenada—Tourist Row.	1:00	4	A-109	One of Baja's best shopping areas, plus a taste of a large Mexican city.
5	La Bufadora.	1:00	5	B-14	Intriguing ocean blowhole and fine coastal views. 14-mile side trip.
6	Adobe ruins of mission at El Rosario.	0:30	4	C-55	1.6-mile side trip to ruins overlooking Rio del Rosario.
7	Excellent desert vegetation.	0:30	3	C-63	Northern edge of Sonoran Desert vegetation region. First *cirios*.
8	Cataviña Boulder Fields.	0:15	2	C-157	Geologically interesting boulder fields and fine desert vegetation.
9	Scammon's Lagoon— Whale-watching. (A drive, and boat trip at Puerto Lopez Mateos (Chapter 22) may be substituted.)	3:00	8	E-208	Major whale calving area. 16-mile side trip. Consider overnight stay.
10	San Ignacio.	0:45	3	E-74	One of Baja's most charming towns. Historic church, square and palms.
11	Tres Virgenes Volcano and lava flows.	0:15	2	E-42	Lava flows adjoining hwy. Excellent specimens of elephant trees.
12	Santa Rosalia.	2:00	6	E-0	Historic church, copper smelter, French buildings, hotel and harbor.

TRANSPENINSULAR HIGHWAY POINTS OF SPECIAL INTEREST TOUR
Points 29 and 30 are along Highway 19

NO.	POINT OF INTEREST	HRS	PTS	KM	COMMENTS
13	Mulege.	2:00	6	F-136	Savor the town and visit the historic prison and restored mission church.
14	Microwave radio tower and fine scenic view.	0:30	4	F-124	Excellent views of the Sea of Cortez. A 3/4-mile side trip.
15	Loreto.	1:00	5	F-197	Historic town—Site of the mother mission. Visit church and museum.
16	Nopolo.	0:30	2	G-111	Visit the hotel and tennis courts in this developing resort area.
17	Puerto Escondido.	0:30	2	G-94	Baja's best natural harbor. Trailer court and developing resort area.
18	Vista point north of La Paz.	0:10	1	H-35	Views of La Paz, Llano de La Paz, Sea of Cortez and islands.
19	La Paz.	4:00	6	H-0	Tour the downtown area and waterfront. Good shopping and hotels.
20	El Triunfo.	1:00	4	J-162	Historic silver mining town. Visit old smelter and cemetery.
21	Santiago.	1:30	5	J-85	Pleasant town and site of a Jesuit mission. Visit the zoological garden.
22	Tropic of Cancer monument.	0:05	1	J-82	Stop and stretch your legs as you enter the tropics.
23	San Jose del Cabo.	2:00	4	J-33	Tour the town square, church and developing resort area.
24	Hotel Pamilla.	0:30	2	J-26	One of Baja's finest hotels. Walk in if driving large RV or trailer.
25	Hotel Twin Dolphin.	0:30	2	J-11	Another of Baja's fine hotels.
26	Cabo San Lucas Vista from the Hotel Calinda Beach.	0:20	2	J-6	Celebrate arrival at "Cabo" by viewing the cape from the hotel pool area.
27	Hotel Finisterra.	0:20	2	J-0	A fine hotel plus excellent views of the Pacific and inner harbor.
28	Boat trip to the tip of Cabo San Lucas.	2:00	4	J-0	Hire a glass-bottomed boat to visit the Cabo arch and view tropical fish.
29	Todos Santos. (On Hwy 19.)	1:00	3	Hwy 19	A charming historic town and farming area. Jesuit mission site.
30	Botanical Garden.	0:30	2	Hwy 19	Excellent garden of labeled desert plants. Adjacent to the highway.

GASOLINE STATIONS (PEMEX) ALONG HIGHWAY 1 (North to South)

Tijuana to Ensenada

Tijuana	*Km A-1*
Rosarito	*Km A-34*
El Descanso	*Km A-53*
El Sauzal	*Km A-100*
Ensenada	*Km A-109*

Ensenada to San Quintin

Maneadero	*Km B-21*
Santo Tomas	*Km B-51*
San Vicente	*Km B-90*
Colonet	*Km B-127*
Camalu	*Km B-157*
C. Vicente Guerrero	*Km B-172*
San Quintin	*Km B-190*
C. Lazaro Cardenas	*Km B-193*

San Quintin to the State Line

El Rosario	*Km C-55*
Cataviña	*Km C-174*
Bahía de L. A. Junct.	*Km C-280*
Villa Jesus Maria	*Km D-96*

State Line to Santa Rosalia

Guerrero Negro	*Km E-217*
Vizcaino Junction	*Km E 208*
San Ignacio	*Km E-74*
Santa Rosalia	*Km E-0*

Santa Rosalia to Loreto

Mulege	*Km F-136*
Loreto	*Km F-0*

Loreto to La Paz

Fed. Water Project #1	*Km G-17*
Ciudad Insurgentes	*Km G-0*
Ciudad Constitucion	*Km H-211*
El Cien	*Km H-100*
El Centenario	*Km H-12*
La Paz	*Km H-0*

GASOLINE STATIONS (PEMEX) ALONG HIGHWAY 1 (North to South)

La Paz to San Jose del Cabo via Highway 1

San Antonio	*Km J-156*
Los Barriles	*Km J-110*
Santiago	*Km J-85*
Miraflores	*Km J-71*
San Jose del Cabo	*Km J-33*
Cabo San Lucas	*Km J-0*

LITERS TO GALLONS

Liters	Gallons	Liters	Gallons
1	0.26	40	10.57
2	0.53	50	13.21
3	0.79	60	15.85
4	10.6	70	18.49
5	1.32	80	21.14
10	2.64	90	23.78
20	5.28	100	26.42
30	7.93	150	39.63

1 gallon = 3.78 liters

KILOMETERS TO MILES

Kilometers	Miles	Kilometers	Miles
1	0.62	30	18.6
2	1.24	40	24.8
3	1.86	50	31.0
4	2.48	60	37.2
5	3.10	70	43.4
10	6.20	80	49.6
15	9.30	90	55.8
20	12.40	100	62.0

1 mile = 1.61 kilometers. To convert kilometers into miles, divide by 2 and add 25%

BAJA DISTANCE TABLE

Top line is distance in miles. Bottom line is distance in kilometers. Figures based on use of Highway 1-D between Tijuana and Ensenada.

All distances are over Highway 1 except for the last line, which utilizes the Highway 1 and Highway 19 route between La Paz and Cabo San Lucas.

Tijuana

Ensenada	Colonet	San Quintin	El Rosario	Cataviña	Bahía de Los Angeles Junction	State Line	San Ignacio	Santa Rosalia	Mulege	Loreto	Ciudad Insurgentes	La Paz	

Ensenada — 68 / 109

Colonet — 145/234, 77/125

San Quintin — 185/299, 118/190, 39/61

El Rosario — 223/360, 156/251, 78/126, 38/61

Cataviña — 297/479, 239/370, 157/245, 112/180, 74/119

Bahía de Los Angeles Junction — 363/585, 295/476, 218/351, 177/286, 140/225, 66/106

State Line — 442/713, 374/604, 297/479, 257/414, 219/353, 145/234, 79/128

San Ignacio — 533/860, 466/751, 388/626, 348/561, 310/500, 236/381, 171/275, 91/147

Santa Rosalia — 579/934, 512/825, 434/700, 394/635, 356/574, 282/455, 216/349, 137/221, 46/74

Mulege — 617/995, 549/886, 472/761, 432/696, 394/635, 320/516, 254/410, 175/282, 84/135, 38/61

Loreto — 701/1131, 634/1022, 556/897, 516/832, 478/771, 404/652, 339/546, 259/418, 168/271, 122/197, 84/136

Ciudad Insurgentes — 776/1251, 708/1142, 631/1017, 590/952, 552/891, 479/772, 413/666, 334/538, 242/391, 197/317, 159/256, 74/120

La Paz — 924/1490, 856/1381, 778/1256, 738/1191, 701/1130, 627/1011, 561/905, 482/777, 391/630, 345/556, 307/495, 223/359, 148/239

Cabo San Lucas via Hwy. 1 — 1059/1711, 993/1604, 916/1477, 875/1412, 838/1351, 764/1232, 698/1126, 619/998, 528/851, 482/777, 444/716, 360/580, 285/460, 137/221

Cabo San Lucas via Hwy. 1 & 19 — 1003/1618, 936/1509, 858/1384, 818/1319, 777/1254, 706/1139, 604/1033, 561/905, 470/758, 424/684, 386/629, 302/487, 228/367, 79/128

THE BORDER AREA
AND HIGHWAY 2

This initial chapter of your Grand Tour of Baja begins with an examination of Highways 2 and 2D and the Mexican communities lying along the international border. It is divided into eight sections:

1 — Tijuana

2 — Highways 2 and 2D, Tijuana to Tecate

3 — Tecate

4 — Highways 2 and 2D, Tecate to Mexicali

5 — Mexicali

6 — Highways 2 and 2D, Mexicali to San Luis

7 — San Luis

8 — Algodones

Highway 2 extends from east to west a short distance south of the international boundary. It is a two-lane roadway little different in design standards from most other highways in Mexico. Construction started about 1990 on Highway 2D, which roughly parallels the old road. It is a four-lane, divided, limited-access tollway. Those portions that are complete are shown on the map on page 311.

Large numbers of tourists enter Mexico at the Tijuana-San Ysidro port of entry and simply wish to pass through Tijuana as quickly as possible to head south on Highway 1. If you are one of these, I suggest you read the first two items in the Tijuana section and then proceed to page 351. The two items in question concern entering and leaving Mexico in the Tijuana area.

Tijuana

We North Americans mispronounce the name of many Mexican communities, but our reference to the city of Tijuana as Tia Juana heads the list. I thought the blame could be laid at the door of the Tijuana Brass (A mariachi band from my younger days), but reference to that group's music labels shows the name spelled correctly, and travel books of the 1950s note that the problem already existed for many years. In deference to our long-suffering Mexican friends, let us proceed to the blackboard with chalk in hand and try to get it right. Try saying TEE-WAHNA and you'll sound less like a tourist. Frequent visitors, particularly Californians, simply call it "TJ".

The town of Tijuana did not come into existence until the 1870s, almost three and one-half centuries after the Baja peninsula was discovered, and 175 years after the founding of the first Jesuit mission at Loreto in 1697. Today, with a population of well over 1 million, it's the fourth-largest city in Mexico and is reportedly the fastest growing city in North America.

The portion of the earlier "History" chapter concerning the years after the Mexican-American War will provide the community's background. Its rapid rise to prominence came in the 1920s as the result of prohibition in the United States. Tijuana led the way in attracting visitors from the north interested in gambling, prostitution and the drowning of sorrows in unnumbered saloons. This wicked past is now largely replaced by a modern metropolis with much business activity and more conventional tourist attractions.

Please refer to the "Around Tijuana" map on page 314. Depicted are the main points of interest and principal travel routes of concern to the first-time visitor. Hundreds of lesser streets are omitted. This "highlight approach" will be used for the community maps throughout this book. Detailed maps are available in a variety of publications obtainable at the border and in almost every hotel and other places frequented by tourists.

Entering Tijuana from the North

In approaching Tijuana from the north, you will be led directly into the port of entry from either Interstate 5 or 805. A canopy over the Mexican entry station bears directional signs.

These signs require some tourists vehicles to pull over to the right for a customs inspection. This could change in the future. Drivers wishing to proceed south on Highway 1-D should bear sharply to the left a short distance after the border as the appropriate route circles over the entrance road, and heads west directly adjoining the border fence. Follow the signs for **Rosarito** and **Ensenada**. This route skirts Tijuana and most of its traffic, and in a few miles delivers its users to the Pacific coast in the vicinity of the **Bullring by-the-Sea**.

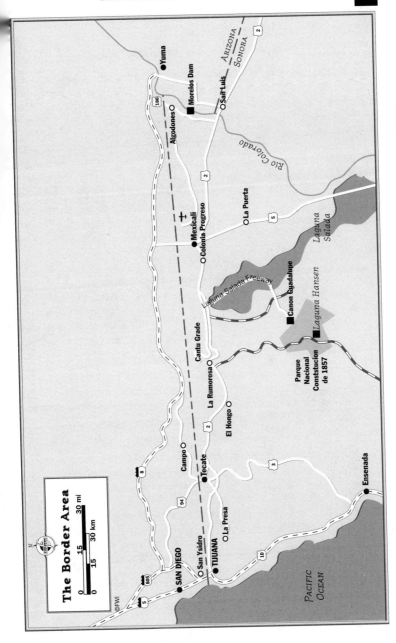

The Border Area

0   15   30 mi
0   15   30 km

©FWI

(Follow the Rio Tijuana signs if you wish to access Paseo de los Heros and Tijuana's better hotels.)

Returning to the U.S.A.

In returning north on Highway 1-D, you may enter the United States at San Ysidro or Otay Mesa. The decision on which crossing point to use must be made at the Highway 1-D offramp at the north end of the town of Rosarito. Here are the advantages and disadvantages of these two alternatives.

San Ysidro

Returning home this way is essentially a retracement of the south-bound Highway 1-D route described previously and in a later section. It is largely a sea level route with few hills. Traffic is modest, as most of the route is on a limited-access toll road. Then brace yourself for lengthy delays while waiting your turn in line at U.S. customs. (See comments in "Returning to United States" section on page 162).

Otay Mesa

This station was opened in 1985 to help alleviate the lengthy delays experienced at San Ysidro. This route to the border is steeper and a bit more complex than that to San Ysidro, but the crossing delays are usually less. I recommend it for everyone. (Travelers with large RVs and trailers will experience heavy traffic in places, but this is the price to be paid for the lesser wait at the port of entry.) Proceed as follows from Highway 1-D to Otay Mesa.

1. Exit Highway 1-D at the north end of Rosarito. The exit sign reads "*Tijuana Libre.*" Drive north on four-lane Highway 1 through hilly terrain. (In the past this road was only two lanes and lengthy delays were caused by slow-moving trucks.)

2. Exit Highway 1 at the top of the grade onto Libramiento Oriente, a four-lane freeway. The exit sign reads "*Garita Otay Mesa/Border Crossing.*" From this exit, it is 3.8 miles to Boulevard Agua Caliente (Highway 2) and an additional 1.7 miles to the bus station turnoff. The freeway ends about one-half mile south of Boulevard Agua Caliente, and heavy city traffic may be encountered from here north to the vicinity of the bus station. Follow signs for the "*Aeropuerto*" along the way.

3. From the bus station, climb up the mesa on a one-way highway to an intersection. Turn right here. The sign reads "*GARITA DE OTAY.*" After 0.6 miles turn left at a similar sign. From this last turn it is 1.2 miles on a six-lane divided boulevard to the border. This all sounds a bit difficult, but try it, you'll like it, and once you have it down, you will never use San Ysidro again.

Visiting Tijuana

If you plan to visit Tijuana for only a short period, why not leave the car behind? There is a 500-car commercial parking lot immediately adjoining the border west of the port of entry on the U.S. side. From the lot, it is about one-half mile over a pleasant walkway to the north end of the Avenida Revolution tourist zone.

As at all the ports of entry, the walking circulation is counter-clockwise, so you will return to the United States on the east side of highway. There are elevated pedestrian walkways over the highway on both sides of the border. Customs delays are usually minimal.

Better yet, take the San Diego Trolley to the border and walk into Mexico. The trolley station is adjacent to U.S. Customs on the east side of the highway. By leaving the car at home you escape the need for Mexican insurance, greatly diminish U.S. Customs delays, and avoid traffic and parking problems. There are plenty of taxis, and the distances to most of the tourist attractions are minimal. Consult the map to locate the following places.

Avenida Revolution

A seven-block stretch of **Ave. Revolution** is the main tourist zone. There are many shops, restaurants and nightclubs. Its northern end is easily reached by the walkway from the border. A few blocks to the west is the principal shopping and business district.

Boulevard Agua Caliente

The **Tijuana Bullring**, **Country Club** and **Agua Caliente Race Track** are all located on the south side of Blvd. Agua Caliente. This same segment of the boulevard also is the location of most of the city's better hotels and motels.

Paseo de Los Heroes

This broad boulevard and several other similar thoroughfares lie south of the Rio Tijuana and are centered around the statue of Cuauhtemoc (the last king of the Aztecs, defender of Tenochtitlan, and for many Mexicans, the original patriot). This is the newest section of the downtown area. There are many businesses, government offices and grassy open areas.

Highway 2 and 2D—Tijuana to Tecate

Tijuana's principal east-west street is Agua Caliente. It is also Highway 2. The route crosses *Presa Rodriquez* (Rodriquez Dam) 14 miles east of downtown Tijuana. Between these two points there is considerable traffic as the highway is also the main four-lane artery for this city and the communities of La Mesa and La Presa. In La Presa, the highway becomes two-lane. East of the dam, traffic is lighter but is utilized by many heavy trucks escaping the tolls required on Highway 2D.

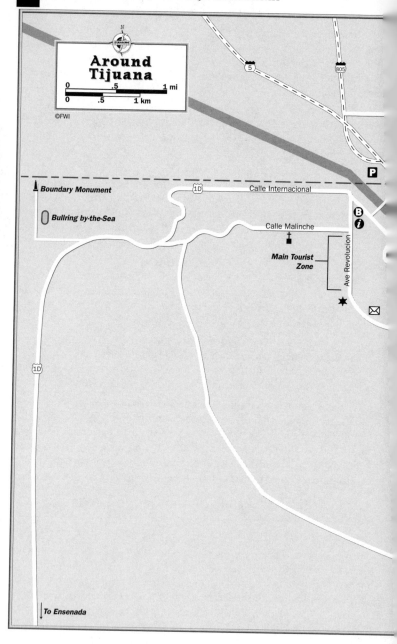

Around Tijuana

0 .5 1 mi
0 .5 1 km

©FWI

Boundary Monument

Calle Internacional

Bullring by-the-Sea

Calle Malinche

Main Tourist Zone

Ave Revolucion

To Ensenada

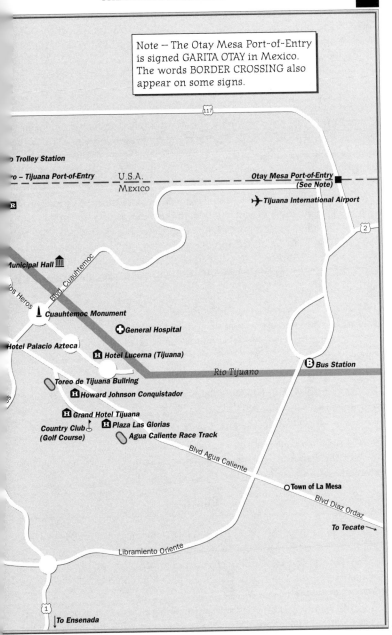

Note – The Otay Mesa Port-of-Entry is signed GARITA OTAY in Mexico. The words BORDER CROSSING also appear on some signs.

117

Trolley Station

o – Tijuana Port-of-Entry **U.S.A.**
– – – **MEXICO**

Otay Mesa Port-of-Entry
(See Note)

Tijuana International Airport

R

Municipal Hall

Blvd. Cuauhtemoc

os Heros

Cuauhtemoc Monument

2

General Hospital

Hotel Palacio Azteca

Hotel Lucerna (Tijuana)

Rio Tijuano

B Bus Station

Toreo de Tijuana Bullring

Howard Johnson Conquistador

Grand Hotel Tijuana

Country Club
(Golf Course)

Plaza Las Glorias

Agua Caliente Race Track

Blvd Agua Caliente

Town of La Mesa

Blvd Díaz Ordaz

To Tecate →

Libramiento Oriente

1

↓**To Ensenada**

Highway 2D is completed between the eastern edge of Tijuana and Tecate. The Tijuana entrance to this toll road is about two miles east of the Otay Mesa port of entry access road (See "Tijuana and Vicinity" map). Highway 2D may be accessed both east and west of Tecate from Highway 2 and south of Tecate on Highway 3.

Km-166

Here the highway crosses the narrow crest of the concrete Rodriquez Dam (*Presa Rodriques*). Natural runoff captured by this structure was Tijuana's principal source of water prior to 1960. The reservoir ran dry in 1961 as the result of rapid population growth and a series of dry years. Runoff is now supplemented by water piped in from La Mision, south of Tijuana on the Pacific coast, and from the Rio Colorado to the east.

From Presa Rodriquez to Tecate, Highway 2 passes through pleasant rolling hills. There is some urbanization, with the flatter lands utilized for farming, grazing and olive orchards. The underlying rock is granite. Note the many hills that are being fractured and eroded into large, light-colored, granite boulders. When these boulders occur adjacent to the highway, they create natural billboards used to advertise political parties and their candidates.

Km-163

Highway 2 is joined at this point by an expressway that bypasses the towns of La Mesa and La Presa. Its western terminus is a short distance south of the Tijuana bus station.

Km-140

At this point lies an interchange between Highways 2 and 2D. Much of Highway 2 between here and Tecate is four-lane.

Km-133—Tecate

Between Tijuana and Tecate, Highway 2 has slowly climbed the western slopes of the Peninsular Range Mountains. A sign at the western edge of Tecate marks the 500-meter (1650 feet) elevation point.

Tecate

Tecate's population of 40,000 is supported by agriculture and growing numbers of assembly plants operating under the *maquiladora* program. It is also the home of the Tecate Brewery. As with other communities in Mexico, it is amazing how a town with this many people is compressed into such a relatively small area.

The community contains several tourist-oriented stores, but its chief attributes for the traveler are the port of entry and the Tecate Brewery. One

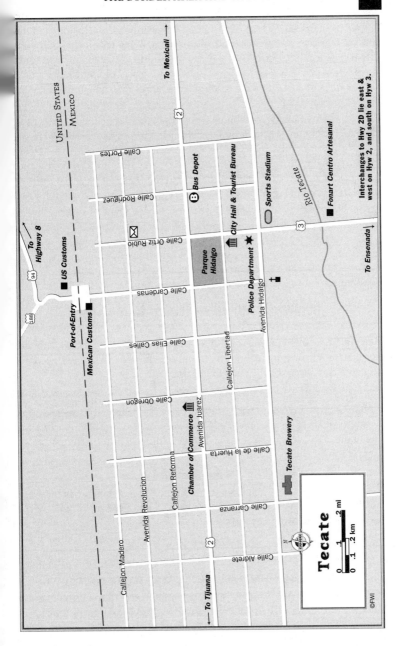

Tecate

To Mexicali →

United States
Mexico

To
Highway 8 ↑

■ US Customs

Calle Portes

■ Bus Depot

City Hall & Tourist Bureau

○ Sports Stadium

Rio Tecate

■ Fonart Centro Artesanal

Interchanges to Hwy 2D lie east &
west on Hyw 2, and south on Hyw 3.

Calle Rodriguez

Calle Ortiz Rubio

Parque
Hidalgo

Police Department

Avenida Hidalgo

To Ensenada →

Port-of-Entry

■ Mexican Customs

Calle Cardenas

Calle Elias Calles

Callejon Libertad

Chamber of Commerce

Calle Obregon

Avenida Juarez

Calle de la Huerta

Tecate Brewery

Callejon Reforma

Avenida Revolucion

Calle Carranza

Callejon Madero

To Tijuana ←

Calle Aldrete

N

0   .1   .2 mi
0   .1   .2 km

©FWI

way to visit the brewery is by traveling on **vintage trains** departing from the U.S. town of **Campo** located a few miles to the northeast on California Highway 94. It is reported that spirits are considerably higher on the return trip after passengers have sampled the brewery's output. Tecate is also located at the junction of Highways 2 and 3. Highway 3 is a very pleasant way to travel south and is the recommended route for tourists returning to the United States from Ensenada.

There is no adjoining community on the U.S. side of the border; thus, there is little commuter traffic and usually little time is spent waiting in line at the U.S. port of entry. Mexican customs and immigration offices are found immediately on the right when entering Mexico. There are also several auto insurance offices within one block of the crossing. Parking is usually available on the city streets. The **Motel El Dorado** lies 0.8 miles west of the Highway 2 and 3 junction on the north side of Highway 2. The **Motel Hacienda** is found 0.7 miles farther along, in the same direction. Tecate has no trailer courts.

A few years ago I was advised by a reliable source that Tecate is the only Baja border town that does not support prostitution, a notable distinction. It may be the only one in the world. I must hasten to add that this bit of information does not reflect my own personal observations.

Highway 2 and 2D—Tecate to Mexicali

East of Tecate, Highway 2 continues to climb gradually upward. Most of the agricultural land has been left behind, to the west. The land becomes steeper and is covered largely with chaparral.

Km-126

Here is an interchange with Highway 2D near the eastern outskirts of Tecate. Construction of Highway 2D between Tecate and La Rumorosa has been limited to overpass structures. The new highway's route roughly parallels Highway 2.

Km-109

At approximately this point, the steeper lands are left behind to the west, and the highway enters a broad plateau with views of the main peaks of the Peninsular Range Mountains to the east.

Km-97

The town of El Hongo lies south of the highway at this point.

Km-80—Vegetational Change

Starting near this point and continuing for the next 20 Km (13 miles), you will see a scattering of Parry pinyon pine trees and low-growing California junipers. This is the best location for observing these species from Baja's highway system. More extensive stands may be viewed by taking the side trip noted below at Km 72. Pinyon pine produces cones containing large nut-like seeds, which are easily gathered when they mature in May. They make good eating and may be found marketed as "Indian Nuts."

THE BORDER AREA AND HIGHWAY 2

SIDE TRIP

Km-72—Road to National Park

A secondary road leaves Highway 2 to the right (south) 0.1 miles east of this point. Immediately west of this junction is a CONASUPO store. This road provides the back-door route to the Parque Nacional Constitucion de 1857, one of Baja's two national parks. The road passes through excellent stands of Parry pinyon pine and numerous unimproved places to camp. Be extremely careful with fire in this area. Pinyon pine burns with great intensity and is very slow to regenerate since its heavy seeds cannot be spread by the wind.

It is 38 miles to Laguna Hanson, the park's principal attraction. This route is recommended only for pickup and van-type vehicles.

Km-68—La Rumorosa

Here, at over 4000 feet in elevation, lies the small town of La Rumorosa. It contains a modest restaurant and a PEMEX station, but is of little other interest to the tourist. Its chief claim to fame is that it lies at the top of the grade. What grade? You will shortly discover: At the eastern edge of La Rumorosa lies the tollgate-interchange for the portion of Highway 2D that was completed in 1995.

The Cantu Grade

East of La Rumorosa you will be making a 15-mile-long descent of the eastern escarpment of the Peninsular Range Mountains. It is the most dramatic segment of highway in the Baja peninsula. This steep and rapid drop, combined with the lengthy and gradual grade to the east, is the peninsula's best demonstration of its fault-block mountain structure. (See "Geology" chapter.)

Although the highway is well-constructed, careful driving is required. Slow-moving vehicles and high winds can be a problem, and snow may be encountered during winter storms. Don't miss the excellent views of the United States to the north, and Laguna Salada and the San Felipe Desert, to the east. Also, note the light blue pipeline north of the highway. It brings water from the Rio Colorado to Tijuana. Pumping stations are in view at the base of the grade and near the conduit's midpoint.

Daughter Barbara poses with the Green Angels at La Rumorosa at the western edge of the Cantu Grande. Note the pinyon pine trees behind the building.

The westbound lanes of Highway 2D have been completed from the northern end of Laguna Salada near **Km-23** to the above-noted tollgate-interchange at the eastern edge of La Rumorosa. Eastbound traffic is limited to using old Highway 2, while westbound traffic could select either route.

The Cantu Grande is Baja's most dramatic segment of highway. Its eastern end lies in the desert, while there are high-elevation pinyon pines to the west.

SIDE TRIP

Km-27—Canyon Guadalupe

A secondary road leaves Highway 2 to the south a short distance west of **Km-27**. *It provides access to Baja's hidden hot spring oasis, Canyon Guadalupe. Nestled in a canyon near the foot of the majestic Sierra de Juarez's eastern escarpment, the oasis has long been a favorite of off-road vehicle fans. Most of the route into the spring has been upgraded to secondary road standards.*

The road roughly parallels the western edge of Laguna Salada for 26.7 miles. At this point, take a branch road to the right through agricultural fields for an additional 7.7 miles to the campground. The last 1.5 miles is steep and rocky and crosses an arroyo several times among granite boulders. This final section of road is clearly not suited for larger RVs. (See **Km-25** *below concerning an alternate route over the lake bed of Laguna Salada.)*

Hot-spring waters (105 degrees) are piped to rock tubs at each campsite set among native fan palms and other desert vegetation. There is also a small store and hot-water pools for swimming. The per-night fee is $15. Call ☎ (714) 673-2670 for reservations. The area is very crowded on weekends and loses some of its ambience. Otherwise, it's a delightful spot. Indian petroglyphs and a small waterfall may be visited by hiking up the canyon farther into the mountains.

SIDE TRIP

Km-25—Laguna Salada

A sign for Playa Laguna Salada marks the junction of a secondary road that leads south for 0.5 miles to the north end of Laguna Salada. Here are located a modest cafe and camping area at the edge of the lake bed. It is a pleasant spot on those few occasions when there is water in the lake. Otherwise, it leaves much to be desired.

From the above-described point one may proceed over "The Laguna Salada Freeway" for a flying 26.2-mile trip over the level lake bed toward Canyon Guadalupe. This route is far smoother and faster than the often washboarded road noted under **Km-27** *above. It joins this latter road near the last 7.7 mile road section into the hot springs. Avoid this trip if there is the slightest hint of recent rain.*

Valle de Mexicali

Approximately halfway between Laguna Salada and the city of Mexicali on Highway 2 lies the agricultural community of Colonia Progreso. This town marks the western edge of the vast Valle de Mexicali agricultural area, which stretches east to the Rio Colorado. It is Baja's largest farming area. The history of its development is contained in the closing section of the "History" chapter. Much of the area along the highway is urbanized.

Highway 5 Junction

Highway 2 joins Highway 5 near the southern edge of the city of Mexicali. (See "Mexicali" map.)

Mexicali

Tourism statistics indicate that Mexicali is the final destination point for 15 percent of the foreign visitors who enter the state of Baja California. The comparable figure for Tijuana is 34 percent and 23 percent for Ensenada. In spite of Mexicali's reasonably high share of total visits, the city has a definite non-tourist flavor. One can only speculate that most visitors are from farming communities in the nearby Imperial Valley and are bent on activities not usually associated with tourism. The economic well-being of Mexicali's 600,000 people rests on industry, agricultural activities in the Valle de Mexicali, and on its being the capital of the state of Baja California.

Mexicali's principal business district adjoins the international border generally southeast from the port of entry. Most of its newer development is taking place in the *Centro Civico-Comercial*, some two miles south of the border. Here are located state and federal office buildings, bus station, bullring and the pink zone (shops, theaters, restaurants, etc.). The city's hotels and motels cluster around the intersection of Boulevard Benito Juarez and Boulevard Justo Sierra.

Tourists entering Mexico at Mexicali and heading south to San Felipe need merely follow Calzada Lopez Mateos (a multilaned boulevard) southeast through town. The railroad lies in the median strip for the first two miles and will serve to keep you on track. Follow the signs for San Felipe. See the next chapter for a full description of the Highway 5 route from Mexicali to the San Felipe area.

Motorists waiting their turn to enter the United States line up east of the port of entry on Avenida Cristobal Colon. This street directly adjoins the border fence and carries one-way, westbound traffic. Travelers returning north might best enter Cristobal Colon at its eastern end (via Benito Juarez and Justo Sierra) to most judiciously assume their place in line.

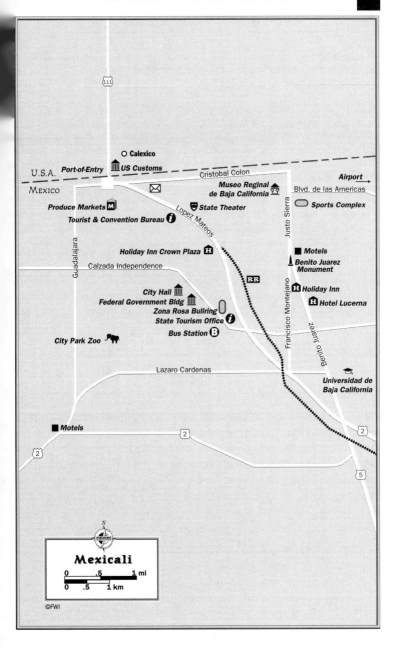

Mexicali

Highway 2—Mexicali to San Luis

The junction of Highways 2 and 5 is near the southern outskirts of Mexicali. The nature of the intersection is shown on the Mexicali map. This is busy industrial area, so drive with care.

It is 65 Km (40 miles) from the above referenced junction to the Rio Colorado and an additional 3 Km (2 miles) to San Luis. From the junction to the river, the entire highway is four-laned, straight and level. In terms of roadside activity it may be divided into three sections:

1. The westerly six miles is lined with numerous industrial buildings. The railroad paralleling much of this section serves these facilities.

2. East of the industrial area, Highway 2 passes through the heart of the Valle de Mexicali agricultural area but, initially, the highway is lined with scores of farm dwellings and garden plots reflecting the nearness of the city.

3. Approximately halfway between Mexicali and the Rio Colorado the city's influence ceases. The highway then passes through pleasant, well-ordered farms watered by an extensive irrigation ditches.

Highway 2 crosses the Rio Colorado on a two-lane toll bridge and enters the state of Sonora.

San Luis

San Luis is a town of 135,000 people in the Mexican state of Sonora. Tourists may enter or leave Mexico here, as at any of Baja's ports of entry. No Mexican car permit is required to pass through this small section of the Mexican mainland en route to the peninsula.

The main street of San Luis is also Highway 2. At the most westerly traffic light a turn to the north will lead to the port of entry only one block away. Cars returning to the United States line up east of the port of entry on the street that directly parallels the border fence. Drivers should access this street several blocks to the east of the above-referenced light to most conveniently locate the end of the line.

San Luis is visited by many tourists from the large city of Yuma, Arizona, 23 miles to the northwest. It contains many shops and other tourist-oriented activities. Mexican immigration offices and insurance outlets are present near the crossing.

Algodones

Algodones is a small farm community located on the international border directly west of the Rio Colorado. It has the most lightly used of Baja's ports of entry. The station is open from 6 a.m. to 8 p.m. Immigration and insurance offices are adjacent to the crossing.

Algodones may be reached from Highway 2 over a level, paved highway that parallels the Rio Colorado. Travel distance is 18.1 miles through pleasant agricultural country. The junction of the two highways is two miles west of the Rio Colorado near **Km-3.** Travelers may stop and look at the Morelos Dam a short distance south of the community. It diverts all of the water used to irrigate the Valle de Mexicali.

THE BORDER AREA
AND HIGHWAY 2

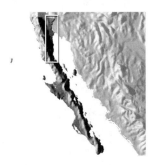

HIGHWAY 5

This chapter describes the Highway 5 route from the international border at Mexicali to its junction with Highway 1 at Laguna Chapala 267.5 miles to the south. Most of this road is constructed to highway standard, but at press time the oiled surface terminated at the community of Puertecitos 180.1 miles south of the border. The southerly 87.4 miles remains to be paved.

In previous editions of this book, I noted that it was reported that this unpaved section of highway would be completed by 1989. In the seven years that have transpired since, nothing new has occurred. For now, this section is heavily washboarded and should be traveled only by pickups, vans and other vehicles designed to take rough treatment.

If, and when, the new highway is completed, it will provide a major alternative to Highway 1 for accessing the southern half of Baja California. People approaching the peninsula from Arizona, Nevada and other states to the north and east will no longer have to travel to, and through, the Tijuana-Ensenada area to head south. The new highway joins Highway 1 near **Km C-229** a point approximately 324 miles south of Tijuana. Almost one-third of the Transpeninsular Highway and the congestion of the two metropolitan areas can thus be bypassed.

Travelers heading south to Baja from northern California, Oregon, Washington and Canada along U.S. Interstate 5 might choose to route themselves from Bakersfield, California, to Mexicali through the Mojave Desert and, believe it or not, bypass "The Jungle," and those delightful monuments to man's insanity, the Los Angeles-San Diego Freeway systems. It is approximately 580 miles from Bakersfield to Lake Chapala via Tijuana and Highway 1, and 607 miles using Highway 5 when entering Mexico at Mexicali. The small additional mileage of only 27 miles should be more than compensated for by safer, easier, faster and more scenic driving conditions.

Even travelers from the Los Angeles area may choose the Highway 5 alternative by traveling east on Interstate 10 toward Mexicali. Those from San Diego can also easily reach Mexicali over Interstate 8. The completion of Highway 5 should thus bring about a dramatic reduction in the use of the Transpeninsular Highway as a route to southern Baja. Tourism in the towns along Highway 5 will increase accordingly.

Highway 5 Overview

Reference to the "Geologic Provinces" map in the "Geology" chapter will show that the portion of Highway 5 between Mexicali and Puertecitos is within the Basin and Range Geologic Province. The western edge of this province is the escarpment of the Peninsular Range Mountains. This steep-faced cliff rises dramatically from near sea level to more than 10,000 feet in elevation. The escarpment is in view from this section of the highway, although in most places its base is obscured by lower intervening ranges of mountains. The latter are typical of the north-south ranges found throughout the Basin and Range Province.

From Puertecitos to Laguna Chapala, the highway passes through the edge of the Peninsular Range Mountains and moderately steep terrain is encountered in many places. Much of this section of road is within sight of the Sea of Cortez. Scenic qualities are thus considerably better than along Highway 1 far to the west.

Most of the area traversed by Highway 5 lies in the rain shadow of Baja's highest segment of the Peninsular Range Mountains, and is thus its driest area. Reference to the "Vegetative Regions" map on page 195 shows that the area's vegetation has been classified as the San Felipe Desert portion of the Sonoran Desert Region. Few of Baja's large and attractive species of desert plants are present here. Plant variety improves west of the Highway 5 junction with the secondary road to Calamajue and is comparable with better plant areas seen along Highway 1.

Mexicali

It is approximately six miles from the Mexicali port of entry to the junction of Highways 2 and 5 over the multilaned Calzada (wide avenue) Lopez Mateos. See the "Mexicali" map on page 323. The accompanying text provides suggestions for approaching the port of entry when returning to the United States and other information about Mexicali.

Valle de Mexicali

Highway 5 is fringed by urban activity for many miles south of its junction with Highway 2, and what was formerly a two-lane road is now a four-lane divided highway south to **Km-27**. The urbanization along the road hides the

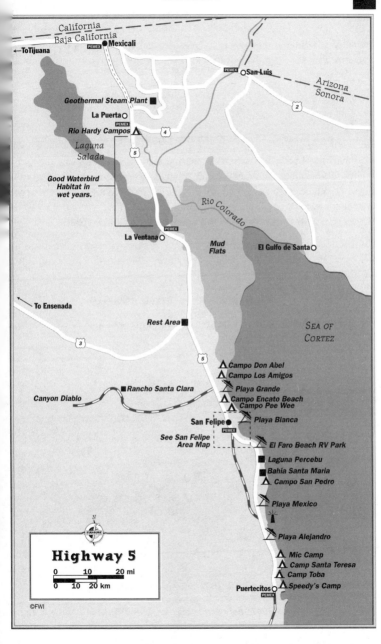

California
Baja California
←ToTijuana
PEMEX ●Mexicali
PEMEX ○San Luis
Arizona
Sonora
②
Geothermal Steam Plant ■
La Puerta○
PEMEX
Rio Hardy Campos ○ △
④
⑤
*Laguna
Salada*
**Good Waterbird
Habitat in
wet years.**
Rio Colorado
PEMEX
La Ventana○
Mud
Flats
El Gulfo de Santa○
To Ensenada
③
Rest Area ■
⑤
SEA OF
CORTEZ
△Campo Don Abel
△Campo Los Amigos
⚓Playa Grande
■Rancho Santa Clara
Canyon Diablo
△Campo Encato Beach
△Campo Pee Wee
San Felipe ●
PEMEX
⚓Playa Blanca
See San Felipe
Area Map
⚓El Faro Beach RV Park
■ Laguna Percebu
■ Bahia Santa Maria
△ Campo San Pedro
⚓Playa Mexico
⚓Playa Alejandro
△ Mic Camp
△ Camp Santa Teresa
△ Camp Toba
△Speedy's Camp
Puertecitos○
PEMEX

N

Highway 5

0   10   20 mi
0   10   20 km

©FWI

HIGHWAY 5

Valle de Mexicali farm lands from the traveler. The agricultural area extend
south to approximately **Km-46**. These lands are irrigated by an extensive se
ries of canals emanating from the *Presa Morelos* (Morelos Dam). This diver
sion extends across the Rio Colorado just south of the international borde
near the town of Algodones.

The history of the valley's development is indicated in the final section c
the "History" chapter.

Km-20—Geothermal Steam

Approximately five miles east of the highway at this point lies the Cerro
Prieto geothermal steam wells and its related electric generating plant. The
facility produces 620 megawatts of electricity, making it the second-larges
producer of geothermal steam energy in the world. It is exceeded only by the
Geysers development north of San Francisco in the United States.

If the air is cool, extensive clouds of water vapor may be seen rising into the
air above the wells. These may be visible during the morning hours but ofter
are absent in the afternoon.

Km-31—La Puerta

A small, Valle de Mexicali farming community with a cafe, store and
PEMEX Station.

*This section of the Rio Hardy is in the level agricultural plain between
Mexicali and San Felipe.*

Rio Hardy and Rio Colorado

The Rio Colorado and its short tributary, the Rio Hardy, roughly parallel Highway 5 on the east from approximately **Km-50** to **Km-72**. During most years there is no water in the Rio Colorado as it is all diverted for domestic and agricultural purposes. During the early 1980s, the Southwest United States experienced heavy rainfall, and water flowed down the Rio Colorado in excess of the storage capacity of its reservoirs. As a result, most of the older "campo" communities along the Rio Hardy were flooded. Now several new campos (including Campo Sonora **Km-55**) have been developed on the river. There are also other campos located easterly from the highway which I have not investigated. These campos advertise bird-hunting and fishing.

Km 72—Laguna Salada

At this point, Highway 5 lies on top of a nine-mile-long levee constructed across the southern end of Laguna Salada. The lake was filled during the flood years referred to above, but in most years there is no water in sight. During wet years, there are many waterbirds and some limited marshlands along the northern shore. The San Felipe Desert vegetation starts south of the lake.

Km-104—Mud Flats

In this vicinity, the desert vegetation is interrupted and the highway passes over the edge of the extensive mud flats that make up the delta area of the Rio Colorado. The mud flats are also closely approached near **Km-111**. These mud areas are up to 15 miles in width and extend easterly from the highway from Laguna Salada to near **Km-174**, a distance of almost 60 miles.

Wildlife experts report that the Rio Colorado delta once consisted of extensive marshlands that made excellent waterbird habitat. Moisture-loving vegetation has now disappeared as a result of the water-regulating effects of the reservoirs upstream along the river. This situation provides another example of mankind's environmental compromises.

SIDE TRIP

Km-141—Junction of Highways 3 and 5

It is 210 km (130 miles) to Ensenada via Highway 3. The easterly portion of this route provides an interesting side trip from Highway 5. It is 28 miles to the base of the majestic escarpment of the Peninsular Range Mountains, through terrain typical of the Basin and Range Geological Province. A further five-mile climb reaches the top of the grade.

SIDE TRIP

The vegetation of this Highway 3 segment of the San Felipe Desert is considerably more interesting than that in view from most of Highway 5. This is particularly true of the five-mile section that climbs up the escarpment. An outstanding stand of barrel cactus is present at the top of the grade.

A fancy picnic area and restaurant were constructed at this Highway 3 and 5 junction in early 1992. I can't conceive of why a picnic area is needed at such a place and will make book that it will be in ruins in a few years.

A roadside residence, cafe and gas station lie about 0.7 miles south of the Highway 3 and 5 junction.

Roca Consag

After proceeding south of the Highway 3 and 5 junction, start looking to the southeast, over the Sea of Cortez, for a view of *Roca Consag* (Consag Rock). It is a steep-sided, isolated pinnacle rising sharply from the sea to a height of 286 feet. It lies approximately due east from San Felipe at a distance of 18 miles offshore. Fishing boats from the town use it as a destination point.

The rock is named in honor of Padre Fernando Consag, one of the most prominent of Baja's Jesuit priests. In 1746, he conducted a maritime exploration of the northern reaches of the Sea of Cortez and the mouth of the Rio Colorado.

Also look ahead for several isolated peaks along the coast of the Sea of Cortez. They lie only a few degrees to the east of the line of the highway. These peaks are situated immediately north of San Felipe. They can be used to judge one's progress in the journey to this community.

Km-172—San Pedro Martir Mountains

At this location, high points on the main ridge of the Sierra San Pedro Martir are approximately due west from the highway. The principal peak is 10,126-foot **Picacho del Diablo**, Baja's highest point. As at other places along Highway 5, the base of the mountain's eastern escarpment is obscured from view by intervening lower ranges.

Picacho del Diablo (the Devil's Pike) lies near the center of the Parque Nacional Sierra San Pedro Martir. The park and its pine and fir forests may best be reached from Highway 1 south of Colonet.

Km-174—Campos

Near this point is the southern end of the Rio Colorado mudflats. The desert vegetation now directly adjoins the sea. As a result, the coast between

ere and San Felipe is lined with a series of campos. (See comments under
an Felipe below.) Each campo is reached over a short dirt road extending
asterly from Highway 5.

Km-180—Canon Diablo

Leaving Highway 5 to the right (west) is the most direct route to Canon
Diablo and Canon Diablito. The two canyons are cut into the steep eastern
escarpment of the Sierra San Pedro Martir. They offer year-round streams,
pools and waterfalls along with a shady camping spot. The road into the canyons is west from Rancho Santa Clara as shown on the Auto Club Baja map.
This a trip of about 32 miles.

Km-191—San Felipe Arch

A large, white, double-arch monument is constructed within a traffic circle
at this point. It marks the entrance to the community of San Felipe.

The double-arch monument at the entrance to San Felipe.

San Felipe

One mile east of the entrance arch on Highway 5 lies another traffic circle.
Highway 5 turns southward at this point. Continue straight ahead for the
town's downtown area. Also located at the traffic circle is one of the town's
PEMEX Stations. Diesel fuel has not been available. It can be obtained at the
diesel storage area at the southern end of the harbor south of town.

The community's main shopping area is located on Calzada Chetumal and
Mar de Cortez within a few blocks of the junction of these two streets. See
the "San Felipe Area" map for the location of the principal hotels and trailer
courts. The RV parks in San Felipe and two others located south of town are

good-to-excellent facilities and are in sharp contrast to most of the campo
described below.

*The dark hill in the photo's left sector is Punta San Felipe. San Felipe and its
harbor are to the right of the point.*

The San Felipe-Puertecitos area is one of Baja's six principal tourist areas.
This is due in large measure to its location only a few miles from the United
States. It can thus be reached on weekend trips and is particularly busy on
holiday weekends. It contains by far the largest concentration of RV parks
and *campos* of any locale in Baja, and serves as a southern extension of the
"snowbird" centers located in southern Arizona. Perhaps the word is spreading among these people that it is safe to travel in Baja, and that with only a
few more miles of driving, one may spend the winter at the seaside and leave
the drab Arizona desert behind.

Perhaps because of this ease of access, some of the area's visitors fall into
the category of what one source describes as an "unruly brand of tourist,"
particularly on three-day weekends. There are long, sandy beaches both
north and south of town. These are an inviting environment for the owners
of motorcycles, dune buggies and other types of off-road vehicles.

Adjoining the beaches are dozens of *campos*. They vary in size but generally
consist of a group of modest residences and trailers owned by *Norte Americanos*. The mandatory decoration for these dwellings appear to be signs ap-
propriated from the highways and other public places north of the border.

It would also appear that ownership of some form of open-air, specially
crafted dune buggy is required equipment. Although I am sure that the great
majority of the *campo* people do not fall in the "unruly" category, the San

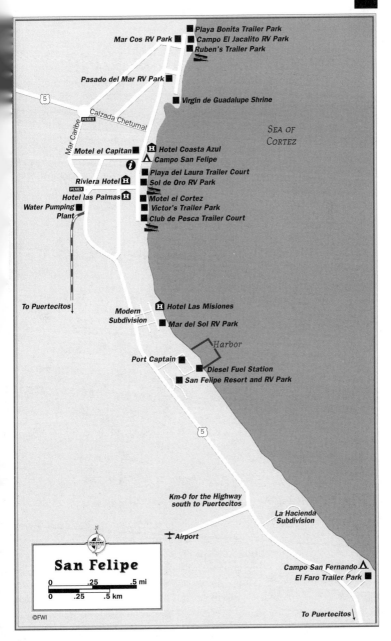

Playa Bonita Trailer Park
Mar Cos RV Park
Campo El Jacalito RV Park
Ruben's Trailer Park

Pasado del Mar RV Park

Virgin de Guadalupe Shrine

SEA OF
CORTEZ

Calzada Chetumal

PEMEX

Mar Caribe

Motel el Capitan
Hotel Coasta Azul
Campo San Felipe

Riviera Hotel
Playa del Laura Trailer Court
Sol de Oro RV Park

PEMEX

Hotel las Palmas
Motel el Cortez
Victor's Trailer Park
Water Pumping Plant
Club de Pesca Trailer Court

To Puertecitos

Hotel Las Misiones

Modern Subdivision
Mar del Sol RV Park

Harbor

Port Captain
Diesel Fuel Station
San Felipe Resort and RV Park

Km-0 for the Highway
south to Puertecitos

La Hacienda
Subdivision

Airport

San Felipe

0   .25   .5 mi
0   .25   .5 km

Campo San Fernando
El Faro Trailer Park

To Puertecitos

©FWI

Felipe-Puertecitos area, without question, has an atmosphere quite different from that found in other parts of the peninsula.

Lying south of San Felipe is a breakwater-lined harbor. It is the home port for many of the shrimp boats that ply the shallow waters of the northern Sea of Cortez. Conventional fishing is good in the area, but launching small boats is complicated by the high tides associated with the constricted upper end of the Sea of Cortez. These may exceed twenty feet and launching ramps are usable only at high tide. There are currently no marinas but one is planned adjoining the above noted harbor (See "San Felipe Area" map).

San Felipe is home for **Tony Reyes Fishing Tours**. This firm charters a large sportfishing vessel that travels to the Midriff Islands, 200 miles south in the Sea of Cortez. For information contact **The Long Fin**, *4010 E. Chapman Avenue, Suite D, Orange CA 92669*, ☎ *(714) 538-8010.*

The Hotel Las Misiones has Punta San Felipe as its background.

San Felipe to Puertecitos

Puertecitos is the approximate dividing point between the Basin and Range Geological Province to the north and the Peninsular Range Province to the south. With few exceptions, the coastline between San Felipe and Puertecitos is formed by level terrain, with almost continuous sandy beaches and shallow offshore depths. Mountains start south of Puertecitos and a majority of the coast consists of rocky bluffs or shingle beaches with deep water close to shore. Both swimming and the launching of small boats at high tide is far more easily accomplished north of Puertecitos.

It is 56.1 miles (paved) from San Felipe to Puertecitos and an additional 87.4 miles (unpaved) from Puertecitos to Highway 1 at Laguna Chapala (total 143.5 miles). Low-water crossings (*vados*) are a common feature along Baja's highways, but no where are they as abrupt as those in some sections of the highway north of Puertecitos. Be prepared to lower your speed to about 30 m.p.h. in driving through these obstructions. The mileage figures below start at San Felipe.

1.1 Miles

The San Felipe seawater pumping plant adjoins the north side of the highway. An old dirt surface road toward Puertecitos leaves the highway directly in front of this facility. After 35 miles, it joins Highway 5. One may visit an abandoned open-pit sulfur mine along the way.

2.7 Miles

A blacktop road leads to the San Felipe harbor and its adjoining industrial park. Note that most vessels are moored along the outer breakwater. This is because there is no water in the inshore portions of the basin at low tide.

6.5 Miles

Highway junction. An oiled-surface highway to the airport runs straight ahead (west). Highway 5 veers to the left (southeast). This is the zero point for kilometer posts between here and Puertecitos.

10.8 Miles

A concrete road leads in a short distance to the El Faro Beach Trailer Park. Its sign boasts that it is the finest resort in Baja, and it does appear to be an excellent facility. Between here and Puertecitos you will encounter dozens of side roads leading to beach-side campos. The most prominent of these are Laguna Percebu, Bahía Santa Maria and Playa Mexico.

56.1 Miles

Arrive at Puertecitos. The paved road ends here. The road to the south is built to highway standards except for a short segment through the community of Puertecitos. The eventual paved highway will no doubt pass a short distance inland.

Puertecitos

This community surrounds a well protected but very shallow natural harbor. There is a boat launching ramp on the north side of the entrance to the cove. Near the head of the cove is the Posada de Orozco, a cafe, RV park and PEMEX station. There is a nearby airstrip.

Puertecitos consists of several hundred homes owned mostly by North Americans. The quality of these structures is generally well above that found in the *campos*, but the community clearly bears the special flavor of the San Felipe-Puertecitos area. It is no doubt the world's leading depository for stolen road signs. No house is complete without one or more. Dune buggie are also in plentiful supply. Perhaps the high point is a very small but prom inent outhouse bearing the delightful label, "Hoppy's El Stinko House."

Puertecitos South to Highway 1

There are a few small resorts between Puertecitos and Highway 1. New signs announcing lots for rent and new *campos* began appearing several years ago, no doubt in reaction to completion of the oiled-surface road south to Puertecitos, and anticipation of its further extension. The road south of Pu ertecitos is too rough to invite many visitors, so this section of Baja will no doubt remain little-changed until the road is surfaced. There are many good places to drive to camp sites on the seacoast over dirt roads from .25 to .5 miles in length. Some of these sites will no doubt be taken over by *campos*, but for now this section of coast has little development. Perhaps the extreme shortage of fresh water in the area will keep it that way. Also there are few good sand beaches. Most coastal areas are rocky, making boat launching and swimming access a bit difficult.

74.6 Miles

Side road to the Huerfanito fish camp and camping area. Fishing boats are for rent.

96.6 Miles

A dirt road leads to the east and in 1.6 miles arrives at the small Punta Bufeo Resort. Most of its buildings are made of stone. Those along the beach are private residences. Inland a short distance is a small but attractive restaurant and several rental cabins.

102.3 Miles

A 0.6-mile-long side road leads to the Papa Fernandez Resort. It offers sev eral modest cabins, concrete boat ramp and fishing pangas for rent. A dirt road leads westerly a short distance to a good camping area at Punta Willard. Papa Fernandez founded his resort many years ago and in spring 1995 was still alive at the age of 100. Stop by and say hello.

106.1 Miles

A 0.8-mile-long secondary road leads to Bahía San Luis Gonzaga and the southern end of a long row of vacation homes with an outstanding sand beach on their eastern flank. A dirt airstrip is on the other side. At the north end of the residential area is Alfonsina's, a modest hotel offering five cot-filled rooms and a restaurant. A higher standard airstrip is immediately south of the above-noted facilities. A gas station and other buildings are west of the road. This Villas Mar de Cortez (Rancho Grande) development has plans for a fancy subdivision, golf course and marina, aimed at serving the private avi-ation flyer. They have made a brave start, but only time will tell.

Highway 5 moves inland at this point and leaves the Sea of Cortez behind. The road passes over relatively level terrain southward to the 120.3-mile point noted below.

116.5 Miles

A low-standard dirt road branches to the east and arrives at the Punta Final development in 9.1 miles. (I have not driven this road.) When visited by sea, I saw a group of about 30 houses and trailers owned by *Norte Americanos,* most of whom arrive by private aircraft on a nearby dirt strip. There was no resort facility. Small boats can be launched at low tide from a sand spit connecting the peninsular shore with a small nearby island.

120.3 Miles

At this point, the highway enters more mountainous terrain. The desert vegetation ahead improves in aesthetic appeal and many granite boulders begin to appear. It is similar, but not of as high a quality, as the Cataviña Boulder Fields area along Highway 1.

SIDE TRIP

129.9 Miles

Here is a road junction now named Coco's Corners in honor of a small enterprise containing a restaurant, RV parking, sodas and auto repairs. It is decorated by various items rescued from the area's trash cans. At this same point a good-quality secondary road branches to the left (north) and arrives at the fish camp of Calamajue in 23 miles. The camp houses the single male fishermen, while families live at a village about a half-mile inland. A few campsites are available on the shingle beach north of the camp.

My trip into Calamajue provided one of the most pleasurable experiences I have had in Baja California. The area's metamorphosed rock provides road-building material that permits a relatively smooth ride with minimal washboarding. In my view, this is the best secondary road in the peninsula. The surrounding mountains are also very scenic and the soil supports a far greater growth of annual plants than most other places.

143. 5 Miles

Junction with Highway 1 near Km C-229. The dry lake bed of Laguna Chapala lies south of the junction point. There is a small café and residence west of Highway 1 near the junction point.

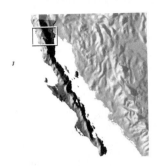

HIGHWAY 3

This chapter describes the two separate sections of Highway 3. They are Baja's most lightly used highways, yet road-construction standards are as good as anywhere in the peninsula. Both sections traverse hilly-to-mountainous terrain and offer good scenery.

Highway 3 Overview

Tecate to Highway 1 Near Ensenada

This 106 Km (66 mile) segment of Highway 3 passes through rolling hills covered with chaparral. Also present are several flat valleys devoted to agricultural endeavors. There are no large communities, and in the spring, the green countryside is pleasant. It resembles the area surrounding the cities of southern California in the United States, but lacks the massive intrusion of urbanization. It has the type of highway scenery one would like to admire on a Sunday drive.

This section of Highway 3 also provides tourists northbound on Highway 1 with the opportunity to cross into the United States at the lightly used port-of-entry at Tecate. I do not understand why anyone who has been to Ensenada—or farther south—would return home any other way. (See "Returning to the United States" page 162.)

Ensenada to Highway 5

Containing 196 Km (122 miles), this section of Highway 3 is almost exactly twice the length of the first segment. It also passes through hilly, and in some places through quite steep terrain. However, most of the route is over relatively gentle plateaus and valleys. There are few communities.

This section of highway offers travelers from the Yuma, Arizona, area a means of reaching Ensenada and the area to the south without passing through San Diego and Tijuana. If your purpose is to see Mexico, why not drive through it, and leave the U.S. freeway system to the less fortunate?

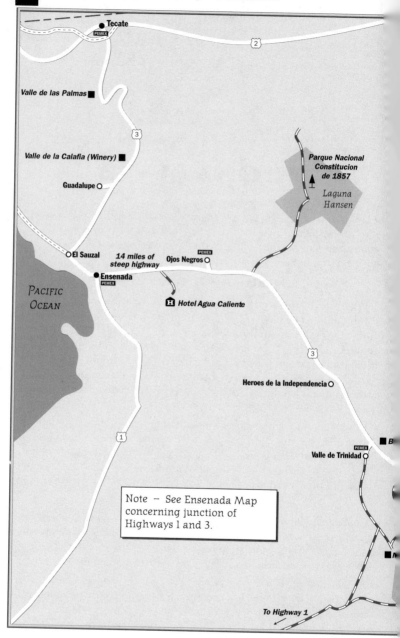

Tecate

Valle de las Palmas ■

Valle de la Calafia (Winery) ■

Guadalupe ○

Parque Nacional Constitucion de 1857

Laguna Hansen

○ El Sauzal

14 miles of steep highway

Ojos Negros ○

● Ensenada

🏨 *Hotel Agua Caliente*

PACIFIC OCEAN

Heroes de la Independencia ○

■ B

Valle de Trinidad ○

Note – See Ensenada Map concerning junction of Highways 1 and 3.

■ M

To Highway 1

HIGHWAY 3

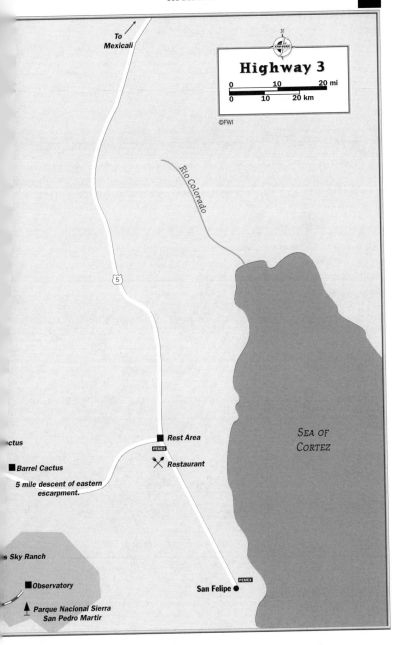

(This Highway 3 alternative will become unnecessary if and when oiling o
Highway 5 from San Felipe south to Lake Chapala is completed.)

Tecate

This community and the route to the Tecate port-of-entry are describec
earlier. Only about one mile of Highway 3 lies within the community. Traffic is moderate to light. Northbound travelers should have little trouble finding the crossing point into the United States. Also there is an interchange
with the 2D four-lane divided highway a short distance south of Tecate so
that one may enter the expressway from the south without going into town.

The hills between Tecate and Valle de las Palmas are made up of granite
rock. The surface areas have been fractured and eroded into thousands of
light-colored boulders. This coloration and erosion pattern is typical of granitic rock areas.

Km-29—Valle de las Palmas

Here is a beautiful valley surrounded by hills. The fields are planted with
grain, grapes and olive and citrus orchards. Farther south, the highway passes through a series of similar valleys.

The Valle de la Calafia is framed in the archways of the DOMECO winery.

Km-76—Valle de la Calafia

This broad, flat valley is planted exclusively with vineyards and is home to
the DOMECO winery. This modern facility produces Pedro Domeco wine.
The overall setting is the match for anything available in the wine country
north of San Francisco in Alta California. There are no public tasting rooms

or organized tours. However, a trip through the plant can be arranged upon request.

Km-79—Guadalupe

The community of Guadalupe lies a short distance to the right (west) of the highway in another valley devoted largely to vineyards. This pleasant spot is the site of the last mission (no ruins) founded in Baja California. It saw service for only six years (1834–1840).

Km-101—Scenic View

The journey from Tecate to the Pacific coast is almost over, and Highway 3 begins its final descent to the sea. In view, ahead, are the Islas Todos Santos. These two rocky islands lie 10 miles offshore, southwest from Ensenada.

Km-105—Junction with Highway 1-D

Highway 3 joins the Highway 1-D four-lane divided highway at the coastal town of El Sauzal. Highway 1-D is a toll road north to Tijuana, but is toll-free from this junction point south into Ensenada.

Junction of Highways 3 and 1 in Ensenada

The second section of Highway 3 starts in the heart of Ensenada at a junction point with old Highway 1. The initial 4 Km of the route proceeds easterly over four-lane Calzada Cortez, one of Ensenada's main business streets. There are several PEMEX stations along the way.

Km-4—Enter Mountains

The flat lands on which much of Ensenada is built terminate near **Km-4**, and Highway 3 begins the longest sustained climb found anywhere on the peninsula's highways. The grade winds upward to near **Km-20**, and after a brief respite it continues to **Km-26**. This steep and curving area can be taxing for vehicles pulling large recreation trailers. This could preclude their owners from using this otherwise fine highway as a route from the Yuma, Arizona, area to Ensenada.

This steep grade near the Pacific coast provides the exception to all other highway crossings of the Baja peninsula. In these other cases the steep section of highway is encountered near the Sea of Cortez coast, where the highway crosses the east-facing escarpment of the Peninsular Range Mountains. The highway climb from west to east is a very gradual one.

SIDE TRIP

Km-26—Agua Caliente

A short distance east of Km 26, the highway reaches the top of the grade and descends into the Valle de Ojos Negros. Exactly at this high point, a dirt road leaves to the right (south) and descends steeply for 5.4 miles to the Hotel Agua Caliente. (See "Hotel Descriptions" section.) The descent is steep but suitable, if recently graded, for most large RVs (other than trailers).

The hotel has large swimming pools fed by hot springs. Camping is permitted in an area of giant live oak trees adjoining the hotel and the Rio San Carlos.

Km-36—Valle de Ojos Negros

Highway 3 enters the western edge of the broad Valle de Ojos Negros (Black Eyes Valley). A short oiled access road heads left (north) at **Km-39** to the farming community of Ojos Negros. It has a PEMEX station. (Nova only during my last visit.) The flat valley continues to near **Km-50**.

Laguna Hansen is framed in Jeffrey pine foliage in the Parque Nacional Constitucion de 1857.

SIDE TRIP

Km-55—Parque Nacional Constitucion de 1857 (Laguna Hanson)

A secondary road leaves the highway 200 yards east of Km-55. It is signed for Laguna Hanson 35 Km. This shallow lake (and the extensive stands of Jeffrey pine surrounding it) are the park's main attractions. It is 22 miles to Laguna Hanson from Highway 3. Although constructed to secondary road standards, the road has some rough spots. The entire route lies in decomposed granite soils and thus is subject to erosion following rain. It is marginal for larger RVs. (See the accompanying map for additional details.)

One may also drive to Laguna Hanson from the north. See Km-72. This northern road is of lower standard than the route from Highway 3, with the most difficult 2.5-mile segment lying in a granite, boulder area just inside the park's northern boundary.

Laguna Hanson contains water following rains; when it is full it provides a pleasant environment. The area surrounding the lake is heavily forested and of gentle terrain. There are minimum-facility campsites at the water's edge along the western shore.

Vegetation

The vegetation east of Ensenada is chaparral typical of the California Vegetative Region. (See "Vegetation" chapter.) East of Valle de Ojos Negros the highway slowly climbs over plateau lands. Near **Km-76** the traveler begins to see low juniper trees and an occasional pinyon pine. This is the lower fringe of the coniferous forest that covers the land in the national park to the northwest.

Km-91—Heros De La Independencia

A small community lies at this point. A PEMEX station (Nova only) is on the east side of the highway.

Km-119—Descent Into Valle de Trinidad

The highway starts a steep descent into the Valle de Trinidad. This is the start of a two-part drop from the mountains into the San Felipe Desert. The second segment takes place east of the valley near **Km-149**. During this first portion, notice the numerous barrel cacti growing on the steep slopes. They are a sign that the highway is rapidly approaching a change in vegetational types.

Near **Km-123** a secondary road bears right (south) to the farming community of Valle de Trinidad. It reaches the town's main street in a short dis-

HIGHWAY 3

tance. At this junction, turn left for 0.5 miles to the PEMEX station. The road to the right leads to one of the back-door entrances to the Parque Nacional Sierra San Pedro Martir. The preferred access route to this park leaves Highway 1 at Km B-140 south of Colonet.

The valley is long and wide, and is filled with orchards and irrigated pastures.

Km 138—Road to Mike's Sky Ranch

A secondary road to the right leads to Mike's Sky Ranch, a resort catering to private flyers. I have not been over this route.

Km-149—Highway Descent

Highway 3 now starts the 4.9-mile second leg of its descent of the eastern escarpment of the Peninsular Range Mountains. As at the first segment, notice the dense stand of barrel cactus. Nowhere else in Baja are such large numbers of these plants in view from the highway. Also present are ocotillo, agave, cardón and other species that are common in Baja's desert areas. The descent represents a vegetational transition from the California Region vegetation, to the west, and the San Felipe Desert, to the east.

Km-157—Vegetation and Geographic Change

Here, at the base of the mountains, are encountered two major changes. The chaparral vegetation of the Peninsular Range Mountains is left behind, to the west, and is replaced with the widely spaced species of the San Felipe Desert. Between here and the Highway 5 junction, the presence of numerous ocotillo plants gives some degree of character to the landscape; yet overall this San Felipe Desert has relatively drab vegetation due to the extreme dryness caused by its location in the shadow of the mountains.

The highway has also entered a typical portion of the Basin and Range Geologic Province. (See "Geology" chapter.) Note that the highway will traverse relatively flat land but that several north-south ranges of mountains project from the plain. Also note the majestic cliffs extending south from the foot of the grade. This is one of the best places in Baja to view the dramatic eastern escarpment of the Peninsular Range Mountains.

Km-196—Junction with Highway 5

Highways 3 and 5 meet at this point in the desert. Fortunately, the inviting Sea of Cortez has been in view from Highway 3 en route to the junction for several miles to the east. While I feel the place is uninspiring, the Mexican Highway Department was inspired in 1992 to build a picnic area and restaurant at the spot. If anyone ever decides to have a picnic here, please let me know.

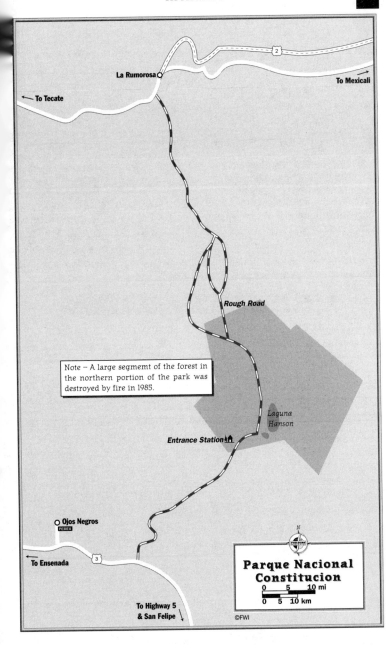

To Mexicali

La Rumorosa

← To Tecate

Rough Road

Note – A large segmemt of the forest in the northern portion of the park was destroyed by fire in 1985.

Laguna Hanson

Entrance Station

O **Ojos Negros**
PEMEX

← **To Ensenada**

To Highway 5 & San Felipe ↓

Parque Nacional Constitucion

0   5   10 mi
0   5   10 km

©FWI

Ocotillo and creosote bush thinly vegetate the San Felipe desert as seen from Highway 3 west of its junction with Highway 5.

THIS NO MAN'S LAND

The conquistadores came with their greed
But Baja California would not concede,

Cortez...Mendosa...Cabrillo...Vizcaino...and more
The riches they sought were not on her shores;

Not even enough food could be found
To feed men and beasts on this arid ground,

Native Pericues and Guaycuras barely survived
and with white man's diseases too many died.

Then missionaries tried but despite their valiant struggle
Many missions remain only as heaps of old rubble,

Padres Kino...Salvatierra...Serra...Ugarte...
Like the conquistadore bands,

Left only their names on this inhospitable land.

—**Ken Reimer**

HIGHWAY 3

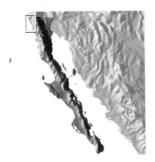

TIJUANA TO ENSENADA

A teeming residential area in hilly Tijuana.

Thousands of Baja buffs find that the peninsula provides a welcome relief from the hectic conditions of the Los Angeles–San Diego metropolitan areas. Many buffs would also agree that decompression takes place in three stages: (1) Tijuana to Ensenada, (2) Ensenada to San Quintin, and (3) south of San Quintin. Described in this chapter is the first stage of relief. It may be undertaken without a doctor's prescription.

Highway 1-D between Tijuana and Ensenada is one of Baja's best highways. It and the older, more or less parallel Highway 1 are described in this chapter.

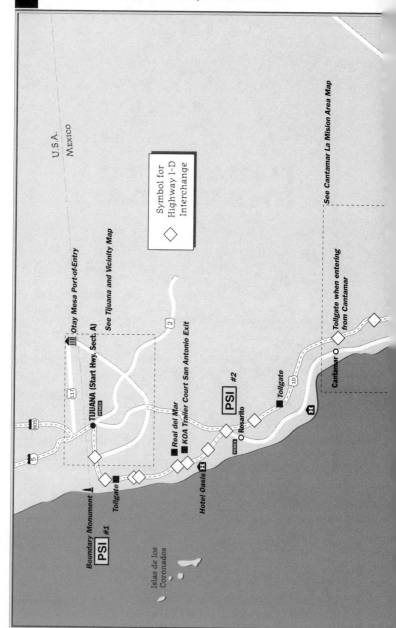

U.S.A.
MEXICO

Symbol for
Highway 1-D
Interchange

Otay Mesa Port-of-Entry

See Tijuana and Vicinity Map

See Cantamar La Mision Area Map

Tollgate when entering
from Cantamar

Cantamar

TIJUANA (Start Hwy. Sect. A)

Real del Mar

KOA Trailer Court San Antonio Exit

PSI #2

Rosarito

Tollgate

Hotel Oasis

Boundary Monument

Tollgate

PSI #1

Islas de los
Coronados

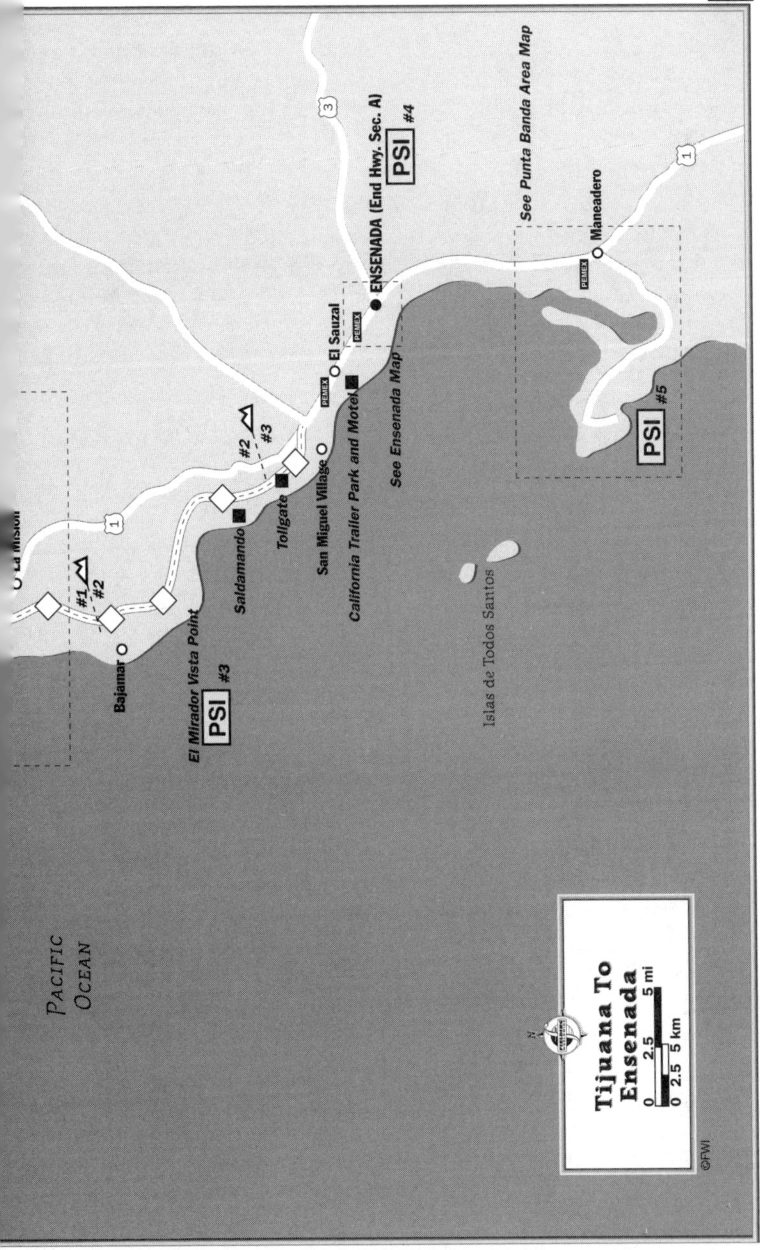

PACIFIC OCEAN

O La Misión

Bajamar O

PSI #2

El Mirador Vista Point **PSI** #3

Saldamando

Tollgate

San Miguel Village O

California Trailer Park and Motel

See Ensenada Map

Islas de Todos Santos

#2 #3

El Sauzal

PEMEX

ENSENADA (End Hwy. Sec. A)

PSI #4

See Punta Banda Area Map

Maneadero O

PEMEX

PSI #5

Tijuana To Ensenada

0   2.5   5 mi

0   2.5   5 km

N

©FWI

Overview of Highway 1-D

Highway 1-D is a four-lane, divided, limited-access toll road. It is signed "*Cuota*," meaning "fare." A toll is collected to use all but short sections at either end. It may be paid in either pesos or U.S. dollars. (There are three tollgates, as shown on the map on page 314.) This route is the fastest, safest and most scenic way to travel between Tijuana to Ensenada.

There are approximately 20 interchanges along Highway 1-D. I say "approximately" in that several of the original interchanges are sometimes closed and new ones are sometimes constructed. In all cases, it is possible to leave the highway and then to re-enter at or near the same point to travel in the same direction. In most places, one may also re-enter to travel in the opposite direction.

Overview of Highway 1

There are three distinct sections of Highway 1. All are built to good two-lane standards. There is no toll on this road so it is signed "*Libre*," meaning "free."

Tijuana to Rosarito

This is the quickest way to travel south for those starting their journey from the vicinity of the bullring on Boulevard Agua Caliente in Tijuana. However, it offers no advantages for the southbound traveler starting at the Tijuana-San Ysidro port of entry who should use Highway 1-D. In contrast, it is my recommended route for returning north as it provides access to the Otay Mesa port of entry. The southernmost 7.3 miles of this route is a four-lane, divided highway. It is described in the "Returning to the U.S.A." section in "The Border Area and Highway 2" chapter.

Rosarito to La Mision

This section of highway passes along the edge of a series of communities made up largely of homes, condominium developments, restaurants and other facilities serving people from north of the border. Unless you are headed for one of these destinations, taking this route offers no advantages to the southbound traveler. This portion of Highway 1 is also heavily used by truckers and others who wish to escape the tolls charged on Highway 1D. Unless you are short on funds, the latter route is by far the better choice.

La Mision to El Sauzal

This is an inland road through the mountains. It provides a pleasant drive through undeveloped countryside but does not offer the excellent scenic vistas of the ocean and coast that are available from Highway 1-D.

The balance of this chapter describes the Highway 1-D route from Tijuana to Ensenada.

Km A-0—Tijuana

After entering Mexico at the San Ysidro port of entry one must drive a circle route bearing left. Follow the signs for Rosarito and Ensenada. After the circle, Highway 1-D proceeds west along the international boundary fence toward the Pacific. See the "Tijuana and Vicinity" map and the "Entering Tijuana From the North" section for more details.

Km A-9—Boundary Monument

PSI
#1

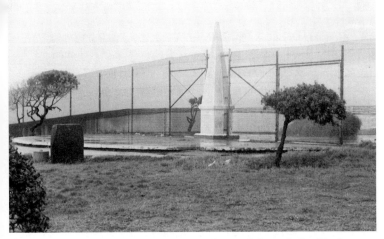

The international boundary monument a few yards from the Pacific Ocean at Tijuana. Sadly, there has to be a chain-link fence between the two countries.

Just prior to **Km A-9** one encounters an interchange signed "*Playas de Tijuana*" as Highway 1-D begins a broad curve from westbound to southbound. The Bullring by-the-Sea is in view near the coast, and its access road is easy to find by taking this offramp.

Immediately north of the bullring and adjacent to the Tijuana lighthouse is the international boundary fence and a 12-foot obelisk commemorating the establishment of the U.S.–Mexican boundary that resulted from the Mexican-American War and the February 2, 1848, Treaty of Guadalupe Hidalgo. While the monument itself is not overly impressive, it has been included as stop No. 1 on the Points of Special Interest Tour. It is a good place to pause and reflect on the history of the two countries and also to relax a moment and celebrate your safe arrival in Mexico's Baja.

The northerly tollgate is located just south of the "Playas de Tijuana" interchange near **Km A-10**.

Km A-11—Islas Coronados

Islas Coronados (Coronados Islands) lie about six miles offshore. These islands are in view for many miles along Highway 1-D, but all four of the two large and two smaller islands can be seen from here, near **Km A-11**.

Km 19.5—Real del Mar

On the inland side of the highway lies the very swank Hotel Real del Mar and an 18-hole golf course.

Km A-22—San Antonio del Mar

The Rosarito KOA trailer court lies on the side of a nicely landscaped hill 0.2 miles east of the highway after taking the San Antonio interchange. It is the closest trailer court to the international border. Most of its sites are rented on a year-round basis, but there is always room for overnighters.

Km A-25—Oasis Hotel and RV Resort

Between the highway and beach lies a fancy hotel and RV complex. It is accessible only from the southbound lanes of Highway 1-D.

Km A-34—Rosarito

Rosarito is a major center of tourist-oriented shops, motels, hotels and restaurants strung out along a lengthy section of old Highway 1. The town adjoins an excellent sand beach. Government statistics indicate that 11 percent of the tourists entering Baja have Rosarito as their destination point. The most visible facilities are the eight-story Quinta del Mar Resort and other high-rise buildings. In the past, Rosarito was a somewhat shoddy looking town, but now its appearance has been greatly enhanced by development of the main street into four lanes, with palm trees planted along the median strip. Seemingly endless stop signs and traffic lights impede progress, so stay on Highway 1-D unless you particularly wish to visit the town. The middle of the three tollgates straddles this highway immediately south of Rosarito.

PSI
#2

The historic **Rosarito Beach Hotel** lies on the beach near the southern end of town. This low-rise building is one of three casinos that operated in the border area during the late 1920s and early 1930s. Many of the rooms have recently been remodeled and a new wing has been added. It is stop No. 2 on the Points of Special Interest Tour.

There are many smaller motels, restaurants and condominiums from Rosarito south to Cantamar. One must travel on non-toll Highway 1 to access this area. This is also the route to use to reach the Hotel Las Rocas and the Hotel New Port Baja.

Km A-53—Cantamar and El Descanso

The Cantamar interchange is the place to exit Highway 1-D to visit the towns of Cantamar and Descanso. At the southern edge of the latter com-

unity are situated large coastal sand dunes that provide an excellent dune
uggy area.

South of the sand dunes, Highway 1-D crosses the Rio Descanso at **Km A-5**. Just south of this kilometer post, look for a large complex of glass green-
ouses inland from the highway. Behind the greenhouses can be seen a small
hurch. This church stands on the site of the Descanso mission established
ere in 1814 by the Dominican Order. It was the next to last of the penin-
ular missions.

Km A-66—La Mision

The La Mision-Plaza del Mar interchange is the place to exit Highway 1-D
o visit the La Fonda Hotel and to take the side trip noted below.

SIDE TRIP

*It is 3.8 miles south and then east on old Highway 1 from the La Mi-
sion-Plaza del Mar interchange to the ruins of the San Miguel de la
Frontera mission. These adobe remains lie within a chain-link fence
in the yard of the La Mision community school. They are directly adjacent to the highway 0.8 miles east from the Rio Guadalupe bridge.
You may also continue south on Highway 1 toward Ensenada. This
drive is through pleasant, undeveloped hill-country but lacks the ocean
views afforded by staying on Highway 1-D.*

Km A-69—Parking Area and Beach

Just north of the Highway 1-D crossing of the Rio Guadalupe estuary is a
50-car parking lot and fine sandy beach directly adjoining the highway. It
gets heavy use on holiday weekends.

Km A-71—Playa Mal Paso

Immediately north of **Km A-71**, a dirt road leaves the highway and shortly
arrives at the residence of the operators of the beach camping area at Playa
Mal Paso. This beach can be reached only from the southbound lanes of the
highway. Extra care is needed in reentering the highway as this is not a regular interchange.

Km A-72—Baja Seasons

Located here is one of the finest trailer courts in Baja operated by **Outdoor
Resorts of Baja**, ☎ *(800) 986-Baja*. It has 137 units, tennis courts, pool,
clubhouse and related facilities. Rates are expensive. The court is directly on
the beach, but Pacific waters are cold this far north. Near the RV park is a
fancy hotel *(villas)* establishment.

Km A-73—La Salina

A short drive south from the La Salina interchange brings one to Playa I Salina beach. The area is under development and it is uncertain what will ur fold.

Km A-75—Geographic Change

You have now reached the northernmost breakpoint between the 19 gec graphic sections encountered along the Transpeninsular Highway. The rela tively flat coastal beaches (Section 1) will be left behind as the highway start a climb into steeper terrain (Section 2). In a few miles, this increase in eleva tion will reward the traveler with excellent vistas of the coastline.

Km A-78—Bajamar Interchange

Immediately west of this interchange lies the Bajamar Ocean Front Go Resort. It contains an 18-hole golf course, the Hacienda las Glorias hotel condos and surrounding residences. There is a pro-shop with restaurant, and bar. Bajamar is one of the finest residential developments in the Baja penin sula. There is little development between Bajamar and the southernmost tollgate at Km A-99 due no doubt to the absence of a domestic water sys tem.

Km A-84—El Mirador Vista Point

An interchange a short distance north of **Km A-84** provides direct access to a parking lot near the cliffs overlooking the Pacific Ocean. There is a restau rant, bar and gift shop. From here, you will be rewarded with the best views of the Pacific coast that are available from the entire Transpeninsular High way. Also in view are the Islas Todos Santos, which lie 12 miles to the south west. These two small islands guard the outer limits of the broad bay on whose shore is built the city of Ensenada. Because of the excellent view, El Mirador is included as stop No. 3 in the Points of Special Interest Tour.

Km A-92 to A-94—Sedimentary Rocks

The majority of the rocks visible in the mountainous areas of the peninsula will be granitic or volcanic. Both of these are igneous rocks. Here, north of Ensenada, the highway cuts clearly display the layering that is the most com mon characteristic of sedimentary rocks. (See the "Rock Type" chart in "Geology" chapter.)

Km A-94—Saldamando

Just past **Km A-94**, a dirt road to the west descends steeply to the residence of the operator of a camping area on the bluffs above a rocky shoreline. Sev eral camping spots have been carved out along the road for about one-half mile south from the residence. They provide excellent views of the ocean but are not well-suited for larger RVs.

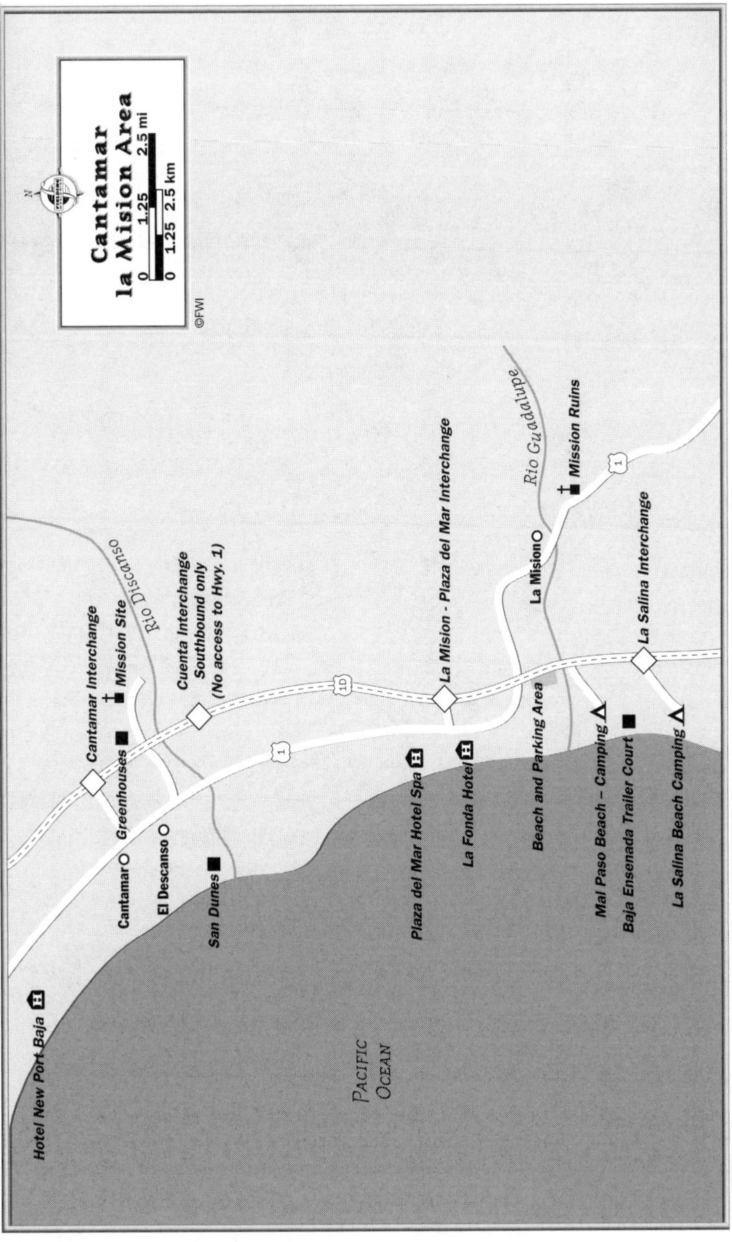

Cantamar
la Mision Area

0   1.25   2.5 mi
0   1.25   2.5 km

©FWI

Hotel New Port Baja

Cantamar Interchange
† Mission Site
Greenhouses
Cantamar ○
El Descanso ○
San Dunes

Rio Discanso

Cuenta Interchange
Southbound only
(No access to Hwy. 1)

Plaza del Mar Hotel Spa
La Fonda Hotel

La Mision - Plaza del Mar Interchange

Rio Guadalupe

La Mision ○

Beach and Parking Area

Mal Paso Beach – Camping △
Baja Ensenada Trailer Court
La Salina Beach Camping △

La Salina Interchange

† Mission Ruins

PACIFIC
OCEAN

The northernmost of the three tollgates on Highway 1-D.

Km A-99—Tollgate and Geographic Change

Near **Km A-99** is situated the southernmost of Highway 1-D's three tollgates. The remainder of the trip into Ensenada is toll-free. Just south of the tollgate is the junction with old Highway 1. The toll station also marks the end of mountainous Geographic Section No. 2. For the next 22 miles the highway passes over flatlands (Section No. 3) surrounding the city of Ensenada.

Immediately south of the tollgate is San Miguel Village. A minimum-facility camping area is present on a level bench near the rocky shoreline.

El Sauzal Area

Approximately 1.5 miles south of the tollgate is the junction of Highway 1-D and Highway 3 and the community of El Sauzal. El Sauzal is one of the largest fishing ports on the Baja peninsula. Note the breakwater-lined harbor that is usually filled with numerous fishing vessels. Adjoining the harbor are a packing plant and related buildings.

Between El Sauzal and Ensenada there are several motels and trailer courts. The latter cater mostly to year-round tenants. One of the better facilities is the California Trailer Park and Motel located about six miles north of downtown Ensenada just north of a large PEMEX plant.

Baja's Sonoran desert has a variety of intriguing cacti.

Baja highway art

Cabo San Lucas is Baja's fishing capital.

Quaint churches are found along many Baja backroads.

Km A-109—Ensenada

Ensenada has an annual Carnaval celebration. Small circuses and carnaval shows are frequently seen in Baja's larger communities.

Ensenada is Baja California's third-largest city with a population of about 170,000. Twenty-three percent of the tourists entering the peninsula have Ensenada as their destination point, making Ensenada second only to Tijuana as a tourist attraction.

To classify Ensenada as a beautiful city would be inaccurate in my view. There are no major beaches and the tourist section of the city is fronted with a busy breakwater-lined harbor. But certainly it is a pleasant place, with a climate similar to San Diego. It gives the one-day or weekend tourist the feeling of having really been to Mexico that somehow does not result from a visit to Tijuana.

Immigration

The Mexican immigration office (signed *Servicios Migrarios*) is located on the left side of the street next to the Port Captain as you enter Ensenada. There are about six parking spots in front of the building. Here is the place to obtain or validate tourists cards if you are heading south of the city, where they are required. A tourist information office is located within walking distance a short distance away. (See the "Ensenada" map.)

Tourist Row

The city's main tourist area centers in and around the section of **Avenida Lopez Mateos** shown on the inset map of the "Ensenada" map. Traffic is usually heavy on this street, so the wise visitor will park along Boulevard Lazaro Cardenas or the streets surrounding the civic plaza.

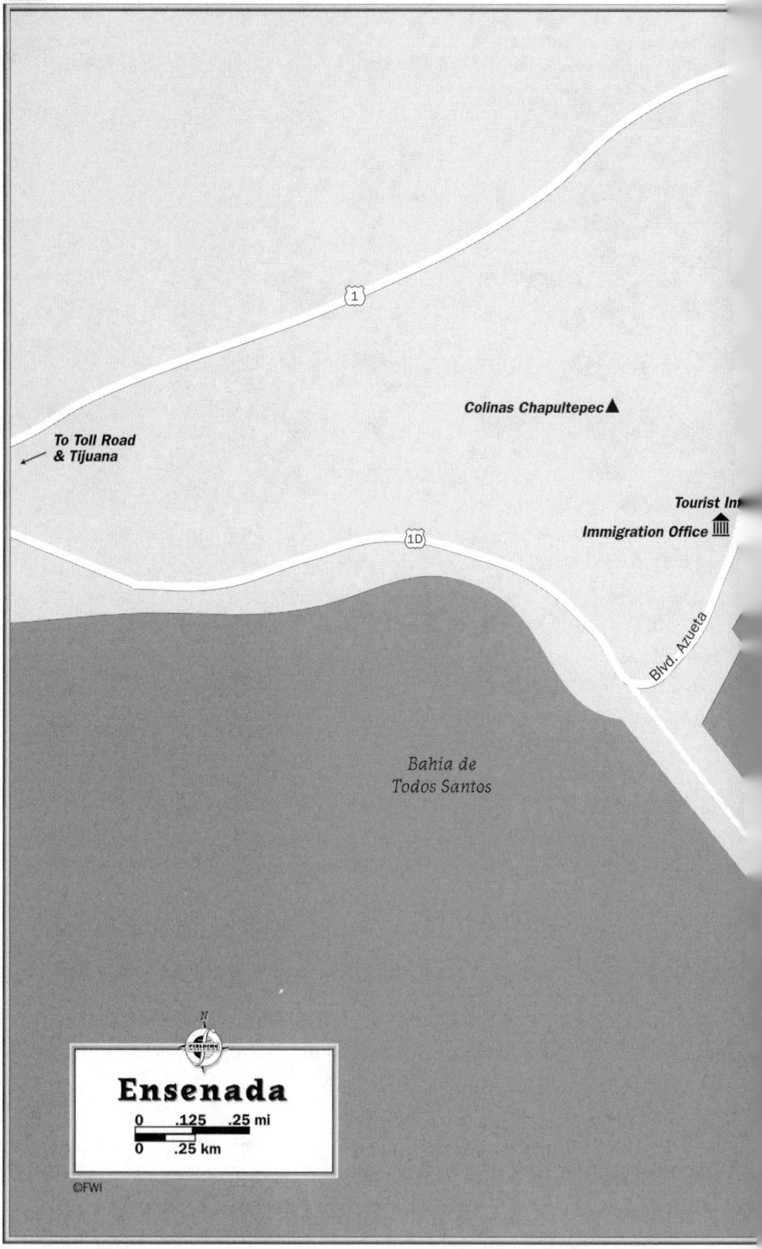

To Toll Road
& Tijuana

Colinas Chapultepec ▲

Tourist Inf

Immigration Office 🏛

Blvd. Azueta

1D

*Bahía de
Todos Santos*

Ensenada

| 0 | .125 | .25 mi |

| 0 | .25 km |

©FWI

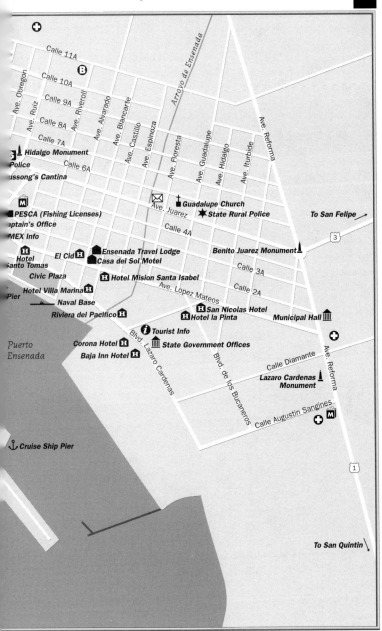

Calle 11A

Calle 10A

Calle 9A

Ave. Obregon

Ave. Ruiz

Calle 8A

Ave. Riveroll

Calle 7A

Ave. Alvarado

Ave. Blancarte

Ave. Castillo

Ave. Espinoza

Arroyo de Ensenada

Ave. Floresta

Ave. Guadalupe

Ave. Hidalgo

Ave. Iturbide

Ave. Reforma

Hidalgo Monument

Police

Calle 6A

ussong's Cantina

PESCA (Fishing Licenses)

aptain's Office

MEX Info

Ave. Juarez

Guadalupe Church

State Rural Police

To San Felipe

(3)

Calle 4A

Benito Juarez Monument

Hotel

El Cid

Ensenada Travel Lodge

Casa del Sol Motel

Calle 3A

anto Tomas

Civic Plaza

Hotel Mision Santa Isabel

Calle 2A

Hotel Villa Marina

Ave. Lopez Mateos

Pier

Naval Base

San Nicolas Hotel

Riviera del Pacifico

Hotel la Pinta

Municipal Hall

Puerto
Ensenada

Tourist Info

Corona Hotel

State Government Offices

Blvd. Lazaro Cardenas

Baja Inn Hotel

Blvd. de los Bucaneros

Calle Diamante

Ave. Reforma

Lazaro Cardenas Monument

Calle Augustin Sangines

Cruise Ship Pier

(1)

To San Quintin

This section of the city is stop No. 4 on the Points of Special Interest Tour. At first glance it may appear to be just another long array of tourist traps. Typical souvenir items are of course in plentiful supply, but there is also much quality merchandise. (I have found the selection to be much better than in La Paz.) If you are a budget-minded person, it is simply foolish not to stock up on Christmas and birthday presents, etc. while in Ensenada. The savings can be substantial.

Also consider visiting the **Riviera del Pacifico** (former gambling casino), the **Santo Tomas winery** at *666 Avenida Miramar*, and, of course, **Hussong's Cantina**. You may find the latter establishment a bit lowbrow, but thousands of beer-drinkers like the place, and the mariachi music is free (unless you are so unwise as to request your favorite song). It was established in 1892 and is still operated by the same family.

Driving Through Ensenada

It is recommended that the Highway 1-D, Lazaro Cardenas, General Agustin route is the best way to travel through the city. These streets are multilaned all the way and traffic is usually moderate. I see no advantages for average tourists in taking the old Highway 1 route unless they are interested in increasing the chances of the culturally rewarding experience of becoming lost.

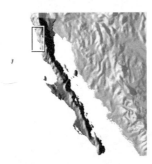

ENSENADA TO
SAN QUINTIN

The Grand Tour now proceeds from Ensenada south to the town of San Quintin and nearby Bahía San Quintin. This 196 Km (122 mile) section of the Transpeninsular Highway is the second decompression step from the Southern California "pressure cooker." There are far fewer tourist accommodations and travelers than you'll find north of Ensenada. However, you will still encounter a series of sizeable towns, much agricultural development, many people and vegetation that still looks much like it does north of the border. You will have to wait until the next chapter to get into the real "magnificent peninsula."

Passing Through Ensenada

There is considerable traffic in Ensenada. I recommend that you enter from the north on Highway 1-D and follow the Lazaro Cardenas-General Agustin route to Highway 1 south of the downtown area. See the "Ensenada" map.

Ensenada to Maneadero

It is 14 Km (nine miles) from Ensenada to Maneadero over a four- and six-lane highway. This section of Highway 1 provides a transition from the freeway to the north and the two-lane road that starts south of Maneadero. The terrain is flat. There is much urbanization from Ensenada to the Estero Beach road. Farther south, there are still some farms and olive orchards. As in other metropolitan sections, the kilometer posts are often missing. Watch for the Joker Motel and Estero Beach turnoff along the way.

Km B-13—Joker Motel and RV Park

A pleasant RV Park adjoins the Joker Motel on the east side of the highway at this point.

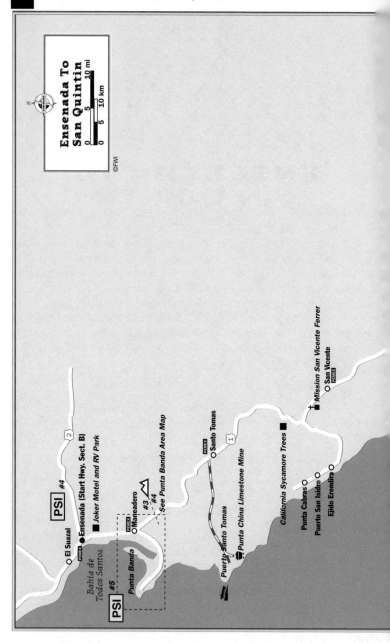

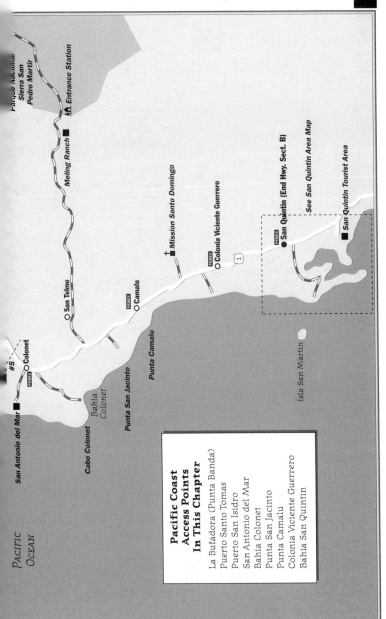

PACIFIC
OCEAN

Parque Nacional
Sierra San
Pedro Martir

▲ Entrance Station

■ Meling Ranch

San Antonio del Mar ■

#5

○ Colonet

PEMEX

Bahía
Colonet

Cabo Colonet

Punta San Jacinto

○ San Telmo

Punta Camalu

PEMEX
○ Camalu

† ■ Mission Santo Domingo

PEMEX
○ Colonia Viciente Guerrero

(1)

See San Quintin Area Map

PEMEX
● San Quintin (End Hwy. Sect. B)

■ San Quintin Tourist Area

Isla San Martin

**Pacific Coast
Access Points
In This Chapter**

La Bufadora (Punta Banda)
Puerto Santo Tomas
Puerto San Isidro
San Antonio del Mar
Bahia Colonet
Punta San Jacinto
Punta Camalu
Colonia Viciente Guerrero
Bahia San Quintin

La Bufadora blowhole draws spectators daily.

SIDE TRIP

Km B-15—Estero Beach

At the 15-Km point, a paved road leaves Highway 1 to the right. (See "Punta Banda Area" map.) A 0.7-mile drive brings one to an intersection. The road to the right leads to El Faro Beach, a residential subdivision. Take the left fork a short distance to the very fine Estero Beach Resort Hotel, trailer court, shops and boat-launching ramp. They lie on the shore of Estero de Punta Banda. The trailer court here is one of the best in the Baja peninsula and is often used as the first-nights stop for large RV caravans heading south.

SIDE TRIP

Estero means estuary. Estero Beach is the northern shore of a sizeable saltwater estuary (Estero de Punta Banda). The western side is a wide, four-mile-long coastal sand spit that protects the estuary from the swells of the Pacific Ocean. Launching small boats is thus an easy matter, but the breaking bar at the mouth of the estero must be negotiated to reach the open ocean. The hotel and its grounds are pleasant and they are worth a visit even if you don't plan to stay. There is ample parking and turnaround area for the large RVs.

SIDE TRIP

Km B-21—Highway 23 and La Bufadora

PSI
#5

Highway 23 branches to the west from Highway 1 in the town of Maneadero (population 11,600) about 200 yards south of a pedestrian overpass. (See "Punta Banda Area" map.) It is a good standard blacktopped highway of some 20 Km (14 miles). The first eight miles cross flat terrain, some of which supports olive orchards and other agricultural fields. The last six miles traverse the sides of precipitous Punta Banda, a narrow, rocky peninsula that projects into the Pacific Ocean.

As the road gains elevation, one is afforded excellent views of the ocean and Ensenada to the northeast. The spouts of the California gray whale also may be seen during the months of its migration from Alaska to Baja's Pacific lagoons. (See "Wildlife" chapter.)

There are several places of interest served by Highway 23 including the La Bufadora blowhole. The commanding views and intriguing blowhole demand that this side trip be placed on the Points of Special Interest Tour.

Numerous souvenir stands have been built along the road near the blowhole, so there is no lack of things to buy. There is parking at La Bufadora, although trailers should not proceed past the restaurant (0.2 miles from La Bufadora) due to the steepness of the parking lot.

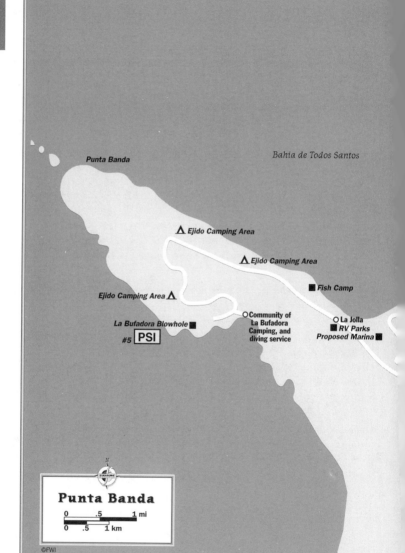

Punta Banda

Bahia de Todos Santos

△ Ejido Camping Area

△ Ejido Camping Area

■ Fish Camp

Ejido Camping Area △

La Bufadora Blowhole ■

#5 PSI

○ Community of
La Bufadora
Camping, and
diving service

○ La Jolla
■ RV Parks
Proposed Marina ■

N

Punta Banda

| 0 | .5 | 1 mi |
| 0 | .5 | 1 km |

©FWI

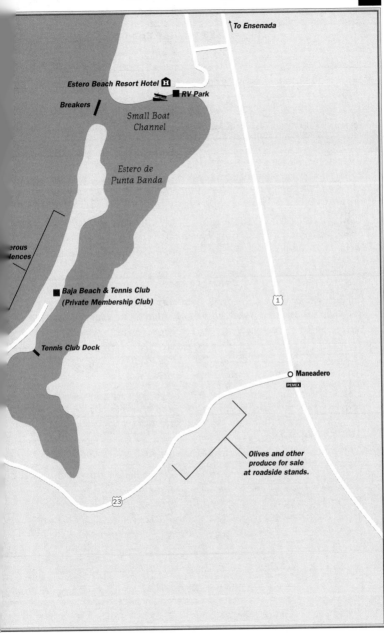

↑ To Ensenada

Estero Beach Resort Hotel ▣

■ RV Park

Breakers

Small Boat Channel

Estero de Punta Banda

erous
ences

■ **Baja Beach & Tennis Club**
(Private Membership Club)

Tennis Club Dock

○ **Maneadero**

PEMEX

Olives and other produce for sale at roadside stands.

(1)

(23)

SIDE TRIP

Punta Banda Barrier Beach

Barrier beaches are low-lying, narrow spits of sand built by wave action along shallow sections of ocean coastline. They are separated from the mainland by saltwater estuaries. Here at about eight miles from Highway 1 is such a formation. An oiled road leads north out the barrier to the Baja Beach & Tennis Club and numerous private residences. A small marina and launch ramp are located a short distance out along this road.

La Jolla

La Jolla is a community made up of several older recreation home subdivisions 14 Km (nine miles) from Highway 1. Lots are very small and many contain trailer houses. There are two RV parks, La Jolla Beach Camp and Villarino RV Park, located on the beach. The former park has a boat launching ramp. The ramp, which provides access to the open Pacific, poses problems at low tide and is unusable in heavy swells.

Campgrounds

There are several gently sloping areas adjacent to the highway near the point where it starts descending to La Bufadora. They provide the sites for minimum-facility campgrounds operated by the members of a local ejido. What you receive for your modest fee in these places is little more than a place to park, but there are excellent views of the ocean. Some of these camps may give way to subdivisions.

There are also RV camping areas and some recreation homes on flat benches above the shoreline cliffs at the head of a cove (Bahía Papalote) east of the La Bufadora blowhole. Because of this cove's rocky nature, it is a popular diving location.

La Bufadora Blowhole

Highway 23 passes over the top of the Punta Banda ridge and descends to the rocky coast on the slope facing southeast. Here you will find a scattering of homes, restaurants, open-air shops, parking areas and a masonry viewing structure adjoining the blowhole. The area is a popular weekend recreation spot for people of the Ensenada area.

SIDE TRIP

There are occasional points along the Pacific Coast where rock formations cause the incoming ocean swells to cast up a spout of water, but La Bufadora (The Roarer) is a blowhole without rival. It consists of a substantial sea-level cave. After observing it for some time, one can readily imagine that it is a living creature. The rhythmic ocean swells impart a breathing cycle to the cave. Water is first taken in. Then, following a pause, it is sprayed back outside by internally compressed air to the accompaniment of a deep roar. Heavy swells cause a large vertical geyser, but La Bufadora puts on a good performance even in calm seas.

Km B-23—Inmigracion

Inmigracion is the Mexican equivalent of the Immigration Service in the United States. Here at the town of Maneadero was the immigration checkpoint where officials issued and validated tourist cards. Their building was one mile south of the Highway 1 junction with Highway 23. There has been no checkpoint here for some five years, but the point is noted in the event it should reappear.

The Transpeninsular Highway has only two lanes from here to the tip of the peninsula, except within some of the larger communities and along the Cabo Corridor between San Jose del Cabo and Cabo San Lucas.

Km B-25—Geographic Change

#3
#4

Here the highway enters Geographic Section No. 4 and initiates a 100-Km (62-mile) journey through moderately steep mountains with numerous intermountain valleys. The area and its chaparral vegetation are similar to those in the mountainous areas in southern Alta California. The brush here in Baja is not as dense as that found north of the border due to the occurrence of frequent, uncontrolled wildfires.

Although the Transpeninsular Highway begins to curve, its grades are moderate and there are many straight, level sections. Its course through this area is reasonably typical of what lies ahead for hundreds of miles, so if what you see here is acceptable you can relax and enjoy the remainder of your trip.

SIDE TRIP

Km B-48—Puerto Santo Tomas

A secondary road signed "La Bocana 26 Km, and Punta China 28 Km" leaves Highway 1 to the right (west). This road is constructed along the foot of the mountains bordering the northern side of the Rio Santo Tomas. It is well constructed but it is not recommended for use by larger RVs.

SIDE TRIP

16.1 Miles

The road to Punta China forks to the left and crosses the Rio Santo Tomas. A 2.9-mile drive brings one to the workers camp at the Punta China limestone mining operation. A short distance to the south, rock is loaded by conveyor belt into barges for shipment to the cement plant in Ensenada. There are nice ocean views along the way.

17.6 Miles

The road arrives at the small village of La Bocana (boca means mouth in Spanish), appropriately located at the mouth of the Rio Santo Tomas. There is a small store and a camping spot with a good view of the ocean. Another nearby campground is operated on a tree-lined meadow adjoining the beach and a marshy lagoon. If the croaking of frogs will keep you awake, consider camping elsewhere.

20.3 Miles

This point brings you to Puerto Santo Tomas, presently the site of a modest fish camp. The small cove provides protection from the ocean swells that crash on the shore only a few yards to the south. Surprisingly, this insignificant cove was a principal port during the missionary period. It served the inland settlement of Santo Tomas. In viewing its waters, picture it containing the ship of Juan Rodriguez Cabrillo, who anchored here during his historic exploratory voyage in 1542.

Within the fish camp is a small cantina and camping is permitted nearby. There is also a narrow, concrete boat ramp facing the open Pacific. Launching boats in heavy swell would not be possible.

Historic Note—The Missionary Trail

Since leaving Ensenada, you have been following the approximate route used by Gaspar de Portola and Padre Junipero Serra on their history-making 1769 expedition north from Loreto to found the first Alta California mission at San Diego. In the ensuing 22 years, Dominican missionaries were to establish three missions along that portion of the route described in this chapter. These were at the present-day towns of Santo Tomas, San Vicente and Santo Domingo. Directions for visiting these sites are given later in this chapter. The ruin of an additional mission near El Rosario is described in the following chapter.

Km B-51—Santo Tomas

Santo Tomas is a small town located in a broad, fertile section of the Rio Santo Tomas. It is the site of a Dominican mission founded in 1791. To view the mission ruins, proceed to the roadside rest stop directly across the highway from the PEMEX Station. Walk several hundred feet north along the east side of the highway. The 50-foot-square ruins may be seen in a pasture near several tall fan palms and 250 feet north of the olive orchard, which contains the **El Palomar Trailer Court**.

All that remains of the Dominican mission founded in Santo Tomas in 1791 are these ruins, visible from the Transpeninsular Highway.

Grapes were cultivated by the missionaries to produce altar wine. Santo Tomas came to lend its name to one of Mexico's most popular wines, although the winery itself has long been located in Ensenada. In the past, much of the valley was planted with grapes. Today, there are relatively few vineyards and most of the land contains olive orchards or is used for grazing. Grape production has been moved to the Guadalupe area along Highway 3, northeast of Ensenada, and the region south of San Vicente to the south along Highway 1.

Today, Santo Tomas offers the tourist a PEMEX station and the El Palomar motel, restaurant and gift shop. Across the highway is the El Palomar Trailer Court. It is a pleasant, shady spot surrounded by olive trees. It provides full hookups, swimming pool and toilet facilities. Beware of weekends when it is heavily used by people from Ensenada.

Km B-72 to B-77—California Sycamore

Highway 1 passes along the stream channel of a moderately steep canyon. Here you can observe numerous California sycamore trees (*Platanus racemosa*), a species commonly found in similar moist locations in Alta California and northern Baja. Note the mottled exfoliating brown and white bark. The broad, sharply lobed leaves fall in the winter months, but many spherical fruiting bodies can be seen dangling from the branches. See the outline of the leaf above.

Many of the canyon walls in this area are composed of granite rocks. They can be identified by their light color. Review the "Rock Type" table in the "Geology" chapter.

SIDE TRIP

Km B-78—Puerto San Isidro Area

Midway between Km B-78 and Km B-79 a blacktop highway leaves Highway 1 to the right (west). It is signed for E.J. Erendira. This is one of the few places you can drive to within a few hundred yards of the Pacific shore on an oiled highway.

The hard-surface highway proceeds along the Rio San Isidro and ends in 12 miles at the farming community of Erendira. It contains small grocery stores, cafe, PEMEX (Nova only) and the 12-unit Motel Erendira near the north edge of town. A secondary road continuing northwest up the coast provides access to the small fishing port of San Isidro. It is 13.3 miles to the port from Highway 1. A reef of rock that projects from the coast provides protection for a fleet of small fishing boats and a boat-launching ramp (concrete surface to the highwater line and then packed sand.). Nearby there is a group of small rental cabins bearing the name Castro's. Boats are available for rent. Across the road is an RV park.

I have driven nine miles north of Puerto San Isidro on a good secondary road. Starting at 1.6 miles north of the port are a series of very nice camping sites on the bluffs overlooking the ocean. At places there are good beaches. At 5.5 miles north of the port is the growing village of Punta Cabras, which is made up largely of Americans. At 5.9 miles is a turnoff to the beach-lined cove at Punta Cabras. The road is a bit rough, but large RVs make it to many of these camping spots.

SIDE TRIP

Km B-88—Mission San Vicente Ferrer

It is a 0.4-mile drive over a low-standard (but passable) dirt road to the ruins of the San Vicente Ferrer mission. This road leaves Highway 1 to the right (west) 0.2 miles south of Km B-88. Drive about 200 feet after leaving the highway and take the left fork, which leads to a parking area adjoining the ruins. A flimsy thatched shelter has been constructed over the crumbling walls of the buildings, but it is falling down and provides pitifully little protection.

SIDE TRIP

Dominican padres founded the mission in 1780 on a low rise a few yards from the Rio San Isidro. It was to become the administrative center for the northern Frontera mission district and headquarters for a garrison of troops.

Km B-90—San Vicente

At this point is the town of San Vicente (population 2500). The only things of interest to the tourist are several stores and a PEMEX station.

Km B-90 to B-107—Llano Colorado

There was little agricultural development on the Baja peninsula prior to the 1940s as the land was controlled by unproductive foreign concessions. Previous travel guides reported only a few families around San Vicente. In contrast, today's traveler will see extensive vineyards, olive orchards and grain fields in the level valley south of San Vicente. (At **Km B-97** is a sizeable cactus farm where prickly pear cactus is cultivated). This is the *Llano Colorado* (the Colorado Plain.) It is interesting to note that while these Mexican lands are only now being developed for agriculture, tracts used for similar purposes in southern California in the United States have long since given way to urbanization.

Km B-125—Geographic Change

#4
#5

Just before entering the town of Colonet, the highway leaves the mountains that started 100 Km (62 miles) to the north. You will now be entering Geographic Section No. 5, the northernmost segment of the Continental Borderlands Province. As you can see, this dividing line between provinces is easy to identify and is typical of others you will encounter to the south.

Highway 1 will now traverse 112 Km (70 miles) of rolling coastal plain with the mountains always in view to the east. The northern portion of the plain is called the *Llano* (Plain) *de Camalu*, and the southern portion the *Valle* (valley) *de San Quintin*. The highway is constructed near the inland portion of the plain, so the ocean is mostly out of sight. These coastal plains are often used for agriculture. These developments extend as far south as El Pabellon Beach at **Km C-15**, much of it occurring since this book was first published in 1986. It is also sad to report that this farming is resulting in serious soil erosion. As many crops are irrigated by drip systems, a majority of the exposed surface soil is relatively dry and easily blown away by strong winds moving onshore from the Pacific ocean. One wonders how long Mexico will be able to continue farming this developing dust bowl.

ROAD CONDITION NOTE: Several secondary road side trips to the Pacific shore are described over the level lands of the Continental Borderlands in this and the following chapter. Soils in this area are fine-grained and become muddy following rain. Local traffic continues during such periods and many ruts and short detours are created. Be very cautious about using these roads for up to 10 days following heavy rain, and expect occasional rough spots long afterwards.

SIDE TRIP

Km B-126—San Antonio del Mar

North of the town of Colonet a secondary road bears west to the Pacific shore. It leaves Highway 1 about 100 yards northeast of the Rio San Rafael bridge, between the bridge and a white church. A small group of residences, San Antonio del Mar is reached in seven miles. There is limited camping area here, but extensive sand beaches and dunes lie in both directions. A great area for those with vehicles capable of traveling over such terrain.

Km B-127—Colonet

South of the Rio San Rafael bridge lies the small farming community of Colonet and its PEMEX station. A considerable agriculture area can be seen on the lands bordering the river.

After passing through Colonet, look south near the western edge of the inland mountains. Here, on clear days, you will see Isla San Martin and a group of volcanic cinder cones lying west of the town of San Quintin. At other times, these peaks may be shrouded in fog or low clouds.

SIDE TRIP

Km B-129—Bahía Colonet

*Near **Km B-129** a secondary road leaves Highway 1 to the right (west) and in 8.1 miles arrives at the southern end of Bahía Colonet on the Pacific coast. The junction is signed for E.J. Villa Morelos.*

The road is constructed along the base of low hills bordering the broad valley of the Rio San Rafael. A lesser-standard road continues south, along the coast, accessing numerous places to camp on the bluffs overlooking the Pacific.

Shown is the largest of the three telescope buildings in the Parque Nacional Sierra San Pedro Martir. Note the gnarled Jeffrey pine tree and the snow remaining from a late March storm.

SIDE TRIP

Km B-141—Parque Nacional Sierra San Pedro Martir

Leading to the left (east) is the main access road to the largest of Baja's two national parks (Parque Nacional Sierra San Pedro Martir) and the highest mountains in the peninsula. The road is signed "Observatorio and San Telmo." The park features extensive Jeffrey pine forests mixed with several other coniferous species. There are many undeveloped places to camp. At the end of the road is an observatory with one large and two smaller telescope buildings. The clearness of the air makes this an excellent point for astronomical observations.

Much of the access road passes over mountainous terrain making a total climb of approximately 10,000 feet. Its construction standards are better than those of most of Baja's secondary roads, but the entire route is through decomposed granite soils that are subject to severe erosion. I have seen this road recommended for use by large RVs and believe that it is suitable for such vehicles (no trailers) if it has been recently maintained. Following heavy storms, this is not the case.

6.0 Miles

Here lies the pleasant farming community of San Telmo.

22.0 Miles

To this point, the road has passed along the edge of a broad valley used for agricultural purposes. The route has been level, with few hills. Now it begins to climb the mountains in earnest.

32.1 Miles

A 0.5-mile dirt road to the right brings one to the Meling Ranch. This is an operating cattle ranch, which also provides very pleasant accommodations for overnight guests. It has a nearby airstrip and has long been a favorite hideout for private flyers. An excellent place to get away from it all.

50.7 Miles

Here are located the park's gate, entrance station and small campground. A modest entrance fee is charged.

65.0 Miles

The living quarters and administrative buildings for the observatory are located here. It is possible to camp at this point, although there are no facilities and little flat ground. Visitors are required to walk the remaining 1.5 miles up to the telescopes.

Km B-150—Punta San Jacinto

A secondary road branches to the right (west) north of **Km B-150**. After about one mile, the road standard decreases, but arrives with no difficulty in 4.1 miles at Punta San Jacinto on the coast. There are endless numbers of places to camp on the low bluffs overlooking the sea in both directions.

Km B-157—Camalu

Camalu is a town of little interest to the tourist except as a source of supplies and for its PEMEX station. In addition, Red Cross volunteers are usually present in the middle of the highway soliciting donations. A contribution will net you a Red Cross sticker for your window, which will save you from a repeat performance on the return trip. Pay up.

SIDE TRIP

Punta Camalu

Immediately north of the Camalu PEMEX station a dirt road leads in 2.3 miles to Punta Camalu. At 1.7 miles along the way, a side road bears left to a fish camp. Keeping right at this point will provide access to numerous good camping spots along the coast.

Adobe ruins of the Dominican mission at Santo Domingo. Here Baja's rich past lies next to the poor dwelling of a present-day Mexican farmer.

SIDE TRIP

Km B-169—Mission Santo Domingo

About 200 yards north of the bridge over the Rio Santo Domingo a side road leaves Highway 1 to the left (east). It leads to the ruins of a mission founded by the Dominicans in 1775. Its photo appears on the first page of Part II. The road is poorly constructed but passes over flat terrain. It is not recommended for larger RVs.

The trip to the mission site and small village of Santo Domingo is 4.9 miles. The ruins lie immediately west of the town's primary school. The full outline of the mission quadrangle is still in evidence, along with several three-foot-thick adobe walls. As with the other missions, the remains lie fully exposed to the elements.

Km B-172—Colonia Viciente Guerrero

Colonia Viciente Guerrero is another small agricultural town. It supports a PEMEX station and two RV parks. The road to these parks leaves Highway 1 to the right (west) 0.2 miles north of **Km B-173**. A sizeable electrical substation lies a short distance south of the junction point. The first park (**Don Pepes**) is close to the highway. The second (**Posada Don Diego**) is 0.3 miles to the west in a pleasant orchard setting. Both have restaurants and full hookups.

SIDE TRIP

From the Posada Don Diego park drive west 2.7 miles to an excellent sand beach backed by dunes. Camping behind the dunes will cut the wind. The road is low standard with many twists and turns; but no problema, *keep heading west and stop short of the water.*

Km B-175—Isla San Martin and San Quintin Cinder Cones

Isla San Martin and the San Quintin cinder cones should now be clearly in view to the right. The island lies some five miles offshore. It is the furthest peak to the right (northwest). It provides a home for several species of marine mammals and is the site of a Mexican fishermen's camp. An anchorage on its southeast shore is a frequently used stopover point for yachts making the passage from San Diego to Cabo San Lucas.

Cultural Note: Fish Camps

The fish camp on Isla San Martin is one of scores of such camps to be found on islands and isolated stretches of coast throughout the Baja peninsula. They consist of one or more shacks made of sheet metal, tar paper,

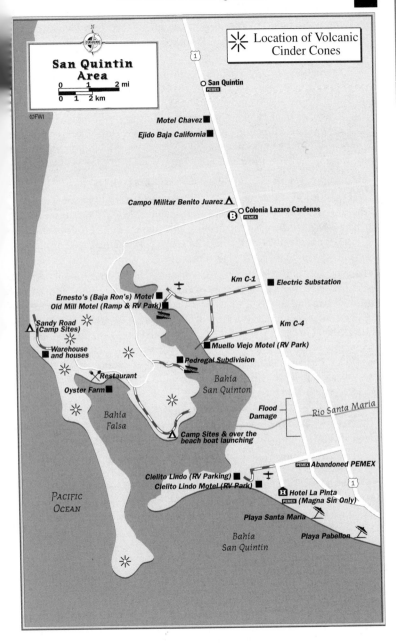

N

San Quintin Area

0   1   2 mi
0   1   2 km

©FWI

Location of Volcanic Cinder Cones

① 1

○ **San Quintin**
PEMEX

■ **Motel Chavez**

Ejido Baja California ■

Campo Militar Benito Juarez ▲
Ⓑ ○ **Colonia Lazaro Cardenas**
PEMEX

Km C-1 ■ **Electric Substation**

Ernesto's (Baja Ron's) Motel ■
Old Mill Motel (Ramp & RV Park) ■

Km C-4

▲ **Sandy Road (Camp Sites)**

■ **Warehouse and houses**

■ **Muelle Viejo Motel (RV Park)**

■ **Pedregal Subdivision**

✕ **Restaurant**

Bahia San Quinton

Oyster Farm ■

Bahia Falsa

Flood Damage

Rio Santa Maria

▲ **Camp Sites & over the beach boat launching**

PEMEX **Abandoned PEMEX**

PACIFIC OCEAN

Clelito Lindo (RV Parking) ■
Cielito Lindo Motel (RV Park) ■
🏨 **Hotel La Pinta**
PEMEX **(Magna Sin Only)**

① 1

Playa Santa Maria

Playa Pabellon

Bahia San Quintin

poles and scraps of other building material. There is little, if any, furniture These crude dwellings provide permanent or seasonal sites for fishing and lobstering operations that are usually outposts for a headquarters cooperative in the larger towns.

Fishing and transportation to and from supply points is done in open, outboard-motor-powered pangas. I have visited dozens of such camps and always found their residents to be friendly, hard working and usually eager to sell a portion of their catch. The location of other fish camps is noted at many other places. Hopefully, you might take the opportunity to pay some of them a visit and gain an understanding of a way of life quite foreign and primitive to most North Americans.

Km B-190—San Quintin

San Quintin and adjoining Colonia Lazaro Cardenas are the southernmost of the towns that dot the coastal plain through which you have been traveling. The area's principal tourist facilities lie to the south off Highway 1 at **Km C-1**, **Km C-4** and **Km C-11**, but you need to make an important decision here in town concerning your vehicle's fuel supply.

The objective is to be able to pass through the remote mountains and desert between El Rosario and Guerrero Negro to the south without exhausting your fuel supply. In past years it was often difficult to obtain fuel within this section (about 400 Km, or 250 miles, in length). Now it is usually available, but you should not count on it. This fueling situation has improved somewhat with the installation of a gas pump (Magna Sin only) at the hotel at Cataviña to supplement the community station. However, in the event of low supplies, the hotel will serve only its guests, and may refuse service to caravans at all times.

Ideally, you would obtain fuel at El Rosario. However, should the stations there be closed or out of fuel, you may have a problem. The prudent plan is to fuel at San Quintin and top off at El Rosario if it is available.

SIDE TRIP

Km B-193—Colonia Lazaro Cardenas and Puerto San Quintin

To the highway traveler, the town of Lazaro Cardenas (population 7600) will appear only as a southerly extension of San Quintin. It is, however, the gateway to Bahía San Quintin.

SIDE TRIP

Puerto San Quintin is a large, shallow, almost totally landlocked estuary. (See the "San Quintin Area" map.) Its northern section is served by a highway-standard, but badly washboarded road. If you are heading south toward the peninsula's tip there is no particular reason to pay a visit here. However, it is a good place to reach the water's edge if the San Quintin area is the destination point of your trip.

The road to the bay leaves Highway 1 to the right (west) near the center of Colonia Lazaro Cardenas at a point about 0.1 miles north of the PEMEX station. There is a military base on the northwest corner. A road sign reads "Bahía Falsa." Bahía Falsa is the westerly arm of the Puerto San Quintin estuary.

A trip of 14 Km (nine miles) over this road will bring you to the shores of the bay. Taking the left fork at this point will bring you in about 2 miles to bay-side camp spots and places to launch small boats over the rocky beach.

The main road continues to the right for two more miles and terminates at a fishing village and warehouse facility on the Pacific shore. En route, you pass by an oyster farm (Campo Ostionero) and small restaurant and drive very close to the bases of the cinder cones you have been seeing from Highway 1. Note the reddish color of these volcanic rocks compared with the light-colored granite you have seen in other areas.

There are places to camp at various places along the bay shore, but they are difficult to access with larger RVs. Lightweight Class-4 boats can be launched over the beach near the fish camp or at boat ramps at the Old Mill Motel and the Pedregal subdivision. You will have to negotiate the shallow bars at the entrance of the bay to reach the open ocean. This entrance is protected from the prevailing northwest swells, but careful attention should be given to the state of the tides and weather.

Km B-196 and C-0—End of Highway Section B

The breakpoint between Highway Sections **B** and **C** lies six Km south of the center of the town of San Quintin.

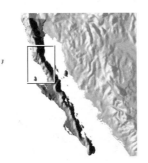

SAN QUINTIN TO THE STATE LINE

The Hotel La Pinta San Quintin is on the beach east of Bahía San Quintin.

Most North Americans who have traveled the Transpeninsular Highway will agree that you really haven't visited the Baja peninsula until you progress south of San Quintin. Once this is done, most of the larger towns will have been left behind, there are substantial areas of open space, and after a few miles the peninsula's fascinating desert vegetation begins to dominate the landscape. A new world emerges. You have entered the final decompression stage in the escape from the land of the freeways to the north.

Roll down the window of your vehicle and take in the fresh air. To hell with the air-conditioner. Wave hello to the Mexicans and stop looking like you expect to be attacked by bandits. This is the "magnificent peninsula." Enjoy.

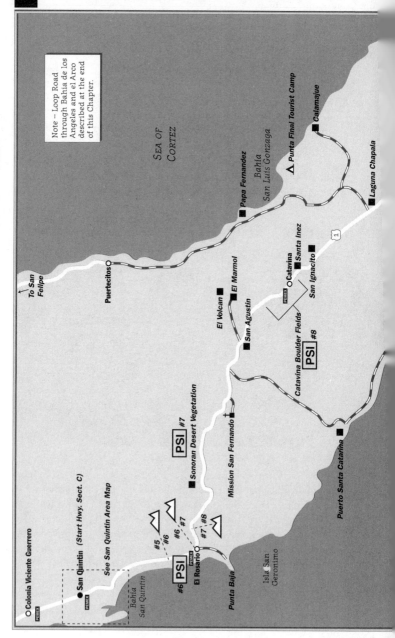

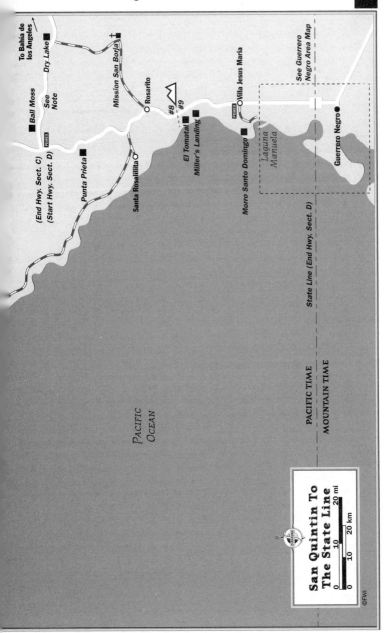

Coastal Winds

It was noted previously that strong coastal winds cause considerable so erosion along the Pacific shore's agricultural areas. These same winds als make conditions less than fully enjoyable in the three San Quintin-area rec reation spots described immediately below. This is particularly true for thos using the RV parks. For this reason most serious Baja travelers head farthe south and one seldom sees long-term visitors in these areas.

Km C-1 and C-4—Bay-Side Motels

A short distance to the west there are three motels located on the low bluff overlooking the eastern shores of Puerto San Quintin. These are **Ernesto's** (**Baja Ron's**), the **Old Mill** and the **Muelle Viejo**. Each has an accompanying res taurant and bar. The Old Mill has been extensively refurbished and include a boat-launching ramp, boat rental and RV park. Similar improvements may occur at the adjoining Ernesto's (Baja Ron's) Motel. All three places provide pleasant spots at the water's edge. Take your pick.

The access road leading to these facilities from the **Km C-1** point on High way 1 has been widened and improved, but the other roads are low-standard affairs running between agricultural fields. (See the "San Quintin Area" map.) These latter roads are not well-suited for larger RVs, particularly in wet weather, when they become next to impassable.

SIDE TRIP

Km C-11—San Quintin Tourist Area

A paved access-road leaves Highway 1 200 yards north of **Km C-11** *and is signed for the Hotel La Pinta. This junction is on a relocated section of Highway 1. After 1.2 miles, you cross the original highway and an abandoned PEMEX station. This highway relocation no doubt throws a slight kink into all the kilometer points to the south and provides the perfect excuse if you find my distance figures slightly in error.*

The area contains the Hotel La Pinta San Quintin (3.1 miles from Highway 1) and the Cielito Lindo Motel and RV Park. They are near an excellent Pacific beach. The Hotel La Pinta is the northern- most of the original parador hotels. I do not find it as nice as the other La Pinta hotels, but it will provide a fair idea of what to expect from its sister facilities to the south. The Cielito Lindo Motel and its adjoin- ing RV park are pleasant places to stay. The old original Cielito Lindo RV park is now little more than a place to park, but it is closer to the beach. The access road to Cielito Lindo can be impassable follow- ing storms.

Km C-15—El Pabellon Beach

Midway between **Km C-15** *and* **C-16** *a dirt road leaves to the right and in 1.2 miles arrives at El Pabellon Beach on the Pacific shore. A 0.3-mile-long strip has been graded paralleling the ocean in imitation of an RV park. In the process, the original coastal dune that once provided some wind protection has been destroyed. I'm sure it is a lovely spot in calm weather. What was once Honey's Camp RV Park is nearby but has been supplanted by the El Pabellon Beach facility.*

Km C-24 to C-41—Pacific Coast

After entering the flat coastal plain at Colonet to the north, Highway 1 now runs some distance inland. Finally, at **Km C-24**, the road approaches the coast and parallels it within 0.25 to 0.5 mile until **Km C-41**. The ocean is in view along much of this section of highway, and there are numerous low-standard dirt roads that may be used to reach camp spots on the low coastal bluffs. Sadly, this relatively unimpressive 10-mile section of road is the only place south of Ensenada where the Pacific Coast is in close view from the Transpeninsular Highway. Your next close encounter with saltwater will be on the Sea of Cortez, more than 200 miles to the south, near Santa Rosalia.

Km C-41—Geographic Change

Km C-41 brings the traveler to the southern end of Geographic Section No. 5. At this point the highway leaves the flat Continental Borderlands Province and reenters the Peninsular Range Mountains. Lying ahead is Geographic Section No. 6, a short 14-Km (nine-mile) mountainous segment ending at El Rosario.

At **Km C-41** the highway starts to wind its way uphill to a plateau area that levels out at **Km C-50** at an elevation of some 800 feet. After a few miles, it then descends rapidly to the town of El Rosario.

Km C-41 to C-55—Vegetation Transition

Much of the original vegetation north of this point has been replaced or heavily modified by agricultural activities. At **Km C-41** the native chaparral becomes more evident, but it shares the hillsides with various types of cactus, century plants and other species normally associated with the desert. You are traveling through a transitional vegetational zone between the California Region to the north and the Sonoran Desert to the south. The full change will become more apparent when the highway crosses to the south of the Rio del Rosario at **Km C-63**.

Km C-55—El Rosario

At the center of the community of El Rosario (The Rosary), the highwa takes an abrupt 90-degree turn to the left (east) and proceeds up the north ern edge of the flat valley lands of the Rio del Rosario. At this turn, a second ary road leaves the highway, to the right, and is the starting point for the tri to the mission ruins and Punta Baja. (See the "El Rosario Area" map.)

There are two PEMEX stations on the highway. Be sure to obtain fuel her unless you are positive you can make it through the mountains and desert t Guerrero Negro. Near the 90-degree highway turn is **Mama Espinosa's Res taurant**. It is famous for its lobster burritos and is well worth a visit.

As recently as the mid-1960s, El Rosario was portrayed as "the end of th line." Roads to the south could only be described as primitive. Mail servic and the weekly bus from Ensenada proceeded no further. The completion o the Transpeninsular Highway in 1973 was to alter El Rosario's place in the sun. Rather than the *end*, the town is now more properly looked upon as the *beginning*, for here the new highway starts its lengthy journey through the interior mountains and deserts of the peninsula.

El Rosario was also the point of beginning for Baja's Dominican friars, for it was here that they established their first mission in 1774, only two years after they took over administration of the peninsula's missionary activities from the Franciscans. It was to be the jumping-off point for the founding of eight additional missions between there and the international border.

The original mission site was upriver from the center of town. In 1882, it was moved about 1.5 miles downstream. Its ruins may be visited as part of the Points of Special Interest Tour. A sign in front of the site notes, "1434 Christian Indians registered between 1774 and 1817. These were supported from products of desert, sea, cattle, sheep, goats, and plantings of cereals im- ported by the Spaniards." Many of these Indians were soon to die in the ep- idemics that accompanied the Spanish wherever they went.

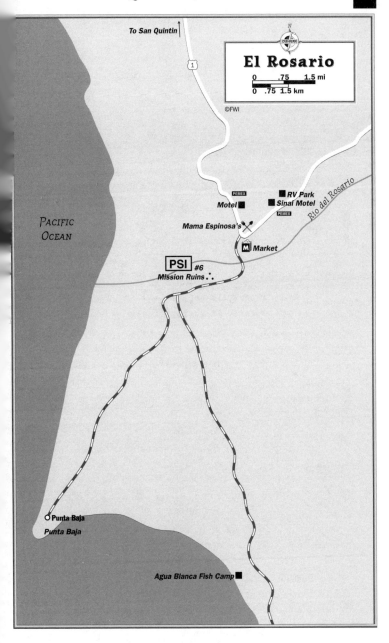

To San Quintin

El Rosario

0   .75   1.5 mi
0   .75 1.5 km

©FWI

N

PACIFIC
OCEAN

PEMEX

Motel

RV Park
Sinal Motel

PEMEX

Rio del Rosario

Mama Espinosa's

M Market

PSI #6

Mission Ruins

Punta Baja
Punta Baja

Agua Blanca Fish Camp

The author's original camper, shown in splendid isolation above the Pacific surf at Punta Baja.

**PSI
#6**

SIDE TRIP

Km C-55—Mission Ruins and Punta Baja

Start at the 90-degree highway turn mentioned in the first paragraph of the section above and drive west, past the market.

0.1 Miles

Junction with dirt road marked on the southwest corner by two sizeable tamarisk trees. Turn left taking this road. Take the left fork at a junction a short distance ahead.

1.0 Miles

Cross the Rio del Rosario. In an earlier edition, I wrote, "On my last visit in 1992 the river had been bridged with an earthen embankment and culvert, but high water may soon deposit these in the ocean." By 1995, the culvert was gone and one had to ford the shallow river.

1.1 Miles

Junction with another dirt road paralleling the south side of the river. Turn right on this road and drive downriver.

1.6 Miles

To the right, on a bluff overlooking the valley, are the ruins of the mission which was founded in 1782. This is stop No. 6 on the Points of Special Interest Tour. Continue past the mission ruins if you are heading for Punta Baja.

SIDE TRIP

2.6 Miles

Junction with dirt road heading 90 degrees to the left. This road goes to Agua Blanca. For Punta Baja, continue straight ahead through agricultural fields.

2.9 Miles

Junction with another dirt road heading 90 degrees to the left. Turn left on this road and promptly begin to climb up the face of a broad ridge.

8.3 Miles

Road breaks out on top of ridge with fine view of Punta Baja and the ocean.

9.6 Miles

Junction with road bearing sharply to the left. Continue straight ahead and remember not to stray onto this road on your return trip.

10.6 Miles

Punta Baja fishing village. Note the one-room schoolhouse, which was constructed in October 1980 by the Del Mar Rotary Club and dedicated to the children of Punta Baja.

11.9 Miles

Punta Baja navigation light, and the tip of the point. Almost all of Baja's navigation lights are now reliable and are powered by solar energy. Note the solar panels atop the Punta Baja light.

Punta Baja is one of the most prominent points of land on Baja's Pacific coast. It provides good protection from the ocean's prevailing northwest swells. For this reason, it is an anchorage used by Mexican fishing craft and yachts making the Baja passage. Small Class-4 boats may be launched over the rocky beach at the village by using a steep road cut through the bluffs by the local fishermen. Because this is the open Pacific, small boats should not stray far from the protection of the point.

From Punta Baja, you can see Isla San Geronimo lying in the Pacific some eight miles to the southeast. It supports a sizeable fish camp. Punta Baja is also a good place to watch for gray whale spouts during the annual migration.

Km C-55 to C-63—Geographic Change
Rio del Rosario Valley

This short eight Km (five-mile) section of Highway 1 passes through the valley of the Rio del Rosario (Geographic Section No. 7). The highway passes along the northern edge of the valley, which has been cleared for agriculture since the arrival of the missionaries in 1774. It is one of the few places in the peninsula where there is sufficient surface water to support crops. During my 1995 visit, most of these crops have been replaced by urbanization.

During heavy rain from late fall tropical storms, the river can become a roaring torrent. The Transpeninsular Highway was opened before many of its bridges were completed. The river crossing at **Km C-63** was the burial ground for many vehicles that tried to cross during such runoff periods. The present 0.5 miles of causeways and bridges are safe and the longest anywhere in Baja.

Km C-63—Geographic Change

After crossing the Rio del Rosario, the highway enters the longest of its 19 geographic sections (Geographic Section No. 8). For 287 Kms (178 miles), the road passes through the mountains and plateaus that are typical of the gentle, westerly slopes of the Peninsular Range Mountains.

To the south, Highway 1 crosses over endless numbers of westerly draining arroyos without the aid of drainage structures. Rainwater and debris must pass over the surface of the highway. To drive over these crossings (*vados*) at high speeds when they contain water or debris is to invite severe tire damage.

In many places the highway passes over broad ridges with good scenic views. Also, there are extensive level stretches through intermountain valleys. In summary, the road conditions are not severe and reflect the relatively gentle terrain of the Peninsular Range's western slope. South of the Rio del Rosario bridge, Highway 1 gains elevation.

The Rio del Rosario crossing also marks a place of climatic, as well as geographic, change. The cool coastal lowlands along the Pacific shore are left behind, and the highway to the south passes through warmer air over the interior deserts. This temperature change is often easy to detect and also results in vegetational changes as noted below.

Km C-63 to C-80—Sonoran Desert
Vegetation

Sonoran Desert vegetation begins after crossing the Rio del Rosario. The brush species you have been seeing to the north are still present, but true desert plants now become commonplace. Among them are century plants and several species of cactus. Baja's unique plant, the *cirio*, comes into view at about **Km C-69**. From **Km C-70** to **Km C-74** the highway passes through a road valley where these plants are numerous. Although many of Baja's desert plants persist all the way to the peninsula's tip, you will see no more rios after leaving Geographic Section No. 8.

At **Km C-80** the desert vegetation is particularly varied and plentiful and by now includes prickly pear cactus, galloping cactus, candelabra cactus, velvet cactus, giant cardón and *cirio.* This is stop No. 7 on the Points of Special Interest Tour. Linger here and seek the assistance of the "Vegetation" chapter in identifying the more common species and in investigating the characteristics of the desert plants that it describes. It is necessary to look at least 100 feet back from the roadside to locate the larger, more interesting desert plants, as plants were destroyed in clearing the land to build the highway.

Shown are adobe ruins of the Mission San Fernando founded by Junipero Serra in 1769. The flat valley behind the ruins provided the pasture which was the reason for founding the mission at this site.

SIDE TRIP

Km C-114—Mission San Fernando

Immediately south of **Km C-114** *a low-standard dirt road leaves Highway 1 to the right (west). It is level but narrow and is not recommended for larger RVs. A journey of three miles will bring you to the ruins of the only mission in the Baja peninsula that was founded by the Franciscan order. If you don't make the side trip, at least pause and reflect that the Portola-Serra expedition passed through this lonely and desolate place in 1769 on its historic journey from Loreto to San Diego. See the story in the "History" chapter.*

SIDE TRIP

The mission site lies on the north side of the Rio San Fernando. This location was selected because it provided good pasturage for the expedition's livestock. It is hard to believe that this remote outpost founded by Junipero Serra was developed by the succeeding Dominicans into the home of some 1500 Indians. These people were decimated by epidemics in the years 1777–80, and by 1818 the mission was abandoned. A local Mexican has a house here and sells mineral samples, etc. to tourists. He indicated that visitors are welcome to camp nearby.

Km C-128—Pacific Coast Loop

Leave Highway 1 to the west just before **Km C-128**. The road is signed for Puerto Santa Catarina—33 Km. The route travels about 35 miles south to Puerto Santa Catarina (the former shipping port for the El Marmol onyx mine—see later description) and then some 100 miles southeast along the coast to Santa Rosalillita. There are several unroaded gaps shown in this route on the AAA Baja map. Actually, there are no gaps. The return road to Highway 1 from Santa Rosalillita is noted in this chapter at **Km D-38**.

This coastal loop offers numerous outstanding camping spots, deserted beaches and spectacular vistas of the Pacific. You may find yourself taking a few wrong turns discovering the main road along the coast, but the ever-present coastline will be your guide. Best travel with a buddy vehicle—breakdowns in this seldom-traveled region would mean a lot of walking.

Km C-140—San Agustin

There is an inoperative government-built trailer court at this point. The toilet and related facilities are abandoned and on one of my visits the gate was locked shut. On other occasions, I have been able to spend the night in its well-landscaped, pull-through trailer spaces.

SIDE TRIP

Km C-144—El Marmol

It is a 9.8-mile side trip over a good secondary road to the famous open-pit onyx mine at el Marmol (Marble), which is known for its unique onyx-block schoolhouse. The mine was the source of onyx that was hauled over 51 miles of rough dirt road for shipment by sea from Puerto Santa Catarina on the Pacific coast. The market for onyx is now greatly reduced because of the development of plastics. Quarried blocks of onyx may be seen lying about the mine area.

SIDE TRIP

One would expect a mine to be deep in the mountains. However, el Marmol is at the foot of the hills and the access road is passable even to larger RVs. The initial six miles is totally flat with the remainder a bit more rolling. The road surface is relatively easy to drive in comparison to most of Baja's secondary roads.

Northeast from the schoolhouse, one can drive about 4.5 miles over rough roads to visit unique El Volcan, a mineral spring where water oozing from the ground results in new deposits of onyx.

The Cataviña Boulder Field and its impressive Sonoran Desert vegetation represent a place that befits the Norte Americano *conception of the Wild, Wild West.*

Km C-157 to C-179— Cataviña Boulder Field

PSI #8

The next 11 Km (seven miles) segment of the Transpeninsular Highway is one of its most scenic and interesting. The highway has been constructed through an area of massive granite boulders and the desert vegetation is excellent. In particular, notice the elephant trees growing from the boulders south of **Km C-169**. This is stop No. 8 on the Points of Special Interest Tour. Most vehicles can pull over at many places along the way. Even larger RVs and trailers can pull off and turn around at a side road and blacktop mixing area a short distance north of **Km C-161** and also at **Km C-163**.

The thousands of rounded boulders that you will see are composed of granite rock. (See the "Rock Type Classification" table in the "Geology" chapter.) Granite is an igneous—plutonic—intrusive rock. All this complicated terminology means that a mass of molten material was cooled *slowl* beneath (inside) the Earth's surface. Because of the slow cooling, identifiabl crystals of various minerals were able to form, and the rocks appear light i color. Pick up a piece of granite, and you can readily see the individual crys tals of quartz, feldspar and mica. Take a piece with you to compare it with the fine-grained, darker colored igneous—volcanic—extrusive rocks tha you will see to the south.

Observe the soil beneath your feet. It is made up of weathered particles o granite rock. This type of soil is universally known as D.G., decomposec granite. It is a road engineer's nightmare, as D.G. soils are subject to severe erosion.

Many tourists ask "Where did the boulders come from?" The answer is that they were manufactured on the spot. Masses of granite rock tend to fracture vertically at the surface. These fractures are weathered by water and freezing temperatures, and the rock mass breaks up into blocks. With further weathering, the blocks are rounded into the boulders that you see.

Km C-171 and C-175—Palm Trees

Within the Cataviña Boulder Field, Highway 1 crosses two substantial arroyos near **Km C-171** and **C-175**. Along these watercourses you will see groves of native *Washingtonia* fan palms. Note that the leaves extend fan-like from the end of each stem. While palms are inhabitants of the desert, most species grow in places such as these arroyo bottoms where there is water near the surface.

Several species of palm are native to the Baja peninsula. However, most of the trees that you will see are date palms introduced by the early missionaries. Date palms are still found in great abundance in such towns as San Ignacio, Mulege and Loreto. The leaves of this species project from both sides along the stem.

Km C-174—Cataviña

Cataviña is a small development located near the highway in the heart of the Cataviña Boulder Field. At **Km C-174**, adjoining the highway, are an RV park, PEMEX station and the attractive Hotel La Pinta Cataviña. The latter is typical of the original parador hotels.

The RV park is also typical of other government camps built throughout the peninsula. The white masonry structures housing the water and electrical outlets make these facilities look like cemeteries from a distance. Some of these courts have been abandoned. The one here was open during my last visit. The PEMEX station has usually been open in recent years, and a second station (Magna Sin only) has been built at the hotel for guests only.

Km C-175—Santa Inez

A blacktop road leaves Highway 1 to the left (east) south of **Km C-175**. It is 0.8 miles to an airstrip and the **Rancho Santa Inez**. The ranch has a small cafe and several low-standard rooms for rent. An area near the cafe has been cleared and is used as an RV parking area. It offers a bit more seclusion than the park at Cataviña.

The Mission Santa Maria, established to the east in 1767, was the last of the chain of outposts built by the Jesuit fathers. At the time, it was the most northerly point of civilization on the peninsula and was the final jumping-off point for the Portola-Serra expedition to San Diego in 1769.

A 14-mile private road was constructed some years ago from Rancho Santa Inez over the peninsular divide to the mission. This road is now in poor repair. Only the end walls and foundations of the mission remain, but its lovely palm canyon and the remote beauty of the area make this a rewarding adventure. Ask for directions at the Rancho Santa Inez.

Km C-187—San Ignacito

Here, across the highway from the **Rancho San Ignacito Restaurant**, is a brass plaque marking the point where the two ends of the Transpeninsular Highway came together, and where work on the road was finished in September 1973.

Km C-206—El Pedregoso

On the right (west) side of the highway can be seen a hill of grotesquely shaped granite boulders. It is named El Pedregoso (the rocky one). It is a boulder field in the process of development.

Km C-229—Highway Junction

The southern end of the road from San Felipe joins Highway 1 at this point. It is built to highway standards, but only the first 56 miles south from San Felipe are oiled.

If ever completed, this highway will become a major new access route from the United States to Baja California. It will bypass all of the 324 miles of Highway 1 to the north of this point. The road is signed to Calamajue (60 Km), a Sea of Cortez fishing community at the end of a branch off the main road.

Km C-231—Laguna Chapala

Highway 1 passes along the western edge of a large dry lake bed (a playa lake), Laguna Chapala. This topographic depression is similar to many found in desert regions where water collects after heavy rains due to lack of a drainage outlet. Prior to the completion of the highway, the road ran across the middle of the lake and provided rock-jostled drivers with a rare opportunity to gather speed. Following rain, the lake bed became a quagmire and vehicles had to be detoured around the eastern perimeter.

Km C-241—A Cardónal

The Transpeninsular Highway passes through an impressive *cardónal*, or forest, of *cardón* (giant cactus). See the "Vegetation" chapter. Also present are numerous ocotillo and *cirio*.

Km C-250—Datilillo

At this point the traveler can see a scattering of datilillo trees. This species is commonplace south to the state line and along the highway to Bahía de los Angeles. Datilillo means *little date*, although the plant is in the lily family and is not related to the date palm. These multitrunked plants closely resemble the Joshua tree found in the deserts east of the Los Angeles basin and in other places in southwestern United States.

Datilillo is one of the dominant plants along the southern portion of Highway 1 described in this chapter.

Km C-280 and Km D-0— Bahía de Los Angeles Junction

This is the break point between Highway Sections C and D and the junction with the highway to Bahía de Los Angeles. The government trailer court here is open for use but there are no operable facilities. The PEMEX station that had been abandoned in the past was open on our last trip.

SIDE TRIP

A loop road leaves Highway 1 at this point and travels 42 miles to Bahía de Los Angeles, south along the Sea of Cortez, and then inland through el Arco to rejoin Highway 1 at **Km E-190**. *Bahía de Los Angeles is an important tourist area. The entire loop is described in a separate section at the end of this chapter.*

Km D-13—Punta Prieta

A detachment of army personnel is based to the right (west) at a place named Punta Prieta. The area to the south is sometimes bathed in fog and low clouds rolling in from the Pacific Ocean. Starting at about **Km D-20**, note that many of the *cirio* trees are draped with flowing lichens, which thrive in the moist air.

Km D-29—Ocean View

From this point on the highway, you will be able to see the Pacific Ocean many miles to the west if it is not obscured by fog. This will notify you that the Transpeninsular Highway is now rapidly approaching the Pacific coast. There will be three opportunities to make side trips to camping spots on the coast between here and the state line.

SIDE TRIP

Km D-38—Santa Rosalillita

Midway between **Km D-38** *and* **Km D-39** *a secondary road leaves Highway 1 to the right (west) for the small fishing village of Santa Rosalillita, which is located directly on the Pacific shore. It is 15 Km to the coast.*

If you turn left (south) after reaching the town you will find places to camp on the bluffs overlooking the Pacific. A little farther along on this same road is a beach where the fishermen launch their boats. Because the waters are very shallow at this point, launching is done with the aid of a trailer made from the rear axle and wheels of a car. It is an interesting operation to watch.

You can also work your vehicle over low-standard roads to the beach in the cove north of the village.

Km D-45—Ball Moss

For a mile or so south of this point, you will see round masses of foliage surrounding the branches of the larger plants. These masses are ball moss. There is a far larger colony on the highway to Bahía de Los Angeles and on numerous secondary roads near the Pacific shore. The nature of this plant described in the "Vegetation" chapter.

Km D-51—Rosarito

The town of Rosarito is of little interest to the traveler, and its PEMEX station and trailer court are abandoned.

Km D-68—El Tomatal

A low-standard road leaves Highway 1 to the right (west) at **Km D-69**. It is 2.9 miles to a camp spot in a grove of date palms at the inland edge of a small lagoon and some 100 yards from the beach. Approximately 0.2 miles past the palms and southeast along the coast is the El Tomatal fish camp. The low-standard road is straight and flat but is not recommended for large RVs.

An even lower standard road branches south from the road to El Tomatal 0.4 miles before reaching the palm grove. This leads in 2.0 miles to Miller's Landing. Take the right fork along the way. Decades ago, Miller's Landing was a shipping point for onyx. Large blocks and many smaller pieces of onyx are scattered about near the shingle beach.

#8

#9

Km D-70—Geographic Change Desierto de Vizcaino

Here, just south of the junction with the road to El Tomatal, is the dividing line between the Peninsular Range Mountains (Geographic Section No. 8) to the north and the Desierto de Vizcaino (Geographic Section No. 9) to the south. The Desierto de Vizcaino is a portion of the Continental Borderlands Province. As in other places, this dividing line between geographic provinces is readily apparent. The highway now leaves the mountains and plateaus and will traverse flat terrain for the next 192 Km (119 miles).

Km D-80—"Living" Fence

Notice that the fences along the highway starting near here are made of posts cut from the datilillo. Densely packed rows of posts also outline the yards of the dwellings in the upcoming town of Jesus Maria. Many of these take root and form "living" fences. This is an example of vegetative reproduction common with desert plants.

Km D-96—Villa Jesus Maria

Villa Jesus Maria (population 500) is a small community adjacent to the highway. I have always found the PEMEX station open here and this is a good place to fill ones fuel tank before traveling north on Highway 1. If you look to the west you will see a small mountain, Morro Santo Domingo, the only one present in this otherwise flat area. Keep it in mind for it will guide you to the coast if you choose to take the side trip described in the following item.

SIDE TRIP

Km D-96—Laguna Manuela

A secondary road to the Pacific at Laguna Manuela leaves Highway 1 to the right (west) at Villa Jesus Maria, 200 yards north of **Km D-96**. *Laguna Manuela is a saltwater estuary lying directly south of Morro Santo Domingo. The first 0.8 miles is a two-lane paved road. At the 0.8-mile point a wide, straight, gravel road veers off to the left and heads directly to the peak of the mountain. Taking this road for an additional 6.4 miles will bring you to the coast near the edge of Laguna Manuela. (Total 7.2 miles.) This road is straight and flat but with a washboard surface.*

Local fishermen launch their boats into the protected lagoon and have developed its waters into an oyster farm. Tourists can find campsites along the shore. The lagoon and adjoining ocean bay are protected from the Pacific swells by Morro Santo Domingo.

The camping spots adjoining Laguna Manuela leave something to be desired. Thus, if you have a four-wheel drive vehicle, you may take an excursion up the steep, sandy road that starts near the masonry buildings at the head of the lagoon and proceed westerly past the lighthouse to Morro Santo Domingo.

This short three-mile drive traverses the cliffs above the Pacific and offers secluded campsites with spectacular views of the surf below.

Km D-128—Paralelo 28 (the State Line)

Starting about **Km D-117**, the huge, 135-foot-tall Monumento Aguila (Eagle Monument) is in view rising above the desert floor. It marks *Paralelo 28*, the 28th parallel of north latitude, and the line between the states of Baja California and Baja California Sur.

Here is located another in the chain of parador developments that accompanied the completion of the Transpeninsular Highway. The **Hotel La Pinta Guerrero Negro** is well-maintained and the adjoining RV park (named **The Dunes**). The PEMEX station and series of semi-underground shops built between the highway's divided lanes are closed. Part of the latter space has been converted into a school. There is now a gas pump at the hotel and there are gas stations in nearby Guerrero Negro. A restaurant called **La Espinita** just north of the point where the highway divides offers free RV parking in an adjacent graded field.

Paralelo 28 is the division point between highway sections **C** and **D**. In the sections to the south, you will encounter the kilometer posts in reverse order (descending numbers heading south). There is also an agricultural inspection station where you will be asked if you have any citrus fruit. It is recommended that you answer "No," and that you be telling the truth.

The village of Bahía de Los Angeles. At the top of the photo, the oiled highway can be seen entering town. The secondary road heading south toward El Arco is visible at the bottom.

Bahía de Los Angeles—El Arco Loop

SIDE TRIP

This subsection of the chapter will detail the loop road starting at the division point between Highway 1 sections **C** *and* **D** *(***Km C-280*** and* **Km D-0***) and ending at* **Km E-190***. It consists of four substantially different segments with a total distance of 181.4 miles.*

(1) The initial 68 Km (42 miles) is a paved highway to the village of Bahía de Los Angeles on the Sea of Cortez. En route it passes through desert vegetation that is varied and interesting. Fuel (no Magna Sin) is normally available at Bahía de Los Angeles.

(2) The second segment is a 1.5-lane secondary road with a fairly rough surface. It connects Bahía de Los Angeles with the El Progreso Ranch area and provides side trips to several places on the ocean. It is easily traveled by pickups and vans, but travel time is slow due to the rough surface.

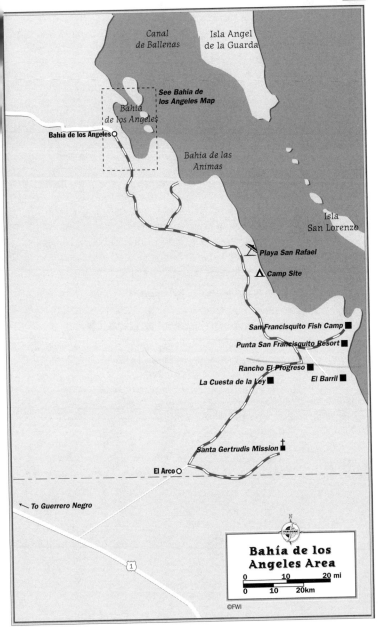

SAN QUINTIN TO
THE STATE LINE

Canal
de Ballenas

Isla Angel
de la Guarda

*See Bahía de
los Angeles Map*

Bahía
de los Angeles

Bahía de los Angeles O

Bahía de las
Animas

Isla
San Lorenzo

⚠ *Playa San Rafael*

△ *Camp Site*

San Francisquito Fish Camp ■

Punta San Francisquito Resort ■

Rancho El Progreso ■

La Cuesta de la Ley ■

El Barril ■

Santa Gertrudis Mission †■

El Arco O

To Guerrero Negro

①

N

Bahía de los
Angeles Area

0   10   20 mi

0   10   20km

©FWI

(3) From El Progreso to the town of El Arco is a narrow, low-standard dirt road. In most places, travel speeds are actually faster than on Segment 2 because of the smooth, sandy roadbed. With one exception, the terrain is relatively level. The exception is La Cuesta de la Ley (Grade of the Law). It poses a segment of steep grades for both directions of travel. My standard-drive pickup made it with no trouble going northeast, but the opposite direction appeared more formidable. As few Mexicans have four-wheel-drive vehicles, it is no doubt passable to standard vehicles in both directions, but be prepared to grit your teeth.

(4) A paved highway was constructed from El Arco to **Km E-190** *on Highway 1 when the latter route was completed. This was no doubt a concession to the community for being bypassed by the new highway. Virtually all of the original layer of paving has disappeared, leaving a moderately washboarded travel surface. Most traffic uses a closely paralleling and smoother-surfaced dirt road.*

Segment (1)

The highway to Bahía de Los Angeles leaves Highway 1 to the left (east).

Km-10—Ball Moss

Starting at this point, you will see hundreds of six- to eight-inch-diameter, ball-shaped masses surrounding the branches of the cirio, datilillo, and other larger plants. This is ball moss. The plant is not a true moss, and it makes its own food through photosynthesis and secures moisture from the air. Ball moss does not penetrate into the tissue of its host, as is the case with mistletoe.

Km-36—Dry Lake

At this point, the highway enters the western edge of a dry lake bed some five miles in diameter. It is nearly surrounded by high, sparsely vegetated mountains.

Km-49 to Km-52—Cirio

Here, near the southern end of the dry lake, is an outstanding array of cirios. The individual plants are large and of many interesting shapes. A good spot for photography.

SIDE TRIP

Km-52—Geographic and Vegetative Changes

At this point, the traveler is rewarded with a vista of the Sea of Cortez and the highway begins its descent to sea level. From the Transpeninsular Highway to here, the terrain has been gentle, as one would expect of the westerly slopes of the Peninsular Range Mountains. Ahead lies the much steeper grade down the eastern escarpment.

There also occurs a prompt change in vegetation. The interesting and varied species of the Vizcaino Desert community are left behind and one enters the less attractive San Felipe Desert community, composed mostly of creosote bush and other low shrubs. This scant plant growth clearly reflects the arid conditions of the rain shadow of the mountains.

Km-58—Ocean View

*A short distance past **Km 58**, Bahía de Los Angeles and its close-in group of protecting islands are arrayed before you. Isla Angel de la Guarda, the second-largest island in the Sea of Cortez, is in the background. These islands combine to make Bahía de Los Angeles an extensive and well-protected boating area.*

Km-61—Punta La Gringa Shortcut

*An old dirt road leaves the highway about 200 yards downgrade (easterly) from **Km-61**. This is the shortcut route to Punta la Gringa. Its travel surface is smother than the main secondary road described in the next paragraph.*

Km-64—Punta La Gringa

To the left is a road junction at the northern edge of the village of Bahía de Los Angeles. (See "Bahía de Los Angeles" map.) You will no doubt wish to proceed straight ahead into town. Should you return to this Punta La Gringa road you will travel over it as follows: (A) 0.8 miles. Branch-road left to the airport. (B) 1.3 miles. Branch-road right to the Brisa Marina and Tony Resendiz RV parks. The former area is used as a campsite, although its rest rooms are not available to the public. It also contains the Sea Turtle Research Station described in the "Wildlife" chapter. (C) 7.8 miles. End of the road near a point of land, Punta La Gringa.

SIDE TRIP

Punta la Gringa has a fine beach where you may camp after paying a small fee. The area has extensive views of the bay and the towering escarpment of the mountains in the background. Many visitors find this a more enjoyable site than the trailer courts in the village.

Km-64—Village of Bahía de Los Angeles

At this point, you enter the village of Bahía de Los Angeles. Here you will find the **Casa Diaz Motel** *and* **Hotel Villa Vitta**. Both of these establishments operate nearby RV parks. **Guerrmo's Trailer Court** lies between these first two. They offer little or no landscaping due to the areas dryness and thus appear austere. Each court offers a hard-surfaced boat launching ramp.

To some people, the Bahía de Los Angeles area suffers in charm because of its scant vegetation. To others, its near-barren mountains are beautiful to behold as the sun casts an ever-changing variety of shadow patterns on their slopes. Also on the positive side are its excellence as a boating and fishing area and the relatively short driving distance from the international border (405 miles).

Bahía de Los Angeles can be particularly hard hit by the strong northern winds common to the upper Sea of Cortez in the late fall and winter. In addition, gale-force winds sometimes flow across the Baja peninsula from the west and strike the village area. Taking to sea in small boats becomes impossible and living conditions become uncomfortable.

Segment (2)

The Segment 2 secondary road leaves the Bahía de Los Angeles village behind (west of) the Casa Diaz Motel. (The mileages noted below start at 0.0 from this point.) The initial three to four miles parallels the shore of Bahía de Los Angeles, where tourists' homes are being constructed. The road then moves inland.

4.6 Miles

A low-standard dirt road heads east at this point, traverses a dirt airstrip and accesses a small group of tourist houses and a good camping area at the southeast corner of Bahía de Los Angeles in about five miles.

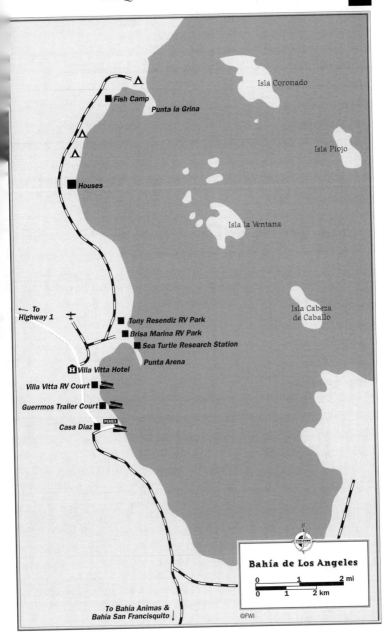

Isla Coronado

Punta la Grina

△

■ Fish Camp

△

△

■ Houses

Isla Piojo

Isla la Ventana

← To
Highway 1

Isla Cabeza
de Caballo

■ Tony Resendiz RV Park

■ Brisa Marina RV Park

■ Sea Turtle Research Station

Punta Arena

H Villa Vitta Hotel

Villa Vitta RV Court ■

Guerrmos Trailer Court ■

Casa Diaz ■ PEMEX

N

Bahía de Los Angeles

0   1   2 mi

0   1   2 km

To Bahía Animas &
Bahía San Francisquito ↓

©FWI

SIDE TRIP

27.6 Miles

Junction with side road to Bahía de las Animas. It is 10.7 miles to the first good camping spots on the edge of the bay and an additional 0.3 miles to the first of two fish camps. Most of this road is little more than two tracks in the sand, but the terrain is level and regularly traveled by standard-drive vehicles. Portions of the route are in an arroyo bottom that can be impassable following rain. At the 7.1-mile point, one has the choice of going straight ahead or turning 90 degrees to the left. The left turn is the proper choice.

There are several good campsites on a narrow sandy beach. Be alert to numerous small stingrays that inhabit the shallow waters at the head of the bay. I was treated to my first, and hopefully last, sting from one of these "moving rocks" while cooling the beer in the ocean (one of the lesser known hazards of alcohol addiction).

41.6 Miles

Spur road east heading toward the coast. In about one mile it becomes very low standard and is best for four-wheel-drive vehicles.

45.6 Miles

A short spur road leads east and in about 0.1 miles arrives at a camping spot at the north end of Playa San Rafael.

47.8 Miles

Spur road east leads in 0.1 miles to a fish camp at the south end of Playa San Rafael.

48.3 Miles

Spur road east accesses campsites on a bluff overlooking a rocky shore. The San Lorenzo Island chain and the south end of Isla Angel de la Guarda are in view from here.

73.7 Miles

Junction with low-standard road to the right (south) leading to Rancho el Progreso. This spur road is the beginning of Segment 3 of the loop route under discussion. However, the main secondary road continues eastward. Taking this latter route you encounter (1) a junction with another two-lane road heading southeast in 0.3 miles (see note below); (2) the junction with the road into the Punta San Francisquito Resort in an additional 11.8 miles. The road then arrives at the Bahía San Francisquito Fish Camp in an additional 0.4 miles. It is thus 86.2 miles from Bahía de Los Angeles to Bahía San Francisquito.

SIDE TRIP

The **Punta San Francisquito Resort** *offers several modest sleeping cabins, central toilet and shower facilities and a small restaurant. It caters primarily to patrons arriving at its nearby dirt airstrip. Aviation and regular fuel are available but they are expensive.*

NOTE—*I have not traveled the two-lane road mentioned above, but it appears that is being built to highway standards. It is no doubt heading toward El Barril, a private residential area on the coast about seven miles distant.*

Segment (3)

Return to the Rancho El Progreso junction noted above at 73.7 miles.

74.3 Miles

The Rancho El Progreso and its well of fresh water lies on the south side of the road.

82.7 Miles

A gate in a cattle drift fence is built at the top of the steep La Cuesta de la Ley (see discussion at the start of this subsection). Between here and the rock corral noted below, much of the road passes through an extensive burned-over area. Travelers must be careful with fire even in the desert.

92.0 Miles

A large rock corral lies adjacent to the road making an unmistakable landmark.

106.5 Miles

At this point, you leave the relatively level terrain and sandy soils prevailing to the northeast and enters rolling hills. The travel surface becomes more rocky.

112.8 Miles

El Arco. In approaching El Arco from the reverse direction (west) one is tempted to turn right in the center of town. The correct course of action is to proceed straight ahead crossing an arroyo, whereupon the road veers to the northeast.

SIDE TRIP

The main peninsular road passed through El Arco prior to construction of the Transpeninsular Highway. Gold was mined in the area by a U.S. company, and during the 1920s more than 1000 people were employed. Gerhard and Gulick's Lower California Guidebook describes the town in 1960 as consisting of two groups of shacks on opposite sides of the arroyo with a population of about 150. By 1989, there had been a modest rejuvenation of the mining industry and the community was the base for a small detachment of federal soldiers. A lonely place for such duty.

Segment (4)

It is 26.6 miles from El Arco to Highway 1. The first six miles southwest from town passes through rolling terrain and one is compelled to drive on the main highway standard road and its washboarded surface. Beyond this point the land is level and the road is closely paralleled by a low-standard dirt road where a smoother surface makes it the most popular route of travel.

139.4 Miles

After many bumpy miles, the loop road joins Highway 1 near **Km E-190**.

STATE LINE TO
SANTA ROSALIA

San Ignacio's famous Dominican-built church.

This chapter will guide you for 221 Km (137 miles) in a journey completely across the peninsula from the Pacific Ocean to the Sea of Cortez. While
very few tourists set out to visit this region, it nevertheless contains some of
Baja's most intriguing points of interest. These include the gray whale-
watching area at Scammon's Lagoon, the interesting town of San Ignacio
with its famous mission, and the major cave-painting area at San Francisco de
la Sierra. Many of Baja's best cave-painting sites are present in the central
portion of the Baja peninsula presented in this chapter. For these reasons, I

415

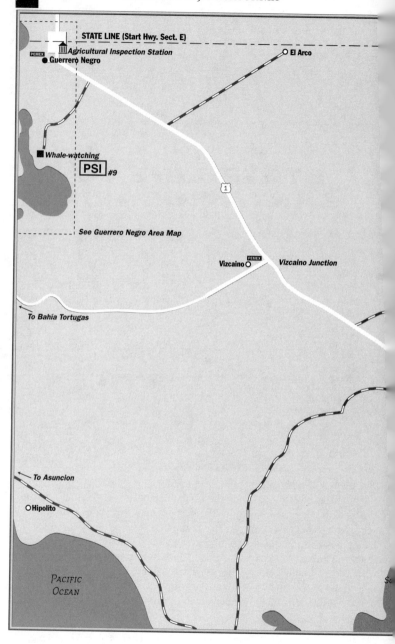

STATE LINE (Start Hwy. Sect. E)

PEMEX

Agricultural Inspection Station

● Guerrero Negro

○ El Arco

■ Whale-watching

PSI #9

1

See Guerrero Negro Area Map

Vizcaino ○ PEMEX Vizcaino Junction

← To Bahía Tortugas

← To Asuncion

○ Hipolito

PACIFIC
OCEAN

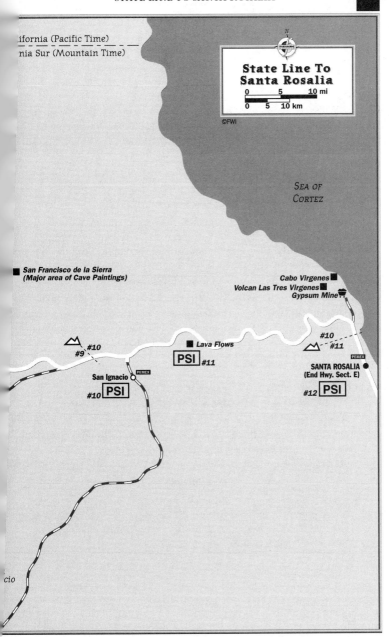

ifornia (Pacific Time)

nia Sur (Mountain Time)

State Line To Santa Rosalia

0   5   10 mi

0   5   10 km

©FWI

SEA OF CORTEZ

■ San Francisco de la Sierra
(Major area of Cave Paintings)

Cabo Virgenes ■

Volcan Las Tres Virgenes ■

Gypsum Mine

⌂ #10
#9

■ Lava Flows

PSI #11

#10 ⌂ #11

San Ignacio PEMEX

SANTA ROSALIA ●
(End Hwy. Sect. E)

#10 PSI

#12 PSI

cio

hope you will not let the lure of the beaches ahead pull you through this re
gion with undue haste.

Km E-217—Guerrero Negro

At this point, Highway 1 veers to the left to begin its journey across th
peninsula. Turn to the right, at the junction here, to enter the town of Gue
rero Negro ("Black Warrior") and its 7200 people. After 1.1 miles you wi
find the **Malarrimo Restaurant** and several motels (several with RV parking) a
on the right (north) side of the road. The **Malarrimo Restaurant** (touris
hangout with live music) is very nice and the motels are modest but ade
quate. Farther into town are a *supermercado* and two PEMEX stations, on
on each side of the road. Remember to pay them a visit before starting th
long trip north on your way home.

Salt Manufacturing

Guerrero Negro is supported largely by the salt-producing industry. Large
segments of the land to the south have been converted into salt-evaporation
ponds, reportedly the largest such operation in the world. Seawater is introduced into these areas. After the sun has baked out sufficient layers, the salt is
trucked to barges waiting at docks located west of town.

The shallow waters of the coastal estuaries near Guerrero Negro are unsuited for large ocean freighters. The barges are thus towed through a channel
into the ocean and then to the shores of Isla Cedros some 70 miles away.
Here, at a deepwater port, the salt is transferred into gigantic mounds, where
it awaits reloading into large ore carriers.

SIDE TRIP

Puerto Venustiano Carranza

*A wide, two-lane road with a packed sand surface turns right
(north) from the main street of Guerrero Negro in front of the salt
company's headquarters near the western edge of town. Travel over
this road, as follows:*

1.1 Miles

*Another wide, two-lane, dirt road leads to the left (southwest). Stay
straight ahead for Puerto Venustiano Carranza. The road to the left
leads in 6.8 miles to the gate of the salt-barge loading facilities on
Scammon's Lagoon (visitors are not normally encouraged).*

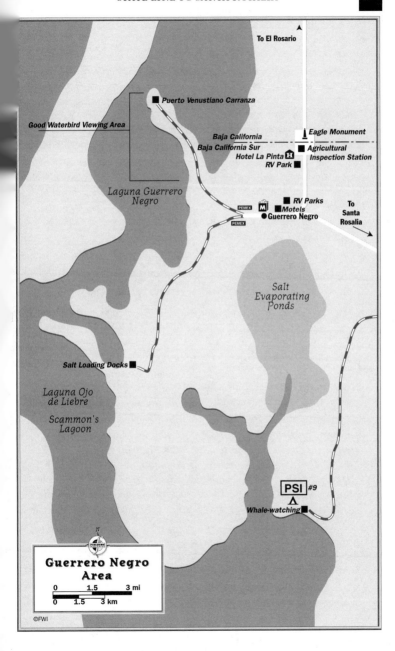

To El Rosario

Puerto Venustiano Carranza

Good Waterbird Viewing Area

Eagle Monument

Baja California
Baja California Sur
Hotel La Pinta
RV Park

Agricultural
Inspection Station

*Laguna Guerrero
Negro*

PEMEX

RV Parks
Motels
Guerrero Negro

To
Santa
Rosalia

PEMEX

*Salt
Evaporating
Ponds*

Salt Loading Docks

*Laguna Ojo
de Liebre*

*Scammon's
Lagoon*

PSI #9

Whale-watching

N

**Guerrero Negro
Area**

0	1.5	3 mi
0	1.5	3 km

©FWI

SIDE TRIP

6.9 Miles

Arrive at the long-abandoned port facility that extends into Laguna Guerrero Negro. Mating gray whales may be present in this lagoon, but in some years they are unable to enter because the entrance is blocked with sand. I have not been able to view the whales from the dock area during my visits as they tend to congregate some distance away near the lagoon entrance. Whale-watching trips by boat are usually available and arrangements may be made at the motels and RV parks in Guerrero Negro.

Bird lovers will wish to take this side trip to Puerto Venustiano Carranza, regardless of the presence of whales, as the road passes through 5 miles of excellent saltwater marshlands. The road lies atop a massive, 10-foot-high fill, so you can look down on the birds. See the "Wildlife" chapter.

SIDE TRIP

Km E-208—Scammon's Lagoon

Laguna Ojo de Liebre (Scammon's Lagoon) is one of the major breeding grounds for the California gray whale. Visiting the whales is stop No. 9 on the Points of Special Interest Tour.

The whales are normally present from the end of December to early April. See the "Wildlife" chapter for details concerning the whale, Scammon's Lagoon and for observational techniques. Whale-watching boat service usually operates from the Scammon's Lagoon camping area. Reservations are not normally required.

A sign on Highway 1 marks the junction with the road to Scammon's Lagoon 100 yards north of **Km E-208**. *It reads "Laguna Oro de Liebre." It is 15 miles to the edge of the lagoon over a flat, natural-surface road that is graded through the desert. The road may be washboarded, but it is occasionally graded with equipment owned by the salt company.*

Members of a local ejido collect a small fee for camping at the edge of the lagoon. The ejido also operates the whale-watching boats. Facilities are limited to crude outhouses, but the area is kept clean, and the road from the highway is signed at points where you might go astray.

SIDE TRIP

I recommend that you plan to camp overnight if you take this jour-
ney. It is a long trip in and out, and you need to let the sight and
sounds of the whales make a proper impression, otherwise, you will be
disappointed if you rush in and out.

Km E-190—Road to El Arco

Between **Km E-189** and **Km E-190**, a road branches to the left. This is the
southern end of the Bahía de Los Angeles–el Arco loop road described earlier. The mining town of El Arco is located some 26.6 miles to the east, at
the base of the mountains that can be seen in this direction.

The fishing village and small cove at Punta Eugenia

SIDE TRIP

Km E-144—Vizcaino Junction and Road to Punta Eugenia Area

There is a growing cluster of homes, a PEMEX station and the
Kaadekaman RV Park where a blacktopped highway leaves Highway
*1 to the right (west) exactly at **Km E-144**. (See the "Punta Eugenia*
Area" map.) It is 5.4 miles to the turnoff to the village of Vizcaino.
Vizcaino is surrounded by orderly plantings of grape vines and fig
and citrus trees. It is a good place to visit to see the Mexican people
turn the desert into a productive farming area.

West of the Vizcaino junction, the oiled surface continues for an additional 16.5 miles. Farther west, to Bahia Tortugas, the road has been constructed to highway standards, but is not yet oil-surfaced. (The same is true of a 23.8-mile branch road leading to Asuncion.) The oiled surface has not been extended on this road for several years, and what the future holds is anybody's guess. For now, most of the roads shown on the map are usable by large RVs, although there is some washboarding. But, because of the relatively long distances involved, the area currently receives little vehicular tourist traffic. However, the town of Bahia Tortugas is a major stopping and fueling point for yachts making the Baja passage. Its people are thus well accustomed to U.S. and Canadian visitors.

Much of the road from **Km E-98** *on Highway 1 to Punta Abreojos has been completely rebuilt and is about six miles shorter than the old route. This road and most others shown on the "Punta Eugenia Area" map do not have a surface of rough imported gravel as do most other secondary roads in Baja. The travel surfaces are thus relatively smooth.*

Each coastal town shown on the map is a sizeable community with schools, fish-packing plants and power-generation facilities. There is a PEMEX station at Bahia Tortugas. A major water line has been constructed from wells near Vizcaino to all the coastal towns.

While many of the roads pass over flat desert lands, the coastline is mountainous, picturesque and offers many places to camp. The only tourist facilities are the small **Vera Cruz Motel** *at Bahia Tortugas and the minimal facility resort named* **Campo Rene** *on the shores of Estero Coyote. For an extended trip, make a complete loop starting at the Vizcaino junction and ending at* **Km E-98** *on Highway 1. Also, take the side road to Punta Eugenia.*

Pinturas Rupestres (Cave Paintings)

Several signs along Highway 1 south of Guerrero Negro call attention to Baja's cave paintings. As a result, I have included a brief overview of this subject at the end of this chapter. The peninsula's most accessible area of paintings is noted below.

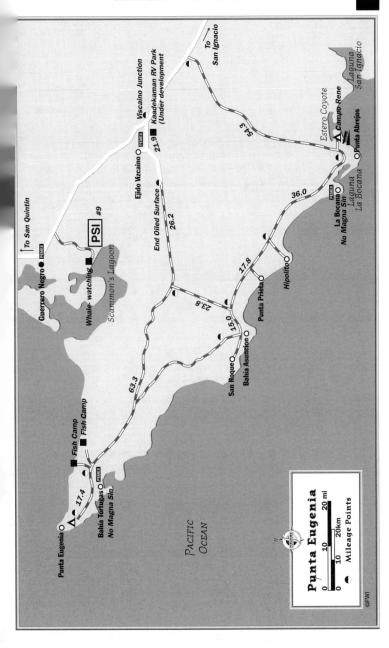

SIDE TRIP

Km E-119—San Francisco de la Sierra

*Between **Km E-118** and **E-117** a secondary road leaves Highway 1 to the left (east) and may be seen climbing the mountains to the northeast. A sign reads "San Francisco de la Sierra 37 Km—Pinturas Rupestres."*

6.0 miles

After a six-mile drive across level terrain, the road moves steeply into the mountains. After about one mile there are several places where one may camp in the rugged mountains with their fine views and desert vegetation. The road ahead was constructed to good secondary standards, but was badly eroded by a major storm during the winter of 1993–94. The damage becomes worse as the road gains elevation, with the last 3.5 miles being the worst due to steep side-slopes. I made it with little trouble in my 19-foot van, but caution is clearly in order until such time as repairs are undertaken.

16.4 miles

At this point is an interpretative sign that notes that the area is administered by the Instituto Nacional de Antropologia e Historia.

21.4 miles

At this point is Cueva del Raton (Rat Cave). It is located directly along the road, but a guide must be secured from the village ahead. High-quality development of the cave is under way.

23.0 miles

The small village of San Francisco and the camp for workers developing the cave painting exhibits.

Km E-98—Road to Punta Abrejos

Heading south at this point is the road to Punta Abrejos and Campo Rene. (See discussion of this road earlier in this chapter.)

#9

#10

Km E-84—Geographic Change

Highway 1 has slowly gained in elevation, and in the vicinity of **Km E-84** the eastern edge of the Continental Borderlands blends with the beginning of a low pass through the Peninsular Range Mountains. This dividing line between geographic provinces is not as sharp as in other places, but it will soon be apparent that the highway has left the flat plains behind and enters more rugged terrain.

Km E-74—San Ignacio

The town of San Ignacio lies in a lava rimmed valley filled with palm trees. The town square is in the trees to the left of the church.

There is a PEMEX station near the junction of the paved side road into the town of San Ignacio. (A "Magna Sin" pump is also present at the Hotel la Pinta.) Directly behind the station is another of the government-constructed trailer courts. I have always found it to be in operation.

SIDE TRIP

San Ignacio is one of Baja's most charming towns and is surrounded by date palms introduced by the Jesuits more than 200 years ago. It is stop No. 10 on the Points of Special Interest Tour. Even the largest of RVs can make this trip and head back to the highway by circling the town square. However, to minimize traffic congestion, I suggest that trailers be parked near the hotel and their occupants walk the last few hundred yards.

It is 1.4 miles from Highway 1 to the town square. En route, you will pass RV parks in the palms, and the **Hotel La Pinta**. *My favorite spot for camping is in the palms near a small pond west of the* **El Padrino RV Park**. *Here is one of the few places to go swimming in the desert. In past years the area was operated as an RV park, but is now undeveloped. No one has objected to my using it, but this could change.*

The town square is typical of such public places found throughout Spanish America. Here and elsewhere they are called el zocalo (the public square). At the west end of the zocalo is Mision San Ignacio, one of the finest churches in all of Baja. Originally established by the Jesuits in 1728, the mission was for 24 years the northernmost mission. At one time it served some 5000 Indians. The present thick-walled stone church was completed many years later by the Dominicans, in 1786.

The square is completely shaded by six massive Indian laurel trees (Arbol de la India) with trunks three to four feet in diameter. You will find smaller examples of this broad-leafed evergreen tree along the waterfront at La Paz and in many other places.

NOTE—The northern termini of the rough-surfaced secondary road leading in 32 miles to Laguna San Ignacio is shown on the "San Ignacio" map. Laguna San Ignacio is then linked by roads of various standards to the town of La Purisima. From here a paved highway leads south to Ciudad Insurgentes. This entire San Ignacio to Ciudad Insurgentes route may eventually be a paved highway.

Km E-71—School Buildings

To the right of the highway notice the modern, one-story school building. Most of the schools you will see in Baja offer primary education only. Here is one of an increasing number of *secundaria-tecnico* facilities built during recent years to improve the educational standards of rural Mexico. See the discussion of education in the "Our Developing Country Neighbor" chapter.

Km E-67—Volcan Las Tres Virgenes

After passing east of **Km E-67**, you will see a massive mountain ahead and to the left of the highway. This is the 6547-foot-high Volcan las Tres Virgenes (Three Virgins Volcano). It was known to have erupted in 1746 and to have emitted smoke in 1857. When an area's principal mountains are dominant, isolated peaks such as Las Tres Virgenes, it is a good sign that you are viewing mountains of volcanic origin.

Starting near San Ignacio, you pass through an area made up of volcanic rock. Refer to the "Rock Type Classification" chart in the "Geology" chapter. This igneous-volcanic-extrusive rock is called basalt and is formed when molten material is extruded at or near the surface of the Earth. Because it cools rapidly, the rock is fine grained as no recognizable crystals have time to form. Note the reddish color typical of these formations. In some places, basalt is honeycombed with small holes formed by pockets of gas trapped at the

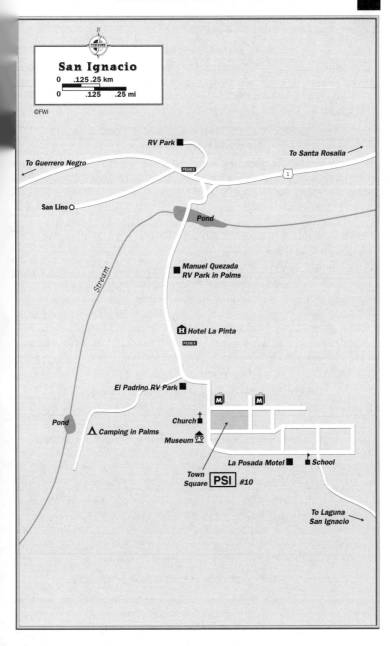

San Ignacio

0   .125 .25 km
0   .125   .25 mi

©FWI

RV Park

To Guerrero Negro

To Santa Rosalia

PEMEX

1

San Lino

Pond

Manuel Quezada
RV Park in Palms

Hotel La Pinta

PEMEX

El Padrino RV Park

M   M

Church

Pond

△ Camping in Palms

Museum

La Posada Motel   ■ School

Town
Square   PSI   #10

To Laguna
San Ignacio

time of solidification. Thus, from a distance, an observer can come to believe that basalt is coarse, rather than fine-grained.

Km E-62—Datilillo

The datilillo is one of the most characteristic of the plants of the Sonoran Desert. The stand visible here in the mountains is the most robust seen anywhere along the Transpeninsular Highway. It is mixed with other attractive plant species.

Km E-42 to E-38—Lava Flows and Elephant Trees

For several miles the Transpeninsular Highway passes through an area of recent lava flows originating on the sides of Volcan las Tres Virgenes. Here, at stop No. 11 on the Points of Special Interest Tour, I suggest that you pull over and take a closer look at these flows. A good turnout is just east of **Km E-41**. There are very few places along the highways of North America where you will have this opportunity. Walk a few feet out onto a flow. There are few environments where you will have such a feeling of complete desolation.

Ironically, this most hostile of growing sites provides the preferred environment for the thick-trunked elephant tree *(Pachycormus discolor)*. Some individuals growing on these flows are three feet in diameter at the base, and they are the sole vegetation. In nearby deep-soiled areas, you will find a species of very similar appearance but which is only distantly related to the trees on the lava flows. This is *Bursera microphylla*. (See the "Vegetation" chapter for descriptions.) The fact that these two species look so much alike is a dramatic example of convergent evolution, as was discussed in that chapter.

Km E-35—Geographic Note

It is here that Highway 1 starts its descent down the steep, east-facing escarpment of the Peninsular Range Mountains. Contrast the considerable drop in elevation you will experience on the highway ahead to the almost effortless climb that has taken place over the gentle western slope behind you. See the "Geology" chapter.

The dominant, dome-shaped mountain lying ahead is Cabo Virgenes (Virgin Cape). It marks the northern limits of the relatively gentle coastal lands through which you will be passing in the miles ahead and which contain the most extensive tourist area on the Sea of Cortez. The ruggedness of Cabo Virgenes and the mountains to the north forced highway engineers to route the Transpeninsular Highway across the peninsula through the pass.

Km E-17—Sea of Cortez Vista

Highway 1 renews its steep descent at this point. A section of highway known as "The Devil's Grade" lies ahead. It is the most dangerous section of mountain highway in Baja. At **Km E-17** the traveler is treated to the first sigificant view of the Sea of Cortez. In nine more kilometers, you will be at its shore.

Directly ahead you can also see the first of many offshore islands that rim the peninsula's eastern shore. This is Isla Tortuga (Turtle Island). Like its mainland neighbors, it is also an extinct volcano, most of which lies below the surface of the sea.

Km E-8—The Sea of Cortez at Last

At long last, after a journey of 920 Km (572 miles) from the international border, the Transpeninsular Highway overlooks the shore of the Sea of Cortez, then turns south toward Santa Rosalia. This is the end of Geographic Section No. 10 and the northern end of the gentle coastal lands lying along the Sea of Cortez.

Prior to reaching **Km E-7**, a dirt road leaves Highway 1 to the north. It provides access in 2.3 miles to an open-pit gypsum mining operation. The area is worth a visit only if you are interested in this industrial activity. Visitors must secure a pass from the mine office in Santa Rosalia.

The town of Santa Rosalia has a breakwater-lined harbor.

Km E-0—Santa Rosalia

Santa Rosalia has received mixed reviews from previous travel book writers. Some even have said that it has little interest to the tourist. Nothing could be further from the truth, and I have placed this town of 10,200 people on the Points of Special Interest Tour as stop No. 12.

Admittedly, it may not be a pretty place, for Santa Rosalia was an industrial town where there is little vegetation and the surrounding hills bear the scars of more than a century of copper and manganese mining. But for uniqueness and historic interest it is hard to surpass.

Santa Rosalia's famous metal church is surrounded by many of the town's old wooden buildings.

I said *was* an industrial town, as the old smelter closed, probably for the last time, about 1990. During my 1992 visit, it was being extensively rebuilt, but even a retired forester such as myself could see that this was probably socialistic nonsense. It was. During my last visit, I interviewed a mining engineer who is investigating the possibility of reprocessing the numerous mine tailings in the area, so future smelting activity may still occur in Santa Rosalia.

The church interior has prefabricated iron panels that are easy to observe.

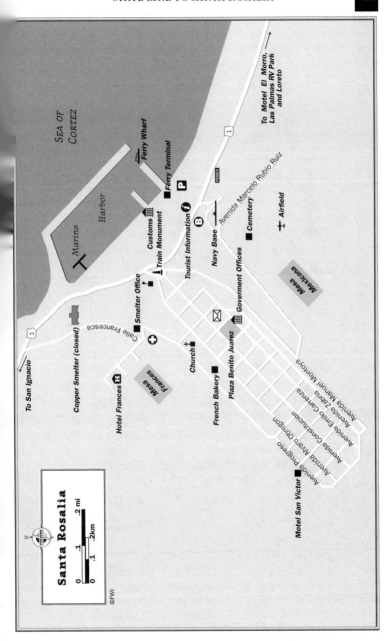

Santa Rosalia

N

0   .1   .2 mi
0   .1   .2km

©FWI

SEA OF CORTEZ

Ferry Wharf

Ferry Terminal

P

Harbor

Marina

Customs

Train Monument

Tourist Information *i*

To Motel El Morro, Las Palmas RV Park and Loreto

1

PEMEX

Avenida Marcelo Rubio Ruiz

B

Navy Base

Cemetery

Airfield

Smelter Office

Goverment Offices

Mesa Mexicana

To San Ignacio

1

Copper Smelter (closed)

Calle Francesca

Church

Plaza Benito Juarez

Mesa Frances

Hotel Frances

French Bakery

Avenida Constitución

Avenida Emilio Carranza

Avenida Zarria

Avenida Manuel Montoya

Avenida Alvaro Obregón

Avenida Progreso

Motel San Victor

STATE LINE TO
SANTA ROSALIA

The town was built by the French (see the "History" chapter for Santa Rosalia's background as a mining center) and as a result almost all of its buildings are made of imported lumber rather than masonry. Many have broad verandas, and the houses along the three main streets are closely packed in orderly lines. It is an interesting community. (During my last visit, the town had sprouted two traffic lights. Horrors, the place is going to hell.)

Smaller vehicles can be driven into town, but trailers and large RVs should be parked along the highway or in the parking lot at the ferry dock. Do your sightseeing on foot. I recommend you proceed as follows:

1. Walk about on the streets in the main section of town and notice the architecture and wooden construction of the buildings.

2. Visit the unique church designed by Gustave Eiffel (builder of the Eiffel Tower in Paris). It was constructed from prefabricated galvanized iron—the building was originally destined for a humid African country where resistance to termites was needed.

3. Starting in front of the church, proceed up the steep road that winds its way up to the Mesa Frances (French Mesa). Here you will find a broad street lined with large wooden buildings. Take note of the mining company office across from the hospital. Visit the **Hotel Frances**, which has been recently remodeled and reopened after several years of being closed. Outside the hotel, note the adjacent brick tunnel leading from the smelter to the smokestack high above town.

4. Look over the breakwater walls that form the harbor. They are made from blocks of slag left over from the smelting process. A small marina was completed about 1987, which attracts boaters, most of whom cross the Sea of Cortez from San Carlos near Guaymas on the mainland shore.

5. If you can get inside the old smelter, it is worth a visit. It contains an old French clock and loads of decades-old machinery.

Pinturas Rupestres (Cave Paintings)

Signs bearing the term "*Pinturas Rupestres*" began appearing along Highway 1 south of Guerrero Negro starting about 1993. *Pinturas* is the Spanish word for "paintings," but I have had a bit more difficulty translating *Rupestres*. My Spanish-English dictionary indicates the word means "rupestrian," a definition that doesn't move one too far along the road to enlightenment. In biology this term refers to "growing on or living among rocks." It is thus likely that *Pinturas Rupestres* refers to a variety of prehistoric rock art that includes but is not limited to cave paintings. As Baja is most famous for her cave paintings, I will equate the two terms in this discussion until corrected by some irate professor.

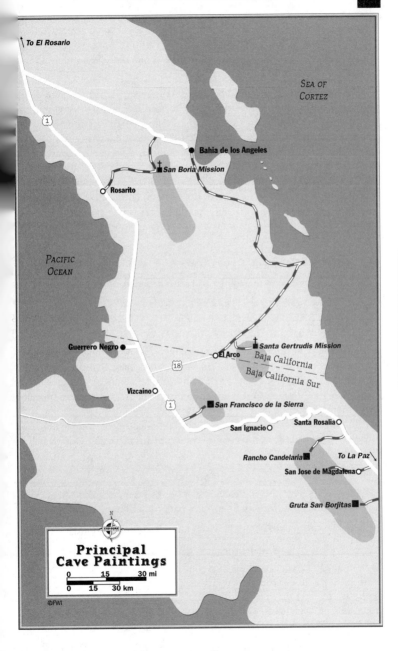

To El Rosario

SEA OF
CORTEZ

1

Bahia de los Angeles
† San Borja Mission

Rosarito

PACIFIC
OCEAN

† Santa Gertrudis Mission

Guerrero Negro
18
El Arco
Baja California
Baja California Sur

Vizcaino
1
San Francisco de la Sierra
San Ignacio
Santa Rosalia
Rancho Candelaria
To La Paz
San Jose de Magdalena
Gruta San Borjitas

N

**Principal
Cave Paintings**

0   15   30 mi
0   15   30 km

©FWI

Examples of rock art may be found the full length of the Baja peninsul, but the largest concentration of cave paintings appear to be concentrated the four areas shown on the "Principal Cave Painting Areas" map accomp, nying this discussion. These areas encompass some of the Peninsular Range most rugged mountains.

Baja's cave paintings began to be noted in literature in the late 19th centu ry, but they were brought to the public's attention by mystery writer Er Stanley Gardner. Garner mounted two expeditions in 1962 and visited se eral rock art sites including the one that is now considered Baja's best an that bears his name (Garner Cave or Cueva Pintada). Baja's caves are simila to those hosting the so-called "cliff dwellings" of the Pueblo Indians i southwestern United States. These are generally shallow linear depression running along the face of near vertical mountain cliffs. Baja's cave painting are often spectacular and depict human figures and animals. They extend fo hundreds of feet in length and are up to 30 feet in height. Colors are red black, white and occasionally yellow.

Visiting the Cave Paintings

There are several ways to arrange to visit Baja's cave paintings.

San Ignacio

Reference to the accompanying map will show that the town of San Igna cio lies near Highway 1 in the heart of the cave painting country. In past years, I have been informed that arrangements could be made to visit rock art sites at the **La Posada Motel**. While the details may change, the patient traveler can no doubt arrange for guide service at a variety of places in San Ignacio. A well-designed museum related to rock art adjoins San Ignacio's famous church. Unfortunately the display labels were all in Spanish and there was no handout material. Perhaps this will change in the future, especially considering the fact that most of the museum's prospective visitors will be English-speaking tourists.

Mulegé

My past visits have also indicated that trips to rock art sights could be ar ranged by contacting the hotels and RV parks in and near Mulegé.

A cave painting site may also be visited as noted at **Km 189** on page 436.

San Francisco de La Sierra

Travelers can drive directly to the vicinity of Baja's best cave sites by taking the Side Trip noted earlier in this chapter. Guided tours to backcountry sites can be arranged at the village of San Francisco de la Sierra. One of the added attractions of a visit to this area is outstanding desert mountain and vegeta tive scenery. Trips into the backcountry also feature delightful palm canyons.

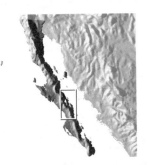

SANTA ROSALIA TO LORETO

The restored mission church at Loreto boasts a fine historical museum housed in an adjoining building.

This chapter describes the Sea of Cortez central coast, one of the six principal tourist areas introduced in "The Big Picture." It contains the peninsula's most heavily used beachside camping areas and the towns of Mulegé and Loreto. Highway 1 passes over a series of coastal benches and low hills lying at the base of the steep eastern escarpment of the Peninsular Range Mountains. This section of the mountains is called the Sierra Giganta (the Giant Range) and will treat you to the best views from the Transpeninsular Highway.

435

The fuel situation has improved along the Central Coast in recent year There are PEMEX stations at Santa Rosalia, Mulegé and Loreto. In additio there is a new, easy-to-access station about three miles south of Mulegé o Highway 1. It is no longer necessary to enter the constricted street of th community to obtain fuel at the town station.

Km F-195—Hotel El Morro

On the cliffs overlooking the Sea of Cortez is the **Hotel El Morro**. It has ; very nice restaurant.

Note the navigation light tower on the small rocky islet lying 200 yards off shore from the motel. You should become familiar with these aluminun towers and their solar-powered lights if you plan to use a boat in the Sea o Cortez. They are to be found in scores of locations and are reliable aids to navigation.

Km F-193—RV Park Las Palmas

There has long been need for a trailer park near Santa Rosalia since many people like to settle down for the night after the long journey through the desert to reach the Sea of Cortez. Also it is quite easy to spend many hours prowling about the historically interesting town and an overnight visit is often just what is needed.

This need has now been met a short distance south of Santa Rosalia by the **RV Park Las Palmas** and cafe. Since its origin about 1992, is has been extensively landscaped and is becoming one of Baja's most pleasant RV parks.

Km F-190—State Prison

There are no signs on the large building at this point, but there is little doubt about its function. There is relatively little crime in Baja California, but obviously there is some.

Candelaria

Six miles south of Santa Rosalia (between **Km 188** and **189**) a secondary road signed for Santa Agueda 13 Km leaves Highway 1 to the west. The village of Santa Agueda is reached in about seven miles. The additional 20 miles to the Rancho Candelaria is lower-standard road along an arroyo bottom. Ask at the ranch for a guide for a walk to nearby Indian cave paintings.

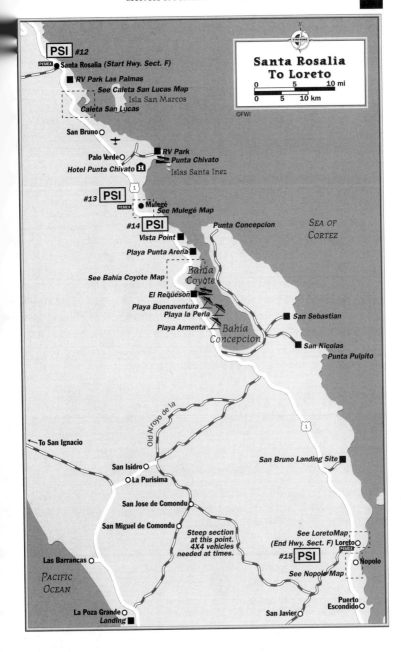

PSI #12

PEMEX ● Santa Rosalia (Start Hwy. Sect. F)

■ RV Park Las Palmas

- - See Caleta San Lucas Map

Isla San Marcos

Caleta San Lucas

San Bruno ○

✈

Palo Verde ○

■ RV Park

Hotel Punta Chivato ⌂ ■ Punta Chivato

Islas Santa Inez

#13 **PSI**

PEMEX ● Mulegé

See Mulegé Map

#14 **PSI**

Vista Point ■

Playa Punta Arena ■

See Bahía Coyote Map

Bahía Coyote

El Requesón ■

Playa Buenaventura ⌂

Playa la Perla

Playa Armenta *Bahía Concepcion*

Punta Concepcion

SEA OF CORTEZ

■ San Sebastian

■ San Nicolas

Punta Pulpito

Santa Rosalia To Loreto

0   5   10 mi
0   5   10 km

©FWI

N

Old Arroyo de la

← To San Ignacio

San Isidro ○

○ La Purisima

San Jose de Comondu ○

San Miguel de Comondu ○

Steep section at this point. 4X4 vehicles needed at times.

Las Barrancas ○

PACIFIC OCEAN

San Bruno Landing Site ■

1

See Loreto Map
(End Hwy. Sect. F) Loreto ○ PEMEX

#15 **PSI**

○ Nopolo

See Nopolo Map

La Poza Grande ○
Landing ■

San Javier ○

Puerto Escondido ○

SIDE TRIP

Km F-182—Caleta San Lucas

A dirt road leaves Highway 1 to the left (east). In 0.4 miles you will reach the shores of a shallow cove protected from the sea by a rocky bar. This is Caleta (little cove) San Lucas. Here you will find the **San Lucas RV Park** *at the water's edge. A military detachment lies southwest from the park. A small restaurant is located nearby to the south.*

Near the cove's southern end, another dirt road leaves Highway 1 at **Km F-180** *and accesses many fine palm-shaded campsites along the shore. See "Caleta San Lucas" map.*

Isla San Marcos

Isla San Marcos is in view offshore from this general area. Notice the light color of the land at the south end of the island. This light area is the barren slope of an open-pit gypsum mine. The workers' village, the mill and port facilities can be seen north of the mine. Gypsum is one the softest of minerals, and the San Marcos variety is light yellow in color. Many of the town's buildings have been constructed from foot-thick blocks of compressed gypsum, despite the fact that you can scratch it with your fingernail. Walking through this almost totally yellow town is an interesting experience.

Km F-173—San Bruno

The small dirt-street town of San Bruno is in view on the shore to the left (east). A drive of 0.5 miles over a secondary road accesses a small RV park (**Coasta Serena**) occupied largely on a full-time basis and for this reason I have not included it in the earlier list of RV parks. The town is fronted by a good sandy beach. It is a good place to wander about and view a small, rural Mexican town that has had minimal impact from tourism.

Km F-162—Santa Rosalia Airport

A jet airport and 1.6-mile oiled access road were completed east of this point in fall 1988. It was designed to serve Santa Rosalia to the north and Mulegé to the south, but it has seen almost no use. Such projects illustrate one of the characteristics of a centralized, socialistic form of government. The international airport at Loreto and the resort area at Nopolo to the south are vastly underutilized. And yet here, someone contemplated a repeat performance. Perhaps new hotels and other tourist facilities will follow. Time will tell. In the meantime, the tarmac makes a fine RV parking area if you can negotiate with the military people that guard the strip from being used for illicit purposes. They use the terminal building as their barracks.

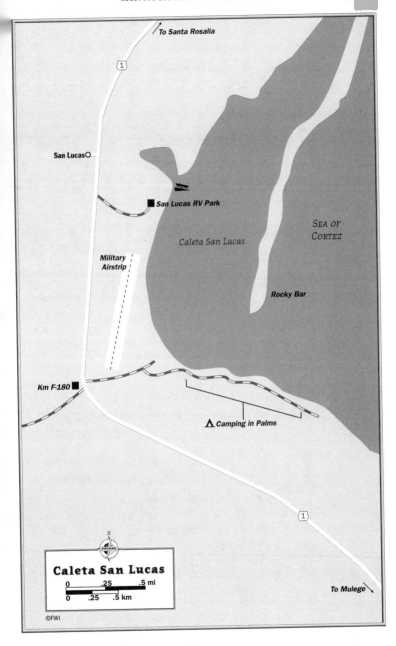

To Santa Rosalia

San Lucas○

San Lucas RV Park

Caleta San Lucas

Sea of Cortez

Military Airstrip

Rocky Bar

Km F-180

△ Camping in Palms

N

Caleta San Lucas

0   .25   .5 mi

0   .25   .5 km

©FWI

To Mulege

The isolated Hotel Punta Chivato is north of Mulegé.

SIDE TRIP

Km F-156—Punta Chivato

A sign at this road junction indicates that it is 20 Km to Punta Chivato. The small community of Palo Verde lies along the highway. Taking this secondary road left (east) from Highway 1 leads in 4.5 miles to a point where a lesser-standard road branches right to Punta Chivato. The very nice **Punta Chivato Hotel** is reached after a total of 12.8 miles, with an RV park at the water's edge just an additional 0.6 miles away. (See inset map on the "Santa Rosalia to Loreto" Map). In the past, the access-road suffered from chronic washboardi-tis, but since the hotel acquired a grader, the entire road has been graded every two weeks. Large RVs and trailers make it on a regular basis.

Km F-136—Mulegé

Again, as at Santa Rosalia, I suggest that you take an hour or two and visit another of Baja's historic and intriguing communities. It is stop No. 13 on the Points of Special Interest Tour. The two towns have little in common except that the river along which Mulegé is built bears the name Rio Santa Rosalia. Santa Rosalia is also the name of Mulegé's famous mission.

PSI
#13

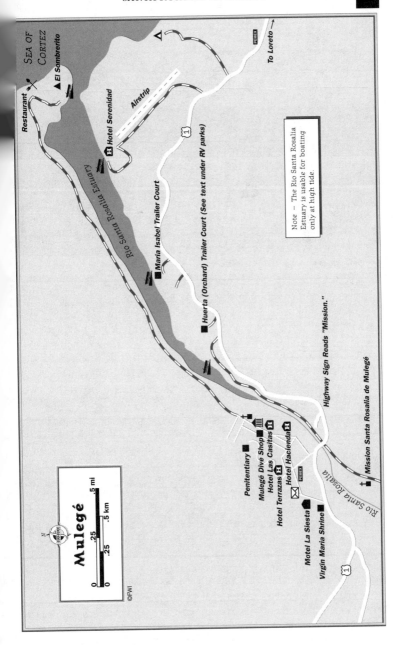

SEA OF CORTEZ

El Sombrerito

Restaurant

Rio Santa Rosalia Estuary

Airstrip

H Hotel Serenidad

1

To Loreto

Maria Isabel Trailer Court

Huerta (Orchard) Trailer Court (See text under RV parks)

Note – The Rio Santa Rosalia Estuary is usable for boating only at high tide.

Penitentiary

Mulegé Dive Shop

Hotel Las Casitas

Hotel Terrazas

Hotel Hacienda

Motel La Siesta

Virgin Maria Shrine

Highway Sign Reads "Mission."

Mission Santa Rosalia de Mulegé

Rio Santa Rosalia

1

Mulegé

N

0   .25   .5 mi

0   .25   .5 km

©FWI

The historic federal prison at Mulegé.

Town Center

The center of this community of 3100 people is reached from a road leaving Highway 1 west of the highway bridge shown on the "Mulegé" map on page 441. The town's streets are narrow so it is best to leave the big RVs and trailers near the highway. Obtain gasoline at the PEMEX station three miles south of town on Highway 1.

If you drive into town, park near the **Hotel Las Casitas** and savor the community on foot. Keep in mind that you are viewing a place that was founded 60 years before the first Europeans discovered San Francisco Bay. Be sure to visit the massive, thick-walled federal prison. It looks like a structure you would find in the Sahara Desert manned by the French Foreign Legion. It is no longer an active prison and is operated as a museum. The prison was famous for being operated on the honor system. The inmates worked or visited in town during the day but were required to return for the night. Misconduct by one prisoner was considered an infraction by all, and all were punished. It was no doubt a very orderly place.

If you have a small vehicle, drive down the dirt road along the palm-lined north bank of the river and visit the site of the Hotel Vista Hermosa. (At press time it was closed.) True to its name, it offers *avista hermosa* (beautiful view) of the mouth of the Rio Santa Rosalia, the Sea of Cortez and a small hat-shaped hill that could only be named *El Sombrerito* (The Little Hat). In October 1847, this hill witnessed a battle during the Mexican-American War between local patriots and forces from the U.S. sloop *Dale*. See the "History" chapter.

RV Parks

The southeast side of the Rio Santa Rosalia is the main tourist area at Mulegé. It may be reached by driving under the highway bridge at the southeast end of the main section of town, or directly from the highway. There are two large RV parks among the palms along the river. They have boat ramps usable at high tide only. There is another smaller RV park adjoining the **Hotel Serenidad**. (The owner of the **Huerta RV Park** advised us that his park is being converted to permanent facilities and that the RV park will be relocated south of Highway 1 and west of the highway bridge.)

Mission

From under the highway bridge, drive upstream for 0.4 miles on a dirt road through palm groves along the southeast bank of the river to the restored Mission Santa Rosalia de Mulegé. The towers of the church can be seen while crossing the bridge and from the highway entering town from the north. Here, Jesuit missionaries founded their fourth mission in 1705, only eight years after they established themselves on the peninsula in 1697. It originally served an Indian population of some 2000 people.

Walk to the vista point on top of a point of rock located a few feet behind the mission. From here you can look over a sea of palm trees, a small reservoir, and the agricultural area upstream from downtown Mulegé.

The restored mission church on the banks of the Rio Santa Rosalia at Mulegé was founded in 1705 by the Jesuits. The church was originally built in 1766 and has been remodeled many times.

South of Town

At **Km F-132** a dirt road will bring you in 0.5 miles to the **Hotel Serenidad**. This attractive facility is located near the mouth of the river and directly adjacent to a dirt surface airstrip. Many of the hotel's patrons arrive by small private aircraft. Adjacent to the hotel is a small RV park.

Near the mouth of the river, and hidden from view by the hotel, is the Fisherman's Landing boat launching ramp. One must drive around three sides of the hotel on a narrow dirt road to arrive at the ramp. Boaters need to time their launching with the state of the tide as there is no water at the ramp when the sea is at low ebb.

About 0.1 miles south of the road to the Hotel Serenidad, another side road leaves to the left (east). After passing through the remains of a former dumping ground, this road arrives in 0.4 miles at a camping spot on a long sandy beach. It was here that my wife and I camped for 10 days on our first trip to Baja and fell in love with the peninsula. We both agreed we had never had such a relaxing vacation. After returning to the hectic life of the city, it was several days before I was aware that I was no longer smoking a pipe that up until now had been a constant fixture in my mouth. I have never touched it again.

Km F-131—Pemex Station

This station was constructed about 1990 to relieve traffic congestion caused by the old station on Mulegé's narrow streets.

The entrance to Bahia Concepcion as seen from the vista point at PSI stop No. 14.

Km F-126—View of Punta Concepcíon

You are now approaching Bahía Concepcíon, the largest protected body of water on the Sea of Cortez. To the southeast from this point on the highway, you can see Punta Concepcíon, the northern tip of the peninsula that forms the eastern shore of the bay. The channel into Bahía Concepcíon lies between this peninsula and the promontory supporting a microwave tower, which is in view ahead and to the left.

Near this same point on the highway, a dirt road leaves to the left and in 0.4 miles arrives at a camping spot on the low bluffs above a shingle beach. There are also several other dirt roads heading toward the Sea of Cortez between the new PEMEX station and the vista point noted below. I have not explored these, so help yourselves.

SIDE TRIP
Km F-124—Vista Point

PSI
#14

There are few good vista points directly along Highway 1. I have therefore included a visit to the microwave tower, noted above, as stop No. 14 on the Points of Special Interest Tour. It is signed for "Est. Microonades (Microwave Station) Tiburones." The last word on each microwave sign along the highway is the name of the individual station. In this case Tiburones *means sharks.*

The cobblestone road to the tower begins with two moderately steep switchbacks, which are in view from the highway. These are the main problem spots on the 0.8-mile drive to the tower. Because of these switchbacks and the lack of places to pass oncoming vehicles, this trip is not recommended for large RVs. If you make the trip, you will find good turnaround spots at the end of the road or in a low saddle about 100 yards before reaching the tower. You will be rewarded with fine views of the entrance to Bahía Concepcíon and the coastline.

Km F- 121—Villa de Mulegé

It is 1.6 miles to the beach and a *palapa*-type, private subdivision. There is a natural surface boat-launching ramp.

Km F-119—Playa Punta Arena

To the left, a dirt road leads to the sandy beach camping areas at **Punta Arena** (**Sand Point**). The mileages to the area's two RV parks are shown at the top of the "Bahía Coyote Area" map. I recommend that you proceed to the **Santispac** area at the northern end of Bahía Concepcíon if you have not visited this region before. However, should the crowds of people that are normally found there not be to your liking, you can consider Punta Arena as an alternative. There are usually fewer campers and the beach is excellent. Its negative features are the bumpy access road and its exposed location, which provides little protection from the northerly winds that prevail in the early winter months.

Km F-114 to F-108—Bahía Coyote

Bahía Coyote. The island in the foreground is Isla Blanca. The J-shaped beach above and to the right of the island is Playa Santispac.

Bahía Coyote is the wind-protected bay lying at the northwest corner of the much larger Bahía Concepción. It is the most heavily used camping and boating area in the entire Baja Peninsula. In recent years, the number of tourists visiting Baja has declined sharply, but the beach camping areas at Bahía Coyote have been packed as usual. Most of these camping areas have no facilities other than crude outhouses. RVs simply line up at right-angles a few feet from the beach.

There are five sections of the Bahía Coyote area, each served by a short side road from Highway 1. They are described in the order they are encountered along the highway from north to south. The exact operating conditions of these campgrounds varies from year to year, but at most beaches you will be charged a daily fee. At some places, this will entitle you to the use of a beach-side shelter called a *palapa*. They are made from poles and grass mats.

Playa Santispac (Km F-114)

Standing at the beach at Santispac, one can readily come to the conclusion that most weary travelers from north of the border shout, "This must be the place!" when they arrive at Santispac, for during the winter the beach is usually lined with vehicles of every description. Many travelers stay here for ex-

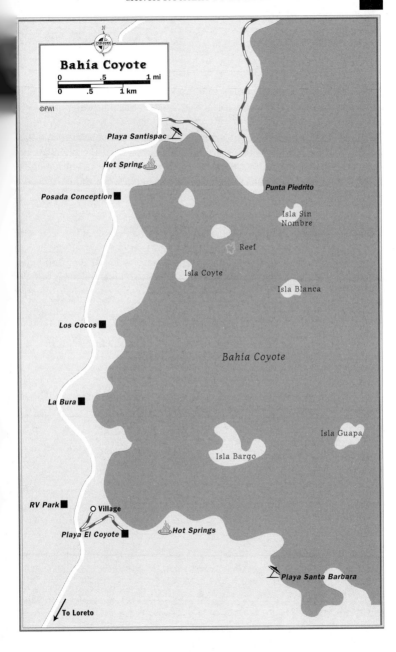

Bahía Coyote

Playa Santispac

Hot Spring

Punta Piedrito

Posada Conception

Isla Sin Nombre

Reef

Isla Coyte

Isla Blanca

Los Cocos

Bahía Coyote

La Bura

Isla Guapa

Isla Bargo

RV Park ■ ○ Village

Playa El Coyote

Hot Springs

Playa Santa Barbara

To Loreto

©FWI

tended periods, others make it a one-night stopping point. Expect a bus influx of vehicles every evening and a sudden torrent of departees afte breakfast. Be careful using the steep approach road and guard against th possibility of tipping over at its junction with the highway. Larger trailer rig sometimes have to take a run to return to the highway.

Shoreside vegetation has long ago yielded to the onslaught of campers However, the protected cove is excellent for windsurfing, water-skiing and swimming, and **Baja Tropicales**, offers kayak rentals. There is a small restaurant, and your modest camping fee helps keep the area clean. A short walk to the west of the main beach, on a trail along the base of the highway, will bring you to a natural hot spring. Thus, if you enjoy beach-bumming in close proximity to many other friendly folks doing the same thing, then your first assessment will prove correct and, in fact, *this must be the place.*

Posada Concepcíon (Km F-112)

Posada Concepcíon is the domain of those who became enamored with this part of the world and decided to stay. Located here is a subdivision of winter homes and numerous trailer houses supplemented with adjoining grass-mat shelters. There is also an RV and boat storage area. You can arrange to park your RV by the day, but the permanent residents have the best locations.

Los Cocos (Km F-111)

The access road from Highway 1 is 0.3 miles in length and leads to a fine beach and camping area with many *palapas.*

La Burra (Km F-109)

Another good camping beach that is in full view from the highway. The access road leaves directly at the **Km F-109** sign.

Playa El Coyote (Km F-108)

The southernmost of the Bahía Coyote camping spots is a beach that bears the same name. A few feet after the side road leaves the highway, turn right and proceed along the water's edge and in 0.5 miles you arrive at an excellent beach. At the far (south) end of this camping area, a trail leads some 100 yards to a hot spring near the water's edge. This is my favorite of the Bahía Coyote camping areas. There is a sizeable trailer park on the other side of the highway, but it is very lightly used.

Approximately one mile southeast from Playa el Coyote is another fine beach in a deep cove at Playa Santa Barbara. This cove provides an excellent picnic or camping site for small boat owners who can load up their gear and escape the crowded conditions at the other camping areas that rim Bahía Coyote. It is only a short distance over the protected waters of the bay from any of these areas.

"Siesta'neath the sun" at Playa Coyote.

Bahía Concepcíon (Southwestern Shore)

For many years there were no waterfront tourist areas along the shores of Bahía Concepcíon south of Bahía Coyote. (Recall that sites at Bahía Coyote are reasonably well-protected from the winter wind.) There were several reasons for this lack of development, including the fact that this southwestern area is subject to brisk northerly breezes funneling down the length of Bahía Concepcíon during the winter months. However, the area started to build up early in the 1990s, and now contains several of the better tourist areas on Bahía Concepcíon. While this section of shoreline can be a bit windy and chilly during the winter, this very condition becomes a blessing as the weather turns hot in spring and summer.

Playa Buenaventura (Km F-94)

The development here is probably the nicest on Bahía Concepcíon. The owner is an excellent craftsmen who has fashioned a small low-rise hotel to standards not often found in Baja. Use of the adjoining RV park is restricted to its limited number of developed units, thus avoiding the sardine-like conditions often found at Bahía Coyote. There is an adjoining restaurant-bar and a well-constructed boat launching ramp. These facilities are directly in view from Highway 1.

El Requeson (Km F-92)

El Requeson (see photo on page 63) is a small island lying between **Km F-93** and **Km F-92**. At low tide it is connected to the mainland by an isthmus of sand. The higher portion of this isthmus provides a fine camping spot, and it

and the island form a small, well-protected but shallow bay. A good spot fo
launching Class-4 boats over the beach. The entire area is in view from th
highway, and the approach road is less than 0.1 miles in length.

Playa La Perla (Km F-91)

A short distance north of **Km F-91** a short dirt road leads to a waterfron'
camping area with *palapas.*

Playa Armenta (Km F-91)

Playa Armenta is a small beach lying on the north side of a point of lav‹
rock. It is fully exposed to the prevailing northerly wind but is a good camp‹
ing spot during calm weather. The approach road is 0.6 miles in length and
leaves Highway 1 between **Km F-91** and **Km F-90**. The beach cannot be seen
from the junction point, but it and the approach road are in full view from
the highway, a short distance to the south, should you care to look it over
before driving in.

Additional Camping Sites

Spur roads lead to several camping sites at (1) 200 yards north of **Km F-88**,
(2) north of **Km F-85**, (3) north of **Km F-84**, (4) just south of **Km F-82**, and (5)
near **Km F-80**. These are not as good as other areas along Bahía Concepcíon,
but some of us can suffer some shortcomings in exchange for not being
herded into the larger, more developed areas. Some of these sites will no
doubt be developed sites in the future.

SIDE TRIP

Km F-77—Bahía Concepcíon (South and East Shore)

A dirt road leaves Highway 1 between **Km F-77** *and* **Km F-76** *and
closely follows the south shore of Bahía Concepcíon. The terrain at the
southern end is extremely low and flat. After a rain, the road in this
vicinity becomes slick and impassable, but in dry weather, travel is
easy. There are numerous spurs that provide access to camping spots at
the water's edge. A second, parallel road branches inland about 0.25
mile in from the highway. It traverses higher ground and is preferable
in wet weather.*

*The area's principal shortcoming is that it is fully exposed to the
northerly winds that funnel between the mountains that rim Bahía
Concepcíon on both sides. Near the junction with Highway 1 lies an
abandoned, cemetery-like RV parks that have been previously mentioned. It was no doubt a victim of these windy conditions. A small
group of trees a few yards east of the park provides one of my favorite
camping spots. As the weather heats up with approaching summer, the
breeze here makes this a very pleasant location.*

SIDE TRIP

At the southeast corner of Bahía Concepción the traveler is offered three choices of travel. Two roads proceed easterly to San Sebastian and San Nicolas on the Sea of Cortez shore. I have started out on both of these routes but turned back after several miles feeling they were a bit marginal for a standard drive pickup. I have been to both areas by sea and they are two of the most attractive of Baja's hidden coastal Shangri-las.

A third road runs at the water's edge along the full length of the eastern shore of Bahía Concepción and passes over the divide ridge to the Sea of Cortez. At this point, one may explore the extensive ruins of an abandoned manganese mine or take a trail north to Punta Concepción. Much of this road is suitable for standard drive vehicles, but there are rough spots making extra traction advisable.

Km F-77—Cardon

The flat plain lying along the southern and eastern shore of Bahía Concepción (just south of **Km F-77**) supports one of the finest *cardonals* (forests) of giant cardón cactus in view along the entire Transpeninsular Highway. It is a good area for photographing Baja's largest desert plant.

Km F-68—Sierra Giganta

The base of the Sierra Giganta has been some distance inland since the Peninsular Range Mountains were crossed north of Santa Rosalia. South of **Km F-68**, the range's steep eastern escarpment is closer to the coast and will provide you with the best mountain scenery in view from the Transpeninsular Highway. Note the characteristic saw-toothed silhouette of the mountains.

SIDE TRIP

Km F-60—Road to La Purisima

At this point, a secondary road leads right (west) to the historic towns of San Jose de Comondu, San Isidro (61 Km) and La Purisima (65 Km), and eventually to Cuidad Insurgentes. It provides one of the most interesting backroad adventures in Baja. The full route is described at the end of this chapter.

Km F-21—San Bruno Landing Site

From this portion of Highway 1, the Sea of Cortez is in view about six miles to the east. A low section of coast lies between mountains to both the north and south. It is along here that Padre Francisco Kino and Isidro de Atondo made their attempt to found a colony in 1683. This effort lasted only 19 months but was a key step to the permanent settlement made i Loreto 14 years later in 1697. (See the "History" chapter.) The dirt road t the area leaves the highway just north of **Km F-20**.

Km F-6—Scenic View

Prior to **Km F-6** one can see the town of Loreto and its thousands of dat palms lying along the shore at the eastern edge of a sizeable coastal plain. The large island south of town is Isla Carmen. The smaller island off it southwest tip is Isla Danzante, with Puerto Escondido hidden along the peninsular shore to the west. It is apparent, toward the south, that the Sierra Giganta is sweeping to the coast and the offshore islands appear to be its sea ward extension.

PSI #15

Km F-0 and G-120—Loreto

Whenever you have visited a locality long enough ago to be considered an old-timer, you must be prepared for the disappointments brought about by change. Much of Baja is changing rapidly, but it is particularly apparent at Loreto (population 17,300). While the town is the oldest permanent Spanish settlement in all of the Californias, in the past Loreto has never been among Baja's most charming. Its flat terrain made it easy to design the town in conventional and uninspiring square blocks.

Shown is the boat-launching ramp and breakwater-lined harbor at Loreto. The open boats in view are different models of the Mexican panga.

But for about 10 years Loreto has undergone a considerable face-lift of new streets, buildings and other facilities. All this effort has finally transformed Loreto into a pleasant community. Even its western fringe (shown as

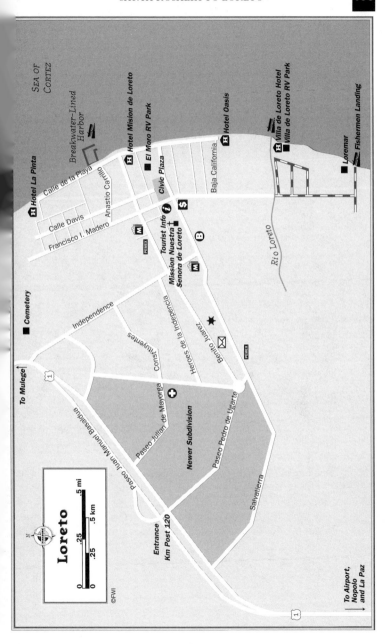

SEA OF CORTEZ

Breakwater-Lined Harbor

H Hotel La Pinta

Calle de la Playa

Calle Davis

Francisco I. Madero

Anastio Carrillo

H Hotel Mision de Loreto

El Moro RV Park

Civic Plaza

Baja California

H Hotel Oasis

Villa de Loreto Hotel

Villa de Loreto RV Park

Loremar

Fishermen Landing

Tourist Info

Mission Nuestra
Senora de Loreto

Río Loreto

Cemetery

Independence

Constituyentes

Heroes de la Independencia

Benito Juárez

To Muleg

To Airport, Nopolo and La Paz

Paseo Julían de Mayorga

Newer Subdivision

Paseo Pedro de Ugarte

Salvatierra

Entrance
Km Post 120

Paseo Juan Manuel Basque

Loreto

N

0   .25   .5 mi

0   .25   .5 km

©FWI

"Newer Subdivision" on the "Loreto" map), which was planned to be an e
tensive recreation home subdivision, contains a few newer homes. Rece
improvements included construction of a small breakwater lined harbc
boat-launching ramp and parking area that incorporates the old town pier
its northerly leg. In addition, the old dirt surface waterfront street has bee
replaced by a handsome, hard-surfaced boulevard, complete with palm tree

Loreto finds a place on the Points of Special Interest Tour as stop No. 1!
Drive into town and peruse the civic plaza. The mission church and the ac
joining historical museum are the most important places you should visi
The present church is the successor to Baja's original mission founded i
1697.

*An aerial view of Loreto. The town dock has now been expanded into a small
breakwater-lined harbor. The sizeable three-story building on the shore to the
left is the Motel Mission de Loreto.*

Loreto is where it all began—from this base, Junipero Serra started his expedition to settle Alta California. Loreto served as the military presidio, the
residence of the father superior of the peninsula's missions and the seat of its
civil government until 1829. In that year, the town was essentially destroyed
by a hurricane and the capital moved to La Paz. Loreto drifted into oblivion,
but has now been given a new birth by the tourist industry. There are good
RV parks and hotels at various locations. See the "Loreto" map.

The beautiful valley of the Arroyo La Purisma is between the communities of San Isidro and La Purisma.

Loop Road to La Purisima and Ciudad Insurgentes

SIDE TRIP

Described from north to south in this subsection of this chapter is a 111.6-mile loop road from **Km F-60** *on Highway 1 to Ciudad Insurgentes. The route is shown on the map on the facing page.*

The principal reasons for traveling this loop are as follows: (1) to visit the historic and picturesque towns of La Purisima-San Isidro and San Jose de Comondu-San Miguel de Comondu; (2) to access sites for launching kayaks and other small boats near the north end of the Magdalena Lagoon System; (3) to access Bahía San Juanico on the Pacific Ocean (the latter area is one of Baja's better surfing locations); and (4) to take advantage of an alternative to Highway 1 in making the round-trip journey up and down the Baja peninsula.

The Baja peninsula offers several small communities that affect travelers consider to be places that look like Mexican towns ought to look. Among the best of these are San Ignacio, Mulegé and Todos Santos. But each of these has been modified to one degree or the other by the presence of highways and the onslaught of tourism. The best advice I can offer is to say "You ain't seen nothin' yet" until you visit the four towns noted in the paragraph above.

The road from **Km F-60** *to San Isidro-La Purisima is a secondary road through mountainous terrain but it is readily negotiable in pickups and vans. It is not suited for larger RVs. The 70.1 miles of road from La Purisima to Ciudad Insurgentes is a paved highway through level terrain.*

Km F-60

The loop road leaves Highway 1 to the west 0.1 miles south of **Km F-60***. The sign at this junction indicates it is 65 Km to La Purisima. The mountainous peninsular divide, approximately 1500 feet in elevation, is reached in about eight miles. West from here the roadbed lies in reasonably gentle terrain but can be badly damaged after heavy rains. Another 1500-foot pass is encountered at the 31.5-mile point, whereupon the road descends steeply into the valley ahead. This is the steepest grade on the entire loop.*

Approximately 13 miles southwest from Highway 1 on the secondary road to San Isidro one encounters the junction with the old canyon road along Arroyo de la Purisima to San Isidro. Taking this 24-mile-long route offers a scenic challenge with numerous arroyo crossings. Near its eastern end the road encounters the Rancho Ojo de Agua, which is where the water rises that is eventually channeled into the palm-covered valleys at San Isidro and La Purisima.

32.7 Miles

Encounter a T-intersection (straight ahead to San Isidro). The left branch is a single-lane, 19.5-mile, secondary road to San Jose de Comondu. It is readily passable to pickups and vans, but travel speed is slow due to its rough, rocky surface. San Jose de Comondu and San Miguel de Comondu lie about two miles apart along a palm-shaded valley surrounded by steep lava cliffs.

Jesuit padres established their fifth mission in 1708 at Comondu Viejo. It was moved to San Jose de Comondu in 1737. The present stone chapel is reported to have been the missionary's house. San Miguel de Comondu is the site of a 1714 visiting station and cattle ranch for the San Javier mission to the southeast.

Taking off to the southeast from San Jose de Comondu is a 26-mile-long road to San Javier that passes through high desert terrain. (San Javier and its remarkable mission church are described in the next chapter.)

An aerial view of La Paz

Baja 1000 Off Road Race

Island in Sea of Cortez

Kayaking on the Sea of Cortez near Loreto

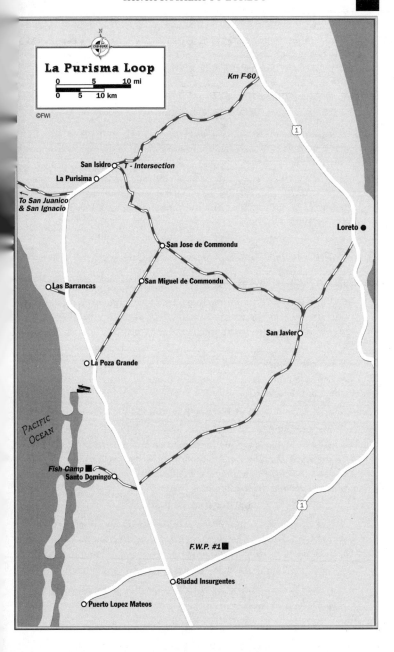

La Purisma Loop

N
FIELDING

| 0 | 5 | 10 mi |
| 0 | 5 | 10 km |

©FWI

Km F-60

1

San Isidro○ *T - Intersection*
La Purisima ○

← To San Juanico
& San Ignacio

Loreto ●

○ San Jose de Commondu

○ San Miguel de Commondu

○ Las Barrancas

San Javier ○

○ La Poza Grande

PACIFIC
OCEAN

Fish Camp ■
Santo Domingo ○

F.W.P. #1 ■

1

○ Ciudad Insurgentes

○ Puerto Lopez Mateos

A 23.8-mile secondary road runs from San Miguel de Comondu to the highway standard road near La Poza Grande. I have not taken this road, but I believe it would make a good route for proceeding south and avoiding the return trip to San Isidro. Something has to be left for the adventurous traveler.

35.1 Miles

Town center of San Isidro (population 1000). At the east end of town a road forks to the north and crosses the Arroyo de la Purisima. A short distance farther, a second road branches to the right, providing access to numerous places to camp in the desert. There are few campsites in the valley itself that are not a part of someone's home or garden. The road between San Isidro and La Purisima was oil-surfaced in 1995.

37.6 Miles

Center of La Purisima. It is approximately a six-mile drive through the two towns of San Isidro and La Purisima. The majority of the area is a valley some half-mile in width, completely covered with palms and other trees and numerous garden plots. Surface water runs in the stream, and the overall atmosphere is most pleasant. We have observed no tourist-oriented facilities in either San Isidro or La Purisima.

From this point to Ciudad Insurgentes, the paved highway is marked with kilometer post signs and these will be noted during the balance of this side trip.

41.5 Miles (Km-107.5)

At this point the paved road bears southward at a junction with a good-standard secondary road leading north to San Juanico. I have been informed that this road may eventually be improved to highway standards north to San Ignacio, but that it is not a high priority project. I have not driven this road.

54.5 Miles (Km-87)

A good standard secondary road leads in 5.2 miles to a solar experimental area. This sizeable facility built by the Mexican government was abandoned during my last visit.

69.4 Miles (Km-64)

A secondary road branches to the northeast and accesses San Jose de Comondu in 23.8 miles.

SIDE TRIP

72.4 Miles (Km-61)

A two-lane oiled road branches to the west and in two miles arrives at the community of La Poza Grande. From the extreme southwestern edge of town at the end of the oiled road, a low-standard but level dirt road leads in 3.8 miles to a good landing and campsite (San Jorge) at the northern end of the Magdalena Lagoon System. Kayaks and small car-top boats may be launched over the shore for trips south through the lagoons. There are a few confusing side roads on the way to the lagoon, but perseverance—and the maintenance of a generally southwest direction—will bring one to the water's edge. (San Jorge is shown mistakenly as being northwest of La Poza Grande on the AAA Baja map.)

92.4 Miles (Km 27.5)

A paved road branches to the west and arrives in two miles at Santo Domingo and its PEMEX station. From this community it is 11.9 miles over a low-standard but level dirt road to a fishing and clamming village near the mouth of Boca de Santo Domingo. A concrete lighthouse marks the spot. Kayaks and car-top boats may be launched here for trips along the Magdalena Lagoon System. There are numerous branching roads along the way so this trip may involve some wrong turns and doubling back.

96.0 Miles

This is the approximate dividing line between desert vegetation to the north and agricultural fields to the south. The farming area extends the remaining 15 miles to Ciudad Insurgentes.

110.1 Miles (Km 1.5)

A paved highway to the right leads in 24.6 miles (34 Km) to Puerto Lopez Mateos. Because of this town's importance as a whale-watching center it is described as a side trip from Ciudad Insurgentes in the next chapter. As of my last visit, there were no tourist-oriented services in this community other than whale-watching panga service.

111.6 Miles (Km-0)

Ciudad Insurgentes and the Transpeninsular Highway.

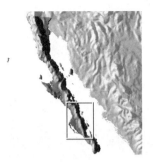

LORETO TO LA PAZ

The giant Dove of Peace statue marks a major road junction as one enters La Paz from the west.

Baja's Central Coast Tourist Area continues for 36 Km (22 miles) south of Loreto. It ends near Ligui on the shore of Ensenada Blanca. From this point south to La Paz, there are several interesting and challenging side trips, but the journey along Highway 1 itself is one of the peninsula's least inspiring.

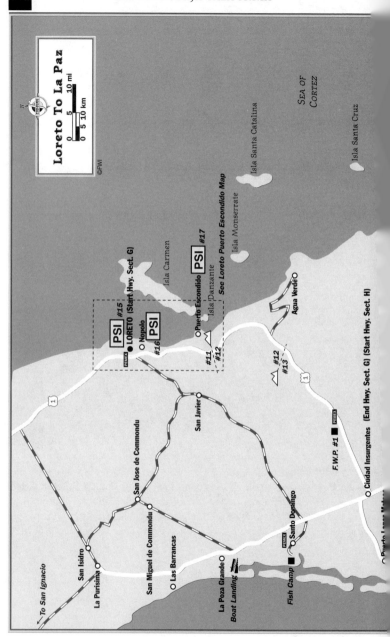

Loreto To La Paz

0   5   10 mi
0   5   10 km

©FWI

SEA OF CORTEZ

Isla Santa Catalina

Isla Santa Cruz

Isla Carmen

Isla Monserrate

PSI #17

Puerto Escondido

Isla Danzante

See Loreto Puerto Escondido Map

PSI #15

LORETO (Start Hwy. Sect. G)

● Nopolo

PSI #16

#11 #12

#12 #13

Agua Verde ○

(End Hwy. Sect. G) (Start Hwy. Sect. H)

F.W.P. #1

○ Ciudad Insurgentes

San Jose de Commondu

San Javier

To San Ignacio

San Isidro

La Purisima

San Miguel de Commondu

○ Las Barrancas

La Poza Grande ○
Boat Landing

Santo Domingo

Fish Camp

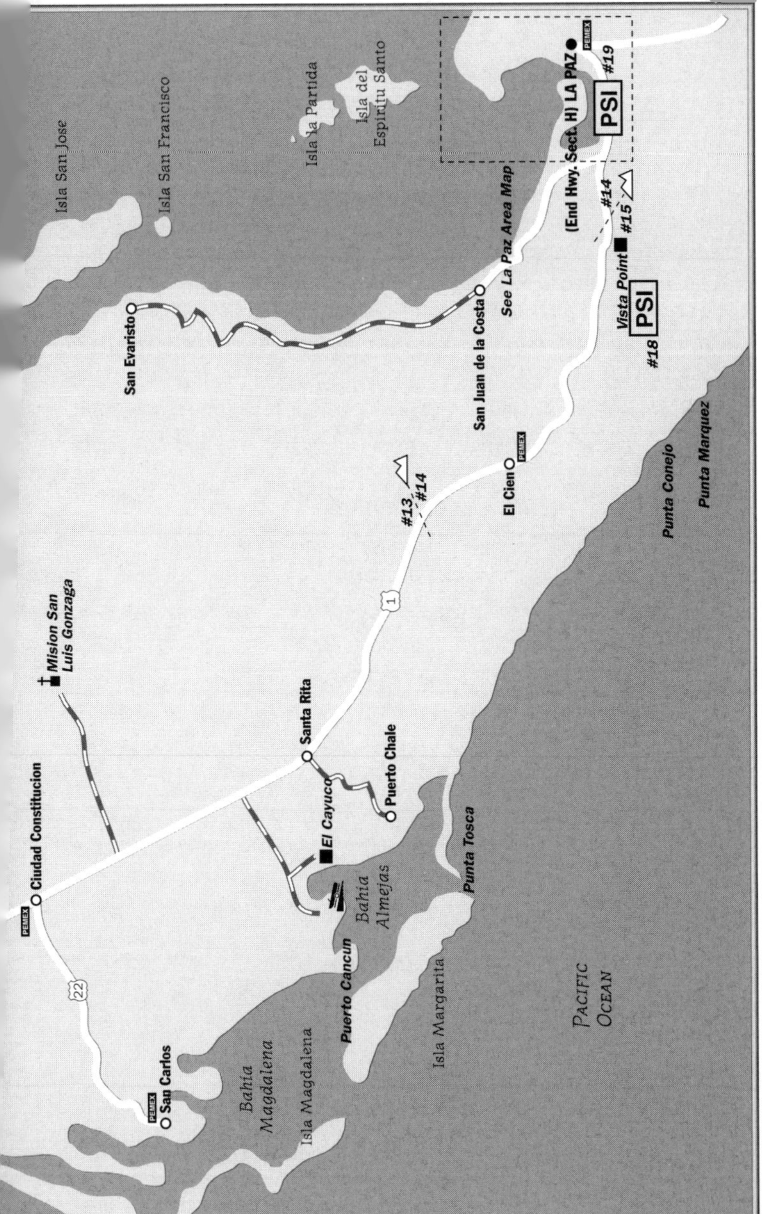

Isla San Jose

Isla San Francisco

Isla La Partida

Isla del Espíritu Santo

(End Hwy. Sect. H) LA PAZ ●

PEMEX #19

PSI

#14

#15

Vista Point ■ #15

PSI

#18

See La Paz Area Map

San Evaristo ○

San Juan de la Costa ○

El Cien ○

PEMEX

#13

#14

1

22

Ciudad Constitucion ○

PEMEX

San Carlos ○

PEMEX

† Mision San Luis Gonzaga ■

Santa Rita ○

■ El Cayuco

Puerto Chale ○

Puerto Cancun

Bahía Almejas

Bahía Magdalena

Isla Magdalena

Isla Margarita

Punta Tosca

Punta Conejo

Punta Marquez

PACIFIC OCEAN

SIDE TRIP

Km G-118—San Javier

To the right (west), a secondary road leaves Highway 1 and crosses the Sierra Giganta to the village of San Javier (32 Kms). In the vicinity of this community the Jesuits founded their second mission in 1699, only two years after landing in Loreto. In 1744, they began construction of a stone church at San Javier, which today is a small village of some 300 people. The building's stone masonry and its lava rock ornamentation are truly remarkable considering its location in what was one of the world's most remote and primitive places. Still in use today, it represents Baja's finest and best-preserved of the Jesuit missions.

The access road is well-constructed, but its steep grades and rough surface make it best suited for lightly loaded vans and pickups. It passes through scenic mountain terrain.

9.4 Miles

Cross stream channel. A good camping spot.

12.5 Miles

Rancho Las Parras. A pleasant oasis of grape vines, figs, olives and citrus trees.

13.7 Miles

Top of the divide after having climbed the steep eastern escarpment of the Sierra de la Giganta. The Sea of Cortez has been in sight to the east for some time.

19.4 Miles

Junction with a road to San Jose de Comondu. Steep grades and erosion reduced this road to four-wheel-drive status 10 miles to the west in 1986, but I have talked with people who made it through with no problem since that time.

23.1 Miles

San Javier.

Km G-117—Loreto Airport

An oiled road leaves Highway 1 to the left (east) and arrives at the Loreto airport in 0.7 miles. Here you will find a parking lot, modern waiting room and an international airfield serving aircraft from the United States and the Mexican mainland. These facilities provide air access to Loreto, Nopolo and Puerto Escondido. NOTE—**Aero California Airlines** has had scheduled flights

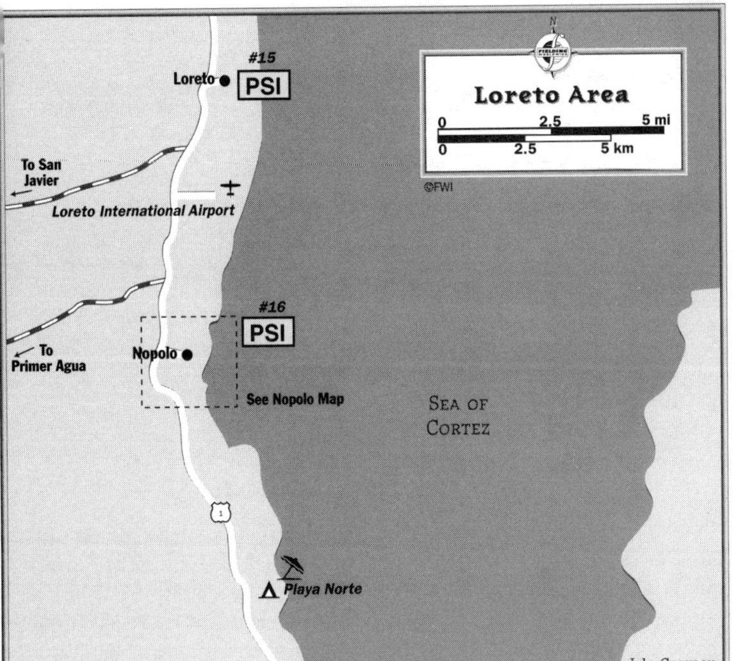

Loreto Area

0   2.5   5 mi
0   2.5   5 km

©FWI

Loreto **#15** PSI

To San Javier

Loreto International Airport

To Primer Agua

Nopolo **#16** PSI

See Nopolo Map

SEA OF CORTEZ

1

Playa Norte

Isla Carmen

El Juncalito

Puerto Escondido **#17** PSI

Nautical Village Development

Tripui RV Park

Tripui Beach

Isla Danzante

Ligui

#11
#12

Ensnada Blanca

here for several years, but at times in the past there has been no commerci.
air service.

Km G-114—Primer Agua

Between **Km G-113** *and* **Km G-114** *is a large electric transformer station. A secondary road leaves to the west, directly south of the station,
and leads in 4.1 miles (7 Km) to Primer Agua. Here, near the base of
the Sierra Giganta, lies a delightful oasis watered by a ditch-diverted
stream. FONATUR has developed the area as a nursery to supply or-
namental trees and shrubs for its developments. Trails lead through
beds of a large variety of plants being reproduced from cuttings. There
is also a pool of water and an adjoining barbecue area. It is a pleasant spot to visit if you are staying in the Loreto-Puerto Escondido
area. It is open to the public on a charge basis.*

**PSI
#16**

Km G-111—Nopolo

Prior to 1977, this section of coast was a deserted beach providing isolated
camp spots for a few people seeking solitude. Now you will find a 0.5-
square-mile area laced with well-landscaped roads waiting to serve future
tourists. This is the FONATUR development at Nopolo. It has attracted
very little attention and lags far behind similar developments at Cabo San
Lucas and San Jose del Cabo to the south. For this reason it is a pleasant, un-
hurried place to visit.

There are about 20 very nice residences and the **Loreto Inn Hotel**, one of the
peninsula's most charming hotels. I have visited this facility on many occasions, and while it has rarely been full, everyone present seemed quite happy.
Across from the hotel are a large number of tennis courts and related facilities that it was hoped would attract international competition. An 18-hole
golf course and a fancy club house (**Campo de Golf**) are also completed. Only
the future knows the eventual success of this substantial undertaking, but
certainly it will be one of the few places in Mexico where the tourist can
enjoy golf, tennis, watersports, a fine hotel and excellent scenery all at one
location.

Nopolo is stop No. 16 on the **Points of Special Interest Tour**. The hotel is
worth a visit, and I believe a circle drive through the area will give you a quick
vision of what the future holds for Baja. Even the largest of RVs can easily
make this tour. On occasion, tourists have been permitted to camp along the
excellent sandy beach (**Playa Nopolo**) at the south end of the Nopolo development, where a cobblestone road built parallel to the beach provides a good
parking area. Each time I visit, the camping situation is different.

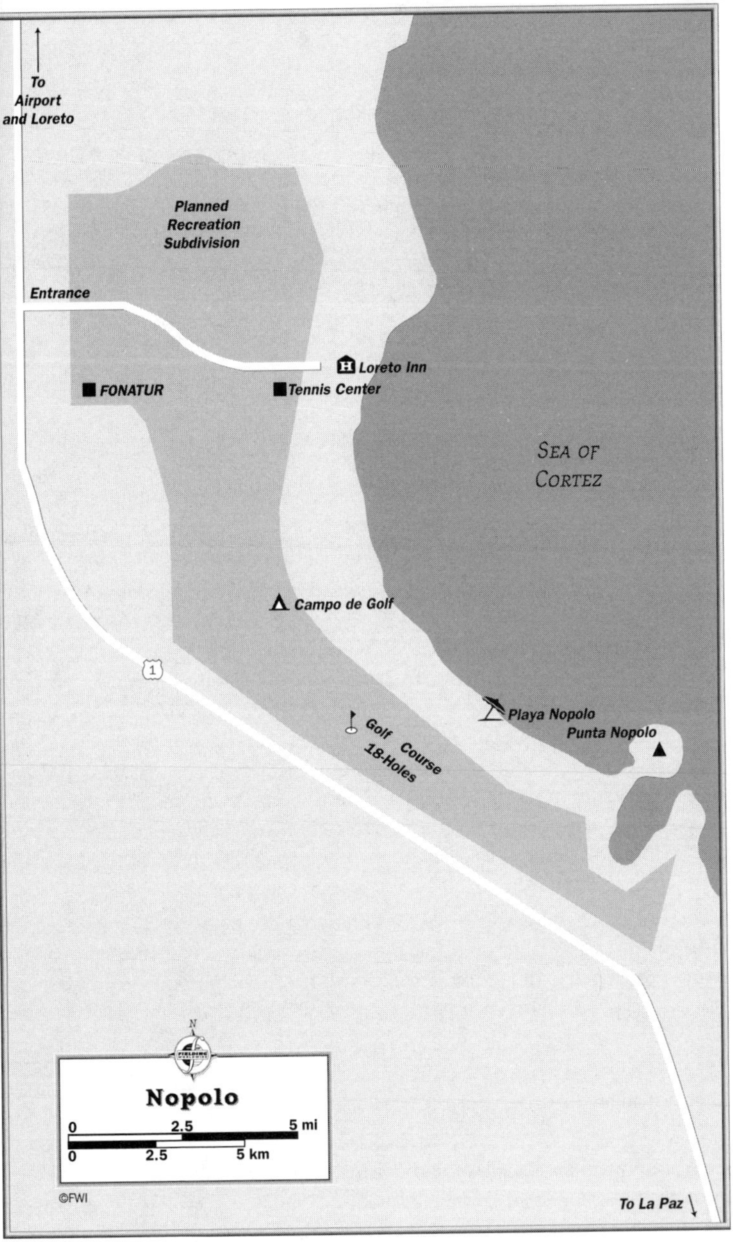

To
Airport
and Loreto

Planned
Recreation
Subdivision

Entrance

■ *FONATUR*

🏠 *Loreto Inn*
■ *Tennis Center*

SEA OF
CORTEZ

⛰ *Campo de Golf*

🏴 *Golf Course
18-Holes*

⛵ *Playa Nopolo*
Punta Nopolo
▲

①

Nopolo

| 0 | 2.5 | 5 mi |
| 0 | 2.5 | 5 km |

N
FIELDING

©FWI

To La Paz ↘

Km G-103—Playa Norte

Playa Norte is a part sand and part shingle beach providing camping spot about 150 yards east of the highway.

Km G-97—El Juncalito

A low-standard road leaves to the left (east) at this point. This road shortly divides with the left branch leading to the seaside village of el Juncalito. Proceeding straight ahead brings one in 0.5 miles to a grove of palms and a fine sandy beach. You may camp among the palms or along the 0.25-mile-long beach. (I am advised that FONATUR plans some type of development here, so look for the possibility of change.)

PSI #17

Km G-94—Puerto Escondido

Take the paved side road at this point 0.6 miles to Tripui and 0.9 miles farther to the inner harbor area. This is **PSI** stop No.17.

The shore of the almost totally landlocked bay at Puerto Escondido (Hidden Port) was long one of Baja's most heavily used camping spots. The area was then taken over by FONATUR for a massive Pueblo Nautico (Nautical Village). Planned for construction were hotels, dockside condominiums, a marina and other attractions. However, the past eight years have seen very little progress, and the only usable facility is a concrete boat ramp. One could conclude that the balance of the development was an ill-conceived project from Mexico City. (God bless socialism.)

Tripui RV Park

Many tourists regretted the passing of Puerto Escondido's beachside camping area. But at least, here at Puerto Escondido, you can find an excellent replacement facility—an outstanding, attractively landscaped RV park was constructed nearby and complemented with a swimming pool, showers, restrooms, laundry facilities, restaurant, store, small motel and sports facilities. While not at the water's edge, it offers splendid views of the Sierra Giganta and is surrounded by attractive desert vegetation.

The sad part is that the **Tripui RV Park** has now been totally converted to full-time tenants with a guard at the gate to keep the rest of us out. Short-term RVs are relegated to a relatively small fenced-in parking area next to the road. So depending on your point of view, you will either love Tripui or hate it.

Should a less expensive beachfront spot be more to your taste, return north to el Juncalito, or drive south to Ensenada Blanca near Ligui.

Tripui Beach

A good gravel road leaves the oiled highway into Puerto Escondido to the right at the west end of the fence surrounding the Tripui RV Park. In about 1.5 miles this road leads to a secluded camping area near the shore. During ur last trip, the access road had been gated shut, supposedly by orders from ONATUR. Obviously the Tripui RV Park benefits by this closure. All amping outside established RV parks has been eliminated in the Cape Area or several years, and this may be what is occurring here. What the future holds is open to question.

Canyon Hiking

Directly across Highway 1 and north of an electrical substation from the blacktopped entrance to Puerto Escondido is a low-standard dirt road paralleled by a power line. In 0.9 miles, this road will bring you to a water pumping station at the base of the Sierra Giganta. There is a small turnaround area here, but you should leave large vehicles behind. Park at this spot and hike into the steep-walled canyon that dissects the cliffs a few yards north of the pumping station.

There is no developed trail, but once you are between the steep cliffs it is impossible to lose your way. It takes 20 to 30 minutes of hiking along a cascading stream to arrive at a point where further progress is impeded by massive boulders. The rocks and canyon walls are of volcanic origin, and the stream bed is an enticing realm of small pools, palm trees and other vegetation. Take along your bathing suit and enjoy an hour or so in this delightful rock-walled oasis.

Ensenada Blanca features small off-lying islands. Note the steep face of the mountains directly along the shoreline.

Km G-84—Ligui (Ensenada Blanca)

A small schoolhouse and other buildings are located to the left (east) of Highway 1 north of **Km G-84**. This is Ligui. A low-standard dirt road leaves

the highway and in 1.9 miles arrives at the fishing village of Ensenada Blanc
located on a fine, sandy beach. An even lower standard road continues fo
some 1.1 miles around the edge of Ensenada Blanca to camping spots at th
water's edge. There are also several spur roads to similar beachside hideaway
between the highway and the village. These roads are level but unimproved

Ligui is the southernmost area of level land on the Central Coast Touris
Area that began north of Santa Rosalia. Confronted with this topographic
situation, the Jesuit missionaries located the Ligui mission here in 1705
only six years after arriving on the peninsula. It became the jumping-of
point for missionary trails leading into the mountains of the interior and
south along the coast, but the mission itself lasted only 16 years.

#11

#12

Km G-83—Geographic Change

The Sierra Giganta's presence at the Sea of Cortez coast forces the
Transpeninsular Highway to ascend the steep eastern escarpment (Geographic Section No. 12). The road is winding, but grades are moderate, and
the traveler is rewarded with fine mountain scenery, the last to be seen for
many miles. This dramatic and rapid climb up the eastern face of the Peninsular Range Mountains, and the level and lengthy descent lying ahead on the
western side, provides the best examples you will see of the fault-block
mountain structure presented in the "Geology" chapter.

South of this point, **Km G-83**, the eastern coastline of the peninsula is steep,
rocky and majestic. It is best viewed by boat or from small private aircraft.
However, portions of the area can be enjoyed by taking the side trips to
Agua Verde and San Juan de la Costa described in this chapter.

Highway 1 passes through the mountains of Geographic Section No. 12 west of
Ligui.

Km G-63—Agua Verde

A secondary road heads left (south) from Highway 1 between **Km G-63** *and* **Km G-64** *to the small fishing village of Agua Verde. Taking all or a portion of this 24-mile side trip will allow you to enjoy a portion of the dramatic eastern side of the Sierra Giganta, an area that is viewed by very few tourists.*

10.9 Miles

You are greeted with an outstanding view of the Sea of Cortez, offshore islands and the coastal mountains. There is a flat area for camping some 200 yards prior to reaching this vista for those who do not wish to proceed farther. The road to this point passes over rolling desert lands and can be traveled by most RVs.

The road ahead makes a steep, four-mile descent down the face of the eastern escarpment. I recommend that you park your vehicle at the vista point and walk ahead for 0.2 miles to a place where the road descending the mountain is in view. From this spot, you can also look to the south and see a large pinnacle rock lying several hundred feet offshore. This is Roca Solitaria. It marks the entrance to the anchorage at Agua Verde. Having located this landmark and looked over the road, you can judge how far you will have to travel to Agua Verde and can make your decision as to whether to proceed. I alert you that it is not a suitable trip for large RVs or any vehicle that tends to be top-heavy. However, if the road is in good repair it makes a fine trip for those in pickup trucks, vans and other smaller vehicles.

14.6 Miles

You have reached the bottom of the grade and can start worrying about the return trip. A short distance ahead, a side road veers sharply to the left and in 200 yards arrives at a camping spot on a bluff overlooking the sea.

16.8 Miles

A side road leads for 0.5 miles to a camping spot along the banks of an arroyo near a shingle beach. There are also several other side roads that I have not explored between this point and the Agua Verde village.

25.4 Miles

Arrive at Agua Verde. You will find this village to be one of the most primitive in Baja, but one most abundantly supplied with goats. The new road built in the early 1980s will no doubt bring much change to Agua Verde.

Km G-64 to G-45—Volcanic Mountains

This section of the highway is relatively flat but passes through massiv mountains of volcanic rock. This is a good place to stop and examine thes igneous volcanic rocks if you have not done so before. See the "Rock Classi fication" chart in the "Geology" chapter. Note their dark reddish color, fin grain and the numerous pockets formed by gases trapped in the molten mas as it cooled.

Km G-45—Geographic Change

It is here that you might ask, "What happened to the other side of the mountain?" You have arrived at the end of Geographic Section No.12, and the western side of the mountains simply blend with the Continental Borderlands Province ahead. This section of the province is the *Llano de Magdalena* (Magdalena Plain). It is Geographic Section No. 13. You will be passing over its flat terrain for the next 164 Km (102 miles).

Looking ahead on clear days, you will be able to see the mountains that rim the outer edges of Bahías Magdalena and Almejas on the Pacific coast. At other times they, and the entire Magdalena Plain, may be shrouded in fog and low clouds. The straight stretch of highway between **Km G-39** and **Km G-32** points directly at this range.

Km G-17—Federal Water Project No.1

An easily accessed PEMEX station lies at this point and serves the agricultural area you have just entered. Here, or at Villa Insurgentes, are good places to fuel on the return trip north in order to avoid the congestion often encountered at the stations at Loreto and Mulege.

Zona de Neblina

At several places along the highways in this area you will see signs reading "*Zona de Neblina.*" *Neblina* means fog and you are being alerted to the fact that layers of fog will sometimes restrict visibility. The fog also brings moisture to the desert plants. Many of the larger species become festooned with lichens and ball moss (see the "Vegetation" chapter). This situation may be seen along any of the side roads leading from Highway 1 to Bahía Magdalena.

Km G-0—Ciudad Insurgentes

At this point, Highway 1 makes a 90-degree turn to the south. You have now reached the breakpoint between highway sections **G** (Km-0) and **H** (Km 234) and the edge of the town of Ciudad Insurgentes. A PEMEX station lies on the south side of the highway, a short distance east of this turning point. There is another PEMEX station in town on the west side of the main street.

Cuidad Insurgentes, a town of some 18,500 people, lies near the center of one of the largest agricultural areas in Baja. As noted in the "History" chaper, development here did not begin until 1933. Prior to this time, most of the peninsula's lands were encumbered with various foreign-dominated leases that produced little more than speculation. It is easy to understand why the Mexican government has, until recently, wanted to maintain control over all the country's enterprises.

Puerto Lopez Mateos is on the Magdalena Lagoons. The group of large buildings along the shore is the fish-processing plant noted in the text. Whale-watching tours leave directly to the left of the cannery. The community itself lies within the trees farther inland.

SIDE TRIP

Puerto Lopez Mateos

Cuidad Insurgentes is the starting point for a side trip to Puerto Lopez Mateos on the 70-mile-long coastal lagoon lying north of Bahía Magdalena. It is the most convenient site for viewing the California gray whale in Baja California. (Scammon's Lagoon is also popular, but access is over a lengthy dirt road.) See the "Wildlife" chapter for information about the gray whale.

From the Highway 1 90-degree turning point noted above, travel north through Cuidad Insurgentes for 1.5 miles. At this point, a blacktop highway leads to the left (west). It is 24.6 miles to Puerto Lopez Mateos.

Upon arrival at the port, proceed around the north side of the waterfront fish processing plant. Here is a public parking area from which you may sometimes view the whales. (This area is closed at night, but you may camp in a not-too-inviting area immediately outside.) Pangas are for hire to take you for a closer encounter with these marine giants at their calving areas about five miles distant.

SIDE TRIP

Small boats and kayaks may also be launched over the beach for camping adventures along the lagoon. There is abundant bird life in addition to the whales. (Guided whale-watching trips to Puerto Lopez Mateos are available in La Paz.)

Km H-211—Ciudad Constitucion

Km H-211 marks the center of the largest community in the Llano Magdalena agricultural area. Ciudad Constitucion has a population of 35,000. Upon entering town from the north, look for a small traffic circle on the right with a statue at its center. This is the junction with Highway 22, which leads to Bahía Magdalena and the port city of San Carlos. (See Side Trip below.)

Also north of town near **Km H-213** is **Manfred's RV Park and Austrian Restaurant**. It was started by Manfred Roschker and his wife Ida about 1994 and represents a marvel of two people's efforts. The well-landscaped park provides a long needed RV rest-stop between the Sea of Cortez coast and La Paz. (**The Campestre La Pila** noted below leaves a bit to be desired.) The restaurant bears Manfred's name, but let's face it, Ida does the cooking.

South of the Highway 22 junction the main street of town turns into a palm-lined boulevard. There are two PEMEX stations on the west side of this boulevard. Two blocks south of the Highway 22 junction you will cross Olachea street. On the northeast corner lies a three-story concrete building housing the **Hotel Maribel**. Two blocks east on Olachea is the smaller Hotel Casino. These are adequate facilities for an overnight stay, but are not of the luxurious variety. There are also other motels along the main street.

At **Km H-209** south of town a dirt road leads to the right (west) and in 0.6 miles arrives at the **Campestre La Pila Trailer Court**. This facility has full hook-ups. It is located adjoining a working farm and a large grassy area with swimming pools, picnic tables and showers.

SIDE TRIP

San Carlos (Bahía Magdalena)

It is 57 Km (35 miles) to San Carlos, a town of some 5,000 people, and the shores of Bahía Magdalena over straight and level Highway 22. There is a statue within a small traffic circle at the junction point. I recommend visiting this area if your principal aim is to take advantage of the best waters for using small trailer boats on Baja's Pacific coast. If, instead, you are seeking the best camping locations or hotels, you will be better served in other places.

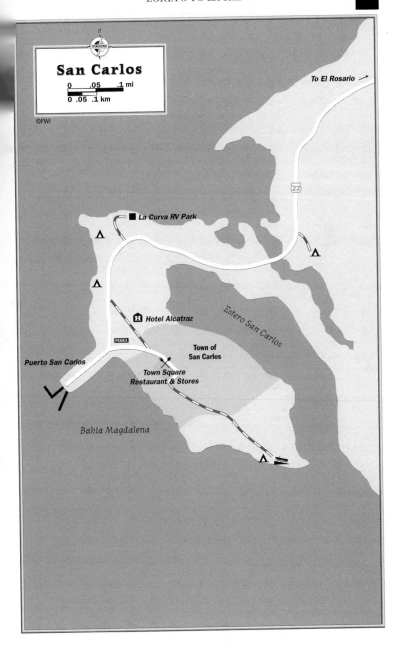

San Carlos

0   .05   .1 mi
0 .05 .1 km

©FWI

To El Rosario

La Curva RV Park

Estero San Carlos

Hotel Alcatraz

PEMEX

Town of
San Carlos

Puerto San Carlos

Town Square
Restaurant & Stores

Bahía Magdalena

SIDE TRIP

At Km 52 (about three miles prior to reaching San Carlos) is a massive square building from which projects a stubby smokestack. This is the most recent of Baja's three power-generating plants. Its fuel is delivered by ship to the port of San Carlos, and then through a short pipeline to the plant. The building and its many lights provide a prominent landmark.

As you approach San Carlos, you will to see marshy areas, and the town itself is located on an island. These features are indicative of the fact that the western edge of the Continental Borderlands is sinking into the sea.

After arriving at the edge of San Carlos, you can see a sizeable wharf that has been built many hundreds of yards into the shallow waters of Bahía Magdalena to a point where deep-draft ships can be accommodated. This dock and its warehouses are the shipping points for cotton, grain and other agricultural products grown in the interior. San Carlos and Ensenada to the north are the only deepwater commercial ports on the peninsula's Pacific coast. The PEMEX station is near the landward end of the port facility.

Bearing left at the PEMEX station, it is 1.7 miles through town to what is indicated as the Las Palapas RV Park on the map. Proceed into town, pass by the eastern side of the town square, and take the road paralleling the shore. The Las Palapas RV Park was originally constructed as a tourist facility many years ago, but its former rental cabins have more recently served as homes for Mexican fishermen, a house of ill repute, and recently we found them deserted. Whatever the future holds, the nearby beach is where most RV-owners and campers make their headquarters in the San Carlos area. Boats may be launched at mid to high tide at a nearby ramp. Be careful in picking your spot as some high tides will put your vehicle awash.

Km H-195—San Luis Gonzaga

 Just south of **Km H-195**, a secondary road leaves Highway 1 to the east. It is signed for a large dam named *La Presa Iguajil*, which is about 21 miles distant. From the dam, a road runs south to a grove of palms sheltering the stone Mision de San Luis Gonzaga and a ranch whose owners serve as caretakers for the mission.

San Luis Gonzaga was founded in 1737 and was the 15th of Baja's Jesuit missions. Its oasis-like setting is a welcome relief from some of the most barren landscape in the peninsula. Numerous other roads proceed easterly into

ıe mountains from here, one of them reaching the Sea of Cortez shore at
an Evaristo.

SIDE TRIP

Km H-173—Puerto Cancun

*You may have always longed to take your wife to exciting Cancun
in Mexico. Here is your chance. Perhaps she will not notice that this is
not the exotic resort area on the Caribbean coast. In any case, she will
be consoled knowing that accommodations are less expensive camping
here on the shore of Bahía Almejas.*

The secondary road to Puerto Cancun north of **Km H-173** *is straight,
wide, level and washboarded. At the 13.0 mile-point a one-lane secondary road leads in 2.5 miles to the El Cayuco fishing village. It is a
bit on the dirty side and camping space is limited unless you can negotiate low-standard sandy roads along the shore.*

*Puerto Cancun is 19.9 miles from Highway 1. There are good
camping spots on the bluffs above the beach west of the village. Almejas
means clams, and there is no better place to find them than in the extremely shallow waters of Bahía Almejas here at Puerto Cancun. Low
tide exposes sandy clamming grounds over one-half mile in width.*

Km H-169—Magdalena Mountains

Here, near a large microwave tower, is an excellent view to the west of the
mountains that rim the outer edges of Bahías Magdalena and Almejas. (Although on some days they are hidden in fog and low clouds.) A gap in this
range is the two-mile-wide entrance to the bay from the Pacific Ocean.
While passing through this rocky portal by boat, one is reminded very much
of the Golden Gate at San Francisco. San Francisco Bay and Bahía Magdalena are the two finest natural harbors in the Californias.

SIDE TRIP

Km H-157—Puerto Chale

*Highway 1 makes a 45-degree turn to the left at the very small town
of Santa Rita. At this turn is a junction with the secondary road to
Puerto Chale. Puerto Chale lies on an estuary at the edge of Bahía
Almejas. Here are located a small fishing village and an experimental shrimp farm. It is 14.6 miles to the water's edge over a straight,
level road.*

Km H-120—Geographic Change

South of Santa Rita on Highway 1, the totally flat terrain through which you have been passing comes to an end and the land begins to roll. The highway slowly gains elevation, and the Llano de Magdalena merges indistinctly with the gentle western slopes of the Peninsular Range Mountains. Thus, **Km H-120** is only an approximate dividing line between geographical sections. In a few miles, however, it is apparent that you have left the plains of Geographic Section No. 13 and are in the plateaus of Section No. 14. You will travel through this region for the next 89 Km (55 miles).

The terrain in this section is composed of sandstone, shale and other sedimentary rocks. Notice the horizontal banding of the rock layers in the highway cuts and surrounding hills.

Km H-100—El Cien

El Cien is a small village whose chief claim to fame for the tourist is a PEMEX station, the only one between Ciudad Constitucion and La Paz. Appropriately, El Cien (*cien* means 100 in Spanish) lies exactly at the 100-kilometer point.

Km H-82—Pacific View

Near **Km H-82** there is a tall microwave tower. From this point, you can see the Pacific Ocean far to the west. There will be other such views between here and the **Km H-35** Vista Point ahead. A short distance south, near Km H-80, a side road leads to the coast at El Conejo. The coast is relatively uninviting in this area. Beginning south of the Magdalena Mountains and stretching for more than 100 miles to Todos Santos, the shore is basically one long sandy beach backed by monotonous low plains. The Pacific swells break heavily, making swimming and boating hazardous.

Km H-35—Vista Point

On the right, near Km H-35, is a small monument bearing a cross. Even the largest RVs can pull over here at **Points of Special Interest Tour** stop No. 18 and enjoy one of the most rewarding views in Baja.

1. The vista point lies near the edge of the plateau area through which you have just passed. Lying below, to the south, stretches the Llano de La Paz, the southernmost portion of the Continental Borderlands Province. At this narrow point the peninsula is almost divided in half, providing clear evidence to geologists that it has been stretched linearly as noted in the "Geology" chapter.

2. South of the plain lie the massive granite Sierra de la Laguna in the Cape Area.

LORETO TO LA PAZ

A monument bearing a cross lies alongside the highway at PSI Stop No. 18. A visit here awards the traveler with fine views of the Sea of Cortez.

3. To the northeast is Bahía de La Paz, a broad indentation in the Sea of Cortez. At the water's edge, near the base of the Sierra de la Laguna the city of La Paz is in view.

4. Several miles into the Sea of Cortez rest Isla Espiritu del Santo and Isla la Partida. The two islands appear as one. They provide many snug coves frequented by yachts. Here, and on the other Sea of Cortez islands to the north, the ocean-cruisers are free from the activities of the peninsula's road builders.

Km H-31—Geographic Change

At approximately this point, the highway leaves the plateau lands (Geographic Section No. 14) and enters the level Llano de La Paz (Geographic Section No. 15).

Km H-27—Sierra Giganta

From a slight rise in the highway near **Km H-27**, one may look to the north and see the southern terminus of the escarpment of the Sierra Giganta. This is the end of the steep-faced coastal mountain range that started at Ligui. Visible is a light pinkish band of volcanic ash. This band is not level, as viewed from here. Rather, it slopes downward below the earth's surface at its inland end, providing yet another indication of the downward westerly tilt of the fault-block mountain structure.

Km H-21

At this point is a government agricultural inspection station where you will be required to stop. They are looking for citrus fruits.

This picturesque view is between Highway 1 and San Juan de la Costa.

SIDE TRIP

Km H-17—San Juan de la Costa

A trip to, and beyond, the phosphorus-mining community of San Juan de la Costa is your second opportunity to experience the steep coastal section of the Sierra Giganta at close range (the first was at Agua Verde to the north). The road is oiled the first 26 miles into San Juan de la Costa and is constructed to highway standards but not yet paved for an additional 32.7 miles. The route offers some of the best coastal scenery in view from any of Baja's highways.

1 Mile

In approximately one mile from Highway 1, an oiled road leaves to the right and accesses the Centro de Investigaciones Biológicas de Baja California Sur, a modern scientific facility of laboratories and offices. The scientists' principal interests lie in the high-country area of the Sierra de la Laguna south of La Paz, and the Vizcaino Desert region just south of the state line to the north. Of particular interest is the fact that the area on either side of the access road has been fenced for many years and one may see the desert vegetation free from the effects of recent grazing.

12.5 Miles (Km-19)

The oiled road crosses the level Llano de La Paz and arrives at the base of the towering Sierra Giganta escarpment.

14.3 Miles (Km 23)

This point is the end of the flat plain and the site of an abandoned highway work center. Nearby are campsites behind a coastal dune fronted by a fine sandy beach. There are additional places to reach the coast between here and San Juan de la Costa by detouring at points where the road dips to cross arroyos.

25.0 Miles (Km 39)

The main, but unpaved, road veers to the right toward the village of San Evaristo (population 500). The paved road continues straight ahead for one mile into San Juan de la Costa. This community is a mining company town with scores of homes built in neat rows on a level area several hundred feet above the sea. There is a CONASUPO grocery store, but no other tourist facilities.

I do not recommend the trip toward San Evaristo for larger RVs. (Mileages continue to be from Highway 1 and do not include the side trip into San Juan de la Costa.)

SIDE TRIP

27.7 Miles

At this point, you arrive at the dock-and-conveyor system used to load ocean-going ore carriers. Inland are the processing facilities where raw earth containing about 10 percent phosphorus is enriched to 30 percent by leaching with seawater. After a freshwater rinse, it is dried for shipping and is used as fertilizer.

The road ahead for the next three miles is extra-wide and well-maintained, but is heavily used by ore-carrying equipment except on weekends. Between here and mileage point 57.7, the road is constructed to highway standards but is not yet oiled. There are several places to camp on the coast in the shadow of the magnificent Sierra Giganta mountains.

57.7 Miles

End highway standard road. Pickups and vans can readily make it ahead an additional 1.2 miles to a camping spot near a shingle beach. Beyond that point the road is best suited for four-wheel-drive vehicles. In the past I have traversed this road in my standard drive pickup complete with camper, but on my last trip, the surface had been badly eroded. Look for additional highway standard construction in this area in the future.

73.8 Miles

Arrive on the beach near the small fishing village of San Evaristo, another of the ocean-cruiser's hideaways captured by the road builders.

Km H-17—El Comitan

Immediately east of the highway to San Juan de la Costa, a dirt road leads to the left (north). In 0.8 miles, it arrives at a beachside camping spot at the western end of Ensenada de Aripes.

Km H-17—Ensenada de Aripes

From the San Juan de La Costa junction to La Paz, Highway 1 passes along the southern edge of a large lagoon Ensenada de Aripes. The lagoon is separated from the Sea of Cortez by a spit of land whose eastern end is a sand bar that is awash only at low tide.

The city of La Paz and all of its tourist facilities are located along this almost fully enclosed body of water. The location protects the area from the open sea, but some tourists find that the lagoon's beaches, the quality of the water and its overall aesthetic appeal are not as high quality as available in other areas. Please keep this situation in mind when evaluating the La Paz ourist accommodations presented in the balance of this chapter. In spite of these somewhat negative comments, La Paz is my favorite city in all of Mexico, and I am not alone in this assessment.

Km H-15—El Centenario

Adjoining Highway 1 near the shallow western end of Ensenada de Aripes is the small community of El Centenario. At the eastern edge of town are two RV parks. The first bears the name **City View RV Park**. It is one of the original government-constructed parks with desert-plant landscaping. As its name implies, it offers a good view of La Paz over the water. On a sandy beach a bit closer to La Paz lies the pleasant **Oasis de Aripes RV Park and Restaurant**. These are the only two RV parks directly on the water's edge in the La Paz area. Between **Km H-12** and **Km H-11** east of El Centenario is a PEMEX station with plenty of room for large RVs. It is a good place to avoid the often hectic conditions at the stations in La Paz.

Km H-9—La Paz Airport

A blacktopped highway leads to the right for two miles to the La Paz Airport. This was the first of southern Baja's international airfields. It has modern terminal facilities. There is almost continual urban development from this junction into the center of La Paz.

Km H-7—Dove of Peace Statue

Just past **Km H-7** is a large, white, concrete statue of a bird. My notes say its a seagull, but for a city named La Paz (The Peace) it must be a dove. It marks the junction of the old highway along the La Paz waterfront (to the left), and the newer divided bypass highway that skirts much of La Paz (to the right). Proceed accordingly. I don't know which of these routes is the official Highway 1, but I give the distinction to the old route on the map of La Paz. One branch of this bypass highway brings one to the western end of Isable la Catolica (see "La Paz" map) while the other joins Highway 1 south of La Paz and south of the Highway 1 junction with Highway 286. This latter route avoids almost all the developed area of La Paz.

Km H-6—Tourism Department

Between **Km H-6** and **Km H-5** is the office of the *Coordinador Estatal de Turismo Baja California Sur*. Stop here for maps and travel information. There is another office downtown, but parking is limited.

Km H-4—La Paz RV Parks

There are four RV parks in La Paz. **The Casa Blanca** and **El Cardón** lie south of the highway near **Km H-4**. **The La Paz Park** and the **Aguamarina** are located near, but not on the water front close to the high-rise **Hotel Gran Baja**. See the "La Paz" map.

Km H-0—La Paz

At last, the Transpeninsular Highway arrives at the city of peace, La Paz. was here that Hernan Cortez stepped ashore on May 3, 1535, only 43 yea after Columbus discovered the Americas. See the "History" chapter.

La Paz is a clean, modern city of 140,000 people and the capital of the sta of Baja California Sur. A walking tour of its waterfront and downtown area stop No. 19 on the **Points of Special Interest Tour**. While the city is growing i population, the downtown area is nicely settled down and there is little c the hectic growth apparent at Cabo San Lucas.

There are several fine resort hotels where sun worshippers can hibernate in definitely. I strongly recommend them as destination points. However, submit that if you choose a hotel in La Paz for your vacation, you should d so at least in part to enjoy the city itself—its weather, shopping, culture an friendly people. If you are more interested in simply relaxing on the beach o around the swimming pool of a fine resort hotel, you probably will be mor content at one of the fine hotels at the tip of the peninsula.

Near the heart of the downtown area, and across the street from the beach is the **Hotel los Arcos** and its affiliated **Cabanas de los Arcos**. The restaurant is excellent, and while the Los Arcos is slightly less luxurious than some of the other hotels, it is located where you can readily enjoy the downtown area. **The Hotel Perla** is also located downtown on the waterfront, but is a less-auspicious establishment. In addition, there are a number of less expensive but fully acceptable hotels in or near the downtown area. **The Hotel Gardenias** is perhaps the best of these.

The pool area of the La Concha Beach Resort.

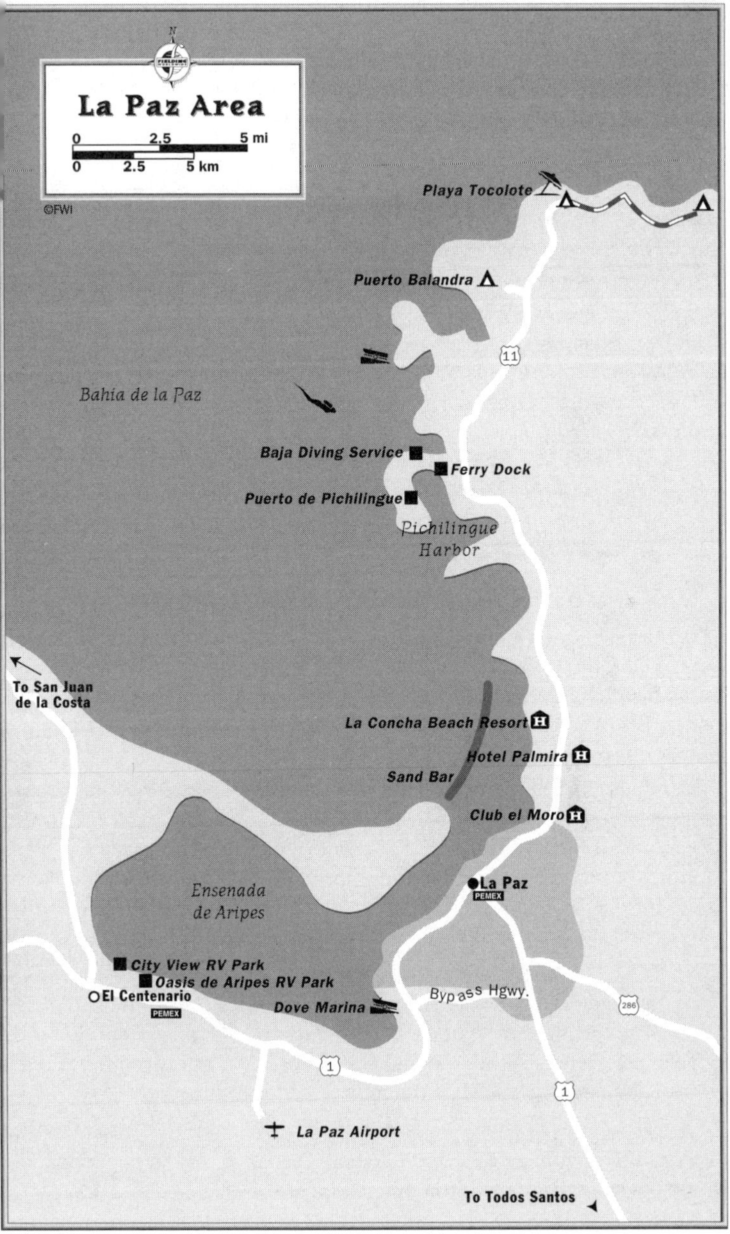

La Paz Area

N

0   2.5   5 mi
0   2.5   5 km

©FWI

Playa Tocolote

Puerto Balandra ▲

Bahia de la Paz

11

Baja Diving Service ■
■ **Ferry Dock**
Puerto de Pichilingue ■

Pichilingue Harbor

←
To San Juan de la Costa

La Concha Beach Resort 🏨

Hotel Palmira 🏨

Sand Bar

Club el Moro 🏨

●**La Paz**
PEMEX

Ensenada de Aripes

■ **City View RV Park**
■ *Oasis de Aripes RV Park*
○**El Centenario**   **Dove Marina** ■
PEMEX

Bypass Hwy.

286

1

1

✈ **La Paz Airport**

To Todos Santos ◀

The tall building west of the downtown area on the waterfront is the **Hotel Gran Baja**. Nearby on the beach is the charming **Hotel La Posada**. North of town on the highway to Pichilingue are the **Club el Morro**, the **Hotel Marina**, the **La Concha Beach Resort** and the **Araiza Inn Palmira**. The latter is nicely landscaped but is separated from the beach by the highway.

SIDE TRIP

Pichilingue

Highway 11 travels 23 Km (14 miles) north from downtown La Paz to Pichilingue, which derived its name from the Dutch pirates who roamed the area in the 17th century.

As the long and narrow channel leading from the Sea of Cortez to La Paz is not suited for deep-draft vessels, port facilities have been developed at the well-protected harbor at Pichilingue. Various industries requiring access to the sea are located in an industrial park surrounding the harbor. Also located here are (1) the terminal and parking lot for the ferries from La Paz to Mazatlan and Topolobampo, and (2) a new passenger terminal developed to lure ocean-cruise ships into La Paz.

Puerto Ballandra and Tecolote

To the north of Pichilingue there is presently almost no development. Here, facing the open Sea of Cortez are two beach areas heavily frequented by the people of La Paz on weekends. They also make good camping spots for tourists. These places are reached by taking a continuation of Highway 11 that was completed in 1991.

The new highway noted above was obviously constructed in anticipation of the development of a major new resort area—drawings of which adorn the office walls of the coordinator of tourism—but I have been advised by the coordinator that these plans have now been dropped in favor of lower-key facilities for the local citizens. Is it possible one of Baja's great beaches will be spared from the hotel builders?

4.4 Miles

Four-plus miles north of Pichilingue an oiled side-road to the left leads in 0.3 miles to the inner edge of the cove at Puerto Ballandra. (Continue ahead to Tecolote.) The shallow waters of the cove allow safe swimming, but at low tide its waters recede several hundred feet from the road.

5.7 Miles

At this point, you arrive at the beach at Tecolote. It is far superior to the one at Puerto Ballandra, although it is exposed to the wind and open sea.

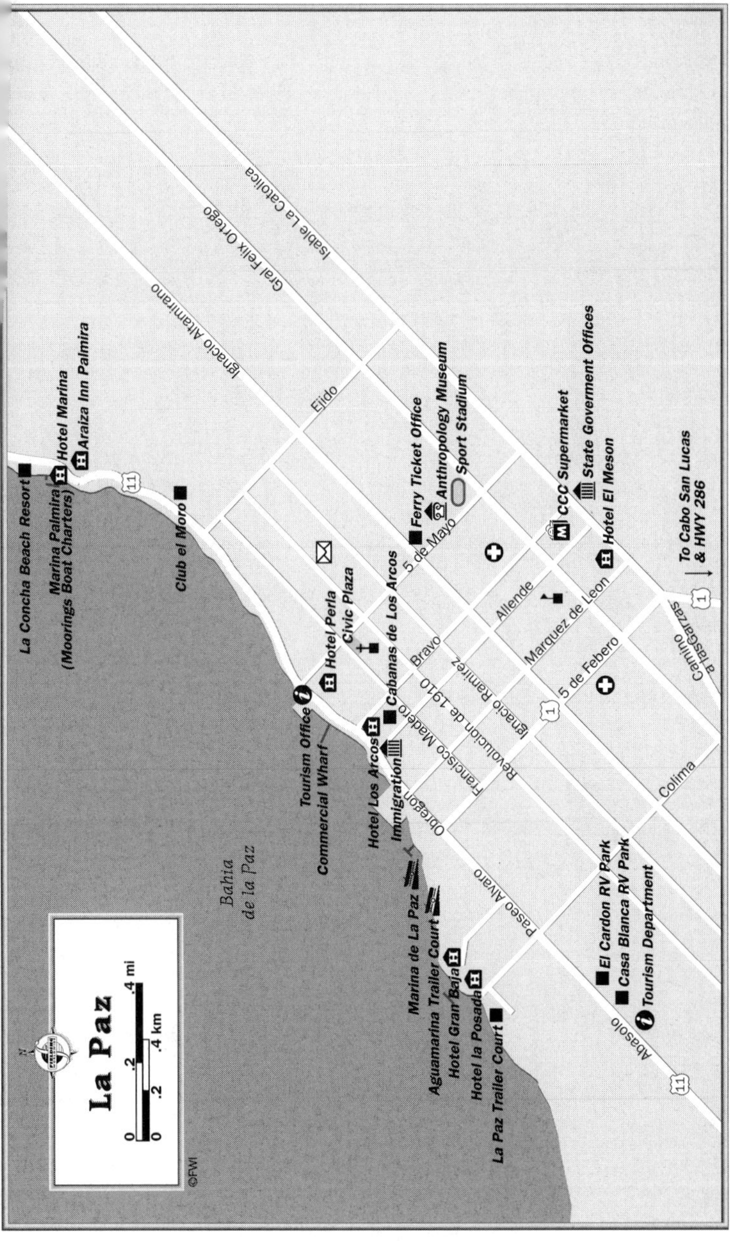

La Paz

N

La Concha Beach Resort

Hotel Marina
Marina Palmira
(Moorings Boat Charters)
Araiza Inn Palmira

Club el Moro

Bahia de la Paz

Isable La Católica
Gral Félix Ortego
Ignacio Altamirano
Ejido

Hotel Perla
Civic Plaza

Ferry Ticket Office
Anthropology Museum
Sport Stadium

5 de Mayo

Tourism Office

Cabanas de Los Arcos
Calle de Los Arcos

Commercial Wharf

Hotel Los Arcos
Immigration

Francisco Madero
Revolución de 1910
Ignacio Ramírez

Obregón

Bravo

Allende

Marquez de Leon

5 de Febero

CCC Supermarket
State Goverment Offices

Hotel El Meson

To Cabo San Lucas
& HWY 286

Paseo Alvero

Marina de La Paz

Aguamarina Trailer Court

Hotel Gran Baja

Hotel la Posada

La Paz Trailer Court

Colima

El Cardon RV Park
Casa Blanca RV Park

Tourism Department

Camino

Abasolo

©FWI

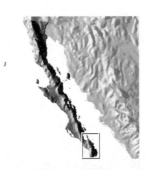

LA PAZ TO SAN JOSE DEL CABO VIA HIGHWAY 1

Recreation vehicles line the bluff overlooking Bahía de los Muertos.

After traveling 1483 Km (922 miles) from the international border, your Grand Tour begins the final leg of the journey to the Cape Area at the peninsula's tip. The scenery lying ahead is a considerable improvement over the rather unimpressive plains and low plateaus north of La Paz, as both of the highways to the south pass through or around the Sierra de la Laguna. The vegetation is also some of the most impressive to be encountered on the peninsula.

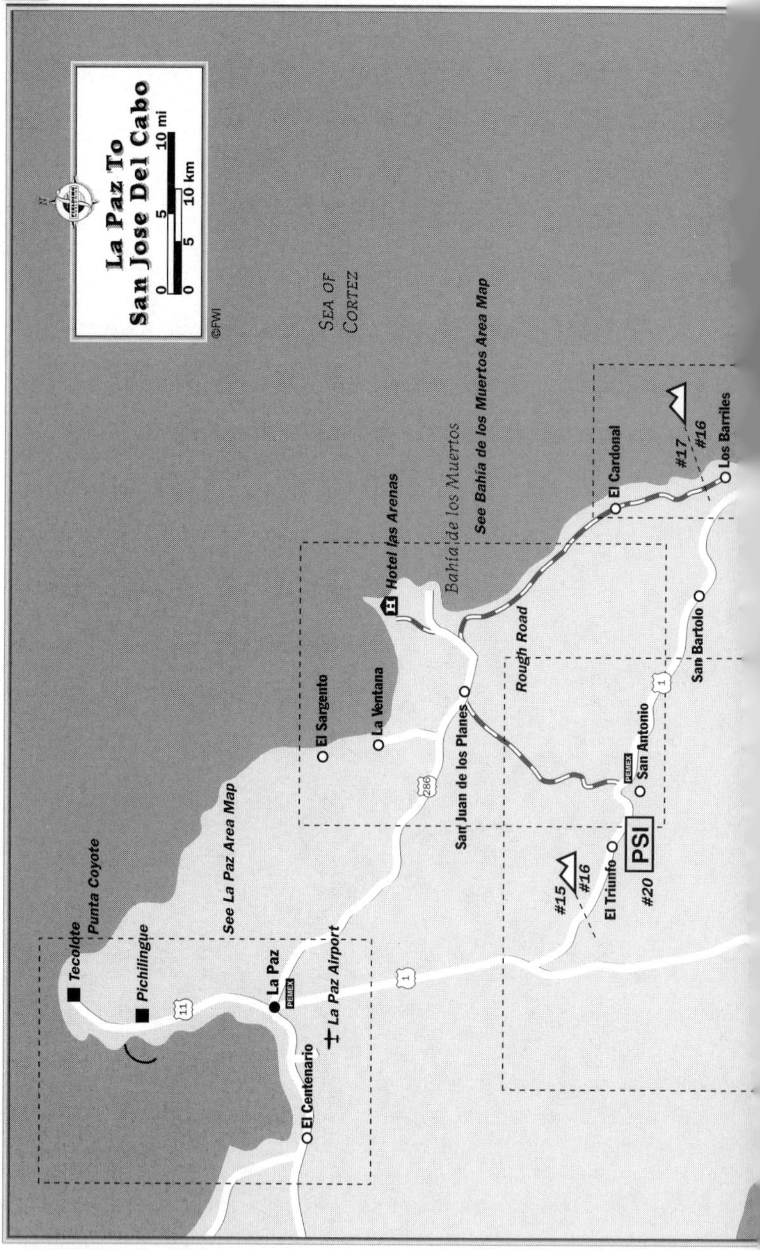
La Paz To San Jose Del Cabo
0 5 10 mi
0 5 10 km
©FWI
Sea of Cortez
Tecolote
Punta Coyote
Pichilingue
See La Paz Area Map
La Paz
PEMEX
La Paz Airport
El Centenario
11
1
286
El Sargento
La Ventana
Hotel las Arenas
Bahía de los Muertos
See Bahía de los Muertos Area Map
San Juan de los Planes
Rough Road
El Cardonal
Los Barriles
#17
#16
San Bartolo
San Antonio
PEMEX
PSI
#20
El Triunfo
#15
#16

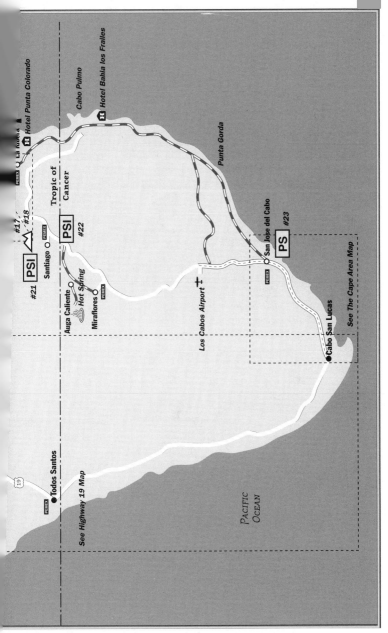

Camping South of La Paz

Many of the locations along Highway 1 south of La Paz that were on popular beachfront camping areas have been usurped for residential a commercial purposes. This is particularly true in the "Corridor" betwee San Jose del Cabo and Cabo San Lucas, where the last free beach-campin area was closed to the public in 1991. It is also true in the Buena Vista-Lo Barriles area. If beach camping is your objective, you need to consider takin one of the side trips described in the present chapter. Excellent beach cam ing, and beach-side RV parks, are also available along Highway 19 on the P cific coast.

Passing Through La Paz

On entering La Paz from the west, keep to the right at the Dove of Peac Statue. Taking this route will bypass the downtown section of La Paz.

SIDE TRIP

Highway 286

The residential areas of La Paz are rapidly spreading to the south, so the junction of Highways 1 and 286 falls within the city. Be alert for the highway sign to S.J. de los Planes and position your vehicle to en-able you to turn left from the busy, multilaned road. The junction is 1.3 miles from the intersection of 5 de Febrero and Forjadores Blvd. It is 58 Km (36.5 miles) to Bahía de los Muertos.

Highway 286 is constructed through highly erosible granite soils. Thus, each side of the road has been provided with concrete-lined ditches to allow rainwater to run off without damage to the travel surface.

Km-24

Highway 286 climbs through a region of low hills and reaches its maximum elevation near this point. As you descend to the east an ex-cellent view unfolds and you will be able to see the Sea of Cortez and the southern end of mountainous Isla Cerralvo lying seven miles off the shoreline. For several miles on either side of the summit one may see elephant trees and other diminutive trees that make up the Arid Tropical Forest noted in the "Vegetation" chapter.

SIDE TRIP

Km-37

A paved highway leads left (north) to the small towns of La Ventana **Km-7** *and El Sargento* **Km-11**. *There is a good camping spot on the beach at the north end of La Ventana in a grove of palm and mesquite trees. Now that the access road to this area has been paved, development is occurring between the two communities and eventually they will merge. A low-standard road branches to the east between* **Km-6** *and* **Km-7** *(1.2 miles south of the warehouse in La Ventana) and in 0.5 miles arrives at an excellent camping beach. I am advised that this road extends eastward to the Hotel las Arenas but is best suited for four-wheel-drive vehicles due to sandy conditions. During winter, all of these locations are exposed to the prevailing northerly winds.*

Km-41

Between **Km-40** *and* **Km-41** *a secondary road leads right (south) 14.3 miles to the town of San Antonio at Highway 1. It provides the opportunity of traveling south without returning to La Paz.*

Km-43

Highway 286 passes through the center of the town of San Juan de los Planes. This community is the center of an agricultural region.

Km-48

The paved surface ends near the town of Agua Amarga. The road farther eastward is constructed to the same standard as the balance of Highway 286 but was not paved in 1995.

Km 55

About 0.1 miles west of **Km 55** *a low-standard but level road leads left (north) for 3.5 miles to the* **Hotel las Arenas**. *This is a first-class resort serving many guests who arrive in small private aircraft, but it was closed in 1995. A short distance prior to reaching the hotel another road branches to the left and in 1.2 miles arrives at good camping spots on a sandy beach near a lighthouse.*

Km-58

Arrival at Bahía de los Muertos. The name means "The Bay of the Dead," but there could not be a more pleasant spot, with camping along a low bluff overlooking the beach. The beach has reasonable protection from the prevailing northerly winds. My favorite spot is on the floor of a long-abandoned warehouse at the northern end of the area.

Km J-185—Highway 19 Junction

Highway 1 from La Paz to its junction with Highway 19 traverses the eastern edge of the Llano de la Paz. The highway is straight and level. At the junction you have a choice of two paved highways to Cabo San Lucas: 185 Km (115 miles) via Highway 1, or 128 Km (80 miles) over the shorter Highway 19. If this is your first trip to the area I recommend that you travel south on one route and return on the other. If you simply wish to proceed to Cabo San Lucas in the easiest manner, take Highway 19. It is shorter, does not require climbing over the Sierra de la Laguna, and there are fine views of the Pacific Ocean.

A great majority of larger RVs and commercial trucks now travel to the Cape area over Highway 19. This has removed almost all of the slow-moving traffic that once was a problem on Highway 1. The latter route is now far more enjoyable for recreation travel than it was in the past.

#15

#16

Km J-172—Geographic Change

Southeast from the Highway 19 junction, the Llano de la Paz (Geographic Section No. 15) begins rising to meet the mountains. At **Km J-172** the plains come to an end and the highway enters the Sierra de la Laguna (Geographic Section No. 16). You will be traveling in the mountains until arriving at the coast at Los Barriles; however, most of the curves and steeper grades are encountered during the first 17 Km (10 miles).

Decomposed Granite

The Sierra de la Laguna is composed of granitic rocks. If you will remember the discussion about the Cataviña boulder fields in an earlier chapter, you will recall that granite rock breaks down into a very granular soil referred to as "D.G." (decomposed granite). "D.G." erodes readily. To complicate matters, the Cape Region receives much of its rainfall from intense storms related to tropical cyclones. The area's roads suffer heavy damage during such storms. I have always found Highway 1 to be in good repair, but you may encounter washouts and detours when using lower-standard roads. Be particularly cautious during and following heavy rains.

Cape Region Vegetation

Upon entering the Sierra de la Laguna, the characteristics of the Cape Region's Arid Tropical Forest vegetation become readily apparent. In the mountains between **Km J-170** and **Km J-50**, several species of low-growing trees become dominant, although many desert species are still present. The white-barked palo blanco is very abundant. This plant community has been described as an "impoverished tropical jungle." South of **Km J-50**, the trees are replaced by a variety of low shrubs, but the overall amount of vegetation remains far more dense than in the Sonoran Desert to the north.

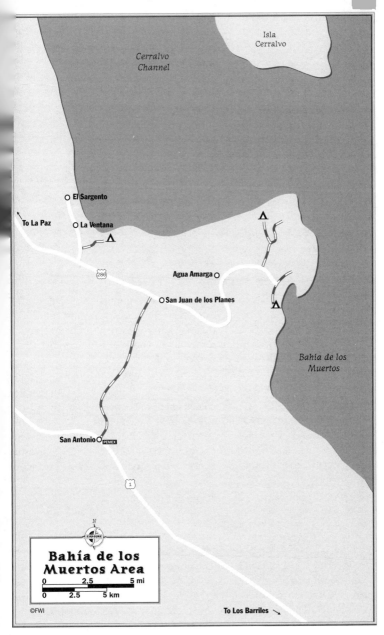

The mining ruins at the town of El Triunfo.

PSI #20

Km J-164—El Triunfo

The mining community of El Triunfo (The Triumph), population 400, and its neighboring town of San Antonio lie in one of Baja's most historic areas. El Triunfo was the site of a cattle ranch in the early Jesuit period, and in 1748, silver was discovered in the mountains south of San Antonio. Many years later, in 1862, silver and gold were also located at El Triunfo. Believe it or not, the sleepy little town that you see today soon was to have a population of 10,000, making it the largest community in the southern peninsula.

El Triunfo is stop No. 20 on the **Points of Special Interest Tour**. Even large RVs can pull off the highway near the church. Take a short walk to the ruins of the old smelter. The smokestacks are clearly in view from the highway. A few hundred feet southeast of the larger stack lies a brick-walled enclosure containing 13 above-ground crypts. These reportedly contain the remains of U.S. miners.

Be careful as you wander about—present-day miners are using arsenic to reprocess the old mine tailings, in order to obtain what little metal remains. These areas are fenced and signed.

Km J-159—Scenic View

Between **Km J-159** and **Km J-158**, look out over the mountains to the plains around San Juan de los Planes. The Sea of Cortez and huge Isla Cerralvo also are in view on clear days. The island is separated from the mainland by a narrow channel. The arid tropical-forest vegetation is well developed in this area.

Km J-156—San Antonio

San Antonio (population 800) is a pleasant little town situated along the bottom of a sizeable arroyo. The town square and church lie 0.3 miles upstream to the south. There is a PEMEX station on the highway that I have found closed on some of my visits. About 0.1 miles prior to reaching the PEMEX station, an oiled road leaves Highway 1 to the left (north). This is the beginning of the secondary road leading to San Juan de los Planes. After traveling on this road for 0.1 miles, it takes first a sharp left, and then a sharp right turn near a high voltage electric tower. Failure to make these turns will place you on the old, lower-standard road that runs through the northern portion of San Antonio.

In 1748, silver mining started five miles south of here in the mountains at a place called Santa Ana. Look south into the rugged terrain and recall that Santa Ana was the site of one of the most important meetings in the history of the American West. In 1768, Jose de Galvez, personal representative of the King of Spain, made Santa Ana his headquarters. From here he sent for Junipero Serra, the newly arrived head of the Franciscan missionaries, and at this most unlikely of places the two men drew up the plans for the expeditions that resulted one year later in the founding of the missions in Alta California.

In 1828, Baja California's capital at Loreto was destroyed by flooding. Two years later the seat of power was moved to La Paz. During the brief interim, San Antonio served as the capital city.

Km J-128—San Bartolo

The town of San Bartolo (population 500) lies along the highway above the banks of a deep canyon. The area contains numerous palms and a variety of large hardwood trees, a sight not often seen in Baja. Note the many light-colored granite rocks in view along the highway and contrast them with the darker basalt found to the north in the Sierra Giganta. Produce stands along the highway are a good place to stock up on fresh fruits and vegetables.

Km J-112—Geographic Change

#16
#17

Highway 1 arrives at the eastern edge of the Sierra de la Laguna (Geographic Section No. 16) and begins a short journey south along relatively level coastal flats (Geographic Section No. 17). The Sea of Cortez is in full view.

The Los Barriles-Buena Vista area is on the East Cape.

SIDE TRIP

Km J-110—Los Barriles

A good standard oiled road bears left (east) 0.2 miles north of **Km-J-110**, *and Highway 1 swings to the south down the coast. Taking the former road brings you in a short distance to the hotels and RV parks in los Barriles. (See the "Los Barriles–Buena Vista Area" map.) The oiled surface ends a short distance beyond Los Barriles, but the road proceeds farther north up the coast as follows:*

9.1 Miles

Arrive at the very pleasant **Hotel Punta Pescadero**, *adjoining recreation homes, and a paved airstrip. The resort's fishing fleet is moored in a shallow bight to the south. There is a steep pitch a short distance prior to arriving at the hotel but it does not pose a major problem.*

13.7 Miles

The small village of El Cardónal is located at this point. The town lies on a level plateau above the Sea of Cortez and contains the **El Cardónal Resort**, *a modest motel and RV park. From El Cardónal, the campers on the beach at Bahía de los Muertos to the north are clearly in view. A road continues north from here to San Juan de los Planes, but some of those who have used it report that portions are suitable only for the most rugged of four-wheel-drive vehicles. More recently, I have been informed that the locals use it with regular vehicles as their shortcut to La Paz. In either case, all agree its a rough road.*

The roadside monument at the Tropic of Cancer is between Buena Vista and San Jose del Cabo.

Km J-108—Buena Vista

The community of Buena Vista lies along the shores of the Sea of Corte and blends together with adjacent Los Barriles. To the left near **Km J-106** is short side road to the **Rancho Buena Vista**, a very pleasant resort hotel. A few yards south of the turnoff to the Rancho Buena Vista, a secondary road lead 0.5 miles to the right (west) up the hill to the Flag Monument. From there you can enjoy a good view of the coast in both directions.

A road leaves the highway to the left 0.2 miles near **Km J-105** for the **Hotel Buenavista** and a subdivision development. From here south, Highway 1 starts to turn inland. At **Km J-104** another dirt road signed for the Rancho Leonero bears to the left (east) and in 1.6 miles reaches the **Capilla RV Park** on the beach. It is 4.1 miles on this same road to the **Rancho Leonero Hotel** (see the "La Ribera Area" map).

#17
#18

Km J-93—Geographic Change

At this point, Highway 1 leaves the flat coastal area (Geographic Section No. 17) and starts a 60-Km (37-mile) journey over low hills and plateaus (Geographic Section No.18) between two ranges of mountains. To the right is that section of the Sierra de la Laguna that was the location of revolutionary battles from 1913 to 1915.

Km J-93—East Cape Loop

An oiled highway leaves Highway 1 to the left (east) for the small coastal village of La Ribera, which is reached in 7.7 miles. This town is the northern terminus of a 100-Km (62-mile) road along the coast leading to San Jose Del Cabo. This road, referred to in this book as the "East Cape Loop," is described in a separate subsection at the end of this chapter.

PSI
#21

SIDE TRIP

Km J-85—Santiago

A blacktop road joins Highway 1 on the right (west) and leads to the historic town of Santiago, a pleasant village supported by small farms and ranching. It is stop No. 21 on the **Points of Special Interest Tour**. *Here the Jesuits founded their 10th mission in 1724. While the mission was maintained until 1795 (71 years), no traces of it remain.*

Santiago was one of the sites of the 1734 Pericue Indian revolt described in the "History" chapter. The missionary padre, two soldiers and an Indian were killed here, and the uprising caused temporary abandonment of all the missions in the Cape Area and La Paz.

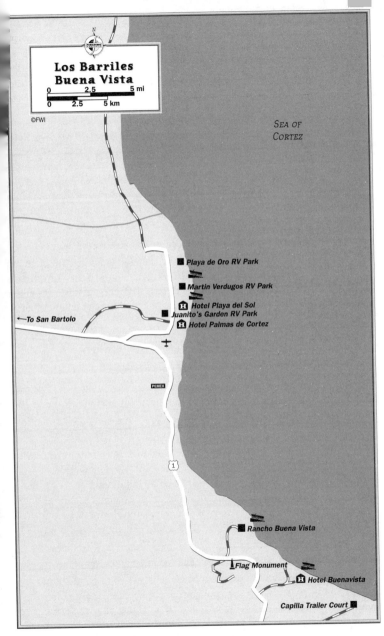

SIDE TRIP

The town square and PEMEX station are 1.5 miles west of the highway. Proceed through the square, bear left and take the main, tree-lined street to visit the charming Hotel Palomar, a museum and the only zoological garden in Baja California. (See description in the "Wildlife" chapter.)

Agua Caliente

Continuing westerly past the zoological garden in Santiago is an 11-mile-long road to the town of Miraflores noted below. Near the midpoint between Santiago and Miraflores is the village of Agua Caliente. Take a dirt road west from Agua Caliente to its end (about 2.5 miles) where you will be rewarded by a scenic camping spot in a canyon beside a large pool of water. A nearby hot spring fills a cement tub for your soaking enjoyment. There are other roads in this general area accessing the base of the Sierra de la Laguna.

Km J-82—Tropic of Cancer

There is nothing fancy about the concrete sphere located by the road on the right, but most people from Canada and the United States never have the opportunity to stand exactly on the Tropic of Cancer (23 degrees north of the equator). This is stop No. 22 on the **Points of Special Interest Tour**. I suggest you pause and stretch. You are now entering the world's tropical zone. The sun moves in its yearly course between the Tropic of Cancer and the Tropic of Capricorn in the southern hemisphere.

Km J-71—Miraflores

A PEMEX station is located here at the junction of Highway 1 with a blacktop road that leads in 1.4 miles to the small town of Miraflores.

Km J-44—Los Cabos Airport

The southernmost of Baja's international airports is reached in 0.6 miles over a blacktop road leading right (west). This is the entry point for tourists bound for the Cape Area and the Buena Vista area. There is a modern terminal, parking and ample ground transportation including numerous car rental agencies. The airport has been expanded so as to accommodate jumbo jets. The airport is accessed by an overpass structure over Highway 1 and the remainder of the road to Cabo San Lucas is a four-lane divided highway. The Cape Area has entered the Big Time.

Km J-33—San Jose del Cabo

San Jose del Cabo marks the last geographic breakpoint. The highway remaining ahead passes along a section of coastal benches and low hills. The community of San Jose del Cabo is one of Baja's most interesting and is well worth a visit. It is described in more detail in the next chapter.

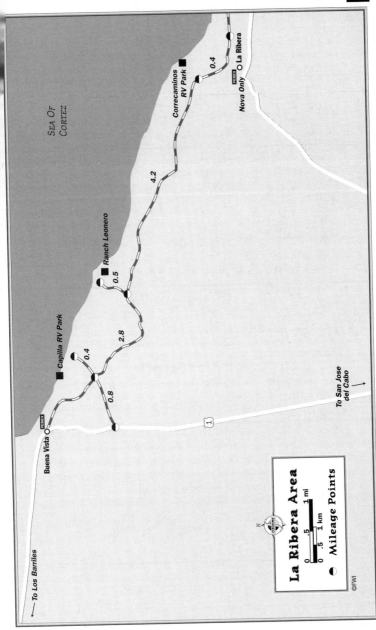

SEA OF CORTEZ

To Los Barriles

Buena Vista

Capilla RV Park

Ranch Leonero

Correcaminos RV Park

La Ribera

Nova Only

To San Jose del Cabo

0.4

4.2

0.5

2.8

0.4

0.8

1

N

La Ribera Area

0   .5   1 mi
0   .5   1 km

● Mileage Points

©FWI

Shown is the Bahía los Frailes Area along the East Cape Loop. Cabo los Frailes is the prominent point of land in the top-right portion of the photo.

East Cape Loop

SIDE TRIP

This subsection describes the road that closely follows the southeast coast of the cape from Highway 1 south to San Jose del Cabo. The loop as described below is an oiled highway from Highway 1 to the town of Ribera, and a secondary, often badly washboarded dirt road from there to San Jose del Cabo.

In spring 1992, a new highway was being pushed south from La Ribera inland, roughly paralleling, the above-noted secondary road. Seven miles of hard-surface had been completed and many additional miles were almost ready for oiling. By 1995, these additional miles had been paved but the new highway had not yet reached the hotel at Bahía los Frailes. I have been informed by the coordinator of tourism in La Paz that work on the remainder of the highway would be completed soon. Time will tell whether this actually occurs. What is presented below will no doubt be badly outdated in a short while, but it is the best I can offer at this time.

SIDE TRIP

The old secondary road of the East Cape Loop is built through an area of decomposed granite; thus it is subject to severe erosion damage in the event of storms. On my most recent trip, there was clear evidence that the eroded spots were being currently repaired. There are no steep grades, and barring storm damage there is nothing to stop larger RVs from making the complete trip. However, its overall length, the potential for severe erosion damage and the roughness of the road surface will make it uninviting for the owners of most such vehicles. Taking relatively short excursions into the camping spots that are concentrated at either end of the loop present alternatives to making the entire trip.

0.0 Miles

The East Cape Loop begins at the Transpeninsular Highway just south of **Km J-93**.

7.0 Miles

Highway junction. The new highway noted above bears right a short distance prior to **Km-11** at the outskirts of the town of La Libera. Stay straight ahead for La Ribera and the balance of the route described below.

7.7 Miles

Staying straight ahead brings one to the park in the small village of La Ribera. Continue straight ahead and drive down a slope toward the sea.

7.8 Miles

At the base of the slope is a T-intersection with the road to the left (north) leading to Buena Vista. At 0.4 miles along this road on the right is the **Correcaminos RV Park** nestled in a mangrove orchard. It is one of Baja's more pleasant RV parks and is only a short walk from the beach.

Turn right (south) at the T-intersection down the coast and at 8.2 miles pass a PEMEX station (Nova only) on the right.

8.9 Miles

Road junction near a grove of tamarisk trees. The main road proceeds straight ahead. Taking a 90-degree turn left toward the coast offers a slightly longer loop route, but it provides access in 2.6 miles to an excellent camping area along the northern edge of a lagoon bordered with low trees. A sand dune separates the camping area from an excellent sandy beach, and in an additional 1.6 miles one reaches the gate to the very pleasant **Hotel Punta Colorado**.

SIDE TRIP

25.3 Miles

Arrive at spur road to Cabo Pulmo. There is a large area for RV parking at this point. The waters of Bahía Pulmo to the south of Cabo Pulmo support the only live coral reefs in the Sea of Cortez. It is thus a popular diving area.

28.3 Miles

A 0.9 miles spur leads to a ranch and camping area at the south end of Bahía Pulmo. This is the windy side of Cabo Frailes during the winter season.

30.4 Miles

A short spur road leads to the fine sandy beach at Bahía los Frailes. The point of land to the north (Cabo los Frailes) provides some protection from northerly winds. Located here is the small but comfortable **Hotel Bahía los Frailes**. *It is used as a headquarters for those interested in acquiring a home in the nearby residential subdivision, but transient visitors are also welcome.*

South of Bahía los Frailes the road narrows but has numerous sizeable cuts and fills. It is these fill sections that provide the East Cape Loop Road with its weak links because they are narrowed by erosion after storms. Proceed with caution.

44.8 Miles

A side road leaves the East Cape Loop here and joins Highway 1 near the Los Cabos Airport in 23 miles. From here to the lighthouse at San Jose del Cabo, I have observed more than 30 places to camp near the water's edge, every one of them with one or more groups of people. Most of these are relatively small areas located by the sea below where an arroyo crosses the road. Some are on fine sand beaches, others on the bluffs overlooking the water. Access to these sites is most often over low-standard "trails" where one can become mired down in the sand. Freedom has its price.

62.0 Miles

The East Cape Loop formally ends here, only a few feet from the lighthouse on the hill south of San Jose del Cabo. The road forks at this point, but either branch takes you through the small community of La Playa that lies on the east bank of the Rio San Jose. It is two miles from here, across the riverbed, to the boulevard south of the civic plaza at San Jose del Cabo. The junction is near the fire station and a tall microwave tower. If you plan to drive from San Jose del Cabo north on the East Cape Loop and have some difficulty getting started, look for the lighthouse and work your way to it as your point of departure.

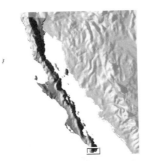

THE CAPE AREA

Along the Cape Area coastline, the Hotel Palmilla lies on the prominent point of land (Punta Palmilla), at the left edge of the photo. Cabo San Lucas can be seen in the distance at the photo's top right-hand corner.

Cape Area Summary

That portion of the Baja peninsula lying along its southern tip is known in English as "The Cape Area." A cape is defined as "a piece of land projecting into a body of water; promontory; headland." Thus, a good case can be made that the cape in question here is the entire southern end of the peninsula. However, in Spanish the region is referred to as "Los Cabos," that is, The Capes (plural). Is there more than one cape?

The famous Cabo San Lucas is the only really dramatic promontory in the area, with Punta Palmilla to the east being far less dramatic. More likely the

507

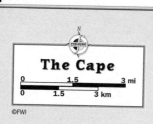

The Cape

0   1.5   3 mi
0   1.5   3 km

©FWI

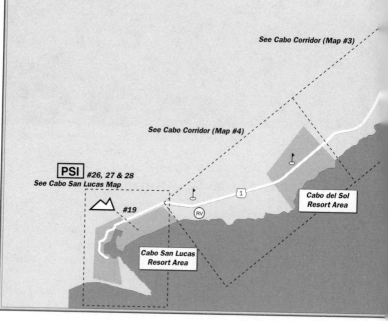

See Cabo Corridor (Map #3)

See Cabo Corridor (Map #4)

PSI #26, 27 & 28
See Cabo San Lucas Map

#19

Cabo del Sol
Resort Area

Cabo San Lucas
Resort Area

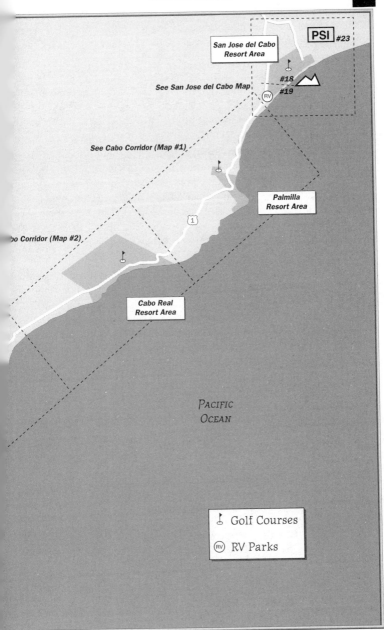

San Jose del Cabo
Resort Area

PSI #23

See San Jose del Cabo Map

#18
#19

RV

See Cabo Corridor (Map #1)

Palmilla
Resort Area

1

bo Corridor (Map #2)

Cabo Real
Resort Area

PACIFIC
OCEAN

Golf Courses

RV RV Parks

plural term "Los Cabos" refers to the two towns of Cabo San Lucas (Cape Saint Luke) and San Jose del Cabo (Saint Joseph of the Cape). If I am not correct, I will no doubt be firmly corrected prior to this book's next edition.

In any case, The Cape Area has undergone more change from a recreational standpoint than any area in Baja. During the first few years following completion of the Transpeninsular Highway in 1973 the region contained several first-class hotels catering largely to the general aviation flyer. But the camper was king, and people such as myself lined the beaches under conditions that often were disgraceful from a sanitation standpoint.

Now, camping outside of developed RV parks is a thing of the past. In its place, The Cape Area has become one of the world's finest resort and hotel meccas. I believe that portions of the French and Italian Riviera are superior in overall aesthetic appeal, in part because Baja's desert vegetation is a somewhat austere. But I have never seen the equal of The Cape Area hotels. Perhaps with another decade or so of development and landscaping, the southern tip of the Baja peninsula will be unrivaled as the *world's* best resort area.

To complete this summary, I refer you to the comments made in the "Resort Areas" section concerning San Jose del Cabo, Cabo San Lucas and the intervening area known as the Cabo Corridor. The points of interest presented in the balance of this chapter are shown on six maps as depicted on the facing map. Keep in mind that the four Cabo Corridor maps are not aligned in a true north-south direction as are most of the maps in this book.

The church at the civic plaza at San Jose del Cabo features a mosaic over the entrance that depicts the 1734 Indian uprising.

Km J-33—San Jose del Cabo

San Jose del Cabo is a town of 10,000 people and the last geographic breakpoint. If you are approaching from the north on Highway 1 and are in rush to reach the coast and Cabo San Lucas, stay straight ahead on the divided highway that passes west of the center of town. However, I suggest you turn left at the PEMEX station and take the three-sided loop through own. (See the "San Jose del Cabo" map). San Jose del Cabo is stop No. 23 on the **Points of Special Interest Tour**. This hard-surface loop will bring you back to Highway 1, near the coast, with no problems.

The town's history is one of the richest in the peninsula and includes the activities of the early Jesuit mission, visitations by numerous ships and famous captains, and an intensive battle in the Mexican-American War. The statue in the civic plaza is that of Naval Lieutenant Jose Antonio Mijares, who died here in 1847 while defending the town from takeover by the United States. Visit the church on the west side of the plaza. It was built in 1940 on the final site of the mission originally founded in 1730. A tile mosaic over its entrance depicts the slaying of the mission priest during the Indian uprising in 1734.

Most of the town's major hotels are located along an outstanding beach south of town. The **Hotel Presidente Inter-Continental Los Cabos** is at the western edge of the coastal lagoon lying at the mouth of the Rio San Jose. There can be no more historic spot on the peninsula. The original 1730 mission was located between here and the cemetery, and the fresh water entering the lagoon was of critical importance to the crews of ships plying Pacific waters.

To the west of the Presidente are three additional hotels. Inland from these is a golf course and residential and condominium area. All of this is a part of FONATUR's San Jose del Cabo development. A major marina project is planned for the estuary between San Jose del Cabo and the small community of La Playa.

I should note that the major new, privately owned hotel and resort complexes being developed to the west along the Cabo Corridor appear to be having a dampening affect on FONATUR's San Jose del Cabo project. There have been no new hotels constructed here in years, and some of the existing ones are suffering from lack of maintenance. The activity level here is in marked contrast to the feverish pace in evidence along the Cabo Corridor and at Cabo San Luca

The Cabo Corridor

The section of highway between San Jose del Cabo and Cabo San Lucas is referred to as "The Cabo Corridor," or simply "The Corridor." As recently as 10 years ago there was very little development in this area. It is now probably only a matter of a few more years until it will be lined solid with build-

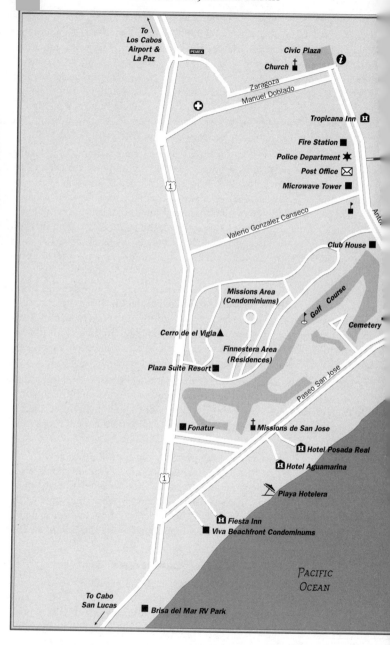

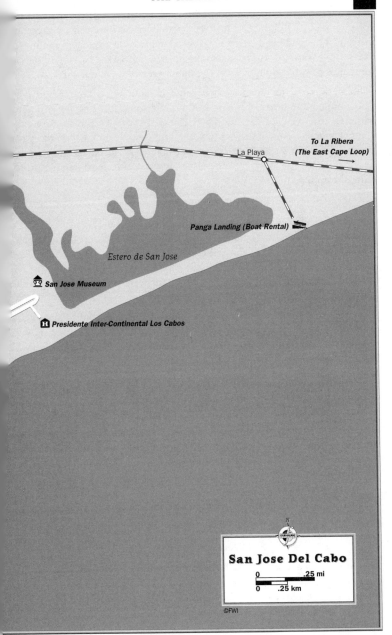

La Playa

**To La Ribera
(The East Cape Loop)**

Panga Landing (Boat Rental)

Estero de San Jose

San Jose Museum

Presidente Inter-Continental Los Cabos

N

San Jose Del Cabo

0   .25 mi

0   .25 km

©FWI

ings. Highway 1 was upgraded to a four-lane divided highway through the Corridor about 1993, easing what was becoming a serious traffic-congestion problem. The road's right-of-way is fenced in most places, so there is limited access to the waterfront. There are now no areas where the parking of RVs or camping is possible along what is the finest stretch of coast in all Baja.

There are often discrepancies between the kilometer addresses noted for various hotels and other sites in locally available literature and the kilometer markings that were present along Highway 1. Perhaps the markings are being changed as part of the roadway upgrading project. The kilometer references given below, and on the accompanying maps, reflect my personal observations. My apologies for the fact that you will have to join me in suffering through some confusion.

Km J-29

On the beach SW of town, near **Km J-29.5**, is the **Brisa del Mar**, one of Baja's most popular RV parks. There are approximately 100 sites complemented by a bar, restaurant and pool. This is the only RV park on the beach in the Cape Area. All the rest are at the western end of the Cabo Corridor near Cabo San Lucas and are some distance removed from the water's edge. Farther to the west along the beach at **Km J-29** is the **Hotel La Jolla**.

The next stop on the **Points of Special Interest Tour** is the **Hotel Palmilla**. Its buildings may be seen near the end of the point of land projecting to sea several miles to the south. This promontory provides the only protection from Pacific Ocean swells in the San Jose del Cabo area.

PSI #24

Km J-28—Hotel Palmilla

Each time I visit Baja I am impressed that a different hotel seems to be the finest in all Baja, but the **Hotel Palmilla** is always in the competition. The drive in from the highway is about one-half mile. There is a small parking lot, but the road is narrow and unsuited for large RVs. This hotel has been here for many years and thus has excellent landscaping.

The Pamillia development is now being greatly expanded and the area is served by a full-fledged interchange over Highway 1. A 27-hole golf course is present north of the highway and many condominiums are scattered about. The area is truly world-class.

Cabo Real

The advertised address for the **Cabo Real** resort area is **Km J-19.5**. However, this 2500-acre development lies along several kilometers of Highway 1. At the eastern extremity near **Km J-24** is the grandiose **Hotel Westin Regina Resort**. Farther west an interchange near **Km J-21** serves the **Hotel Melia**, the smaller **Hotel Casa del Mar** and a nearby golf course. The area north of the

ghway will eventually contain numerous roads and residential develop-
ents. Everything is world-class and is being done on a grand scale.

Km J-15—Hotel Cabo San Lucas

By now you must be aware that I believe my readers will be charmed, as I
m, by Baja's fine hotels. Here is another one that is among the very best.
he **Hotel Cabo San Lucas** was completed in 1962 and is surrounded by excel-
nt landscaping. There is a sizeable parking lot and the road is suitable for
ven large RVs. A very picturesque, small cove (Puerto Chileno) lies westerly
rom the hotel. Near the beach at its head is a large palm-covered structure
ffering diving services. The road to this facility leaves Highway 1 a short
distance westerly from the hotel access road.

Km J-11—Hotel Twin Dolphin

Here is another very fine hotel that may be easily visited by even the larger
RVs. Its landscaping was designed to feature native desert plants. It thus offers a unique atmosphere and has been placed on the **Points of Special Interest
Tour** as stop No. 25. Immediately east of the hotel is Bahía Santa Maria, a
small idyllic cove with a fine sandy beach.

**PSI
#25**

Km J-11—Shipwreck Beach

Near here a dirt road used to lead left (south) for 0.5 miles to an undeveloped camping area on the slopes above a fine beach. The wreck of a sizeable
ship lay stranded on the beach and gave rise to the area's name. This was the
last place in the Cape Area where beach camping and RV parking was permitted. It was finally closed in 1991, reportedly at the insistence of the **Cabo
San Lucas RV Park** owners who wanted the shipwreck crowd as their paying
guests. Pause here to mourn the passing of an era.

Km J-10—Cabo Del Sol

A highway interchange lies just east of **Km J-10** and provides access to the
Cabo Del Sol resort development. Much construction has taken place at this
1800-acre property, including a **Hyatt Hotel**. Also envisioned are three additional oceanfront hotels, three golf courses, a colonial village center, 3400
residences and assorted other amenities. I suspect that the property includes
the Shipwreck Beach noted above. Could it be that there is more money to
be made from Cabo del Sol than from catering to a bunch of American
beach bums? Amazing!

Km J-7—Villa Serena RV Park

At this point in time the **Villa Serena** is the most easterly of several RV parks
lying between here and Cabo San Lucas. The access road is 0.4 miles in
length. When first developed several years ago many of the sites offered fine
ocean views and a pool area fit for a fancy hotel. Unfortunately the best spots

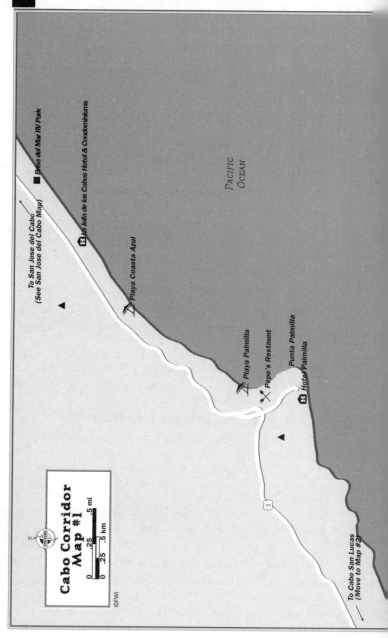

Cabo Corridor
Map #1

0   .25   .5 mi
0   .25   .5 km

©FWI

To San Jose del Cabo
(See San Jose del Cabo Map)

PACIFIC
OCEAN

Boca del Mar RV Park

La Jolla de los Cabos Hotel & Condominiums

Playa Coasta Azul

Playa Palmilla

Pepe's Restaunt

Punta Palmilla

Hotel Palmilla

1

To Cabo San Lucas
(Move to Map #2)

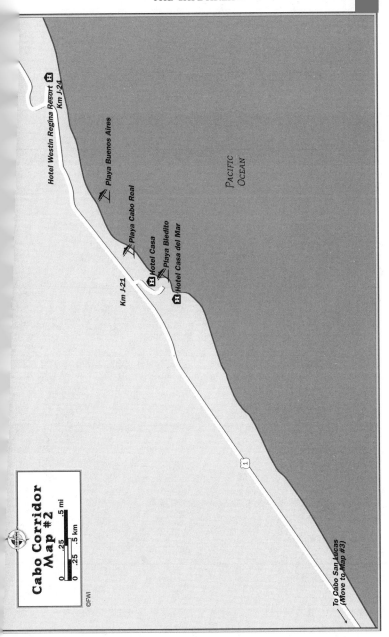

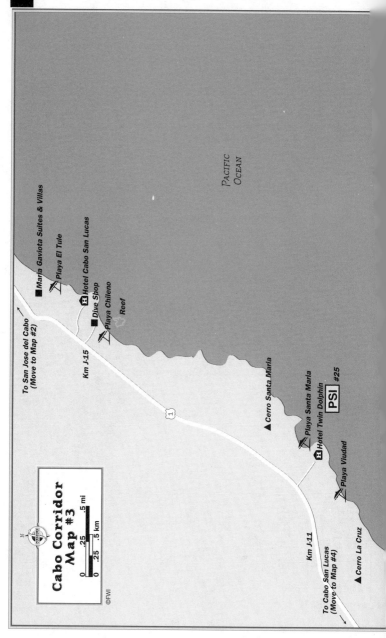

Cabo Corridor Map #3

©FWI

N

0 .25 .5 mi
0 .25 .5 km

To San Jose del Cabo
(Move to Map #2)

Km J-15

Maria Gaviota Suites & Villas

Playa El Tule

Hotel Cabo San Lucas

Dive Shop

Playa Chileno

Reef

PACIFIC OCEAN

Cerro Santa Maria

Playa Santa Maria

Hotel Twin Dolphin

PSI #25

Playa Viudad

Km J-11

To Cabo San Lucas
(Move to Map #4)

Cerro La Cruz

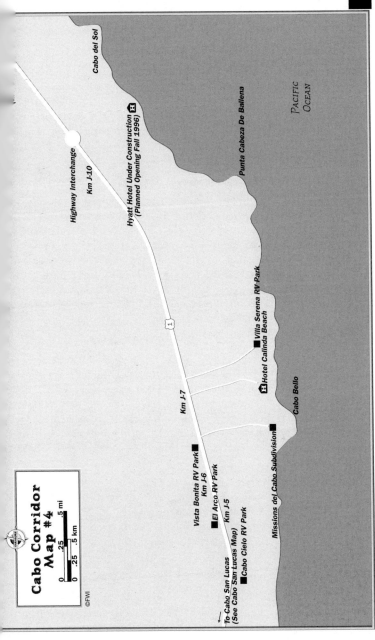

Cabo Corridor
Map #4

©FWI

0   .25   .5 mi
0   .25   .5 km

To Cabo San Lucas
(See Cabo San Lucas Map)

Cabo Cielo RV Park

Km J-5

El Arco RV Park

Km J-6

Vista Bonita RV Park

Km J-7

Missions del Cabo Subdivision

Hotel Calinda Beach

Cabo Bello

Villa Serena RV Park

Highway Interchange

Km J-10

Hyatt Hotel Under Construction
(Planned Opening Fall 1996)

Cabo del Sol

Punta Cabeza De Ballena

PACIFIC
OCEAN

have now been converted to permanent status and the transient sites leav
bit to be desired. The area was still under development in 1995.

Km J-7—Hotel Calinda Beach

A blacktop road leads left for 0.5 mile to the hotel. Most of the times I ha
paid it a visit its name has been changed, so be prepared for something d
ferent. From the **Hotel Calinda Beach**, look westerly across the outer harbor
Cabo San Lucas and see the peninsula's rocky tip. The pool area is super
and one can argue with considerable validity that it has the best view of an
hotel in Baja. The Missions del Cabo subdivision lies just to the west of th
hotel on a promontory of land called Cabo Bello.

Km J-6—Cabo San Lucas Vista

At this point there used to be a simple concrete monument on the left side
of the road. I designated this as **Points of Special Interest Tour** stop No. 2
and recommended that you stop here for an excellent view of Cabo San Lu
cas. Nowadays it might be dangerous to stop along this busy highway, bu
you are still permitted to admire the view and enjoy Baja's most famous land
mark. (Better yet, visit the Hotel Calinda Beach noted above and enjoy a re
laxed view of the Cape.) Let me add my own salute. Congratulations, you
have arrived within site of *Finisterra* (Land's End). I hope you have not been
led too far astray along the way.

Km J-6 to J-3—RV Parks

There are five RV parks with full hookups adjoining the highway between
here and Cabo San Lucas. These are the **Vista Bonita** right (north) of the
highway (it was under construction in 1995 and was not yet open); the **El
Arco** (also right of the highway); the **Cabo Cielo** left of the highway (appeared
closed and somewhat the worse for wear on our last trip), **San Vicente** left of
the highway and **Vagabundos del Mar**, also left of the highway. The latter
court appeared to be the best of the litter during my last visit, but the Vista
Bonita has considerable potential.

Club Cabo RV Park is tucked in along the eastern edge of the Vagabundos
del Mar park. It is reached by turning left (south) of the highway onto a dirt
road just west of **Km J-3**. After a short distance again turn left and in about
0.25-mile, there you are. This park is more secluded than the others and caters to tent campers. An RV park is also being constructed on Paseo del
Pescador in town.

Km J-3.5—Cabo San Lucas Country Club

On the right side of the highway across from the Vagabundos del Mar RV
Park lies the Cabo San Lucas Country Club. This 746-acre development is
planned to include a 36-hole golf course and approximately 1600 home

PSI
#26

tes. Hotels do not appear to be part of the picture here and there is no
cean frontage.

Km J-3—Entering Cabo San Lucas

Upon entering Cabo San Lucas note the junction with Highway 19 on the
ight (north). This highway skirts the community on its eastern edge. A
EMEX station may be found along Highway 19 near the northern edge of
own. Another easily accessible PEMEX station adjoins Highway 1 on the
ight at **Km J-**2.

*The Cabo San Lucas area features the famous Cape, at the right side of the
photo. Additional developments have been made in several areas since this photo
was taken.*

Km J-0—Cabo San Lucas

The zero-kilometer post for the Transpeninsular Highway lies across from
the town square. The latest town entrance sign claims 14,000 people, and
the town is experiencing an enormous expansion of hotels, condominiums
and tourist-oriented shops. In spring 1989, I described the place as hectic
and bathed in construction activities. By 1995, things had settled down, but
Cabo San Lucas will never again be the simple fishing village it once was.

There are many places of interest to the tourist in the Cabo San Lucas area.
Here are some of the more important ones:

The Inner Harbor

It took more than a decade to convert the waterfront area of Cabo San
Lucas into a dredged, concrete-walled inner harbor. And now it has finally

secured a first-class marina filled with the world's fanciest yachts. At the harbor's southern end are open-air gift shops.

Hotel Finisterra

Perched high on the cliffs south of the inner harbor is the **Hotel Finisterra**. It is stop No. 27 on the **Points of Special Interest Tour**. The hotel offers intriguing rock-masonry architecture, and from its entrance way the entire Cabo San Lucas community and harbor area are in view. Be sure to visit the **Whale Watcher's Bar**, where the vista changes to the south and provides a commanding panorama of the Pacific Ocean. The men's rest room is also one-of-a-kind.

Hotel Solmar

If you love the beach, the **Hotel Solmar** is the place. It is in view from the Whale Watcher's Bar at the Finisterra, and its access road starts opposite the ferry terminal.

Hacienda Hotel

Yet another of Baja's very finest hotels adjoins the beach fronting the outer harbor. The **Hacienda Hotel's** access road circles the inner harbor on its eastern side. If you like to swim in the ocean, this is the best place, as the beach here is protected from the main force of the Pacific swells.

Hotel Melia

One of Cabo's newest hotels, the **Hotel Melia**, is done in a "grand style." The hotel lies immediately northeast of the Hotel Hacienda. Again the beach is readily used for swimming.

Mar De Cortez Hotel

A more modest, smaller, but very charming hotel lying in the business area of the community.

Outer Harbor Tour

You have arrived at the town of Cabo San Lucas and have gazed seaward at the jagged finger of rock that forms the cape itself, but you haven't actually been there. The next challenge of the **Points of Special Interest Tour** (stop No. 28) is to visit the natural arch and spires of rock at Land's End. (Stops No. 29 and 30 are along Highway 19.)

There is also a pinnacle of rock in the bay near the cliffs some 0.3 miles south from the inner harbor entrance. Most of this formation lies under water and attracts thousands of colorful tropical fish that are easily viewed with snorkeling equipment or from a glass-bottom boat. Small boats are for hire in the harbor or along the beach, so you may accept this final challenge. Rent one with a glass bottom to see the fish.

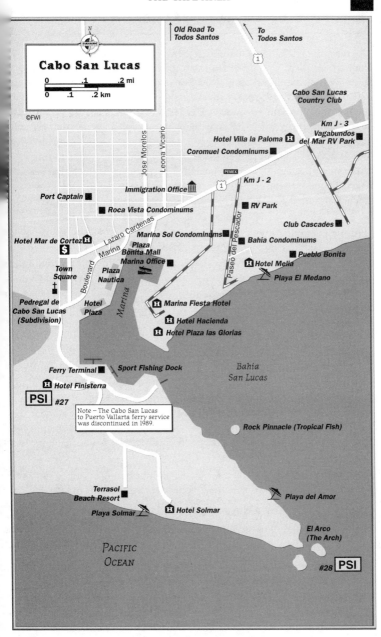

Cabo San Lucas

0 .1 .2 mi
0 .1 .2 km

©FWI

Old Road To Todos Santos

To Todos Santos

Cabo San Lucas Country Club

Km J - 3

Vagabundos del Mar RV Park

Jose Morelos

Leona Vicario

Hotel Villa la Paloma

Coromuel Condominums

PEMEX

Immigration Office

Km J - 2

RV Park

Club Cascades

Port Captain

Roca Vista Condominums

Bahia Condominums

Paseo del Pescador

Hotel Mar de Cortez

Lazaro Cardenas

Marina

Marina Sol Condominums

Plaza Bonita Mall

Marina Office

Pueblo Bonita

Hotel Melia

Plaza Nautica

Boulevard

Town Square

Playa El Medano

Pedregal de Cabo San Lucas (Subdivision)

Hotel Plaza

Marina

Marina Fiesta Hotel

Hotel Hacienda

Hotel Plaza las Glorias

Ferry Terminal

Sport Fishing Dock

Bahia San Lucas

Hotel Finisterra

PSI #27

Note – The Cabo San Lucas to Puerto Vallarta ferry service was discontinued in 1989.

Rock Pinnacle (Tropical Fish)

Terrasol Beach Resort

Playa del Amor

Hotel Solmar

Playa Solmar

El Arco (The Arch)

PACIFIC OCEAN

#28 PSI

THE CAPE AREA

Cape Area Beaches

As recently as about 1980, anyone could leave Highway 1 at almost an point where there was a side road and make one's way to the shoreline t camp and use the Cape's numerous beaches. Rapid development of privat land has made this practice a thing of the past. During one recent trip, noted a sign along the highway at San Jose del Cabo listing 22 beaches tha were open to the public. Each was served by an access road of varying stan dards and its junction with Highway 1 was marked with an "Accesso Playa" (Beach Access) sign. Since then the highway has been upgraded to four lane and some of the signs have disappeared. Thus, getting to the beach is a chal lenge. To assist in this endeavor the following material lists 14 Cape Are beaches and their location is shown on the six maps presented in this chap ter.

From a swimming-safety standpoint, Cape Area beaches can be said to fall into three categories: (1) dangerous, (2) normally safe, and (3) in-between. The "dangerous beaches" lie westerly from the Cabo San Lucas promontory where they are impacted by heavy swells traveling down the Pacific coast. The breaking swells and undertow can be quite strong and swimming can be hazardous. The normally safe beaches lie immediately easterly from the Cape in the protected portions of Bahía San Lucas. This area offers the best shelter from the prevailing Pacific swells.

Most of the beaches presented below fall easterly from Bahía San Lucas and are in the "in-between" class. The prevailing winter season Pacific swells re-fract around Cabo San Lucas causing breaking swell conditions all the way northeast into the Sea of Cortez to near the town of La Ribera. Swell inten-sity becomes less the farther one proceeds northeasterly from Cabo San Lu-cas. However, it must be noted that some of the beaches in this "in-between" area have a good degree of local protection from small points of land, or man-made breakwaters.

During the summer and fall months the entire Cape Area can be impacted by strong southerly winds and all of its beaches will become unsafe.

La Playa (The Beach)

This is the portion of a very long beach accessed by road at the town of La Playa where the local panga fishing fleet makes its headquarters. See the "San Jose del Cabo" map.

Playa Costa Azul (Blue Coast Beach)

Playa Costa Azul is a miles-long beach extending from the western end of the Estero de San Jose to the eastern edge of the bight northeast of Punta Pamilla. It has long-been named Playa Coasta Azul. With the advent of the achfront hotels at San Jose del Cabo, its eastern portion is now referred to **Playa Hotelera** (Hotel Beach). Access is through the hotels, the Brisa del ar RV Park and a variety of other places.

Playa Palmilla (Palmilla Beach)

This is a small section of beach lying in the cove formed easterly from unta Palmilla. During the winter season it is well-protected from refracted wells and is thus one of the safest beaches east of Bahía San Lucas. The each is reached by road just before arriving at Pepe's Restaurant. **Playa almilla** may be seen in the lower right portion of the Cape Area coastline hoto in this chapter.

Cabo Real

Several great beaches lie along the seaward edge of the Cabo Real resort evelopment. A stone breakwater has been built offshore from the Hotel Melia Cabo Real, providing swell protection for **Playa Cabo Real** to the east. To the west of the breakwater a small natural cove has **Playa Bledito** at its nead. In both cases access is via the hotel. For several miles easterly from the notel lies **Playa Buenos Aires**. This beach is now little-used and can be accessed from the hotel. The area is within the Cabo Real resort development property and it is surely only a matter of time before there will be new developments with resulting changes in access. There is also a small beach in front of the Hotel Westin Regina Resort.

Playa El Tule

A small secluded beach, **Playa El Tule** (also known as Surfing Beach) lies near the Maria Gaviota Suites and Villas and is reached over a low-standard road at **Km J-16** at the Puente los Tules (Los Tules Bridge).

Playa Puerto Chileno

This relatively small beach lies southwest from the Hotel Cabo San Lucas. **Playa Puerto Chileno** is reasonably well-protected from refracted swells by a sizeable rocky reef extending at right angles from the coast. The best access is over a road leaving Highway 1 west of the hotel. The road leads to a diving and equipment rental service.

Playa Santa Maria

Playa Santa Maria lies at the head of a classic small, horseshoe-shaped cove (Bahía Santa Maria) just east of the Hotel Twin Dolphin. The beach may be reached from a walkway leading from the hotel parking lot or over a nearby dirt road leading to a small parking area. The cove itself is a protected marine sanctuary.

Playa Las Viudas (Widow's Beach)

Playa las Viudas lies on the western side of the Hotel Twin Dolphin. It reached over a rough 0.4 miles dirt road leaving Highway 1 near **Km J-11**.

Playa El Medano

This is *the* beach at Cabo San Lucas. **Playa El Medano** stretches from the entrance to the inner harbor easterly for about two miles. It is backed by sever major hotels. Access is at the hotels or numerous other places. The farth one proceeds easterly from the inner harbor entrance the more the beach impacted by refracted swells.

Playa del Amor (Lover's Beach)

This is a small beach that extends completely through the rocky spine tha forms Cabo San Lucas. The portion that faces the Pacific side is quite ha ardous for swimming. The Bahía San Lucas side is more sheltered. The loc propaganda claims that you can only get to **Playa del Amor** by boat (hiring ride from the local panga owners is an easy task) but the photo of the Cab San Lucas area in this chapter would suggest that one can "sneak" aroun into the beach from Playa Solmar if the tide is right. But be careful and don' get trapped by a rising tide or increasing swells.

Playa Solmar

This is the wide beach facing the open Pacific shown on the Cabo San Lucas area photo. Swimming is dangerous. Access is through the severa hotel developments built on or near this beach.

Cape Area Fishing

This section is supplemental to the information on fishing in the "Water-sports" chapter.

Fishing Areas

The material presented below relates to the "Cape Area Fishing Grounds" map in this chapter. This map was traced from U.S. Government Nautical Chart 21120, so the relationship between the peninsular coast and the vari-ous "banks" is well represented.

1. Golden Gate Bank

This frequently visited fishing area is 26 nautical miles from the Cabo San Lucas harbor. It is well-known for its marlin and other surface game fish. Taking small trailerable boats this far into the open Pacific is a bit risky. Best use one of the larger charter vessels from Cabo San Lucas.

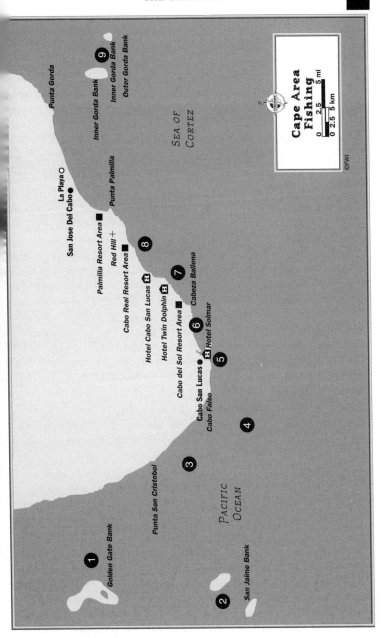

THE CAPE AREA

Cape Area Fishing

0   2.5   5 ml
0   2.5   5 km

©FWI

Golden Gate Bank

San Jaime Bank

Punta San Cristobol

PACIFIC OCEAN

Cabo Falso

Cabo San Lucas

Hotel Twin Dolphin

Cabo del Sol Resort Area

Hotel Cabo San Lucas

Hotel Solmar

Cabeza Ballena

Cabo Real Resort Area

Red Hill

Palmilla Resort Area

Punta Palmilla

San Jose Del Cabo

La Playa O

Punta Gorda

Inner Gorda Bank

Inner Gorda Bank

Outer Gorda Bank

SEA OF CORTEZ

2. San Jaime Bank

This area is some 20 nautical miles from Cabo San Lucas. It is frequent[ly] visited to land marlin, dorado or wahoo. As with the Golden Gate Bank, y[ou] are well into the open Pacific.

3. San Cristobol Ranch

Just north of Cabo Falso, a sandy beach extends a considerable distance t[o]ward Punta San Cristobol. The area offshore from this beach provides goo[d] trolling for wahoo and dorado.

4. Bait Grounds

This is the area where almost all bait is caught by the charter vessels base[d] at Cabo San Lucas. It is approximately 1.5 miles offshore in water 250 t[o] 350 feet deep. Wahoo and schooling dorado may be found in this area.

5. Playa Solmar

The waters off the Playa Solmar and the Hotel Solmar are noted for roost[er] erfish and many small boats troll here.

6. Harbor Entrance

Although most of the better fishing is farther offshore, many large gam[e] fish are found just outside the harbor entrance. Almost all fish in this area are within easy reach using small boats.

7. Shipwreck Beach

Just northeast of the harbor is the Cabeza Ballena Lighthouse. In the area offshore from the light and as far east as Santa Maria Bay (east of the Hotel Twin Dolphin) there is an excellent reef located approximately one mile offshore. This is a productive area for wahoo, dorado and bottom fish. Water depths vary from 125 to 300 feet over the reef.

8. Red Hill (Cerro Colorado)

Red Hill lies just west of Punta Palmilla. Trolling in 200-foot deep waters offshore here often produces good catches of wahoo.

9. Gorda Banks

It is 26 nautical miles east from the Cabo harbor to the Gorda Banks, where one finds excellent bottom fishing along with large grouper and cabrilla. The area is also well-known for producing wahoo and many other species of game fish.

Fishing Charters

Eighteen sportfishing charter fleets are based in the Cape Area. One of these is owned by the **Hotel Palmilla** and is anchored off that hotel at Punta Palmilla. A second is the *panga* fleet that operates off the beach at the town of La Playa east of San Jose del Cabo. All the rest are based in the harbor at Cabo San Lucas. In the future, other fleets may be expected to operate in the protection of new breakwaters at the Cabo Real and Cabo del Sol resort arıs. It is a rare Cabo hotel that does not have a sportfishing desk where boat ·servations may be arranged.

Most *pangas* (22- to 24-foot open skiffs) could be rented for $125 to $150 ·er 5- to 6-hour fishing day. Sportfishing cruiser prices ranged from $235 to 900 per day. Rates include crew, fishing equipment, licenses, ice chest and ·e. Food, drinks and tips are normally extra.

Cape Area Residential Developments

For a variety of reasons, I have never been a fan of second-home subdivisions, condominiums and their numerous cousins. These developments frequently usurp lands that my sense of values feel might best be devoted to other uses available to the general public, and the vast majority of the resultant residential units seem to lie unused while their owners wait to retire. The world is too full of wonderful places to visit without tying myself down to only one locale at vacation time.

Regardless of these negative feelings, I know that Baja's Cape Area is rapidly becoming a major vacation or retirement home capital, with the quality of many of the developments being very high. And it is equally obvious that those who are investing in these developments do not agree with me. For those of you who fall in this category, I offer the following listings (from east to west) of what appear to me to be the most prominent of the modern recreational residence developments. They are good places to start looking if you are a prospective buyer.

1. San Jose del Cabo Area

The land between Valerio Gonzalez Canseco and Peseo Malecon at San Jose del Cabo has been developed to uniformly high standards for second homes and a golf course since about 1985. The Missions Area to the north is largely condominium buildings, while the southerly Finnestera Area is single family homes with well-developed landscaping. In addition, the Missions de San Jose and Viva Beachfront condominiums are shown on the "San Jose del Cabo" map. Condominiums are also apart of the La Jolla de los Cabos development shown on the "Cabo Corridor" map #1.

2. Palmilla Resort Area

Many fancy homes have been built in the vicinity of the Hotel Palmilla for many years. Many more will now be added in the golf club areas on either side of Highway 1.

3. Cabo Real Resort Area

This 2500-acre tract is rapidly being developed into a sizeable community built around its expansive golf course.

4. Cabo del Sol Resort Area

At 1800 acres, this resort area is slightly smaller than Cabo Real, but community of some 3400 residences is contemplated. Again a golf course a central feature.

5. Missions del Cabo

This is a sizeable area that has been under development for many years. I features lots with views of the nearby ocean waters.

6. Cabo San Lucas Area

Approximately 1600 home sites are planned and construction is well unde way at the Cabo San Lucas Country Club on the eastern edge of Cabo Sar Lucas. On the western edge of town is Pedregal de Cabo San Lucas. It lie. on mountainous ground lying west of the old community and has been ir existence for many years. The development lacks a golf course but feature: excellent views of the Pacific Ocean and the topographic uniqueness of a hilly area. These and several other condominium developments are indicated on the "Cabo San Lucas" map.

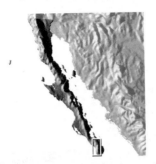

HIGHWAY 19

The northern junction of Highway 1 and Highway 19 is at **Km J-185** on Highway 1. There has long been a road between this point and Cabo San Lucas via Todos Santos and the Pacific coast, but completion of a modern highway took many years. In spring of 1984, the highway was opened to traffic for its full length. Highway 19 is easily traveled by all classes of vehicles and is the shortest and easiest route from La Paz to the tip of the peninsula.

Highway 19 will be described from north to south. Kilometer post numbers proceed in this same direction, with 0 at the Highway 1 junction.

Taking Highway 19 offers the following advantages over traveling to Cabo San Lucas via Highway 1: (A) The 80-mile trip to Cabo San Lucas over Highway 19 is 35 miles shorter. (B) There are no steep mountainous sections such as the Sierra de la Laguna crossing on Highway 1. (C) There are many miles of highway offering fine views of the Pacific Ocean. Water views along Highway 1 are limited. (D) As the Sea of Cortez coast becomes overly hot in the summer the Pacific shore along Highway 19 provides cooler weather.

Km-10—Cape Region Vegetation

You have now driven well into the area of Cape Region Vegetation, as shown on the map in the "Vegetation" chapter. It can be clearly seen that plant growth is far more dense than that encountered in the Sonoran Desert Region. The cardón cactus and many other desert species are still present, but note the dominance of woody shrubs and small trees. Many of the trees are members of the pea family. They all have very small, compound leaves and are armed with numerous spines.

Km-31—Geographic Change

The northerly 19 miles of Highway 19 crosses the flat southern end of the Llano de la Paz, which can be seen stretching endlessly to the northwest. In

sharp contrast, the lofty peaks of the Sierra de la Laguna rise a short distan~
to the southwest. At **Km-31** the highway begins to enter the low hills at t~
base of these mountains.

Km-42—Presa de Santa Inez

At this point a secondary road leaves to the left (east) and in 3.6 miles (
km) arrives at the Presa de Santa Inez (Santa Inez Dam). This large concre~
dam was completed in 1983 to provide flood control and a more dependab~
water supply for the town of Todos Santos.

The church and adjoining civic plaza at Todos Santos.

Km-51—Todos Santos

Enter Todos Santos (population 3,500), one of Baja's most entrancing
towns. Note the trees and agricultural crops in the flat river valley to the
right (west).

Park along the main street near the Hotel California and enjoy the town on
foot. Todos Santos is stop No. 29 on the **Points of Special Interest Tour**. It and
Stop No. 30 are the only points not on Highway 1, but they have been included on the assumption that most travelers will use both Highways 1 and
19 in their visits to the Cape Region. A hurricane went ashore near Todos
Santos on October 14, 1996 and travelers may encounter damage as a result
of high winds and ocean swells. Camping areas along Highway 19 to the
south may also still be recovering from hurricane damage.

Todos Santos was established as a visiting station for the mission at La Paz
in 1724. It became a separate mission in 1734 but was then destroyed in the

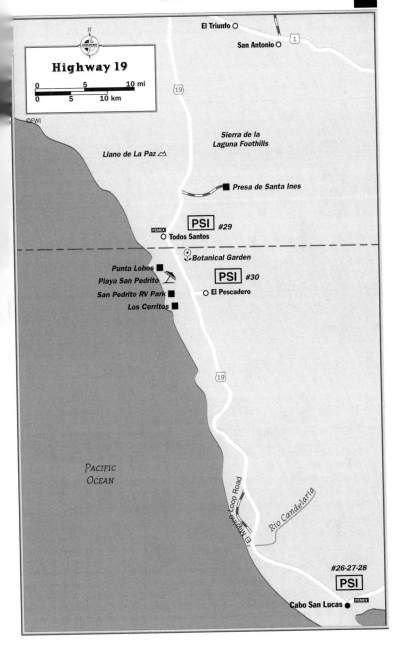

Indian rebellion that started that same year. The site of this original mission
is up the arroyo from the town, but no ruins remain.

Ruins of one of the sugarcane mills at Todos Santos.

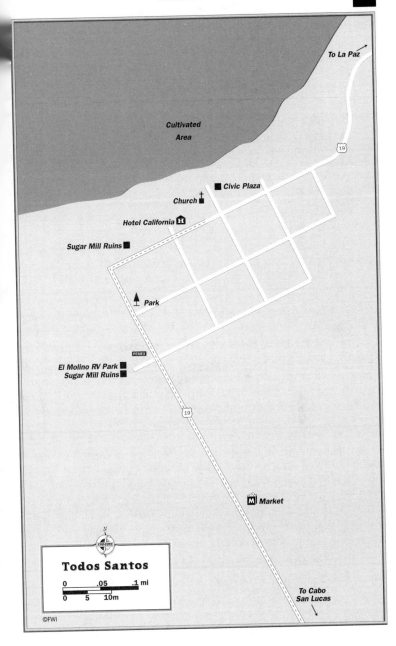

Cultivated Area

Civic Plaza

Church

Hotel California

Sugar Mill Ruins

Park

PEMEX

El Molino RV Park
Sugar Mill Ruins

Market

To La Paz

To Cabo
San Lucas

N

Todos Santos

0   .05   .1 mi

0   5   10m

©FWI

I suggest your visit include the following places:

1. Hotel California. The Hotel California was not built with the modern tourist in mind. Rather, it looks like what a hotel in an isolated western Mexican town should look like: thick walls, tile floors and a balcony rounding its second story. Ownership changed about 1987 and a well-landscaped swimming pool was added to provide a touch of modernism to its charms.

2. The village church, civic plaza and municipal buildings overlook the flat, fertile valley of the arroyo. In the 1950s, the valley was reported to be planted almost entirely with sugar cane. Today, the cane is gone and has been replaced with a variety of other crops. It is a welcome change to look out over abundant greenery after driving through many miles of desert.

3. Overlooking the valley are the ruins of one of the town's sugar mills fringed with a few remnants of cane (see the facing map).

4. Behind the PEMEX station is a well-landscaped RV park that has been converted to all-permanent sites. The park encompasses another of the town's abandoned sugar mills and is appropriately named El Molino (The Mill).

For the first 20 miles south of Todos Santos, Highway 19 passes over gently sloping coastal benches, some of which have been cleared for agriculture.

Km-54—Punta Lobos

The Pacific Coast undergoes a significant geographic change at Todos Santos. North of the village, for over 100 miles, the shoreline is essentially one, long, sandy beach backed by nearly level plains. To the south, the Sierra de la Laguna heavily influences the topography. Here the coast is frequently rocky and steep with mountains towering in the background. It is an attractive region through which to drive.

From Todos Santos, the northernmost of several rocky promontories is in view. This is Punta Lobos. (*Lobo* means wolf in Spanish but refers to sea lions when used in coastal place-names.) Here, 200 yards north of **Km-54**, a dirt road to the right (west) leaves Highway 19, and in one mile arrives at a sandy beach. The local fishermen launch their boats over the beach immediately north of the point. The best campsites are at the end of a spur road near an abandoned building a few hundred yards to the north.

Km-57—Playa San Pedrito

Near **Km-57** a dirt road to the right (west) leads in 1.5 miles to a fine sandy beach, Playa San Pedrito. The junction point is directly opposite the botanical garden described below. The beach is backed by a large grove of native *Washingtonia fan palms* mixed with the introduced coconut palm. The com-

nation of sea, sand and palms makes this one of Baja's most pleasant camp-
ng spots. It is my personal favorite of all those in Baja. It is almost certain to
ll prey to the hotel builders. The area is best suited for smaller vehicles as
he seaward end of the access road is often badly rutted.

**PSI
#30**

Km-57—Botanical Garden

Opposite the road to Playa San Pedrito is the Campo Experimental Todos
Santos. Here has been developed a fine array of desert plants from all regions
of Baja. Many are marked with signs. This botanical garden adjoins the highway and is open to the public at no cost. This is an excellent place to test
whether you have properly identified the plants you have seen along the peninsula's highways. The garden is the final stop on the **Points of Special Interest Tour**. I hope you have visited many of the areas it highlights and that they
have added to your enjoyment of Baja.

The palm-lined beach and cove at Playa San Pedrito.

Km-59—San Pedrito RV Park

A secondary road leaves the highway to the west 0.2 miles north of **Km-59**
and in 1.8 miles arrives at the San Pedrito RV Park. (At the 0.5 mile point a
side road branches the right and travels to Playa San Pedrito as noted at Km
57 above.) This was the first tourist facility built along Highway 19 after it
was completed. There is a restaurant, bar, swimming pool, a large number of
full hookup units and an excellent sandy beach. Tent campers are accommodated along the beach immediately south of the RV area. The RV parking
area is a bit sterile but it will improve when the recently planted palm trees
increase in size. The park's name is a bit confusing, as it is not at Playa San

HIGHWAY 19

Pedrito. According to the official Mexican government topographic ma
Playa San Pedrito is located to the north at **Km-57** as noted above.

Km-60—Rancho Nueva Villa

Many of the level lands between the mountains and sea in this area hav
been cleared for produce farming. About 100 yards prior to **Km-60** is a veg
etable-packing facility. In past years it has also offered vegetables for reta
sales. This was not the case on my last trip, but this business may be resumec
As an alternative, try shopping for fresh produce at the markets in the nearb
town of El Pescadero.

Km-61—El Pescadero

At 0.2 miles north of **Km-62** a paved side road leads to the left (east) to th
village of El Pescadero (population 1200). The name means "the fish dealer." There are many palms and other trees in and around the community. I
is a pleasant town in the heart of the vegetable farming area, but is without
tourist facilities other than a grocery store.

*Shown is the Pacific beach at los Cerritos near Todos Santos. The short point of
land noted in the text lies out of sight to the right and provides wind and swell
protection.*

Km-64—Los Cerritos

A two-lane secondary road leads to the right (west) directly at **Km-64** and
arrives at a fork in the road in 1.3 miles. The left turn brings one to another
of the original government trailer courts. This one is now open and being
improved, but the rest rooms were inoperative on a recent visit. A short trip
on the road to the right terminates at another excellent unimproved camp-

g area near a fine sandy beach. A short point of land provides reasonable
rotection from both wind and swells. There are fine views of the coastline
o the south.

Km-82—Geographic Change

Between here and Todos Santos, Highway 19 has remained within a short
distance of the ocean and passed over mostly level coastal benches. At this
point 0.2 miles north of **Km-82**, the highway gains elevation and moves in-
and over rolling plateau lands. Here is being developed the first of the subdivision tracts that are bound to blight the Highway 19 area in the future.
Such is progress.

Km-94—El Migrino Loop North End

Leading to the right (west) at a point 100 yards north of **Km-94** is the
northern end of a section of the old, dirt-surface coastal road. It loops toward the Pacific and rejoins the Highway 1.7 miles ahead. The loop road is
about 2.5 miles in length and offers several excellent places to camp on low
bluffs overlooking excellent sandy beaches. Near the middle of the loop are
several steep dips. Larger RVs should approach these with caution. (To my
knowledge this loop area has no name, but I call it El Migrino after a ranch
bearing this name located near its southern end.)

There are no further coastal camping spots between here and Cabo San
Lucas. In the previous version of this book I wrote, "This El Migrino area
may become a very popular camping location now that beach sites in the
Cabo San Lucas area on Highway 1 are all taken over by hotels and various
private interests." To my surprise this has not occurred and this excellent
camping area appears to get very little use.

Km-97—Rio Candelaria

About 100 yards north of **Km-97** Highway 19 makes a long, low-water
crossing of the Rio Candelaria. While normally dry, this crossing could cause
problems during and after storms. One might predict that it eventually will
have to be bridged.

Km-97—El Migrino Loop South End

Here, 100 feet south of **Km-97**, is the southern junction of the El Migrino
loop road. Look for a small sign "**Migrino Access a Playa**." The last two times
I have visited this area this southern end of the loop road has been modified
with some of the land placed under agriculture, so you may have to find your
way about by trial and error. In general try to keep to the right (north) to access the camping areas noted above. Bearing left leads to the edge of a large
lagoon area that also offers camping spots.

Rio Candelaria to Cabo San Lucas

Highway 19 climbs inland south of the Rio Candelaria, with the Pacific Ocean occasionally in view in the distance. The vegetation you will encounter from about **Km-110** southward is the best example of the Arid Tropical Forest found along Highway 19. In particular, note the *cardónals* (forests) of cardón cactus and the several species of low-branching trees. Among the largest is the *palo blanco*. Its light bark makes it easy to identify.

Km-124—Cabo San Lucas

At the northern edge of Cabo San Lucas a new section of Highway 1 turns sharply to the left (east) and skirts the edge of the community. Bearing to the right brings one into the heart of town via Jose Morelos (see "Cabo San Lucas" map). A PEMEX station lies near the junction and offers a fueling alternative to the town's other gas station on Highway 1.

Vaya Con Dios

I always hate books that abruptly come to an end without a parting word. While we have never met, we have been companions along the way, and it seems improper to leave without a brief farewell.

I sincerely hope that *Fielding's Baja* has enhanced your journey. My wife Patty and I have worked diligently to bring you what we hope is the best guidebook available for Baja California.

Our greatest joy in producing the book is knowing that we have helped others to more fully enjoy a brief time in their lives. If our paths should cross, please give us a yell so we can say hello. But for now, *vaya con dios.*

ROAD SIGNS

Some Mexican road signs are pictorially self-explanatory and use the diagonal slash to indicate NO (see the No Parking sign). However, the majority simply spell out their message in Spanish as shown on many of the signs in this exhibit.

Bus Stop

Speed Limit in Kilometers

No Estacionarse
(No Parking)

Left Turn Only
(IZQ abbreviates)
(IZQUIERDO)
(DERECHA is right)

VADO
(Dip)

TOPE
It means Bump.
Nobody stops at the stop signs, but
we all slow down at the tope.

Dip in 300 meters

Stop
Keep to the right when
stopping as you are holding up
traffic and the locals need
room to roar by. (NOTE In recent
years I have found Baja drivers a
bit more respectful of STOP signs
than in the past-but not much.)

Yield
Right of Way

ROAD SIGNS

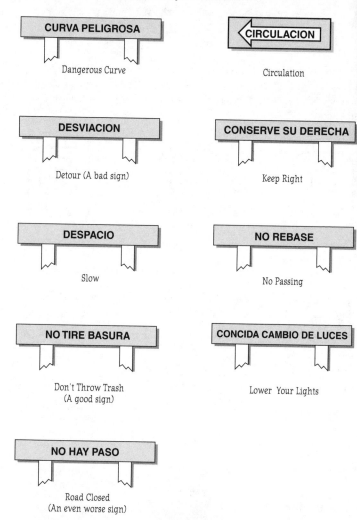

CURVA PELIGROSA

Dangerous Curve

CIRCULACION

Circulation

DESVIACION

Detour (A bad sign)

CONSERVE SU DERECHA

Keep Right

DESPACIO

Slow

NO REBASE

No Passing

NO TIRE BASURA

Don't Throw Trash
(A good sign)

CONCIDA CAMBIO DE LUCES

Lower Your Lights

NO HAY PASO

Road Closed
(An even worse sign)

ROAD SIGNS

INSIDER TIP

Baja's highways are narrow and her drivers are always in a hurry. For safety's sake HOLD DOWN YOUR SPEED.

INDEX

Order Your Guide to Travel and Adventure

Title	Price	Title	Price
Fielding's Alaska Cruises and the Inside Passage	$18.95	Fielding's London Agenda	$14.95
Fielding's The Amazon	$16.95	Fielding's Los Angeles	$16.95
Fielding's Asia's Top Dive Sites	$19.95	Fielding's Malaysia & Singapore	$16.95
Fielding's Australia	$16.95	Fielding's Mexico	$18.95
Fielding's Bahamas	$16.95	Fielding's New Orleans Agenda	$16.95
Fielding's Baja California	$18.95	Fielding's New York Agenda	$16.95
Fielding's Bermuda	$16.95	Fielding's New Zealand	$16.95
Fielding's Borneo	$18.95	Fielding's Paris Agenda	$14.95
Fielding's Budget Europe	$17.95	Fielding's Portugal	$16.95
Fielding's Caribbean	$18.95	Fielding's Paradors, Pousadas and Charming Villages	$18.95
Fielding's Caribbean Cruises	$18.95	Fielding's Rome Agenda	$14.95
Fielding's Disney World and Orlando	$18.95	Fielding's San Diego Agenda	$14.95
Fielding's Diving Indonesia	$19.95	Fielding's Southeast Asia	$18.95
Fielding's Eastern Caribbean	$17.95	Fielding's Southern Vietnam on 2 Wheels	$15.95
Fielding's England	$17.95	Fielding's Spain	$18.95
Fielding's Europe	$18.95	Fielding's Surfing Indonesia	$19.95
Fielding's European Cruises	$18.95	Fielding's Sydney Agenda	$16.95
Fielding's Far East	$18.95	Fielding's Thailand, Cambodia, Laos and Myanmar	$18.95
Fielding's France	$18.95	Fielding's Vacation Places Rated	$19.95
Fielding's Freewheelin' USA	$18.95	Fielding's Vietnam	$17.95
Fielding's Hawaii	$18.95	Fielding's Western Caribbean	$18.95
Fielding's Italy	$18.95	Fielding's The World's Most Dangerous Places	$19.95
Fielding's Kenya	$16.95	Fielding's Worldwide Cruises	$19.95
Fielding's Las Vegas Agenda	$14.95		

To place an order: call toll-free 1-800-FW-2-GUIDE
(VISA, MasterCard and American Express accepted)
or send your check or money order to:
Fielding Worldwide, Inc., 308 S. Catalina Avenue, Redondo Beach, CA 90277
http://www.fieldingtravel.com
Add $2.00 per book for shipping & handling (sorry, no COD's), allow 2–6 weeks for delivery

NEW FIELDINGWEAR!

Now that you own a Fielding travel guide, you have graduated from being a tourist to full-fledge traveler! Celebrate your elevated position by proudly wearing one of these heavy-duty, all-cotton shirts, selected by our authors for their comfort and durability (and their ability to hide dirt). Choose from three styles—radical "World Tour," politically correct "Do the World Right," and elegant "All-Access."

Important Note: Fielding authors have field-tested these shirts and have found that they can be swapped for much more than their purchase price in free drinks at some of the world's hottest clubs and in-spots. They also make great gifts.

WORLD TOUR

Hit the hard road with a travel fashion statement for out times. Visit all 35 of Mr. D.P.'s favorite nasty spots (listed on the back), or just look like you're going to. This is the real McCoy, worn by mujahedin, mercenaries, UN peacekeepers and the authors of Fielding's The World's Most Dangerous Places. Black, XL, heavy-duty 100% cotton. Made in the USA. $18.00.

DO THE WORLD RIGHT

Start your next adventure wearing Fielding's politically correct "Do the World Right" shirt, complete with freaked-out red globe and blasting white type. A shirt that tells the world that within that high-mileage, overly educated body beats the heart of a true party animal. Only for adrenaline junkies, hard-core travelers and seekers of knowledge. Black, XL, heavy-duty 100% cotton. Made in the USA. $18.00.

Name:

Address:

City:

State: Zip:

ALL ACCESS

Strike terror into the snootiest maitre'd, make concierges cringe, or just use this elegant shirt as the ultimate party invitation. The combination of the understated red Fielding logo embroidered on a jet-black golf shirt will get you into the snobbiest embassy party or jumping night spot. An elegant casual shirt for those who travel in style and comfort. Black, XL or L, 100% preshrunk cotton, embroidered Fielding Travel Guide logo on front. Made in the U.S.A. $29.00.

Telephone:
Shirt Name:
Quantity:

To order books or request latest listing phone (800) 355-8635 or (415) 332-8635. Write Baja Bookshelf P.O. Box 203, Sausalito, CA 94965, or contact http://www.sirius.com/~jackbaja on the World Wide Web. E-mail jackbaja@sirius.com

—Fielding's Baja California
Additional copies of the book you are reading are $18.95.

2—Baja Boater's Guide Vol I—The Pacific Coast
By Jack Williams—212 Pages—Soft cover—Glossy Paper—Stitch Binding—$24.95
The boater's bible for Baja waters. 201 photos, (mostly oblique aerials) and 81 charts of every prominent bay, cove, promontory, island and harbor in Baja. Full chapters on Anchoring & Anchorages, Maritime History, Natural History and background about boating along Baja's Pacific coast.

3—Baja Boaters Guide Vol II—The Sea of Cortez
By Jack Williams—264 Pages—Soft cover, Glossy Paper—Stitch Binding—$26.95
Similar information as Volume I but for the Sea of Cortez coast. 254 photos, 97 charts. Volume I is used mostly by ocean-cruisers. Volume II is equally usable by these sailors and the thousands of trailer boaters who use the Sea of Cortez. Both books are marine companions for The Magnificent Peninsula.

4—Sea Kayaking in Baja
By Andromeda Romano-Lax—168 Pages—$13.95
The first comprehensive book on sea kayaking in Baja. Much background material about kayaking along with details on 15 kayak-friendly routes along both peninsular coasts.

5—Launch Ramps of Baja California
By Mike Bales—106 Pages—Soft Cover—$6.95
Black & white photos and full descriptions of every launch ramp (38) in Baja, together with many tips on trailer boating.

6—Boating Guide to Mexico (West Coast Edition)
By John Rains & Patricia Miller—278 Pages—Spiral bound—$39.95
A full color guide covering the entire west coast of Mexico including the Baja peninsula. Contains hundreds of color photographs and some 80 charts. Contains less detail on Baja than the Baja Boater's Guide but is the best book available for the complete Mexican west coast.

7—Cruising Guide to the Middle Gulf
By Gerry Cunningham—174 Pages—Soft cover—$29.95.

Detailed coverage of both coasts of the central portion of the Sea of Cortez including the Midr Islands. Several aerial and sea-level photos. Other excellent guides by Gerry Cunningham for the ea ern shore of the Sea of Cortez are also available. These include Cruising Guide to San Carlos, Cruisir Guide to Bahía de los Angeles and charts for San Carlos, Bahía Kino and Puerto Penasco areas. C for details.

8—The Baja Catch—2nd Edition
By Niel Kelly & Gene Kira—275 Pages—Soft Cover—$19.95

The best Baja fishing manual ever written, with detailed info on where and how to fish. Many ma and illustrations of the most common fish. Based on the exploits of a world class fisherman.

9—Diving Baja California
By Susan Speck—128 Pages—Soft Cover—Glossy paper—$18.95

An authoritative Baja diving guide with 90+ brilliant color photos and color maps. Background mate rial on diving in Baja plus details on where to dive along both peninsular coasts.

10—Marine Animals of Baja
By Daniel Gotshall—114 Pages—Soft Paper—Glossy paper—$20.95

A great asset for sport divers, snorkelers and naturalists. This well respected book contains color pho tos and written descriptions of 150 species of fish and 65 species of invertebrates in Baja peninsula waters.

11—Baja Camping
By Fred and Gloria Jones—296 Pages—5 1/4 x 8 1/2—$12.95

Detailed information about Baja's RV parks and campgrounds (fees—number of units—restroom facilities—access and notes on good and bad features. Comments by the authors about their many years of traveling in Baja.

12—Backroad Baja
By Patti and Tom Higginbotham—128 pages—5 1/2 x 8 1/2—$14.95

Detailed roadlogs of 19 great backroad adventures in the area from Bahía de los Angeles to Ciudad Insurgentes. Complete with maps and background material about each trip.

13—Crossing the Border Fast and Easy
By Paula McDonald—a pocket guide with 196 Pages. $6.95

An amazing little book devoted primarily to giving explicit directions for escaping Baja through the maddening Tijuana-San Ysidro Port-of-Entry plus many tips on the Tijuana area.

14—Cabo San Lucas Handbook
By Joe Cummings
275 Pages—Soft Cover—$14.95

A guide that zeros in on Cabo San Lucas, San Jose del Cabo, the Cabo Corridor and the mountains immediately to the north. Details on accommodations, entertainment, beaches, fishing, shopping, plus hiking trails and remote villages in the mountains.

15—Field Guide to the Gray Whale
By the Oceanic Society—50 Pages—Soft Cover—$5.95

A pocket guide crammed with facts on the gray whale, life-cycle, conservation, & whale watching. Baja is the winter home & calving grounds for the gray whale where they are easily viewed.

BAJA BOOKSHELF

—Baja California Plant Field Guide—2nd Edition
y Norman C. Roberts—309 Pages—Soft Cover—$22.95
HE definitive work on the plants of Baja. Descriptions of 550 plants with 275 color photos. Don't
to Baja without being able to fully appreciate its truly world class vegetation.

7—The Baja Highway—Geology & Biology Field Guide
y John Minch & Thomas Leslie—233 Pages—Soft Cover—$19.95
guide to the geology, wildlife and plant features seen along Baja's main highways, keyed to easy to
d kilometer post signs. Authored by two college professors after 30 years of traveling in Baja.

8—Spanish Lingo for the Savvy Gringo
By Elizabeth Reid—217 Pages—Soft Cover—$12.95
great guide for understanding Spanish as spoken in Mexico. Broken into practical topics such as
Courtesy, Lodging, the Alphabet, Telephoning etc. plus practical info about traveling in Mexico.

19—Into a Desert Place
By Graham Mackintosh—312 Pages—Soft Cover—$14.00
The author's inspiring account of his 3000-mile walk around the coast of Baja. A remarkable true
adventure story complete with 16 pages of full color photos.

20—Back Country Mexico—Guide and Phrase Book
By Burleson & Riskind—311 Pages—Soft Cover—$14.95
A "must book" for getting along in rural Mexico (Baja is as rural as it gets). Culture & lifeways, village
life, rural industries, speaking Spanish, back-country travel.

21—Distant Neighbors
By Alan Riding—385 pages—Soft Cover—$13.00
A nonfiction best seller by a former *New York Times* Bureau Chief. Covers The Mexicans, a concise
historical summary, the political system, economics, social and population problems. Designed to
foster understanding between Americans and Mexicans. Great!

22—How to Buy Real Estate in Mexico
By Dennis John Peyton—204 Pages—5 1/2 x 8 1/2—$19.95
The works on buying property in Mexico; Laws—Trusts—Types of property—Time-shares—Ejido
lands—Property related zones—Much more. The author is one of the few American attorneys
licensed to practice law in Mexico.

23—Baja California Business Opportunities & Retirement Guide
By Tom and Mary Lou Magee—6 x 9—360 Pages—$19.95
A Baja specific book on Mexican culture—Banking, finance & Investment—Business opportunities—
Real Estate—The legal system—NAFTA—Retirement. Written by full time residents of Baja with a
successful public relations and marketing business.

Baja Quest Video
A 60-minute Video by Russ and Jo Ann Hyslop—$19.95
This well done video is a great visual companion for *Fielding's Baja California*. Road logs from the
International border along Highway 1 to Cabo San Lucas. Hwy 19 and several other important side
trips are also included. The film concentrates on historic, natural history and Mexican cultural aspects.
Highlighted are the sights and sounds that make traveling to Baja by road a fascinating adventure.
Ample time is also devoted to the glamourous, world-class resort areas near the peninsula's tip.

International Conversions

TEMPERATURE

To convert °F to °C, subtract 32 and divide by 1.8. To convert °C to °F, multiply by 1.8 and add 32.

Fahrenheit	Centigrade	
230°	110°	
220°		
210°	100°	Water Boils
200°		
190°	90°	
180°	80°	
170°		
160°	70°	
150°		
140°	60°	
130°		
120°	50°	
110°		
100°	40°	
90°	30°	
80°		
70°	20°	
60°		
50°	10°	
40°		
30°	0°	Water Freezes
20°	-10°	
10°		
0°	-20°	
-10°		
-20°	-30°	
-30°		
-40°	-40°	

WEIGHTS & MEASURES

LENGTH

1 km	=	0.62 miles
1 mile	=	1.609 km
1 meter	=	1.2936 yards
1 meter	=	3.28 feet
1 yard	=	0.9144 meters
1 yard	=	3 feet
1 foot	=	30.48 centimeters
1 centimeter	=	0.39 inch
1 inch	=	2.54 centimeters

AREA

1 square km	=	0.3861 square miles
1 square mile	=	2.590 square km
1 hectare	=	2.47 acres
1 acre	=	0.405 hectare

VOLUME

1 cubic meter	=	1.307 cubic yards
1 cubic yard	=	0.765 cubic meter
1 cubic yard	=	27 cubic feet
1 cubic foot	=	0.028 cubic meter
1 cubic centimeter	=	0.061 cubic inch
1 cubic inch	=	16.387 cubic centimeters

CAPACITY

1 gallon	=	3.785 liters
1 quart	=	0.94635 liters
1 liter	=	1.057 quarts
1 pint	=	473 milliliters
1 fluid ounce	=	29.573 milliliters

MASS and WEIGHT

1 metric ton	=	1.102 short tons
1 metric ton	=	1000 kilograms
1 short ton	=	.90718 metric ton
1 long ton	=	1.016 metric tons
1 long ton	=	2240 pounds
1 pound	=	0.4536 kilograms
1 kilogram	=	2.2046 pounds
1 ounce	=	28.35 grams
1 gram	=	0.035 ounce
1 milligram	=	0.015 grain

cm 0 1 2 3 4 5 6 7 8 9 10

Inch 0 1 2 3 4